Wine Report 2005

Tom Stevenson

To Tony & Joan

Best Wishes

Tom Stevenson

DK

"A meaty and original volume."
Joanna Simon, *The Sunday Times*

"If you want to know what's really going on in the wine world, *Wine Report 2004* is a good place to start."
The Independent Magazine

"The perfect companion for a quiet evening in with a few glasses of smoky Spanish red? Oenophiles ... might like to curl up, glass in hand, with Tom Stevenson's excellent new *Wine Report 2004*."
Giles Kime, *The Sunday Telegraph Magazine*

"*Wine Report*'s 380 pages are packed with valuable information, fascinating facts, vintage evaluations and useful recommendations. It should become an annual institution."
Liz Sagues, Grapevine,
The Hampstead & Highgate Express

"If you want the inside track on the global wine industry, with best bargains and top tips, this is the book for you. Stevenson offers a new angle using top wine experts to provide a snapshot of the world market."
The Oxford Times

LONDON NEW YORK MUNICH
MELBOURNE DELHI

For Dorling Kindersley

Senior Editor Gary Werner
Senior Art Editor Sue Metcalfe-Megginson

Managing Editor Deirdre Headon
Art Director Peter Luff

DTP Designer Louise Waller
Production Controller Kevin Ward

Indexer John Noble

Produced for Dorling Kindersley by

Sands Publishing Solutions
4 Jenner Way, Eccles, Aylesford,
Kent ME20 7SQ

Project Editors David & Sylvia
Tombesi-Walton
Project Art Editor Simon Murrell

For Tom Stevenson
Editor Pat Carroll

First edition published in
Great Britain in 2004 by
Dorling Kindersley Limited
80 Strand, London WC2R 0RL

Printed and bound by Graficom, Italy

Discover more at
www.dk.com

CONTENTS

Sex sells, so they say, and no one knows this better than Larry Mawby, the Michigan-based fizz-master *extraordinaire* (see Atlantic Northeast).

I've been tasting his wines for many years and the quality and consistency have improved dramatically. It used to be – how shall I put it? – enthusiastic at best. But the amazing thing about Larry, apart from being able to levitate, is that even his worst sparkling wines have sold out. Other winemakers in the state thought that if Larry can do it, they could too, and within no time at all, almost everyone was selling Michigan fizz. Well, actually they weren't: they were making it, but not selling it. After a few years of watching their stock sit there, a number of wineries asked Larry if he would take it off their hands. He was mulling this over one morning, when the official notification arrived in the post that he could sell wines under the Sex label. Larry nearly spilled coffee over himself because he had half-jokingly applied for permission, not really believing that it would be granted in what is, after all, America's fairly puritanical society. But it was and, all of a sudden, he knew exactly what he could sell as Sex. He took everyone's stock, opened up the bottles, added a dash of red wine to turn the fizz pink, relabelled it Sex, and it has been flying off the shelf as fast as he can stack it! The owners of the other wineries were relieved and grateful that Larry bought the stock from them, but when they saw how quickly it sold, they did not know whether to laugh or cry. As for Larry, he never even knew what the 'pink dollar' was until Sex came along….

New this year

There are two new reports this year: Luxembourg by Danny Kay-lookalike David Furer; and Belgium, Netherlands & Scandinavia by Fiona Morrison and Gert Crum. David Furer is a UK-based American who used to live in Germany, close to the border with Luxembourg, where he has a number of contacts. Fiona Morrison is a Belgium-based Master of Wine, whose husband, Jacques Thienpont, is the owner of Le Pin. It tickled me to think that someone used to drinking the world's most expensive wine would be reporting on the hobby wines of Belgium. I was also impressed that she would bother. After all, she hardly needs the money. Gert Crum is a Dutch wine writer I last saw on a small 12-seater plane in 1992, as we hedgehopped across Poland on our return from visiting wineries in Moldova. Gert was so struck by the experience that he wrote *The Moldovan Wine Adventure* (published by Immerc BV).

These two reports will appear in every edition, but do not expect contributions in the future to be as information-packed as they are this year. Fiona, Gert, and David have been asked to provide one-off overviews as introductions to these relatively unknown wine-producing countries. Future reports will be exclusively news-driven and will include, of course, Top 10s, Vintage Report, and Opinion.

Future editions

It is not just the world of wine that is moving fast – wine consumers are leading ever more hectic lives too, making it increasingly difficult for the twain to meet. The concept of *Wine Report* was so simple it is surprising that it did not already exist. The aim is to provide a one-stop update to what has happened in the world of wine over the previous 12 months. This makes it an ideal resource for the busy wine enthusiast who wants to keep up to speed but does not have the time. It has even caught on in the wine trade itself, which is not surprising since it encompasses many wine enthusiasts. Yet they are often far too busy to keep abreast of much else beyond the products they handle. If anything, the knowledge of most people in the wine trade is distinctly lopsided. They have a good general grounding and probably know a darn sight more about the wines they handle than most high-profile experts, but they also have huge gaping holes. Since the publication of *Wine Report 2004*, I have met many people in the wine trade who had not heard of the book, but not one who could put it down once he or she saw its contents. News is knowledge, and the wine trade is thirsting for it.

But *Wine Report* is ideal for all wine enthusiasts, not just those in the trade. I know of one very famous international businessman who keeps a copy of *Wine Report* in his briefcase, so that he can read the appropriate chapter when flying to different countries. When he dines out the first night, he is already up to speed. He told me that his local contacts raise an eyebrow when he orders one of the Most Exciting or Unusual Finds listed in the report, especially when he can tell them why it is so exciting or unusual. Just knowing the New Up-and-Coming Producers and some of the Grapevine news items that even his local contacts do not know gives him an enormous advantage.

Ideal maybe, but *Wine Report* is never likely to be perfect. There are plenty of gaps to plug. Not just countries such as Morocco and Algeria (which are lined up for the next edition), but even more obscure wine-producing areas like Zimbabwe, Kenya, or the islands of Madagascar, Réunion, and Mauritius (which were supposed to have been covered in both the first and second editions, but proved to be tougher nuts to crack than expected, so the search continues). Or, indeed, minuscule-production countries of the ilk of Malta and Ireland. When they are reported on, readers will know that I am happy with the extent of geographical coverage. I also need a contributor whose remit will pick up on French wine news items that fall beyond that of the regional reports, such as the proposed super-AOCs. René Renou, the director of the Institut National des Appellations d'Origine, has been dubbed 'Superman' for proposing a two-tier appellation system, the upper division of which would be bestowed on wines of "demonstrably superior quality". The good news is the Burgundians are for it, the bad news is the *Bordelais* are not. Still, the good news is not all that good when we read why the Burgundians support the proposal. As Jean-François Delorme, president of the Bureau Interprofessionnel des Vins de Bourgogne, commented: "Of course, all of Burgundy's AOCs would be super-AOCs." … Er, no. If they were, they would not be very super, would they? It would have been good to have a contributor follow this through and perhaps make it central to an Opinion piece, but it is not quite clear how such a report would be structured. Perhaps it should also have a broader brief to include matters of global importance, such as multinational wine companies.

As the reader can discern, there is a lot of tweaking to be done before *Wine Report* is even half-perfect but, as some of the topics covered in this edition illustrate, it should be interesting getting there.

• Wine made from vines grown north of Poland.
• Winery on Bali grows a crop every month.
• Viognier is a no-brainer in Idaho.
• Screwcap arrives in Canada.
• Teetotal Canadian restaurateur has 47,000-bottle wine cellar.
• Bioterrorism threatens Burgundy.
• Red-wine grapes grown in one-third of Germany's vineyards.
• Value of fake Italian wine in US exceeds $541 million.
• 10,000 hectares of vines go missing in Slovenia.
• Wild vines have more sex.
• Black goo found in California nursery.
• Luxembourg wins nine out of 55 gold medals at the Riesling du Monde.

Tom Stevenson

This is not so much a 'How to Use' section as an explanation of the brief that I gave to contributors and the parameters they applied (or did not!).

Contributors

Every contributor to *Wine Report* was my personal choice. For the most part, they are the expert's experts in their various specialist areas. For some regions there are no experts, and I had to twist the arm of the most strategically placed professionals to tackle such reports. There have been small changes in contributors since the first edition, and I imagine there will be more in the future. *Wine Report* has very specific needs, so if some contributors come and go, the going has nothing to do with their expertise on the subject and everything to do with how I expect it to be applied. Ideally, I would like to see no more than one report per contributor (with my Champagne and Alsace reports the only exception), since this would project the desired specialist ambience, but it will take time to achieve.

Opinions expressed by contributors

These are, of course, their own. I am not referring specifically to the Opinion section of each report (which is dealt with separately below), but rather the more general way in which they report a story. For example, the way that François Lefort (Grape Varieties) writes about GMOs could not be further from the way that Monty Waldin (Organic & Biodynamic Wines) covers the subject. I respect both of these contributors' opinions, although I do not agree with either of them. (Anyone interested in my view should look at www.wine-pages.com/guests/tom/gm.htm.)

Reader's knowledge level

Unlike most other wine books, *Wine Report* assumes a certain level of knowledge. Therefore, there are rarely any explanations for technical terms or even references to historical incidents. Readers are expected to know what these terms mean and what the references refer to, or at least have the intelligence and curiosity to look them up.

News and Grapevine items

Regional reports include news affecting the region and its producers, wines, and consumers. This may incorporate gossip and rumour but not marketing or sales stories unless they are of an exceptional or very hot nature. Non-regional reports have their own structure. It should be noted that, for Wine & Health, Beverley Blanning has been specifically commissioned to report the bad news as well as the good and, if anything, to err on the side of the former rather than the latter. I want to give readers as much good health news as possible, but *Wine Report* is for wine enthusiasts and cannot afford to be vulnerable to accusations of selective reporting of this sensitive issue.

Opinion

Contributors have quite a free hand to spout off about anything they feel strongly about, but there are certain categories of opinion that are obligatory. These are, essentially, anything that is currently practised, legally or not, that the contributor believes should not be, and anything that the contributor believes should be happening, but is not. A few contributors found nothing wrong in their regions, which I cannot accept. There is no wine region where everything is right. Contributors should always attempt to balance their criticisms with practical solutions. Readers should expect to see the same opinions repeated or refined in each edition, unless the situation changes, which would be news in itself.

Vintage Reports

Each regional contributor provides an advance report on the very latest harvest (the year before date of publication for the northern hemisphere, the actual year of publication for the southern hemisphere), plus brief updates on the previous five vintages. In the first edition, it was difficult enough to get some contributors to rate vintages on a 100-point scale, but most toed the line. However, everyone was using a different yardstick, so, from the second edition, all vintage ratings conform to the following definitions.

100	No vintage can be accurately described as perfect, but those achieving a maximum score must be truly great vintages.
90–99	Excellent to superb.
80–89	Good to very good.
70–79	Average to good.
60–69	Disappointing.
40–59	Very bad.
0–39	Disastrous.

Vintage ratings should merely be seen as 'betting odds'. They express the likelihood of what might be reasonably expected from a wine of a given year. The higher the rating, the fewer the exceptions; quality and consistency do, to some extent, go hand in hand.

Top 10s

If percentile ratings for vintages did not set the cat among the pigeons, then these Top 10s of producers and wines certainly did. Very few contributors were worried about listing the 10 best of anything, but several were extremely reluctant to put that list in order of preference. Eventually most agreed to do this, but readers might come across the odd list that looks suspiciously as if it is in alphabetical order....

There was no requirement for each Top 10 to be fully utilized. If a contributor truly believes that, for example, only five or six producers or wines deserve a place in a particular Top 10, then that is perfectly acceptable. Furthermore, it was permitted to place the same producer or wine in more than one list. Such coexistence could even apply to the Greatest and Best-Value or Best-Bargain Top 10s.

Prices

All prices in this guide are average retail prices, including tax, per bottle, expressed in the local currency of the country of origin. This is not a buyer's guide; the wines listed are supposed to be the greatest, best-bargain or most exciting or unusual, without restricting the choice to those that happen to be available on any specific market.

Greatest Wine Producers

My guidelines to the contributors made it clear that their choice should be "regardless of status". In other words, even if there is some sort of acknowledged hierarchy, such as Bordeaux's *cru classé* system, the contributor should not feel restrained by it. On the other hand, if a contributor agrees entirely with a perceived hierarchy, there was nothing preventing him or her following it slavishly. Some contributors set themselves their own criteria. Dan Berger, for example, told me that for his greatest producers he had decided: (a) the winery had to be in business for at least 10 years, and production over that period had to have remained substantially the same; (b) the winery had to use substantially the same fruit sources, mainly from owned or leased vineyards, for the last 10 years, and not deviate from a house style; (c) the ownership and winemaking had to be consistent over the last 10 years; and (d) the winery must make at least two wines that have achieved the highest levels of quality without ever deviating from that level, even in a mediocre vintage.

Dan's criteria represent a very professional way of ascertaining greatness, but it is not one that I would impose on all contributors. Furthermore, the term 'greatest' is relative: it does not necessarily mean that the producer is intrinsically great. The best producer in California should be intrinsically great, but although the greatest producer in Belgium must, by definition, be its greatest, in practice it will be no more than 'interesting'. Readers should expect the Greatest Producers list to change the least of all the Top 10s from year to year.

Fastest-Improving Producers

Whether good or bad, reputations tend to stick well beyond their shelf life, which is why this particular Top 10 is probably the most useful. While the rest of the market lags behind, you can benefit from the insider knowledge of *Wine Report*, buying up top-performing wines long before others cotton on and prices increase.

New Up-and-Coming Producers

While Fastest-Improving Producers will probably be well-established wineries that have perked up, this Top 10 focuses on the newer producers that are the ones to watch. In some of the more conservative traditional areas, 'new' will be relative and should perhaps be taken to mean newer or a producer whose wines used to be sold only from the cellar door but have recently become more widely available.

Best-Value Producers

This is self-explanatory.

Greatest-Quality Wines

Each contributor has his or her own method for determining their greatest wines. I am sure that many do as I tend to do, and that is to list the greatest I have tasted within the last 12 months, rather than the greatest wines *per se*. True experts in classic areas will probably have notes on thousands of wines tasted in the last 12 months, and of these there could be 50-odd wines that would justifiably achieve a top score. Most contributors could probably fill their Top 10 Greatest Wines several times over. (Most years I could fill the Top 10 Greatest Alsace Wines twice over with just Zind-Humbrecht's wines.) Thus realistically this should be viewed as merely '10 of the greatest'. Then, of course, we have to put them in order of preference, which can be a real pain. How, for example, is it possible to say whether the greatest red bordeaux is better than the greatest Sauternes, or the greatest Alsace Gewurztraminer better than the greatest Alsace Pinot Gris? If David Peppercorn and I find this difficult, what about Nick Belfrage and Franco Ziliani? The range of wines in Italy is far more complex. So, what most contributors end up with is '10 of the greatest in a less-than-logical order of preference'. This would worry me in any other book, but readers of *Wine Report* are supposed to be sophisticated enough to understand that this is fascinating enough in its own right.

Best Bargains

Although most will be relatively inexpensive, bargains do not necessarily have to be cheap. It is easier to find bargains at lower prices, just as it is easier to find great wines at higher prices, but it is possible to find relative bargains at any price point. In theory, the greatest, most expensive bordeaux could be the number-one Best Bargain.

Most Exciting or Unusual Finds

This could be an unusually fine wine from what is normally a below-standard region, winery, or grape. It might be an atypical wine, or the first of a certain variety or style. Each wine listed will carry a brief explanation of why it is so exciting and/or unusual.

The 100 Most Exciting Wine Finds

Each contributor was asked to submit four wines for consideration for this section of the book, which meant approximately 160 wines. Only contributors for the emerging or more obscure wine regions were allowed to proffer wines from their Greatest Wines. The rest had to select wines from either their Best Bargains or Most Exciting or Unusual Finds, otherwise this section would be stacked with Pétrus, Krug, Romanée-Conti, the quality of which most readers will be aware of, but few can afford. I then tasted the wines blind, grouped by variety or style, culling almost 40 per cent (which is why I limited myself to just two wines from Champagne and two wines from Alsace). Contributors also provided a tasting note, which is followed by my own comment.

Bordeaux

David Peppercorn MW

When it came to reclassifying *cru bourgeois*, the commission charged with this responsibility pulled no punches. Of 419 *crus* that applied to be classified, only 247 succeeded.

DAVID PEPPERCORN MW

Only nine received the *exceptionnel* accolade, compared with 18 in the last unofficial classification in 1978; 87 were *bourgeois supérieurs* and 151 *crus bourgeois*. The nine *crus bourgeois exceptionnels* were Chasse-Spleen (Moulis), Haut-Marbuzet (St-Estèphe), Labégorce-Zédé (Margaux), de Pez (St-Estèphe), Phélan-Ségur (St-Estèphe), Potensac (Médoc), Poujeaux (Moulis), Les Ormes de Pez (St-Estèphe), and Siran

(Margaux). As expected, Sociando-Mallet did not apply – it has consistently achieved prices higher than many well-known *crus classés* on the secondary market for some years. Nor did Gloria apply. But there were surprises. No AOC Médoc had ever been given an *exceptionnel* grade, so Potensac was an overdue signal that there are excellent wines in this AOC. Then, d'Angludet, which I had improved consistently during the 1990s, was classified only as *supérieur*. There will certainly be several châteaux that will be focusing on an upgrade over the next decade. The classification is due to be revised in 12 years' time. The most public complaint came from Jean-Christophe Mau, who bought Château Preuillac AOC Médoc in 1998. Since the samples to

DAVID PEPPERCORN MW When David Peppercorn went to Bordeaux as a Cambridge undergraduate in September 1953, it was the beginning of a lifelong love affair. He became a Master of Wine in 1962 and was chairman of the Institute of Masters of Wine from 1968 to 1970. It was while David was a buyer for IDV (International Distillers & Vintners) in the 1970s that he started writing about wine, making his debut as an author with the award-winning *Bordeaux* (Faber & Faber, 1982). His *Pocket Guide to the Wines of Bordeaux* (Mitchell Beazley) has been updated every other year since 1986 (2002 being the latest edition). David now spends his time travelling, writing, and lecturing. He is married to Serena Sutcliffe MW.

be submitted were for the years 1999 back to 1994, it was perhaps not a great surprise that his improvements had not had time to make an impact.

Sales gloom

The dominant topic among *négociants* is lack of sales. On the other hand, growers are increasingly excited each time they taste their 2003s. They are hoping for higher prices to match what they perceive as exceptional quality. So, how to square the circle? Just to complicate things, while 2002 Left Bank wines sold reasonably well, the supposedly fashionable Right Bank offerings sold hardly at all. A complicating factor is the strong-euro/weak-dollar situation. While the *Bordelais* were talking about the size of the 2002 price reductions, US importers were noting that most of it had been wiped out by currency movements. Since the 2002 campaign, things have got worse. And some producers are now saying that they 'gave away' the 2002s! Fortunately, the pound sterling, while losing some ground to the euro, has proved more resilient than the dollar.

Parker a no-show

For the first time since his *Wine Advocate* put down a marker for the *primeur* market, the great man did not attend the *primeur* tastings at the end of March 2003, citing security concerns after the outbreak of the Iraq war. Nor did he appear during Vinexpo. Finally he came in September and his preliminary scores were being circulated in October. The main impact was to confirm what the market had already signalled, that the Médoc Firsts were at historically attractive prices. These did rise but, with the campaign over by then, the impact was slight.

Grapevine

- **Low acidity levels in 2003** were the subject of a lot of press chatter. Although blanket authorization was given for reacidification, most producers found their musts well balanced, and acidities, which were low at the time of picking, rose during vinification. Reports of the use of reacidification are few and far between.

- **Jess Jackson,** the head of the US firm Kendall-Jackson, has bought Château Lassègue, a St-Emilion *grand cru* in the commune of St-Hippolyte. The château itself is an 18th-century *chartreuse*. Pierre and Monique Seillan, who have worked for Jackson in California for six years but are originally from the region, will be responsible for managing the 23.5-hectare (ha) vineyard, planted with 50 per cent Merlot, 30 per cent Cabernet Franc, and 20 per cent Cabernet Sauvignon.

- **Gérard Persse** has taken his *premier grand cru classé* Pavie and *grand cru classé* Pavie-Decesse off the Place (the Bordeaux market) and is selling direct. He experienced difficulty in selling his 2001s at the prices demanded, and the situation in 2002 was even worse.

There has long been an argument as to when the new wines should be available for tasting by the trade and journalists. The present system of organizing tastings around 1 April was brought in to try to halt the growing anarchy of journalists demanding earlier and earlier dates to steal a march on competitors.

The problem is that in some vintages – 1998 was a good example – this can favour the Merlot-dominated Right Bank but disadvantage the Cabernet-based Left Bank. My own experience suggests that end March/early April is a period when the wines are changing week by week; one could almost say day by day. Whenever I return in May, I notice how much the wines have evolved and that they are much easier to judge, especially Cabernet-based wines. Probably the best time of all for an accurate global picture is the autumn.

However, any change has to take into account the *primeur* campaign, when the wines are placed on the market. This usually takes place in May, often overspilling into June, and sometimes with a few offers in April. The campaign seems to start more and more slowly, much to the frustration of buyers trying to put offers together.

My preferred solution is to delay the tastings for a month, until the first week of May. Some owners say that this would interfere with the campaign, but I believe that it would help to concentrate minds. What is certain is that the wines would taste better and more consistently across the board.

Marketing fails Bordeaux whites

Bordeaux is now producing the best white wines it has ever seen, yet the expensive publicity campaigns seem to do nothing to promote these delicious, modestly priced wines, and production of dry white wine continues to decline.

Grapevine

- **Jean-Hubert Delon** did not put Château Léoville-Las-Cases 2001 on the market because he believed prices were too low. So, when the 2002s came out at significantly lower prices than the 2001s, he was in something of a quandary. Rumours that the two vintages would be offered in the autumn of 2003 have proved ill founded. Will they now be offered before the 2003 *primeur* campaign begins? So far, Jean-Hubert Delon continues to keep us all guessing.

Advance report on the latest harvest
2003

Unusual and extravagant weather patterns now seem virtually the norm, but 2003 really was special. There were more hours of sunshine, higher temperatures, and less rain than usual. Fortunately, September delivered cool, fine weather, which enabled the final ripening for the reds to take place under perfect conditions. Unlike 2002, this is a vintage that has produced exceptional results across the region, along with water-stress problems on the lighter soils.

Prior to the first tastings in April, the impression is that St-Estèphe is exceptional on the Left Bank, with Pauillac and St-Julien not far behind, but Margaux has suffered from stress problems. Pessac-Léognan looks very good. On the Right Bank, St-Emilion and Pomerol talk of some exceptional wines. Vintages such as 1945, 1947, and 1949 are being mentioned.

Yields on the Right Bank are low; 30 hectolitres per hectare (hl/ha) is considered good. In the Médoc, yields of 40–45 hl/ha are quite usual.

Sauternes is exceptional. The whole harvest was mostly gathered over two weeks, and degrees were even higher than in 1990, giving wonderful concentration that is said to rival 1929.

Updates on the previous five vintages
2002

Vintage rating: *Left Bank: 93, Right Bank: 86*
The year that was very nearly a disaster was saved by a classic high-pressure system in September. The Left Bank Cabernets were able to take full advantage of this and very fine wines resulted in Pauillac, St-Julien, and St-Estèphe. Excellent botrytis in Sauternes also means another fine vintage there. But *coulure* had already compromised much of the old-vine Merlot on the Right Bank, and the weather change was just too late to help the Merlots produce top quality. Those with good levels of Cabernet Franc benefited. The dry whites have an attractive fresh fruitiness.

2001

Vintage rating: *Left Bank: 90, Right Bank: 90*
Now they are in bottle, these wines continue to develop well. They are not 2000s (the exceptions prove the rule), but they do have balance, length,

elegance, and breed — even lovely succulent fruit flavours in the best *crus*. They are variable but clearly superior to the 1999s. The dry whites are very fruity and elegant. Sauternes are outstanding, probably the best year since 1990.

2000

Vintage rating: *Left Bank: 98, Right Bank: 98*

Nature managed to provide what the market had prayed for, with an exceptional spell of weather from 29 July until 10 October. Temperatures were above average and there was very little rain, hence the thick skins, which gave very powerful, deep-coloured wines. Features of the year include consistency across the region and the outstanding character and typicity of the wines. The exceptionally high standard of so many of the wines is greater than in 1990 or 1989. Perhaps the potential of the vintage has been better realized than ever before. Unfortunately, Sauternes missed out, yielding about one-third of its normal crop and a quality that is good but not special.

1999

Vintage rating: *Left Bank: 85, Right Bank: 85*

A combination of rain and heat put a premium on vineyard work. A record crop produced a wide variation in quality. Many St-Emilions and *cru bourgeois* Médocs can now be drunk with pleasure, but some St-Emilions show signs of overextraction. The Pomerols are more consistently enjoyable. There are plenty of medium-weight, stylish Pauillacs, St-Juliens, Margaux, and Pessac-Léognans for drinking in four to five years' time. It was the fourth successive fine Sauternes vintage.

1998

Vintage rating: *Left Bank 89, Right Bank: 95*

These are wines of exceptional colour and power, rich in tannins but with an elegant balance. *En primeur*, the Merlots were impressive and seductive, whereas the Cabernets seemed somewhat austere. Yet the Médocs have developed into classic, well-structured wines that improve on every tasting. Many Pomerols and St-Emilions are outstanding, with the marvellous Cabernet Francs giving them added freshness and elegance. The Merlots are dense-textured and opulent. Very fine, rich Sauternes were made in a similar style to 1996.

GREATEST WINE PRODUCERS

1. Château Lafite
2. Château d'Yquem
3. Château Ausone
4. Château Pétrus
5. Château Margaux
6. Château Léoville-Las-Cases
7. Château Lafleur
8. Château Cheval Blanc
9. Château Laville-Haut-Brion
10. Château Tertre-Rôteboeuf

NEW UP-AND-COMING PRODUCERS

1. Château Barde-Haut, St-Emilion
2. Château Laforge, St-Emilion
3. Château Trianon, St-Emilion
4. Château Ste-Colombe, Côtes de Castillon
5. Château Laussac, Côtes de Castillon
6. Château Lezongars, Premières Côtes de Bordeaux
7. Santayne, St-Emilion

FASTEST-IMPROVING PRODUCERS

1. Château Lafite *Very good from 1982 to 1990, but has moved into another gear as of 1996.*
2. Château Ausone *Some of the greatest wines in Bordeaux since 1998; more sensual, yet just as well structured as before.*
3. Château Berliquet *A sea change since Patrick Valette's consultancy from 1998 onwards.*
4. Château Pontet-Canet *Outstanding wines since 1996.*
5. Château du Tertre *Since 1995, the real potential has at last been realized. The 2000 is spectacular.*
6. Château Duhart-Milon *A great leap forward since 1996.*
7. Château Dauzac *André Lurton's team has worked miracles here since 1996.*
8. Château Rouget *New ownership has transformed this fine Pomerol since 1995.*
9. Château Ferrière *This forgotten Margaux has blossomed since a change of ownership in 1992.*
10. Château Smith-Haut-Lafitte *Both red and white wines have made giant strides in the last decade.*

BEST-VALUE PRODUCERS

1. Château Berliquet, St-Emilion
2. Château Sociando-Mallet, Haut-Médoc
3. Château Pontet-Canet, Pauillac
4. Château Langoa-Barton, St-Julien
5. Château d'Angludet, Margaux
6. Château du Tertre, Margaux
7. Château Beauregard, Pomerol
8. Château Doisy-Daëne, Barsac
9. Château Roc de Cambes, Côtes de Bourg
10. Château La Tour de By, Médoc

GREATEST-QUALITY WINES

1. **Château Pétrus 1990** (€1,330)
2. **Château Lafite 1990** (€212)
3. **Château d'Yquem 1988** (€202)
4. **Château Sociando-Mallet 1989** (€43.50)
5. **Château Tertre-Rôteboeuf 1990** (€90)
6. **Château Pichon-Longueville-Lalande 1985** (€103)
7. **Château Latour 1985** (€176)
8. **Château Léoville-Las-Cases 1988** (€60.50)
9. **Domaine de Chevalier Blanc 1988** (€58)
10. **Château Pichon-Longueville-Baron 1989** (€112)

BEST BARGAINS

1. Château de Pez 1999 (€26)
2. Château de Cruzeau Blanc 2001 (€9)
3. Lafleur de Quinault 1999 (€20)
4. Carruades de Lafite 1996 (€28.50)
5. Château Sociando-Mallet 1997 (€29.50)
6. Château Sigalas-Rabaud 1997 (€28.50)
7. Château Beauregard 1999 (€19)
8. Château Roc de Cambes 1997 (€18)
9. Château Smith-Haut-Lafitte Blanc 2001 (€35)
10. Château Dauzac 2000 (€21)

MOST EXCITING OR UNUSUAL FINDS

1. **Château Lezongars L'Enclos 2000** (€8.75) *A wonderfully seductive, modern claret from a Premières Côtes property transformed by a dedicated English family.*

2. **Château de Roques Sauvignon Blanc 2002** (€6) *Forget about the usual Bordeaux straight Sauvignons, this is fruity and full in the mouth without any 'cattiness'. It is beautifully made. From the Iles family vineyard in the Premières Côtes.*

3. **Château d'Aiguilhe 1999** (€12) *This is Stephan von Neipperg's (of Canon La Gaffelière and La Mondotte fame) new Castillon venture. It combines vivid, crunchy fruit with spicy oak to give pleasurable drinking now and the ability to age.*

4. **Reignac 1999** (€18) *After a decade of hard work, this modest Entre-Deux-Mers vineyard has produced this irresistible old-vine cuvée.*

5. **Château Pillot 2000** (€7) *Bordeaux is not the easiest place to run an organic vineyard, and at present they are few and far between. This modestly priced sample seems to have everything you could reasonably wish for.*

6. **Château Bonnet 2002** (€10) *My cast-iron standby for a quality, dry white wine when travelling in France!*

7. **Château Brown Blanc 2000** (€18) *This well-placed, recently revived Pessac-Léognan vineyard is now producing a white wine to rival some of the big names but at a far more modest price.*

8. **Clos Marsalette Blanc 2001** (€9) *A really delicious Pessac-Léognan from Stephan von Neipperg's first Left Bank venture. It shows his touch with whites is as sure as with reds.*

9. **Château Rochemorin Rouge 1997** (Pessac-Léognan) (€14) *From a vineyard reclaimed from the forest by André Lurton in the mid-1970s. The deliciously seductive fruit and velvety texture show what is possible with mechanical harvesting.*

Grapevine

• Haut-Brion created a new record when picking for the 2003 white wines (Haut-Brion Blanc and Laville-Haut-Brion) began on 12 August, easily their earliest harvest. Yields were 50 per cent above those of 2002.

Bioterrorism threatens the availability of domaine-bottled Burgundy in the USA.

With label approval required for every single wine in every single export order, and myriad different rules and regulations in every single individual state, exporting to the US was complicated enough. The new rules brought in by the Bioterrorism Act are likely to make it so complicated that, except for large volumes of merchant wine, it will not be worth the time and paperwork involved.

CLIVE COATES MW This has implications not only for the growers and brokers on the spot, but also for auction houses and other merchants who export Burgundy to the US from Britain. It should be pointed out, however, that this has nothing to do with any residual anti-French feeling left over from the Iraq war. The act applies as much to wild-boar salami from Tuscany as it does to Nuits-St-Georges.

Law of averages

With a cautiousness that seems almost excessive, the wine *syndicats* in the Côte d'Or (please note this does not cover Chablis, the Côte Chalonnaise, Mâconnais, or Beaujolais) have agreed on a new system, giving individual growers more responsibility for restricting yields. The new benchmark will be the Rendement Moyen Décennal (RMD), or 10-year average. For instance, the permitted maximum yield for village and

CLIVE COATES MW is the author of *Côte d'Or* (Weidenfeld & Nicolson, 1997), which has won various awards, including Le Prix des Arts et des Lettres from the Confrérie de Tastevin, "the first time that a book on wine and a non-Burgundian have been so honoured for 30 years". He is also author–publisher of the award-winning fine-wine monthly magazine *The Vine* (for a free sample issue, contact www.clive-coates.com). Clive's new book, *The Wines of Bordeaux*, is published by Weidenfeld & Nicolson.

premier cru Gevrey-Chambertin is 47 hectolitres per hectare (hl/ha) or 470 over 10 years. Growers will be allowed to vary yields up and down, making it easier for them to adjust to climatic conditions, by a maximum of 3 hl, provided the total does not exceed 470 hl over 10 years.

Split ends

It is a sad but inevitable fact of Burgundian life that very frequently, subsequent to the retirement of Papa, the domaine is split, particularly if there are two or more male children. We have seen this recently at Daniel Rion in Prémeaux, to cite one example. Three more such fractures occurred in 2004: at Lucien Boillot et Fils in Gevrey-Chambertin, Gérard Chavy et Fils in Puligny-Montrachet, and Michel Colin-Déléger et Fils in Chassagne. Prepare yourself for new domaine names: Louis Boillot, Pierre Boillot, Jean-Louis Chavy, Alain Chavy, Philippe Colin, and Bruno Colin.

Grapevine

• **Jacques, Marquis d'Angerville,** has died at the age of 75. Angerville's father, proprietor of a 15-ha estate in Volnay, was one of the pioneers of domaine bottling alongside Henri Gouges and Armand Rousseau before World War II. Jacques was a member of several wine committees and president of the Institut Universitaire de la Vigne et du Vin: a *grand homme du vin*. Burgundy has lost a great man.

• **Faiveley gains a toehold** in the Côte de Beaune south of Corton for the first time. Michel Jaboulet-Vercherre entrusted the farming of several of his family vineyards some years ago to Maison Jadot. One of these, the 2.4-ha monopoly Beaune Clos de L'Ecu, has now been sold to Faiveley.

• **Christophe Perrot-Minot** of Morey-St-Denis continues to expand. He acquired the Vosne-Romanée domaine of Perrin-Rossin in 2001. This will be supplemented with Gevrey-Chambertin, Les Cazetiers, and more Chambolle-Musigny *premier cru* this year.

• **Laurent Ponsot** has bought the 3-ha Chambolle-Musigny domaine of Léni Volpato. As well as Chambolle in

Les Chabiots and Les Feusselottes, Volpato was renowned for his very old-vine Bourgogne Passetoutgrains, one of the few really successful versions of this Gamay-Pinot Noir blend.

• **To add to his 7-ha Mâcon domaine** based in Milly-Lamartine, Dominique Lafon has acquired another 7 ha of Chardonnay vines elsewhere in the Mâcon-Villages. "This now brings me up to a size that is properly economic," he says.

• **Patrick Rion** (Domaine Michelle et Patrick Rion) has bought the lease of the Nuits-St-Georges *premier cru* Clos St-Marc, a vineyard formerly exploited by Bouchard Père & Fils. The deal also enlarges Rion's holding in the neighbouring Les Argillières.

• **In the Prémeaux sector** of the Nuits-St-Georges appellation, 2004 was the first vintage following the surrender of the lease of the *premier cru* Clos de la Maréchale by Faiveley to its owners, the family of Jacques-Frédéric Mugnier of Chambolle-Musigny. This increases the Mugnier domaine from 4 to 11 ha.

SINGING IN THE RAIN

Ten years ago, at the time of the 1993 harvest, the American critic Robert Parker was in Burgundy sampling the 1992s. It rained. Into his 1992 report he dropped a PS: 1993 is a disaster, he pronounced.

As it happened, despite this rain – and it should be noted that very few harvests in Burgundy are rain-free – the 1993 vintage turned out rather well; indeed, it is the best red-wine harvest between 1990 and 1999. Although Parker has been unable to change his mind – he marks the vintage 76 in the Côte de Nuits and 68 in the Côte de Beaune – those on the spot, as well as French and British wine writers, have always had faith in the vintage. A comprehensive 10-year-on tasting in Burgundy in June 2003 confirmed that they were right: the reds are splendid (the best still need keeping), and the top whites are now more interesting than the 1992s.

BIODYNAMIC GROWTH

While on the one hand it is not surprising that Burgundy, of all wine regions perhaps the most individualistic, should possess more biodynamists per head than elsewhere, the fragmentation of the vineyards makes the application of the system very difficult. Nevertheless, the rush to convert to biodynamism is becoming more and more evident.

Pioneered by those such as Jean-Claude Rateau in Beaune, Lalou Bize-Leroy in Vosne-Romanée, Anne-Claude Leflaive in Puligny-Montrachet, Pierre Morey and Dominique Lafon in Meursault, and the Domaine du Comte Armand in Pommard, more and more domaines are doing trials or going fully biodynamic. Rossignol-Trapet has joined cousin Jean-Louis at Domaine Jean & Jean-Louis Trapet in Gevrey-Chambertin. Others include Domaine Charles Thomas in Nuits-St-Georges, Michel Lafarge in Volnay, and the young Emmanuel Giboulot in Beaune.

VIN DE MERDE

Readers of *Wine Report 2004* may remember the court case that resulted from *Lyon Mag*'s quote from wine critic François Mauss that Beaujolais was a *vin de merde* (shit wine). This was brought by the association of Beaujolais producers. A judgment in January 2003 fined the magazine €350,000. This was reduced on appeal to €113,000, when the Beaujolais producers announced that they would not pursue the magazine for the damages awarded but only for their costs (€2,800). *Lyon Mag*, however, is fighting on. The principle of press freedom is at stake. It is appealing to the Minister of Justice in Paris and will take its case to the European Court of Human Rights if necessary.

Fifty years ago, Beaujolais, like its white-wine equivalent Muscadet, was a wine of no pretension, served by the glass or the carafe in countless bars and bistros throughout France. What the French got, delivered in bulk for the most part, was the genuine article: light in weight, fresh and fruity, one-dimensional, cheap.

Enter a man called Georges Duboeuf – a man of ambition. He had the bright idea of investing in a mobile bottling unit. He travelled round sniffing out the best growers and offering them a 'domaine' bottling facility. It was not long before he graduated from being a broker to being a wine merchant. At the same time, the local wine associations came up with the idea of competitive wine tastings. There was one in Villefranche, another in Mâcon. Duboeuf wines won most of the prizes going.

These prize-winning wines, and the rest of the top wines selected by Duboeuf and other local quality wine merchants, such as Trénel and Louis Tête, plus the ever-increasing number of individual domaines, were (and still are) very good wines. They sold for higher prices, which they deserved. But then the prices of other Beaujolais *cru* wines began to rise. It was not long before the price of all Beaujolais had gone up too. The difficulty became that, while a top Moulin à Vent, for instance, merits an €8.50 price tag, most simple Beaujolais is not worth the €4–4.50 being asked for it today. Beaujolais is no longer the cheap quaffing wine it used to be.

Beaujolais produces around 1.4 million hl a year. Of this, 650,000 hl is simple Beaujolais, from the limestone south, not the granitic north. In 2002, around 480,000 hl was made into Beaujolais Nouveau. The trouble with the straitjacket of forcing a wine into becoming something drinkable two months after the harvest is that in a good year it is a waste of good wine, and in a bad vintage the wine is sour and unpleasant anyway. There are few things worse than unripe Gamay. However, Beaujolais hasn't had a bad vintage since 1984, so grape maturity should not be a problem.

The vast majority of ordinary Beaujolais is *nouveau* or almost *nouveau* in style and comes from the cooperatives. While there are some very good co-ops, perhaps too many do not produce enough good wine. If merchants are prepared to bottle and market this dross, they as well as the producers are to blame. They cannot really object if outsiders consider it crap.

2003

The 2003 vintage will be small, uneven, and atypical in character. But there could be some magnificent red wines. As elsewhere in France, the hot, dry summer of 2003 produced an unprecedentedly early harvest. It started on 11 August in the Beaujolais, the 19th in the Côte d'Or, and the 25th in Chablis: the earliest since 1822 (or 1555, according to one report). The white wines, not surprisingly, have a tendency to be heavy and alcoholic. Consumers will probably prefer the greater freshness found in the 2002s. The best of the red wines come from the Côte de Nuits, picked in September after the heat wave had relaxed its grip and after some much-needed rain. These are rich, concentrated, alcoholic wines, with spicy, exotic flavours not often found in Burgundian Pinot Noirs. Acidities are low, in some cases too low.

The first opportunities to sample the 2003s, at the time of the Hospices de Beaune auction in November 2003 and four months later, at the Grands Jours de Bourgogne (March 2004), have confirmed what many feared. The vintage is uneven; flavours resemble more Côte Rôtie than the Côte d'Or, lacking Pinot finesse; and some have the astringent tannins of 1976. Alcohol levels exceed 14 per cent and acidities are low. Nevertheless, according to Roland Masse, manager of the Hospices de Beaune, quoted in November 2003, this is a "great vintage". My advice is to take this opinion with a large pinch of salt.

The harvest, though, is tiny: 35 per cent less than 2002, which itself was smaller than normal. Prices have risen, but not excessively. The market remains slack.

Updates on the previous five vintages

2002

Vintage rating: 85 (Red: 86, White: 85)

The 2002s, now in bottle and on the market, have abundantly lived up to their early promise. The reds are ripe, fresh, and succulent; the whites lush, balanced, and full of fruit. Only at the very top levels does 2002 not quite pull it off: 2002 La Tâche is not 1999 La Tâche. But elsewhere, from generic Bourgogne upwards, 2002 scores highly and prices have remained reasonable. This is a consistent vintage geographically. The wines are medium in structure and will come forward alongside the 2001s, after the 2000s, and before the 1999s, in the case of the top reds.

2001

Vintage rating: *75 (Red: 80, White: 70)*

Unlike 1999, but similar to 2000, the health of the fruit of the average- to large-sized 2001 harvest gave cause for concern, making it vital to sort through and eliminate the unripe and rotten. The vintage is quite good, but variable, for whites. The quality at merchant level differs considerably between their own-domaine wines and those made from bought-in grapes and wines, while the best growers' wines are more than competent, yet lack real backbone, intensity, and definition. These are wines for the short term. They are better − or at least more consistent − in Meursault than Puligny-Montrachet and Chassagne-Montrachet; best of all in Corton-Charlemagne. The red wines are better than the whites, except in Volnay (due to hail). Quality gets progressively better as you journey north.

2000

Vintage rating: *76 (Red: 70, White: 81)*

With the exception of a miserably cold July, 2000 was a warm and sunny year, and this led to an early, average- to large-sized harvest. Just as it began, the weather changed and, though it cleared up later, this had a material effect on the wines. The white grapes could be gathered relatively unscathed and in general are as good as − and in some cellars in Meursault better than − 1999. In contrast to 1999, quality here is better and more consistent than in Puligny or Chassagne. The better wines have depth and grip and will last well. Village wines will be ready from 2005/6, *premiers crus* two years later, *grands crus* from 2009/10.

The reds are soft, juicy, for the most part very pleasant, especially to drink early − along the lines of the whites − but not serious. They get progressively better as one journeys north from Santenay upwards, and are best of all in Gevrey-Chambertin.

1999

Vintage rating: *88 (Red: 90, White: 85)*

A heaven-sent vintage, not only fine quality in both colours, but abundant in quantity. After a fine summer, the harvest was early and the fruit so healthy that in most cases no sorting was necessary. The red wines are fullish and show sumptuous, ripe, pure, concentrated fruit, with ripe tannins and a very long, complex finish – the vintage of the decade. The best will not begin to come round until 2008 or so. Indeed, the vintage as a whole will probably go into its shell in a while and not show very well for a few years. The whites are richer than the 2001s, but in some cases not as elegant. I find them best in Chassagne-Montrachet and most variable in Meursault. Both reds and whites of the Côte Chalonnaise are also fine, but it is 2000 that is the greater vintage in Chablis.

1998

Vintage rating: *78 (Red: 83, White: 73)*

This was a small and very good vintage for red wines, though some have somewhat dry tannins, and the wines are currently a bit adolescent. Gevrey-Chambertin is the most variable of the main villages. Drink the best from 2005 onwards. Frost at Easter reduced the size of the crop, its depredation being most felt in the Meursault *premiers crus*. As a result, this is the most variable village for white wines. These, in any case, do not have the flair of the reds. The majority are now ready.

Grapevine

- **Bouchard Père & Fils** is building a brand-new winery in the Zone Industrielle in Savigny-Lès-Beaune. Neighbours Bichot will take over Bouchard's old (1985) premises opposite the Château de Beaune.

- **Château de Pommard** has been sold. Following talks with the Cathiards of Bordeaux's Château Smith-Haut-Lafitte, which led nowhere, Jean-Louis Laplanche, owner of this 21-ha estate, has sold it to Maurice Giraud, a property developer. Giraud has plans to restore the château and renovate the *cuverie*. Laplanche remains as wine adviser.

- **In the short time** since Nicolas Potel set up on his own, following the death of his father Gérard in 1997 and the sale of the family's Pousse d'Or domaine, he has rapidly created a high reputation for his *négociant* wines. But he overbought. Financial rescue has come in the form of a tie-up with Cottin Frères, proprietors of Nuits-St-Georges-based merchants Labouré-Roi. Potel retains freedom over his choice of wines and is hoping to convert more and more of his purchases into fruit rather than wine over the next few years.

GREATEST WINE PRODUCERS

1. Domaine de la Romanée-Conti
2. Domaine Leroy
3. Domaine Comte Georges de Vogüé
4. Domaine Armand Rousseau
5. Domaine des Comtes Lafon
6. Domaine Anne Gros
7. Domaine Jean Grivot
8. Maison Louis Jadot
9. Domaine Leflaive
10. Domaine Ramonet

FASTEST-IMPROVING PRODUCERS

1. Maison Nicolas Potel
2. Domaine Bertagna
3. Chanson Père & Fils
4. Domaine Prince Florent de Mérode
5. Domaine Jean & Jean-Louis Trapet
6. Domaine Lucien Jacob
7. Domaine Gilles Remoriquet
8. Domaine Alain Michelot
9. Domaine Hervé & Cyprien Arlaud
10. Domaine Gilles Bouton

NEW UP-AND-COMING PRODUCERS

1. Domaine Bruno Lorenzon
2. Domaine Saint-Jacques
3. Domaine Arnaud Ente
4. Domaine David Duband
5. Domaine Michèle & Patrice Rion
6. Domaine de la Vougeraie
7. Domaine du Vicomte Liger-Belair
8. Domaine Vincent Dancer
9. Domaine François & Vincent Jouard
10. Domaine Martelet de Cherisey

BEST-VALUE PRODUCERS

1. Maison Jadot, Beaune, for its Moulin-à-Vent, Château des Jacques
2. Domaine Saumaize-Michelin
3. Domaine Mathias
4. Domaine Bruno Lorenzon
5. Domaine Saint-Jacques
6. Domaine A & P Villaine
7. Domaine Lucien Muzard & Fils
8. Domaine Vincent Girardin, for his Santenay Rouge and Blanc
9. Domaine Jean-Marc Pavelot
10. Domaine Marc Colin & Fils

GREATEST-QUALITY WINES

For keeping:

1. **La Tâche 1999** Domaine de la Romanée-Conti (€115)
2. **Richebourg 1999** Domaine Anne Gros (€110)
3. **Charmes-Chambertin 1999** Domaine Denis Bachelet (€50)
4. **Meursault Perrières 2000** Domaine Jean-François Coche-Dury (€45)
5. **Chevalier-Montrachet La Cabotte 2000** Maison Bouchard Père & Fils (€55)

For drinking:

1. **Chambertin 1990** Domaine Armand Rousseau (€110)
2. **Richebourg 1990** Domaine Jean Gros (€115)
3. **Clos de Vougeot 1985** Domaine Jean Gros (€80)
4. **Chassagne-Montrachet Grandes Ruchottes (white) 1995** Domaine Ramonet (€60)
5. **Meursault Perrières 1995** Domaine des Comtes Lafon (€75)

BEST BARGAINS

1. **Mercurey Rouge Les Champs Martin Cuvée Caroline 1999** Domaine Bruno Lorenzon (€16)
2. **Rully Blanc Clos Saint-Jacques 2002** Domaine Saint-Jacques (€10)
3. **Rully Blanc Les Pucelles 2002** Domaine Jacquesson (€12)
4. **Savigny-Lès-Beaune La Dominode 1999** Domaine Jean-Marc Pavelot (€15)
5. **Chablis Fourchaume Vieilles Vignes 2000** Domaine Gérard Tremblay Domaine des Iles (€10.50)
6. **Mâcon La Roche Vineuse Vieilles Vignes 2001** Domaine Olivier Merlin (€8.40)
7. **Saint-Aubin Les Charmes (white) 2002** Domaine Marc Colin & Fils (€15)
8. **Pommard Clos des Boucherottes 2002** Domaine Coste-Caumartin (€19)
9. **Maranges Clos Poussots 2002** Domaine Contat-Grangé (€9.90)
10. **Santenay Les Charmes Dessus (red) 2002** Domaine Claude Nouveau (€11)

MOST EXCITING OR UNUSUAL FINDS

1. **Bourgogne Blanc Cuvée Oligocène 2002** Domaine Patrick Javillier (€8) *This is a generic wine from soil exactly the same as that found in Meursault. And it tastes like it, too.*
2. **Irancy Vieilles Vignes 2002** Domaine Anita, Stéphanie & Jean-Pierre Colinot (€9.50) *Irancy lies southeast of Auxerre and produces the best red wines of the Côte Auxerroise. This is a delicious vibrant example of Pinot Noir.*
3. **Maranges Clos de la Boutière Cuvée Vieilles Vignes 2001** Domaine Edmond Monnot (€9.10) *An intensely flavoured wine from the very bottom of the Côte d'Or.*
4. **Bourgogne Rouge 2002** Domaine Michel Lafarge (€7.50) *This is from vines just 10 m (33 ft) from AOC Volnay and is, not unexpectedly, rather better than the vast majority of village wines.*
5. **Bourgogne Rouge 2002** Domaine Ghislaine Barthod (€7.50) *From soil similar to that of Chambolle-Musigny, but on the wrong side of the road.*
6. **Marsannay Rosé 2002** Domaine Bruno Clair (€10) *Pinot Noir makes lovely rosé. This is the best example.*
7. **Morgon Côte de Py 2001** Domaine Louis-Claude Desvignes (€8) *Proper Beaujolais (not the wishy-washy nouveau stuff) from the best grower in the most distinctive cru in the region.*
8. **Nuits-St-Georges Clos de L'Arlot Blanc 2002** Domaine de l'Arlot (€32) *A rare white wine from the Côte de Nuits. It has little to do with a Meursault. Enjoy its individuality.*
9. **Santenay Blanc Les Hâtes 2002** Domaine René Lequin-Colin (€11.50) *A delicious plump honeysuckle-flavoured wine from a village better known for its red wines.*
10. **Morey-St-Denis Blanc Les Monts-Luisants 2002** Domaine Ponsot (€30) *Largely from very old Aligoté, and no malolactic. Unique!*

Champagne

Tom Stevenson

Champagne houses reneged on their promise to stop trading in *sur lattes* among themselves.

TOM STEVENSON

According to the chairman of one house, the demand for *sur lattes* was so strong in the first two months of 2004 that the price rose by 7 per cent over that period to peak at €8.50, despite a supposed ban being implemented on 1 January 2004. When each bottle costs, on average, €1.50 to disgorge, *dosage*, label, and case up, and some champagnes were being retailed for less than €10 at the time, it is clear that these *sur lattes* are not being sold as buyer's own-brands or supermarket fantasy labels. Only *grandes marques* have sufficient premium to make a profit on such expensive *sur lattes*. Yet, in March 2003, as revealed in *Wine Report 2004*, the Union des Maisons de Champagne (UMC) voted "unanimously to ban all *sur lattes* transactions among *négociants* as from 1 January 2004".

If the UMC vote was unanimous, why would any of its members wait for a signature on a piece of paper? Why not just keep their word? As the head of one house told me: "The houses agreed for the regulation to be promoted, but as long as it is not in force, they're free to do as they please. It's like cheating on your fiancée before marriage: it is not adultery, just indecent. You should know about *Champenois* morality by now...."

TOM STEVENSON has specialized in champagne for 25 years. *Champagne* (Sotheby's Publications, 1986) was the first wine book to win four awards, and it quickly established Tom's credentials as a leading expert in this field. In 1998, his *Christie's World Encyclopedia of Champagne & Sparkling Wine* (Absolute Press, revised 2003) made history by being the only wine book ever to warrant a leader in any national newspaper (*The Guardian*), when it published a 17th-century document proving beyond doubt that the English used a second fermentation to convert various wines, including still champagne, into sparkling wines at least six years before Dom Pérignon even set foot in the Abbey of Hautvillers. Tom's annual Champagne Masterclass for Christie's is always a sellout.

Free-market threat

The Syndicat Général des Vignerons (SGV) engaged itself in a hectic schedule of meetings to brainwash growers on an almost daily basis during the first three months of 2004. Philippe Feneuil, *président* of the SGV, and Patrick le Brun, his heir apparent, attempted to sell the flawed proposals of the Cap 2004 Commission. This working party was set up to find a solution to Champagne's perennial problem of supply and demand (see Opinion). With sales of almost 300 million bottles and a maximum sustainable yield for a fully planted Champagne region of 310 million, there is very little room to increase sales. Simply to maintain these sales, the houses, which own just 12 per cent of the vineyards yet sell 70 per cent of all champagne, need to purchase two-thirds of the grapes that growers harvest every year. Until 1989, an interprofessional contract strictly regulated this by rationing each house with a proportion of grapes based on its previous year's sales, as well as dictating the price per kilo that must be paid. But the market was liberalized in 1990, and the Bricout–Delbeck affair (see last year's *Wine Report*) was seen, by some, as a manifestation of the excesses of a free market.

Grapevine

- *Vins sur lattes* **will act** as a 'safety valve' for houses and growers who opt for the cartel's closed market, according to Patrick le Brun, who should be president of the SGV by the time this edition of *Wine Report* is published.

- **Laurent-Perrier** has taken over the Château Malakoff group, which includes Beaumet, Oudinot, and Jeanmaire, plus 50 hectares (ha) valued at between €500,000 and €700,000 per hectare. The Michelin-starred La Briqueterie was part of the deal, and there is much discussion in-house about whether this should remain or be sold on.

- **The Lombard family** has sold Cazanove to the privately owned Rapeneau group (GH Martell, Mansard-Baillet, Château de Bligny). Well-placed sources say losses from *sur lattes* deals with Bricout/Delbeck forced the sale.

- **The low-profile** but unstoppable privately owned Alain Thienot group (which includes Joseph Perrier and Marie Stuart, as well as its eponymous brand) took over Malard (George Goulet, Gobillard, and Malard) and moved more into the limelight by purchasing Canard-Duchêne from LVMH. Jean-Louis Malard remains in day-to-day control of his old company in addition to being made chairman of Canard-Duchêne.

- **So many rumours** surround the collapse of Daniel Prin (Binet) that it is difficult to discern the truth. Some say that Binet had debts running to millions of euros and this was the precursor of Bricout's trouble, while others claim that Bricout owed Prin a lot of money. Even more intriguing is the rumour that Marie Le Pen, the daughter of you-know-who, would take over Binet. It is said that this rumour was started by the National Front party itself.

- **Taittinger's new Prelude cuvée** is a non-vintage blend of exclusively *grand cru* wines from Avize and Le Mesnil-sur-Oger for 50 per cent Chardonnay, and Bouzy and Ambonnay for 50 per cent Pinot Noir.

The SGV wanted a return of the interprofessional contract, but the EU no longer permitted such restrictive practices and has also outlawed price fixing, so Cap 2004 was set up to seek an EU-friendly solution. This involved forming a non-profit *groupement de producteurs* in which growers would pledge an agreed proportion of their crop. They would then contract with the houses who had agreed to buy only from the *groupement* at a fixed price. Those growers who decided not to supply the *groupement* would be able to sell only to houses that are not contracted to purchase from the *groupement*. At SGV meetings throughout the region, growers were given the impression that this insidious cartel was a done deal and that they were either in or out. Under such pressure, the show of hands, it is said, was often more than the requisite 80 per cent minimum, but many growers changed their minds in the following days, as they discussed the implications with one another.

There was a lot of public posturing by Feneuil and Yves Bénard, *président* of the UMC, who were billed as some sort of dynamic duo on a mission to rescue Champagne, but although Bénard publicly supported

Grapevine

• **Philipponnat** has sold the old Abel Lepitre building, and is now building new facilities in Mareuil-sur-Aÿ, which will be operational for the 2004 harvest. Charles Philipponnat explained: "This will enable us to carry out all vintage operations within an 8-km (5-mile) radius of our vineyards, in one single location, much to my relief. It is a big step towards ever-increased control of quality. The *cuverie* will also include space for up to 500 barrels. Clos des Goisses is already 35–45 per cent wood and will stay that way; vintages are 15–20 per cent wood and will increase to about 30–35 per cent; non-vintage is 5–10 per cent and will increase to 20–25 per cent. We shall ferment, then keep reserve wines in all barrels, thus wooding up to 2,000 hectolitres."

• **Champagne has just requested** INAO to study whether its vineyards should be expanded. The idea is not to expand outwards, but to see whether any of the holes in the lacework of vineyards that currently comprise AOC Champagne deserve to

be planted. Some villages simply did not apply for AOC status because none of their inhabitants was interested in viticulture at the time. Yet some of these villages have slopes that are intrinsically superior to those of their AOC-classified neighbours. The expansion of AOC Champagne is therefore a very good question, but now is the wrong time to ask it. This question should have been addressed 10 years ago, when there was a slump in sales and the *Champenois* could not be accused of cynically expanding the AOC to fulfil the demands of a growing market. The findings of this special INAO commission will not be known until 2006/7.

• **Young Dominique Demarville** has almost single-handedly rescued the quality and reputation of Mumm since becoming *chef de caves* in 1998 (and being primarily responsible for making the wines since 1996). He has been justly rewarded by a promotion to wines and vines director, responsible for viticulture and vinification at both Mumm and Perrier-Jouët.

Cap 2004, I do not think he ever thought it stood a cat in hell's chance of taking off. He was playing the diplomat because he knew that, whatever happened, from this proposal to a completely free market, the future of Champagne would depend on a good working relationship with the growers. Thus he had to appear to go the extra mile. I am not sure that even Feneuil believed it could work. Was it a coincidence that the hectic schedule of village meetings occurred just before he was to retire from the SGV to take up politics? The Cap 2004 Commission definitely believed in it but does not understand that a minority free market cannot live side by side with a majority cartel. The free price would soar, making it impossible for small and medium-sized houses outside the cartel to compete. One by one they would fall by the wayside, to be picked up and asset-stripped by the bigger brands. Perhaps this was part of the SGV's strategy and the reason why the LVMH and Vranken groups were thought to be solidly behind Cap 2004. But it would require a unanimous vote by the UMC, including those who would be left outside the cartel, which would have been suicidal, hence Bénard's scepticism.

Grapevine

• **Jean-Marc Pottiez** gets the last laugh. Pottiez was head-hunted by Nicolas Feuillatte in 1994 and almost quadrupled sales in seven years, but the growers thanked him by giving him the boot. Apparently he had spent too much of their money in the process. How sweet then that he should land the top job at Jacquart, which used to be a bigger brand than Feuillatte, and Pottiez will take great delight in making sure it regains the lead.

• **New winemakers appointed** include Michel Fauconnet, who has been Alain Terrier's deputy at Laurent-Perrier for the last 20 years and took over as chef de caves in early 2004. Although Terrier has stepped down from this post, he remains in overall charge of grape supplies for the group and has been promoted to Laurent-Perrier's board of directors. He has also been made chairman of the recently acquired Château Malakoff. Jean-François Barrot has retired from the post of chef de caves at Ruinart, to be replaced by Jean-Philippe Moulin, formerly the technical

director at Mumm and Perrier-Jouët. Odillon de Varenne has moved from Deutz to Henriot, while Michel Davesne, who made his name producing excellent vintages at Champagne Palmer, took his place as chef de caves at Deutz.

• **Jacquesson** turned the NV concept on its head when it replaced its old non-vintaged Perfection Brut with Cuvée No. 728, which aims to make the "best possible Champagne" each year, rather than maintain a consistency of style. The 728 is 2000-based, thus the 2001-based will be 729 and so on. It would have been much simpler had they started with Cuvée 2000, 200, 00, or suchlike. The first few years might be easy for devotees to work out, but they will soon have to get out a calculator to add 1,272 (if they can remember) to the cuvée number to work out the base year.

• **Piper-Heidsieck** has launched no fewer than four new wines: Brut Divin (Chardonnay), Rosé Sauvage (low dosage), Cuvée Sublime (demi-sec), and an NV version of its classic Cuvée Rare.

The reason champagne sales have a cyclical history, going from boom to bust and back to boom again, is due partly to achieving worldwide fame when the Industrial Revolution created new money, and partly to the intrinsic imbalance of vineyard ownership. The pop of a champagne cork and liveliness of its bubbles captured the imagination of the nouveau riche and suited their celebratory lives. They quickly made champagne the most chic drink in London, Paris, and New York, doubling its sales. Ever since, champagne has been inextricably linked to success, thus extremely sensitive to the mood of consumers. This makes fluctuations in sales inevitable, and any well-organized industry could cope with that (as champagne has been doing by emphasizing that it is a wine first, thus building up more regular consumption). But these fluctuations will always be a factor, and the imbalance of vineyard ownership creates tensions in supply and demand that convert what would otherwise be relatively harmless fluctuations into damaging booms and busts.

It should be possible for houses to buy vineyards directly. In theory, there is nothing stopping anyone buying any land in France, but in practice, Champagne's stricter adherence to certain controls ensures that the growers maintain their 88 per cent ownership of the vineyards, despite selling only 20 per cent (30 per cent including cooperative sales) of all champagne. The only way for a house to acquire more vineyards is to take over ailing companies that owned land prior to the Contrôle des Structures, which forbids any firm from farming more than 15 ha, owned and rented. Such restrictions in a supposedly free country are astonishing, and for Champagne they have encouraged the industry's polarization, since fewer companies attempt to grab a larger share of the same slice of the cake.

There is nothing wrong, and everything right, with a house having the right to buy or rent vineyards, but as long as they are prevented from doing so, the more pressure will be placed on supply and demand at the most crucial moments. So deep rooted is the *Champenois* attachment to their *patrimoine* that few families would consider relinquishing ownership, but I cannot imagine the *Champenois* ever allowing those who would sell to do so. Thus the imbalance in ownership will remain and the cycle from boom to bust will continue, and the *Champenois* must now realize there is no one else to blame but themselves.

2003

Picking commenced on 25 August (21st in the Aube), thanks to the pan-European heat wave – the earliest Champagne harvest since at least 1822, when records began. And with 50 per cent of the potential crop destroyed by spring frosts, it was also the smallest harvest since 1981. The second crop, from buds that developed after the frost, was substantial. Although this is a common phenomenon in Champagne, the second crop rarely ripens – and almost never on a region-wide scale. It is known in *Champenois* dialect as the *bouvreu* ("for the birds"). I have known only two ripe second crops – in 1989 and, to a lesser degree, 1990 – but neither was of the scale of 2003. Although the variation in quality was noticeable, the cream of the second crop was often just as ripe as the first harvest, but with distinctly superior acidity.

The grapes were exceptionally clean (Champagne normally being prone to rain at harvest time and thus a high incidence of rot) and, as might be expected, very ripe (10.6 per cent on average), but there were concerns over low acidity and disproportionately high pH readings. In fact, the pH readings were the worst ever. Generally, the pH for champagne should not be more than 3.0-something and, providing the grapes are physiologically ripe, the lower the number the better. But whereas the average for each of the last three decades has been good, and going in the right direction – downwards (3.07 in the 1970s, 3.06 in the 1980s, and 3.04 in the 1990s) – the last five years have averaged a worrying 3.13, with 2003 hitting no less than 3.28, with some wines as high as 3.7! However, the recent trend to high average levels is far more disturbing than individual wines of often higher pH because, as the best wines of Champagne's ripest, low-acid vintages (1976, 1959, 1947, and 1929) have demonstrated, if the high pH is in harmony with all the other properties in a base wine, the potential exists for a champagne of extraordinary quality. Having tasted a number of 2003 *vins clairs*, it is obvious that some truly special champagnes will be produced, albeit mixed in with a motley crew of the weird and ugly. The *vins clairs* of Jacquesson best reflected 2003's sumptuous richness, while Krug and Roederer displayed exceptional acidity for the year. Considering the small size of the crop and proportionately greater scarcity of Chardonnay, it is understandable that a number of houses might not release a standard vintage, but any producer who has not done his or her best to make a small volume of pure 2003, even if for in-house use only, will live to regret it. Especially if 2003 is an indication of what Champagne might expect on a more regular basis from global warming and they have no library bottles to learn from.

Updates on the previous five vintages

2002

Vintage rating: *85–90*

This is without doubt a vintage year and a very special one too, marked by the *passerillage* that reduced the crop in some vineyards by up to 40 per cent and endowed the wines with the highest natural alcohol level since 1990 (which itself was the highest since 1959). It is definitely a Pinot Noir year, with Aÿ-Champagne the most successful village. There are some fine Chardonnays, but in general they are less impressively structured and lack acidity. Not that the Pinot Noirs are overblessed with acidity. Low acidity is a key feature of this vintage, with *vins clairs* tasting much softer than their analyses would have us believe.

2001

Vintage rating: *35*

Dilute, insipid, and unripe. Anyone who declares this vintage needs their head testing.

2000

Vintage rating: *80*

Virtually vintage-quality ripeness, but more of a good non-vintage year. However, there are a lot of *Champenois* who believe that 2000 is a magical number, so we can expect more declarations from this year than it really deserves. Even so, good, even great, champagne can be made in almost any year if the selection is strict enough, and with so many 2000s likely to be marketed, there should be plenty of good bottles to pick from. Some special wines, like Clos des Goisses and Jacquesson Dizy 1er Cru Corne Bautray, will be great.

1999

Vintage rating: *80*

Vintage-quality ripeness but the worst acidity and pH levels Champagne has seen for a couple of decades. Some very good champagnes will no doubt be made through strict selection, but with fewer producers likely to declare, the number will probably be much lower than for 2000. Chanoine's new vintaged Tsarine Rosé and Drappier's Grande Sendrée are the only 1999s with true finesse encountered so far.

1998

Vintage rating: *85*

The 1998s and 1997s are not dissimilar to the 1993s and 1992s respectively, which means this vintage is in theory not quite as good as 1997. But although 1993 was not as good as 1992 on paper, the former actually produced significantly more superior champagnes than the latter, so who knows which way 1998 will swing? Indeed, some of the 1998s are already quite impressive, and a number of *Champenois* winemakers rate this vintage above the 1997s.

GREATEST WINE PRODUCERS

1. Krug
2. Pol Roger
3. Billecart-Salmon
4. Louis Roederer
5. Bollinger
6. Deutz
7. Jacquesson
8. Gosset
9. Pierre Gimonnet
10. Vilmart

FASTEST-IMPROVING PRODUCERS

1. Mumm
2. Bollinger
3. Duval-Leroy
4. Bruno Paillard
5. Pannier
6. Mailly Grand Cru
7. Philipponnat
8. Vve Devaux
9. Moët & Chandon
10. Vilmart

NEW UP-AND-COMING PRODUCERS

1. Henri Giraud
2. Serge Mathieu
3. Fluteau
4. Bruno Paillard
5. Audoin de Dampierre
6. Chanoine's Tsarine range

BEST-VALUE PRODUCERS

1. Charles Heidsieck
2. Serge Mathieu
3. Henri Mandois
4. Duval-Leroy
5. Alfred Gratien
6. Bruno Paillard
7. Lanson
8. Louis Roederer
9. Drappier
10. Piper-Heidsieck

GREVINE-PEUR SENSE

- **Billecart-Salmon's** new single-vineyard champagne, Le Clos Saint-Hilaire, was spoiled only by its lack of *dosage*. I am surprised it is still not understood in some quarters that not only does champagne need at least a little sugar for the Maillard reactions (which contribute to the complex aromas produced after disgorgement), but it is also essential for ageing with grace and finesse. Drink on purchase; do not age.

- **Paul Vranken** surprised his critics by selling more Pommery in 2003 without dropping the price. The consensus was that, in order to meet bank repayments for the purchase of Pommery, he would have to cut prices, but sales increased 14.2 per cent in volume, compared to 18.2 per cent in value.

GREATEST-QUALITY WINES

1. **Vieilles Vignes Françaises 1996** Bollinger (€325)
2. **Dom Pérignon 1996** Moët & Chandon (€95)
3. **Cristal Rosé 1996** Louis Roederer (€300)
4. **Brut Vintage 1988** Krug (€150)
5. **Cristal 1996** Louis Roederer (€150)
6. **Cristal 1997** Louis Roederer (€150)
7. **Noble Cuvée Blanc de Blancs 1996** Lanson (€80)
8. **Gold Label 1996** Lanson (€27.50)
9. **Comte de Champagne 1996** Taittinger (€100)
10. **Amour de Deutz Blanc de Blancs 1997** Deutz (€95)

BEST BARGAINS

1. **Gold Label 1996** Lanson (€27.50)
2. **Cuvée Rare NV** Piper-Heidsieck (€35)
3. **Mis en Cave 1998 NV** Charles Heidsieck (€25)
4. **Brut Millésime Grand Cru 1996** Pommery (€25)
5. **Brut Millésime 1996** Guy Cadel (€14.30)
6. **Brut Rosé 1997** Deutz (€50)
7. **Tsarine Rosé 1999** Chanoine (€29.95)
8. **Cuvée Victor Mandois 1998** Henri Mandois (€19)
9. **Millésime 1996** Collard-Chardelle (€17.10)
10. **Blanc de Blancs 1998** Louis Roederer (€55)

MOST EXCITING OR UNUSUAL FINDS

1. **Gold Label 1996** Lanson (€27.50) *Like gargling with razor blades, this is the most definitive and the best-value 1996 on the market.*
2. **Joyau de Chardonnay 1989** Boizel (€49) *Rare to find such mature blanc de blancs commercially available, especially when it is impeccably preserved.*
3. **Millésime 1996** Collard-Chardelle (€17.10) *A stunning find from hitherto unknown grower, not least because it has extraordinarily rich, huge flavours and massive acids for its 50 per cent Meunier content (plus 25/25 Chardonnay/ Pinot Noir). Great potential complexity, and it has the focus and finesse, too.*
4. **Brut Cuvée No. 728 NV** Jacquesson (€25) *Guaranteed not to be consistent! See Grapevine, p.33.*
5. **Réserve Brut NV** Michel Loriot (€12.50) *Not up to Jacquesson's Le Clos 1998 but superior to its Le Clos 2000, this is the best pure Meunier champagne I have tasted in the past 12 months.*
6. **Brut Sélection NV** Pehu-Simonet (€12.50) *The huge mouthful of fruit is the result of being vinified in used – not new – oak.*
7. **Rosé Sauvage NV** Piper-Heidsieck (€20) *A riot of fruit with a luminous pink colour!*
8. **Grand Siècle Alexandra Brut Rosé 1997** Laurent-Perrier (€220) *Why jump from 1990 to 1997? Because Alain Terrier made far too much 1990 and it has only just sold out. This might not be as great a vintage in general terms, but this cuvée is superior to the 1990 Alexandra and has a better-balanced dosage.*
9. **Divin Blanc de Blancs NV** Piper-Heidsieck (€25) *Not many pure Chardonnay champagnes are fruity guzzlers that are ready to drink as soon as they hit the shelf, but Piper's first blanc de blancs is precisely that.*
10. **Brut Blanc de Blancs NV** Petit-Camusat (€12.50) *A pure Pinot Blanc rarity.*

It's official: Alsace wines are sweet! The hot debate in *Wine Report 2004* was the sweetness of Alsace wines and the difficulty that consumers face when trying to discern whether a wine is dry, particularly a *grand cru*.

TOM STEVENSON

The simple solution was to introduce an obligatory dry wine designation. The very worst thing that could have been done was to emphasize the sweetness factor, yet that is precisely what has been done. All wines with a minimum residual sugar of 12 grams per litre (9 g/l for Riesling) must now be labelled *moelleux*. If a wine has more than 6 g/l of total acidity, the minimum residual sugar rises to 18 g/l. The Sec designation is permitted but not obligatory. What difference does it make? Defining minimum residual sugar content for a sweet designation does not mean that all those not qualifying are in fact dry, so the introduction of *moelleux* has reduced, not solved, the problem. From a global perspective, emphasizing which wines are sweet, rather than dry, further erodes the traditional reputation of Alsace wine.

Côte de Rouffach rules, okay!

Clause 10 of the new French labelling laws requires all village and other local designations to be included in the original AOC edict and to adhere to restrictive criteria agreed with INAO (Institut National des Appellations d'Origine). For the Côte de Rouffach, which was established by Jean-Claude Rieflé in 1988, this will mean:

TOM STEVENSON specializes in champagne but he is equally passionate about Alsace. In 1987 he was elected a *confrère oenophile* of the Confrérie Saint Etienne, when he was the sole person to correctly identify a 50-year-old wine made from Sylvaner. In 1994, his 600-page tome *The Wines of Alsace* (Faber & Faber, 1993) won the Veuve Clicquot Book of the Year award in the United States.

- Located on 430 hectares (ha) in the villages of Pfaffenheim, Rouffach, and Westhalten (this represents 40 per cent of the total AOC Alsace land within these three villages, and encompasses the *grands crus* of Vorbourg and Steinert);
- Delimited on *lieux-dits* single vineyards;
- Only Riesling, Gewurztraminer, Pinot Gris, Pinot Noir, or Muscat allowed;
- Maximum yield of 72 hectolitres per hectare (whites), 65 hl/ha (reds);
- Higher natural potential alcohol;
- No Vendange Tardive (VT) or Sélection de Grains Nobles (SGN) allowed.

A few years ago, there were proposals for more than 70 village or local appellations, but this had dropped to just 34 by the deadline in February 2004. Just one-third of these had prepared dossiers good enough to show to INAO. It is expected that the appellations should know by the summer of 2004 whether they are accepted, but at the time of writing the favourites were Rouge d'Ottrott, Riesling de Wolxheim, Vallée Noble, and, of course, Côte de Rouffach.

Grapevine

- **Over 10,000** *lieux-dits* could be allowed under new labelling regulations that allow all individually named vineyards registered in each village *cadastre* to be indicated an AOC wine, without any superior production criteria. This has caused problems in Alsace because such wines would cohabit with *lieux-dits* adhering to stricter rules under the so-called *appellation intermédiaire* between AOC Alsace and AOC Alsace Grand Cru. All clouds have silver linings, and this one is the threat of 10,000 *lieux-dits*, which has kick-started renewed interest in resolving the *appellation intermédiaire* (the Alsace Hierarchy project), an issue that had effectively been put on the back burner. At least the matter will now be resolved once and for all.

- **Sylvaner is now allowed** full *grand cru* status if grown on the Grand Cru Zotzenberg in Mittelbergheim.

- **An assemblage of different varieties** has been granted *grand cru* status for the Grand Cru Altenberg de Bergheim, although Jean-Michel Deiss of Domaine Marcel Deiss had already

been selling such wine in anticipation of it becoming legal.

- **At long last,** the growers of Ammerschwihr's Kaefferkopf have been given the go-ahead for *grand cru* application, providing they restrict the vineyards to be classified to a much smaller area than that delimited by tribunal in 1932. The sticking point has always been that the tribunal had recognized the historical tradition of many growers using two or more of the officially designated varieties (Gewurztraminer, Riesling, Muscat, Pinot Gris, and Pinot Blanc) and the AOC Alsace Grand Cru regulations stipulated pure varietal wines only (not including Pinot Blanc). However, Deiss proved to be an irresistible force in the fight for allowing a blend of varieties for Altenberg de Bergheim, and when INAO caved in, they could no longer say no to Kaefferkopf.

- **Diminishing importance** of the grape variety was officially confirmed by its reduction in size on the label to half that of the appellation text as from the 2004 harvest.

If the trade and media are to understand the *grands crus*, then CIVA (Conseil Interprofessionnel des Vins d'Alsace) must initiate the process. At annual tastings in major export markets, the *grand cru* wines are to be found, higgledy-piggledy, by this variety and that on a producer-by-producer basis. The result is pandemonium. The only way to discern the differences between *grands crus* is to focus on one grape variety at a time, and since Riesling is the most sensitive to *terroir*, CIVA should start with that. Sugar masks the finer differences, so no SGN, no VT, and none of the sweeter *grands crus*. Just dry and off-dry styles, set up as a stand-alone tasting, *grand cru* by *grand cru*, with the wines lined up in order of residual sweetness, even though there should not be any that are actually sweet. The next year, Muscat, followed by Tokay-Pinot Gris, and finally Gewurztraminer, then back to Riesling and so on. This should have started long ago, but better late than never.

Ban residual sugar in chaptalized wine

If a wine has to be chaptalized, it should be dry (residual sugar of less than 5 g/l would be a generous limit). This would not prevent anyone from selling wine with residual sweetness, but any such sweetness should be the natural product of the grapes harvested. If this is not acted on, it will not be because the producers do not want it. Everyone I spoke to about this proposal told me it was both necessary and workable.

Grapevine

• **The 7th World Riesling Competition** was held in Strasbourg on 9 February 2004. Only two Premier Gold Medals were presented (Grand Cru Pfersigberg 2002 Emile Beyer and Grand Cru Steinert 2002 Pierre Zink).

• **Rumours that Kuentz-Bas** was up for sale were correct, sadly, but it was JB Adam that took over, rather than a cooperative or Pierre Sparr. The wines have been going downhill for a while, but those Kuentz-Bas presented at the Journées 2003 des Grands Crus d'Alsace in November 2003 were so bad that they can only get better.

• **Who's who?** With so many producers bearing the same surname, it is important to note when some change, since even a knowledgeable consumer could easily confuse them for a new or different producer. These changes include Robert Baltzinger of Gertwiller, which is now Samuel Baltzinger; François Uhl of Epfig, which is now EARL Du Hertenstein; François Kieffer et Fils of Itterswiller, which is now François et Vincent Kieffer; GAEC Maetz of Rosheim, which is now Carine et Materne Maetz; and Martine et Jean Rapp of Dorlisheim, which is now Jean et Guillaume Rapp.

2003

The Vosges are usually Alsace's blessing, bleeding off the rain and rendering its sheltered vineyards drier and sunnier than almost anywhere else in France. In 2003, however, the Vosges merely exacerbated the heat wave and drought experienced elsewhere. According to CIVA, it was the hottest summer since 1540, and they really do have records going back that far. Rainfall was virtually nonexistent (11.4 cm between May and September) and temperatures were relentlessly hot – at one point exceeding 40°C for almost two weeks continuously. There is no doubt, therefore, that 2003 was an exceptional and extraordinary vintage, but apart from Pinot Noir and a handful of anomalies, the quality will be neither exceptional nor extraordinary. Picking started on 25 August for Crémant d'Alsace, 8 September for AOC Alsace and AOC Grand Cru, and 15 September for VT and SGN. Generally, older vines fared better than younger ones. Vineyards on lighter soils suffered the most. North-facing vines excelled, with a number of growers contemplating extending these plantations, especially if 2003 is a wake-up call for global warming (average temperatures in Alsace have increased by 0.6°C in the past 10 years), rather than an anomaly. The heat and drought stress caused many vines to shut down their metabolic systems during *véraison*, especially Riesling, which does not like hot weather and stopped for 10 days or more. Remarkable as it might seem for a hot year, some Riesling even failed to ripen fruit beyond the 8 per cent achieved prior to shutting down. This will be a benchmark vintage for Pinot Noir, while the most affected category of wine will be Crémant d'Alsace, because its primary grape variety, Pinot Blanc, was too concentrated, too alcoholic, and much too low in acidity for anything other than a still wine. Some atypically superb Muscats have been made, but much of the Gewurztraminer curiously ripened without changing colour and had exceptionally thick skins. According to Olivier Humbrecht, such Gewurztraminer grapes were sugar ripe but not physiologically ripe. "In a year like 2003," Olivier told me, "it was more like a New World red-wine harvest than Old World white. Although most growers had picked the greater part of their crop by mid-September, the grapes were not physiologically ripe until mid-October. We had a little rain in late September, after which the vine's metabolism started to recover, adjusting the balance of its fruit, even producing very tiny amounts of malic acid."

Updates on the previous five vintages

2002

Vintage rating: *88 (Red: 85, White: 89)*

Although there is some variability in quality, the best 2002s have the weight of the 2000s, but with far more focus and finesse. Riesling definitely fared best and will benefit from several years' bottle-age, but Gewurztraminer and Muscat also performed well. The Gewurztraminers are very aromatic with broad spice notes, whereas the Muscats are exceptionally fresh and floral. Pinot Gris was less successful. Some extraordinary SGNs have been produced.

2001

Vintage rating: *90 (Red: 88, White: 90)*

Most growers rate 2000 over 2001, but size is not everything, and this vintage has the finesse and freshness of fruit that is missing from most of the 2000 bruisers. The hallmark of the 2001 vintage is a spontaneous malolactic that endowed so many of the wines with a special balance. You hardly notice the malolactic in the wines – it is just a creaminess on the finish, more textural than taste, and certainly nothing that can be picked up on the nose. Although I'm an avid fan of non-malolactic Alsace wine, this particular phenomenon left the fruit crystal clear, with nice, crisp acidity.

2000

Vintage rating: *80 (Red: 90, White: 80)*

A generally overrated, oversized vintage, but with a few stunning nuggets. Lesser varieties, such as Sylvaner and Pinot Blanc, made delicious drinking in their first flush of life but have since tired. The classic varieties lack finesse, although some exceptional VTs were made. Excellent reds should have been made, but many were either overextracted or heavily oaked.

1999

Vintage rating: *80 (Red: 80, White: 80)*

An easy-drinking vintage that has started to tire.

1998

Vintage rating: *88 (Red: 80, White: 88)*

Still drinking beautifully, particularly for Riesling. Not great longevity, but a very good medium-term developer.

GREATEST WINE PRODUCERS

1. Domaine Zind-Humbrecht
2. Domaine Weinbach
3. Trimbach (Réserve and above)
4. Marcel Deiss
5. René Muré
6. André Kientzler
7. Ostertag
8. Hugel (Jubilée and above)
9. Léon Beyer (Réserve and above)
10. JosMeyer

FASTEST-IMPROVING PRODUCERS

1. JosMeyer
2. Jean Becker
3. Hugel
4. Ostertag
5. Lucien Albrecht
6. Paul Blanck
7. Albert Boxler
8. André Rieffel
9. Antoine Stoffel
10. Albert Mann

NEW UP-AND-COMING PRODUCERS

1. Lucien Albrecht
2. André & Rémy Gresser
3. J-P & J-F Becker (Jean Becker's organic range)
4. Bruno Sorg
5. Albert Boxler
6. Albert Mann
7. Antoine Stoffel
8. Nicolas Simmler
9. Louis Freyburger
10. Cave Vinicole de Hunawihr

BEST-VALUE PRODUCERS

1. JosMeyer
2. Jean Becker
3. Lucien Albrecht
4. René Muré
5. Rolly Gassmann
6. Schoffit
7. Meyer-Fonné
8. Jean-Luc Mader
9. Paul Blanck
10. Hugel

GREATEST-QUALITY WINES

1. **Riesling Clos Ste-Hune 1998** Trimbach (€120)
2. **Riesling Grand Cru Hengst VT 1995** JosMeyer (€38)
3. **Pinot Noir Burlenberg 2000** Marcel Deiss (€28)
4. **Grand Cru Schoenenbourg 2000** Marcel Deiss (€59)
5. **Riesling Grand Cru Geisberg SGN 2001** André Kientzler (€90)
6. **Riesling Grand Cru Sommerberg Vieilles Vignes 2002** Albert Boxler (€18)
7. **Gewurztraminer Vieilles Vignes 2002** Claude et Georges Humbrecht (€6.70)
8. **Riesling Grand Cru Sonnenglanz VT 2002** Jean Becker (€15.30)
9. **Riesling Grand Cru Schlossberg 2002** Paul Blanck (€15.30)
10. **Gewurztraminer Wintzenheim 2002** Domaine Zind-Humbrecht (€26)

Grapevine

• **Pierre Frick** became the first person in Alsace – and, probably, the world – to give up using corks not for screwcaps or synthetic stoppers, but for stainless-steel crown caps (your humble beer-bottle caps). Frick has never been shy of taking the lead. He has been an organic producer since 1970, became biodynamic in 1981, and has not chaptalized any of his wines since 1989. He even bottles one or two wines without any sulphur every year.

BEST BARGAINS

1. **Gewurztraminer Vieilles Vignes 2002** Claude et Georges Humbrecht (€6.70)
2. **Gewurztraminer Grand Cru Pfingstberg 2002** François Schmitt (€7.70)
3. **Tokay-Pinot Gris 2002** Antoine Stoffel (€6.10)
4. **Gewurztraminer 2002** Antoine Stoffel (€6.10)
5. **Riesling Schlossreben 2002** Nicolas Simmler (€6.90)
6. **Pinot Gris 2002** Alfred Meyer (€7.80)
7. **Gewurztraminer Grand Cru Pfersigberg 2002** Bruno Sorg (€12)
8. **Gewurztraminer 1997** Pierre Meyer (€9.10)
9. **Pinot Gris Grand Cru Rosacker 2002** Cave Vinicole de Hunawihr (€9.65)
10. **Gewurztraminer Grand Cru Zinnkoepflé 2002** Domaine Léon Boesch (€14.20)

MOST EXCITING OR UNUSUAL FINDS

1. **Muscat VT 2001** Jean-Marc & Frédéric Bernhard (€18) *A late-harvest Muscat of exceptional finesse and beautiful botrytized complexity.*
2. **Riesling SGN 1989** Fernand Engel (€20) *An SGN for this price would be unusual enough, but it is also 15 years old and exquisitely matured!*
3. **Gewurztraminer VT 1990** Léon Beyer (€17) *Mature Gewurztraminer is rarely commercially available, particularly when it has aged so gracefully, with the potential to improve further over the next 5–10 years.*
4. **Grand Cru Schoenenbourg 2000** Marcel Deiss (€59) *A very sweet assemblage of varieties.*
5. **Kaefferkopf 2002** Marcel Freyburger (€7.70) *A luscious, medium-sweet, budget version of Deiss's Schoenenbourg from the soon-to-be grand cru of Kaefferkopf.*
6. **Tokay-Pinot Gris Grand Cru Gloeckelberg SGN 2001** Koeberlé-Kreyer (€34) *The best Pinot Gris SGN I have tasted in many a year, and relatively inexpensive for the quality.*
7. **Tokay-Pinot Gris 2002** André Kientzler (€8) *A totally dry Pinot Gris that needs at least three years to build up spicy bottle aromas.*
8. **Riesling Grand Cru Moenchberg 1983** André & Rémy Gresser (€25) *An amazing 20-years-plus dry Riesling.*
9. **Gewurztraminer Grand Cru Eichberg 1990** Albert Hertz (€17) *This wine illustrates how low-acid, high-pH Gewurztraminer ages gracefully, with the alcohol and phenolics replacing acidity's role in providing length.*
10. **Sylvaner 2002** Agathe Bursin (€7.80) *Although not allowed to say so on the label, this was grown on the Grand Cru Zinnkoepflé. It is one of the freshest, most exciting, dry-tasting (despite residual sugar of 14g/l) Sylvaners I have ever come across, with its unusually ripe yet light and refreshing fruit.*

Loire Valley

Antoine Gerbelle

The Loire has been shaken by two liquidations –
Cave Saint Florent and Besnard.

ANTOINE GERBELLE

In 2003, these traders went out of business
with debts of €17 million, a large proportion
of which was owed to local producers. *L'affaire*
made headlines not just because it was very
painful for all the producers who were never
paid for their wine, but also because it
finished in front of the Angers court.

The story began in March 2002, when
Jean-Claude Beunard set up Cave Saint
Florent. In an effort to capture a large market
share, he bought generic wines and sold them at very low prices to
supermarkets and discount stores – prices so low that they were actually
below cost. The court quoted some examples: "Muscadet was sold at
€1.06 in Lidl, whereas the cost price was €1.21. Red Anjou was sold at
€1.08, with a cost price of €1.25." It was inevitable that a business run
on these lines would eventually be unable to pay its suppliers.

The people involved in the affair are Jean-Claude Beunard, manager of
Cave Saint Florent, Daniel Macé, manager of Besnard, and eight brokers,
including Bernard Sécher (former chairman of Sécher Frères, which was
liquidated in 2000). Before his business folded, Jean-Claude Beunard's
company was number two in sales volume in the Loire Valley. He has
been barred from managing a company for 10 years and has been
ordered to refund €1 million.

ANTOINE GERBELLE is a journalist and author of guides specializing in the
wines of France, including *Wine Roads of France* and *Wines and Vineyards of Character
and Charm in France*. He also contributes to the prestigious *La Revue du Vin de France*
and is coauthor of the *Guide des Meilleurs Vins à Petits Prix*, the third edition of
which was published in September 2003.

In addition to the losses sustained by the producers, this policy of very low prices has resulted in damage to other Loire merchants' profits, since companies were faced with the unenviable choice of falling into line and accepting much-reduced profits or losing their markets altogether.

Rescue plan for Muscadet

The vineyards of Nantes are financially in bad shape. Growers are anxious about the generic Muscadet market, apart from the damage inflicted by the bankruptcy of Cave Saint Florent (see lead story). Muscadet sales fell 12 per cent in 2001/02 and 27 per cent in 2002/03. The AOC authorities have consequently been granted EU approval to pull up 500–600 hectares (ha) of Gros Plant vines, which are low quality. At the beginning of 2004, the Interprofessional Committee of the Wines of Nantes (CIVN) announced a plan to control the production of Muscadet. M Liebeau, the president, announced that volume would be restricted to 630,000 hectolitres (hl) and the potential vineyard area would be reduced to about 2,000 ha. Between 500 and 1,000 ha of Gros Plant will be removed out of a total of 2,000 ha.

Rocky bubbles

Loire sparkling wines have been in trouble for several years. In Saumur, sales dropped by 9.2 per cent during 2003. There is great potential for developing a thriving market for sparkling wine from the Loire, especially in exports, but Loire sparklers have lost market share to Crémant d'Alsace, now the second-largest producer after Champagne.

Patrice Monmousseau, chairman of the Saumur house Bouvet-Ladubay, proposes that a marketing campaign should be launched to promote Loire sparkling wines rather than spreading a limited budget over different appellations. It remains to be seen whether the sparkling-wine houses have the means or the will to invest in such a move. "The Saumur companies are in the hands of large groups, and one wonders whether they are really concerned with the area," said Guillaume Roussy, vice president of the union of Saumur Brut.

Grapevine

• **The Nantes trader** Donatien Bahuaud and his Touraine counterpart Pierre Chainier, creators of a joint company two years ago called Bahuaud-Chainier Loire Premium, announced a split in the summer of 2003. Jointly, they had a turnover of €30 million and sold 13–14 million bottles per year, making them the number two in the Loire Valley, but they have decided to go their separate ways. Pierre Chainier, however, seems ready to go into partnership with another operator in Anjou or Nantes.

SHEER CHENIN

Rendez-Vous du Chenin was held at the Abbaye du Fontevraud, near Saumur in the Loire Valley, in July 2003. The object of this new annual event is to put the international spotlight on Chenin Blanc, which is often perceived as a lesser-quality grape variety. This competition was not welcomed by all the producers in the Loire, many of whom were concerned that any focus on the grape variety would undermine the reputation of their appellations. The Syndicat of Vouvray producers even went as far as to urge their members not to enter or be associated with Rendez-Vous du Chenin. However, of the 214 wines entered for the event, 80 per cent came from France, and most of these were from the Loire, including Vouvray. The remainder came mostly from South Africa, although entries were also received from Australia, Morocco, and New Zealand. Three-quarters of the 50 judges were French, and of the best 49 wines selected, 35 (71 per cent) came from France (all but one from the Loire), 12 from South Africa, and one each from Australia and New Zealand. The best dry Chenin from the Loire included Château de Varennes 1997, Savennières (Vignobles Germain); Cuvée Rémus 2000 Domaine de la Taille aux Loups, Montlouis; and Domaine Langlois-Château Vieilles-Vignes 2001, Saumur.

In the demi-sec and sweet sections, all 22 selected were from the Loire, and most of these came from the Layon Valley, with Robineau Sélection de Grains Nobles 2001, Domaine du Petit Métris les Tétuères 1997, Domaine Chupin Prestige 1996, and Patrick Baudouin SGN 1999 all standing out. Apart from Layon, the most impressive sweet wines included a pair of Vouvrays from Prince Poniatowski (Aigle Blanc 1990 and Clos Baudoin 1990).

Grapevine

• **Nantes growers** know that they will continue to suffer poor returns in spite of a plan to pull up a fifth, or even more, of the vineyard area. They now wish to join forces with the wine areas of Touraine, Anjou, and the other wines of the Loire, something they had previously refused to do. The CIVN is trying to join Interloire, an organization covering the other Loire areas. Interloire, for its part, has made reorganization of the Nantes vineyard a condition of the Nantes producers joining. At the same time, Interloire is aware that the €1.2 million Nantes promotional budget would make a significant addition to its own budget of €5.6 million. If agreement can be reached, all 4,700 wine producers of the Loire basin will soon find themselves in the same organization.

• **The Loire** has its first premier cru. Coteaux du Layon Chaume, which was given the name only in the 2003 vintage, is now called Chaume Premier Cru. This is the first time that the INAO (Institut National des Appellations d'Origine) has awarded the term premier cru to a wine from the Loire Valley. This small appellation produces 1,700 hl per year, with 28 estates making the wine in 2003.

Advance report on the latest harvest

2003

This was an atypical year, with climatic conditions upsetting vineyard practices. The reduced harvest was exceptional and quality is potentially outstanding, with high sugar levels. The wines will have a marked personality and will be easily identified as 2003. Cabernet Franc reds have seldom been so rich. They have intense colour and fairly low acidity. The exceptional maturity of the components will ensure balanced wine.

The dry white wines of Chenin are rich and powerful. The maturation process will have to be directed at maintaining freshness (no malolactic). There is no botrytis in late-harvested grapes, but a very high proportion of grapes dried by overripeness – some are approaching 30 per cent. The weather during this vintage, the best since 1989, was more like the south of France than the Loire.

Updates on the previous five vintages

2002

Vintage rating: 93 *(Red: 96, White: 90)*

Sauvignons are quite ripe, the Muscadets are of rare exception and there are great Chenins: this is a superb year for dry whites, better than 1996. These are excellent wines for ageing. The reds, which are healthy, solid, and lively, are equal to the 1996s or slightly lower in quality. Their limiting factor is, sometimes, reduced potential longevity, yet they are better than the average quality of the reds produced further south in France.

2001

Vintage rating: 90 *(Red: 90, White: 89)*

The dry whites, Chenin and Sauvignon, are better than in 2000, but not as exceptional as the 2002s, and they should be drunk up. The Pinot Noirs of Sancerre et al are extremely average, as indeed are the Cabernet Francs, most of which should be consumed between now and 2009. Generally, Bourgueil and Chinon will outlive Saumur-Champigny and St-Nicolas de

Bourgueil. As for sweet wines with noble rot, this is the best year since 1997 in Anjou and Touraine. However, the greatest successes are in Coteaux du Layon and Quarts de Chaume.

2000

Vintage rating: *87 (Red: 88, White: 85)*

Both the Cabernet Franc and Pinot Noir reds are ready to drink, in a soft style with gentle blackberry fruit. They look like the 1997s, but with more freshness of fruit. The whites are more heterogeneous, with Savennières (for Chenin) and Sancerre (for Sauvignon) the greatest successes.

1999

Vintage rating: *76 (Red: 73, White: 79)*

A poor-quality year, with reds and dry whites at best fruity, but more often diluted and precocious. Only a handful of growers succeeded in producing wines of exceptional standard. Even more difficult for sweet white wines.

1998

Vintage rating: *82 (Red: 82, White: 82)*

A large harvest of average quality, due to a lack of sun at the end of the summer. Apart from rare exceptions, this year did not provide wines of any longevity in red or white, dry or sweet (which were spoiled by grey rot). The most successful wines were simple and best enjoyed young.

GREATEST WINE PRODUCERS

1. Domaine Didier Dagueneau (Pouilly Fumé)
2. Domaine de la Coulée de Serrant (Savennières)
3. Domaine Huet (Vouvray)
4. Clos Rougeard (Saumur-Champigny)
5. Domaine Alphonse Mellot (Sancerre)
6. Domaine Yannick Amirault (Bourgueil & St-Nicolas de Bourgueil)
7. Domaine du Clos Naudin (Vouvray)
8. Domaine Philippe Alliet (Chinon)
9. Domaine de la Sansonnière (Anjou & Bonnezeaux)
10. Château Pierre Bise (Anjou, Savennières & Coteaux du Layon)

FASTEST-IMPROVING PRODUCERS

1. Domaine de Roche Neuve (Saumur-Champigny)
2. Domaine François Chidaine (Montlouis)
3. Château de Villeneuve (Saumur-Champigny & Saumur)
4. Domaine de Bellivière (Jasnières & Coteaux du Loir)
5. Domaine des Sablonettes (Anjou & Coteaux du Layon)
6. Domaine Vincent Pinard (Sancerre)
7. Domaine de l'Ecu (Muscadet de Sèvre-et-Maine)
8. Domaine Henry Pellé (Menetou-Salon)
9. Domaine Pierre Soulez (Savennières)
10. Domaine de la Taille aux Loups (Vouvray & Montlouis)

NEW UP-AND-COMING PRODUCERS

1. Domaine de la Monnaie (Savennières)
2. Domaine Sebastian David (St-Nicolas de Bourgueil)
3. Le Domaine Le Briseau, Christian Chaussard (Coteaux du Loir & Jasnières)
4. Domaine de la Puannerie (Touraine)
5. Domaine du Regain (Anjou)
6. Domaine Emile Balland (Coteaux du Giennois)
7. Domaine Olivier Cousin (Anjou)
8. Les Vignes de l'Ange Vin, Jean-Pierre Robineau (Coteaux du Loir & Jasnières)
9. Domaine de la Garrelière (Touraine)
10. Domaine Stéphane Cossais (Montlouis)

BEST-VALUE PRODUCERS

1. Domaine Didier Dagueneau (Pouilly Fumé)
2. Domaine Alphonse Mellot (Sancerre)
3. Domaine de la Coulée de Serrant (Savennières)
4. Domaine Huet (Vouvray)
5. Domaine de la Sansonnière (Anjou & Bonnezeaux)
6. Clos Rougeard (Saumur-Champigny)
7. Domaine Philippe Alliet (Chinon)
8. Domaine Yannick Amirault (Bourgueil & St-Nicolas de Bourgueil)
9. Domaine du Clos Naudin (Vouvray)
10. Château de Fesles (Bonnezeaux)

GREATEST-QUALITY WINES

1. **Pouilly Fumé Silex 2001** Domaine Didier Dagueneau (€46)
2. **Bonnezeaux Mellerese Premières Tries 1997** Château La Varière (€40)
3. **Chinon Coteau de Noiré 2002** Domaine Philippe Alliet (€15)
4. **Sancerre Edmond 2002** Domaine Alphonse Mellot (€33)
5. **Bourgueil La Petite Cave 2002** Domaine Yannick Amirault (€13)
6. **Chinon Blanc Croix Boissée 2000** Domaine Bernard Baudry (€15)
7. **Vouvray Moelleux Réserve 1996** Domaine du Clos Naudin (€22)
8. **Coteaux du Loir Vignes Centenaires 2002** Domaine de Bellivière (€17)
9. **Vin de Pays du Jardin de la France Provinage 2002** Domaine Henry Marionnet (€38.50)
10. **Domaine Germain Anjou La Chapelle 2002** Château de Fesles (€12)

BEST BARGAINS

1. **Muscadet de Sèvre-et-Maine Les Gras Mouton 2002** Domaine la Haute Févrie (€4.40)
2. **Saumur-Champigny Les Terrages 2002** Domaine René-Noël Legrand (€5.50)
3. **Coteaux du Layon 2001** Domaine des Grandes Vignes (€7)
4. **Coteaux du Layon Sélection de Grains Nobles 2001** Domaine Michel Robineau (€14)
5. **Vouvray Moelleux 2002** Domaine François Pinon (€7.50)
6. **Chinon Réserve du Trompegueux 2001** Château de Saint Louand (€5.50)
7. **Menetou-Salon 2002** Domaine Arnaud Lejus (€6)
8. **Quincy Le Rimonet 2002** Domaine Joseph Mellot (€5.50)
9. **Anjou la Potardière 2001** Domaine des Chesnaies (€6.90)
10. **Gros Plant 2002** Domaine Bruno Cormerais (€2.30)

MOST EXCITING OR UNUSUAL FINDS

1. **Vin de Table La Goule 2002** Domaine des Griottes (€5.90) *A blend of very old Anjou vines (Grolleau, Cabernet, and Pineau d'Aunis), neglected because they are outside the AOC area. Very fruity and easy drinking.*
2. **Touraine Sauvignon Vinifera Franc de Pied 2002** Domaine Henry Marionnet (€11) *Some of the best producers in France are planting without rootstocks. Here is a Sauvignon franc de pied, very frank, very pure, with perfect elegance.*
3. **Saumur 2001** Château Yvonne (€18) *A pure, dry Chenin matured for 18 months in oak with the care worthy of the biggest Chardonnay in the Côte de Beaune. Very fatty, long, and sharp at the same time.*
4. **Coteaux du Layon Grains Nobles 1998** Domaine Patrick Baudouin (€33) *This producer never chaptalizes these sweet natural wines, even in the difficult year of 1998. This is a sweet white with fantastic freshness.*
5. **Anjou Noël de Montbenault 2001** Domaine Richard Leroy (€12) *Anjou whites are often too heavy when they are vinified in barrel. Here is an example showing the opposite, with a certain raciness.*
6. **Vin de Pays du Jardin de la France Ligeria 2001** Adeâ Consules (€33.80) *A garage wine that blends the two Cabernets, the Merlot and the Côt, all coming from soils very distant from each other in the Loire Valley. Matured for 20 months in new barrels, it is a solid, velvety, long red that remains fresh on the finish.*
7. **Châteaumeillant 2002** Domaine du Chaillot (€6) *Loire Gamays are rarely excellent. This one, from an area close to Sancerre, is a terrific discovery: superbly fruity and generous.*
8. **Vin de Table Vert de l'Or 2001** Domaine des Baumard (€6) *A white resulting from the Verdelho of Madeira, which has been planted experimentally in this Anjou vineyard. Not very high in acidity, fatty and mellow, it resembles a dry white port.*
9. **Vin de Pays du Jardin de la France Cépage Oublié 2002** Domaine Henry Marionnet (€8.70) *Made with Gamay of Bouze, a hybrid Gamay with black juice (not the Gamay with white juice used commonly for Beaujolais, for example), this wine has good colour, slightly animal flavours, and rough tannins.*

The poor quality of the 2002 vintage in the southern Rhône Valley has led two well-known estates to declassify their crop.

OLIVIER POELS

The difficult decision was taken after fermentation in April 2003. The overall unsatisfactory quality of the wine led the Brunier brothers to discard their red Châteauneuf-du-Pape Vieux Télégraphe 2002 rather than produce a substandard product. This very sensible and courageous decision has to be lauded when its significant financial impact is considered. A few days later, another top-rated domaine in Châteauneuf-du-Pape, Château de Beaucastel, also announced that it would not produce a 2002 vintage. Considering the dreadful conditions under which picking was carried out, one wonders why no other producer followed the example of these two top estates. It's noticeable, though, that many *cuvées spéciales*, or 'plot selections', will not be released in the 2002 vintage.

At the same time, the selling price per barrel of some Rhône appellations is due for a serious increase. In May 2003, the merchant rate per litre for 2002 Côte Rôtie was €11 – an increase of 10 per cent over the previous year. Quite a paradox for a very average vintage: good wines are hard to find, the price hits the roof, and finally the bottles won't sell because of absurd retail prices.

OLIVIER POELS is a journalist at *La Revue du Vin de France* and a member of the Comité de Dégustation. He also produces wine programmes for French TV channel LCI and is coauthor of the *Guide Malesan des Vins de France*.

New *cuvée* for Chapoutier

A new *sélection parcellaire*, or single-vineyard *cuvée*, has been launched by Michel Chapoutier. The famous producer of Tain l'Hermitage completed his range of the different aspects of Hermitage with a new red wine: Les Greffieux, a small parcel located just under Le Méal. The vineyard is more than 60 years old and produces only 3,000 bottles of pure and concentrated wine. The first vintage, 2001, is selling for about €110. Michel Chapoutier has been developing his strategy of producing single-vineyard *cuvées* since 1990. These wines – Hermitage de l'Orée, Le Pavillon, L'Ermite, and Le Méal – are extremely limited in availability and expensive due to very low yields.

Découverte discovers success

The second Découverte en Vallée du Rhône wine festival in March 2003 was a great success. More than 780 exhibitors presented over 4,000 wines to 20 tasting panels, each of which addressed a different *terroir* of the region. This wine fair has become an important meeting place for winemakers and professionals seeking an opportunity for a detailed overview of the quality of the wines and the potential of the region.

Guigal's Ex Voto

Marcel Guigal achieved his long-held dream of buying a parcel in Hermitage two years ago. In 2003, to celebrate, he made two new *cuvées*, a red and a white, called Ex Voto. This exceptional wine is made from the best parcels: Les Murets and Hermite for the white; Bessards, Greffieux, Hermite, and Les Murets for the red.

New label for Bernard

Louis Bernard has expanded its wine range with a new label, Grande Réserve. The wines currently available are from Costières de Nîmes and Lirac. Louis Bernard is now installed along the river Durance, in Caumont-sur-Durance, in an outstandingly beautiful property, the Chartreuse de Bonpas.

• **The Côtes du Rhône website** (www.rhone-wines.com) was revamped in 2003. Organized into eight sections, the site has the latest news and information on different wine routes in the region.

• **Gabriel Meffre** has built a new bottling plant on its site in Gigondas with a storage capacity of 24 million bottles.

There is a French fable about a frog who would like to become as big as a bull. The moral of this story is that, no matter what he does or how hard he tries, he will only ever be a frog. For several years in the southern Rhône Valley there has been a trend towards high extraction and the use of new oak in an effort to bulk out wines to win medals and get high ratings in blind tastings. However, these techniques do not compensate for lack of work in the vineyard or the low potential of the *terroir* itself. Many of these wines will dry out – they will die as they age or simply be overheavy.

Tavel lagging behind

Considering their high prices, the most prestigious Rhône *rosé* wines often fail to fulfil expectations. The easy market means that there is no incentive for many Tavel winemakers to produce great wines. High yields, lack of maturity, and rough-and-ready vinification all lead to one conclusion: the wines are not good enough. Exceptions such as Domaine de la Mordorée and Domaine d'Aquéria show Tavel's real potential.

Double standards?

In recent years, the massive spread of *cuvées spéciales* – produced from the best plots, the oldest vines, and the best barrels – has become a cause for concern. Although these very expensive bottles are often excellent, the higher-volume wine produced by the same domaine can be of questionable quality. The true potential of a domaine cannot be judged solely on a few hundred 'super-*cuvées*'.

Grapevine

• **AOC Côtes du Rhône** has designed a new marketing strategy in a bid to boost retail and export sales. As of spring 2004, bottle labels will include a description of the wine: "Fruity" or "Full-bodied". This extra, if brief, information is expected to help the buyer when it comes to wine selection.

• **Two Côte Rôtie plots** uncultivated since 1914 are now linked by a 160-m (525-ft) monorail. The hill incline, which is 60 per cent in some areas, made the land impossible to work. The initiative was the brainchild of neighbours Gilles Barges and Antoine Montez.

2003

The north had one of its earliest vintages. The south needed more patience due to ripening being delayed by lack of water. The rainfall deficiency – up to 50 per cent in some places – and the exceptionally scorching heat have resulted not only in historically low yields, but also in a grape profile never seen before. The combination of very high sugar richness and low acidity baffled many winemakers, leaving them wondering how to proceed. The critical question was whether to add acid to the must, but acidification in the cellar has never been a good idea. Unusually, and surprisingly, acidity levels have risen naturally in the tanks during fermentation. Contrary to common belief, the 2003 vintage will be a vintage for expert winemakers. Those who have chosen the right options in the vineyard and the cellar will produce stellar wines. In some places, the harvest was the earliest ever seen. Since it produced small quantities of grapes, there will not be a lot of wine available. The scene is set for a marked increase in price, bearing in mind that the 'written-off' 2002 vintage is still hard to sell. The 2003 wines have achieved high alcohol levels and have very rich and mature tannins. This will be a vintage to keep.

Updates on the previous five vintages
2002
Vintage rating: *70 (North: 70–75, South: 55–60)*
Dramatic rainfall destroyed a large part of the harvest, especially in the Vaucluse region. An average vintage in the north.

2001
Vintage rating: *86 (North: 88–92, South: 80–85)*
A solid vintage in the north. Some wines are too acid and coarse, but the best are powerful and long. Some problems of dilution and tartness in the south.

2000
Vintage rating: *88 (North: 85–90, South: 85–90)*
Good but supple wines, with a lot of fruitiness in both parts of the valley. Most of the wines will not age very long.

1999

Vintage rating: 92 (North: 85–95, South: 90–99)

The vintage in the south is less powerful than 1998, but the balance of many Châteauneuf-du-Papes is superb. The wines are soft-structured and will age wonderfully in under 10 years. This is also a great year in the north, particularly for Côte Rôtie, which enjoyed its best vintage since 1990.

1998

Vintage rating: 92 (North: 85–90, South: 95–99)

An excellent and very powerful vintage in the south, above all at Châteauneuf-du-Pape. The wines must be kept in the cellar for years. A good, rather than great, year in the north, with some Hermitage wines not as impressive in bottle as they were during the first tasting from barrel.

GREATEST WINE PRODUCERS

1. Jean-Louis Chave (Hermitage)
2. Château d'Ampuis (Côte Rôtie)
3. Château de Beaucastel (Châteauneuf-du-Pape)
4. Tardieu-Laurent (Cuvées Vieilles Vignes)
5. M Chapoutier (Hermitage, Châteauneuf-du-Pape)
6. Paul Jaboulet (Hermitage La Chapelle)
7. Clos des Papes (Châteauneuf-du-Pape)
8. Domaine du Vieux Télégraphe (Châteauneuf-du-Pape)
9. Château Grillet (Château Grillet)
10. Réserve des Célestins (Châteauneuf-du-Pape)

FASTEST-IMPROVING PRODUCERS

1. Vins de Vienne (northern and southern Rhône)
2. Domaine Georges Vernay (Condrieu, Côte Rôtie)
3. Delas Frères (all northern Rhône)
4. Domaine de la Présidente (Châteauneuf-du-Pape)
5. Domaine Gourt de Mautens (Côtes du Rhône)
6. Domaine de Marcoux (Châteauneuf-du-Pape)
7. Pierre Coursodon (St-Joseph)
8. Domaine de la Mordorée (Châteauneuf-du-Pape)
9. Domaine de la Janasse (Châteauneuf-du-Pape)
10. Domaine Gabriel Meffre (southern Rhône)

NEW UP-AND-COMING PRODUCERS

1. Domaine Eric Rocher (St-Joseph)
2. Domaine Jean-Michel Stephan (Côte Rôtie)
3. Stéphane Pichat (Côte Rôtie)
4. Emmanuel Darnaud (Crozes-Hermitage)

BEST-VALUE PRODUCERS

1. Cave des Vignerons d'Estézargues (Côtes du Rhône)
2. Domaine la Réméjeanne (Côtes du Rhône)
3. Domaine de l'Oratoire Saint-Martin (Côtes du Rhône)

4 Château Val Joanis (Côtes du Lubéron)

5 Louis Bernard
(Côtes du Rhône)

6 Marcel Richaud
(Côtes du Rhône-Villages)

7 Alain Graillot (Crozes-Hermitage)

8 Domaine Les Goubert (Gigondas)

9 Domaine Lafond-Roc-Epine (Tavel)

10 Château Mourgues du Grès
(Costières de Nîmes)

GREATEST-QUALITY WINES

1 **Hermitage 2000** Jean-Louis Chave (€130)

2 **Côte Rôtie La Mouline 2000** E Guigal (€300)

3 **Châteauneuf-du-Pape Chaupin 2000** Domaine de la Janasse (€60)

4 **Châteauneuf-du-Pape Vieilles Vignes 2000** Domaine de Marcoux (€100)

5 **Hermitage Le Pavillon 2000** M Chapoutier (€130)

6 **Hermitage Les Bessards 1999** Delas Frères (€100)

7 **Condrieu Coteau de Vernon 2001** Domaine Georges Vernay (€40)

8 **Châteauneuf-du-Pape Cuvée des Cadettes 2000** Château la Nerthe (€50)

9 **Châteauneuf-du-Pape 2001** Château de Beaucastel (€40)

10 **Hermitage 2001** Tardieu-Laurent (€60)

BEST BARGAINS

1 **Costières de Nîmes 2001** Château des Nages (€5.30)

2 **Côtes du Rhône 2001** E Guigal (€6)

3 **Costières de Nîmes Terre d'Argence 2002** Château Mourgues du Grès (€8)

4 **Côtes du Rhône Grande Réserve 2001** Louis Bernard (€8)

5 **Côtes du Rhône Villages Domaine la Montagnette 2001** Cave des Vignerons d'Estézargues (€6)

6 **Côtes du Rhône 2002** Domaine de la Janasse (€5.50)

7 **St-Joseph 2001** Pierre Coursodon (€11)

8 **Crozes-Hermitage Chaubayou 2001** Domaine Eric Rocher (€8.50)

9 **Côtes du Rhône Villages Cairanne 2002** Marcel Richaud (€10)

10 **Gigondas 2001** Domaine Les Goubert (€11)

MOST EXCITING OR UNUSUAL FINDS

1 **Côtes du Rhône Rasteau 2001** Domaine Gourt de Mautens (€25) *Outstanding quality for the appellation. Gets better every year.*

2 **Lirac Cuvée de la Reine des Bois 2001** Domaine de la Mordorée (€20) *Who says that Lirac is a 'small' appellation? This wine is better than a lot of Châteauneuf-du-Pape.*

3 **Côtes du Rhône Dimanche d'Octobre en Famille 1999** Domaine de la Présidente (€50) *A fabulous expression of Viognier made from very low yields. Late harvest but totally dry.*

4 **Hermitage Vin de Paille 2000** M Chapoutier (€70 per half-bottle) *Very rare (only 3,000 half-bottles produced). An incredible nectar-like wine.*

5 **Châteauneuf-du-Pape Réserve des Célestins 1995** Henry Bonneau (€150) *The 1995 vintage is now in bottle. This new chef d'oeuvre of the master is a unique expression of Châteauneuf-du-Pape.*

avoie

Few skiers heading to Courchevel or Val d'Isère notice the exit to the sleepy village of Cevins. But, if they looked, they might see a steep, terraced, south-facing slope lined with wooden posts dominating the village.

WINK LORCH

These are the recently established vineyards of the new Domaine des Ardoisières, which produces Vin de Pays d'Allobrogie.

June 2003 saw the official inauguration of Domaine des Ardoisières, established by well-known Savoie *vigneron* Michel Grisard, owner of the biodynamic Domaine Prieuré Saint Christophe in Fréterive. It followed six years of planning, persuasion, and hard graft. Grisard's dream was to rescue the hillside and restore the vineyards, abandoned since the early 1980s. Before the technically difficult job of taming this steep and wild landscape could begin, agreement had to be reached with more than 400 landowners for an area of under 10 hectares (ha). Fortunately, the village mayor and most of the villagers were keen to restore the terraces, dry-stone walls, and even the *sartos* (vineyard cabins).

Domaine des Ardoisières (meaning 'slate quarry') lies mainly on solid rock of mica-schist, a type of slate, and it proved initially too hard to work using organic techniques. However, conversion is well under way now that the oldest vines are four years old. A total of 5 ha is currently planted, with two more planned, though plantings made in 2002 were badly

WINK LORCH is a wine writer and educator with a passion for the mountains and a chalet in the Haute Savoie. She is a past chairman of the Association of Wine Educators and has contributed to several books, including Time-Life's *The Wine Guide*, *The Global Wine Encyclopedia*, and Le Cordon Bleu's *Wine Essentials*. Wink particularly enjoys enthusing about wines from vineyards in sight of snowcapped mountains, whether the Andes, the Alps, or the Jura. She divides her time between the UK and the French Alps.

affected by the 2003 drought. About three-quarters is planted to white varieties, with Altesse and Jacquère dominating, along with Roussanne, Pinot Gris, Chardonnay, Mondeuse Blanche, and Malvoisie. The most planted red variety is Persan, with a smaller amount of Mondeuse.

An old village house has been bought for future use as a vinification cellar and visitor sales centre. Tourism is considered important and already there are organized vineyard walks in summer. The first vintage in 2002 was small and the 2003 vintage even smaller due to the drought. However, in 2002, three blended Vin de Pays d'Allobrogie were made: Améthiste, a red; Schiste, a light dry white based on Jacquère; and the flagship Quartz, based on Altesse. A late-harvest wine is planned too. The Quartz 2002 showed good weight and potential, with a really stony flavour. Should the project prove a success, it is possible that other hillsides further up the Tarentaise Valley may be planted in the future.

Jura pioneer dies

Henri Maire, founder of Jura's largest domaine and *négociant* house, died in November 2003, aged 86. Maire is credited by many as the person who did most to revive and promote the Jura region after World War II. Writer Gerald Asher, who imported Henri Maire's wines to the UK in the 1960s, commented, "The region owes a great deal to him."

After inheriting his father's small vineyards in 1939, Maire gradually built up the family estate to its current 300 ha, nearly 20 per cent of the total Jura region. In 1950, he launched a sparkling wine with the not-so-crazy brand name Vin Fou, making it a household name in France through distinctive roadside advertisements. He was media-savvy and known for his stunts, even promoting *vin jaune* at the Tour d'Argent in Paris by donating a barrel to age in their cellars.

Officially retired in 1985, Henri Maire remained involved in the company until 1996 and could be seen checking out new technology at trade shows well into his 80s.

ORGANIC GROWTH

Three large Jura estates are now worked organically: from 2003, Domaine Pignier, with 15 ha, has been in conversion to biodynamic viticulture; Domaine de la Pinte (30 ha) and Domaine A et M Tissot (32 ha) both now have full Ecocert certification, with Stéphane Tissot also exploring biodynamic methods. Together with several smaller estates, this gives an estimated 110 ha of Jura vineyards now farmed organically, about 7 per cent of the total area, more than double the average for France. Antoine Pignier, recently appointed president of the Comité Technique Viticole in Jura, comments that, with the marnes soil (a type of heavy clay) and steep slopes, working the soil organically provides more stability and vines are looking healthier as a result. In Savoie, Domaine Belluard in the Ayze *cru*, inspired by Michel Grisard, has converted half of its vineyards (more than 6 ha) to biodynamic viticulture, and Gilles Berlioz in Chignin is making waves with his first organically certified Chignin Bergeron 2002 from 1.2 ha.

TESTING TIME FOR CHÂTEAU-CHALON

Permitted for release only in 2004, Château-Chalon 1997 is the first vintage to undergo compulsory testing (*agrément*) before release by an approved and trained committee of tasters, under the auspices of the INAO (Institut National des Appellations d'Origine). President of the Château-Chalon syndicate Denis Bury believes that this has already had a positive effect on quality. More *vignerons* now employ a laboratory to monitor the progress of their wines during their six years in barrel *sous voile* (under a film of yeast), so very few rejections are expected. All 17 wines submitted to the first tasting in December 2003 were approved. Other *vins jaunes*, also compulsorily aged for six years and three months, do not go through this testing, having, like all AOC wines, simply been tested a few months after harvest. The president of the Jura Comité wants to see what improvements there are in Château-Chalon before suggesting to the INAO that all *vins jaunes* should go through this process.

Grapevine

• **The VDQS Vin du Bugey statute** has been rewritten in the hope that this will hasten the area's application for promotion to AOC. Vin du Bugey is currently top of the INAO list of France's VDQS regions in line for promotion.

• **The AOC Crépy Syndicat** has applied to the INAO for the right to include the term "Vin de Savoie" on the label. Apparently no one knows where Crépy is, despite it being one of the region's oldest appellations.

• **Two Savoie domaines** are up for sale. Pierre Boniface, a well-known Apremont producer and one of the few exporters, wishes to sell his estate and small *négociant* business, but a buyer has yet to offer the right price. Meanwhile, Domaine G & G Bouvet continues to trade actively, despite Madame Bouvet's assertion last year that the future of the business was in question.

At present, many Jura wines are labelled with the simple AOC (Arbois, Côtes du Jura, or Etoile) but no mention of grape variety or, even more importantly, style. This is a big problem, especially if the sales and reputation of these wines are to extend beyond the very local market. Many white wines are still made in the traditional oxidized, or partly oxidized, style – aged under *voile* (a layer of yeast similar to *flor* and essential for *vin jaune* production). Others are made in the more conventional, fresher, burgundian way of topping up barrels or vats completely. Some producers name the former style *typé* or *tradition* and the latter *floral*, but there is no agreed standard term and the two styles of wine taste completely different. Some producers do not state the grape variety either, so the wine may be Chardonnay, Savagnin, or a blend of the two. Current appellation laws permit the naming of a single variety, but not a blend. No term will please all producers, but a solution must be found to eliminate the current confusion and this may well involve full cooperation between regional wine bodies and the INAO. Rumours are rife that meetings are being held between the more modern producers and the local official bodies on this subject. It is certain that something must be changed soon, whether it is a compulsory back-label explanation or a completely new appellation system for white wines.

Straw law needs to be flexible

The rules on *vin de paille* production need to be reviewed to give growers more flexibility. At present, *vin de paille* is required to have a minimum of 14.5 per cent alcohol (actual, not potential) and three years in oak. This limits the styles that can be produced and often results in unbalanced wines. Indeed, some producers have produced a similar style of wine, but outside the auspices of the appellation. If the appellation is to survive, the law should specify only minimum potential alcohol at the pressing stage and back labels should be used to describe the style.

Pressure mounts on bad producers

The quality of wines sold by some local *négociants* and small growers in Savoie is still too low, bringing down the image of the area. The tourist market (principally the winter-sports visitors) is all too easy to satisfy with thin, acidic wines to wash down a fondue or *tartiflette*. The worst quality is to be found in the largest and best-known *crus* of Apremont and Abymes. The Comité Interprofessionnel has taken steps to improve this by invoking the INAO initiative to check systematically on yields in the vineyards at the *véraison* stage, by taking the new AOC *agrément* laws seriously, and by practising random sampling in local shops and restaurants. This is none too soon, but still not strict enough. With the French wine consumer becoming more demanding, Savoie needs to be very careful to maximize its potential. The culprits should listen carefully to the views of proprietors of the leading quality estates.

Cerdon authenticity under threat

Cerdon VDQS, the sparkling *rosé* from the Bugey region, may currently be made either by the *méthode traditionnelle* or the *méthode ancestrale*. Since Cerdon is the only quality *rosé* sparkling wine to be made by the *méthode ancestrale*, the region is officially seeking to promote this by phasing out *méthode traditionnelle* wines by 2008.

However, the large Boisset-owned Varichon et Clerc in Seyssel currently sells only *méthode traditionnelle* Cerdon but, confusingly, also markets Pellin Rosé Vin Mousseux Demi-Sec, labelled "Méthode Ancestrale" and made from bought-in (probably Loire) Gamay. Elsewhere in the region, many carbonated *rosé vins mousseux* are made from grapes bought outside and sold side by side with Cerdon. If the Cerdon appellation is to mean anything, this practice should be stopped.

Grapevine

• **Jean-Paul Crinquand,** a leading grower of the Arbois cooperative, took on the presidency of the Comité Interprofessionnel des Vins du Jura in April 2003 for a three-year term. He sees his main task as uniting the different personalities, and he believes that, with so many different wine styles already, producers should not seek to market new styles that are not traditional to the area.

• **The very early harvest** meant that many Jura producers pressed grapes for *vin de paille* twice in 2003, once for the 2002 vintage in January/February, and then again for the 2003 vintage in October/November.

• **The beautiful Château du Lucey** in Jongieux, owned by the head of the Casino supermarket chain, is to take over more than 2 ha of old Mondeuse and Altesse vineyards for the 2004 vintage. This will take the total holding of this estate, created in 1992, up to 5.5 ha of Altesse, Mondeuse, and Pinot Noir.

• **Percée du Vin Jaune 2005,** the biggest annual Jura wine festival, celebrating the newly released 1998 *vins jaunes*, will take place over the weekend of 5–6 February 2005 in the village of St-Lothain.

Jura – A hot wind during the heat wave of August gave an unprecedented 3 per cent increase in potential alcohol in the week 3–10 August. Harvest started soon after, around five weeks earlier than average – the earliest harvest since 1822. Chardonnay grapes were too ripe for Crémant du Jura, but, on the other hand, the extraordinarily healthy grapes were ideal for making *vins de paille* and a greater quantity than usual may be produced. However, overall quantities are extremely small, having been reduced in many places by frost damage earlier in the year, as well as localized hail. Production is, on average, 30 per cent down. For Trousseau and Poulsard, the small amount of juice in the grapes gave deeper colours and more powerful flavours than normal, posing an interesting potential. The quality of Chardonnays will depend partly on site (ironically, the best-exposed having suffered most) and the cellar-handling of acidity levels. The development of Savagnin wines, including *vins jaunes*, remains the big unknown in this unusual year. The Jura normally markets its wines after several years of ageing, whether in barrel *sous voile* or topped up, but the 2003s could well be ready sooner than anyone expects.

Savoie – With harvest almost completed during the last fortnight of August, this normally overwet region suffered badly in places from drought and heat. Raisining on the vine was a big problem in certain well-exposed sectors, such as the rockier parts of Chignin (especially Bergeron), Chautagne, and the south-facing Marestel slope in Jongieux, where new plantings were badly hit. However, some good wines should have been made, providing growers had the facilities and ability in the cellar to cope with the heat at harvest and to handle the low acidities, with adjustments where appropriate. In view of the superbly healthy grapes in the vineyard, one *vigneron* commented ironically that the chemical companies selling antirot treatments would lose profits, but EDF (Electricité de France), providing electricity for refrigeration, would have done very well. Average quantity is down about 15 per cent, but some areas are down by as much as 40 per cent. Bergeron and Altesse are likely to be patchy, but occasionally excellent in quality; Jacquère will be for very early drinking, but the reds could well be winners for short-term drinking.

Updates on the previous five vintages

2002

Vintage rating: 83 (Jura: 88, Savoie: 77)

Jura – After a difficult summer, the north wind dried the grapes at the end of August and a period of fine weather in autumn gave overall good quality, if not great quantity. Nearly all varieties showed both good natural ripeness and high acidity levels. This bodes well for *vin jaune* in the future. Trousseau reds and Chardonnays are already tasting excellent, with good weight and balance.

Savoie – Three weeks of fine, warm weather, accompanied by a cold north wind from late September, saved the harvest, following a relatively cool and wet August. Later varieties Jacquère and Mondeuse fared best, though there is variation in Mondeuse. Altesse suffered from rot in places and is also varied, though better in the Jongieux area, including the best-known Roussette *cru* Marestel. Bergerons are fairly early drinking. Overall a fairly good vintage, but not spectacular.

2001

Vintage rating: 67 (Jura: 69, Savoie: 64)

Jura – A generally difficult, fairly small, and variable vintage. However, good weather at the end of harvest should produce some decent *vin jaune*, though no AOC Château-Chalon, because this was declassified. For the rest of the wine styles, there is much variation, but those who made a severe selection have made elegant and balanced Chardonnays and Savagnins.

Savoie – A difficult year for many, with some mildew and intermittent hail storms in places reducing quantities. It was cool at the start of September. Better producers who carried out careful selection at the vine have produced reasonable wines across the board, but it was a medium-quality vintage for all the varieties and especially difficult for reds.

2000

Vintage rating: 82 (Jura: 81, Savoie: 83)

Jura – A rather cool summer gave, in the end, a good-quality vintage overall, with attractive fruit characteristics, reasonable structure, but some lack of concentration, often due to high yields. Enjoy these wines before the 1999s.

Savoie – A good year overall, with good yields, too. There was concentrated Bergeron and Altesse, but a lack of weight and structure in Mondeuse has resulted in quick-maturing reds.

1999

Vintage rating: 85 *(Jura: 90, Savoie: 80)*

Jura – An extremely sunny year gave the highest sugar levels ever seen in most varieties, great fruit concentration, and good yields, too. There were excellent overall results, especially for Chardonnay. It may lack the high acidity for real long-term ageing.

Savoie – Some variation, but overall a good year, with both Roussette and Mondeuse capable of ageing well.

1998

Vintage rating: 77 *(Jura: 79, Savoie: 75)*

Jura – Though this year was spoilt by rain in September, most producers were able to harvest a reasonable, healthy crop. Somewhat light, but well-balanced wines overall.

Savoie – Difficult spring and summer weather conditions gave relatively light, early-drinking wines, although it is an overall decent vintage.

GREATEST WINE PRODUCERS

Jura
1. Domaine André et Mireille Tissot
2. Domaine Labet
3. Jacques Puffeney
4. Domaine Berthet-Bondet
5. Domaine Baud Père et Fils
6. Jacques Tissot
7. Jean Rijckaert

Savoie
1. Domaine Prieuré Saint Christophe
2. Domaine Louis Magnin
3. André et Michel Quenard

FASTEST-IMPROVING PRODUCERS

Jura
1. Domaine Pignier
2. Daniel Dugois
3. Frédéric Lornet
4. Domaine de la Pinte

Savoie
1. Domaine Jean Vullien et Fils
2. Jean-Pierre et Jean-François Quenard
3. Jean-Pierre et Philippe Grisard
4. Patrick et Annick Quenard

NEW UP-AND-COMING PRODUCERS

Jura
1. Domaine de la Renardière
2. Domaine Ganevat
3. Domaine de la Tournelle
4. Domaine Ligier Père et Fils

Savoie
1. Domaine Gilles Berlioz
2. Domaine Saint-Germain
3. Domaine Genoux
4. Château de Lucey

BEST-VALUE PRODUCERS

Jura
1. Daniel Dugois
2. Domaine Rolet Père et Fils
3. Château Béthanie, Fruitière Vinicole d'Arbois

Savoie
1. André et Michel Quenard
2. Domaine Dupasquier
3. Edmond Jacquin et Fils
4. Domaine de l'Idylle
5. Pierre Boniface
6. Cave du Prieuré
7. Eugène Carrel et Fils

GREATEST-QUALITY WINES

Jura
The two Château-Chalons need a minimum of 10 years' ageing; other wines can be drunk soon or kept.
1. **Château-Chalon 1996** Jean Macle (€27)
2. **Château-Chalon 1996** Domaine Berthet-Bondet (€27.60)
3. **Arbois Chardonnay Les Graviers 2001** Domaine André et Mireille Tissot (€13)
4. **Côtes du Jura Chardonnay Les Varrons 2001** Domaine Labet (€10)
5. **Arbois Savagnin 2000** Jacques Puffeney (€12)
6. **Côtes du Jura Vin de Paille 1999** Domaine Pignier (€20 per half-bottle)
7. **Côtes du Jura Chardonnay Les Grandes Teppes Vieilles Vignes Bouteille Antique 2000** Domaine Ganevat (€11)

Savoie
1. **Roussette de Savoie 2002** Domaine Prieuré Saint Christophe (€15)
2. **Vin de Savoie Arbin Mondeuse Vieilles Vignes 2001** Domaine Louis Magnin (€10.50)
3. **Vin de Savoie Chignin Bergeron 2002** Domaine Gilles Berlioz (€15)

BEST BARGAINS

Jura
1. **Crémant du Jura Brut NV** Richard Delay (€5.50)
2. **Côtes du Jura Fleur de Chardonnay 2001** Domaine Labet (€8)
3. **Arbois-Pupillin Trousseau 2001** Domaine de la Renardière (€7)

Savoie
1. **Vin de Savoie Chignin Bergeron 2002** Domaine Jean Vullien et Fils (€6.50)
2. **Vin de Savoie Chignin Mondeuse 2002** André et Michel Quenard (€4.65)
3. **Vin de Savoie Chignin Bergeron 2002** André et Michel Quenard (€7.35)
4. **Vin de Savoie Arbin Mondeuse l'Authentique 2002** Domaine Genoux (€6)
5. **Roussette de Savoie Château de Monterminod 2002** Jean Perrier et Fils (€6.60)
6. **Vin de Savoie Pinot 2001** Domaine Dupasquier (€5)
7. **Vin de Savoie Gamay Vieilles Vignes 2002** Edmond Jacquin et Fils (€5.20)

MOST EXCITING OR UNUSUAL FINDS

Jura

❶ **Arbois Chardonnay Cuvée Aigrefeu 1999** Daniel Dugois (€8) *Made only every four years, this superb Chardonnay is aged for four years in foudres that have been meticulously maintained and topped up. Its concentration and flavours justify the continuing use of foudres for Chardonnay in the Jura.*

❷ **Arbois Savagnin Vendange de Novembre 1997** Jacques Tissot (€26 per half-bottle) *Made from grapes left to dry on the vine and affected by light botrytis, this is totally different from Jura's vins de paille. With the classic balance of a high-quality dessert wine, it was aged in barrel for several years.*

❸ **Arbois-Pupillin les Terrasses 2001** Domaine de la Renardière (€10) *In the difficult 2001 vintage, Jean-Michel Petit selected this pure Savagnin to make in a fresh, nonoxidative style, providing a lovely lemon-rind character and excellent balance.*

❹ **Arbois Trousseau 2002** Domaine André et Mireille Tissot (€10.50) *Low yields and careful handling of the fickle Trousseau variety by Stéphane Tissot have produced a most unusual Jura red of excellent cherry colour and fruit intensity.*

❺ **Arbois Traminer 2002** La Cave de la Reine Jeanne (€8.50) *The Savagnin variety is from the Traminer family, hence the rather cheeky naming of this off-dry, ripe white wine made by Stéphane Tissot from old vines of Savagnin for his négociant company.*

❻ **Arbois Solstice 2001** Domaine de la Tournelle (€11) *This is made from Savagnin grapes harvested one month later than usual and vinified into a dry wine in old barrels, then matured and topped up for two years.*

Savoie

❶ **Idylle Vin de Savoie Arbin Mondeuse Prestige 2002** Domaine de l'Idylle (€8) *This Mondeuse has not been near an oak barrel; instead, the Tiollier brothers selected good fruit and used microoxidation to provide a soft, approachable style – just what Mondeuse needs to popularize it further outside the region.*

❷ **Roussette de Savoie Altesse Château St-Philippe 2000** Domaine Jean Vullien et Fils (€10) *If the Altesse fruit is good enough, it can take oak barrels – as proved by this wine aged for 10 months and put through malolactic.*

❸ **Vin de Savoie Apremont Symphonie des Rocailles 2002** Pierre Boniface (€6.75) *Made from Chardonnay blended with Jacquère and Altesse, this is vinified and matured in oak with bâtonnage. The end result gives a weightier character than most Apremonts, and one that will age better, too.*

❹ **Vin de Savoie Malvoisie 2002** Edmond Jacquin et Fils (€6) *Only a couple of producers are experimenting with the so-called Malvoisie variety (no relation to others in the world), an old Savoie grape that is said to be identical to the red Veltliner of Austria. It ripens easily, and here at Jacquin, with their meticulously clean winemaking, the aromatic, almost exotic character is encouraged to shine through.*

Alain-Dominique Perrin, managing director of Cartier and the owner of Château Lagrézette, ruffled many a feather when he announced his views on Cahors wines to the American press.

PAUL STRANG

"People like to talk about the 'typicity' of Cahors; it makes me laugh. Modern Cahors has only existed since about 1960 and, with few exceptions, the wines have been bad. Auxerrois [local synonym for Malbec] is a difficult grape, but it's a noble one. If we can master it, we can make great wine. I'm fascinated by the experiment." Here Perrin sounds as if he claims credit for rescuing Cahors single-handed, which has upset the natives no end. Nor were the local growers whom he had insulted much impressed when he tried to push through reforms that would oblige them to dig up their family vineyards and replant elsewhere in the AOC. This was a classic example of Parisian big business failing to understand the syndicalist spirit of proud *vignerons*, for whom land ownership is a totem of family continuity. His powers of persuasion having failed, Perrin has resigned all his positions in Cahors and threatened to take his Château Lagrézette out of the appellation altogether and market his wines as *vins de pays*. If he does, some might consider this a tragedy; others might breathe a sigh of relief.

PAUL STRANG is recognized as one of the leading experts on the wines of southern France, where he has had a home for over 40 years. He is the author of *Wines of Southwest France* (Kyle Cathie, 1994), which was shortlisted for the Drink Book of the Year by the Glenfiddich Awards. Another book, *Take 5000 Eggs* (Kyle Cathie, 1994) deals with the markets, fêtes, and fairs of southern France, and was also shortlisted for Glenfiddich in 1997.

Searching for traditional grape varieties

Lavilledieu-du-Temple is not France's best-known VDQS appellation, although it dates back more than 50 years. It almost disappeared after the disastrous frosts of 1956, when no wine was declared for four years. The huge *cave* that had been built for the pioneering cooperative became a centre for making wines from neighbouring districts.

Today the dormouse appellation has woken up, largely through the efforts of the dedicated management of Gil Bénac and Xavier Briois. Since 2000, they have put Lavilledieu back on the map, supported and encouraged by the experimentally minded president of the growers' *syndicat*, André Magnac.

Apart from its range of quaffable wines of all colours, the *cave* at Lavilledieu deserves special praise for its research into forgotten grape varieties. Before Bénac joined the *cave*, he had worked on applied research for the Bordeaux Institute. After his arrival at Lavilledieu in 1998, it was decided to investigate and replant pre-1956 grape varieties, perhaps 100 plants of each of the most interesting. The few surviving growers were questioned and small parcels of interesting *cépages* identified.

Grapes that are now mature enough for winemaking are Prunelard, a relative of the Cot, giving deeply coloured wine and a bouquet of plums in brandy, firm on the palate, and with quite substantial weight; Blanc Vert, producing pale juice, not much of a bouquet but lively on the palate, suggesting Granny Smith apples, low in alcohol, but interesting as a potential blending wine with, say, Ondenc or even Viognier on account of its good acidity and vivacity; and finally Milgranet, a clear and agreeable red wine to look at, if a little light in colour, but with spice and fruit in abundance (reminiscent of Duras), probably in need of strict yield control to make a viable product.

• **Didier Dagueneau** installed himself in the Jurançonnais more than two years ago and seems thrilled with his first effort in the tricky 2003 vintage. Many will be waiting to taste the wines with keen anticipation. Didier is, of course, better known as the *enfant terrible* of the Loire, where he has managed to take the cat's pee out of Pouilly-Fumé.

• **Never one to rest on his laurels,** Alain Brumont has now opened his flagship Château Montus as a luxury hotel. The château, derelict until he built a dedicated *chai* for it, is off the main road south to Tarbes from the Gers and is surrounded by vines. "Discreetly opulent" is how one commentator puts it.

UP IN THE AIR

Last year the vineyards of Fronton were under threat from the French government's project to build the second-largest French airport. This would have meant the death of the whole appellation. Fortunately the authorities saw sense and withdrew the idea following massive lobbying. Their attention has now switched to the Gaillac area. The latest plan is to put the airport on the other side of the river Tarn from the town of Rabastens, at the very southern end of the appellation area. This might not cause quite the same havoc to Gaillac as it would have done at Fronton, but it would nevertheless be an act of fearful vandalism to French wine heritage and to beautiful Rabastens itself. Once again, local opinion is up in arms. One wonders what the aviation ministry has against wine, when there are thousands of hectares of flat land to the south and west of Toulouse where the new airport would hardly be noticed, if indeed one is needed at all.

Grapevine

• **Tonus is the name of a new wine** that Brumont has launched as "a revolutionary kind of new Madiran". Cross-examination of the sales staff reveals that it is actually a rebranding of the excellent Domaine Meinjarre, a value-for-money blend of wines from young grapes at Montus and Bouscassé. At the other end of the scale, La Tyre, though still very young, is as yet unbroachable as well as unaffordable (€70). Some Madiran fanciers with neither patience nor unlimited funds might prefer the *tradition* wines of the Capmartin brothers, Denis's (Château Barréjat) at a modest €3.20, Guy's (Domaine Capmartin) at €3.90.

• **Diversification seems to be** the buzz word of the year. The Verhaeghe brothers at Château du Cèdre in Cahors are contemplating going into the *négociant* business, travelling in the reverse direction to those big Cahors names who started life as *négociants* and became growers almost as a sideline (Vigouroux, Rigal, Perrin). Pascal seemed uncertain when I asked him whether he was contemplating franchising the Cèdre name. I would have thought his wine too good to make that sort of risk sensible.

• **Patrick Ducournau in Madiran,** having invented the technique known as *microbullage* (the injection of tiny quantities of oxygen into tank or barrel to avoid the necessity of racking and also to hasten the softening of red wines), has gone into the oak-chip business. The chips are not, of course, to be used in Madiran or any other French AOC, where their use is forbidden, but for the benefit (?) of those countries where there is a market for them. A surprising development for a winemaker whose own use of oak is so masterly.

Sometimes the winemakers of the southwest give the impression that they are some 50 years behind the rest of the world, and their results are often all the more endearing for that. Now it seems that they have just discovered new oak barrels. Since news has not yet filtered through that the trend today is against overoaking wines, some growers are producing huge, hefty, floorboard-tasting *cuvées* in the belief that this is what the world wants. The paradox is that the biggest difficulty in the southwest is to persuade producers that their wines are becoming more rather than less accessible. Unfortunately, they are encouraged by the press and critics in France, who, while decrying the trend towards excessive use of wood, overextraction, and excessively hard tannins, award stars and medals to just that style of wine. Of course that does not happen anywhere else, does it?

Solidarity in fragments

A spirit of solidarity and cooperation within and between the disparate regions of the southwest seems further away than ever. Having noted last year the need for these mostly small growers to pool resources to make an impact on the world scene, one can only view with dismay a situation where Duras, Buzet, Marmande, Cahors, Irouléguy, and Bergerac (and its subappellations) are no longer members of the Comité Interprofessionnel des Vins du Sud-Ouest. It is hard to know whether this reflects the obstinate independence of the growers or the quality of the direction of the Comité.

Shop still closed

Meanwhile, in Gaillac and Cahors in particular, many growers are still unhappy about the capricious way in which appellation tasting committees grant or deny their *agrément*. This can be part of a policy (declared or not) of moulding the image of an area in the direction of the kind of wines that the great and the good are themselves producing. In other, 'happier', appellations there seems to be much more consistency.

Advance report on the latest harvest
2003

Rain during the winter restored the water table, which had been depleted by the dry summer and autumn of 2002. However, Easter marked the beginning of the long drought, some areas having no rain at all until the end of September and consistent high temperatures from May onwards. The buds broke early, and flowering was both precocious and healthy. The whole cycle was weeks ahead of the normal schedule. The weather was sometimes also cruel; there were spring frosts and hailstorms in mid-August. Quantity is sharply down. Production in Gaillac was about half that of a normal year. The fruit was often ripe, sometimes overripe, well ahead of proper phenolic development, and acidity levels were precariously low. Grapes harvested early are likely to have produced short-lived wines of low colour but good fruit and alcohol. Rain came at the end of September – just enough to restore some acidity levels to grapes not yet harvested. Quantity is well down everywhere. In theory, prices should rise, but it is doubtful whether the market will stand sharp increases.

There is some hope for late-picking areas such as Marcillac, Jurançon, and Madiran, though even in Madiran picking started in early September. Sweet wines by *passerillage* rather than botrytis might be the most successful in this difficult year, which held out such high hopes but has delivered so little.

Updates on the previous five vintages
2002

Vintage rating: *Cahors and westwards 85; eastwards 75*
The split rating says it all. The mid-September Indian summer produced a sudden surge in the vine cycle west of the A20, the red wines enjoying an uprush in sugar levels and quick malolactic fermentations that set in almost as soon as the first fermentations were over. Fourteen degrees ABV became the norm, quite exceptional for the Malbec grape in particular. Sweet white wines everywhere will be well above average. In Fronton, Gaillac, and Marcillac, the picture was much more patchy, with cold, grey weather in August and early September.

2001

Vintage rating: *88*

This was an excellent year, with drought conditions for most of the summer and ideal picking conditions. Low acidity and high alcohol sometimes caused problems, so the wines may not keep as long as the 2000s.

2000

Vintage rating: *85*

Generally a very good year, especially for the sweet whites of Jurançon, Gaillac, Monbazillac, and Saussignac. Reds have good balance and promising tannins.

1999

Vintage rating: *78*

This was a mixed vintage, especially in those areas of the deep southwest that were caught by August hail. (There was no Château d'Aydie in Madiran, for example.) There were few sweet wines from the Bergerac appellations. Elsewhere it was a fair to middling year.

1998

Vintage rating: *90*

This was an excellent year everywhere, with both reds and whites extremely successful. However, with the exception of oak-aged Jurançons, most dry whites will be past their best.

GREATEST WINE PRODUCERS

1. Clos de Gamot (Cahors)
2. Château Lamartine (Cahors)
3. Tour des Gendres (Bergerac)
4. Château du Cèdre (Cahors)
5. Châteaux Montus and Bouscassé (Madiran)
6. Clos des Verdots (Bergerac)
7. Domaine de Berthoumieu (Madiran)
8. Domaine Cauhapé (Jurançon)
9. Clos Bacqueys (Côtes du Marmandais)
10. Les Très Cantous (Gaillac)

FASTEST-IMPROVING PRODUCERS

1. Domaine de Causse-Marines (Gaillac)
2. Domaine des Costes (Pécharmant)
3. Château les Miaudoux (Saussignac)
4. Domaine Bordeanave (Jurançon)
5. Domaine Cosse-Maisonneuve (Cahors)
6. Domaine Arretxea (Irouléguy)
7. Domaine Laffont (Madiran)
8. Domaine de la Bérengeraie (Cahors)
9. Château de Masburel (Montravel)
10. Clos Fardet (Madiran)

NEW UP-AND-COMING PRODUCERS

1. Domaine de Saint-Guilhem (Fronton)
2. Domaine de la Chanade (Gaillac)
3. Domaine Bernet (Madiran)
4. Château Mascaaras (Madiran)
5. Château la Reyne (Cahors)
6. Domaine de Gineste (Gaillac)
7. Château Jonc Blanc (Bergerac)
8. Domaine des Cailloutis (Gaillac)
9. Domaine de Cause (Cahors)
10. Château d'Arlus (Gaillac)

BEST-VALUE PRODUCERS

1. Les Producteurs Plaimont (Côtes de Saint-Mont)
2. Château Plaisance (Fronton)
3. Clos de Coutale (Cahors)
4. Domaine du Cros (Marcillac)
5. Château Les Ifs (Cahors)
6. Domaine Labranche-Laffont (Madiran)
7. Les Vignerons Réunis des Côtes de Buzet (Buzet)
8. Domaine de Larroque (Gaillac)
9. Château le Roc (Fronton)
10. Domaines Lapeyre and Guilhémas (Béarn)

Grapevine

• **English growers** David and Sarah Meakin have won an award from *Guide Hachette* for their Domaine du Merchien in the Coteaux du Quercy. Their wine had already been noted in *Wine Report* as one of the discoveries of the year.

GREATEST-QUALITY WINES

1. **Château Montus 1995** Madiran (€32)
2. **Cuvée Madame 1997** Château Tirecul-la-Gravière, Monbazillac (€65)
3. **Quintessence du Petit Manseng 1990** Domaine Cauhapé, Jurançon (€50)
4. **Vignes Centenaires 1985** Clos de Gamot, Cahors (€20)
5. **Chapelle Lenclos 1991** Madiran (€22)
6. **Vin d'Autan 1989** Vignobles Plageoles, Gaillac (€40)
7. **La Gloire de Mon Père 1998** Tour des Gendres, Bergerac (€28)
8. **Clos des Verdots 1998** Bergerac (€25)
9. **Cuvée Particulière 1998** Château Lamartine, Cahors (€30)
10. **Château du Cèdre 1998** Cahors (€20)

BEST BARGAINS

1. **Domaine de Merchien 2001** Coteaux du Quercy (€6)
2. **Château d'Arlus Mauzac 2001** Gaillac (€4)
3. **Rouge Tradition 2001** Domaine Capmartin, Madiran (€3.90)
4. **Lo Sang del Païs 2001** Domaine du Cros, Marcillac (€4)
5. **Classique 2001** Château Plaisance, Fronton (€6)
6. **Rouge Tradition 2001** Château Barréjat, Madiran (€3.20)
7. **Château de Palme 2001** Fronton (€5)
8. **Château Miaudoux Sec 2001** Bergerac (€5)
9. **Coteaux de Glanes 2002** Vin de Pays du Lot Rouge (€4)
10. **Château Latuc 2000** Cahors (€6)

MOST EXCITING OR UNUSUAL FINDS

① Clos Saint-Jean 2000 Cahors (€20) *A tiny 1.5-hectare (ha) vineyard belonging to the Jouffreau family of Clos de Gamot fame, planted on almost vertical slopes between the causse and the river valley. One hundred per cent Auxerrois (Malbec). Destined to go fast to the top of the Cahors tree.*

② Château Palvié 2001 Gaillac (€8) *Another recent vineyard, this one planted by the Bézios family on the Premières Côtes to the north of the town. At last an important red Gaillac. Two parts of Syrah and one of Braucol combine to produce a wine that has some Rhône and Bordeaux characteristics but remains essentially Gaillac. There is an oaked version too (€12).*

③ Marcillac 2001 Claudine Costes et Eric Vinas (€4.50) *These growers have much improved their viticulture and winemaking techniques during the last year or two. Their wines rank with the best of this small appellation.*

④ Delire d'Automne Doux 2001 Domaine de Causse-Marines, Gaillac (€18 per 50-cl bottle) *Patrice Lescarret on the AOC system: "The only weapon capable of protecting us from the attacks of barbarians has become a wretched repressive machine, obstructive and sterile." His wines are no less colourful than his language. This one is 100 per cent Ondenc, of which there are only 4 ha or so in the whole appellation.*

⑤ Lavilledieu-du-Temple Milgranet 2002 Cave Coopérative de Lavilledieu-du-Temple (€6) *A trial production from an experimentally revived grape variety of prephylloxera times. (See Searching for traditional grape varieties.)*

⑥ Tonus 2001 Domaines Bouscassé and Montus, Madiran (€8) *The rebranded version of Domaine Meinjarre, Alain Brumont's best value-for-money line in AOC Madiran. (See Grapevine.)*

⑦ Le Vin Est une Fête Rouge 2001/2 Domaine Elian da Ros, Côtes du Marmandais (€6) *A terrific everyday drinking wine from a prestigious producer who has played such a large part in making Marmande famous for wine as well as tomatoes.*

⑧ Domaine de Laulan Sauvignon 2002 Côtes de Duras (€6) *More of a rediscovery than a discovery. Gilbert Geoffroy has been making his pure Sauvignon (in both oaked and unoaked versions) for 20 years and more, but he has recently seemed to move into a higher gear.*

⑨ Château du Cèdre Viognier 2002 Vin de Pays du Lot (€12) *A delicious venture into dry white wine from Pascal Verhaeghe, who has to market it as vin de pays because there is no such thing as white Cahors – yet.*

⑩ Domaine de Perchade-Perrouchet (all colours) 2002 Tursan (€6) *The Dulucq family are extraordinarily successful as Davids in making and marketing their Tursan wines in face of the competition from the Goliath Tursan cooperative and from master chef Michel Guérard.*

This year the spotlight falls on Limoux. The rules have been changed and many exciting growers have been attracted to the region.

PAUL STRANG

Of the three appellations for sparkling wine, Crémant de Limoux has been the most esteemed due to its content of up to 40 per cent Chardonnay and Chenin Blanc. This produces a finer sparkling wine than Blanquette de Limoux, which is heavily dependent on the local Mauzac grape, with the Chardonnay and Chenin Blanc restricted to a maximum of just 10 per cent. From the 2003 harvest onwards, Crémant de Limoux's finesse factor will be further enhanced by the increased contribution of Chardonnay and Chenin Blanc, which may be as high as 90 per cent (of which Chenin Blanc must represent 20–40 per cent of the global blend) and the inclusion of up to 10 per cent Pinot Blanc. The Mauzac is restricted to a maximum of 10 per cent and thus could be ignored altogether. The intention may be to create a bigger differential between the Crémant and other Blanquettes.

It is not hard to find in this the influence of Champenois and Burgundian newcomers to the region, attracted by the suitability of the *terroir*, particularly the land on the higher ground to the south and west of the region, where Chardonnay has proved such a success. Jean-Louis Denois, for whom nobody had a good word at one time, set the pace for this. Since then he has been joined by Burgundian *négociant* Antonin Rodet and by the Mâconnais partnership of Christian Collovray and Jean-Luc Terrier of Château d'Antugnac, who are making a delicious pure Chardonnay.

PAUL STRANG is recognized as one of the leading experts on the wines of the south of France, where he has had a home for many years. His most recent book is *Languedoc-Roussillon: The Wines and Winemakers* (Mitchell Beazley, 2002).

At the same time, an AOC for red Limoux has been newly created, admitting growers who have hitherto been limited to the production of *vins de pays*. The qualifying *encépagement* must be at least 50 per cent Merlot; Cot, Syrah, Grenache, and Carignan and the two Cabernets are other grapes allowed. To rank as AOC, the wine must be made from at least three of these seven grape varieties. This will suit properties like Antugnac well, though their surprisingly delicious pure Alicante wine will have to remain a *vin de pays*.

Greenland

Who ever heard of a biological cooperative grower? The excellent Sieurs d'Arques establishment has one on its books. Christian Meuser, who is German by birth, fell in love with the hill country of Limoux. He saw the prospects of an isolated vineyard where biological practice could be conducted somewhere in the outback without the risk of contamination by non-biological growers and farmers.

St-Sernin is miles from anywhere and here Meuser bought and planted 7 hectares (ha) or so of Mauzac, Chardonnay, and Chenin Blanc at a height of over 400 metres. Christian has no *chais*, so he sends all his grapes to Sieurs d'Arques, whereby hangs this tale. The French supermarket chain Carrefour, which was promoting a range of bio wines at the time, asked the co-op to vinify Christian's wine separately, provided he became fully bio. The co-op agreed. However, Carrefour was eventually bought out by an American concern, which dropped the bio range. Christian would have been left high and dry but for the Rothschild family, who had bought a lot of his wine at the Toques et Clochers auction. Since Christian had been invited by Mondavi (no less) to go to California and make wine for him, it is not surprising that the co-op has kept the arrangement going. It means not only that his wines have to be vinified and bottled separately, but also supervised by Ecovert, of which he is a fully paid-up licence holder.

All change!

Limoux is not the only area to have its rules changed. We now have a white Collioure, whereas the appellation was previously limited to red and *rosé* wines. Grenache Gris and Blanc will be the mainstay grape varieties, plus Malvoisie, Macabeu, Marsanne, Roussanne, and Vermentino. The permitted area covers 1,000 ha and it has taken the growers 12 years to get the new appellation through.

Also in the Roussillon, where the rules are already complicated enough, we have a new Roussillon Aspres appellation, where Syrah and/or Mourvèdre will be compulsory from 2004. Aspres is the area to the north of the Tech, the most southerly of the three Roussillon rivers, almost in the shade of Mount Canigou.

St-Chinian has sprouted two *crus* of its own, both in the north of the appellation, in the hills on either side of the river Orb. To the west, Berlou (home to Domaine Rimbert as well as an excellent cooperative) covers just its own commune, while Roquebrun on the east bank also takes in the communes of Vieussan to the north and St-Nazaire-de-Ladarez to the east, where Domaine Borie-la-Vitarèle flourishes.

Finally, the emergence of the grouping of *crus* and *terroirs* under the name Grès de Montpellier (red wines only) has finally been accomplished for the vintages of 2002 onwards. The component vineyards comprise Vérargues, St-Christol, St-Drézéry, Sommières, La Méjanelle, and St-Georges d'Orques.

Grapevine

• **AXA is one of France's biggest** financial institutions. Christian Seely, MD of its wine-investment arm (which already owns Pichon-Longueville-Baron, Suduiraut, Pibran, Cantenac-Brown, Petit-Village, and La Tour Pibran in France, as well as Disznókő in Hungary and Quinta do Noval in Portugal), had previously purchased Domaine Ste-Hélène (30 ha) between Caux and Pézenas. Now, though, he has added the neighbouring property of Château Belles Eaux (60 ha), giving AXA 90 ha of prime Syrah, Mourvèdre, and Grenache. Bernard Magrez (Pape-Clément and Fombrauge) and Gérard Depardieu, not content with their acquisition at Aniane, have also bought vineyards in the Côtes de Malepère. Magrez also has a château called L'Oustric near Carcassonne. The family of Baron Philippe de Rothschild, in addition to its partnerships with Sieurs d'Arques (Baron'Arques), also owns Domaine Limbert in Limoux.

• **The commercial launch** of Faugères brandy, currently being made experimentally, has been delayed until the end of 2004 at least, because the quality of the brandy has turned out to be much better than expected. By 2008 at the latest, growers will be marketing an *hors d'age* brandy in any format, bottle shape, or label they wish to use. In the 19th century there were 1,000 distilleries in the department of Hérault alone, so this will be an interesting revival of an old product.

• **Aimé Guibert** seems to be gradually handing the reins at Daumas Gassac to the next generation, though Madame Guibert seems unlikely to be the least influential voice at a family board meeting. London saw the launch of a new top *cuvée* named after Emile Peynaud, who first identified Aniane as an ideal *terroir* for Cabernet Sauvignon. The new wine is all Cabernet and is raised in wholly new oak. At the launch, cask samples could hardly be tasted through the wood, and the wine will clearly need several years to come round.

Syrah is a noble grape variety. It was grown in Languedoc-Roussillon as a minority grape long before the present renaissance of the region. Since then it has been promoted by the wine authorities and by the French media to the point where it is regarded as almost a *sine qua non* in any serious wine. There are obvious dangers in this, despite the undoubted qualities of the grape. Syrah is particularly liable to hydric stress in prolonged drought, a misfortune that affects young vines in particular and also vines in shallow ground where the roots are not able to plunge deep enough to gain access to moisture. There is also the risk that it will cuckoo out the other grape varieties grown in the deep south, become a ubiquitous mono-*cépage* and thus cause a standardization of taste and style in an area that can at the moment justly pride itself on its diversity. Grenache and Carignan grow well in Pic-St-Loup, La Livinière, and Roussillon Aspres, but these three *crus* are gradually pushing up the compulsory Syrah levels to the point where other grapes are minority supporters only.

Hierarchies and heresies

We don't have a word in English for *hierarchisation*, but in France it is the buzz word of the year. They feel in the Languedoc that a level playing field for all is not helping to promote the better wines. The subdivision of existing appellations and even *crus* of existing appellations into smaller units seems to suggest to many people the way ahead. But care needs to be taken not to penalize growers who, through an accident of geography or *terroir*, may not qualify for a superior *cru*, even if they are making wine that is better than many who do.

In Minervois there is just one single interior subappellation called La Livinière, covering certain *terroirs* within a smallish radius of the village. Many of the best Minervois wines come from here, but the mere existence of one sole inner *cru* suggests that growers outside the privileged area are, by definition, less worthy than those within it, when this is far from the case.

For example, Jean-Baptiste Senat at Domaine Saint-Sernin has his vines in the village of Trausse. This is just outside the area of

La Livinière, but, even if it were within it, Senat would still not qualify for the La Livinière label because he has little Mourvèdre and no Syrah at all (one, the other, or both in combination being obligatory up to a total of 40 per cent). He says he cannot grow Syrah because his soil is too sandy. Nevertheless, his wines are excellent. He is not resentful about his exclusion because one result of the new *cru* is that it is the only area in Minervois where Americans and Bordelais will buy land, which is pushing up prices, while vineyards at Trausse are much cheaper.

Co-ops improve

Notable progress has been made by a number of cooperatives in the south, of whom one can single out Les Maîtres Vignerons du Faugérois, Les Vignerons du Pic (St-Loup), the Caves at Roquebrun and Berlou in St-Chinian, the Cave at Montpeyroux, the better wines from Les Vignerons Catalans (itself a grouping of cooperatives), the well-known Mont Tauch, especially for its Fitous, and the smaller Caves at Tautavel and Terrats in the Roussillon. But the laggards are sadly still in the majority.

No change in grape varieties

If the cooperatives have been listening, the wine authorities have not. There is still little sign of liberalization of the rules on grape varieties outside the areas where new appellations have been created (see above).

Grapevine

• **Costières de Nîmes growers,** hardly helped by three difficult vintages in the past five, are having problems with the image of their appellation. Ambitious properties such as Château de Beck are finding it hard to get the prices they want for their wines and may in future operate under the Vin de Pays banner. This is all very well for those who can afford a publicity budget or who are what the French call *médiatique*, but for more modest producers life may become harder rather than easier. Part of the difficulty is that the Costières fall between two wine-growing stools, being seen as neither quite Languedoc (which they are politically) nor Côtes du Rhône (which they are stylistically). A pity, because there are some really good-value wines here.

• **Marselan, a grape variety** promoted by the Union des Caves Coopératives (UCCOAR) in the Aude, is a cross of Cabernet Sauvignon and Grenache. There are only 20 ha of this plant, so it is not surprising that it has taken 40 years for the resulting wine to become available in the UK. A varietal version is made by Domaine Jordy near Lodève, and a blend of the grape with equal quantities of the two Cabernets by Domaine Les Quatre Pilas at Murviel-lès-Montpellier.

Advance report on the latest harvest
2003

In general, winter rains made up for the lack of water the previous year, but, outside the previously flooded areas, only just. Warm weather set in at Easter, bringing early budding and flowering of the grapes. Warmth developed into excessive heat during the summer, but there were storms to relieve the water shortage to a certain extent. Vines planted in deep soils will have done best. The main problem was the fierce sun, with temperatures often at 40+ °C for days on end. In many places the fruit was grilled on the plant by the heat of the sun. Halfway through the cycle, drought prevented the sap from rising in the plants, causing the fruit to remain small, but concentrated, with tough skins. Sugar levels developed early, picking in Roussillon (Gauby) starting in the first few days of August, but the problem is going to be low acidity levels. The harvest took place in torrid heat, and even growers with the most sophisticated cooling equipment found it difficult to keep temperatures under control. The virtues of nighttime harvesting were well demonstrated. The growers on the higher ground, where cooler night air often restores the capacity of the vine to resist excessive sun heat, will have done best – in Pic-St-Loup, Montpeyroux, and the hinterland of Roussillon especially. Syrah vines, especially those recently planted, suffered sometimes from hydric stress and, while Mourvèdre enjoyed the heat, there was not enough moisture coming from the sea. The traditional Grenache, Carignan, and Cinsault may have succeeded best. Growers seem undecided whether this was an absolutely fantastic year or one that will ultimately yield generous fruity wines but for early drinking. Red and white wines seem equally to have profited/suffered by the exceptional conditions. This is a year in which the skills of the winemaker in the *chais* may determine quality. Quantity is dramatically down for the second year running.

Updates on the previous five vintages

2002

Vintage rating: *83 (60 in the flooded areas)*

Away from the areas (Costières de Nîmes, Grès de Montpellier especially, and parts of Pic-St-Loup) affected by floods or heavy rain in early September, the vintage has turned out better than first expected. The best wines may well come from areas able to profit from the Indian summer, which rescued the harvest after a cool growing season. Collioure and Banyuls did well, as did Roussillon generally, as well as the inland areas of Aniane and Montpeyroux, which pick later than some others. Quantities were down on previous years, and in general the quality was below that of the two preceding years.

2001

Vintage rating: *90*

Exceptional throughout the region. A heat-wave summer produced very ripe fruit (perhaps too ripe in those cases where it has been at the expense of acidity), good sugar levels, and plenty of natural concentration. Reds and whites were equally successful, though the production of white table wine in the region is very much a minority business (about 5 per cent). The quantity was down on 2000. Everywhere east of Béziers needed a good year to offset the floods of 1999 and the disasters of 2002. The best vintage since 1998, and some wines will be better than that.

2000

Vintage rating: *86*

A very good, abundant year. The weather was cool until the middle of July, thereafter very hot – sometimes too hot for Syrah, which is liable to stress if allowed to dry out. There was an unusually large discrepancy between harvesting times in the hot seaside vineyards and the cooler properties on the *coteaux* – up to a month for the same grape varieties. There was some disparity in sugar levels, too, and the quality was more variable than in 2001. Notable successes in this vintage were Banyuls, Collioure, Fitou, St-Chinian, Faugères, and Pic-St-Loup. Some wines will keep longer than the more forward 2001s.

1999

Vintage rating: 80

There were some disasters through wet harvest times in the east. The Costières are weak and watery, with some growers declassifying altogether, and Pic-St-Loup had some trouble too. However, further west there were many successes. The Aude had a particularly good year, Corbières and Minervois often making wines quite as good as, sometimes better than, 1998. In a variable year, it is difficult to give an overall high rating, although many producers surpass the 80 score with ease.

1998

Vintage rating: 90

It is hard to find a disappointing wine from this vintage, which was excellent just about everywhere. Long drought conditions favoured most varieties, but overall it was a year for the traditional Carignan, Cinsault, and Grenache, rather than the so-called *améliorateurs*, such as Syrah and Mourvèdre, which sometimes did not produce the phenolic levels hoped for. There were plenty of drying winds throughout the season and ideal harvesting conditions. The wines will not be over their peak in 2005, and the best will keep longer, especially those raised in new wood.

GREATEST WINE PRODUCERS

1. Domaine Gauby (Calce, Roussillon)
2. Domaine Canet-Valette (St-Chinian)
3. Roc d'Anglade (Coteaux du Languedoc)
4. Domaine Sarda-Malet (Perpignan, Roussillon)
5. Domaine Ferrer-Ribière (Terrats, Roussillon)
6. Domaine Jean-Michel Alquier (Faugères)
7. Domaine d'Aupilhac (Montpeyroux)
8. Domaine Peyre-Rose (St-Pargoire)
9. Coopérative d'Embres-et-Castelmaure (Corbières)
10. Mas de Champart (St-Chinian)

FASTEST-IMPROVING PRODUCERS

1. Clos Marie (Pic-St-Loup)
2. La Terre Inconnue (St-Christol)
3. Pierre Clavel, Mas de Périé (Grès de Montpellier)
4. Luc Lapeyre (Minervois)
5. Clos de l'Anhel (Corbières)
6. Mas des Brousses (Coteaux du Languedoc)
7. Domaine Gardiès (Vingrau, Roussillon)
8. Domaine Bertrand Bergé (Fitou)
9. Mas de Martin (Coteaux du Languedoc)
10. Domaine d'Escourrou (Cabardès)

NEW UP-AND-COMING PRODUCERS

1. Domaine La Madura (St-Chinian)
2. Domaine Saint-Sernin (Minervois)
3. Olivier Pithon (Calce, Roussillon)
4. Domaine Villa Maria Fita (Fitou)
5. Mas Foulaquier (Pic-St-Loup)
6. Château de Beck (Costières de Nîmes)
7. Domaine des Morets (Tautavel, Roussillon)
8. Clos de l'Oum (Bélesta, Roussillon)
9. Clos de Gravillas (St-Jean-de-Minervois)
10. Château Bassanel (Minervois)

BEST-VALUE PRODUCERS

1. Mas de Séranne (Aniane)
2. Domaine La Tour Boisée (Minervois)
3. Coopérative Aiméry Sieurs d'Arques (Limoux)
4. Mas des Chimères (Terrasses de Larzac)
5. Domaine de l'Arjolle (Côtes du Thongue)
6. Domaine du Tabatau (St-Chinian)
7. Domaine du Vieux Relais (Costières de Nîmes)
8. Domaine Comps (St-Chinian)
9. Domaine de Cabrol (Cabardès)
10. Château de Jonquières (Montpeyroux)

GREATEST-QUALITY WINES

1. **Grand Vin Rouge 1988** Mas de Daumas Gassac (€30)
2. **Muntada 2000** Domaine Gauby (€30)
3. **Le Soula Blanc 2002/Rouge 2001** Domaine Gauby (€28)
4. **Clôt de Taillelangue 1999** Le Casot de Mailloles (€20)
5. **La Grange des Pères Rouge 1998** (€30)
6. **Le Prieuré de Saint-Jean-de-Bébian Rouge 1998** (€28)
7. **Cuvée Nicolas 2001** Domaine de Barroubio, St-Jean-de-Minervois (€32 per half-bottle)
8. **Clos des Cistes 1998** Domaine Peyre Rose (€38)
9. **Capitelle de Centeilles 2001** Clos des Centeilles (€18)
10. **Léon Barral Rouge 2001** Domaine Léon Barral, Faugères (€12)

BEST BARGAINS

1. **Domaine du Clos Perche 2001** Coteaux du Languedoc St-Christol (€3)
2. **Roque-Sestières Vieilles Vignes Blanc 2002** Bérail-Lagarde, Corbières (€6)
3. **Domaine de la Reynardière Rouge 1998** Faugères (€6)
4. **Domaine de Reilhe Rouge 2000** Coteaux du Languedoc (€7)
5. **Château Saint-Jacques d'Albas Rouge 2001** Minervois (€6)
6. **Domaine Fontanel Tradition Rouge 2001** Côtes du Roussillon (€6)
7. **Cellier de Trouillas Tradition Rouge 2001** Côtes du Roussillon (€4)
8. **Domaine de Limbardié Rouge Classique 2002** Coteaux de Murviel (€6)
9. **Domaine du Météore Rouge 2002** Faugères (€5)
10. **Château L'Etang des Colombes Rouge 2002** Corbières (€6)

MOST EXCITING OR UNUSUAL FINDS

1. **Cuvée Los Abuelos 2001** La Terre Inconnue, Vin de Table (€26) *Mistaken by the owner of Château Rayas (Châteauneuf-du-Pape) on a visit for one of his own wines. Pure Grenache, reaching 15 per cent.*

2. **La Chapelle San Roch Blanc 2002** La Préceptorie de Centernach, Vin de Pays du Val d'Agly (€8) *One of the first to mature of the new breed of high-altitude dry whites from Roussillon.*

3. **Domaine Cros 2002** Vin de Table (€5) *A rare and eccentric blend of Piquepoul Noir, Alicante, Aramon, and Carignan. A real song of the terroir from an experimental grower in the Minervois.*

4. **Les Terrasses Blanches 1998** Domaine des Schistes (€12) *An extraordinary oxidized wine in the style of a vin de voile. Nutty and golden, but still dry. Reminiscent of a Montilla, but unfortified. From a top-flight Roussillon grower.*

5. **Aspiran Noir 2002** Domaine Navarre, Vin de Table (€8) *From a grower in St-Chinian. A rare varietal from this ancient grape variety. Pale, completely charming, fluid, relatively light in alcohol (12 per cent), fruity and mineral.*

6. **Château Maurel-Fonsalade Felix Culpa 1997** (€18) *A happy mistake now repeated deliberately each year, caused by M Maurel leaving some heat under a cask of Syrah. Vinified in open vats with pigeage and a touch of Grenache in the blend, this big wine will keep for 10 years and will be superb with red meats and stews.*

7. **Marselan 2001** Domaine Jordy (€14) *Unblended example of this rare cross between Grenache and Cabernet Sauvignon (see above).*

8. **Mas Haut Buis, Costa Caoude 2001** Coteaux du Languedoc Rouge (€25) *Way up on the Larzac plateau, this property enjoys a partly oceanic, partly Mediterranean climate. Raised from 50 per cent Syrah, 30 per cent Grenache, and 20 per cent Carignan, with 60 per cent in new barrels and 40 per cent in tank.*

9. **La Clape Rouge Elevé en Fût de Chêne 1999** Château de Marmorières (€9) *Exciting because this is such a little-known but excellent property, quite one of the best in this terroir. A lightly oaked (one year or older barrels) blend of Carignan (50 per cent), Syrah (30 per cent), and Grenache (20 per cent).*

10. **L'Evêque Petit Manseng 2002** Domaine de Condamine, Vin de Pays (€16) *A new late-harvested wine from Guy Bascou, ubiquitous consultant as well as winemaker.*

Grapevine

• **The little appellation** of St-Jean-de-Minervois, a moonscape where the soil is almost entirely chalk, is becoming home to a number of enthusiastic growers seeking the quiet life; quiet, because St-Jean is on a road to nowhere in the hills separating Minervois from St-Chinian. Visitors to the region should lose no time in seeking out small-time properties such as Domaine de Gravillas and Le Petit Domaine de Gimios, where artisanal Muscat, unfortified as well as fortified, is made to a high standard, and where the welcome is as good as the wine.

The best of the *vins de pays*, especially in the south of France, continue to provide an outlet for myriad wines that do not conform to appellation regulations.

ROSEMARY GEORGE MW

While it is true that *vins de pays* do have to meet some criteria, these are less restrictive than those of the appellations, and if you choose to make *vins de table*, the limitations on what you may or may not do are even less curtailing. The downside is that you may put virtually no information on the label, just your name and a name for the wines, but no vintage and certainly no details of provenance other than a postal code. Nonetheless, questioning and experimentally minded producers are finding the *vins de table* category perfectly acceptable for their requirements. However, it does help if their name is already known as a producer of quality. So we have Domaine Cazes in Rivesaltes producing the appropriately named Libre Expression, a pure Macabeu. The wine was originally destined for Rivesaltes, but reached a natural 16 per cent all on its own and consequently the necessary alcohol for the appellation was never added. Another nonconformist is Domaine Rimbaud in St-Chinian. His first vinification of some very old Carignan vines proved problematic with a stuck fermentation; the resulting wine did not conform to the required analysis norms for St-Chinian and consequently was refused its *agrément*. Le Chant de Marjolaine,

ROSEMARY GEORGE MW was lured into the wine trade by a glass of The Wine Society's champagne at a job interview. Realizing that secretarial work was not for her, she took the wine-trade exams, becoming one of the first women to qualify as a Master of Wine in 1979. She has been a freelance wine writer since 1981 and is the current chairman of the Circle of Wine Writers. Rosemary is the author of nine books, including *Chablis*, *French Country Wines*, *The Wines of New Zealand*, and *The Wines of the South of France*. Her next book, *Walking through the Vineyards of Tuscany*, is due for publication in spring 2004.

with a poorly disguised vintage masquerading as a lot number, is just one example of the extraordinary creativity that abounds in the south of France.

Nor are such activities confined to the Midi. Olivier Humbrecht MW, of the reputable Alsace house of Zind Humbrecht, has fallen foul of the Institut National des Appellations d'Origine (INAO) for planting Chardonnay, which is allowed in Alsace only for Crémant d'Alsace. Olivier, however, wanted to give some more flavour to his Pinot Blanc and Pinot Auxerrois and, for a number of years, sold the wine as plain Pinot d'Alsace. But then somebody told the authorities and the INAO intervened, initially by examining the possibility of allowing Chardonnay for still wines in Alsace, but ultimately deciding against it. There is no doubt that politics and bureaucratic restrictions come into play here. If Chardonnay were to be allowed in Alsace, growers in other parts of France would want to plant Riesling and Gewurztraminer, and that the INAO does not want.

• **An area to watch** is a small part of the Collines Rhodaniennes, around the village of Seyssuel, near the town of Vienne. Although the vineyards are on the opposite side of the Rhône from Côte Rôtie, they enjoy the same south-facing aspect on steep hillsides and the same granite soil. Indeed, when the appellation of Côte Rôtie was created in 1947, the growers at the time were given the option of joining the appellation but preferred the then-soft option of continuing to make *vin de table*. The leaders in this small quality region are a group of three growers, all with vines in St-Joseph, Condrieu, and Côte Rôtie, namely Pierre Gaillard, Francois Villard, and Yves Cuilleron, who work under the name of Les Vins de Vienne. They have planted 10 hectares (ha) of Syrah and one of Viognier, for Sotanum and Tabernum respectively. Since 2003, their successful example has been followed by other producers from the Rhône Valley, namely Alain Paret and Max Chapoutier, among others, ensuring that Seyssuel is a name we are likely to hear more of.

• *Copeaux*, or oak chips, continue to prove contentious. Officialdom deems that they are not allowed, while some producers consider them to be permitted, but only for *vins de pays*, and even then for only a small 5 per cent of your total production, and not before you have filled in the necessary forms and obtained the relevant permit. If you are making inexpensive *vins de pays*, the use of chips is no bad thing, but, like anything, it needs to be done properly. As with *barriques*, there is a world of difference between cheap chips and expensive chips.

• **Changes to the list** of *vins de pays* include the promotion of the distinctive Vin de Pays de la Haute Vallée de l'Orb, covering higher-altitude vineyards behind Faugères, near Bédarieux, to appellation status. For the moment, the dossier is *en cours*, as the French so elegantly say. Meanwhile, the creation of the red appellation of Limoux will have elevated wines made from Merlot and Cabernet, while Pinot Noir will continue as a Vin de Pays de la Haute Vallée de l'Aude. The creation of the appellation of white Collioure will result in the disappearance of some of the more characterful white *vins de pays* from Domaine de la Rectorie, since they have become Collioure Blanc.

MORE NAME GAMES

In Roussillon, Vin de Pays Catalan, Vin de Pays des Vals d'Agly, and Vin de Pays des Coteaux de Fenouillèdes have all been incorporated into the all-embracing Vin de Pays des Côtes Catalanes. This seems particularly unfortunate in the case of the Coteaux de Fenouillèdes, which was beginning to establish a reputation for itself, with considerable outside investment and interest repaying dividends in wine quality. The list of potential headline-making projects includes Jean-Luc Thunevin of St-Emilion fame with a local grower, Jean-Roger Calvet; Stéfan d'Arfeuille from Pomerol at La Feuillade; two Plumpton College graduates at La Pertuisane; Olivier Pithon from the Loire Valley; and a partnership of local growers, Eric Laguerre of Domaine des Cistes with Gérard Gauby and the British wine merchant Richards Walford at Le Soula. All are realizing the fantastic potential of fabulous old, low-yielding Grenache vines, so we can look forward to some wonderful flavours with a concentration and depth quite unlike anything that usually comes from the vins de pays of Roussillon, or indeed from the appellation of Côtes du Roussillon. The problem revolves around politics – yet again. All over the Midi, the village cooperatives are important players in the wine scene, but there are no cooperatives making Coteaux de Fenouillèdes – and therefore nobody with sufficient political clout to defend the unique potential of the area in the face of bureaucracy.

STALL OVER NATIONWIDE *VIN DE PAYS*

Politics is never far from the French wine scene, and certainly the rumblings over the course of the past few months about a putative Vin de Pays de France, as a varietal wine, are beset by political machinations at every level. If you had to draw up the lines, this is an argument between Vin de Pays d'Oc and the potential producers of *vin de pays* in the Gironde. At the moment, no *vin de pays* is produced in the Gironde; the lowest recognized category is the humblest quality of Bordeaux, which covers the whole department. However, it is a well-known secret that a not-inconsiderable amount of Merlot and Cabernet Sauvignon from the Languedoc allegedly travels north to add some fruit and ripeness to some of the leaner vintages of the Gironde. But if a new category of *vin de pays* were to allow for varietal wines to come from all over France, the producers of Vin de Pays d'Oc, who have most successfully marketed varietal wines to meet the competition of the New World, would lose their commercial edge. Needless to say, they are not at all happy at the prospect and, consequently, are defending their corner energetically, so far with success. Doubtless the political machinations will continue to rumble for a while yet, but for the moment Vin de Pays des Cépages de France is in abeyance.

Irrigation is a 'mute' point in the Midi. It is allowed for *vins de pays*, but not for appellation wines, and not during August, although that is when the inspectors go on holiday. If linked to strict controls on yields, why not allow it for both categories?

More nonsensical is the official attitude towards the numerous late-harvest wines of the Midi – not the *vins doux naturels*, but the late-picked wines that may be the result of raisined grapes or even – occasionally – of noble rot. The political clout of the Alsatians within the INAO is such that the term *vendange tardive* is effectively forbidden. Marc Benin of Domaine de Ravanès in the Coteaux de Murviel found himself in court and fined for labelling late-picked Ugni Blanc as *vendange tardive*. Currently the term *vendanges surmûries* is tolerated, and more often than not bottles bear the long-winded description: "Moût partiellement fermenté, issu de vendanges passerillés". Do not be put off by the terminology; the wines are delicious, but clearly they need to be given some legal definition.

Grapevine

• **The 2003 harvest** was one of the earliest on record, with many producers starting in mid-August. More significantly, it was the second year running in the Midi that production was down, by as much as 50 per cent in some cases. This means that there is strong demand for some grape varieties, particularly Sauvignon and Chardonnay, while Cabernet Sauvignon is more stable. Sauvignon from the Loire Valley is also enjoying high demand, especially because Sauvignon de Touraine has risen in price in recent months. In fact, the differences between the two are not so distinct. What is more serious is that the village cooperatives need a certain amount of wine to cover their overheads. If there is another short harvest in 2004, some village cooperatives may well face bankruptcy. Hitherto a popular solution has been the fusion of two neighbouring cooperatives to address the need to market their wines more effectively.

• **The roll call of *vins de pays*** is far from fixed; they come and go. Vin de Pays de Pézenas in the Hérault has been suppressed and incorporated into the adjoining Vin de Pays de Caux, Caux being a village near Pézenas. Presumably, with Pézenas now one of the possible *terroirs* of the Coteaux du Languedoc, there was the possibility of confusing the appellation and the *vin de pays*.

Several of these producers are known for their appellation wines, as well as for vins de pays, which may form only a small part of their production.

GREATEST WINE PRODUCERS

1. Domaine de Trévallon, Bouches du Rhône
2. Domaine Gauby, Côtes Catalanes
3. Mas de Daumas Gassac, Hérault
4. Domaine la Grange des Pères, Hérault
5. Domaine Routas, Var
6. Domaine de Clovallon, Oc
7. Domaine Vaquer, Côtes Catalanes
8. Domaine de l'Arjolle, Côtes de Thongue
9. Domaine Grassa, Côtes de Gascogne
10. Producteurs Plaimont, Côtes de Gascogne

FASTEST-IMPROVING PRODUCERS

1. Jean-Louis Denois, Oc
2. Domaine de la Marfée, Hérault
3. Mas des Chimères, Coteaux du Salagou
4. Domaine Magellan, Côtes de Thongue
5. Domaine la Croix-Belle, Côtes de Thongue
6. Domaine Fontcaude, Oc
7. Domaine Belles Pierres, Oc
8. Domaine Aupilhac, Mont Baudile
9. Domaine la Grange des Quatre Sous, Oc
10. Domaine de Ravanès, Coteaux de Murviel

NEW UP-AND-COMING PRODUCERS

1. Les Vins de Vienne, Collines Rhodaniennes
2. Domaine Lalaurie, Coteaux de Narbonne and Oc
3. Domaine Camp-Galhan, Duché d'Uzès and Oc
4. Domaine Perdiguier, Coteaux d'Enserune
5. Domaine Fougeray de Beauclair, Hérault
6. Domaine Virgile Joly, Hérault
7. Mas de l'Ecriture, Oc
8. Domaine Rimbaud, Vin de Table (St-Chinian)
9. Zind Humbrecht, Vin de Table (Alsace)
10. Pascal Jolivet, Jardin de la France

BEST-VALUE PRODUCERS

1. Domaine de la Chevalière, Oc
2. Domaine de Valmoissine, Gorges de Verdon
3. Domaine Cazes, Côtes Catalanes
4. Abbotts, Oc
5. Mas Montel, Gard and Oc
6. Domaine Perdiguier, Coteaux d'Enserune
7. Cave de Tain l'Hermitage, Collines Rhodaniennes
8. Maurel Vedeau, Oc
9. J & F Lurton, Oc
10. Producteurs Plaimont, Côtes de Gascogne

Grapevine

• **Gérard Depardieu** has settled into the Midi and picked his first grapes – Syrah, Grenache Noir, and Carignan – from his 2.4-ha vineyard outside Aniane in the Hérault. Look out for Le Secret des Templiers 2003, which will be released in 2005, after 18 months of oak ageing.

GREATEST-QUALITY WINES

1. **Domaine de Trévallon Rouge 2001** Vin de Pays des Bouches du Rhône (€45)
2. **Cuvée Emile Peynaud 2001** Mas de Daumas Gassac, Vin de Pays de l'Hérault (€100)
3. **Mas des Chimères Blanc 2001** Vin de Pays des Coteaux du Salagou (€7.50)
4. **Les Pomarèdes 2001** Domaine de Clovallon, Vin de Pays d'Oc (€15.50)
5. **Les Aurièges 2001** Domaine de Clovallon, Vin de Pays d'Oc (€15.50)
6. **Chloé 2001** Jean-Louis Denois, Vin de Pays d'Oc (€15)
7. **Les Collines Rouge 2001** Domaine Magellan, Vin de Pays des Côtes de Thongue (€8.50)
8. **Zind Z001** Zind Humbrecht, Vin de Table (€16.90)
9. **Sotanum 2001** Les Vins de Vienne, Vin de Pays des Collines Rhodaniennes (€28)
10. **Domaine la Grange des Pères Rouge 2001** Vin de Pays de l'Hérault (€45)

BEST BARGAINS

1. **Prélude d'Hiver 2000** Domaine de Saint Lannes, Vin de Pays des Côtes de Gascogne (€5.50)
2. **Chardonnay 2000** Dominique Laurent, Vin de Pays d'Oc (€10)
3. **Cuvée Jericho 2002** Mas Montel, Vin de Pays d'Oc (€6.50)
4. **Merlot 2001** Domaine de Granoupiac, Vin de Pays d'Oc (€6)
5. **Chardonnay 2002** Domaine la Grave, Vin de Pays des Hauts de Badens (€4.30)
6. **Symphonie 2001** Domaine de Perchade, Vin de Pays des Landes (€4.30)
7. **Vin de Pays des Coteaux de Glanes 2002** Cave de Glanes (€3.80)
8. **Merlot 2001** Domaine Lalaurie, Vin de Pays des Coteaux de Narbonne (€5.50)
9. **Marsanne Vin de Pays des Collines Rhodaniennes Blanc 2002** Cave de Tain l'Hermitage (€3)
10. **Les Filles de Septembre Viognier 2002** Gérard et Fils, Vin de Pays d'Oc (€5.90)

• The sale of **Domaine de la Baume** by Australian giant BRL Hardy to American conglomerate Constellation Wines has been followed by a further sale. Domaine de la Baume now belongs to Les Grands Chais de France, one of France's largest producers, the owner of the popular brand JP Chenet, and the single biggest buyer from the cooperatives of the south. The acquisition of Domaine de la Baume is likely to give their business a new emphasis in that they now control some of their grape sources.

• In the **Loire Valley**, the current hot potato is the suggestion of changing the name of the all-embracing Vin de Pays du Jardin de la France to Vin de Pays des Vallées de la Loire. Some of the big players believe that Jardin de la France does not mean much to the average wine drinker and they would like an identity, or brand, more closely linked to the Loire. Meanwhile, Merlot has been added to the grape varieties allowed in Vin de Pays du Jardin de la France and Syrah has been included in Vin de Pays des Côtes du Condomois.

• As a result of the deluge that affected the vineyards of Les Baux just before the 2002 harvest, the quality is generally very dilute. Eloi Durbach of Domaine de Trévallon will not offer any 2002; will others be as quality conscious?

MOST EXCITING OR UNUSUAL FINDS

1 Libre Expression 1996
Domaine Cazes, Vin de Table
(€14.50 per 50-cl bottle) *A pure
Macabeu, with a honeyed nose
and intriguing rich but dry palate:
16 per cent but certainly did not
taste like it, and a vin de table
since alcohol has not been added
to turn it into AOC Rivesaltes.*

2 Vendange d'Octobre 2000
Mas de Bellevue, Vin de Table (€20)
*From a leading producer of
Muscat de Lunel; made from
raisined grapes, with some
botrytis but no additional alcohol.
Beautifully unctuous, but less
concentrated than a fortified wine.*

3 Viognier Roussanne 2002
Domaine Camp-Galhan, Vin de Pays
du Duché d'Uzès (€6.40) *Some
wonderful leafy fruit in an unusual
and successful combination.*

4 Moelleux de Muscat 2002
Château Stony, Vin de Pays d'Oc
(€6.70) *Another unfortified Muscat,
this time from Frontignan. Rich and
complex, but not obviously sweet.*

5 Cépage d'Antan 2000 Domaine
Fougeray de Beauclair, Vin de Pays
de l'Hérault, (€12) *Literally, a grape
variety of yesteryear; Terret Blanc
was once grown almost exclusively
for the production of Noilly Prat.
With some burgundian treatment,
this shows just how intriguing a
grape variety it is and illustrates
the potential of the traditional
grape varieties of the Midi.*

6 Domaine Virgile Joly 2001
Vin de Pays de l'Hérault (€12)
Dry spicy fruit from the Midi,
*from the only independent
grower in the cooperative-
dominated village of St-Saturnin.
His first vintage was 2000.*

7 Attitude Pinot Noir 2002
Pascal Jolivet, Vin de Pays du Jardin
de la France (€9) *The first vintage
of Pascal Jolivet's red partner to
his highly successful white Attitude,
with raspberry fruit and the
freshness of a northern Pinot Noir.*

8 Marselan 2002 Devereux,
Vin de Pays de l'Aude (€4.50)
*A new grape variety, a cross
between Cabernet Sauvignon
and Grenache, with some
cheerful berry fruit and a
touch of Midi spice.*

9 Ampelidae Sauvignon 1998
Vin de Pays de la Vienne (not
available; €8 for the 2002, which
could age as well as the 1998)
*A beautifully aged honeyed
Sauvignon, akin to a white Graves,
from a vineyard north of Poitiers.
A surprise that a humble vin de
pays should age so well. Normally
this would come within the VDQS
of Vin du Haut Poitou.*

10 Le Chant de Marjolaine 2001
Domaine Rimbert, Carignan Vieilles
Vignes Vin de Table (€9.10)
*Another wine that does not
conform to appellation regulations
and was consequently demoted
to vin de table status. The vintage
masquerades as a discreet lot
number and the palate is rich
and raisiny.*

Germany

Michael Schmidt

"Chardonnay the Pretender is dead.
Long live King Riesling!"

MICHAEL SCHMIDT

Resounding throughout the fraternity of wine journalists for some time now, this message is still slow to catch on with the consumer abroad. However, in the Heimatland, supplies of the finest Riesling are already being rationed. But what of that other German great – Spätburgunder? The 2003 German edition of *Parker's Wine Buyer's Guide* caused more than a little consternation by calling it a grotesque and ghastly wine, though his continual repetition of this judgment since 1988 has done little to deter the pilgrimage to the red-wine temples of the Ahr, Pfalz, and Baden.

Tremendous progress has been made since the mid-1980s, when Werner Näkel first began operating in Burgundian mode, swiftly followed by others who realized that the moderate climate in their vineyards put them in a favourable position for making first-rate Pinot Noir. The results of their efforts have been well rewarded by the home supporters plus a small bunch of knowledgeable foreign disciples. But 20 years down the line, some of the gurus of international wine writing still dredge up the old myth that there are no challengers in Europe to Burgundy and that only Oregon, bits of California, New Zealand, and Australia provide any real competition.

Perhaps they think that Adeneuer, Meyer-Näkel, Cossman-Hehle, Fürst, Keller, Huber, Schneider, Johner, Becker, Bernhart, and Rebholz are the line-up of the latest German football side, but their Pinot Noir wines

MICHAEL SCHMIDT runs his own wine school (www.wineschmidt.co.uk) in Surrey and Hampshire. He is a judge at the International Wine and Spirit Competition and has worked as a consultant on a number of publications, including assisting in the selection of recommended wines for the German chapter of *Sotheby's World Wine Encyclopedia* and *The New Sotheby's Wine Encyclopedia* (DK, 1988–2001).

could throw down the gauntlet to many a Côte d'Or *premier cru*. With most of the vineyards in family ownership for decades, if not centuries, these guys know their *terroir*, are blessed with plenty of old vines, and 20 years of *barrique* experience have given them an edge that many of the New World Pinot fashionables would find hard to compete with.

Sceptics might ask how wines of such amazing quality can remain so unknown beyond German borders. The answer lies in the question – they are well known within!

Frühburgunder revival

And then there is Frühburgunder, Germany's very own variation on the Pinot Noir theme. Thought to be an indigenous mutation of the noble red Burgundy grape, it enjoyed a period of relative popularity in the first half of the 20th century, until the arrival of less fickle and higher-yielding crosses nearly led to its extinction. However, once the great postwar thirst had been quenched with floods of Müller-Thurgau and Portugieser, a new generation of German growers turned their attention to the strength of their own vineyards. In the Franconian village of Bürgstadt, the young Paul Fürst discovered a tiny parcel of neglected Frühburgunder vines and over the next 20 years managed to rekindle that variety to what can now only be called cult status. His success did not go unnoticed, as demonstrated by the recent surge from 44 hectares (ha) countrywide in 1994 to an estimated 150 by 2003.

Many believe that, given a grower's full dedication, Frühburgunder is capable of surpassing Spätburgunder in quality, though never in quantity. Under the right conditions, Frühburgunder produces higher must weights, deeper colour, and a less pronounced acidity, resulting in more powerful, velvety wines. The vine is very picky and thrives only on poor, lightly structured soils, but, if afforded total commitment, it will reward winemakers with a product worthy of ageing and highly suitable for extended *barrique* maturation.

Not many among his colleagues would deny Fürst the accolade of the Grand Master of Frühburgunder and, as such, he is qualified to define the quintessential requirement for the grape's success: very restricted yields, definitely lower than 50 hectolitres per hectare (hl/ha), and as low as 27 for very special wines such as his own Bürgstadter Centgrafenberg "R" 2001. Other producers to look out for are Meyer-Näkel, Kreuzberg, Stodden, the Mayschoss/Altenahr cooperative from the Ahr region, and Neiss, Wilker, and Kuhn from the Pfalz, though several new pretenders are showing promise.

ACID TEST

The high temperatures and low rainfall of the 2003 season created Mediterranean conditions in German vineyards, leading to an unprecedented reduction of acids in ripe grapes. At the end of August it became clear that the country's wine industry would have no option but to apply for permission to use acidification techniques usually available only to wine producers in southern Europe. On 1 October, a concession was granted that allowed the addition of concentrated natural grape acids for the acidification of musts up to 1.5 grams per litre (g/l) and another 2.5 g/l maximum for wine. Any use of the technique had to be registered and was restricted to the 2003 vintage. The most important implications of acidification are a greater protection against undesirable microorganisms and volatile acidity, as well as prevention of malolactic fermentation in white wines naturally low in acids. The EU directive also states that musts/wines registered for acidification may not be chaptalized.

GERMAN GREAT GROWTHS IN LONDON

The first presentation of German great growths on foreign soil took place in London on 15 September 2003. More than 100 wines from the top tier of the premium growers' (VDP) own classification were on show at the German ambassador's residence. With few exceptions, the whites of the 2002 vintage showed a high standard, while the handful of 2001 reds did little to convince visitors of the country's true Spätburgunder potential. Exhibitors struggled manfully, but not always successfully, with the heat to present their wines at the right tasting temperature. The Rheingau, Franken, and the Pfalz were well represented, while some other famous regions kept a low profile. As expected, the highest-calibre wines were Rieslings. Most impressive were Wittmann's Westhofener Morstein, Bürklin-Wolf's Forster Ungeheuer, Ökonomierat Rebholz's Siebeldinger im Sonnenschein, and the Hochheimer Domdechaney from Domdechant Werner. The most convincing performance by a non-Riesling was put in by the Schlangenpfiff Weißer Burgunder from the Münzberg estate of Godramstein.

AHR JOINS GREAT-GROWTH CLASSIFICATION

In August 2003, the VDP members of the Ahr region finally agreed to join the three-tier classification model for great growths adopted by other regional VDP branches. Fifteen vineyards were selected to become part of the *crème de la crème* of German sites under the *Große Gewächse* statute. Only wines made from Spätburgunder and Frühburgunder with a minimum must weight of 90 degrees *Oechsle* qualify for inclusion in the top category. Growers making use of the *Großes Gewächs* designation for their red wines will no longer be able to use the name of the vineyard for their Riesling wines. This is bound to accelerate the further demise from the valley of a variety once regarded as the great white hope of the Ahr.

GERMANY SEES RED

According to a report published in November 2003 by the Federal Office for Statistics (Statistisches Bundesamt), the share of red-wine-producing vines in Germany rose to 31.5 per cent in 2002. Out of a national total of 103,000 ha, the area covered by red-wine grapes amounts to 32,380 ha, with nearly 10,500 ha occupied by Spätburgunder, and almost 7,000 ha by Dornfelder, while Portugieser, Regent, and others account for the balance. Over the past five years, the nation's red-wine consumption has increased from 43 per cent to 51.8 per cent, and no less than 30 per cent of this is German wine. To their credit, German consumers appear to be prepared to pay more for reds from their own country than for any other wine.

GLASS WORKS

No less a personage than the president of the VDP, Michael Prinz zu Salm-Salm, is advocating a revolutionary new wine-bottle closure as an alternative to cork. A glass stopper is fitted into the neck of the bottle with the aid of a small plastic ring at its lower end to provide an airtight and wine-tight closure. In Salm's view, the Vino-lok, developed by American manufacturer Alcoa, offers three considerable benefits: it is totally taste-neutral, it can be used to reseal the bottle, and it has a greater aesthetic appeal than screwcaps or crown caps. Despite the lack of research concerning the long-term implications of the closure, several top producers have shown great enthusiasm and 70,000 bottles of VDP wine from the 2002 vintage were sealed using the glass invention.

Grapevine

• **Cabernet Carbon,** Cabernet Cortis, Cabernet Carol, Monarch, Prior, and Baron are the names of six new fungus-resistant varieties planted on a 25-ha site at the Federal Institute for Viticulture (Staatliches Weinbauinstitut) in Freiburg on an experimental basis. The trial also includes a white variety called Helios.

• **For many years,** considerable confusion reigned among the customers of Bruno Schmitt and Paul Schmitt, two VDP member estates in the Franconian village of Randersacker. One chose to name his estate Weingut Trockene Schmitts,

while the other referred to his as Schmitt's Haus der Trockenen Weine. Their decision to merge was helped not only by the fact that they are brothers, but also by their shared belief in complete fermentation of their wines without the use of chaptalization or backblending.

• **Reichsrat von Buhl,** a top Pfalz estate steeped in tradition, has put a new man in charge of wine production. Jan Kux was brought in to revive the slightly flagging ship, having made a name for himself at the estate of Schloss Wackerbarth, in the Sachsen region.

Germans now drink more red wine than white, and the mass producers have risen to the challenge. A relative newcomer of 30 years, Dornfelder has exploded on to the domestic scene with almost 7,000 ha in 2003, propelling it straight into the number-two spot of German black-grape plantings. Soft tannins and great intensity of colour make this variety an ideal candidate for the production of attractive, easy-drinking reds, but the emergence of a flood of thin and stressed wines prompted remedial action by the German Wine Institute and the government of the State of Rheinland-Pfalz. In the summer of 2003, legislation was pushed through to raise the minimum requirements for the variety to 68 degrees *Oechsle* and 12 per cent of alcohol to promote and maintain the image of Dornfelder as a dry quality wine. This measure was not welcomed by the large-volume producers and eventually led to the resignation of Werner Hiestand, the long-standing president of the Rheinhessen winegrowers' association, who was castigated for his support of the new law by some of his own members.

It does not take much to work out the motives of the fervent protesters. Since the recent legalizing of irrigation in German vineyards, some growers of Dornfelder had made such liberal use of water that they managed to obtain yields of up to an incredible 400 hectolitres per hectare (hl/ha). As a consequence, the diluted grapes barely reached the previous pitiful minimum must weight requirement of 60 degrees *Oechsle*, capable of producing no more than 9.5 per cent alcohol in the finished wine. This shortcoming could easily be remedied with the addition of the necessary quantities of sugar before fermentation, raising alcohol levels to a more respectable 12 per cent plus. Using every loophole in the law to combine practices never meant to be combined, it finally became possible to supply supermarkets and discount chains with a flood of German red wine that could compete with the low-cost offerings from France, Italy, and the New World. German wine law urgently needs to address the issue of yields, and there is no reason why irrigation, just like acidification, could not be regulated on a yearly basis.

Great wines must be natural

The top prize taken by Karl Heinz Johner for his vacuum-condensation-assisted red wine raises important questions. Although EU law has permitted must concentration as an alternative to chaptalization for some years now, its use in Germany has been as recent as 1998 and restricted to a trial basis only. Johner's estate was, in fact, one of the chosen few to be allowed to experiment with various winemaking techniques involving reverse osmosis and vacuum condensation under strictly controlled conditions. However, the trail that his Baden Spätburgunder Qualitätswein SJ 1999 blazed at one of the most prestigious events on the wine competition circuit, *Vinum* magazine's 2001 Deutscher Rotweinpreis, only added to the demand that such technology should be available to all. With the competition results on one hand and EU acceptance on the other, it was almost impossible for the authorities to refuse, and in July 2002 the German wine law was adapted to give its official blessing to must concentration. But will this be good for German wine?

Having worked with both the vacuum distillation of must and removal of water molecules by high-pressure filtration, Johner is encouraged by the positive results and thinks that their application will benefit German wine in the long run. One important question is, however: will other producers employ these methods with the same conscientious approach or just see them as another technical aid to compensate for a lack of effort in the vineyard? If the latter happens to any degree, the perpetrators could be in for a shock, since Johner believes that only musts from ripe and healthy grapes can gain from concentration. If inadequate raw material is used, its shortcomings are more likely to be emphasized than disguised.

The proponents of must concentration must be grateful for the summer of 2003, when ideal grape-ripening conditions made any use of the technology superfluous for that vintage, taking the heat out of the argument, at least temporarily. The hot weather brought its own problems at the opposite end of the scale, with worryingly low acidity levels. The authorities dealt with this conundrum in a far more sensible manner by allowing producers to use acidification, but for this vintage only. Instead of giving *carte blanche* for must concentration, could this issue not have been decided on a year-to-year basis as well?

Advance report on the latest harvest
2003

Healthy, sugar-laden grapes were the result of the driest and warmest growing conditions in Germany since 1540. All sorts of records were broken, with the starting gun for the harvest fired in early August, 102 degrees *Oechsle* for a *spätlese* reported by the middle of that month, the first *trockenbeerenauslese* grapes gathered at the end of September, and the earliest frozen berries for *eiswein* picked on 24 October. Several growers recorded must weights of over 300 degrees *Oechsle* for their TBAs, with Mosel estate Markus Molitor bringing in some grapes at a new all-time high of 331. First indications of an exceptional vintage were the unusually early budburst at the beginning of April and flowering of the vines in the first days of June, three weeks ahead of schedule. Over the whole growing period, temperatures were 3°C above the long-term average. Harvest conditions were ideal and most grapes brought in achieved at least *spätlese* level. Mainly due to the lack of precipitation, quantity was down by 20 per cent to an estimated 8 million hl total. Vintage of the century? In principle, yes, the fruit is there, but much depends on how producers manage to balance the high alcohol potential with reduced acidity levels.

Updates on the previous five vintages
2002

Vintage rating: *94*

Germany generally enjoyed an even growing season with an almost-perfect balance of sunny days and rainfall until the end of September. The ripeness level of grapes was 10–12 days ahead of normal when the autumn deluge arrived, so most of the grapes for *Qualitätswein bestimmter Anbaugebiete* (QbA) and *kabinetts* had already been picked. Growers going for premium-quality wines faced nail-biting times, but lessons learned from the difficult 2000 vintage paid off. A green harvest at most estates had reduced the number of bunches by some 20 per cent, giving rot very little opportunity to spread, and this preventive measure was helped by the generally cool autumn temperatures. In November and December, patient growers were rewarded with grapes of *auslese*, *eiswein*, and *trockenbeerenauslese* quality.

2001

Vintage rating: *92*

Favourable weather conditions until the end of August led to well-advanced degrees of ripeness, but hopes for an outstanding vintage were somewhat dampened by September rains. However, a sun-blessed October dispelled fears of rot and the continuation of fine weather right into November rewarded patient growers with *auslese* grape material. The majority of the harvest total weighed in at *kabinett* level. Red-wine producers in the Ahr, Pfalz, Baden, and Württemberg reported an almost-perfect balance of phenolic and sugar ripeness. The Rheingau was less fortunate, with severe hailstorms devastating some of the crop in October. One of the earliest harvests ever of frozen grapes for *eiswein* took place at a few sites in the Nahe on 11 November, though almost all other regions were more than adequately compensated by a big, five-day freeze in mid-December, producing must concentrations of up to and above 200 degrees *Oechsle*.

2000

Vintage rating: *70*

It may have been a miracle vintage in Bordeaux, but no such luck in Germany. Any expectations after an optimal cycle up to July were dashed by rainfall throughout the summer. Subsequent swelling and bursting of the grapes led to an early onset of rot in September, accelerating at a rate that defied the efforts of all but the most meticulous growers to salvage any healthy material. Only continuous removal of rotten bunches and severely selective hand-picking at the final stage produced a small number of fine wines, while the less fussy mechanical harvesters stood every chance of devouring grapes already affected by acetic bacteria. An average of more than 100 hl/ha for the country's vineyards will not have advanced the cause of German wine.

1999

Vintage rating: *85*

The early harvesters of mass-production wines had to face the consequences of a rainy September, with diluted raw material more often than not affected by rot. Premium-quality growers who thinned their crop during the wet period benefited from a golden October. At the top end, there were excellent Rieslings in the Mosel, Rheingau, and Mittelrhein, and fine reds from almost all varieties.

1998

Vintage rating: *88*

Early flowering and an extremely hot August laid the foundation for
high expectations, only to be spoiled by continuous autumn rainfall.
The end result of this large harvest was surprisingly good, but only
where the principles of strictly selective picking had been employed.
Two periods of sustained frost allowed for fair quantities of *eiswein*.
It was a large-volume harvest.

GREATEST WINE PRODUCERS

1. Keller (Rheinhessen)
2. Emrich-Schönleber (Nahe)
3. Fritz Haag (Mosel)
4. Dr Loosen (Mosel)
5. Ökonomierat Rebholz (some red, Pfalz)
6. A Christmann (Pfalz)
7. Egon Müller-Scharzhof (Saar)
8. Dönnhoff (Nahe)
9. Rudolf Fürst (red and white, Franken)
10. Meyer-Näkel (red only, Ahr)

NEW UP-AND-COMING PRODUCERS

1. Weingart (Mittelrhein)
2. Josef Leitz (Rheingau)
3. Gerhard Aldinger (red and white, Württemberg)
4. Andreas Laible (Baden)
5. R & C Schneider (red and white, Baden)
6. Bernhart (red and white, Pfalz)
7. Didinger (Mittelrhein)
8. Vollenweider (Mosel)
9. Wagner-Stempel (Rheinhessen)
10. Fürst Löwenstein (Franken)

FASTEST-IMPROVING PRODUCERS

1. Markus Molitor (Mosel)
2. Dr Wehrheim (Pfalz)
3. Deutzerhof-Cossmann-Hehle (mainly red, Ahr)
4. Grans-Fassian (Mosel)
5. Wittmann (Rheinhessen)
6. Bürklin-Wolf (Pfalz)
7. Horst Sauer (Franken)
8. Knebel (Mosel)
9. Knipser (mainly red, Pfalz)
10. Bernhard Huber (red and white, Baden)

BEST-VALUE PRODUCERS

1. Didinger (Mittelrhein)
2. Bernhart (Pfalz)
3. Manz (Rheinhessen)
4. Korell-Johanneshof (Nahe)
5. Weingart (Mittelrhein)
6. Loewen (Mosel)
7. Michel (Baden)
8. Horst Sauer (Franken)
9. R & C Schneider (Baden)
10. Winzergenossenschaft Mayschoss-Altenahr (Ahr)

GREATEST-QUALITY WINES

1. **Dalsheimer Hubacker Riesling Trockenbeerenauslese 2001** Keller, Rheinhessen (€160 per half-bottle)
2. **Zeltinger Sonnenuhr Riesling Eiswein 1998** Markus Molitor, Mosel (€62.90 per half-bottle)
3. **Nackenheimer Rothenberg Riesling Auslese Goldkapsel 2002** Gunderloch, Rheinhessen (€35)
4. **Spätburgunder R Auslese Trocken 1999** Bernhart, Pfalz (€33.50)
5. **Bürgstadter Centgrafenberg Frühburgunder Trocken "R" 2001** Rudolf Fürst, Franken (€54)
6. **Westhofen Morstein Riesling Trocken Großes Gewächs 2002** Wittmann, Rheinhessen (€23)
7. **Godramsteiner Schlangenpfiff Münzberg Weißer Burgunder Spätlese Trocken Großes Gewächs 2002** Münzberg, Pfalz (€17)
8. **Laumersheimer Kirschgarten Dornfelder Trocken Barrique 1999** Knipser, Pfalz (€15.50)
9. **Escherndorfer Lump Silvaner Auslese Trocken Großes Gewächs 2002** Horst Sauer, Franken (€17)
10. **Ürziger Würzgarten Riesling Kabinett 2002** Dr Loosen, Mosel (€8.80)

BEST BARGAINS

1. **Schweigener Sonnenuhr Gewürztraminer Spätlese Trocken 2002** Bernhart, Pfalz (€6.80)
2. **Bopparder Hamm Feuerlay Riesling Spätlese Halbtrocken 2002** Didinger, Mittelrhein (€5.50)
3. **Kreuznacher Paradies Riesling Auslese 2002** Korrell-Johanneshof, Nahe (€7)
4. **Escherndorfer Lump Silvaner Spätlese Trocken 2002** Horst Sauer, Franken (€8.80)
5. **Becksteiner Tauberklinge Müller-Thurgau Trocken 2001** Tauberfränkische Winzergenossenschaft Beckstein, Baden (€1.99)
6. **Großkarlbacher Burgweg Scheurebe Trockenbeerenauslese 1996** Knipser, Pfalz (€28.62 per 50-cl bottle)
7. **Riesling Trocken 2002** Mosbacher, Pfalz (€4.70 per litre bottle)
8. **Grossheppacher Steingrüble Sauvignon Blanc 2002** Klopfer, Württemberg (€4.70)
9. **Ingelheimer Rotes Kreuz Spätburgunder 2001** Arndt F Werner, Rheinhessen (€6.50)
10. **Rigodolum Sekt Riesling Brut 2000** Römerhof, Mosel (€8.50)

MOST EXCITING OR UNUSUAL FINDS

1. Brüsseler Spitze, Kleinbottwarer Oberer Berg Muskattrollinger Eiswein 2001 Graf Adelmann, Württemberg (€69.60 per half-bottle) *Coaxed from a very rare variation of the red Trollinger grape, this voluptuous sweetie is marked by distinct Muscat aromas and refined elderflower scent.*

2. Laumersheimer Kirschgarten Dornfelder Trocken Barrique 1999 Knipser, Pfalz (€15.50) *The essence of Dornfelder tamed by three years in barrique.*

3. Duca XI Dunkelfelder Cabernet Sauvignon 2001 Egon Schmitt, Pfalz (€15.30) *Artisan and noble in perfect harmony for one of Germany's finest reds.*

4. Chardonnay Spätlese Trocken 2002 Ökonomierat Rebholz, Pfalz (€18) *Can Germany make world-class Chardonnay? Yes!*

5. Schloss Proschwitz Frühburgunder Beerenauslese 2000 Schloss Proschwitz, Sachsen (€35) *Who would think of turning a red rarity into an even rarer dessert wine at the northern fringe of European winemaking? A risk rewarded by total success.*

6. Großkarlbacher Burgweg Gelber Orleans Eiswein 1996 Knipser, Pfalz (€32.84 per half-bottle) *A phoenix rises from the ashes. And they said Gelber Orleans was extinct!*

7. Reicholzheimer First Schwarzriesling Spätlese Trocken 2001 Schlör, Baden (€13.50) *Pinot Meunier, but not as we know it. Easy-drinking red with substance.*

8. Regent Trocken Barrique 2001 Egon Schmitt, Pfalz (€10.20) *With the help of a little wood, Schmitt once again coaxes a great red out of a lowly hybrid.*

9. Sauvignon Blanc Spätlese Trocken 2002 Beurer, Württemberg (€10.50) *Fresh, lively, with delicate elderflower scent, this proves the wisdom of revoking the outlaw status of this variety.*

10. St Laurent Trocken "B" 2001 Gerhard Klein, Pfalz (€7.50) *Do they want to upset Parker? Even with a modest variety at a low price, the bandwagon of successful German reds keeps rolling!*

Grapevine

• **Gerhard Roth** from the Franconian estate of the same name has found a way to improve the heat resistance of new plantings by growing different types of clover between the young vines. The quick and abundant growth of the clover's roots uses up all the water near the surface, forcing the vines to dig deep fast to find their own supplies. Three-year-old plants in clover-clad soil showed considerably less heat stress in the 2003 drought conditions than 10-year-old vines without clover company.

• **A secret weapon** against the dreaded TCA was revealed at a bordeaux tasting held by the German wine magazine *Alles über Wein* in Hamburg. Sommelier Hendrik Thoma used a conveniently corked bottle of Château Lafite 1986 to demonstrate the incredible powers of clingfilm. Dipped into the wine, it eliminated all traces of the offending odour. Unfortunately, it also removed a number of other extracts, making the wine clean but unrecognizable as Lafite.

The Unione Italiana Vini has given its blessing to wholesale price rises of between 8 and 15 per cent for wines distributed to supermarkets, which control 60 per cent of Italy's wine sales.

NICOLAS BELFRAGE MW   FRANCO ZILIANI

This is to offset losses arising from two short vintages in a row causing up to 30 per cent increases in the cost of grapes and wines. Of course, materials and a contraction of the wine market at home and abroad, due in part to the strong euro and the weak dollar, are also part of the equation. Exports of Italian wines in the first quarter of 2003 fell by 17 per cent and indications are that things are getting worse, not better, which raises the question: is putting prices up really the right strategy?

NICOLAS BELFRAGE MW was born in Los Angeles and raised in New York and England. He studied in Paris, Siena, and London, taking a degree at University College London in French and Italian. Nick has been specializing in Italian wines since the 1970s and became a Master of Wine in 1980, the first American citizen to do so. He is the author of the double-award-winning *Life Beyond Lambrusco* (Sidgwick & Jackson, 1985), *Barolo to Valpolicella* (Mitchell Beazley, 1999), and *Brunello to Zibibbo* (Mitchell Beazley, 2001). Nick is a regular contributor to *Decanter* magazine and *Harpers Wine & Spirit Weekly*.

FRANCO ZILIANI is a freelance writer who has specialized in Italian wines since 1985. He is a regular contributor to the Italian periodicals *A Tavola*, *Merum*, *Go Wine*, and *AIS Lombardia News*, as well as the weekly magazine *Il Corriere Vinicolo*. He is responsible for the journalistic side of *WineReport* (www.winereport.com), a weekly e-zine exclusively dedicated to Italian wines, and is a regular contributor to *Harpers Wine & Spirit Weekly* and Californian magazine *Wine Business Monthly*.

Sceptical about Italian prospects

Emilio Pedron, CEO of Italy's number-one heavyweight in the production field, Gruppo Italiano Vini (GIV), expressed the view in a recent interview that "certain categories of Italian wine have priced themselves out of the market". This applies not just to the DOCGs and 'Super' wines, he reckons, but also to more popular products like Pinot Grigio, Valpolicella, Bardolino, and Chianti, which, despite the uninspired quality of the 2002 vintage, have increased prices still further.

"Italian wine must absolutely take cognizance of the fact that we are in a phase of international overproduction, there being considerably more wine on offer than existing markets can absorb, leading to a general lowering of prices and to a new competitiveness at all quality levels. I hope that Italian wine is aware of the risks it is running. Otherwise," he warns, "foreign buyers will no longer promote our wines, undermining decades of work to improve quality. If that happens, it will require years, huge investment, and enormous efforts to regain the lost market position. This, then, must be our hour of sacrifice, of good sense, and of responsible action at every level."

GIV bucks the trend

Gruppo Italiano Vini (Fontana Candida, Bigi, Melini, Santi, Lamberti, Nino Negri, GIV Sud) has announced a record turnover for 2002 of €245 million, which was a 5 per cent increase over the previous year. This takes account of healthy figures from overseas subsidiaries Frederick Wildman of New York and Gruppo Carniato Europe of Paris, in addition to the €160 million notched up by the Italian group. According to GIV, this makes it Italy's leading wine-based business.

Fair few rivals

Ten years ago there was just one Italian wine fair, the annual Vinitaly in Verona around Easter. Then, with the upmarket Merano shindig, now firmly established in early November, there were two. A couple of years ago Turin got in on the act, later in November, with the Salone del Vino at Fiat's former premises at Lingotto Fiera. But the atmosphere at the 2003 occasion was *triste*, with major names and whole regions failing to subscribe and nary an international journalist or buyer (well, hardly any) in evidence; and rumours abounded of an abandonment, or a move to Rome. Now Turin's big rival, Milan, is hoping to fill that gap with the proposed MiWine fair, commencing in June 2004 and manifesting every other year in alternation with Vinexpo.

DRINK OR DRIVE?

Until 2003, to be breathalysed in Italy you practically had to fall out of your car when stopped by the *carabinieri*, who were interested only in your documents. The Berlusconi government has now introduced breathalysers galore, policemen hiding outside restaurants and bars at night, and a points system for various driving offences that has seen numerous aggrieved Italians lose their licences in the past months. But the ingenious Italian *ristoratore* has come up with a riposte in the form of Operazione Buta Stupa (Operation Open Bottle). The idea is simply to encourage customers to take unfinished bottles home in a tasteful bag, rendering respectable something that until now would have seemed mean.

FIZZICAL EDUCATION

At the end of June 2003, an international symposium on sparkling wines of the *metodo classico* was held at the Agrarian Institute at San Michele all'Adige in Trentino. Titled Traditional and Sparkling Wines of the Third Millennium, the symposium took place under the aegis of the OIV (Office International de la Vigne et du Vin). The most significant result was a positive vote on a proposal to create an international study centre for sparkling wines under the patronage of the OIV, with headquarters at San Michele all'Adige. The institute's role would be to analyse the world situation relating to bottle-fermented sparkling wines: viticulture, oenology, microbiology, law and regulation, and economics. A request will be made to all relevant countries and production zones, such as Champagne and Cava (which have already indicated their interest in the project), to join the Centre and collaborate with it, having the status of 'observer'.

STILL A NOVELTY

Beaujolais Nouveau may have lost much of its erstwhile glitter, but Italian Vino Novello, released on the first Thursday of November, is an evolving success. Production in 2003, according to estimates issued by the Istituto Vino Novello Italiano, rose from 18 million to 19 million bottles, while the average price has also gone up by almost 6 per cent to €4.58 per bottle. Sixty-two per cent of Novello is produced in the north, with more than half of this coming from Veneto. Cavit is the most important producer of Novello, with more than one million bottles. At 675,000 bottles, Cavit's Fiori d'Inverno is the number-one bestselling Novello brand, after which comes Banfi's Santa Costanza (550,000 bottles), the Sicilian Corvo Novello (500,000), and Pasqua's San Zeno Bardolino (450,000). No fewer than 59 different grape varieties may be used for the production of Italian Novello, but Merlot is the most popular, followed by Cabernet and Sangiovese, then in significantly smaller quantities, such grapes as Montepulciano, Corvina, Barbera, Rondinella, Teroldego, and Marzemino.

The drought of 2003, following the precipitation-plagued 2002 campaign, has highlighted certain aspects of what it is to be a wine producer in 21st-century Europe. While England enjoyed its best vintage since Roman times, basking in well-nigh Burgundian conditions, Italy – and especially northern Italy – moved that much closer to North Africa. If it is like this in 2003, what is it going to be like in 2020? 2050? Will viticulture still be viable? While total 'Saharification' of Italy seems unlikely, growers are going to have to start thinking now about how they will cope with climate change in the coming decades.

Most important of all is the question of irrigation. At present, the various DOC laws are a little vague on this subject, contenting themselves for the most part with an interdiction on any 'forcing techniques' on the vine. Generally, the interdiction has been taken to mean no irrigation unless the plant itself, as distinct from this year's crop, is under severe stress: *irrigazione di soccorso*, or first aid, although some rules specifically forbid any form of watering. Yet more and more producers today (30 per cent of the total, according to estimates) are equipping their vineyards against drought, often on the (perfectly valid) pretext that recently planted vines with ill-developed root systems will not withstand extreme conditions.

Ezio Rivella, one of the wise elder statesmen of the Italian wine scene, has gone on record as saying: "It is absurd that certain wine regulations should still be based on the belief that irrigation means higher production. Today this concept is out of date, since the regulations themselves set the limits for production per hectare and the parameters of the wines produced, not to mention the further self-imposed restrictions on the part of quality-conscious growers. The drought of 2003 is the shining proof that it is time to review those regulations that forbid any form of irrigation. Indeed, a rational and timely intervention at certain periods of the vegetative cycle often perceptibly enhances wine quality."

Other considerations linked to climate change will have to do with techniques of encouraging root establishment and possibly even transplanting vine types acclimatized to hot, dry conditions to more northerly growing zones. However, most of the traffic of that sort to date has been in the reverse direction, with French varieties like Chardonnay and Cabernet being planted – with considerable success, it should be added – as far south as Sicily.

"Untypical" wines rejected

The absurdity that more or less kicked off the whole disastrous defiance of Italian wine law in the 1970s, when official tasting commissions used to refuse DOCs to wines because they were "untypical" (in other words, too good to be considered on a par with the prevailing rubbish), is amazingly still with us. Cesconi's Traminer Aromatico 2002 (see the Most Exciting or Unusual Finds list), the best of its type by a mile, was recently denied the dubious accolade of official blessing and had to be reduced to IGT status. As long as the authorities display their ignorance and incompetence in this way, Italy will continue to struggle to command international respect.

Update

Overconcentration remains a problem in Italian wines, especially at the top end, where uniqueness is still sacrificed to international acceptability. In weak vintages like 2002, the temptation to concentrate is especially strong. In a vintage like 2003, however, it is not only unnecessary but would be ludicrous.

The best thing one can say about the practice of passing off, as in the case of Grandarella producing an Amarone in all but name, is that the practice has not spread in the past year.

Grapevine

• **The Cavit group of Trento,** representing 13 cooperatives in Trentino, was recently confirmed as the second-biggest Italian wine group (after GIV), with a turnover in the last financial year of €197.8 million, up 26 per cent on the previous year. Exports accounted for a massive 79 per cent of the total, with Pinot Grigio by far the strongest performer.

• **Italian companies are expanding** into wine ventures in Eastern Europe and beyond. Following Antinori's lead in Hungary, Miroglio of Alba (a textile group) has invested in the Sliven region of Bulgaria, Castello della Paneretta of Chianti in Romania, and Baroncini of San Gimignano in Georgia, while Campari is cultivating 200 hectares (ha) in China.

• **Campari is to invest** a further €500 million expanding the wine and spirits sector. The most important alcoholic beverages group in Italy, and sixth in the world, Campari took over the 500-ha estate of Sella & Mosca of Sardinia in 2001. In the summer of 2003, Campari coughed up €11.3 million to complete the purchase of Bersano Riccadonna of Piemonte, makers, among other products, of the volume sparkler President. Further takeovers are planned, provided that they feature, in the words of CEO Signor Cippo, "Italian wine estates of strong image with good growth potential".

2003

After 2002, shortest on quantity for 50 vintages and short on quality too, 2003 had nowhere to go but up. Quantity-wise, it must be said, the upward movement was almost imperceptible – around 3 per cent in the north, nearer to 1 per cent nationally – bringing further upward pressure to bear on prices that really need to go down. Quality-wise, however, there was a great improvement. Grapes were universally sound. The main problems were drought – there was virtually no rain from April until the end of the harvest, barring a couple of isolated and brief summer storms – and heat, which caused some raising and excessive degrees. Ripening was also very precocious in most parts, with whites being picked in the first half, even the first week, of August, prompting one grower to complain that there was no longer any such thing as a summer holiday. On the other hand, high grape-sugar values were often reached before the polyphenolic substances were ripe, so balance became a major factor. Those waiting for the tannins to come round suffered from excessive sugar levels and low acidity, while those who picked early ran the risk of green flavours.

Nonetheless, there were raves about quality, with comparisons with 1997, and even 1947, being bandied about. The Nebbiolo growers of Barolo and Barbaresco were generally ecstatic, as were producers of big, lush Barbera. The picture was the same right across the north, with red-wine producers showing distinctly more enthusiasm than white specialists. Thus, the growers of Valpolicella were delighted, especially since production was up around 10 per cent on 2002, while the enthusiasm of Soave makers was less intense, some even saying that 2002, despite the rot problems, was better. In Friuli and Alto Adige, quality producers were happy enough, however, especially those specializing in big, rich wines of a sort more associated with the New World.

Updates on the previous five vintages

2002

Vintage rating: *75 (Red: 70, White: 80)*

In retrospect, from certain points of view, not as bad as we thought a year ago, nor certainly as bad as the international pundits have painted it. In Piemonte, it's true, many Barolos/Barbarescos were produced in tiny quantities or not at all, due to hail damage or general lack of ripeness, but Nebbiolos of lesser denominations, as well as Barberas and Dolcettos, often benefited from the addition of grapes from great vineyards normally reserved for the *crus*. A similar comment could be made in Valpolicella – wines not as big as usual but drinking nicely now. As for whites, some growers in Soave were declaring 2002 to be the best year for a decade, and indeed there was plenty of freshness and nerve, if less alcohol, in whites of other northern zones: Gavi, Alto Adige, and Friuli.

2001

Vintage rating: *92 (Red: 94, White: 90)*

The first year of the new millennium had points of excellence to rival those of the previous six. There were predictions of Barolos and Barbarescos at the highest quality levels, possibly capping the achievements of the previous six years. Other Piemontese wines were excellent too, with Barberas and Dolcettos of great concentration and structure. Nebbiolo (Chiavennasca) in Valtellina was also splendid. Very good year, too, for the whites of Friuli and for the Soaves of Veneto, as well as for reds of Valpolicella.

2000

Vintage rating: *88 (Red: 90, White: 86)*

A very hot year more or less everywhere, giving rise to wines of great concentration and power, albeit lacking a bit in subtlety. An excellent year for the Pinot Neros of Alto Adige, but also very good for the aromatic varieties Sauvignon and Gewürztraminer throughout the northeast. In Alba, Barolo, Barbaresco, and Barbera recorded the sixth excellent vintage in a row, the previous historical record being a mere three (1988, 1989, and 1990). The Amarones of Valpolicella enjoyed ideal conditions in the post-harvest drying period, so we can expect some superb wines.

1999

Vintage rating: *94 (Red: 96, White: 92)*

An extraordinary year in the classic Alba zone (Barolo, Barbaresco, Barbera, and Dolcetto). The Barolos are seen by some to be superior to the great 1996s, and on a par with 1989 and 1982, which are legendary. Great year in Friuli, too, with white wines of particular elegance and freshness. In Valpolicella, a few problems with rain at vintage time, but the wines are still very good.

1998

Vintage rating: *83 (Red: 81, White: 85)*

A good, if not great, year. Wines of real elegance and balance were made in Piemonte. Barolos and Barbarescos in some cases are better than the 1997s, at least for drinkability. Rain during picking caused problems in Valpolicella, but the wines turned out to be more than respectable. A good year for whites.

GREATEST WINE PRODUCERS

1 Bruno Giacosa (Barolo & Barbaresco)
2 Giacomo Conterno (Barolo)
3 Aldo Conterno (Barolo)
4 Angelo Gaja (Barbaresco)
5 Roberto Voerzio (Barolo)
6 Allegrini (Valpolicella)
7 Lis Neris (Friuli Isonzo)
8 Tenuta San Leonardo (Trentino)
9 Borgo del Tiglio
   (Colli Orientali del Friuli)
10 Ca' del Bosco (Franciacorta)

NEW UP-AND-COMING PRODUCERS

1 Enzo Boglietti (Barolo)
2 Eraldo Viberti (Barolo)
3 Claudio Viviani (Valpolicella)
4 Cesconi (Trentino)
5 Poderi Colla (Piemonte)
6 Ciabot Berton (Barolo)
7 Matijaz Tercic (Friuli)
8 Le Fracce (Oltrepò Pavese)
9 Anselma (Barolo)
10 Zuani (Friuli)

FASTEST-IMPROVING PRODUCERS

1 Tommaso Bussola (Valpolicella)
2 GD Vajra (Barolo)
3 Foradori (Trentino)
4 Massolino (Barolo)
5 Ca' Rugate (Valpolicella)
6 Pra (Soave)
7 Coffele (Soave)
8 Malvira (Roero)
9 Paitin (Barbaresco)
10 Corte Sant'Alda (Valpolicella)

BEST-VALUE PRODUCERS

1 Il Cascinone (Acqui Terme)
2 Michele Castellani (Valpolicella)
3 La Riva dei Frati (Valdobbiadene)
4 Tiefenbrunner (Alto Adige)
5 Franz Haas (Alto Adige)
6 Gianni Voerzio (Barolo)
7 Camerano (Barolo)
8 Barale Fratelli (Barolo)
9 Cavallotto Fratelli (Barolo)
10 Produttori del Barbaresco
   (Barbaresco)

GREATEST-QUALITY WINES

1 **Barolo Rocche di Falletto 1999**
Bruno Giacosa, Piemonte (€90)

2 **Barolo Cascina Francia 1999**
Giacomo Conterno, Piemonte (€90)

3 **Barolo Cannubi Boschis 1999**
Sandrone, Piemonte (€75)

4 **Barolo Monprivato 1999**
Giuseppe Mascarello,
Piemonte (€60)

5 **Barbaresco Martinenga
Camp Gros 1999** Marchesi
di Gresy, Piemonte (€55)

6 **Amarone Vigneto Alto 1999**
Tommaso Bussola, Veneto (€85)

7 **San Leonardo 1999** Tenuta
San Leonardo, Trentino (€50)

8 **Barbera d'Asti Superiore
Mongovone 2001**
Elio Perrone, Piemonte (€30)

9 **Franciacorta Cuvée Annamaria
Clementi 1996** Ca' del Bosco,
Lombardy (€65)

10 **Studio di Bianco 2001**
Borgo del Tiglio, Friuli (€40)

BEST BARGAINS

1 **Barolo Bussia Dardi le Rose
1999** Poderi Colla, Piemonte (€35)

2 **Barolo Sorano di Serralunga
d'Alba 1999** Ascheri, Piemonte
(€35)

3 **Barolo Serralunga 1999**
Fontanafredda, Piemonte (€25)

4 **Barbera d'Asti Rive 2001**
Araldica Vini Piemontesi,
Piemonte (€15)

5 **Valpolicella Classico Superiore
Ripasso 2000** Michele Castellani,
Veneto (€15)

6 **Soave Classico Superiore Ca'
Visco 2002** Coffele, Soave (€12)

7 **Alto Adige Chardonnay
Linticlarus 1999** Tiefenbrunner,
Alto Adige (€15)

8 **Soave Classico 2002**
Pra, Veneto (€12)

9 **Erbaluce di Caluso La Rustia
2002** Orsolani, Piemonte (€12)

10 **Barbera d'Alba 2002**
Enzo Boglietti, Piemonte (€12)

MOST EXCITING OR UNUSUAL FINDS

1 **Recioto della Valpolicella
Classico TB 2000** Tommaso
Bussola, Veneto (€50) *Bussola
achieves an almost impossible
concentration with this wine. The
grapes are dried for nearly six
months before pressing, without
losing fruit or balance. An
outstanding alternative to port.*

2 **Roncùs Bianco Vecchie Vigne
1999** Roncùs, Friuli (€24) *A blend
of three native Friulian grapes –
Malvasia (70 per cent), Tocai
Friulano (20 per cent), and Ribolla
Gialla – vinified in 20-hl barrels
where it remains for 12 months,
followed by 24 months in stainless
steel on the fine lees, then eight
months in bottle.*

3 **Pinot Nero Hausmannhof
Riserva 2000** Haderburg, Alto
Adige (€20) *Italy is not known
for Pinot Noir production except
for a few sites in Alto Adige, which
is hardly Italy. Producer Alois
Ochsenreiter makes this from
organically grown grapes and
with scrupulous attention to
Burgundian methods.*

4 **Traminer Aromatico 2002**
Cesconi, Trentino (€12) *The young
Cesconi brothers are the best
white-wine producers in Trentino
today. Twenty years ago, although
the village of Tramin is just up the
road in Alto Adige, no one was
making Traminer at an international
level. Easily the best of its type in*

Italy, this wine was denied the DOC for lack of typicity (too damn good!).

❺ Ormeasco le Braje 2001 Lupi, Liguria (€12) *Ormeasco is a historic Ligurian synonym for Dolcetto, but the wine is distinctively Ligurian rather than Piemontese in style, coming from slopes between forest and riviera, between scrub and mountain, combining all sorts of intriguing herb and fruit aromas.*

❻ Langhe Nebbiolo 2000 Aurelio Settimo, Piemonte (€12) *Unlike Barolo and Barbaresco, this Nebbiolo is vinified and aged (12–18 months depending on the year) exclusively in stainless steel, so that the tannins are all grape tannins and the aromas, too, are of the grape.*

❼ Dolcetto di Dogliani San Matteo 2001 Eraldo Revelli, Piemonte (€8) *A good illustration of why the village and confines of Dogliani are particularly famed for Dolcetto, which may be only third in the Piemontese red-grape hierarchy but here explores dimensions to which other Dolcettos can only aspire.*

❽ Barbera d'Asti Superiore Passum 2000 Cascina Castlet, Piemonte (€24) *Mariuccia Borio is a creative spirit among whose innovations is this Barbera from slightly dried grapes, giving the wine more concentration and viscosity, with something of the aroma of Valpolicella passito but the acidity and smooth tannins of Barbera.*

❾ Bianco Breg 1999 Gravner, Collio, Friuli-Venezia Giulia (€40) *Probably the most independent thinker in Italian wine, Gravner believes in white wine for extended ageing and is not afraid of strange blends or even a touch of oxidation. This is a mix of Sauvignon, Chardonnay, Pinot Grigio, and Riesling Italico.*

❿ Collio Bianco Vigne 2002 Zuani, Friuli (€17) *Another Friulian blend, this time combining Tocai, Chardonnay, Pinot Grigio, and Sauvignon. Patrizia Felluga, sister and erstwhile colleague of Roberto Felluga of the house of Marco Felluga, has struck out on her own with amazing success.*

Grapevine

- **Marta Galli** died in May 2003. She was a pioneer of the rebirth of Valpolicella and one of the first women involved in wine. Walter Allegrini, 55, elder brother of Franco and Marilisa Allegrini of Valpolicella fame, died of a heart attack while swimming on holiday on 20 July 2003. Ezio Voyat, probably the best-known producer of the small Alpine enclave of Valle d'Aosta, died in November 2003. He was particularly famous for his outstanding Moscato di Chambave, a sweet wine from dried Muscat grapes.

- **Pornassio,** or Ormeasco di Pornassio, is a new DOC in the province of Imperia, in western Liguria. The Ormeasco grape is a variant of Dolcetto dating back hundreds of years. Until now, this wine has gone under the title Riviera Ligure di Ponente Ormeasco. The name Pornassio refers not to what you might be thinking but to a particularly prized subzone within that area.

The most significant recent development in central Italy has been the call by certain Tuscan producers to move away from the relative anarchy of the IGT Super-Tuscan culture towards the official Chianti Classico DOCG status.

In the spring of 2003, six of the top central Tuscan producers signed a cooperation charter aimed at promoting their territory above their own production, putting Chianti Classico DOCG wines at the top of their lists image-wise and price-wise. In their determination to stress *terroir*, they have even eschewed the extra prestige of the description Riserva, which makes no reference to the land. The protagonists, who hope their movement will encourage other producers, are Castello di Brolio, Castello di Ama, Fonterutoli, Il Palazzino, La Massa, and Le Corti. Considering that Tuscany's postwar fame has been built on its outstanding Super-Tuscans,

NICOLAS BELFRAGE MW   FRANCO ZILIANI

NICOLAS BELFRAGE MW was born in Los Angeles and raised in New York and England. He studied in Paris, Siena, and London, taking a degree at University College London in French and Italian. Nick has been specializing in Italian wines since the 1970s and became a Master of Wine in 1980, the first American citizen to do so. He is the author of the double-award-winning *Life Beyond Lambrusco* (Sidgwick & Jackson, 1985), *Barolo to Valpolicella* (Mitchell Beazley, 1999), and *Brunello to Zibibbo* (Mitchell Beazley, 2001). Nick is a regular contributor to *Decanter* magazine and *Harpers Wine & Spirit Weekly*.

FRANCO ZILIANI is a freelance writer who has specialized in Italian wines since 1985. He is a regular contributor to the Italian periodicals *A Tavola*, *Merum*, *Go Wine*, and *AIS Lombardia News*, as well as the weekly magazine *Il Corriere Vinicolo*. He is responsible for the journalistic side of WineReport (www.winereport.com), a weekly e-zine exclusively dedicated to Italian wines, and is a regular contributor to *Harpers Wine & Spirit Weekly* and Californian magazine *Wine Business Monthly*.

while many continue to associate anything with the name Chianti in it as representative of the bad old days, it is a bold move.

Meanwhile, Baron Giovanni Ricasoli-Firidolfi, owner of Castello di Cacchiano at Gaiole in Chianti and newly elected president of the Consorzio Gallo Nero, has also emphasized that "*terroir* constitutes our true, indeed our sole, added value, the only factor that distinguishes us from our ever more aggressive international rivals. The territory of Chianti Classico, its evocative power, and its culture should be associated with the product in all our communications."

Faking it

According to the Italian research institute Nomisma, there exists a massive and growing market for false Italian consumables (pasta, oil, cheese, and wine) in the US. The market value of the phoney 'Italian' wine alone is estimated at a mind-boggling $541 million, some 10 per cent of the total wine market, of which $21 million are supposedly for products of controlled denomination. This represents a figure substantially higher than that achieved by the genuine product (around $397 million). The almost unbelievable figures highlight the importance of pursuing efforts to achieve maximum traceability, systems by which products may be traced by accompanying documentation back to their point of origin.

The problem of phoney wine also exists at home. The trial of 12 people accused of falsifying bottles of Sassicaia started in February 2004 in Pisa. In 2002, agents of the Guardia di Finanza (tax police) sequestered 20,000 bottles of phoney Super-Tuscan as well as 6.5 million bottles of fake Chianti Classico. Meanwhile, in a raid on offices in Palermo, L'Ispettorato Centrale Repressione Frodi (ICRF, Italian Fraud Squad) seized documents revealing that some 60,000 hectolitres (hl) of Sicilian IGT Pinot Bianco and Pinot Grigio had been sent to wineries in the Veneto, where the ICRF assumes it would be transformed into fashionable and more expensive DOC Pinot Grigio.

Does this demonstrate that the system of traceability is working? Perhaps, but who can say how many undetected fake bottles are still out there? And how can we tell what is what? In a paraphrase of the witticism "If all else fails, read the instructions", it looks as if we may ultimately be forced to fall back on the evidence of our taste buds.

GREAT EXPECTATIONS?

Marchese Nicolò Incisa della Rocchetta's estate at Bolgheri, Tenuta San Guido, has announced the birth of a third wine to follow the legendary Cabernet Sassicaia and the Merlot/Cabernet blend Guidalberto. This is Le Difese, 80–90 per cent Sangiovese, the rest Cabernet. The wine will initially be produced in very small quantities – 7,000–8,000 bottles – and is destined for limited distribution at a (relatively) modest price of €8–10. Indeed, the whole operation seems to be very *sotto voce*. "I can't think", said the Marchese, "why so much expectation should have built up over this wine. A little cousin for Sassicaia? We shall see – for the time being sales have been limited to the Bolgheri area."

Il Terriccio, another major producer of the Maremma, has also widened its list. At the higher end, it has launched Castello del Terriccio, a Syrah/Mourvèdre/Petit Verdot blend priced between the expensive and exclusive Cabernet/Merlot Lupicaia and the Cabernet/Merlot/Sangiovese Tassinaia. At the other extreme, it has introduced Capannino, 90 per cent Sangiovese with a splash of Cabernet and Merlot, unoaked and surprisingly moderately priced at around €5 ex cellar. Is this, together with Sassicaia's (relative) cheapie, more evidence of the crisis descending on Italian wines, forcing even the greatest downmarket to rustle up turnover?

UP POMPEII

The wine of the ancient Romans is reborn in Pompeii. Using an updated version of the technology that was current at the time of the catastrophic eruption of AD79, the famous Campanian producer Mastroberardino has come up with a limited edition (1,721 bottles) of Villa dei Misteri. The project began in 1996 with Mastroberardino planting an experimental vineyard of 200 square metres, provided by the Pompeii authorities, to eight varieties thought to have existed in Roman times. Later, three indigenous but not necessarily Roman varieties – Piedirosso, Sciascinoso, and Olivella – were chosen to make a wine suitable for modern consumption, the methods of planting (high density, plants supported by chestnut stakes) being analogous to those used two millennia ago. The first six bottles were sent to President Carlo Azeglio Ciampi; the rest will be sold at auction.

BACKING FOR INDIGENOUS VINES

Cabernet Sauvignon, Cabernet Franc, Merlot, Syrah, Chardonnay, Sauvignon Blanc, and even Semillon have been planted in Puglia at a frantic rate, mainly by producers from the north. This inrush of international grapes threatens to push numerous indigenous varieties towards second-class status, if not outright extinction, which is why the move by the authorities of Regione Puglia, in favour of the rediscovery and encouragement of its native grapes, is to be applauded. A €20-million package has been agreed to restructure old vineyards and to plant new ones with indigenous varieties "whose validity has been amply demonstrated". Such grapes include Primitivo, Negroamaro, Uva di Troia, Fiano, and Greco, but also lesser-known ones like Susumaniello, Pampanuto, Ottavianello, and Aleatico, which are only just in the process of being rediscovered.

SICILY FUNDS VINE RESEARCH

The Sicilian regional authorities are following those of Puglia in financing a study of vines native to the island, setting aside €2 million to study the properties not only of well-known varieties like Nero d'Avola, Nerello Mascalese, Inzolia, Grecanico, Cataratto, and Frappato, but also other less familiar ones such as Maialina, Dunnuni, Albarello, Nocera, and Nivureddu. The project will be overseen by the ubiquitous Professor Attilio Scienza, of the University of Milan, in collaboration with the University of Palermo and the Istituto Regionale della Vite e del Vino. A 50-hectare (ha) site has been selected in the province of Ragusa. The Regione Sicilia has already spent some €76 million between 2000 and 2002, plus a further €21 million in 2003, on restructuring vineyards. So far, 11,000 ha have been reconverted, and there are requests from growers to restructure a further 11,500 ha.

LOOKING FOR CULPRITS

Following a recent request by the Chianti Classico Consorzio for the EU to investigate whether the exponential growth of Australian wine on European markets has been favoured by the practice of dumping, the EU's restrictive controls on planting have once again come under the spotlight.

The Consorzio alleges that the Aussies have been selling on certain markets below cost, citing the fact that, between 2002 and 2003, exports of Australian wines to Germany rose by 83 per cent, whereas Italian wines on that market have slumped heavily recently. Australian exports have been helped by a 31 per cent reduction in price, bringing the cost per litre down to €1.60. The Tuscans maintain that this came about as a result of a cartel between the principal Australian exporters seeking to create a situation of commercial imbalance between their products and those of their European competitors.

However, has this situation not been brought about, at least in part, by the freedom of New World producers to plant where, what, and when they like, compared with the near impossibility of obtaining planting rights even in classic European zones? Is the Common Agricultural Policy (CAP) – with its disastrous policy of subsidizing overproduction, encouraging every kind of fiddle from the petty to the mega-mafioso, and leading to mass uprooting and the interdiction on further planting – not the real culprit behind the increasing imbalance between production costs in old Europe and the rest? Is it not time to stop wasting taxpayers' money, throw wine production open to market conditions, taking due safeguards against practices like dumping, and allow the producers themselves to decide what's right for them?

While oak excess continues to a large extent, a notable improvement was seen in some 1999 classics, released in 2003, compared with those of 1998 and 1997. Perhaps because producers are beginning to get the message that great oak is everywhere and great wine comes only from specific locations, they seem to be reining back. Let us hope the message spreads.

Illicit blending has also declined somewhat, with the decision by some of the main offenders to reclassify their dodgy wines as IGT rather than DOC or DOCG. Producers are more concerned about the possibility of being rumbled by DNA testing.

The pundits still wield much power and producers continue to go in fear of their august judgment. However, there is perhaps a move towards seeing that a producer's long-term interest is served more by being different, even unique, than by following a general standard.

Price rises are easing back as producers take note of the alarming strength of the euro and the accumulation of unsold high-priced wine in world warehouses. Reality is beginning to sink in.

Grapevine

- **In November 2003**, it was announced that all producers of Vino Nobile di Montepulciano, Montalcino, and Chianti Classico will now come under the control of their respective consortia, whether or not they are paid-up members. These are powers that the consortia have been seeking for some time, and while the advantages in terms of organization and consistency can be appreciated, it is hard to avoid the suspicion that undue pressure might be applied for renegades to return to the fold (or else?).

- **Celebrated sparkling-wine producer** Guido Berlucchi has followed Ferrari, Italy's biggest champagne-method producer (4.5 million bottles per annum), and other famous names, such as Gaja, Frescobaldi-Mondavi, and Antinori, into the Maremma, at Bolgheri. In early August 2003, with an investment of some €6–7 million, Berlucchi purchased Caccia al Piano, a 19-ha estate on the Bolgherese road between Castagneto Carducci and Bolgheri.

- **The aromatic sweet red sparkler** Vernaccia di Serrapetrona (no relation to any other Vernaccia) is one of the world's most unusual wines, yet it has become the first wine of the Marche to achieve DOCG status. No doubt it will be joined, when the producers get their act together, by two or three others, notably the far more important Verdicchio dei Castelli di Jesi, as well as by Verdicchio di Matelica and Rosso Conero.

Advance report on the latest harvest
2003

The drought in the centre and south was as severe as it was in the north, but, curiously, the further south you went, the less it seemed to matter, presumably because they are more used to going months without rain at baking temperatures. In quantity terms, overall production was more or less on the same level as the year before, which itself was much reduced. Some suffered more than others, however. Tuscany and the Marche were 15 per cent down on 2002 and 25–30 per cent down on the five-year average, while in the deep south – Puglia, Sicily – they were up a bit on 2002, although still down on average. So, again, upward pressure on prices, just at the worst time. On the other hand, qualitatively it seemed at first like chalk and cheese compared with 2002, with healthy grapes abounding (some raisining, but no rot) and high, sometimes too high, sugar levels. The best wines in 2003 will tend to come from the most mature vineyards, which favours the more traditional zones like Puglia and Abruzzo rather than the dynamic 'new' zones like parts of Tuscany, where so much replanting has been taking place over the past decade or so. The result has been that many root systems are not sufficiently established to withstand the onslaught of unremitting heat and water stress (unless irrigated – see Opinion in the Northern Italy section).

As time passes, it is becoming more apparent that 2003, while characterizable as 'great' for some, was not so for others. White wines were in many cases more balanced, certainly lighter and fresher, in 2002 than 2003. Reds were full of colour and substance but, in some cases, if picked too early – and it was generally an extraordinarily early vintage – not quite balanced, with tannins not fully mature. Perhaps the best news concerns the Sangioveses of Tuscany, which, at the top, be they Brunello, Vino Nobile, or Chianti, will be superb.

Updates on the previous five vintages

2002

Vintage rating: *73 (Red: 67, White: 79)*

The shortest vintage in quantity for 50 years, qualitatively 2002 has proved not as bad as predicted. White wines like Verdicchio are fresh and fragrant, with plenty of nerve. Sangiovese in Tuscany had a poor time of it, but there is so much Merlot and Cabernet these days that they can compensate. Lower-than-average temperatures, plenty of rain, and freak weather conditions made a mess of things along the east coast, but modern techniques saved a lot that would have gone down the pan in 1992.

2001

Vintage rating: *93 (Red: 93, White: 93)*

A good year virtually everywhere. Marginally better, perhaps, than 1997, although that vintage received much more hype. Perhaps 2001 was less anomalous than 1997, with wines more in the mainstream but at a higher-than-normal level, whereas 1997s in retrospect seem almost too ripe, too much of a good thing. In Chianti Classico the level was very good from the start, and the emerging wines confirm that it is a year of excellent aroma, concentration, and balance. In the south, Puglia and Sicily enjoyed ideal conditions. All in all, a very satisfactory outcome for both whites and reds.

2000

Vintage rating: *85 (Red: 88, White: 82)*

A very hot year, with a dry summer, giving rise to wines that are concentrated and potent, but lacking in elegance, with a slightly baked character – especially in central Tuscany. In some places the vegetation was temporarily arrested by the heat, yielding alcoholic wines with unripe tannins. On the east coast and south, where the varieties are more used to coping with such conditions, everything went swimmingly. As a rule, though, better for reds than whites.

1999

Vintage rating: *77–83 (Red: 77–83, White: 77–83)*

An extraordinary year in Tuscany, probably the best of the decade despite the excellence of 1990 and 1997 (and which, on its own, would rate 97 points). Tuscan classics of wonderful balance, with depth of colour, good but not excessive sugar levels, beautifully ripe tannins, and plenty of extract. Not so great, however, east of the Apennines and down south, where – particularly in Puglia – rains arrived just at vintage time to wash away the promise.

1998

Vintage rating: *88 (Red: 88, White: 88)*

This is a good year, at first discounted because it was compromised by vintage-time rains in central Tuscany, but becoming more appreciated. Chiantis have grace and balance rather than power, and Brunellos are surprisingly drinkable, without loss of character, compared with the 1997s and 1999s. Seen by some as the best year of the decade for the wines of the Tuscan Maremma (which, on its own, would rate 96 points). The east and south did well too. A good year for whites.

GREATEST WINE PRODUCERS

1. Antinori (Tuscany)
2. Castello di Ama (Tuscany)
3. Felsina (Tuscany)
4. Fontodi (Tuscany)
5. Tenuta San Guido Sassicaia (Tuscany)
6. Querciabella (Tuscany)
7. Castello del Terriccio (Tuscany)
8. Valentini (Abruzzo)
9. Tasca d'Almerita Regaleali (Sicily)
10. Argiolas (Sardinia)

FASTEST-IMPROVING PRODUCERS

1. Mastroberardino (Campania)
2. Villa Cafaggio (Tuscany)
3. Tenute Silvio Nardi (Tuscany)
4. Tenuta Valdipiatta (Tuscany)
5. Rivera (Puglia)
6. Castello di Volpaia (Tuscany)
7. Marramiero (Abruzzo)
8. Castello di Cacchiano (Tuscany)
9. Librandi, Ciro' (Calabria)
10. Paternoster (Basilicata)

Grapevine

- **Giovanni Ricasoli,** president of the Consorzio Gallo Nero, has officially voiced concern about a trend that environment-conscious producers have been muttering darkly against for years – to wit, the unbridled spread of housing and industrial property in places of outstanding beauty. Especially spoiled has been Panzano, which lies on a hilltop in the centre of the growing zone. Vagliagli and Chiocchio are other beauty zones becoming eyesores.

NEW UP-AND-COMING PRODUCERS

1. Salcheto (Tuscany)
2. Podere Collelungo (Tuscany)
3. Montepeloso (Tuscany)
4. Terre de' Trinci (Umbria)
5. Sabbionare Paolini (Marche)
6. Il Molino di Grace (Tuscany)
7. Pieri Agostina (Tuscany)
8. Luigi Rubino (Puglia)
9. Mille Una (Puglia)
10. D'Alfonso del Sordo (Puglia)

BEST-VALUE PRODUCERS

1. La Vite/Monteschiavo (Marche)
2. Barberani (Umbria)
3. Contesa di Rocca Pasetti (Abruzzo)
4. Accademia dei Racemi (Puglia)
5. Masseria Monaci (Puglia)
6. Agricole Vallone (Puglia)
7. Odoardi (Calabria)
8. Santadi (Sardinia)
9. Camigliano (Tuscany)
10. Terre Cortesi Moncaro (Marche)

Grapevine

• **Primitivo** (aka Zinfandel, aka Crljenak Kastelanski) may no longer be considered the poor cousin of Puglia. Used for decades as a high-octane blending wine to be exported by the shipload to places like Sete in France, Primitivo is today increasingly used to make wines of superior quality and price: Visello from Rubino, Torcicoda from Tormaresca, Dunico from Masseria Pepe, Casaboli from Barsento, and Taras from Albano Carrisi, to name a few. Nor has this phenomenon gone unnoticed in the centre and north of Italy, with names like Antinori, Zonin, Pasqua, and GIV moving in. Sales are booming despite swiftly rising prices, with production of DOC Primitivo di Manduria up to 63,000 hl, with a turnover of €4 million.

GREATEST-QUALITY WINES

1. **Brunello di Montalcino 1998** Salvioni, Tuscany (€80)
2. **Brunello di Montalcino 1998** Canalicchio di Sopra, Tuscany (€55)
3. **Camartina Chianti Classico 2000** Querciabella, Tuscany (€60)
4. **Chianti Classico Riserva 2000** Villa Cafaggio, Tuscany (€35)
5. **Aglianico del Vulture Vigna Caselle Riserva 1998** d'Angelo, Basilicata (€20)
6. **Messorio 1999** Le Macchiole, Tuscany (€80)
7. **Brunello di Montalcino 1999** Gianni Brunelli, Tuscany (€50)
8. **Turriga 1999** Argiolas, Sardinia (€40)
9. **Chianti Classico Siepi 2001** Castello di Fonterutoli, Tuscany (€50)
10. **Saffredi 2001** Le Pupille, Tuscany (€55)

BEST BARGAINS

1. **Montepulciano d'Abruzzo 2000** Ciavolich, Abruzzo (€6)
2. **Capannino 2002** Castello del Terriccio, Tuscany (€8)
3. **Chianti Classico Riserva 1999** Casa Sola, Tuscany (€9)
4. **Carminio IGT Salento 2001** Carrozzo, Puglia (€10)
5. **Brindisi Rosso Vigna Flaminio 2000** Vallone, Puglia (€7)
6. **Verdolino 2002** Casa d'Ambra, Campania (€8)
7. **Alcamo Bianco 2002** Conte Ruggero Foraci, Sicily (€7)
8. **Ischia Rosso Per' e Palummo 2002** Cenatiempo, Campania (€10)
9. **Rosso di Montalcino 2000** Lisini, Tuscany (€12)
10. **Brunello di Montalcino 1998** San Carlo, Tuscany (€25)

MOST EXCITING OR UNUSUAL FINDS

1 **San Martino IGT Toscana 2000** Villa Cafaggio, Tuscany (€40) *One hundred per cent Sangiovese from a single vineyard, made like a cru classé claret. Nothing unusual about that, except that it could be labelled Chianti and isn't, in defiance of the trend back to the DOCG noted earlier.*

2 **Primitivo di Manduria Memoria 2000** Consorzio Produttori Manduria, Puglia (€7) *A Primitivo that expresses the authentic, untamed soul of the grape from an exemplary cooperative with 300 members.*

3 **Montepulciano Cerasuolo Pie delle Vigne 2002** Cataldi Madonna, Abruzzo (€10) *Montepulciano is a grape with so much colour that hardly any maceration suffices to give a healthy colour to the famous Abruzzese rosatos called Cerasuolo. This 100 per cent Montepulciano is from first-selection free-run juice.*

4 **Verdicchio dei Castelli di Jesi Classico Nativo 2001** Monteschiavo, Marche (€10) *Made from grapes left on the vine a couple of weeks after full maturation, vinified and bottled without filtration to retain maximum flavour.*

5 **Verdicchio dei Castelli di Jesi Classico Superiore Cuprese 1991** Colonnara, Marche (€11) *Just to show how versatile the Verdicchio grape is, this is a wine that, having been vinified and aged entirely in stainless steel, has retained its liveliness after several years in bottle.*

6 **Esino Bianco 2002** Montecappone, Marche (€12) *This wine could qualify as a Verdicchio dei Castelli di Jesi, but the producer has preferred to slot it in under the newly created and as yet ill-defined Esino DOC. It represents the fresh, youthful style of the remarkable Marchigiano grape.*

7 **Rosso Enrico Vallania Cabernet Sauvignon 1999** Terre Rosse Vallania, Romagna (€18) *From an ancient strain of Cabernet Sauvignon present since time immemorial in the hills of Bologna, a strain selected by the late Enrico Vallania, this wine is produced only in great years. It is aged 3–4 years in stainless steel, no wood.*

8 **Vermentino di Gallura Superiore Aghiloia 2002** Cantina del Vermentino, Sardinia (€8) *Vermentino di Gallura DOCG must have a minimum alcohol level of 13 per cent, without which it can appear thin and unbalanced, but with which it can be full of dry, fruity-floral flavour.*

9 **Efeso 2001** Librandi, Calabria (€25) *Made from the Calabrian variety Mantonico, often reserved for sweet wines, this is vinified and matured in barriques under the auspices of the Piemontese oenologist Donato Lanati.*

10 **Vin Santo Recinaio 1998** Sangervasio, Tuscany (€50) *Tuscan Vin Santo comes in every style from (practically) dry-sherry-like to rich, sweet, and sticky. This is one of the best of the latter style.*

After a gestation period of eight years, the new Spanish national wine law was published on 26 June 2003.

JOHN RADFORD

The first change since the 1970 law (pre-democracy), it was cautiously welcomed by wine producers, particularly those in emergent and *vino de la tierra* (VdlT) areas. The main changes are listed below.

Table wines

VdM – *vinos de mesa*: no change – no region, grape, or vintage may be named on the label.

VdlT – *vinos de mesa con derecha a la mención tradicional vino de la tierra*: encompasses the old VdlT, *vino comarcal*, and *VdM de* [province/region name] classifications. All VdlT regions are (fairly lightly) regulated by a local *asociación*, and most of these belong to the national grouping AVIMES, which looks after and promotes VdlT zones.

Quality wine

VCIG – *vinos de calidad con indicación geográfica* (VQIG – *vi de qualitat amb indicació geográfica* in Catalan): a new category aimed at VdlT zones seeking promotion to quality-wine status. Regulation will be tougher than VdlT but lighter than DO, and the regulator will be known as an *órgano de gestion* (OG – management committee). This is seen as being roughly equivalent to the VDQS classification in France and is likely to become a stepping stone from VdlT to DO for many regions.

DO – *denominación de origen* (*denominació d'origen* in Catalan): as before, but VCIG wines must wait for at least five years before asking for promotion to DO status; still regulated by the *consejo regulador* (CRDO).

JOHN RADFORD is a writer and broadcaster with 30 years' experience of the culture, landscape, architecture, food, and wine of Spain. He is the author of *The New Spain* (Mitchell Beazley), which won four international awards in 1999, and a new edition of which was published in the spring of 2004. He is also the author of *Rioja* (Mitchell Beazley), published in autumn 2004.

DOCa – denominación de origen calificada (DOQ – *denominació d'origen qualificada* in Catalan): as before, but DO wines must wait at least 10 years before asking for promotion to DOCa status.

DO de pago – for single estates within or without existing DO(Ca) zones of exceptional quality. As predicted in the last edition of *Wine Report*, these have now passed into national law. Some very small *DOs de pago* may be exempted from regulation by the OG or CRDO that administers their area.

New definitions for ageing wines

These will be subject to the approval of the appropriate *asociación*/OG/ CRDO. VdlT and all quality wines can use the following terms:

noble – 12 months in cask (600 litres maximum) or bottle;

añejo – 24 months in cask or bottle;

viejo – 36 months, with a marked oxidative effect.

Quality wines only can use the following terms:

crianza – red: 24 months with at least six in cask (330 litres maximum, down from 1,000 litres); white/*rosado*: 12 months with at least six in cask;

reserva – red: 36 months with at least 12 in cask and the rest in bottle (not tank); white/*rosado*: 24 months with at least six in cask and the rest in bottle (not tank);

gran reserva – 60 months with at least 18 (down from 24) in cask and the rest in bottle; white/*rosado*: 48 months with at least six in cask and the rest in bottle (as before).

Promotion of wines

This hit the headlines in Spain: taxpayers' money being used to promote wine drinking. The Health Ministry would like to reverse the pattern of static wine consumption and increasing beer and spirit consumption. Money will be available only under certain circumstances:

• Recommending moderate and responsible consumption;

• Informing the public of the benefits of wine within the Mediterranean diet;

• Improving the sustainable development of vine cultivation;

• Emphasizing historical, traditional, and cultural aspects of Spanish wine;

• Improving knowledge about Spanish wines throughout the countries of the EU and third countries.

Irrigation

This will be permitted (by national or regional government) on a case-by-case basis, especially in areas with low rainfall, but always with the aim of preserving the vegetal cycle and ecosystem of the vine, and to increase quality in the wine.

OTHER CHANGES

In addition to the changes on the previous pages, there are also alterations to viticultural and vinicultural regulations and aspects of wine terminology, as well as safeguards for regional and local identities. The main visible change that the consumer should see during 2004/5 is probably going to be the gradual evolution of VdlT zones into the new VCIG category.

DUEROS DUEL

CRDO Ribera del Duero has brought a case against the small VdlT zone of Arribes del Duero in the province of Zamora. This area is on the Spanish side of the river Duero, which forms the Hispano–Portuguese border for about 100 km (62 miles) of its length. Arribes del Duero became a VdlT zone in 1992, but it took 10 years for Ribera del Duero to decide the names were too similar and that Arribes would have to change theirs, losing the word 'Duero' and replacing it with, perhaps, Fermoselle, the main town in the area. What had happened in those 10 years, of course, was that Ribera del Duero wines had rocketed to international stardom, with prices to match. In addition, the new Durius Bodega (ARCO-Bodegas Unidas with the Marqués de Griñón as consultant) has been completed and turned in its first vintage (2003) in Arribes del Duero. Perhaps the prospect of something at Griñón quality levels has got them worried in Roa de Duero. The court should have handed down its decision in the summer of 2004. Regardless, Arribes plans to apply for VCIG status as soon as possible.

CASTILLA Y LEÓN CHASES EXPORTS

The country wines of Castilla y León are starting to flex their muscles and are trying to get into export markets: at the Salón Internacional del Vino in Madrid, in October 2003, several emergent regions were exhibiting and chasing export business. Interestingly, they are not attempting a side-door entry with Tempranillo, Garnacha, or international varieties (although these are represented), but majoring on what grows locally, including Rufete and Juan García, both grapes that have had potential for rather a long time but that are now starting to show some progress as winemaking practices improve. Names to look for include VdlT Arribes del Duero (but see above for a possible name change), particularly the wines of the co-op. Nuestra Señora del Castillo's 2001 Condado de Fermosel (80 per cent Juan García, 15 per cent Tempranillo, 5 per cent Rufete, with three months in American oak) offers mind-boggling quality at a retail price of €2. In addition, land prices in the neighbouring regions of Castilla y León are now so high that *bodegas* active in these regions are looking at the potential of VdlT areas, especially with, perhaps, the prospect of promotion to the new VCIG category in the near future. One such is Bodegas Arzuaga from Ribera del Duero, which has established Bodegas La Colegiada in Lerma.

BODEGAS Y BEBIDAS OPENS NEW *BODEGA*

Bodegas y Bebidas opened its new Juan Alcorta *bodega* in time for the 2003 vintage. In keeping with the trend in Rioja and other high-profile areas, tourism played a part in its design, with the inclusion of a purpose-built visitors' centre with a dining room, a tasting room, meeting rooms, and, of course, a shop. The new complex covers 40,000 sq m (48,000 sq yds), and the fermenting hall has every modern contrivance: gone are the days when it was hip to have a computer controlling your tanks. Now every tank (all 140 of them) has its own computer, all of which report to a mainframe in the winemaker's office. ByB is using the new *bodega* as an opportunity to step up the quality of its wines, including using grapes from a property it owns in Quel, which, in spite of being in the Rioja Baja, is the region's highest vineyard, at 750 m (2,460 ft). Winemaker Elena Adell San Pedro has introduced two new wines: La Finca and Alcorta, both 1998 *reservas* in the classic Rioja mould, with the second being reserved for the on-trade.

GrapeVine

- **Another ARCO-Bodegas Unidas** project is underway in Alfaro (Rioja Baja) at the Dominio de Susar (although, confusingly, it keeps changing its name). The group bought the *bodega* and its vineyards several years ago and spent some considerable time retraining the vines, which had been *en vaso* and are now trained on the Smart-Dyson principle. The attraction was that these vineyards are classified as experimental, so, as well as the usual Riojano suspects, there are also plantations of Syrah, Merlot, and Cabernet Sauvignon. The rules governing experimentals in Rioja are complex, but the winemaker at Susar, Carmelo Angulo Bernedo, has a cunning plan. He believes that, within a few years, he will be able to put a varietal Merlot on the market and label it Rioja. In the meantime, the wines made at Susar are no longer being called Enartis but have been renamed Marqués de la Concordia. The Enartis name will be reserved for the *tête de cuvée* wines across the group.

- **A recent visit to the three DOs** in the province of Zaragoza threw up some tremendous wines made from plantations of, particularly, old-vine Garnacha, many of which had been neglected for years. Interestingly, the co-op *bodegas* are at the forefront of the wave, grouping themselves together to pool marketing, turning themselves into limited companies (with the former members as shareholders), and, most importantly, paying for the grapes on a sliding scale according to the health and the age of the vineyard. Bodegas y Viñedos de Jalón in Calatayud, for example, is paying some of their growers €1 a kilo for grapes from 100-year-old vines. Their Castillo de Maluenda (40-year-old vines) is €1.80 ex cellar, and their latest wine is called Navritum (80-year-old vines), which costs €5 ex cellar. There is no tradition of high prices here and the value for money is quite outstanding. Expect to see a lot more from Calatayud, Campo de Borja, and Cariñena.

Last year I wrote about inappropriate ageing in oak for wines that don't have the extract to cope with it; dirty old barrels that should be burned and replaced; inappropriate irrigation (now legal in individual cases); and asset-stripping of individual varieties to the detriment of a *bodega*'s mainstream wines. These are all matters that still need to be addressed.

The question of yields is also a perennial one. To give an example: in 2000, Rioja was massively overproduced, resulting in swimming pools of thin, uninteresting wine. The CRDO declassified thousands of litres, but it didn't make much difference because a lot of the wine within the system was exactly the same quality as the wine that had been declassified. Rioja was thought to have learned its lesson, and 2002 and 2003 were more normal harvests. In 2003, there were predictions of a big and good harvest, but the very hot weather in August and September put paid to those. However, the CRDO set a maximum production of 118 per cent of base yield at harvest time and, in the event, the region yielded 432 million kg of grapes which, at a *rendimiento* of 72 per cent, can produce 311 million litres of wine, which is actually more than the production in 2000 (and an 80 per cent increase since 1993). This would be the biggest harvest ever, although there is no certainty that all *bodegas* will make the maximum amount of wine or that the CRDO will not declassify some of the production. But what's the point of having a maximum yield if you're not going to stick to it? Indeed, there are those who would suggest that Rioja would do better to think about lowering its maximum yields (currently 62 hectolitres per hectare [hl/ha] for whites and 47 hl/ha for reds) and enforcing them more rigorously. Neither Rioja nor Spain is alone in this, of course.

Grapevine

• **The first vintage** (2001) of a new project by Codorníu (of Cava fame) is on the market: a white (Chardonnay) and two reds (Tempranillo/Cabernet Sauvignon and Tempranillo/Merlot). It's made by a subsidiary company called Bodegas Nuviana in Belver de Cinca in the VdlT Valle del Cinca (mentioned in passing in last year's *Wine Report*). The zone, created in 1996, covers 11 villages around Fraga. The river Cinca is a tributary of the Ebro, flowing south from the Pyrenees via Barbastro in the province of Huesca (not far from DO Somontano). The wines show promising quality but probably need another couple of vintages to reach their full potential.

Advance report on the latest harvest

2003

High levels of summer heat right across Spain brought the harvest forward by anything up to 10 days. Parts of Rioja suffered very badly, with some of the vines simply shutting down their stomata in the heat with resultant damage to the grapes. Vineyards with irrigation survived the best. In the south, Jerez reported an excellent-quality vintage. Penedès harvested excellent reds with the exception of Syrah, which had suffered from the heat, and quantity is down almost everywhere to about 90–95 per cent of the five-year average. On the whole, the south did better than the north again, perhaps because southern vineyards are more hardened to extremes of heat.

Updates on the previous five vintages

2002

Vintage rating:
northeast: 60, southwest: 80
The 2002 vintage in Spain divided roughly into a southwest/ northeast divide, with the former having the better time of it. Damp conditions in Catalonia extended to rain during the harvest with resultant rot, while in the south La Mancha picked very healthy fruit in excellent conditions.

2001

Vintage rating: *90*
Excellent quality throughout Spain, with Rioja and Ribera del Duero showing particularly well, and the south (La Mancha, Valdepeñas, etc) making what may become some very long-lived wines. Good whites, too, particularly in Rías Baixas and Rueda, for early drinking.

2000

Vintage rating:
generally: 60; better estates and Penedès: 70–80
Better in the south than the north. Rioja produced a vast, dilute, and unattractive vintage. Those *bodegas* that green-harvested and hand-selected made some good wines, but they were in the minority. Some of the better estates and Penedès fared better than most.

1999

Vintage rating: 70

Generally a good, if not outstanding, year with a substantial minority of wines with *reserva* potential and a very few (the single estates again) with very good wines. In the meantime, some early-released *crianzas* have developed a thread of acidity, which is rather prominent, but what few *reserva* wines have been released show rather better.

1998

Vintage rating: 80–90

A very good year in the north, with considerable potential for *reserva* quality and above in Rioja (the biggest vintage ever) and Ribera del Duero. Both of these are now showing well at *reserva* level, as are Valdepeñas and Penedès.

Grapevine

• **Work continues apace** at Marqués de Riscal in Elciego on the new corporate headquarters designed by Frank Gehry of Guggenheim Bilbao fame. The new centre should be completed by the end of 2004/early 2005 and will include a visitors' centre, hotel, restaurant, shop, and much else, instantaneously becoming the top tourist attraction in Elciego (population 995).

• **Eyebrows were raised** by the news in May 2003 that La Rioja now has a *vino de la tierra* zone, called Valles de Sadacia. Named after the river Cidaco (a tributary of the Ebro and called Sadacia in Roman times), the vineyards are around Alfaro, Calahorra, Pradejón, and Quel in the Rioja Baja. There are only five members of the *asociación* (the VdlT equivalent of a *consejo regulador*), of which two – Bodegas Castillo de Maetierra and Bodegas Peñuela – actually make wine. There are 60 ha of vines, and the wine must be a minimum of 85 per cent Moscatel de Gran Menudo (Muscat of Alexandria) and may be dry, sweet, or anything in between. Previously, Rioja had shown no interest in VdlT wines and at least one *bodega* has been trying to get Muscat-based wines (which have a long tradition in these parts) admitted to the DOCa Rioja for years. This is seen by some as a first step.

• **DO Priorat** (the Catalan spelling is now standard on all bottles) has now been promoted to DOCa, although the Catalan expression DOQ – *denominació d'origen qualificada* – is being used on bottles and labels, applying it retrospectively to all current bottlings, so wines as old as 1999 may be seen with the DOQ epithet. On the quality front, new and exciting *bodegas* producing fabulous (and fabulously expensive) wines continue to reach the market.

GREATEST WINE PRODUCERS

1. Alejandro Fernández (Ribera del Duero, La Mancha)
2. Peter Sisseck (Ribera del Duero)
3. Álvaro Palacios (Priorat, Bierzo)
4. Mariano García (Ribera del Duero, Castilla y León)
5. Vega Sicilia (Ribera del Duero)
6. Carlos Falcó (Dominio de Valdepusa, Rioja, Castilla y León)
7. Telmo Rodríguez (*ubique*)
8. Miguel Torres (Penedès, Catalunya)
9. Costers del Siurana (Priorat)
10. Contino (Rioja)

FASTEST-IMPROVING PRODUCERS

1. Juan Alcorta (Rioja)
2. Bodegas Langa (Calatayud)
3. Vinos de Bierzo Co-op
4. Bodegas La Cerca (Méntrida)
5. Co-op Vinícola del Priorat
6. Lezaun (Navarra)
7. Co-op Agrícola Falset-Marca (Priorat)
8. Castillo Perelada (Empordà-Costa Brava)
9. Parés Baltà (Penedès)
10. Celler Vall-Llach (Priorat)

NEW UP-AND-COMING PRODUCERS

1. Sangenís i Vaqué (Priorat)
2. Ripoll Sans (Priorat)
3. Dominio de Tares (Bierzo)
4. Señorío de Andión (Navarra)
5. Celler Ardèvol i Asociats (Priorat)
6. Macaya Siglo XXI (Navarra)
7. Bodega Rejadorada (Toro)
8. La Perla del Priorat
9. Lezaun (Navarra)
10. Joan Simó (Priorat)

BEST-VALUE PRODUCERS

1. Bodega San Alejandro Co-op (Calatayud)
2. Bodegas y Viñedos de Jalón (Calatayud)
3. Monte Amán (Ribera del Arlanza)
4. Manuel Martínez Meroño (Campo de Cartagena)
5. Arribes del Duero Co-op
6. Bodegas Camino del Villar (Navarra)
7. Bodegas La Cerca (Méntrida)
8. Covinca (Cariñena)
9. Castillo de Capmany (Empordà-Costa Brava)
10. Luís Gurpegui Muga (Rioja)

GREATEST-QUALITY WINES

1. **Clos Monlleó 2000** Sangenís i Vaqué, Priorat (€49)
2. **Doix 2001** Mas Doix, Priorat (€48)
3. **Viña Izadi Expresión 2001** Viña Villabuena, Rioja (€45)
4. **P3 2002** Dominio de Tares, Bierzo (€36)
5. **Aia 2001** Miquel Oliver, Pla i Llevant de Mallorca (€13.20)
6. **Grandes Añadas 2001** Artadi, Rioja (€87)
7. **Villaester 2001** Villaester, Ribera del Duero (€24)
8. **Fagús 2001** Coto de Hayas, Campo de Borja (€18)
9. **Viña Tondonia Blanco 1987** López Heredia, Rioja (€15)
10. **Recaredo Brut Reserva NV** Recaredo, Cava (€20)

BEST BARGAINS

1. **Monte Ducay Cariñena Crianza 2000** Bodegas Gran Ducay (€2.50)
2. **Pago de Campean Barrica 2001** Co-op El Soto, Tierra del Vino de Zamora (€2.80)
3. **Condado de Fermosel Roble 2001** Bodega Ocellum Durii, Arribes del Duero (€2)
4. **Las Rocas de San Alejandro 2002** Co-op San Alejandro, Calatayud (€2)
5. **Gavión Tinto Joven 2002** Co-op Viña Escuderos, Tierra del Vino de Zamora (€2.60)
6. **Viña Perguita Crianza 1999** Fernández de Arcaya, Navarra (€4)
7. **Casa de la Viña 2000** Casa de la Viña, Valdepeñas (€3.74)
8. **Pago de Valleoscuro 2001** Bodegas Otero, Valles de Benavente (€4)
9. **Azabache 2000** Co-op Viñedos de Aldeanueva, Rioja (€4.77)
10. **Viña Acedo Blanco 2002** Bodegas La Emperatriz, Rioja (€4.25)

MOST EXCITING OR UNUSUAL FINDS

1. **Finca Sanguijuela Acinipo 2001** Bodega Friedrich Schatz, Sierras de Málaga (€30) *Astonishing and beguiling organic Andaluz take on a grape (Lemberger) more normally found in Württemberg.*
2. **Tinto Lerma Crianza 2000** Bodegas La Colegiada, Ribera del Arlanza (€5.50) *Powerful, high-level winemaking unique in Ribera del Arlanza, but the bodega does belong to a parent company (Arzuaga) in Ribera del Duero.*
3. **Alizán Elite 2000** Alizán Bodegas y Viñedos, Tierra del Vino de Zamora (€6) *Just a lovely wine with 12 months in American oak, made to exacting standards at a very reasonable price.*
4. **Finca Sandoval 2001** Finca Sandoval, Manchuela (€20) *Made by one of Spain's foremost wine writers, Victor de la Serna, this single-estate Syrah/Monastrell continues to improve every year.*
5. **Partal 2001** Crianza Bodegas Balcona, Bullas (€4.65) *One of only a handful of bodegas making a fist of the Monastrell in Bullas – excellent value and a bodega with promise.*
6. **Monte Armantes 2002** Co-op San Gregorio, Calatayud (€10) *This was a cask sample of what will become the 2002 reserva (release January 2006): impressive quality from this ever-improving bodega in all its wines, but this particularly.*
7. **Marqués de la Concordia Hacienda de Susar 2001** Dominio de Susar, Rioja (€34) *The experimental Rioja from Dominio Susar, complete with Cabernet Sauvignon, Merlot, and Syrah as well as Tempranillo – a stunner.*
8. **Viña San Román 2000** Bodegas Maurodos, Toro (€24) *Only the second vintage from the (Mariano) García family's new property in Toro – exceptional quality that will no doubt improve further as the vineyards mature.*
9. **Viña Norte Vendímia Seleccionada 2001** Bodegas Insulares-Tenerife, Tacoronte-Acentejo (€20) *The first really world-class red wine from the Canary Islands; mainly Listan Negro from phylloxera-free vines, beautifully made with 12 months in oak.*
10. **Vino Naranja NV Bodegas Oliveros, Condado de Huelva** (€3.50) *To try to inject some interest into wines from the Condado, Miguel Oliveros makes a lightly fortified Zalema with Seville orange skins marinated in it. Surprisingly, not unpleasant.*

There are happy faces in the sherry towns, but one has heard rumours of upturn before. Brandy sales, which provide a lot of the profit, have gone down, but that is shrugged off; they are expected to rise again.

JULIAN JEFFS QC

Sherry sales have been going up, though not very much as yet. However, there are signs that the wine is becoming more fashionable in major export markets. This has been spurred on by an increasing awareness that sherry really is one of the greatest wines in the world. Why has this happened? Partly, no doubt, the pendulum of taste, which always swings. Partly the burgeoning local market, which has been exploited particularly well by the *bodegas* of Sanlúcar with their fabulous manzanillas. Partly travel, which has introduced holiday-makers in Spain to the delights of well-chilled finos and manzanillas, has helped to introduce tapas bars to the UK, and has shown how well sherry goes with food. Partly by the move towards modern packaging and marketing. But not least by the very fine wines that are now available.

JULIAN JEFFS QC became a Gray's Inn barrister in 1958, attained Queen's Counsel in 1975, and retired from practice in 1991, although he continued as a Deputy High Court Judge until 1996. His love of sherry began in 1956, when he was a sherry shipper's assistant in Spain, and this led to a passion for writing when *Sherry* (Faber & Faber) was published in 1961. He began a two-year stint as editor of *Wine and Food* in 1965, the same year that Faber & Faber offered him the post of general editor for its radically new Wine Series. Over the next 40-odd years he commissioned many of the most respected, long-lasting, and definitive works on wine. He held this position until 2002, when Faber & Faber sold the Wine Series to Mitchell Beazley. Julian has been chairman (1970–72), vice president (1975–91), and president (1992–96) of the Circle of Wine Writers, winning the Glenfiddich Wine Writer award in 1974 and 1978. His books include *The Wines of Europe* (Faber & Faber, 1971), *The Little Dictionary of Drink* (Pelham, 1973), and *The Wines of Spain* (Faber & Faber, 1999).

The cheap, profitable, easy-to-drink wines of the past did no end of damage to the image. Fine, mature wines of all classes are well on the way to putting this right, and any multinational that ignores them does so at its peril. They will never make bulk sales, any more than first-growth clarets will, but they give something to aspire to and people are beginning to pay high prices for them. Vintage sherries can fetch astronomic prices at auction. Younger and less expensive wines of top quality, such as finos and manzanillas, offer fantastic value and people are at last beginning to realize it. They are learning that sherry is the cheapest great wine in the world.

Advancing age of old sherry

The new designations are rapidly making headway. The two for very old wines are VORS, *Vinum Optimum Rare Signatum* or Very Old Rare Sherry (minimum age of 30 years), and VOS, *Vinum Optimum Signatum* or Very Old Sherry (minimum age of 20 years). Bottles may be labelled with the words, the initials, the age, or all three.

Acquiring the new designations involves a lot of expense, since samples have to be supplied for tasting, analysis, and even a form of carbon-14 testing. There is also a maximum shipping quota. The red tape and expense involved mean that smaller quantities of wine that could qualify are often not submitted. However, many shippers do find applying for the designation very worthwhile and *Wine Report 2004* listed 18 shippers and 47 wines, all of which continue, but Williams & Humbert has changed two of the names: Amontillado Solera Especial (VORS) has become Jalifa, and Pedro Ximénez Solera Especial (VOS) has become Don Guido. Now there are two more shippers and 11 new wines. The new shippers are Osborne, with Pedro Ximénez Viejo (VORS), and Sandeman, with Amontillado Royal Esmeralda (VOS), Oloroso Royal Corregidor (VOS), and Pedro Ximénez Royal Ambrosante (VOS). Bodegas Tradición has added Amontillado Tradición (VORS); José Estévez has added Oloroso Don Gonzalo (VOS) and Oloroso Solera 1842 (VOS) (both Valdespino wines); and Bodegas Hidalgo-La Gitana (formerly Vinícola Hidalgo) has added Amontillado

Solera Especial (VORS), Amontillado Vaedro (VORS), Palo Cortado Hidalgo (VORS), and Oloroso Vaedro (VORS).

The new designations agreed in 2003 for 12- and 15-year-old wines have not yet caught on, but several shippers are thinking about it and it is safe to say that there will be some new entries for the next *Wine Report*.

Getting the balance right

In the 1980s there was serious overproduction and the sherry vineyards were the only ones in Spain where prices were going down instead of up. Something had to be done, so the authorities commissioned a report by Price Waterhouse, which showed that between 1980 and 1988 the vineyards had produced 27.5 per cent more must than required, following frenetic planting because sherry sales had been rising and the shippers projected the graph up and up. Instead, sales fell. As a result, the vineyard area declined from 21,874 hectares (ha) in 1982 to 10,359 ha in 2002, a reduction of more than 50 per cent. At least things have now stabilized. Perhaps the pendulum has gone a bit too far: there is plenty of wine in an average harvest, but there can be a shortage in a poor one.

The reduction in vineyard area has also been reflected by a reduction in stocks. In the late 1970s, shippers were holding too much wine, with stocks of 4.1 million hectolitres (hl) in 1978. By 1999, shippers' stocks had reduced to 2.7 million hl. At the moment, supply and demand, in terms of vineyards and stocks of sherry, seem to be pretty much in balance. If demand goes up, however, this situation could change.

Grapevine

• **El Puerto de Santa María** is getting a facelift. It used to be a rather dishevelled little town with well-kept *bodegas* and crumbling palaces. The palaces are crumbling no longer but are being turned into beautiful apartments. The *bodegas* are being rationalized. Once, many of the Jerez houses had *bodegas* there for maturing light finos, but they have learned how to do that in Jerez. El Puerto is still very good for light finos, though, as customers of the local *bodegas* are learning to their joy; and Luis Caballero, who owns Lustau, has now moved his *soleras* around so that all the finos are matured in El Puerto, and wines of all the other categories are matured in his fine Jerez *bodegas*.

• **Bodegas Tradición,** having built up remarkable *soleras* of old wines, is now selling them. They are worth seeking out.

• **Sanlúcar de Barrameda** has transformed itself. Old buildings have been ripped down and new blocks built, and some of the resulting profits have been put into wine. There have been casualties, though, notably the old house of Manuel de Argüeso (not to be confused with the flourishing Herederos de Argüeso), which was retained by the Valdespino family when they sold out to Estévez and has now been closed down. Some of the buildings are being redeveloped, but one of the most beautiful old *bodegas* has been bought by Pedro Romero and will be put to good use.

The decline in popularity of sherry can be blamed in part on the poor quality of some of the cheap wines shipped. The *consejo regulador* passes all the wines that are sold, and it does a good job in taking wines at random off bottling lines to compare with the approved control sample, but it would do a better job if some of the poorer wines were rejected outright. Recently, the office went through a period of limbo, but now there is a new administrator, César Saldaña, and it is hoped that he will give it bite.

Sweet-sherry vineyards

In the past, some of the sweetening wines used in blending were made with the aid of invert sugar. This is a natural product that did no harm at all, but it is not allowed under EU regulations, so, as in other European wine-growing areas, rectified concentrated must (in Spanish, *mosto concentrado rectificado*) has to be used instead. At present, this comes from vineyards of little wine potential in the centre of Spain. It would make more sense, surely, to grub up some of these vineyards and replant some of the vineyards that lie fallow in Jerez, since this would give the sherry industry scope for expansion when demand rises again.

Grapevine

• **There can be no doubt** that packaging matters. The shippers are at last realizing this and, one after another, are adopting modern-looking labels that help to dispel the myth that sherry is for old fogies. Sánchez Romate led the way and González Byass soon followed. Watch the rest.

• **Jerez is never** without its rumours. Sandeman is no longer a multinational and has been bought by the Portuguese Sogrape Group of Mateus Rosé fame, which is said to be more interested in port than in sherry. At least one takeover approach has been talked of. There has also been speculation about Williams & Humbert, which is half-

owned by the Dutch group Koninklijke Ahold, whose financial difficulties have been well publicized. Will it have to sell off some of its assets?

• **The fine old firm** of Wisdom & Warter, which has been owned for many years by González Byass, has disappeared from the middle of Jerez and now has an office block next to the González Byass fermentation *bodegas* on the road to El Puerto, where it operates separately, though its wines have been taken into the González *bodegas*. Its *bodegas* have been sold to Sánchez Romate, which has enabled that firm to expand next door instead of having to build new premises.

For sherry, vintage assessments per se are not particularly relevant because very little sherry is sold with a vintage year (añada sherry) and it is not released for 20 years or more. However, sherry lovers should be interested to know how much sherry has been topping up the various *soleras* in recent years, and whether the quality of these wines has been good or bad. After a series of rather disappointing vintages, sherry has been blessed with three very good ones in a row. Note that the maximum yield allowed is 80 hl/ha in the best vineyard area (the Zona Superior) and 100 hl/ha in the rest.

Advance report on the latest harvest

2003

A yield of 64 hl/ha provided a total of 134,000 butts of new wine for all the sherry *bodegas*. Rainfall was above average at 760 mm (30 in). Quality: after a hot summer, maturity was good (though overripe in a few vineyards), with an alcoholic strength of 12 per cent.

Updates on the previous five vintages

2002

Vintage rating: 95
A yield of 64 hl/ha provided a total of 137,888 butts of new wine for all the sherry *bodegas*. Rainfall: 594 mm (23 in). Quality: good maturity with an alcoholic strength of 11 per cent.

2001

Vintage rating: 95
A yield of 72 hl/ha provided a total of 152,102 butts of new wine. Another early vintage. Rainfall: 474 mm (18½ in). Quality: exceptional – the grapes had a perfect level of maturation.

2000

Vintage rating: 90
A yield of 65 hl/ha provided a total of 135,542 butts of new wine. Rainfall: 639 mm (25 in). Quality: good.

Grapevine

- **One of the best** boutique *bodegas* is Rey Fernando de Castilla, run by Jan Pettersen, a Norwegian who used to be export director at Osborne. He started with brandies (very good ones), but has been steadily building up *soleras* of fine wines. He is currently selling fino, amontillado, palo cortado, oloroso, and Pedro Ximénez in 50-cl bottles with modern labels.

1999

Vintage rating: 85

A yield of 75 hl/ha provided a total of 157,525 butts of new wine. Rainfall: 245 mm (9½ in). Quality: good.

1998

Vintage rating: 85

A yield of 73 hl/ha provided a total of 154,705 butts of new wine. Rainfall: 702 mm (27½ in). Quality: good.

GREATEST WINE PRODUCERS

1. González Byass (including Croft and Wisdom & Warter)
2. Bodegas Osborne
3. Emilio Lustau/Luis Caballero
4. Allied Domecq España (Domecq and Harvey)
5. José Estévez (Valdespino and Real Tesoro)
6. Bodegas Williams & Humbert
7. Bodegas Barbadillo
8. Hidalgo-La Gitana
9. Sandeman
10. Garvey/José de Soto

FASTEST-IMPROVING PRODUCERS

1. Delgado Zuleta
2. Dios Baco
3. Emilio Hidalgo
4. Herederos de Argüeso
5. Hijos de Rainera Pérez Marin
6. M Gil Luque
7. Pedro Romero
8. Sánchez Romate Hermanos

NEW UP-AND-COMING PRODUCERS

1. Bodegas Pilar Aranda
2. Bodegas J Ferris
3. Bodegas Tradición
4. Bodegas Rey Fernando de Castilla
5. Herederos de Argüeso
6. Gaspar Florido Cano

7. Juan Carlos Gutiérrez Colosia
8. M Gil Luque
9. Pilar Plá Pechovierto (El Maestro Sierra)
10. Torre Dama (Miguel Gómez)

BEST-VALUE PRODUCERS

1. Bodegas Williams & Humbert
2. Emilio Lustau
3. José Estévez
4. Wisdom & Warter

GREATEST-QUALITY WINES

1. **San Léon** Herederos de Argüeso (€5.20)
2. **Tio Pepe** González Byass (€5.90)
3. **Coquinero** Osborne (€5.60)
4. **Pastrana Manzanilla Pasada** Hidalgo-La Gitana (€7.80)
5. **Del Duque Amontillado Muy Viejo Aged 30 Years** González Byass (€32)
6. **1730 Palo Cortado** Pilar Aranda (€38.60)
7. **Oloroso Sibarita Aged 30 Years** Domecq (€48)
8. **Oloroso Solera Especial Dry Sack** Williams & Humbert (€20)
9. **Matusalém Aged 30 Years** González Byass (€32)
10. **Solera 1842 Aged 20 Years** Valdespino (€70)

BEST BARGAINS

1. **Matusalém Aged 30 Years** González Byass (€32)
2. **Bailén** Osborne (€9)
3. **Amontillado Seco Napoléon** Hidalgo-La Gitana (€6)
4. **Oloroso Seco Napoléon** Hidalgo-La Gitana (€6)
5. **Jerez Cortado** Hidalgo-La Gitana (€17)
6. **Fino del Puerto** Gutierrez Colosia (€3.50)
7. **Manzanilla Las Medallas** Herederos de Argüeso (€3.50)
8. **Don Fino** Sandeman (€6.60)
9. **Fino** Valdespino (€4.27)
10. **Pedro Ximénez Viejo Napoléon** Hidalgo-La Gitana (€8)

MOST EXCITING OR UNUSUAL FINDS

1. **1970 Añada Oloroso** González Byass (€85) *Is this the shape of things to come? Perfectly mature and bottled at its peak, this shows the glories that an oloroso can reach.*
2. **Vintage Collection Palo Cortado 1962** Williams & Humbert (€250 estimated auction price) *Hard to get but enormously worth the effort. If left to develop without blending, sherry can show remarkable complexity, especially if it is a palo cortado, and no wine shows it better than this.*
3. **Palo Cortado P-D-P** Osborne (€95) *Palo cortado is normally bottled dry and shows remarkable subtlety, between an amontillado and an oloroso. Slightly sweetened, as this is, it can be a superb dessert wine – rare and wonderful.*
4. **Royal Esmeralda** Sandeman (€25) *The blend of this wine has changed over the years. It used to be rather sweet but now it is dry and a VOS. This amontillado really shows the quality of the solera from which it is drawn.*
5. **Oloroso Solera Su Majestad** Valdespino (€160) *A magisterial old oloroso, worthy of its royal title and its very high price.*
6. **Apóstoles Very Old Palo Cortado** González Byass (€33) *With a certified age of 30 years, it is not surprising that it has cast off its origin as a fino.*
7. **Antique Oloroso** Fernando de Castilla (€24) *An oloroso of the highest quality but not too old: it is old enough to show the stylishness of a fine oloroso, but its flavour is not overwhelming.*
8. **Amontillado Viejo Pastrana** Hidalgo-La Gitana (€26) *There are not many single-vineyard sherries and this is one of them, kept apart because of its exceptional quality. Amontillados from Sanlúcar are lighter and more delicate than those from Jerez or even from El Puerto, but its great maturity gives this one plenty of flavour.*
9. **Old East India Sherry** Lustau (€17) *The name is full of nostalgia. It used to be applied to wine matured by being shipped to the East Indies and back. This is no longer done, but the name is justly applied to a mature, sweet blend that gives a good idea of what our ancestors used to drink.*
10. **Lustau Moscatel Las Cruces** (€31) *Moscatel has been rather eclipsed by the grander, sweeter Pedro Ximénez but, when fully mature, it is a sweet wine of elegance and charm with a real Moscatel flavour.*

He is not Portuguese, but Professor Michael Porter's name is now well known throughout Portugal.

As one of the founders of the US-based Monitor Group, he carried out an extensive study on the Portuguese economy for the government in 2002, in which he identified the wine industry as a key 'cluster', or sector, for future growth. A year later, ViniPortugal, one of two generic bodies responsible for promoting Portuguese wines, commissioned a further in-depth study of the wine sector at a cost of €500,000.

RICHARD MAYSON

Porter's conclusions should be a wake-up call for everyone involved in the industry. First he writes that there is "no explicit strategy shared by the cluster as a whole" and that "most of the industry leaders are of the belief that each company has its own unique view on where future opportunities lie". Furthermore, the sector has, in the past, followed "the path of least resistance", with most wine sold on the local market and only 14 per cent (in 2001/02) exported. Of the wine that is exported, "much goes to consumers who are easy to sell to (that is, expatriate communities and ex-colonies), as opposed to those that will return the highest value". This

RICHARD MAYSON writes and lectures on wine, dividing his time between London, Portugal, and a family business in the Peak District. He speaks fluent Portuguese, having been brought up in Portugal, and is regarded as one of the most respected authorities on port, sherry, madeira, and the wines of Spain and Portugal. His interest in the subject goes back to his university days, when he wrote a thesis on the microclimates of the vineyards of the Douro Valley. His books include *Portugal's Wines & Wine Makers* (Ebury Press, 1992), *Port and the Douro* (Faber & Faber, 1999), and his latest work, *The Wines and Vineyards of Portugal* (Mitchell Beazley), which was published in 2003. He is currently preparing a second edition of *Port and the Douro*, a third edition of *Portugal's Wines & Wine Makers*, and a new book on the wines of Madeira.

strategy (if it can be called such) is hugely risky at a time when domestic consumption is declining (per capita consumption has halved in 20 years), expatriate groups are becoming naturalized, and ex-colonies (such as Brazil) look to competitive wine-producing neighbours like Argentina and Chile. He concludes that "as currently configured, the most likely outcome for the Portuguese wine industry is at best slow growth driven by gradual upgrading of local demand, with some considerable downside risk".

There is much in Porter's report that makes gloomy reading (see Opinion), but he does map a way forward for Portugal. "In the higher end of the premium and superpremium range [€7–12], there is strong untested belief that Portugal is competitive on the price–quality scale as compared to both New World and Old World wines … a consumer would have to pay a premium of 50 per cent or more to purchase such a wine from France or Italy." Having put this forward as the 'sweet spot' for the industry, Porter then goes on to identify the UK and the US as the markets most suited to Portuguese export needs.

The Monitor report has met with a mixed reception in Portugal and it is questionable whether any action will be taken. Investment is needed for promotional activity in the UK and the US, yet recent years have seen these budgets continually cut. However, ViniPortugal is following up Porter's conclusions by commissioning two further detailed reports on the UK and US markets.

Who shrank the vineyards?

The total area of land under vine has declined from 267,000 hectares (ha) to 216,000 ha in a decade, according to statistics released by Eurostat. The only part of the country to show an increase was the Alentejo, where the area under vine has grown by 30 per cent. Reflecting the trend towards larger vineyard holdings and better-quality wine, the total number of wine producers in Portugal has decreased from 367,000 to 247,000. Eurostat highlights Italy and Portugal as the countries that have done the most to restructure their vineyards over the past decade.

TOP OF THE WORLD

An international tasting panel placed four Portuguese red wines among the world's best at a blind tasting held in Lisbon in November 2003. The winning Portuguese wines included two from the Douro (Quinta do Vale Meão 2000 and Niepoort's Charme 2000) and two from Estremadura (Quinta de Pancas Premium 2000 and Quinta do Monte d'Oiro, Homenagem a António Carqueijeiro 1999). The wines were selected from a line-up of 30 red wines, 15 from Portugal and 15 from the rest of the world. Other winning wines included Pétrus 1997, Château Cheval-Blanc 1997, Château Mouton-Rothschild 1998, Chapoutier's Hermitage Pavillon 1996, and Ridge Monte Bello 1997. Although several leading Spanish wines were included in the tasting, the Portuguese press was quick to point out that none of them made it into the final dozen. The jury included Michel Bettane, editor of *La Revue du Vin de France*, José Penin, director of the Spanish magazine *Sabaritas*, Joshua Greene, editor of *Wine and Spirits Magazine* in the US, Peter Moser, editor of *Falstaff* in Austria, and this author from the UK. The tasting was organized by the Portuguese Academy of Gastronomy in association with Atlantis Crystal.

KING OF THE CASTELÃO?

The IVV's (Instituto da Vinha e do Vinho) inventory of principal grape varieties lists the red Castelão grape as the most planted variety in Portugal. Castelão (sometimes known by its nickname Periquita) covers an area of nearly 16,000 ha, mostly on the Setúbal peninsula (Terras do Sado), the Ribatejo, and Estremadura. It is followed closely by the white Fernão Pires with 15,100 ha, mainly in the Ribatejo and Estremadura but also in the Beiras (Bairrada and Dão), where it is known as Maria Gomes. Touriga Franca (formerly Touriga Francesa), the most planted port grape, comes in third place, with 9,600 ha. The other most important grapes are as follows (with the main regions in which they are planted in brackets):

Baga: 8,100 ha (red, Bairrada and Dão);
Aragonez/Tinta Roriz: 7,300 ha (red, mostly in the Douro and Alentejo);
Vinhão: 6,800 ha (red, Vinho Verde);
Síria (also known as Roupeiro and Codega): 6,500 ha (white, mostly in the Douro and Alentejo);
Tinta Barroca: 5,500 ha (red, Douro);
Trincadeira: 5,000 ha (red, mostly Alentejo and Ribatejo);
Loureiro: 4,500 ha (white, Vinho Verde).

It is surprising that one of Portugal's best grape varieties, Touriga Nacional, doesn't make it into the top 20, although it is one of the most highly regarded port grapes and is increasingly widely planted in other regions. No international grape varieties are sufficiently widespread to register on the inventory.

Portugal has been the next best thing to happen on the world wine scene for as long as I can remember, but, though sales have barely budged, much has improved over the past two decades. Since Portugal joined the EU in 1986, large sums of money have been poured into new wineries and, more recently, vineyards. Portugal is undoubtedly capable of making world-class red wines, but there is a great deal more to be done. Professor Michael Porter's Monitor report (which excludes port and madeira) exposes the structural weaknesses at the heart of the Portuguese wine industry. With expressions like "a serious lack of critical mass on its export markets", "Portuguese wines are often lost in the 'Rest of the World'", and "a lack of strategy" resulting in no "collective sense of the national and regional brands that constitute Portuguese wine", Porter paints a sadly truthful picture. Portugal's principal problem is one of extreme fragmentation. Average production per producer is just 39 hectolitres (hl), compared with 4,200 hl in the US and 2,500 hl in Australia. There are, Porter estimates, only 14 companies big enough to maintain major export relationships with more than one market and, of these, 11 are cooperatives. Portugal's wine exports are split between a large number of different markets, with only 29 per cent of the total selling to its top three export markets (compared with 74 per cent from Australia, 59 per cent from Italy, and 54 per cent from France). As things stand, this makes it difficult for Portugal to concentrate its limited resources promoting wine. On top of this, there is scant cooperation between wine-exporting companies or even the main generic bodies charged with promoting Portuguese wine. Unless the movers and shakers in Portugal develop a viable strategy to target key markets and, most importantly, see this strategy through, Portuguese wines will remain the next best thing on the world wine scene for years to come.

Update

Although the perilous state of Portugal's economy has put pressure on pricing, the price–quality imbalance reported in *Wine Report 2004* remains a serious issue. With producers able to demand substantially higher prices in the domestic market than they can get on export markets, there remains little incentive to export. This point was not directly picked up by Michael

Porter's Monitor Group, which identified the premium and superpremium sectors as the motor for growth. Although Portugal is now producing some outstanding, world-class wines at this level, they are still virtually unknown in export markets, and high prices are a barrier for even the most adventurous of consumers. Despite the recession, many Portuguese restaurants continue to be particularly greedy with their pricing.

• **Led by Sir Cliff Richard,** the Algarve is undergoing a revival as a wine-producing region. Although the co-ops at Portimão and Tavira have been forced to close due to a lack of members, the co-op at Lagoa has gained a new lease of life with the release of a varietal Syrah called Salira. There is also a new wine (Quinta do Morgado da Torre) from Alvor (DOC Portimão), a region that had about 25 wine producers in the mid-20th century. Sir Cliff's Adega do Cantor ('Singer's Winery'), which is strategically located behind Algarve Shopping at Guia near Albufeira, opened for business with the 2003 harvest.

• **The Alentejo has overtaken** Vinho Verde as the most popular wine on the domestic market, according to data from AC Nielsen. The Alentejo's market share has almost doubled from 17.6 per cent to nearly 34 per cent in just four years. Vinho Verde's market share remains static at around 32 per cent.

• **A new wine museum** has been built at Anadia in Bairrada at a cost of €4 million.

• **The tower** at the centre of the Esporão estate, which also appears on the eponymous wine labels, has been restored to its original medieval appearance. The 'new tower' was opened in September by the minister of culture, Pedro Roseta.

• **Wine glasses for Portuguese wines** have been launched by glassmaker Atlantis Crystal. Working alongside Portugal's largest winemakers, Sogrape, Atlantis has designed different glasses for wines from the Douro, Dão, and Alentejo.

• **Unicer,** famous to all who visit Portugal as the brewer of Super Bock beer, is now producing a range of wines from the Douro, Terras do Sado, and Alentejo, as well as Vinho Verde. The latest wines to join the range are a red and a white from the Alentejo called Planura.

• **The Torres Vedras** cooperative in Estremadura, once the largest in the country, has filed for bankruptcy.

• **Quinta do Monte d'Oiro,** a new winery in Estremadura, was opened in 2003 by the president of the republic, Jorge Sampaio.

Advance report on the latest harvest
2003

The winter was abnormally wet, but this replenished the water table after the previous year's drought. Apart from localized outbreaks of downy and powdery mildew in the north of the country, the season began well, with even temperatures during flowering. There was a short burst of heat in mid-June, but the turning point came at the end of July, when the entire country sustained nearly three weeks of extreme heat. Temperatures rose daily to exceed 40°C and remained above 30°C during the night. Photosynthesis slowed and the maturation process came to a standstill. By the start of September, the harvest was under way throughout much of southern Portugal, but sugar readings remained unusually low. However, as the warm weather continued, sugar levels suddenly rose, increasing from a potential of 11 per cent ABV to 15 per cent in a week, according to one grower. Timing was everything, and those who got it wrong made unbalanced wines with high pH and surprisingly low alcohol. Apart from some light rain at the end of September, the weather remained fine well into October and growers in the north of the country completed the harvest under clear skies. The Alentejo, Dão, and parts of the Douro suffered the worst heat damage, whereas Bairrada enjoyed its best and most trouble-free vintage for a decade. The best wines will tend to be those from late-ripening varieties. Aragonez/Tinta Roriz and Trincadeira suffered particularly from loss of acidity, whereas Alfrocheiro (in the Alentejo and Dão) and Touriga Nacional resisted the heat and ripened more evenly. With the exception of reds from Bairrada and parts of the Douro, wines from 2003 are likely to be forward and early maturing. Yields are expected to be above average.

Updates on the previous five vintages
2002

Vintage rating: 65

After one of the driest summers on record, many vineyards in the interior and south were suffering from extreme stress. Fortunately, the summer passed without the excessive heat that sometimes shrivels the berries, and in early September the grapes were generally in good condition. In the Ribatejo, Alentejo, and Douro Superior, picking began in early September, whereas growers in the rest of the country held off until the middle of the month. But on Friday the 13th (an inauspicious date), it began to rain and did not let up for five days. The unsettled weather continued into October, spelling disaster for Bairrada and Vinho Verde, where many growers watched their grapes rotting on the vine. Some excellent wines were made in the Douro by those who harvested early (see Port Vintage Report), and there are small quantities of good wine from the south. But, for most producers, 2002 is a vintage they would rather forget.

2001

Vintage rating: 85

With ground-water supplies replenished during winter and fine weather during flowering, the 2001 harvest produced a hefty crop – the largest since 1996 – and seems to have matched quantity with quality. In the north, an unusually cool and variable August led to uneven ripening, but warm weather in early September saved the day and some high sugar readings were recorded. In the Alentejo, torrential September rain brought sugar levels down, but Moreto (usually an insipid grape) was still harvested at a potential 14 per cent ABV.

2000

Vintage rating: 95

Much of the flowering took place in adverse conditions, and by late May it looked as if 2000 would be the third small harvest in a row. However, warm weather continued into October, allowing for near-perfect harvest conditions. Bairrada, the Douro, and Dão produced some exceptional wines.

1999

Vintage rating: 75

Poor weather conditions, including the remains of Hurricane Floyd, affected the north coast: Bairrada and much of Dão were particularly badly affected. Those areas inland and to the south where the grapes were picked before the rain made some excellent wines. It was a good year for the Castelão grape on the Setúbal Peninsula, but, in the Douro, what looked like a miracle vintage was destroyed by rain at the last minute.

1998

Vintage rating: 60

With reduced yields in the north of the country, 1998 looked set to produce minute quantities of potentially outstanding wines, following a period of unrelenting summer heat. However, just as picking began, rain swept in from the Atlantic. Grape sugars were diluted and the old, interplanted vineyards of the Douro, Dão, Bairrada, and Vinho Verde were devastated by rot. The south fared much better, and good wines were made, albeit in small quantities, in the Ribatejo, Alentejo, and the Setúbal Peninsula.

GREATEST WINE PRODUCERS

1. Niepoort
2. Quinta do Vale Meão
3. Quinta do Crasto
4. Quinta do Monte d'Oiro
5. Prats & Symington
6. Sogrape
7. Esporão
8. Quinta do Roriz
9. Luis Pato
10. João Portugal Ramos

BEST-VALUE PRODUCERS

1. Adega Co-operativa de Pegoes
2. DFJ Vinhos
3. Dão Sul
4. Falua
5. Venâncio da Costa Lima
6. Sogrape
7. JP Vinhos
8. Casa Santos Lima
9. Herdade do Esporão
10. Caves Aliança

FASTEST-IMPROVING PRODUCERS

1. Caves Aliança
2. Quinta de Pancas
3. Quinta do Carmo
4. Quinta Vale Dona Maria
5. Real Companhia Velha
6. José Maria da Fonseca
7. Borges & Irmão
8. Caves Dom Teodósio

GREATEST-QUALITY WINES

1. **Quinta do Vale Meão 2000** Douro (€45)
2. **Vinha da Ponte 2000** Quinta do Crasto, Douro (€70)
3. **Charme 2000** Niepoort, Douro (€50)
4. **Maria Teresa 2001** Quinta do Crasto, Douro (€70)
5. **Chryseia 2001** Prats & Symington, Douro (€40)
6. **Homenagem a António Carqueijeiro 1999** Quinta do Monte d'Oiro, Vinho Regional Estremadura (€60)
7. **Batuta 2000** Niepoort, Douro (€60)
8. **Barca Velha 1995** Ferreira, Douro (> €100)
9. **Quinta do Monte d'Oiro Reserva 1997** Estremadura (€40)
10. **T de Terrugem 2000** Caves Aliança, Alentejo (€60)

NEW UP-AND-COMING PRODUCERS

1. Lavradores de Feitoria
2. Poeira (Jorge Moreira)
3. Quinta da Chocapalha
4. Companhia das Quintas
5. Quinta do Ventozello
6. Quinta das Hidrangeas
7. Monte da Ravasqueira
8. Kolheita das Ideas
9. Quinta do Silval
10. Bago de Touriga

BEST BARGAINS

1. **Conde de Vimioso 2001** Falua, Vinho Regional Ribatejano (€4)
2. **Alabastro 2001** Caves Aliança, Vinho Regional Alentejano (€3.50)
3. **DFJ Caladoc/Alicante 2001** DFJ Vinhos, Vinho Regional Estremadura (€4)
4. **Colheita Seleccionada 2001** Quinta de Cabriz, Dão (€3)
5. **Padre Pedro 2001** Casa Cadaval, Vinho Regional Ribatejano (€3.50)
6. **Terra Boa 2001** Caves Aliança, Vinho Regional Trás-os-Montes (€2)
7. **Fontenario de Pegões 2001** Co-op Sto Isidro de Pegões, Palmela (€3)
8. **Pancas 2000** Quinta de Pancas, Vinho Regional Estremadura (€4)
9. **Quinta de Chocapalha Cabernet Sauvignon 2001** Vinho Regional Estremadura (€6)
10. **Encostas de Estremoz Touriga Nacional 2002** Maria Joana Castro Duarte, Vinho Regional Alentejano (€5)

MOST EXCITING OR UNUSUAL FINDS

1. **Charme 2000** Niepoort, Douro (€50) *Dirk Niepoort's aim of making a burgundian style of wine in the Douro has worked: dense and concentrated, yet supple and succulent.*
2. **Vinha Maria Teresa 2001** Quinta do Crasto, Douro (€60) *From a well-exposed plot of vines planted c.1915, a rich, well-polished red with layers of ripe, liquorice intensity.*
3. **Premium 2000** Quinta de Pancas, Estremadura (€45) *A blend of the best grapes from an excellent estate. The blend varies according to the year. This deep, dense red combines richness, spice, and finesse from Touriga Nacional and Syrah.*
4. **Pape 2000** Quinta de Pellada, Dão (€23) *Proof that the Dão region can make outstanding red wine: floral aromas (violets) followed up by wonderfully ripe, spicy fruit with judicious use of new oak.*
5. **Duas Quintas Reserva Especial 1999** Ramos Pinto, Douro (> €100) *This superintense red aged in second-fill barrels lets the fruit talk. Massive concentration – the very essence of the Douro.*
6. **Esporão Touriga Nacional 2001** Alentejo (€12) *Touriga Nacional is capable of making great wine outside the Douro: floral, ripe, and minty, with lashings of blackcurrant fruit.*
7. **Granjó Late Harvest 2002** Real Companhia Velha, Douro (not yet released; half-bottles) *Made from Semillon grapes grown at high altitude and picked with botrytis at the end of October. Tastes of fresh apricots with a wonderfully rich, honeyed texture. The welcome revival of an old brand.*
8. **Três Bagos 2001** Lavradores de Feitoria, Douro (€7) *A fine, well-balanced red with port-like red berry fruit made from wines blended from the Douro's three subregions: Baixo Corgo, Cima Corgo, and Douro Superior.*
9. **Alicante Bouschet 2002** Esporão, Alentejo (€12) *Soft, chewy, fleshy wine from a grape that crops up fairly frequently in the Alentejo but is so often overlooked elsewhere.*
10. **Dorna Velha Tinta Barroca 2000** Quinta do Silval, Douro (€4.50) *Soft, easy-going, and inexpensive red from a grape that is rarely bottled as a varietal.*

After months of bargaining, a single professional body, the Instituto do Vinho do Douro e Porto (IVDP), has finally been created to govern and represent the interests of both port and Douro wine producers.

RICHARD MAYSON

The new organization is a fusion of several bodies – the Instituto do Vinho do Porto (IVP), the Comissão Interprofissional da Região Demarcada do Douro (CIRDD), and the Casa do Douro (CD). The IVDP will now have sole responsibility for the control and guarantee of both port and unfortified Douro wines. With this merger, the IVDP will act as an interprofessional body, bringing growers and shippers together to decide future strategies and policies for the port and Douro region. The government section of the IVDP will be responsible for controlling and certificating port and Douro wines. The IVDP will also take full control of the *beneficio*, the annual authorization of how much grape must may be fortified to make port in any one year.

The creation of this organization leaves two other official organizations in the sector. The Port Wine Shippers' Association (AEVP) will continue to act as an independent body defending the interests of its member

RICHARD MAYSON writes and lectures on wine, dividing his time between London, Portugal, and a family business in the Peak District. He speaks fluent Portuguese, having been brought up in Portugal, and is regarded as one of the most respected authorities on port, sherry, madeira, and the wines of Spain and Portugal. His interest in the subject goes back to his university days, when he wrote a thesis on the microclimates of the vineyards of the Douro Valley. His books include *Portugal's Wines & Wine Makers* (Ebury Press, 1992), *Port and the Douro* (Faber & Faber, 1999), and his latest work, *The Wines and Vineyards of Portugal* (Mitchell Beazley), which was published in March 2003. He is currently preparing a second edition of *Port and the Douro*, a third edition of *Portugal's Wines & Wine Makers*, and a new book on the wines of Madeira.

companies, many of whom now produce both port and Douro wine. The Régua-based CD, which has been at the centre of a long-running scandal and is heavily in debt (see Opinion), will continue to hold and maintain the *cadastro*, or register of growers, in the Douro and represent their interests.

IVM backs quality madeira

The newly revitalized Instituto do Vinho da Madeira (IVM) has been working with thousands of small growers during 2003 to improve the quality of their grapes. The minimum sugar level at which grapes can be accepted is a potential alcohol level of 9 per cent, but this had not been enforced for some years. The IVM has followed this with a campaign to promote lower yields of disease-free grapes through a series of public meetings in the main grape-growing districts on the island.

The Douro counts the cost of tourism

A total of €1.7 billion is to be spent on improving access to the Douro Valley over the next five years, including the modernization of the famous railway line that runs alongside the river. According to Miguel Cadilhe, president of the API (Associação Portuguesa para o Investimento), this public investment is essential for the growth of quality tourism in the region. One plan is to increase the use of the steam trains that have been running up the Douro during the summer months. This is unlikely to prove popular with growers with land adjoining the railway, where sparks from trains have set a number of vineyards on fire.

Port exports down – and up

Port exports fell by 2.8 per cent in 2002, with a significant drop in sales to traditional markets like Holland, Belgium, and France. However, newer premium markets like the US and Japan registered an increase in sales of more than 20 per cent. Of a worldwide total of 8.6 million cases, 1.2 million fell into the definition of 'special categories', an increase of 31.3 per cent over the year. This figure is somewhat distorted by the fact that reserve (ruby) wines were included alongside vintage, LBV, colheita, and aged tawnies for the first time in 2002.

The 2003 harvest has been overshadowed by the confused political situation in the Douro. In the winter of 2002/03, the government moved to sort out the 14-year saga of the Casa do Douro (CD), and the result is the single new IVDP. This long-overdue streamlining of the Douro's institutions was cautiously welcomed by the shippers until it was revealed that the cash-strapped government intended to relieve itself of its collective guarantee of the CD's debts, estimated at €110 million. The CD holds substantial stocks of port, which the government is using as collateral against the debt, planning to release them onto the market over a 10-year period. Most of the CD's wines are old tawnies of doubtful quality and the wines have been grossly overvalued. Shippers find it difficult to see a natural outlet for these wines and are worried that they could destabilize the market if they are sold too cheaply.

In the meantime, the 2003 *beneficio* has been cut by as much as 20 per cent. The authorities have claimed that this reflects the amount of unsold wine from the poor 2002 harvest that is still sitting in cooperatives, but it seems that the CD scenario could also be playing a part. The reduction in *beneficio* would not be so significant if the 2003 harvest was expected to be poor or small, but it provided both quality and quantity. Since the cut has been applied more or less equally to all classes of vineyard, it puts paid to any pretence that the system has to promote quality. The *beneficio* is used increasingly as a subsidy for small growers and a part of the Douro's social-security system. It has prevented many shippers from fully replenishing stocks of premium ports, the so-called 'special categories' that form an increasingly important part of their businesses.

Grapevine

• **In the wake** of the general declaration of 2000, 2001 was never expected to be a widely declared vintage. However, in a pattern that has developed over the last decade, a number of second-label and single-*quinta* wines have been declared, including Fonseca Guimaraens, Niepoort's Secundum, Taylor's Quinta da Terra Feita and Quinta de Vargellas, Delaforce's Quinta do Corte, Dow's Quinta Senhora da Ribeira, Churchill's Quinta da Gricha, and Cockburn's Quinta dos Canais. Noval Nacional, Poças, and Rozès have each declared a vintage port from 2001.

• **The 2003** *beneficio* was set at 107,900 pipes, a reduction of 20 per cent on the previous year's total of 135,000 pipes (one pipe = 550 litres).

2003

Port – The people of the Douro are generally accustomed to heat, but 2003 brought complaints from the most seasoned inhabitants. There was a burst of extreme heat in mid-June followed by three weeks of sustained heat from the end of July, when the thermometer rose well above 40°C on a daily basis throughout the region. Fortunately, by and large, the vines were able to cope. An exceptionally wet winter replenished the water table, and most vineyards did not visibly suffer from heat stress. At the start of September, sugar readings were still surprisingly low and some growers were tempted to pick before the grapes were physiologically ripe. In the Cima Corgo, picking began around 15 September and was under way throughout the region by the 26th. In the intervening period, *Baumé* levels rose rapidly, with Tinta Barroca, the sweetest of the port grapes, registering 16°+. Apart from some light rain towards the end of the month, the fine, warm weather continued until the end of the harvest. Yields were above average and, given the remarkable ripeness of the grapes, ports of a very high standard were made throughout the Douro region. One leading shipper has already stated that 2003 could be considered a "text-book year" for good port production. A vintage declaration is possible in the spring of 2005.

Madeira – An exceptional year, with a large production of healthy, generally disease-free grapes. The dry summer led to almost unheard-of problems in the vineyards of São Vicente on the north side of the island, where some vines were seen suffering from heat stress. It was an excellent year for Tinta Negra Mole and Verdelho, both of which registered good levels of ripeness. For Verdelho it was the best harvest for 10 years. Both Sercial and Bual produced some good wines, but for Malvasia it was a year with low production and some localized disease problems.

2002

Vintage rating: *Port: 70, Madeira: 85*

Port – After a good start, bouts of torrential rain from mid-September continuing well into October made 2002 a stop-start vintage. Old, interplanted vineyards in the Baixo Corgo were particularly badly affected by rot. However, those who managed to pick before the rain set in have small quantities of good, possibly outstanding, wine. Although it is still too early to be certain, some producers in the Cima Corgo and Douro Superior should have sufficient quantities of high-quality wine to make a single-*quinta* declaration early in 2004.

Madeira – This vintage saw a large production and particularly good-quality Tinta Negra Mole on the south side of the island and excellent quality with large volumes of Bual from Calheta at the extreme west. Bual and Tinta Negra Mole in the Campanário district in the southwest suffered from a difficult vintage due to persistent fog in the last four weeks or so before the vintage. Inconsistent Malmsey and Sercial. Verdelho was excellent but limited in volume.

2001

Vintage rating: *Port: 85, Madeira: 75*

Port – After one of the wettest winters since records began, mild, humid conditions led to an early budburst in March. From April onwards, the weather cleared and only 110 mm (4⅜ in) of rain fell until the end of August. With flowering taking place under optimum conditions and the ground-water supplies thoroughly replenished, there was a large crop. Temperatures were uneven during August, but rain at the end of the month helped to swell the grapes prior to the harvest, which, for most, began on 17 September. Yields were up by 30 per cent on 2000 in the A/B-grade vineyards. Overall, 2001 proved to be a useful year in which a number of single *quintas* produced some fine vintage ports for drinking over the medium term.

Madeira – There was a big production of Tinta Negra Mole, but the volume of Malmsey suffered due to *coulure* at flowering. Sercial and Verdelho from the northern vineyards suffered from particularly bad weather during flowering, which resulted in a greatly reduced vintage for these two varieties. Bual did not suffer as much, and volumes were normal.

2000

Vintage rating: *Port: 95, Madeira: 85*

Port – Low yields helped to make some wonderfully concentrated wines, perhaps not as overtly rich as the 1994s, but with more poise and harmony than 1997. A fine vintage combined with some truly excellent wines made for a universal declaration.

Madeira – There were good-quality Bual and Tinta Negra Mole on the south and west of the island, and a very small crop of excellent-quality Verdelho from Camara de Lobos on the south of the island.

1999

Vintage rating: *Port: 75, Madeira: 95*

Port – A potentially outstanding vintage became no more than good to mediocre, because of Hurricane Floyd. Nonetheless, small quantities of excellent wine were made by those who managed to avoid the rain, and several single-*quinta* wines were declared.

Madeira – Not only was the overall quality very high, but it was one of the largest crops of the last 10 years. Sercial and Bual were especially excellent.

1998

Vintage rating: *Port: 80, Madeira: 80*

Port – Unsettled weather took the shine off what could have been an outstanding vintage. Wines from a number of single *quintas* were declared, the best being from those upstream who, in general, managed to pick before the rains.

Madeira – A small vintage of good quality, particularly for Bual.

GREATEST WINE PRODUCERS

1. Quinta do Noval (port)
2. Fonseca (port)
3. Graham (port)
4. Taylor (port)
5. Niepoort (port)
6. Henriques & Henriques (madeira)
7. Barbeito (madeira)
8. Dow (port)
9. Blandy (madeira)
10. Warre (port)

FASTEST-IMPROVING PRODUCERS

1. Croft (port)
2. Poças Junior (port)
3. Delaforce (port)
4. Barbeito (madeira)
5. Quinta do Infantado (port)

NEW UP-AND-COMING PRODUCERS

1. Quinta do Ventozello (port)
2. Quinta do Vale Dona Maria (port)
3. Quinta do Roriz (port)
4. Quinta do Silval (port)
5. Quinta do Tedo (port)

BEST-VALUE PRODUCERS

1. Smith Woodhouse (port)
2. Martinez (port)
3. Sandeman (port)
4. Justino Henriques (madeira)
5. Gould Campbell (port)

GREATEST-QUALITY WINES

1. **Quinta do Noval Nacional 2000** (€1,750)
2. **Fonseca Vintage Port 2000** (€100)
3. **Graham's Vintage Port 2000** (€100)
4. **Blandy's Terrantez 1969** (€105)
5. **Quinta do Noval Vintage Port 1994** (€105)
6. **Taylor's Vintage Port 1992** (€115)
7. **Delaforce Vintage Port 1992** (€55)
8. **Fonseca Vintage Port 1985** (€60)
9. **Ramos Pinto 30-Year-Old Tawny** (€50)
10. **Niepoort's 20-Year-Old Tawny** (€40)

BEST BARGAINS

1. **Gould Campbell Vintage Port 1991** (€35)
2. **Graham's Malvedos 1992** (€30)
3. **Skeffington Vintage Port 1994** (€35)
4. **Quinta do Vale Dona Maria 2000** (€30)
5. **Henriques & Henriques 15-Year-Old Bual** (€35)
6. **Warre's Traditional LBV 1994** (€20)
7. **Quinta do Passadouro Unfiltered LBV 1997** (€15)
8. **Barbeito Veramar 5-Year-Old Bual** (€12)
9. **Dow's Crusted Port (bottled 1998)** (€16)
10. **Graham's LBV 1996** (€10)

MOST EXCITING OR UNUSUAL FINDS

Note: includes other Portuguese fortified wines.

1 **Magalhães Quinta do Silval 2000** (€40) *Wonderful, superripe vintage port from a family-owned quinta (not to be confused with Silval from Quinta do Noval). Topped Decanter's single-quinta port tasting in 2003.*

2 **Barbeito Boal Colheita Cask 81a 1995** (€25 per 50-cl bottle) *A nervy, medium-bodied madeira with perfect poise from a single 620-litre cask of French oak. Only 888 50-cl bottles were filled in September 2003.*

3 **Fonseca Quinta do Panascal 1991** (€35) *From a year when Fonseca (and Taylor) decided against a full vintage declaration, a massive wine with great length and depth that has proved to be among the best wines of the vintage.*

4 **D'Oliveira's Reserva Boal 1922** Pereira d'Oliveira (€150) *Ethereal perfumed aromas and deliciously concentrated with a tang of tawny marmalade.*

5 **Quinta do Noval Colheita 1974** (€25 per half-bottle) *Fine, delicate caramelized fruit. Soft, smooth, and silky port from a shipper not normally known for colheitas.*

6 **Skeffington 1994 (bottled as Davy's Vintage 1994)** (€35) *Dense, opulent vintage port, powerful with great focus and length. A relatively inexpensive port from a very fine vintage.*

7 **Blandy's Alvada Madeira** (€8 per 50-cl bottle) *A deliciously soft and approachable blend of Bual and Malvasia.*

8 **Churchill's Dry White Port** (€12) *Consistently good, wood-aged dry white port with the nutty character of a 10-year-old tawny. Why don't more port shippers make white port this way?*

9 **Trilogia Setúbal** José Maria da Fonseca (€120) *A blend of cask-aged Moscatel-based wines from the 1900, 1934, and 1965 vintages. Incredible concentration.*

10 **Monte Seco Madeira** Henriques & Henriques (€8 per 50-cl bottle) *A pale, bone-dry apéritif that is slightly nutty and remarkably refreshing served chilled or over ice.*

Grapevine

• **Barros Port** has been given a new look. The familiar – if somewhat staid – white stencilled bottles have been replaced by new bottles with distinctive bulbous necks and gold stencilled lettering. Wren & Rowe was the brand consultant for the new design, which was inspired by an old handmade bottle.

• **The Symington family** won more medals than any other wine producer in the world in the 2003 International Wine Challenge held in London.

Between them, wines from Graham, Dow, Warre, Smith Woodhouse, Quinta do Vesúvio, and Symington associate the Madeira Wine Company won a total of 11 gold medals. On top of this, Charles Symington was presented with the Fortified Wine Maker of the Year trophy.

• **A new annual Master of Wine award** will be given by Quinta do Noval to the candidate with the most outstanding performance as a communicator in all parts of the MW examination.

One exceptionally hot and dry year does not mean that the climate is getting permanently warmer. However, if global warming were to become a reality, what would it mean for UK winemakers?

STEPHEN SKELTON MW

Many of the varieties grown here – Müller-Thurgau, Reichensteiner, Bacchus, Huxelrebe, Madeleine x Angevine 7672, plus many others, which together account for about 75 per cent of the total area under vine – would have to be replaced with traditional cool-climate varieties such as Sauvignon Blanc, Chardonnay, and Pinot Noir. Whether growers would grub up their vines wholesale and reinvest is another question. The growers of the future who will benefit are those who took the plunge a few years ago and planted Chardonnay and Pinot Noir, as well as those with favourable sites who have always pushed at the limits of varieties and already have suitable varieties – especially the better reds.

A (new) wave of vineyards for Kent and Sussex

English Wines Group (trading as New Wave Wines) proposes to "plant up to 200 acres (81 hectares [ha]) of new vines in the Kent/Sussex area" per

STEPHEN SKELTON MW established the award-winning Tenterden Vineyards in 1977 and made wine there for 22 years. His wines have won the Gore-Browne Trophy for the Best UK Wine on three occasions. He is currently a consultant to a number of UK vineyards and wineries. Stephen was a director of the United Kingdom Vineyards Association (UKVA) between 1982 and 1998 and chairman from 1998 until 2003. Having written on wine, winemaking, and viticulture since 1986, he published *The Vineyards of England* in 1989 and rewrote and updated this work under the new title of *The Wines of Britain and Ireland* (Faber & Faber, 2001). This book won the André Simon Award in 2002. Stephen became a Master of Wine in 2003, also winning the Mondavi prize, which is awarded to the candidate gaining the highest marks in the written part of the examination.

year for the next five years. The UK currently has about 750 ha of productive vines and New Wave buys grapes from about 100 ha. It also has about 25 ha of its own vineyards. An expansion of a possible 1,000 acres (400 ha) in the next five years would be a massive increase in output and would require a similar rise in sales.

New Wave managing director Frazer Thompson is looking for fruit growers with spare land to plant vineyards that will then be put under a grape-purchase contract. New Wave is willing to pay the growers a sum equal to a 30-year repayment of the full capital cost of planting the vineyard. This payment would cover all the costs of establishing the vineyard (apart from the land itself) and would be a valuable addition to the annual income from grapes sold to New Wave. What has prompted this fit of expansionism? Frazer believes that global warming is pushing our summer temperatures up and making grapes sweeter, yields higher, and wines better, and he is fearful that, with sales growing at 30 per cent per annum, New Wave will face a shortage of grapes.

Grapevine

• **Barnsole in East Kent** has gained quality or regional wine status for all its wines. Winemaker John Danilewicz's first red wine is made mainly from Rondo and Dunkelfelder and is given a short spell in barrel. In future years, some Regent and Frühburgunder (an early Pinot Noir clone) will be added to the blend. The yield in 2003 was excellent, with high natural sugar levels, good colour, and clean grapes.

• **Success in competitions** seems to be a spur to growers when it comes to expansion. Sam Linter, winemaker at Bookers, says an additional 18 acres (7.29 ha) of vines will be planted by the end of 2006. Varieties such as Rondo, Dornfelder, Chardonnay, Pinots Noir and Gris, and Merlot have been chosen for their ability to produce quality wines that win awards. Almost all Bookers' wines have achieved quality and/or regional wine status, and its Dark Harvest 2001 (a Rondo blend) was the only English red to win a medal at the 2003 International Wine and Spirit Competition (IWSC). The 2003 harvest was excellent, with superb colour and fine fruit character in the reds.

• **Castle Vineyard** must be the only workers' cooperative vineyard in the UK. The 35 members do all the work, each contributing £50 a year, and take home the produce – on average 60 bottles a year each. The 2003 harvest was excellent, despite frost in April, and sugar levels were the best ever recorded. Triomphe (an old French–American hybrid) weighed in at 13.3 per cent potential alcohol.

• **Warden Abbey,** Bedfordshire's only commercial vineyard, enjoyed its best year ever. Its Bacchus 2001 was voted East Anglian Wine of the Year and it harvested 17 tonnes of very ripe grapes from 4.5 acres (1.8 ha) of vines. Sugar levels were good, at 9–11 per cent potential alcohol.

• **UK-grown organic wines** are fairly rare. Seddlescombe is the market leader and continues to plant some interesting varieties. Regent was its best-performing variety in 2003, and Seddlescombe has planted a further 500 vines to keep up with demand. The vineyard has also planted Solaris, another modern disease-resistant hybrid. All the wines are made to Soil Association rules.

TELLY-HO!

TV chef Rick Stein has made Bob Lindo of Camel Valley in Cornwall one of his 'food heroes'. The vineyard and its wines will feature in Stein's next BBC series. Another 6,000 vines were planted in 2003: Pinot Noir, Dornfelder, and Rondo. The year was as good for Cornwall as it was for the rest of the country: at Camel Valley, Seyval Blanc, Reichensteiner, Kerner, and Würzer all made 12 per cent potential alcohol. In three weeks, the winery handled 120 tonnes of its own and contract customers' grapes.

THE ICE QUEEN COMETH

It seems perverse to celebrate the production of an 'icewine' in a year when the news was all about the hot summer, but Tony Skuriat of Eglantine Vineyards is doing just that. His North Star 2001 is made by freezing and then gently pressing Madeleine x Angevine 7672. The wine, which has an actual alcohol content of 11 per cent and enough sugar left to produce another 8.5 per cent, is lusciously sweet, but with enough acidity to leave a lingering exotic fruitiness on the palate. It won gold in the regional competition, a silver medal at the IWSC, and bronze in the United Kingdom Vineyards Association (UKVA) competition.

PLUMPING FOR SECOND BEST?

Plumpton College – the UK's only viticultural and winemaking college – continues to expand and develop. Müller-Thurgau planted in 1965 is being replaced with Chardonnay, Pinot Meunier, and the successful red variety Rondo. Two new instructors, one from New Zealand and the other from Australia's Yarra Valley, have joined the team to help students produce wines. More than 20 tonnes of grapes were crushed in 2003, the college's largest harvest to date. It is just a pity that, since it proposes to market its wines under the UK Table Wine appellation, its labels cannot carry vintage, varietal, or vineyard names. Is the college afraid of having its wines assessed for quality and regional wine status?

Grapevine

• **With new winemaker** Peter Morgan at the helm, aided by French oenologist Jean-Marie Jacquinot from Epernay, Nyetimber had a fabulous 2003 harvest with yields up at 35 hectolitres per hectare (hl/ha) and potential alcohols coming good at 10.5 per cent and 11.6 per cent. The quality is reported to be excellent ("Gorgeous," says the Frenchman) and acids superb. The harvest was two to three weeks earlier than usual, 100 per cent clean, and the only 'dry' harvest any of the pickers could remember. One innovation is that, at long last, Nyetimber will be opening its doors to customers every Friday afternoon.

• **Heart of England Vineyard** enjoyed its best harvest to date in 2003. A total of 12 tonnes of grapes was picked from around 3 acres (1.2 ha). Owner David Stanley thinks that 2003 "could well mark the coming of age of English wine". Its Oberon 2002 (70 per cent Rondo, 30 per cent Triomphe) won Wine of the Year in the regional competition, plus a gold medal. Heart of England will plant 5,000 vines in 2004.

The result of the great English wine-labelling debate is that growers wishing to have their wines labelled using vintage, varietal, and vineyard names will have to have their wines certified by either quality or regional wine schemes. Wines certified by the schemes will be tested and tasted and can be expected to be of a guaranteed level of quality. Wines not submitting themselves to the schemes will have to be labelled as 'UK Table Wines' and will not be able to state the variety or the vintage.

The Department for Environment, Food and Rural Affairs (DEFRA) was unable to accept that vineyard names would be restricted to quality and regional wines only, owing to a nonsense in the regulations stating that only wines grown and made on the same agricultural holding can bear vineyard names. Since many UK vineyards have their wines made under contract at local wineries and some vineyards are sited away from their wineries, DEFRA decided that this was a minefield they dared not cross. This means that all three categories of UK-grown wines – quality, regional, and table – will be allowed to bear the same headline vineyard name – something that is expressly forbidden under EU wine regulations (watch this space!). DEFRA was also unable to accept the industry's proposals that sparkling wines should be treated in a similar way, thus English/Welsh 'quality sparkling wine' remains an untasted and untested category, whereas English/Welsh 'quality wine' will have been through the testing/tasting procedure. Logical or what?

Grapevine

- **Ickworth Vineyard** is the only commercial vineyard on National Trust soil (at Ickworth House in Suffolk). Its Earl's Bishop Reserve won two gold medals in the East Anglian regional competition – the first time a red wine has ever won gold. It has also just launched a traditional-method sparkling wine called Suffolk Pink, made from Auxerrois and Pinot Noir.

- **RidgeView Estate,** the UK's second most important sparkling-wine producer, was one of the few vineyards that suffered from frost in 2003. Although the Chardonnay was in the woolly bud stage, it was still too cold for it to show anything green, so damage was kept to a minimum. Spraying with Antistress (a liquid polymer that covers the vines in a thin protective film) also helped. Yields were slightly lower than the usual 4 tonnes per acre, but sugar and acid levels were superb. Potential alcohol levels were 10–11 per cent, and acids were around 13 grams per litre (g/l) for Chardonnay and 10.5 g/l for the Pinots. These figures may not mean much to a layman, but any grower in Champagne would have been overjoyed to see them.

2003

An amazing year for UK winemakers. Although a few growers reported a sharp frost in mid-April, most had a trouble-free spring. Flowering was on time and was accompanied by largely dry and warm weather. The summer weather was great, with temperatures hitting 35°C (high 90s F), but the autumn was the clincher. September and October were very warm, sunny, and almost completely dry. Grapes were harvested at unheard-of sugar levels, with potential alcohol levels of 11–13 per cent in many vineyards. Initial fears that acids would drop away to leave flabby, short-lived wines were unfounded, and most growers report ideal sugar/acid balances in their wines. All competent growers appear to have made extremely good wines, with reds and sparklings from traditional varieties (that is, traditional champagne varieties) the stars. It was certainly the best year for red varieties that anyone can remember. Not only were sugars high and acids balanced but tannins were ripe, and instead of the usual rush to get wines off the skins and into barrel, winemakers were able to let them sit and soak for a few more days. The wines are (at the time of writing) still young and unbottled, but I have tasted some really interesting Rondos and Pinot Noirs and a couple of Regents that would not look out of place among some from much warmer climes. Although 2003 was probably an abnormal year (despite most growers hoping it was a foretaste of things to come), there can be no doubt that its wines – especially its reds – will live on as a reminder of a glorious year for UK wine growers.

Updates on the previous five vintages
2002

Vintage rating: *83 (Red: 82, White: 85)*

The overall crop was smaller than average, but an Indian summer resulted in exceptional quality, especially with the harder-to-ripen varieties, such as Chardonnay, and the successful red varieties: Pinot Noir, Rondo, Regent, and Dornfelder. Natural sugar levels, which usually languish around 7–9 per cent, were well up into double figures in many cases. Several winemakers made completely natural wines – that is, without chaptalization.

2001

Vintage rating: *79 (Red: 75, White: 82)*

On balance, this was a very fair year. No spring frosts and a good flowering combined to produce a larger-than-average crop. Temperatures were higher in 2001 than for centuries and this was reflected in an early harvest of clean, ripe grapes. Reds had more colour than usual, and the generally tough-to-ripen varieties, such as Riesling and Pinot Blanc, did well. Chardonnay and Pinot Noir for sparkling wine put in a good performance and this should be reflected in the quality of the wines.

2000

Vintage rating: *73 (Red: 70, White: 75)*

This was a cooler-than-average year with a very wet harvest. Whites fared better than reds, and sparkling wines should be good. The best will keep, but the majority should be drunk within two years.

1999

Vintage rating: *77 (Red: 76, White: 77)*

Average yields and a warm summer helped most winemakers produce some interesting wines, especially with varieties such as Bacchus and Seyval Blanc. Harvesting conditions were fine and dry, allowing grapes to hang slightly longer than usual.

1998

Vintage rating: *81 (Red: 77, White: 85)*

Vineyards in the west of the country fared better than those in the east, which suffered from some spring frosts. Sugar and acid levels were average and the specialist sparkling-wine producers reported excellent results. Varieties such as Bacchus and Schönburger produced very fresh, fruity wines with ideal acid/alcohol balance.

GREATEST WINE PRODUCERS

1. Nyetimber
2. RidgeView Estate
3. New Wave Wines
4. Camel Valley
5. Denbies
6. Valley Vineyards
7. Three Choirs
8. Sharpham Estate
9. Breaky Bottom
10. Wickham

FASTEST-IMPROVING PRODUCERS

1. Bothy
2. Astley
3. Davenport
4. Heart of England
5. Sandhurst
6. Eglantine
7. Tiltridge
8. Warden Abbey
9. Wyken
10. Mersea

NEW UP-AND-COMING PRODUCERS

1. Oatley
2. Barnsole
3. Great Stocks
4. Plumpton College
5. Meopham
6. Beeches Hill

BEST-VALUE PRODUCERS

1. New Wave Wines
2. Three Choirs
3. RidgeView Estate
4. Camel Valley
5. Valley Vineyards

GREATEST-QUALITY WINES

1. **Classic Cuvée 1996** Nyetimber (£18)
2. **Chapel Down Brut Rosé 2001** New Wave Wines (£12.99)
3. **Cuvée Merret Fitzrovia Rosé 2000** RidgeView Estate (£18.95)
4. **Dart Valley Reserve 2001** Sharpham Estate (£6.99)
5. **Curious Grape Pinot Blanc 2001** New Wave Wines (£6.99)
6. **Cuvée Merret Knightsbridge Blanc de Noirs 1999** RidgeView Estate (£18.95)
7. **Nyetimber Classic Cuvée 1995** Nyetimber (£19.50)
8. **Cornwall Pinot Noir Sparkling 2001** Camel Valley (£19.95)
9. **Bacchus 2001** Camel Valley (£8.45)
10. **Curious Grape Pinot Noir 2000** New Wave Wines (£12.99)

BEST BARGAINS

1. **Chapel Down Vintage Brut 1997** New Wave Wines (£9.99)
2. **Dart Valley Reserve 2001** Sharpham Estate (£6.99)
3. **Curious Grape Pinot Blanc 2001** New Wave Wines (£6.99)
4. **Seyval Oaked 2002** Tiltridge (£5.95)
5. **Flint Valley 2001** Denbies (£4.99)
6. **Tenterden Rosé NV** New Wave Wines (£4.99)

MOST EXCITING OR UNUSUAL FINDS

1. **Limney Sparkling 1999** Davenport (£12) *Great acidity and fine balance.*
2. **North Star 2001** Eglantine (£15 per half-bottle) *Unctuous and treacly – is this English?*
3. **Aluric de Norsehide Sparkling Rosé 1999** Chilford Hundred (£14.95) *Real strawberries and raspberries.*
4. **Curious Grape Bacchus Reserve 2001** New Wave Wines (£8.99) *Really good fruit flavour – acid drops and elderflowers.*
5. **Fumé 1998** Valley Vineyards (£8.49) *Oak and yeast; malolactic fermentation at its best.*
6. **Curious Grape Seyval Blanc 2002** New Wave Wines (£6.99) *Such a fruit-filled wine from such a plain variety.*

For this report's first appearance in *Wine Report*, we have been asked to provide brief overviews of Belgium, the Netherlands, and Denmark. Our report in future editions will be much shorter!

FIONA MORRISON MW   GERT CRUM

Belgium

Although vines have been planted in Belgium since the 14th century, its wine production today amounts to only 100,000 hectolitres (hl) of wine per year, which is, for comparison's sake, less than one-quarter of the yield of Chinon in the Loire. In the Middle Ages, Belgium belonged to the vast holdings of the Duchy of Burgundy, and vineyards existed around the major southern towns of Leuven, Diest, and Aarschot. The great frosts of the 17th century led to more profitable potatoes replacing vines as the crop of preference, but viticulture continued throughout the 18th century. Wars and Napoleon dealt the final blows to Belgian viticulture at the

FIONA MORRISON MW has spent more than 20 years in the wine trade around the world and speaks several languages. She became a Master of Wine in 1994 and is now a freelance wine journalist and lecturer. She has a weekly wine column in the Brussels weekly *The Bulletin*, and is a columnist for *Wine & Spirits*. She is married to Jacques Thienpont, a wine *négociant* and owner of Le Pin in Pomerol; they divide their time between Bordeaux and Belgium, making, tasting, and promoting wine.
GERT CRUM is one of the best-known wine writers in the Netherlands. He is the author of several books, including titles on Burgundy and Champagne. A freelance writer, he regularly contributes to several leading publications, including *Alliance Magazine*, *Résidence*, and *Perswijn*. He has his own website (www.wijnplezier.nl). Gert's latest book, published in 2004 in four languages, is about Domaine de la Romanée-Conti. He is grateful for the help of René van Heusden, a Dutch wine writer who lives in Belgium.

beginning of the 19th century, since when it has taken more than 150 years for viticulture to resurface in the Flemish part of the country. The first modern-day vineyards were planted in the 1970s, but it is only recently that two appellations (VQPRD) were created, both in the Flemish part of the country: Hagelandse Wijn, created in 1997 in the Flemish Brabant region around the university town of Louvain; and Haspengouwse Wijn, created in 2000 in eastern Limburg, near the Dutch border. There are nine producers in Hageland covering 30 hectares (ha) of vineyard, and six producers in Hespaye with 25 ha.

These appellations are set up along the same guidelines as the French system, with limits on yields and grape varieties, strict rules on production methods, and compulsory chemical analysis and blind wine tasting of the wines submitted. Belgium produces primarily white wines (90 per cent of total production) from 15 authorized grape varieties, including Müller-Thurgau, Pinot Gris, Chardonnay, and Riesling, plus various crosses such as Ortega, Optima, Siegerrebe, and Würzer.

The wines are Germanic in style, the best featuring pure fruit, good acidity, and clean, fresh structure. It is still too early to distinguish differences in *terroir* because there are so many different styles of winemaking and different grape varieties. Apart from these two appellations, there are hundreds of small growers in Flanders and Walloon who are making wines.

One of the driving forces in the modern appeal of Belgian wines was the Van Rennes family, a wealthy Dutch family that owns the Genoels-Elderen castle in the Hespaye region, 10 km west of the Dutch border. Castle archives revealed 18th-century vineyards planted on the estate and remains of old drainage ditches, vineyard parcels, and walls, so it was a natural part of the restoration work to replant the vineyard in 1992. The estate is now the largest in Belgium with 16 ha under vine, planted with Chardonnay and Pinot Noir. Joyce Kekko-Van Rennes is the Burgundy-trained winemaker. She claims the soil is similar to the limestone slopes of Champagne and Burgundy, and she makes still and sparkling wines as well as a grape brandy in an impressive modern winery. These are the only Belgian wines that have, as yet, competed successfully on the international market.

The newest wine project is an ambitious vineyard at Domaine du Chenoy, near Naumur in Walloon. Here, Philippe Grafé has planted 10 ha of vines on south-facing slopes and restored a nearby farm with temperature-controlled vats, a laboratory, and a tasting room. He has chosen German hybrids such as Regent and Merzling for their resistance to disease, damp, and cooler growing conditions. Belgian winemaking is becoming professional.

Among other Belgian wines of note is a sparkling wine made by the Luppens family of Domaine Soniën in Overijse, just outside Brussels, from grapes grown in greenhouses. In the Hainault region, Montpellier-trained Raymond Leroy makes a very drinkable sparkling wine from Chardonnay grapes grown in chalky limestone soil. In another part of the Hainault, an old mining area, the soil is dark schist with mineral deposits. At the Château de Trazegnies, some fairly complex white wines are produced from a blend of Pinot Noir, Müller-Thurgau, Riesling, and Pinot Gris, among others.

Belgian wines are well regulated and overseen by the Belgian Wine and Spirit Association, which controls the appellation laws and organizes the blind tastings each year. The association has noted a definite improvement in wine samples submitted in recent years and a better understanding of winemaking and preserving techniques, which has resulted in fewer flawed wines.

The Netherlands

The Netherlands now has a union of vine growers: Het Wijngaardeniersgilde. There are 117 registered vine growers, 30 of whom are professionals, each with a vineyard of 1 ha or more, making a total of about 50 ha of productive vines. This area produces about 2,000 hl of wine, which is about 270,000 bottles. Since the Netherlands had only a handful of commercial producers five years ago, this is remarkable growth, which is set to continue if the climate continues to get warmer.

Of course this is peanuts in comparison to other countries. The Netherlands is not a wine-producing country in any true sense and will never have the vine acreage of Spain or the image of France. But it is a huge development after two centuries of no activity whatsoever. Vines used to grow in the deep south of the Netherlands, on the hills of Zuid-Limburg, and in the valley of the river Maas around Maastricht, but all such activities were prohibited during the French occupation under Napoleon.

The first vines since Napoleon's time appeared in 1967, when Frits Bosch planted vines on the southeast slope of the Pietersberg, south of Maastricht. He started his own tiny vineyard, Slavante, as a hobby. A few years later, in 1970, Hugo Hulst planted vines next to his apple orchard on the wonderfully situated Louwberg in the Jekervalley, also south of Maastricht. At first, production was very small, but it was a professional operation from the start, with commercial ambitions. Nowadays, the family cultivates a vineyard of 6.5 ha and produces nearly 70,000 bottles of white wine a year. The success story of this estate, the Apostelhoeve, is not the only one. Most are in the deepest south of the country, in Zuid-Limburg, but there are also some in Brabant or even further north.

The Dutch Wine Institute, an independent body, has been established to support and promote viniculture in the Netherlands, and the Dutch government has issued a list of permitted grape varieties. There is great debate among wine producers about the best varieties for Dutch conditions. Many growers, taking advice from the University of Wageningen, have planted modern resistant varieties such as Regent, Phoenix, and Rondo, but results are better with wines made from Riesling, Rivaner, Pinot Blanc, Auxerrois, Gewürztraminer, Müller-Thurgau, Pinot Gris, and even Pinot Noir. Bacchus, Kerner, and Reichensteiner also do well.

Denmark

Viticulture in Denmark, despite being so far north, does exist. The vineyards are very small and are mainly run as a hobby, but there are about 20 commercial growers, of whom six are already selling wine, with the rest planning to have wines on the market in a few years. There are currently about 25 ha of vineyards, mostly in the south. The upper limit for Danish vineyards has been set by the EU at 99 ha. If commercial production goes beyond this limit, the agreement with the EU will have to be renegotiated.

The oldest wine producer in Denmark is Lars Hagermans of Domain Aalsgaard in Alsgårde. He first planted in 1975 and now has 0.5 ha with Ortega, Madeleine Angevine, Siegerrebe, and Kerner. Frederiksborg is principally a wine-trading firm, but it also produces some wine; in 2000, 1,000 vines were planted. Torben Andreasen and Jens Michael Gundersen started Dansk Vin Center, near Rådhuspladsen, in 1999; they now have 3 ha of vines. Gundersen formerly owned Domæne Bacchus, which he began in 1994.

Vinperlen of Bjarne Thougaard in Gislinge is serious, though very small. Some red wine and a tiny amount of white are produced. The red, Bjarnanette Rouge, is a blend of Regent, Dornfelder, and Rondo, which is chaptalized and fermented in a stainless-steel tank, then matured for a short while in French oak barrels. There is ambition here.

FUNKY BIO WINES

The Hageling-Bio estate in Tirlemont, 60 km south of Brussels in the Hagelandse Wijn appellation, is producing the first Belgian organic wine. The tiny, 0.7-ha vineyard is planted with Müller-Thurgau, Kerner, Pinot Noir, Dornfelder, and Sirius grapes, which have the right to be labelled VQPRD, and various experimental grapes, such as Bianca, Orion, and Regent, which are used for table wines. Some 5,000 bottles are produced in a good year. The estate is run by the enthusiastic Hugo Bernar, and his best wines are his funky, lively table wines, such as Orion 2001, Regent 2002, and Bianca 2002.

NEW APPELLATION

The first appellation in Walloon, the French-speaking part of Belgium, is due to be created in April 2004. It is VQPRD Côtes de Sambres et Meuse and applies to wines coming from a region near Liège, where vines are grown between the Sambres and Meuse rivers. There are an estimated 56 growers in Walloon covering 20 ha of vines, 45 of which are eligible for consideration for the new appellation.

BELGIUM GOES GARAGE

Belgium is to get its first garage wines. Amateur winemaker Marc de Brouwer, in Uccle, the residential neighbourhood of Brussels, is giving lessons in vine growing, pruning, and winemaking to other hobbyists. Many of these are passionate amateurs with no more than a few ares of vines (1 are = 0.01 ha), making a small amount of wine in their garages for the delight of a few friends and tourists. Plans are in the works for these wines to be grouped together under the labels *vlaams streekwijn* for the Flemish products and *vins de pays des Jardins de Wallonie* for the Walloon.

FRUITY NEW BLEND

Mathieu Hulst of the Apostelhoeve estate near Maastricht launched Cuvée XII Apostelhoeve, a blend of Pinot Gris, Auxerrois, and Müller-Thurgau, in 2003. This is the estate's first blended wine. Hulst tried including Riesling in the blend but found that it did not work, even with levels as low as 5 per cent. The wine is unoaked – there are no barrels at Apostelhoeve. Cuvée XII is fruity and supple, with more body than the varietals.

Grapevine

- **The Belgian Sommeliers Association** organized its first tasting of Belgian wines in 2004. More than 30 different producers showed their wines to universal enthusiasm. Many top sommeliers were persuaded to add Belgian wines to their lists for the first time.

- **Genoels-Elderen** in the Hespaye region is the first Belgian producer to export wine to such faraway destinations as Japan, Canada, and Scotland. Their Chardonnay Gold is a frequent medal winner at the World Best Chardonnay Competition.

Until now Dutch wine has been more of a curiosity than a serious business. Only a few producers are really ambitious and make interesting wines – and then much depends on the weather. Most wines are blends, since producers have to maximize ripeness and sweetness as well as acidity (which is never a problem) to produce a balanced wine. Even in a nearly tropical year such as 2003 most Dutch wines do not achieve real quality. There is no room for euphoria. Dutch vine growing and winemaking still have a long way to go.

Belgian beer: commitment required

Wine growing has become the cult hobby of this nation of wine lovers – in fact, this amateurish approach has hindered the growth of quality wines until recently. The quality of wines is improving rapidly, even if the area of planted vineyards remains tiny. Belgian wine growers need to take wine production more seriously and address questions of temperature control and hygiene if their wines are going to have any lasting impact. At the moment, most Belgian wine is purchased at the cellar door, but, gradually, the best wines are finding their way onto the wine lists of top restaurants and wine bars. Who knows – they may one day become cult bottlings, like Belgian beers?

Grapevine

• **Plans are afoot** to create a third appellation in Flanders, around the town of Ypres, where the vineyards will no doubt vie with war cemeteries as tourist attractions. No name has yet been mooted.

• **The weather** during the past few summers in the Netherlands has been more Burgundian than Dutch. Extra sunshine and higher temperatures have increased the growing season from around 300 days at the beginning of the 1990s to more than 320 in 2003.

• **Peter Lorenzen** won the Dansk Vinskue wine competition, which is officially recognized by the EU, in 2003. Lorenzen is a horticulture teacher who has been growing vines near Odense since 1991. His winning wine was a blend of Madeleine Angevine, Sylvaner, and two new cold-resistant crosses, Veldze and Reform.

• **In 2003, wine was produced** for the first time at Château Lille Gadegård, on the island of Bornholm in the Eastsee, which is in the far east of Denmark, slightly north of Poland. The wine was produced from 2,000 vines (Rondo, Yvonne, and Jesper Paulsen), which were planted in 2000, and yielded 1,500 kg of grapes, producing 900 litres of red wine, which was fermented in stainless steel and matured in barrels of Limousin oak.

GREATEST WINE PRODUCERS

1. Wijnkasteel Genoels-Elderen (Belgium)
2. Wijngaard Karthuizerhof (Belgium)
3. Apostelhoeve (Netherlands)
4. Lindener (Belgium)
5. Domaine Meerdael (Belgium)
6. Hoeve Nekum (Netherlands)
7. Hagelander (Belgium)
8. Kapittelberg (Belgium)
9. Domaine Aalsgard (Denmark)

FASTEST-IMPROVING PRODUCERS

1. Wijnhoeve Boschberg (Belgium)
2. Wijnhoeve Elsenbosch (Belgium)
3. Château Lille Gadegård (Denmark)
4. Daems & Zonen (Belgium)
5. De Linie (Netherlands)
6. Apostelhoeve (Netherlands)
7. Domain Templeberg (Belgium)

NEW UP-AND-COMING PRODUCERS

1. Peter Colemont (Belgium)
2. Guy Geunis (Belgium)
3. Bjarne Thongaard (Denmark)
4. Domaine du Chenoy (Belgium)
5. Domaine de Blaireaux (Netherlands)
6. Vinperlen (Denmark)
7. Vitis (Belgium)
8. Hageling (Belgium)
9. Stokhemer Wingert (Netherlands)
10. Wijngaard Annendaal

BEST-VALUE PRODUCERS

1. Hoeve Nekum (Netherlands)
2. Wijnkasteel Genoels-Elderen (Belgium)
3. Daems & Zonen (Belgium)
4. Fromberg Estate (Netherlands)
5. Wijngaard Karthuizerhof (Belgium)

GREATEST-QUALITY WINES

1. **Chardonnay 2002** Peter Colemont, Belgium (€15)
2. **Chardonnay Goud 1999** Wijnkasteel Genoels-Elderen, Belgium (€21)
3. **Chardonnay Blauw 2001** Wijnkasteel Genoels-Elderen, Belgium (€9.90)
4. **Cuvée XII 2002** Apostelhoeve, Netherlands (€10)
5. **Riesling 2002** Apostelhoeve, Netherlands (€9)
6. **Méthode Traditionnelle Sparkling Wine NV** Domaine Meerdael, Belgium (€12)
7. **Brut Mousseux NV** Soniën, Belgium (€11)
8. **Blanc Sec 2002** De Linie, Netherlands (€9)
9. **Reichensteiner 2002** Fromberg Estate, Netherlands (€8.25)
10. **Pinot Noir 2002** De Linie, Netherlands (€9.10)

BEST BARGAINS

1. **Riesling 2002** Hoeve Nekum, Netherlands (€8)
2. **Blanc Sec 2002** De Linie, Netherlands (€9)
3. **Chardonnay Wit 2001** Wijnkasteel Genoels-Elderen, Belgium (€7.50)
4. **Chardonnay Blauw 2001** Wijnkasteel Genoels-Elderen, Belgium (€9.90)
5. **Reichensteiner 2002** Fromberg Estate, Netherlands (€8.25)

MOST EXCITING OR UNUSUAL FINDS

1. **Gadegård** Château Lille, Denmark (75 Kroner) *On Bornholm island, the Paulsens produce a red wine from the Rondo grape aged in oak.*
2. **Méthode Traditionnelle NV** Guy Geunis, Belgium (€12) *Good range of sparkling wine, especially the Blanc de Noirs, which holds its head high in international competition.*

For this report's first appearance in *Wine Report*,
I have been given special dispensation to provide
an overview of Luxembourg.

DAVID FURER

This lesser-known wine-producing country is nestled between France, Germany, and Belgium. Its vines stretch for 42 km along the left bank of the Moselle – from the pink dolomite limestone vineyards of Wasserbillig in the north, to the softer, keuper marl vineyards of Schengen in the south. These vineyards generally face south to southeast, with 1,250 hectares (ha) in production in 2003. Luxembourg's wines have taken a cue from its people, who are discreet, even withdrawn, compared to their larger, noisier wine-producing neighbours. The most ancient, neutral, and traditional of Luxembourg's grapes is Elbling – once the staple of Germany's Sekt industry. Thankfully, this variety is on the decline, as is Rivaner (Germany's Müller-Thurgau), although it is still Luxembourg's most prolific grape. Chardonnay is on the increase, primarily for sparkling-wine production. The remaining varieties of Auxerrois, Riesling, Gewürztraminer, and the full flight of Pinots (Gris, Blanc, and Noir) should remind the reader of Alsace. Plantings of Pinot Noir have increased from 1.5 ha in 1982 to just over 80 ha today. While this should not make the Burgundians run for cover, it does signal a shift in climate as well as consumer tastes.

Due to long-standing agreements between the three wine-producing groups (cooperatives, merchants, and independents), there exists no

DAVID FURER, a Certified Wine Educator and Advanced Sommelier, is a writer and judge for wine magazines including *Decanter*, *Drinks Buyer*, *Harpers*, *Santé*, *Wine International*, and *Wine Business Monthly*. He has lectured to the trade, conducted staff training, and led wine classes at the University of Chicago and the London Wine Academy. He also lectures to consumers in Germany. Generic trade organizations from Spain, Germany, and France have retained his services as a consultant.

open market in wine grapes, no spot buying. Domaines de Vinsmoselle, a group of six cooperatives established in 1966, dominates the Luxembourg wine industry, with 60 per cent of total production. The balance is split almost evenly between the Fédération des Producteurs-Négociants (six members, 18 per cent of output) and the Organisation Professionnelle des Vignerons Indépendants (51 private wineries, 22 per cent of output). Quality, whether good, bad, or indifferent, can be found at all levels, with no one group dominating quality wine production.

Vineyards organized, wines not

Luxembourg's wine-governing body, the Institut Viti-Vinicole (IVV), is nearing the end of its restructuring of the region's vineyards. This commenced 12 years ago and has been conducted along similar lines to Germany's *Flurbereinigung*, with 80 per cent currently completed, and a final goal of 90–96 per cent. Most growers have benefited from these changes and are pleased with the results. However, the IVV is drawing the ire of many producers for its inflexibility over the acceptance of developing wine styles. The IVV has time and again refused to allow the release of a wine simply because it has not adhered to the tasting committee's preconceived idea of what a Moselle wine should be, or because they think a producer may be releasing a wine either too early or too late. Nearly every year, one of the greatest 'offenders' is the young Charles Decker, who often encounters difficulties because his wines are naturally concentrated or well aged. The fact that Decker has been awarded more medals at international competitions than any other Luxembourg producer for the very same wines is, in his view, proof enough that the IVV is too parochial and needs to re-examine its benchmarks if the country's wines are to be taken seriously outside its own borders.

IVV sidestepped

In 1988 Domaine et Tradition was set up by seven wineries to exceed what was considered to be seriously low quality criteria by the IVV. This strategy of guaranteeing higher standards has been copied by others outside the original seven, most notably Cep d'Or, with its Signature Terroirs et Cépages. Even the massive Vinsmoselle cooperative has offered financial incentives for growers to produce healthier, riper grapes. If the IVV cannot get its head around what it discerns as atypical styles, it has at least accepted the need for higher quality criteria, which it intends to introduce in 2005. Domaine et Tradition may have rested upon its well-deserved laurels for a few years, but it is now poised to up the ante before the IVV catches up.

Luxembourg wines are in a precarious yet hopeful place in their development. The 2003 vintage is on everyone's lips here as the one that will thrust Luxembourg onto the world stage. Those growers who watched yields will soon be offering dry Riesling and Pinot Gris that could rival some of the finest examples of Alsace and Germany. Production of vast volumes of slightly sweet and neutral Elbling and Rivaner (up to 140 hectolitres per hectare [hl/ha] before the maximum 20 per cent *rendement de base*) for mass consumption is now waning due to a diminishing consumer base that is drinking better and less. However, there are still too many growers who are harvesting noble varieties at yields that are far too high to deliver the quality that consumers now demand. This problem is exacerbated by the difficulty of having foreign pickers on standby, with no work to provide them between the Elbling/Rivaner period of harvest and the later-ripening Rieslings and Pinots. This has usually resulted in growers feeling pressurized to pick their noble varieties before perfect ripeness. All growers who are serious about producing high-quality wine

Grapevine

• **Cep d'Or's innovative Federwaeisen**, a new-style Rivaner, ran into difficulty in 2003 for its early release date, as did Cep d'Or's Auxerrois Sur Lie, for lying too long on its lees.

• **Fifth-generation** Remerschen winemaker Yves Sunnen and his sister Corinne Cox-Sunnen are soon due to become Luxembourg's first biodynamic growers. They began to convert their 4.5 ha to biodynamic viticulture in 2000. To complete their vineyard consolidation and qualify, they need only avoid residue from neighbouring vineyards that are sprayed by helicopter.

• **Remich's Mathis Bastian** has been ostensibly organic for generations but chooses not to advertise it. The five-year-old modern tasting room set among the vines could have been

lifted from California. Mathis Bastian's serious, complete wines are some of the few high-quality Luxembourg non-sparkling wines available in the English-speaking world.

• **The relaxing Hôtel des Vignes** in Remich is not only perched on the top-class Primerberg vineyard, but it also makes its own Riesling Grand Cru from the site and serves this in its gourmet restaurant.

• **Charles Decker** continues to blaze his own trail. Most recently he locked horns yet again with the IVV over a 2000 Crémant that was deemed atypical and unacceptable for a Marque Nationale. While this writer was not mad about it, he believes that this sort of gate-keeping should be done away with or severely modified to allow for stylistic differences.

from noble grape varieties must divest themselves of Elbling and Rivaner, or Luxembourg will never raise its international profile.

Fair's fair

Most wine producers show their wines at May's Foire Internationale du Luxembourg, inevitably rushing the latest vintage to market before the wines are ready to be bottled. They must resist this urge if they are to convince customers that their better wines need time to mature.

Appealing to younger consumers

The long-established cheap-and-cheerful image of Luxembourg wines in Germany, Belgium, and at home must be vigorously combated. The IVV and the various federations must continue to improve, not only in the vineyards and wineries but also in marketing their wines to younger and more affluent consumers. Producers have to acknowledge that the domestic consumer now has greater mobility and myriad choices when shopping. The traditional domestic customer base is growing younger and holds little allegiance to Luxembourg's wines. Rather than sell off land or hide in their shells, Luxembourg's producers would be well advised to exploit their unique soils and marginal climate by lowering yields, increasing vine density, and opening up their better wines to less reductive cellar-management techniques.

Grapevine

● **A vineyard classification** by the IVV in cooperation with the German Weather Institute is under way. Climatic mapping will advise growers on the most appropriate varieties for their vineyards and could, in time, lead to a *grand cru*-type classification. For the moment, however, better matching of grapes to soils should encourage greater ripeness, which is of prime importance in this northerly wine region.

● **Luxembourg won nine** of the 53 gold medals awarded at Strasbourg's 2004 Riesling du Monde, plus 27 of the 84 silver medals. In view of the competition from such famous Riesling areas as Alsace, Austria, Germany, and, to a lesser extent, Australia, such convincing success must bode well for this unheralded corner of the wine world.

● **Convinced that his wines benefit** from bottle-ageing, Cep d'Or's Johnny Vesque initiated a programme to allow sommeliers no-cost reserves of wines to purchase a year or two after initial release. So far only mild interest has been shown.

● **Marc Gales** finally opened his gleaming new sparkling-wine facility in Ellange in 2003. More high-tech than the facilities boasted by most champagne houses, more than 1 million bottles of Luxembourg's 6 million sparkling wines will pass through these doors each year.

● **April 2003** saw Luxembourg stepping into the modern era by establishing a wine-marketing office. Former hotel marketer Nathalie Reckinger is working to improve the reputation of Luxembourg wines through various media, including the www.luxvin.lu website.

2003

As throughout the rest of Europe, a very long, hot, and dry summer made for very ripe grapes with low natural acidity, particularly for those who did not take care in the vineyard. This was the first year Luxembourg was allowed to acidify, so winemakers inexperienced with this method may see disharmony in their wines, especially at the early stages. Auxerrois was completely harvested by the end of September, which allowed for some acid retention, but green pip tannins may have entered into the wines due to lack of full physiological maturity. Sugar ripeness gave high potential alcohol, although the concentration of flavours in this unique vintage keeps one's perception of the typically elevated residual-sugar levels found in some wines in check. A few difficult Pinot Blancs and Pinot Gris, but most will offer great pleasure for the near to mid-term. The relatively late-picked varieties Riesling and Pinot Noir are outstanding. They have, surprisingly, maintained their regional character despite the intense heat of summer. There are many expressive *vendanges tardives* and some terrific icewines for near-term consumption.

Updates on the previous five vintages

2002

Vintage rating: 92

Though ripe, the high acidity levels of many 2002s meant longer fermentation periods for some, especially along the more northerly, limestone-influenced soils. Since nearly all work in Luxembourg is done in steel tank, this translates to what are now very reduced wines. Pinot Blanc, Riesling, Auxerrois, Gewürztraminer, and Chardonnay are all interesting to great. Most Pinot Gris and Pinot Noirs rank as only okay, since they are tending towards leanness. Good icewines were harvested in early January.

2001

Vintage rating: 85

Extremely hot and cold summer periods alternated with much rain through September, devastating the quality for earlier ripeners. The best grapes were harvested mid-October through to early November. Many Rieslings are classic, exhibiting crisp freshness and intriguing fruit; they will need years to open. Good Pinot Blanc and Gewürztraminer, as well as the icewines harvested in December.

2000

Vintage rating: *68*

Wines throughout the region are marked by an intense, darkish colour and high minerality. Initially it was cool in late June and early July, with a hot latter half of summer in which hail burst through in early August, causing scattered damage. Hopes for a classic, though short, harvest were dashed when rains hammered the region for three weeks beginning mid-September. The result was grey rot for those who did not spray. Most wines are showing plenty of dilution or are going over, although a few pleasant surprises can be found. Icewines were generally unsuccessful due to rot problems.

1999

Vintage rating: *88*

A hot summer shifted to rain in early September, encouraging botrytis. Late September brought hot and humid weather again, lowering acidity and maintaining the botrytis. Botrytis-dominated Pinot Gris is atypical for the region. Severe selection was necessary for clean wines. Many easy-drinking wines are available now. There are also some fine late-harvest Gewürztraminers. Some icewine from 20 December gave a very fresh, Germanic style, while others harvested in late January show more dried fruits and glycerol-based notes, as in Alsace.

1998

Vintage rating: *90*

As in Germany, it was difficult to get ripe grapes, and late-picked wines were best. Rigorous fermentations helped reduce the greenish notes, allowing for greater aromatics and balance. Many wines are still exhibiting earthy aromas and finishes, and have yet to open. There are outstanding Auxerrois and Pinot Gris in the north, with huge fruitiness and minerality. *Vin de garde* wines predominate due to the intense minerality and acidity; classic, crisp Rieslings are good for the cellar. The very high-acid icewines should take at least a decade to come around.

GREATEST WINE PRODUCERS

1. Mme Aly Duhr & Fils
2. Domaine Mathis Bastian
3. Charles Decker
4. Alice Hartmann
5. Duhr Frères
6. Bernard-Massard (for Clos des Rochers and Domaine Thill Frères)
7. Caves Gales
8. Krier Frères
9. A Gloden & Fils
10. Domaines de Vinsmoselle

FASTEST-IMPROVING PRODUCERS

1. Domaines de Vinsmoselle
2. Caves Sunnen-Hoffmann
3. A Gloden & Fils
4. Cep d'Or
5. Alice Hartmann

NEW UP-AND-COMING PRODUCERS

1. Alice Hartmann
2. Charles Decker
3. Caves Sunnen-Hoffmann
4. Cep d'Or
5. Steinmetz-Jungers

BEST-VALUE PRODUCERS

1. Domaines de Vinsmoselle
2. Mme Aly Duhr & Fils
3. Cep d'Or
4. Domaine Mathis Bastian
5. Jean Schlink-Hoffeld
6. A Gloden & Fils

GREATEST-QUALITY WINES

1. **Wellenstein Foulschette Riesling 1999** Domaine Mathis Bastian/Domaine et Tradition (€7)
2. **Puits d'Or Riesling Vin de Glace 1999** Mme Aly Duhr & Fils (€27 per half-bottle)
3. **Pinot Blanc Remerschen Kreitzberg 2002** Charles Decker (€9.50)
4. **Wormeldange Koeppchen Riesling Vendanges Tardives 2002** Alice Hartmann (€22 per half-bottle)
5. **Wormeldange Koeppchen Riesling *** 2002** Alice Hartmann (€12)
6. **Clos Mon Vieux Moulin Auxerrois 1989** Mme Aly Duhr & Fils/Domaine et Tradition (€15)
7. **Gewürztraminer Moelleux 2002** Clos des Rochers (€8 per half-bottle)
8. **Clos du Paradis Auxerrois 1997** Mme Aly Duhr & Fils (€29)
9. **Wellenstein Foulschette Pinot Gris 2002** Domaine Mathis Bastian/Domaine et Tradition (€7)
10. **Pinot Blanc 2002** Clos des Rochers/Domaine et Tradition (€7)

BEST BARGAINS

1. **Wormeldange Nussbaum Riesling 2001** Mme Aly Duhr & Fils (€6)
2. **Ahn Hohfels Pinot Gris 1997** Mme Aly Duhr & Fils (€7)
3. **Wellenstein Foulschette Pinot Gris 2002** Domaine Mathis Bastian/Domaine et Tradition (€7)
4. **Wellenstein Foulschette Riesling 1999** Domaine Mathis Bastian/Domaine et Tradition (€7)
5. **Crémant Brut NV** A Gloden & Fils (€7)
6. **Crémant Brut 2001** Cep d'Or (€8)
7. **Schengen Markusberg Gewürztraminer 2002** Domaines de Vinsmoselle (€6)
8. **Pinot Blanc 2002** Clos des Rochers/Domaine et Tradition (€7)
9. **Clos Mon Vieux Moulin Auxerrois 1989** Mme Aly Duhr & Fils/Domaine et Tradition (€15)
10. **Jubilee Crémant Brut NV** Caves Gales (€8)

MOST EXCITING OR UNUSUAL FINDS

1 Gris de Gris Vin de Table 2002 A Gloden & Fils (€6) *The Gloden men claim to have made the first-ever Luxembourg still white made from Pinot Noir. While challenging on its own, it would be a good thirst-quencher on a Moselle summer night alongside a plate of barbecued pork.*

2 Wormeldange Koeppchen Riesling *** 2002 Alice Hartmann (€12) *Harvested at the remarkably low 30 hl/ha from terraced vines during the second week of November, showing what severe pruning and meticulous winemaking can bring. Fermented dry. Stunning.*

3 Crémant Brut NV Alice Hartmann (€14) *Not unusual for its 50 per cent Riesling composition, but for the Riesling icewine that comprised the liqueur d'expédition. Full-bodied, oaky, and very atypical for Crémant de Luxembourg.*

4 Gewürztraminer Moelleux 2002 Clos des Rochers (€8 per half-bottle) *Proprietor Hubert Clasen expressed modest surprise at this unexpected gem. Shows great elegance, complexity, and agreeability for this oft-maligned grape.*

5 Muscat Ottonel 2002 Charles Decker (€9) *Decker's widely popular Muscat is the region's Muscat benchmark. I'm not sure why, though, because the simple Muscat à Petit Grains x Chasselas cross leaves me not quite cold, but distinctly cool.*

6 Pinot Gris Vin de Glâce 2002 Caves Gales/Domaine et Tradition (€33 per half-bottle) *The first Luxembourg producer to commercialize a Pinot Gris icewine harvested this vintage at 170 degrees Oechsle. The high residual sugar keeps the 14 per cent alcohol in check for this mid-term fruit bomb.*

7 Coteaux de Grevenmacher Chardonnay 2002 Domaines de Vinsmoselle (€7) *Aged in barrique from grapes sourced primarily from chalky soils surrounding this cosy wine village, this is not overwhelmingly oaky and it offers plenty of red-apple and peach flavours at a nice price.*

8 Clos du Paradis Auxerrois 1997 Mme Aly Duhr & Fils (€29) *Harvested at the crazy-low 20 hl/ha, Abi Duhr has fashioned Luxembourg's most expensive dry wine with impressively high minerality and acidity, framed by lush 100 per cent new barriques.*

9 Auxerrois Sur Lie Coteaux de Stadtbredimus 2002 Cep d'Or (€5) *Six months on the lees adds aromas and mineral length to what can often be a boring grape.*

10 Pinot Blanc Vin de Paille 2002 Charles Decker (€35 per half-bottle) *Showing its intense, youthful sweet/sour disparity over 14 per cent alcohol, Decker has challenged himself, as well as others, with this style new to Luxembourg. Excellent and expensive.*

Grapevine

• **Vinsmoselle** is developing a gastronomy wine project with its young growers to encourage them to produce low-yielding fruit of 25–50 hl/ha (the average for total production is 120 hl/ha; even the average for noble varieties is 96 hl/ha). Initial reports are that the cost/benefit ratio is still unbalanced.

Demand for quality wines has been growing in Switzerland for the last few years, and winemakers are beginning to focus more on quality than quantity.

CHANDRA KURT

Producers are realizing that they cannot keep reproducing the wine styles of their parents' generation. New World wines have had a strong influence on the tastes of the younger generation of wine drinkers, who are looking for concentrated, fruity wines with medium acidity.

Quantity-wise, production levels are down in the vineyards. The government initiated a vine-pull scheme in 2003 to replace the common but unattractive Chasselas grape with more distinguished varieties. Sauvignon Blanc, Viognier, Pinot Gris, and Chardonnay are whites to watch out for. Pinot Noir, Merlot, Syrah, and local specialities such as Humagne Rouge, Cornalin, and Gamaret make very interesting red wines. Malbec has also been planted recently and the first results are very encouraging.

Swiss drink less

According to the Weinhandelskommission, Zurich, wine consumption in Switzerland dropped from 306 million litres to 301 million litres in 2003, giving an annual average consumption of 41.5 litres per head. Consumption of Swiss wine fell, while imports increased. Foreign wine is important to the Swiss, since indigenous production covers only 40 per

CHANDRA KURT is the author of several wine books, including the bestseller *Weinseller*, which she has been publishing for six years. She is also a freelance wine writer and contributes on a regular basis to several leading publications, including *Finanz und Wirtschaft*, *Schweizer Familie*, and *Hotel + Tourismus Revue*. As a wine consultant she works for Swiss International Airlines and several Swiss retail institutions.

cent of annual consumption. Switzerland, which imports some 1.8 million hectolitres (hl) of foreign wine each year, constitutes an attractive market for wine-producing regions all over the world and ranks first in the world for imports of foreign wines per inhabitant (nearly 26 litres per year per person). Sixty per cent of imported wine comes from France and Italy.

New wine promotion body

Until now, Switzerland has never had an agency to coordinate the promotion of Swiss wine inside and outside the country. The SWEA (Swiss Wine Exporters' Association), founded in 1958, promoted exports but was criticized for the standard of wine it exhibited at international events. A change to the agricultural law (Landwirtschaftsgesetz) in 2003 allocated SF 5 million (£2 million) for the promotion of Swiss wine. Another SF 6 million (£2.4 million) came from the SBW (Schweizer Branchenverband Wein). A new company, Swiss Wine Communication, will be responsible for distributing this money and coordinating promotional events at home and abroad.

Sales of California wine fall

The sales of California wine in Switzerland have dropped by about 10 per cent. Caves Mövenpick, one of the leading distributors, has experienced a 7 per cent decrease in turnover. "We aren't getting any new customers for these wines. They prefer to buy Australian brands, more so than South American," said CEO Ueli Eggenberger. There are two reasons: consumers do not like Bush's Iraq policy, and they are no longer willing to pay the constantly increasing prices. Distributors forecast that prices of California wines will start to drop, promotions of big brands will increase, and middle-range wines (SF 20–35, £8–14) will disappear altogether. Easy to sell are cheap US brands up to SF 15 (£6) and, conversely, top wines such as Opus One.

Grapevine

• **The wine trade** is going through a time of change and rationalization. Too many small wine shops and wine producers are trying to survive in a limited marketplace. Even with average wine consumption running at 41.5 litres per head, there are far too many wine suppliers (more than 2,000). It is likely that in the next couple of years about 30 per cent will either close or merge with other companies.

Swiss wine producers are most comfortable at home and are very slow to change their traditional behaviour. As a result, only a few producers show their wines in other countries or enter international competitions, although the quality of Swiss wine is improving all the time. Top wines from the Valais, the Grisons, or the Italian area – especially Merlot, Pinot Noir, and Syrah – could get high marks in blind tastings. Winemakers, however, seem reluctant to follow this path. Another problem is that producers prefer to represent their own area rather than promote Swiss wine as a whole. This attitude is not helping the Swiss brand to grow internationally.

Yet for international tasters there is so much to discover about Swiss wines. Once you have tasted the best, it is difficult to understand why these wines are not better known. The good producers are making wine in classic European styles. You will taste Pinots that could have come from Burgundy and Syrahs as good as any in the Rhône Valley.

La Côte advertising

The two wine giants Schenk (Rolles) and Uvavins (Morges) have launched a national advertising campaign for wines from La Côte. Lower prices and better quality would improve matters much more than a publicity campaign.

Cult status needed

Switzerland has a problem that denies its best wines the sort of international fame they truly deserve: no famous winemakers. Despite a lot of really great Swiss wines, there is no outstanding personality who is able to act as an ambassador for the industry in general. The norm in Switzerland is to behave like everybody else, rather than be an individualist like Angelo Gaja or Robert Mondavi. Apart from Daniel Gantenbein in Fläsch, no Swiss winemaker has understood how to create a cult following for his or her wines, let alone realize the value of such fame. Even if every single wine in the country happened to be world-class in quality and available in the most limited quantities, the image of Swiss wines would still be mediocre. Swiss wines need cult status, and to achieve that the industry needs its most talented winemakers to strut their stuff.

Advance report on the latest harvest
2003

What a year! Never were Swiss newspapers so interested in a vintage as in 2003. An unusually hot, dry, and long summer will be remembered not only as the vintage of the century but also the one with the highest press coverage. Quality is expected to be extraordinary. Pinot Noir reached an average 106° *Oechsle*, Riesling x Sylvaner 83°. In general, most of the varieties had *Oechsles* over 100, a quality level not seen since 1947. It was also a very early harvest – a month earlier in the Grisons. Most Swiss vineyards finished their harvest by the end of August and all the grapes were in by the end of September. Due to the special sugar and ripeness status of the grapes, some producers will be unsure about the best way to vinify. So, although it is a very special and promising year, the results will not be seen for a couple of years. Some winemakers are convinced that New World winery experience would be necessary to make the best wine in 2003. Nevertheless, there is intense public interest in the 2003 vintage and many wines have already sold out via subscription.

Updates on the previous five vintages
2002
Vintage rating: 94

Quality varies from good to excellent, with wines that are more elegant than full-bodied. In some regions, the quantity dropped by as much as 30 per cent over 2001, which illustrates that a lot of growers are reducing quantity to increase quality.

2001
Vintage rating: 92

A climatically difficult year produced a small crop of variable quality. In the Valais, the quality was very good indeed, while it was just average for the rest of the Romandie. It was excellent in Schaffhausen and the Grisons, too.

2000

Vintage rating: *98*

A large harvest of exceptional quality for both red and white wines in all parts of Switzerland. Those who called 1997 the vintage of the century have had to revise their judgment, because 2000 was even better! The very best wines came from the Grisons and the Romandie.

1999

Vintage rating: *90*

A large harvest of variable quality. The Valais and Vaud both turned out good reds but average whites. The quality was very poor in Geneva, but very good in Italian-speaking Switzerland, and even better in east Switzerland and the Grisons.

1998

Vintage rating: *88*

French-speaking Switzerland showed the greatest differences in quality. Pinot Noir of the Valais was average to good, Gamay good, and white wines very good. The Vaud and Geneva had average-quality wines, while the Grisons ranged from good to excellent. In the Ticino, the quality was good, but not special.

GREATEST WINE PRODUCERS

1. Daniel & Martha Gantenbein
2. Hans Ulrich Kesselring
3. Georg und Ruth Fromm
4. Jean-René Germanier
5. Adriano Kaufmann
6. Luigi Zanini
7. Werner Stucky
8. Daniel Huber
9. Christian Zündel
10. Charles et Jean-Michel Novelle

FASTEST-IMPROVING PRODUCERS

1. Thomas und Barbara Studach
2. Peter Wegelin
3. Baumann Weingut
4. Weinkellereien Volg
5. Guido Brivio
6. Domaine Cornulus
7. Anna Barbara von der Crone
8. Weingut Schmidheiny
9. Domaine de Balisiers
10. Domaine Grillette

NEW UP-AND-COMING PRODUCERS

1. Christian Hermann
2. Didier Joris
3. Philippe Dariely
4. Romain Papilloud
5. Sergio Monti
6. Paolo Visini
7. Meinrad Perler
8. Lorenzo e Enrico Trapletti
9. Bernard Cavé
10. Domaine de la Rochette

BEST-VALUE PRODUCERS

1. Provins
2. Weinkellereien Volg
3. Familie Zahner
4. Zweifel Weine
5. Hermann Schwarzenbach
6. Weingut Saxer
7. Domaine de la Pierre Latin
8. Vins Rouvinez
9. Serge Roh
10. Philippoz Frères

GREATEST-QUALITY WINES

1. **Pinot Noir 2002** Daniel & Martha Gantenbein (SF 46)
2. **Rosso del Ticino 2001** Luigi Zanini (SF 89)
3. **Ermitage Grain Noble 2000** Marie-Thérèse Chappaz (SF 44 per 50-cl bottle)
4. **Chardonnay Barrique Otelfingen Reserve 2002** Zweifel Weine (SF 25)
5. **Pinot Gris 2002** Schlossgut Bachtobel (SF 24)
6. **Malanser Pinot Noir Barrique 2002** Georg und Ruth Fromm (SF 19.50)
7. **Conte di Luna 2001** Werner Stucky (SF 48)
8. **Montagna Magica 2001** Daniel Huber (SF 50.50)
9. **Humagne Rouge 2001** Jean-René Germanier (SF 33)
10. **Syrah Vieilles Vignes 2000** Simon Maye (SF 28)

BEST BARGAINS

1. **Riesling x Sylvaner 2002** Hermann Schwarzenbach (SF 10.50)
2. **Riesling x Sylvaner Truttiker Weiss 2002** Familie Zahner (SF 10)
3. **Charme Spumante Brut NV** Vini Angelo Delea (SF 15)
4. **Vétroz Grand Cru 2002** Caves de la Madeleine (SF 14)
5. **Chasselas 2002** Domaine Grillette (SF 10.50)
6. **Räuschling 2002** Turmgut (SF 15)
7. **Fendant de Sierre 2002** Cave St Mathieu (SF 12)
8. **Fendant La Perle du Valais 2002** Domaine Mont d'Or (SF 12.80)
9. **Riesling x Sylvaner 2003** Weingut Davaz (SF 11)
10. **Garanoir de Satigny 2002** Domaine du Paradis (SF 10.95)

Grapevine

• **A bid to revive protectionism** for Swiss white wine was made by the five cantons of the French part of Switzerland – Freiburg, Genf, Neuenburg, Wallis, and Waadt. Since protection was abolished in 2001, 36 per cent more foreign white wine has been imported, and the average price of white wine has dropped by 13 per cent. The government refused the request, saying that globalization is not to blame for falling sales of Swiss white wine.

MOST EXCITING OR UNUSUAL FINDS

1 Heida Gletscherwein 2002 Chanton Weine (SF 22.80) *Produced from the highest vineyard in Europe, at 1,150 m (3,800 ft) above sea level. A very crisp and fresh wine that shows the potential of the Valais.*

2 Completer Barrique 2002 Peter und Rosi Hermann (SF 25) *A traditional wine from the Grisons. Because of its high acidity, it is not for everybody. Keeps for ages.*

3 Fläscher Schiller 2003 Weingut Davaz (SF 11) *Rare wine from the mountain area of the Grisons. Usually sells out very quickly.*

4 Mitis Amigne 2001 Jean-René Germanier (SF 27) *The most famous Swiss sweet wine.*

5 Paien 2002 Simon Maye (SF 32) *Again, a concentrated example of the high-level quality of the wines from the Valais.*

6 Riesling 2001 Daniel & Martha Gantenbein (SF 28 per half-bottle) *The second vintage of Gantenbein's new baby. This Riesling shows a lot of residual sugar and is a beautiful dessert wine.*

7 Viognier 2002 Domaine Grillette (SF 19.50) *One of the first wineries that became famous for Viognier in Switzerland.*

8 Sauvignon Blanc Les Curiades 2002 Dupraz et Fils (SF 14.50) *Such freshness and typical aromas give this wine an international image. You would never guess it comes from Switzerland.*

9 Malbec/Pinot Noir 2001 Weingut zum Sternen (SF 23) *Malbec, planted in 1997, produces a concentrated wine dominated by fruit.*

10 Fragolino NV Vini Angelo Delea (SF 9) *Red sparkling wine from an American hybrid that grows only in the Italian part of Switzerland.*

With 2002 and 2003, Austria could not have had two more stylistically contrasting vintages.

DR PHILIPP BLOM

Both are excellent, but while 2002 showed elegance and acidity, the hot and dry 2003 will be remembered for the perfectly ripe, perfectly healthy grapes and for the concentration of the fruit. First tastings also show a surprisingly balanced acidity. The intense sun presented new challenges in the vineyard, and many growers resorted to partial leaf canopies to protect the grapes from sunburn.

There is some debate in Austria about whether 2003 was a freak year or a taste of things to come, and some leading growers, among them Willi Bründlmayer and Toni Bodenstein (Prager), are actively thinking about how the wine landscape might change if temperatures continue to rise and seasons become more extreme. With earlier budding and a longer vegetation period, Grüner Veltliner and Riesling will have to be vinified accordingly. Riesling has less trouble with hotter temperatures, while Grüner Veltliner tends to broaden out and lose its finer aromas if the effects of the warm weather are not countered very consciously in both the vineyard and the cellar.

Some more daring colleagues, especially in the Burgenland, are betting on hotter vintages by planting classic hot varieties such as Cabernet Sauvignon and Syrah, which have not yet proved their worth against

DR PHILIPP BLOM is a freelance writer and journalist (*Wine & Spirits Magazine, Decanter, Vinum, Vinaria, La Revue du Vin de France, Amateur de Bordeaux*). His book *The Wines of Austria* was published by Faber & Faber in 2000. Other publications include *To Have and to Hold: An Intimate History of Collectors and Collecting* (Allen Lane, 2002; Penguin paperback edition, 2003) and *Encyclopédie* (Fourth Estate, 2004). He lives in Paris.

Austrian red varieties, especially Blaufränkisch. Stylistically, too, 2003 will be a challenge. If the previous vintage demonstrated that elegant and focused wines can rise to true greatness in Austria, the effects of the hot summer demand considerable craftsmanship and conviction.

Changeable?

When it was announced that the Freie Weingärtner Wachau, often called 'the world's best cooperative', had put its fate in the hands of a new director, many eyebrows were raised. Until then, two young codirectors, Fritz Miesbauer and Rainer Wess, had built on the work of their predecessors and energetically pushed the 800-odd participating growers for ever-better grape qualities, as well as realizing an ambitious renovation programme. They reaped the benefits in international critical praise and a surge in exports, but their constant vigilance made them few friends within the cooperative. The divorce was swift but not amicable, and the growers chose as their successor Roland Grossinger, the brother of a former chairman of the cooperative board and an appointee whose previous experience lies in selling sparkling wines.

Whether Grossinger has the will, and the clout, to continue the previous line of uncompromising quality remains to be seen. The two former directors, meanwhile, have gone their own ways: Rainer Wess as perhaps the first true *négociant-éleveur* in the Wachau, making wines exclusively from bought-in grapes; Fritz Miesbauer as director of the Weingut der Stadt Krems, a medium-sized producer in neighbouring Kremstal, where he just might succeed in waking this immensely promising region from its profound slumber.

Grapevine

- **The Master of Wine course** will be offered by the Austrian Wine Academy in Rust, in conjunction with the Institute of Masters of Wine in London, from February 2004.

- **The Styrian winery Polz** has become one of the region's, and the country's, largest producers by buying one of its main local competitors, Tscheppe, and leasing it back to the former owners, who had to sell due to insolvency.

- **Exports continued to grow rapidly** in Austria in 2002. For the first time, exports exceeded pre-1985 levels both in volume (45 per cent) and value (16 per cent). The proportion of red wines exported rose by 22 per cent.

- **Aristocratic Burgenland estates** Esterhazy and Halbturn, after many a year of genteel slumber, have now started major programmes of investment and building.

Increasingly, blockbuster wines with up to 15 per cent alcohol are a thing of the past. Many producers have understood that they are, to quote one, "too vulgar, too easy to make", and most top producers are now turning away from this style, aided by two vintages, 2001 and 2002, which favoured more elegant, balanced wines. Red wines have especially benefited from this. Now it remains to be seen whether the hot 2003 will produce fewer overly heavy red wines than 2000.

The modification in the styles of some Austrian wines is not only due to the influence of two cool years, however. After the great wave of renewal and revolution, there has been a noticeable return to roots. Having experimented with new vines and vinification methods, many producers and regions are now formulating the core values of their area and are intensifying their investigations of *terroir* and traditional wine styles. Riesling and Grüner Veltliner in Lower Austria and Chardonnay (locally called Morillon) and Sauvignon Blanc in Styria are increasing their dominance as leading white varieties, with a sprinkling of aromatic varieties such as Muskateller and Traminer, especially for the sweet wines of Lake Neusiedl. Among the red varieties, the star is undoubtedly Blaufränkisch, which shows immense potential, as well as perfect suitability for the climate of the Burgenland, with, to a lesser extent, Pinot Noir (which still holds lots of potential) and Zweigelt as supporting varieties.

Discussions about the introduction of an appellation system keep the issue alive and help to develop the essential wine styles of the country.

Grapevine

• **With more and more** outstanding red wines produced in Austria, the identity of Austrian red wines, which have less of a tradition than the great white or sweet wines, is still a focus of discussion and trial. One experiment in particular seems very promising: a series of wines called Moric, made by the Velich brothers (Neusiedlersee) with bought-in grapes from 35- to 100-year-old Blaufränkisch vines in Neckenmarkt and Lutzmannsburg of Middle Burgenland. Taking their cue from burgundian village wines, Heinz and Roland Velich are trying to make authentically regional wines from indigenous grapes, without artificial concentration and with the greatest possible awareness of *terroir* character. The 2002 vintage shows considerable promise.

2003

It is always dangerous to mumble prophetically about a vintage of the century, especially if the century is only three years old, but 2003 certainly was an exceptional year, comparable only, older growers say, to 1947. An early heat wave swept over the country after Easter and, except for a cool week each during May and August, four searingly hot months followed. Hailstorms in mid-May devastated parts of the Vienna vineyards and reduced yields there drastically, but otherwise conditions were ideal. The hot and almost rain-free summer caused the plants to build up a considerable advance on the normal vegetative cycle, despite the fact that some younger vines suffered. In view of the almost Mediterranean climatic conditions – the Styrian capital of Graz recorded top temperatures of 40°C (104°F) – many growers used overhanging leaf canopies to provide the grapes with foliage 'parasols' to prevent sunburn. The competition between vines and other plants in the vineyard also had to be limited to a minimum in 2003.

The vineyards on the eastern banks of Lake Neusiedl were harvested from 20 August – earlier than ever before. During the last week of August, the weather suddenly changed and temperatures dropped as low as 10°C (50°F). Cool nights during a September Indian summer slowed down physiological ripening. The virtual absence of rain until mid-October ensured the perfect health of the grapes. Harvests in Lower Austria were finished in the third week of November and the cool nights gave good acidity.

Early tastings show Riesling and Grüner Veltliner surprisingly balanced with great concentration, promising a vintage that is, although very different in style from 2002, another classic year. Chardonnays and the Thermenregion grapes thrived, but in some instances Sauvignon Blanc suffered from heat stress. The only white-wine growers less happy about the almost-perfect health of the grapes were sweet-wine growers, who had either managed with minimum botrytis or chose to bet more heavily on icewines than in previous years. Red wines were still fermenting at the point of writing, but the quality, especially of 'hotter' varieties such as Blaufränkisch, Cabernet Sauvignon, Merlot, and Syrah, was excellent, with perfectly ripe tannins. Pinot Noir (often tending to a certain fatness here) may be almost overripe.

Updates on the previous five vintages

2002

Vintage rating: 92 *(Red: 90, White: 93, Sweet: 83)*

After an almost-ideal summer, torrential rains in mid-August caused the collapse of many terraced vineyards in the Wachau and catastrophic floods in Lower Austria. Despite these misfortunes, grape qualities were uniformly very good throughout Austria. Red wines are well balanced with ripe tannins, and the prevalent botrytis was good news for nobly sweet wines.

Styrian growers made expressive Sauvignon Blancs and Chardonnays, and in Lower Austria this difficult vintage proved to possess the seeds of true greatness for producers who practised rigorous grape selection and who harvested late. Wonderfully balanced Rieslings and, to a lesser extent, Grüner Veltliners, especially in the Wachau and the Kamptal, show great elegance, depth, and enormous potential. In the best cases, this is a classic vintage.

2001

Vintage rating: 89 *(Red: 91, White: 89, Sweet: 85)*

The never-ending September rain (Vienna saw only four clear days in as many weeks) made the harvest very work-intensive, since healthy grapes had to be sorted. Two frosty periods in December, finally, allowed an icewine harvest. This is a year that vindicates conscientious vineyard work and good vinification, where wines are marked by clarity and balance. The reds are less powerful than 2000, but possess more charm. A good crop of botrytis wines was harvested, too. Generally, these wines will evolve quite quickly.

2000

Vintage rating: 91 *(Red: 85, White: 92, Sweet: 88)*

With little rain in November and above-average temperatures, the perfect conditions were created for late-harvest wines. This was an extraordinary vintage for red wines, with record must weights and dark colours, though many growers let themselves be seduced into thinking they could produce competition-winning wines when it was actually not easy to balance the alcohol and tannins in the more concentrated wines. With their punch and body, this has been declared a great red-wine vintage, though I personally think too many are over the top. For white wines, this was an almost perfect year, with big Grüner Veltliners and Rieslings in Lower Austria and Chardonnays in the Burgenland ideally suited for *barrique* treatment. Styrian growers also harvested wines of great concentration and harmony.

1999

Vintage rating: *94 (Red: 88, White: 96, Sweet: 90)*

This was a wonderful year for dry white and red wines. Red wines show good structure and deep fruit, with less tannin than the 2000s, which are usually rated more highly in Austria. The best producers made beautifully balanced 1999 reds, especially with Blaufränkisch, Zweigelt, and Pinot Noir. White wines in Lower Austria reached great purity, equilibrium, and concentration, with less alcohol than 1998, but a more pronounced acidity than 2000. These are wines expressing varietal character and *terroir* to perfection, ideal for ageing, but often already approachable. In the Wachau and the Kamptal, especially, this was a great year. Beautiful whites were also made in the Burgenland, where the Chardonnays in particular show excellent fruit and well-integrated wood. Styria produced deep and expressive Sauvignon Blancs and Morillons (Chardonnays).

1998

Vintage rating: *85 (Red: 78, White: 87, Sweet: 80)*

A late harvest brought grapes that were almost overripe, with high sugars, resulting in wines that are very high in alcohol (up to 15 per cent), low in acidity, and less clearly profiled than those of 1997.

Grapevine

• **Austria has suffered** from a dearth of big and reliably high-quality producers. Now, with avant-garde wineries shooting up everywhere in Austrian wine-growing areas, the commercial and ownership structures are following suit and several large quality producers are consolidating their positions. Until now there were only a few traditional middle-sized quality producers (Willi Bründlmayer and Jurtschitsch, for instance), while the large houses were undistinguished and exclusively mass-oriented, with the notable exception of the Freie Weingärtner Wachau. Now a new generation of winemakers and entrepreneurs is putting the cat among the pigeons. The famous Burgenland sweet-wine producer Alois Kracher used to make his wines on 7 hectares (ha) a few years ago, but now he owns or buys from 30 ha. In a neighbouring village, Gernot Heinrich has realized an ambitious vision and is vinifying wines from 90 ha of vineyards (from 12 ha five years ago), while the irrepressible Polz family in Southern Styria now owns or controls 105 ha of vineyards. Other successful growers work in partnerships, such as Manfred Tement, FX Pichler, and the late Tibor Szemes with their red *cuvée* Arachon, or as *négociants*, such as Heribert Bayer with his In Signo Leonis label.

GREATEST WINE PRODUCERS

1. Alzinger (Wachau)
2. Willi Bründlmayer (Kamptal)
3. Hirtzberger (Wachau)
4. Knoll (Wachau)
5. Kracher (Neusiedlersee)
6. FX Pichler (Wachau)
7. Pöckl (Neusiedlersee)
8. Prager (Wachau)
9. Tement (South Styria)
10. E Triebaumer (Neusiedlersee-Hügelland)

BEST-VALUE PRODUCERS

1. Kurt Angerer (Kremstal)
2. Willi Bründlmayer (Kamptal)
3. Walter Buchegger (Kremstal)
4. Knoll (Wachau)
5. Schloß Gobelsburg (Kamptal)
6. Roman Pfaffl (Weinviertel)
7. Peter Schandl (Neusiedlersee-Hügelland)
8. Heidi Schröck (Neusiedlersee-Hügelland)
9. Ludwig Hiedler (Kamptal)
10. Platzer (South-East Styria)

FASTEST-IMPROVING PRODUCERS

1. Josef Gritsch (Wachau)
2. Ludwig Hiedler (Kamptal)
3. Karl Lagler (Wachau)
4. Undhof Salomon (Kremstal)
5. Mittelbach (Tegernseehof, Wachau)
6. Franz Proidl (Kremstal)
7. Engelbert Prieler (Neusiedlersee-Hügelland)
8. Weingut der Stadt Krems (Kremstal)
9. Söllner (Donauland)
10. Velich (Neusiedlersee)

GREATEST-QUALITY WINES

1. **Grüner Veltliner Vinothekfüllung Smaragd 1990** Knoll (€45)
2. **Riesling Wachstum Bodenstein 2002** Prager (€30)
3. **Grüner Veltliner Kellerberg Smaragd 1995** FX Pichler (€50)
4. **Cuvée No 8 Zwischen den Seen 1995** Kracher (€50)
5. **Riesling Singerriedel 1995** Hirtzberger (€45)
6. **Riesling Lyra 1997** Bründlmayer (€25)
7. **Riesling Steinertal 1997** Alzinger (€23)
8. **Chardonnay Tiglat 1997** Velich (€50)
9. **Blaufränkisch Perwolff 2000** Krutzler, South Burgenland (€35)
10. **Morillon Zieregg 2000** Tement (€28)

NEW UP-AND-COMING PRODUCERS

1. Kurt Angerer (Kremstal)
2. Josef Bauer (Donauland)
3. Heribert Bayer (Thermenregion)
4. Günter Brandl (Kamptal)
5. Walter Buchegger (Kremstal)
6. Johann Donabaum (Wachau)
7. Meinhard Forstreiter (Wachau)
8. Toni Hartl (Thermenregion)
9. Alois Höllmüller (Wachau)
10. Bernhard Ott (Traisental)

BEST BARGAINS

NB: Prices are ex cellar.

1. **Grüner Veltliner Spies 2002** Kurt Angerer (€9.60)
2. **Grüner Veltliner Novemberlese 2002** Günter Brandl (€9.50)
3. **Grüner Veltliner Kreutles 2002** Bäuerl (€9.20)
4. **Ruster Ausbruch Pinot Cuvée 2001** Feiler-Artinger (€19)
5. **Riesling Rosenberg 2002** Bernhard Ott (€6.50)
6. **Riesling Hiesberg 2002** Groll (€6.90)
7. **Gelber Muskateller Ratscher Nussberg 2002** Gross (€9.30)
8. **Grüner Veltliner Alte Reben 2002** Jurtschitsch (€12.90)
9. **Cuvée Rosso e Nero 2001** Pöckl (€15)
10. **Morillon Sulz 2002** Tement (€14)

MOST EXCITING OR UNUSUAL FINDS

1. **Moric 2001** Velich (€37) *A pure Blaufränkisch from old vines, and a beautiful illustration of what this grape can do.*
2. **Grüner Veltliner Kellerberg 2002** FX Pichler (€26.50) *A wine famous for its exotic notes on explosive aromatic extravagance, this vintage shows the Kellerberg and its most famous champion unusually floral and introverted, but equally stunning.*
3. **Viognier 2002** Graf Hardegg (€33) *True to his image as a maverick, Peter Veyder-Malberg vinifies an extraordinary Viognier, showing a rich, almost waxy and exotic nose but, thanks to the Weinviertel climate, enough acidity to preserve elegance and focus.*
4. **Aurum Grüner Veltliner 2002** Josef Ehmoser (€14) *Experiments with barrique-fermented Grüner Veltliner are not always successful, but this example shows that Grüner Veltliner and wood can marry fantastically well.*
5. **Grüner Veltliner Loam 2002** Kurt Angerer (€12.80) *Coming almost from nowhere, Kurt Angerer has produced a stunning series of 2002s. This well-focused Grüner Veltliner shows his style.*
6. **Grüner Veltliner Tradition 2002** Schloß Gobelsburg (€12) *Made in traditional 1940s fashion – with fermentation with ambient yeasts and without temperature control in large, used oak and unfiltered – this wine of days gone by is not a marketing exercise but the result of winemaker Michael Moosbrugger's passion for history.*
7. **Cuvée Zieregg 2002** Domäne Müller (€10.50) *Often underestimated, this South Styrian domaine is one of the region's best – and most dynamic. This cuvée, aromatic yet powerful, of Muskateller, Riesling, Traminer, and Sauvignon Blanc builds on the old tradition of mixed vineyards.*
8. **Zierfandler Mandlhöh 2002** Stadlmann (€13) *No, this is not Zinfandel, but a white grape with great power, grown only in Austria's Thermenregion. With its notes of orange and punch, this is a beast of a wine.*
9. **Traminer Privat 2002** Leithner (€16.80) *A rose garden in a glass, powerful but well balanced.*
10. **Graubaurgunder 2002** Nachbaur (€8) *With only 12 ha, the wine-growing region of Vorarlberg, in the west of Austria, is smaller than many single producers elsewhere, but this Pinot Gris shows that it is wrong to ignore wines from this region.*

Eastern & Southeastern Europe

Dr Caroline Gilby MW

The big story is the expansion of the EU in May 2004 to include the wine-producing nations of Hungary, Cyprus, Slovenia, the Czech Republic, and Slovakia.

DR CAROLINE GILBY MW

The wine industries of these countries have distinctly mixed feelings about the future, as they face loss of subsidies, removal of tariff barriers, and increased competition in their home markets.

In Hungary, Dr George Rasko, president of Royal Tokaji and adviser to the Minister for Agriculture, reckons that Hungary will lose 20–30 per cent of its vineyards in the next 10 years, as the market has to face up to competition from cheap imports from Spain and France. The vineyards on the Great Plain making basic table wines will be unable to compete and many producers are expected to give up. The Hungarian state has been subsidizing new vineyards and replanting until now. Officially these rebates cover 50 per cent of a project's costs, though sources reckon that this can be as much as 80 per cent due to ineffective financial controls. Under the EU support system, subsidies will fall to around 30 per cent and are expected to be more rigorously policed. Hungary has now agreed on the registered vineyard area and quotas for planting rights. No overall expansion will be allowed. The government also has to implement a new wine law by May 2004 to meet EU requirements. Drafts are in circulation for consultation, but the current proposal is reported to be very

DR CAROLINE GILBY MW started her career as a research scientist working on plant tissue culture, but she left to join the wine trade. She became senior wine buyer for a major UK retail chain, covering Eastern Europe. She is now a freelance writer and independent consultant to the wine trade, and served four years on the Wine Standards Board. Caroline also lectures WSET Diploma students on tasting technique, vinification, and wine handling, and judges at international wine shows.

paternalistic, retaining considerable state control instead of devolving this to regional wine associations.

In Cyprus, the future in the EU looks bleak according to Akis Zambartas, MD of Keo, the largest wine company. Subsidies of €300 per hectare (ha) (rising to €550 in poor years) have been paid, along with fixed minimum grape prices (including a 25 per cent margin paid by the government). Producers have also been earning significant subsidies on exported wines, mainly low-cost bulk wine destined for the EU. These subsidies will be abolished from May 2004, though a little support from the EU may be available on a diminishing scale until 2007. The end result will probably be a significant loss of vineyards.

Slovenia sees EU membership as a challenge for its big-volume producers, who produce bulk and variable-quality wine for local consumption. On the positive side, restrictions on bringing in planting materials should be eased.

For Bulgaria and Romania, Europe is the big story too, since in December 2003 the EU confirmed their joining date as January 2007, provided they are ready. The race is on to identify and register vineyards, benefit from EU funding programmes, and bring wine regulations into line.

Grapevine

• **The world's oldest wine** has been found in Georgia, according to Prof Patrick McGovern of the University of Pennsylvania in his book *Ancient Wine: The Search for the Origins of Viniculture* (2003). Analysis of wine residues found in ancient pottery shows that Neolithic humans were making wine 8,000 years ago and deliberately adding antibacterial tree resins to preserve it.

• **Cricova-Acorex in Moldova** has received certification from Swiss company SGS for its organic vineyards from 2003. It has also invested over €700,000 in updated winery equipment and has established two joint ventures with grape-growing cooperatives.

• **Privatization in Crimea** has been abandoned, since wine is the second-largest foreign-currency generator for the regional government.

• **In Ukraine**, the legendary Massandra Winery is expected to open its cellars for another sale from its library collection in spring 2004. The collection contains more than one million bottles dating back to 1775 and its current value is estimated at $150 million.

• **Renowned Bulgarian** winemaking partnership Dimitar Panov and Kapka Georgieva moved from Stork Nest Estates to Boyar Estates' premium Korten Winery for the 2003 vintage.

• **Romania's Recaş winery** hired David Lockley, winemaker at Yonder Hill in Stellenbosch, to help with vinification of red wines in 2003. Substantial investment has also gone into additional cooling capacity, nitrogen blanketing, and tourist facilities.

• **Carl Reh (Romania)** is spending €1 million on new winery equipment in 2004. It will also plant new areas of Sauvignon Blanc and Pinot Grigio to meet booming demand.

• **Dobogó Winery in Tokaj** will make its first dry wine in 2003. The final blend is yet to be decided, but will probably include Furmint, Hárslevelű, and Muscat.

DOLLARS TO RESTORE TOKAJI GLORY

Across Eastern Europe, foreign money and foreign know-how are the driving forces in improving wines and vineyard management. Hungary's Tokaj region has been the main recipient of high-profile foreign cash. This trend has continued with the grand opening of a new state-of-the-art winery by Árvay in October 2003. Connecticut-based expats Christian and Andrea Sauska have invested US$4 million as part of their aim to "bring back the glory days of Tokaji". They chose to work with Janos Árvay both for his forward-thinking attitudes and the parcels of over 100 ha of vines he has accumulated. Severe crop selection and thinning down to just 700 g (1 lb 9 oz) per vine are key parts of Árvay's approach and are the inspiration behind the brand name Hétfürtös, meaning 'seven clusters'.

FOREIGN INVESTMENT IN BULGARIA CATCHES UP

In May 2003, a multimillion-dollar deal to buy Vinprom Svishtov was announced by a group of private investors led by outspoken Aussie Lou Ghirardello, head of foreign exchange at Deutsche Bank. Now renamed Stork Nest Estates, it is the only winery in Bulgaria with a sizable vineyard holding. There are 428 ha already under vine, with another 300 ready to be planted.

Stork Nest is one of the few Bulgarian wineries that understands the term 'canopy management'. Ghirardello's plan is to produce a wine that will "stop people dead in their tracks". Aussie winemakers Linda Domas and Trevor Tucker have been signed up from the 2003 vintage and have completely scrubbed down the old concrete winery. Early tastings show a

Grapevine

• **The Royal Tokaji Wine Company** has made its first late-harvest wine after years of refusing to consider this type of product. It will be called Áts Cuvée, after the winemaker Karoly Áts, and there will be around 3,000 cases of 2003. Peter Vinding-Diers has not had his contract renewed and is no longer involved with the company.

• **Slovak Tokai?** The EU is ready to consider Slovakia's request for the recognition of the Slovak Tokai trademark. Slovakia has around 900 ha of Tokai vineyards, but Hungary is prepared to recognize only one-ninth of this and has raised objections on the grounds of quality.

• **Viticulture is in a state of crisis** in the province of Kosovo, and the UN has put a support plan in place with the aim of developing a private sector of growers and producers to clear current wine stocks and to improve future quality.

• **Fanagoria winery,** the largest winery within Russia's grape-growing regions, produced its first wine in 2003 from vines imported from France (planted in 1998).

• **Privatization in Moldova continues** with the sale, in September 2003, of Nis-Struguras winery to Russian company Parom Moscow for $1.5 million. In October it was reported that only one offer from an unnamed bidder had been received for the Vinuri-Ialoveni Winery.

welcome improvement in fruit quality and tannin ripeness.

Other deals include the sale of Vini Sliven to Cypriot company Greenlane Consulting (though rumours suggest this may not be the ultimate owner). Boyar Estates sold the assets and wine stocks of Rousse winery to Russian MMVZ (Moscow Inter-Republican Winery) in November 2003 for an unconfirmed €4.6 million (which follows their earlier sale of Vinis Iambol to spirits and rakia producers Peshtera). French group Belvedere, which bought Domain Menada, Oriachovitza, and Domain Sakar in early 2003, recently acquired the export agency Vinimpex from the state for 2.7 million leva. Vinimpex will act as trade agent in a number of export markets for several leading wineries, and it also owns Sophia, the leading Bulgarian brand in Scandinavia. On a much smaller scale, German-based wine importer Ivo Genowski has bought 40 ha near Nessebar on the Black Sea coast for his Santa Sarah 'garage' wines.

MOLDOVA ATTRACTS AMERICANS

Moldova, currently Europe's poorest country, has recently been the recipient of American money. Napoli Enterprises acquired Lion-Gri, one of Moldova's largest producers, in July 2003 and has set about a complete renovation of its wineries and is planting extensive new vineyards. Lion-Gri crushed 30,000 tonnes in 2003 and the Australian consultant Jon Worontshak has been brought in to oversee winemaking. In general, Moldova is finding it hard to attract much-needed foreign investment. Wine accounts for 25 per cent of its export revenues, but, with neo-communists in power, along with allegedly high levels of fraud and bribery, Moldova is a difficult investment environment.

Grapevine

• **Russian mining-to-metals** conglomerate Ariant has purchased control of Russia's most famous winery, the Krasnodar sparkling-wine producer Abrau Durso. It is rumoured that Ariant has also tied up grape supplies covering 50–80 per cent of the region's production. It has also picked up Kuban Vino, which bottles imported bulk wine for the local market, and Mirny winery, a former state wine farm with 600 ha.

• **Turkish wine is to feature** in a new three-nation blend. Chris Cameron of Peppertree Wines in the Hunter Valley will launch his Anzac brand in April 2005, blending Sauvignon Blanc from the 2004 vintage in Australia and New Zealand with Turkish Sauvignon Blanc harvested in September 2004. A red is due to follow in 2006.

• **Cypriot vineyards are shrinking.** The total vineyard area fell from 16,605 ha in 2002 to 15,854 ha in 2003, despite new plantations of 506 ha.

• **British-owned Halewood Romania** has sold its Ceptura winery to a Moldovan company, Vinaria Bostavan.

• **Hungary's famous red-wine area** of Villány plans to introduce an appellation-type system to be called Villányi Eredetvédelmi Rendszer. This is a two-tier system that will be stricter than national law in specifying density of vineyards, varieties, yields, and bottling within the region.

The countries of Eastern and Southeastern Europe must learn to communicate clear, positive messages about their identities and their wines. Few wine drinkers in the West know where these countries are, let alone what their wines are all about. This all comes down to lack of communication.

Stop the bickering

Each country needs to encourage its producers to work together and support each other in the way Australia and New Zealand have done so successfully.

Embrace the future

Looking backwards and inwards is a major failing in most of Eastern and Southeastern Europe and must be addressed. Many Bulgarians, particularly those over 40, still feel life was better under communism. The old industrial grape-processing mentality still comes over strongly in wineries that want to show off their latest heavy machinery. Unlike most wine nations, which whisk visitors straight to the vineyards, international wine judges visiting in June 2003 had to ask to visit a vineyard. In Slovenia, young producers complain that vested interests make it very difficult to join the official tasting-commission panels. Prospective new tasters are required to pass an exam and attend 40 weekly sessions for experience before they can join. In Romania, the Bucharest International Wine Competition in November 2003 caused uproar by awarding the only double gold to a 1974 Furmint, very few bottles of which remain. Several other old wines were also given awards, prompting Vinarte to send back its diploma in protest at a competition that rewards wines that are ancient history for Romania.

Free the wineries

The requirement to impose wine laws in line with the EU brings a real danger of crystallizing winemaking practices as they are now. The wine industries in the former communist bloc are barely a decade old in their current form, and the change from churning out vast quantities of so-so wine to pour down thirsty Soviet throats is still recent. Hungary is still discovering its potential for local varieties like Kadarka, and producers are working with Pinot Noir, Syrah, and Cabernet Franc to identify the country's red strengths. Yet the proposed new wine law seems likely to tie producers in knots. Romania's recently revised DOC laws control minimum sugar levels, permitted varieties, and so on in very specific detail, yet are useful only in selling to the German market. They restrict high-quality varieties like Syrah (which is not an approved grape for Romania) but allow local growers to replant poor-quality hybrids. Steve Donnelly at the English-owned Carpathian Winery finds dealing with regulations and inspections a nightmare.

Divided they fall

Fragmented land holdings and lack of integration remain enormous problems across the region. Privatization in Bulgaria has been disastrous for agriculture and the vines are in a shockingly poor state. Even the area of vineyards is in dispute, with estimates varying wildly from around 90,000 ha to 140,000 ha. Privatization handed back vines in tiny plots to pre-communist-era owners. These are too small to provide a living and often remote from the owners' homes. Lack of know-how, no economies of scale or commercial interest, along with a 'something for nothing' culture result in little attention being paid to fruit quality – and it shows in the wines.

Hope for the future?

The countries in Eastern and Southeastern Europe have an enormous job in front of them. Quality and consistency must be put right, not just by a few icon producers, but across the board. Wineries must learn to work together to promote, educate, and raise awareness of their wines, while government and state regulators need to support go-ahead producers, not tie them up in regulations. The first step is to introduce decent records and encourage vineyard consolidation to allow producers the chance either to control their own fruit or at least to work with growers who are big enough to be professional.

Grapevine

- **An aerial survey** of Slovenian vineyards has been commissioned to get to the bottom of the country's missing vineyards. Official figures suggest 25,000 ha exist, but only 15,500 have been registered.

- **In Croatia,** official statistics claim 59,000 ha of vines, but only 13,000 are reckoned to be in active production, with black-market wines and home consumption accounting for the discrepancy.

Advance report on the latest harvest
2003

A year marked by the hot, dry summer across Europe, with most countries reporting particularly good results for reds and a very early start to the harvest.

In Bulgaria, severe cold spells in April hit harvest volumes in the north of the country; yields in the south were high, so overall yields were average. Quality is reported as very good, with high levels of sugar and polyphenols at harvest, but with unusually high acidity levels. Over the border, in Romania, most of the country was hit by extreme winter cold and April frosts, damaging many vines. Young vines in the western areas of Banat and Mehedinti-Vranju Mare suffered from drought, but the quality is very good. Dealul Mare was badly hit by drought at flowering, causing very poor fruit set on top of frost damage, with hailstorms and heavy rain in the second week of August adding to the problems. Average yields across the country, although some growers were down by 90 per cent in Dealul Mare, with Merlot particularly hard hit.

In Russia, Charles Borden reports that the harvest in Krasnodar is the best in years. The Taman subdistrict harvested almost double last year's total. In Moldova, the 2003 harvest is 25 per cent higher than last year. A good fruit set was followed by a mostly warm summer with some rain in June. Warm days in August were balanced by cool nights, giving very concentrated flavours. Quality is reported as excellent; the vintage is the best in five years.

Slovenia felt the effect of the drought and is generally 5 per cent down on the already-small 2002 vintage, although producers in Brda are 20 per cent down. It was a very early vintage with extremely high-quality reds (the best ever, some say), though some whites suffered from low acidity.

Tokaj in Hungary also suffered from some April frosts, followed by a warm dry season with drought affecting vines on free-draining soils. It was a long picking season, with a lower *aszú* yield than expected, possibly due to a lack of foggy mornings. Generally regarded as a good to very good year, but without the balancing acidity of 1999 and not as rich in sugar as 2000. Very good to outstanding results are reported for dry and late-harvest wines. The rest of Hungary reports excellent reds and intense fruit flavours in whites, though low acidity in some varieties. In Croatia, the harvest was the earliest in the last 100 years. Extreme heat and low rainfall reduced vigour and gave small concentrated berries. Overall, 2003 here is a year with lots of extract, alcohol, and excellent quality.

Cyprus also reports one of the best vintages in recent years and good quantities. In Slovakia, careful canopy management was required to prevent white varieties suffering from sunburn and the drought in August stopped assimilation and delayed ripening. Picking of Riesling in the south of the country was delayed until October, when grapes were in perfect condition. Reports from Ukraine are of a generally poor summer, though western growing areas had a good vintage in both quantity and quality.

Updates on the previous five vintages

2002

Vintage rating: *80 (except Bulgaria, SE Romania)*
(Red: 75, White: 80, Sweet: 85)

A mixed year, ranging from outstanding in Romania's Transylvanian region to below average in areas such as northern Bulgaria and southeastern Romania, which were hit by heavy rains. In Hungary, wines are very concentrated, with whites especially good and reds above average, but Tokaj hopes for a great *aszú* vintage were dashed by rain, although early-harvested wines are very good. In Romania, most wines are very good, although up to 60 per cent of the crop around Murfatlar was rot damaged.

In Bulgaria, the whites are average and reds generally difficult. The vintage in neighbouring Macedonia is also described as difficult and will require careful selection. In Cyprus, quality is good, though down in volume. Unusually, Turkey was hit by rain around harvest, with wines affected by rot. Ukraine has produced promising reds, with good colour and sugar levels around Odessa. In Moldova, 2002 is a very good vintage showing good varietal character. Slovenian production is down, but sugar levels are good and quality high, although there was some rot in early whites.

2001

Vintage rating: *77 (Red: 80, White: 75, Sweet: 75)*

Mould development and poor flavours affected Tokaji wines, although some decent *aszú* wines have been made with ultra-careful selection. Elsewhere in Hungary, early-picked whites and late-picked reds were of sound quality. In Romania it was a good ripe year, while Bulgaria suffered from a second year of drought, reducing crops by as much as 50 per cent. Some producers report good wines, but vines in poor condition shut down and failed to ripen.

2000

Vintage rating: *85 (Red: 85–90, White: 80, Sweet: 90)*

A very good vintage across Hungary, although the wines are maturing quickly due to low acidity levels. In Tokaj, the grapes were blessed with huge sugar levels and great flavours. One of the finest recent vintages in Romania, showing ripe, healthy fruit, balanced acidity, and good keeping potential. A very good year in Bulgaria too, with disease-free fruit and high sugars, though dependent on vineyard management.

1999

Vintage rating: *90 (Red: 85–90, White: 80, Sweet: 95)*

Another classic Tokaji year of excellent quality, with really concentrated *aszú* berries and intense fruit acids giving superb balance, elegance, and keeping potential. Also a very good year for reds in Hungary. Romanian reds are also very good, uniformly ripe with high sugars and good acidity. International red varieties in Bulgaria (especially Cabernet and Merlot) did best in this high-quality vintage.

1998

Vintage rating: *75 (Red: 75, White: 75, Sweet: 75)*

In Tokaj, the *aszú* wines are light in body and quick developing. Not an easy vintage across the rest of Hungary, and difficult also in Bulgaria. In Romania, an extended drought resulted in very tannic, high-acid reds and small quantities.

Grapevine

- **Sixty per cent of wine** imported by Russia is Moldovan, yet random tests in Moscow have revealed that 7 per cent of the wines sampled were not up to Russian state standards and one wine contained artificial colouring E122.

- **Renowned German producer** Egon Müller has released his second vintage of Château Belá Riesling from Slovakia. He says that this is the style of wine he always intended to make – much drier, full-bodied, and intense.

- **Vylyan Winery** reports its first harvest of Syrah from plantings in 2001. The wine is "very beautiful", according to Monika Debreczeni.

- **In Bulgaria, Marc Dworkin** reports that he has made the first vintage from his Bessa Valley project at Ogianovo, near Plovdiv. The vineyard has been planted with Merlot, Petit Verdot, Malbec, and Syrah. Only 6,000 bottles of the 2003 were made.

GREATEST WINE PRODUCERS

Tokaji
1. Szepsy
2. Királyudvar
3. Domaine de Disznókő
4. Royal Tokaji Wine Company

Other wines
1. Edi Simčič (Slovenia)
2. Marjan Simčič (Slovenia)
3. Movia (Slovenia)
4. Atila Gere (Hungary)
5. Château Belá (Slovakia)
6. Vinarte (Romania)

BEST-VALUE PRODUCERS

1. Chateau Vincent (Hungary)
2. Vinarium Szekszárdi (Hungary)
3. Nyakas Winery (Budai) (Hungary)
4. Hilltop Neszmély Winery (Hungary)
5. Carl Reh Winery (Romania)
6. Prahova Wine Cellars (reds only, Romania)
7. Recaş (Romania)
8. Nagyréde Winery (Hungary)
9. Carpathian Winery (Romania)
10. Chapel Hill (Balaton-Boglar Winery, Hungary)

FASTEST-IMPROVING PRODUCERS

1. Stork Nest Estates (Bulgaria)
2. Carl Reh Winery (Romania)
3. Recaş Winery (Romania)
4. Domaine Szeremley (whites only, Hungary)
5. Cricova-Acorex (Moldova)
6. SERVE (Romania)
7. Prahova Wine Cellars (reds only, Romania)
8. Georgian Wines and Spirits Company (Georgia)
9. Keo (Cyprus)
10. Sodap (Cyprus)

GREATEST-QUALITY WINES

Tokaji
1. **Tokaji 6 Puttonyos 1999** Szepsy (16,800 forints, not released)
2. **Tokaji Cuvée 2000** Szepsy (12,600 forints, not released)
3. **Aszú Essencia 1995** Royal Tokaji Wine Company (42,000 forints)
4. **Tokaji Aszú 6 Puttonyos 1999** Domaine de Disznókő (12,000 forints)

Other wines
1. **Duet Riserva 2000** Edi Simčič (Slovenia, SIT 8,500)
2. **Chardonnay Riserva 2000** Marjan Simčič (Slovenia, SIT 2,640)
3. **Pinot Noir 1998** Movia (Slovenia, SIT 6,000)
4. **Cabernet Franc 2000** Bela Vincze (Hungary, 5,000 forints)
5. **Merlot 1999** Tilia (Slovenia, SIT 3,099)
6. **Pinot Gris 2002** Edi Simčič (Slovenia, SIT 3,800)

NEW UP-AND-COMING PRODUCERS

1. Santa Sarah (Bulgaria)
2. Árvay & Co (Tokaji, Hungary)
3. Tilia (Slovenia)
4. Dobogó (Tokaji, Hungary)
5. Maxxima (Bulgaria)
6. SERVE (Romania)
7. GIA (Hungary)
8. Sutor (Slovenia)
9. Damianitza (Bulgaria)
10. Assenovgrad (Swedish Project Wines, Bulgaria)

BEST BARGAINS

1. **Cabernet Sauvignon Sinai Hill 2000** St Donatus (Hungary, 2,500–2,700 forints)
2. **Tokaji Szamarodni 1999** Domaine de Disznókő (Hungary, 3,200 forints)
3. **Merlot 2000** La Cetate (Romania, 160,000–200,000 lei)
4. **Extra Brut 2000** Chateau Vincent (Hungary, 2,100–2,300 forints)
5. **Chardonnay 2002** Budai (Hungary, 960–1,100 forints)
6. **Pinot Noir Reserve 2000** Prahova Wine Cellars (Romania, 135,000–150,000 lei)
7. **Pinot Noir 2003** Recaş Winery (Romania, 90,000–100,000 lei)
8. **Barrel Fermented Chardonnay 2002** Chapel Hill (Hungary, 800–1,000 forints)
9. **Merlot 2000** Cherry Tree Hill (Romania, 635,000–700,000 lei)
10. **Cabernet Rosé 2002** Nagyréde (Hungary, 750–800 forints)

MOST EXCITING OR UNUSUAL FINDS

1. **Cabernet Sauvignon Bin 40 2002** Santa Sarah (Bulgaria, 50 leva) *German-based wine importer Ivo Genowski has set up his own winery in a rented garage. The Bin 40 is supple and appealing, a world away from the harsh green tannins of so many Bulgarian reds.*
2. **Swallowtail Fetească Neagră Gran Riserva 2001** Vinarte (Romania, 380,000 lei) *The Romanians have high hopes of their local Fetească Neagră or 'Black Maiden' grape. Italian-backed Vinarte produces the best example so far.*
3. **Ententa 2001** Assenovgrad (Bulgaria, 25 leva) *Swedish winemaker Lars Torstenson (of Domaine Rabiega in Provence) has been making wines with Bulgarian native grapes since 2001 in a purpose-built micro-winery. This is an impressive, big, but stylish blend of Cabernet, Mavrud, and Rubin.*
4. **Redark Merlot 2001** Damianitza (Bulgaria, 30 leva) *Dramatic, intense Merlot made by Marc Dworkin of Château Bellefont-Belcier in St-Emilion. One of Bulgaria's finest.*
5. **Leonardo Passito 1999** Marjan Simčič (Slovenia, SIT 9,600) *A real labour of love, just 380 half-bottles from 1 ha of Ribolla vines. The grapes are dried for six months and then vinified into this luscious, figgy, complex, sweet wine.*
6. **Kéknyelű 2002** Domaine Szeremley (Hungary, 2,290 forints) *The almost-extinct 'blue stem' grape shows its potential for quality from one of Hungary's most promising white-wine producers.*
7. **Pinot Noir 2001** Tibor Gal (Hungary, 3,500 forints) *Pinot Noir should have great potential in Hungary, and this fragrant, silky, elegant example shows real promise.*
8. **Ryzlink Vlašský Ice Wine 2001** Mikros-Vin (Czech Republic, 813 korunas) *Laski Rizling as never experienced before. Not generally regarded as a grape of much class, but here it shows real intensity.*
9. **Uniqato Rubin 2002** Damianitza (Bulgaria, 20 leva) *A unique Bulgarian cross of Nebbiolo and Syrah, only recently grown commercially. The Bulgarians believe it could be their Pinotage, and this wine shows that it can produce attractive, dark-fruited, velvety wines.*
10. **Pinot Blanc Late Harvest 2002** Kolby (Czech Republic, 210 korunas) *A Pinot Blanc with surprising depth and intensity.*

Until now, teaching about wine in Greece has been based on theory and presented by academics who were gifted but sorely lacking in practical modern winemaking experience.

NICO MANESSIS

Change could not be more timely, since a new, younger generation of applied-research teachers and experienced oenologists has been nominated to key teaching chairs. Among them is George Kotseridis, who teaches at the Agriculture Faculty of Athens University, and Efi Hadjidimitriou, the most highly qualified oenologist of her generation, at Thessaloniki University. Shortly they will be joined by leading consulting viticulturist Stephanos Koundouras, who has several vineyard-driven model ventures to his credit. He will be a lecturer.

It's all Greek to the Americans

The first-ever Greek wine promotion in the US is up and running in the Olympic year, which is crucial for exposure. All About Greek Wine is the brainchild of Sophia Perpera, oenologist and past director of the Greek Wine Federation, who moved to the US two years ago. She has achieved the admirable feat of putting under one roof 16 proactive wineries, mostly boutique estates or medium-sized producers. They have joined forces to promote the image of Greek wine, which is generally

NICO MANESSIS is the author of *The Illustrated Greek Wine Book* (Olive Press, 2000) and the three editions of *The Greek Wine Guide* (Olive Press, 1994, 1995, 1996). He teaches at the Université du Vin in France and has been writing articles on the wines of his native Greece for more than 10 years. Nico is based in Geneva, where he is a member of the Académie Internationale du Vin.

unknown in America. To nobody's surprise, this initiative will be funded by the participating wineries.

A series of tastings and workshops targeting wine-service professionals has now begun in New York, Washington (DC), Atlanta, Aspen, and San Francisco. Real interest has emerged, especially from sommeliers, who have been charmed by food-friendly Greek grape varieties such as white Assyrtiko, Robola, and Rhoditis, and the semi-aromatic Malagousia and Moschofilero. Of the reds, Agiorgitiko and Xinomavro have made an impression – mustering, respectively, descriptions such as "Merlot with spice" and "Nebbiolo with a Pinot Noir nose". There are hopes – tempered with realism – of carving a niche position for quality Greek wine in the important US market.

Isle of dreams

Alexandros Avatangelos, partner in Paris Sigalas's Santorini winery, has planted vineyards on nearby Tinos, another Cycladic island. Situated near the village of Falatado on a 680-m (2,200-ft) plateau, the vineyards have terraced schistous and clay soils totalling 12 hectares (ha). The finest of the Cycladic white varieties, Assyrtiko, is densely planted and trellis-pruned. The red grapes are an inspired choice of Avgoustiatis, Mavrotragano, the obscure dark Thrapsa, and the rare and little-seen Limniona, which has impressive ageing potential. Morning fog shrouds the vineyard in summer before burning off. There is no rush to harvest the first vintage – perhaps in 2007, says Avatangelos, since "we aim to produce no-expense-spared fine wine". Will this important island-vineyard venture start a trend?

Sun god lands in Nemea

Domaine Helios is the name of the latest high-profile winery to open its doors in Nemea, Greece's largest red-wine appellation. A joint venture by veteran vintner George Kokotos and wine-loving banker Mihalis Salas, Domaine Helios is situated at 700 m (2,300 ft) above the village of Koutsi, surrounded by breathtaking views of Mount Killini-Ziria and the Gulf of Corinth. The 1,200-ton-capacity winery has spared no expense. It boasts a helicopter pad and guesthouse accommodation.

From little acorns…

A growing number of schools in and around Thessaloniki have now added winery visits to their outings. Leading the way is Ktima Gerovassiliou, with 3,800 pupils passing through the cellars of this stellar estate in Epanomi each year. Though no tasting is offered, different levels of presentation have been devised according to age groups, which range from 12 to 18. Seniors are shown an in-house video of step-by-step grape-farming and wine-production procedures.

New learning centre

Skouras Wines has built a new 3,500-sq-m (38,000-sq-ft) winery at Panorama Argolidos, on the border of the Nemea appellation. George Skouras, ever the communicator, has focused on education and has built a learning centre for restaurateurs and other wine professionals. The winery is also geared to wine tourism, welcoming groups for tastings, food-and-wine workshops, and other events.

Emery overhauls

Emery Wines, on the island of Rhodes, pioneered wine tourism in the early 1980s. It now receives 300,000 visitors a year, making it Greece's most visited winery. A major overhaul of winemaking equipment at the winery in Emponas, Mount Attavyros, has been carried out. The 1923 distillery, by the port town of Rhodes, has also been converted to a wine centre.

Grapevine

• **Samos Cooperative,** which produces the most-exported Greek wine, Samos Muscat, has encouraged farmer members to convert 15 ha spread throughout the island's terraced and densely planted vineyards to organic viticulture. Two organic labels have been launched: a fortified *vin doux*, with 15 per cent ABV and 200 g of residual sugar per litre, and the dry Dorissa, at 12 per cent ABV.

• **An ampelographic** and genetic study of western Greece's indigenous grape varieties has been commissioned and funded by the Ministry of Development, subsidized by the EU. Carried out by a consortium of researchers, academics, and a leading nursery, the programme aims to save the biodiversity of a rich gene pool.

• **The leading boutique wineries,** which have been building their brands over the past 10 years, have introduced ex-cellar prices. This will modernize the antiquated three-tier system of marketing and distribution by cutting out the wholesaler and selling directly to the retail trade.

Thirty years after the first appellations came into being, and subsequent to huge investments in winemaking equipment, the current generation of gifted winemakers is producing diverse wines in many styles from about 35 of the estimated 300 indigenous grape varieties. Now that the wine industry has (mostly) modernized production, the spotlight is turning to *terroir*: 80,000 ha of *Vitis vinifera* dot the Greek countryside, with a viticulturist's dream of soil types. Limestone on Cephalonia, volcanic ash on Santorini, sand in Amynteo, and schist in Halkidiki are but a few. Much of this rich diversity of soil is the result of seismic activity – for example, the mountains, where some of the best-known wine regions are situated at high altitudes. Though some imported grapes are struggling, indigenous varieties – some with hundreds of years of adapting to local conditions, others with thousands – are rich in mutation.

Work on soil mapping ought to start in two of the finest red-wine appellations – Naoussa and Nemea. In Naoussa, it is essential to map the subregions based on their soils. Naoussa is planted with one grape, the red Xinomavro. The soils of Ghianakohori and Polla Nera are marly conglomerates, Gastra and Fitia are serpentine, and Trilofos clay. All produce wines very different from each other and represent much more than a variation on a theme. Nemea also happens to be a monovariety region planted with Agiorgitiko. Here the vineyard's exposure varies, as does altitude: 350–700 m (1,150–2,300 ft). There is a patchwork of soils: rich-in-oxides red soil in Asprokampos and Ahladia, marl in Koutsi, clay loam in Ancient Nemea, and rocky limestone in Gymno. Not all vineyards and *terroir* are born equal. So, for both these appellations, the next step is the identification of *crus*. Furthermore, Nemea merits a high-Nemea appellation.

Update

Since *Wine Report 2004*, no foreign or joint ventures have materialized. It remains to be seen whether Greece's huge exposure during the Olympic Games will encourage interested parties to invest in the premium sector.

2003

Abundant rain from autumn through spring, with the added bonus of February–March snow, destressed nearly all the vineyards. Though budding got off to a late start, unhurried ripening benefited from a moderate summer with no heat waves. In all but two regions, Naoussa and Goumenissa, both imported and indigenous grape varieties produced exceptionally healthy, ripe, and balanced grapes – some appellations producing wines the likes of which have rarely been seen. The island vineyards of Santorini and Cephalonia are the best. Reduced grape yields in central Crete produced whites and reds showing the unrealized potential of Greece's southernmost island. Muscats from Limnos and Samos are terrific. Eastern Macedonia produced outstanding wines, especially from imported varieties. The finicky, late-ripening Xinomavro, affected by yields that were far too high, struggled to ripen fully in Naoussa and Goumenissa. Re-energized Amynteo experienced the finest vintage since 1994. Nemea, in the Peloponnese, produced deep-coloured fruity wines from the lower-altitude valley subregions. The quality from the hillside vineyards is exceptional. The delicate and aromatic light whites of Patras show uniform consistency and *terroir* expression.

Updates on the previous five vintages
2002

Vintage rating: *80 (Red: 75, White: 85)*

Drama, Kavala, and Epanomi wines are all very good, vibrant, and fruity. Elsewhere, a contrast of extremes was the case. Santorini harvested a fraction of its usual tonnage. Naoussa was a wash-out, with unripeness and widespread rot. Nemea was a disaster, although a couple of higher-elevation vineyards produced healthy grapes, albeit in small amounts and with less colour and body than usual. The unprecedented shortfall resulted in strong domestic demand for red wine, pushing up prices. Mantinia had little rot, good aroma, and satisfactory, if lower, levels of ripeness. Rhodes, which has the most eastern island vineyards, experienced the best vintage in years.

2001

Vintage rating: *89 (Red: 90, White: 89)*
Another very good vintage. Lower yields and higher acidities encouraged wines of notable quality in both colours. Crete, Cephalonia, and Santorini produced superb, crisp, dry whites. Attica vineyards equipped with drip irrigation excelled, following the previous year's heat wave, which had stressed Savatiano vines to their limits. Mantinia had one of its finest harvests, with a quantity and quality not seen since 1998. Standout reds are to be found everywhere. Naoussa wines are delicious, without the overripe jammy fruit found in the previous vintage. Those of Goumenissa are a little less ripe, though delicate. Nemea has produced atypical wines, the best of them characterized by an inspired combination of class and ethereal edge. Balanced Samos Muscats are a delight.

2000

Vintage rating: *90 (Red: 93, White: 88)*
A superlative vintage for red wines, with a rarely seen uniformity of healthy grapes in all regions. Some whites were at the limit of low acidity, but most were concentrated. Vineyards in Mantinia were generally stressed, causing an unusually rapid loss of aroma and fruit. Santorini came up with superb, *terroir*-driven, bone-dry whites, and Crete upped its white-wine profile significantly. In Drama, Merlots were somewhat over the top; elsewhere, they are keepers. Without a doubt, it was one of the greatest Naoussa and Nemea harvests on record, the like not seen since 1994 and 1990. Some Naoussa single vineyards went for broke and harvested overripe grapes, losing the character of their *terroir*. Phenolic maturity in Nemea was perfect. The wines are packed with fruit and the more structured top-notch labels will age up to 12 years. Amber Samos are a shade darker and duller on the palate, due to high temperatures and arid summer conditions.

1999

Vintage rating: *86 (Red: 85, White: 87)*
The quality was more inconsistent than poor. Santorini was mediocre, because this extreme microclimate was deprived of the cooling Meltemi north wind and experienced sporadic rot. Patras came up with good Rhoditis, illustrating that the eastern appellation's potential is being realized. In Mantinia, low levels of maturity confirmed that the 1998 crop was an impossible act to follow. Ktima Mercouri, the leading estate in Ilia, produced

a stunner from 120-year-old vines that could not have succeeded in a richer vintage. The traditional reds from Naoussa are delicately aromatic and will mature faster than those from 2000. Nemea wines are less good and not for ageing. Here the tables were turned for the lower-altitude valleys such as Gymno and Ancient Nemea, which had less frequent harvest showers and have outperformed the better-rated, higher Koutsi vineyards. The Aegean islands of Samos and Limnos produced fragrant wines from Muscat Blanc à Petit Grains and Muscat of Alexandria respectively.

1998

Vintage rating: *89 (Red: 89, White: 88)*

This was a more-than-decent vintage, with good quantity and sound quality. The microclimates highlighted differences. Several appellations made exceptionally good wines. Mantinia scaled new heights with good ripeness levels and very floral wines. A drop in yields in Naoussa made for more concentrated wines, following a series of mediocre harvests. In July, a week-long heat wave reduced the berry size of Agiorgitiko in Nemea, resulting in ultrasmooth tannins in all vineyards. Weather during harvest was near perfect, with dry, warm conditions late into autumn, allowing late-ripening, high-altitude vines to mature fully.

GREATEST WINE PRODUCERS

1. Ktima Gerovassiliou
2. Gaia Wines
3. Ktima Mercouri
4. Oenoforos
5. Biblia Hora
6. Ktima Alpha
7. Parparoussis
8. Sigalas
9. Tselepos
10. Samos Cooperative

FASTEST-IMPROVING PRODUCERS

1. Skouras
2. Gentilini
3. Ktima Pavlidis
4. Ampelones Sakelaridou

NEW UP-AND-COMING PRODUCERS

1. Douloufakis
2. Ktima Mountriha
3. Wine Art Estate
4. Tatsis Bros

BEST-VALUE PRODUCERS

1. Oenoforos
2. Parparoussis
3. Creta Olympias
4. Ktima Mercouri
5. Samos Cooperative
6. Ktima Founti
7. Tsantali
8. Boutari
9. Emery
10. Ktima Roxanne Matsa

GREATEST-QUALITY WINES

1. **Gaia Estate 2001**
   Gaia Wines (€18)
2. **Ktima Alpha White 2003**
   Alpha Estate (€12)
3. **Biblia Hora White 2003**
   Oinopedio (€8.50)
4. **Ktima Alpha Red 2002**
   Alpha Estate (€17.50)
5. **Thallasitis Santorini 2003**
   Gaia Wines (€10)
6. **Santorini Oia 2003**
   Sigalas (€9.50)
7. **Robola 2003** Gentilini (€9)
8. **Patras-Rio Muscat 1999**
   Parparoussis (€14)
9. **Chardonnay 2002**
   Ktima Pavlidis (€9)
10. **Samos Anthemis 1999**
    Samos Cooperative (€7.50)

BEST BARGAINS

1. **Semeli White 2003**
   Ktima G Kokotos (€4.50)
2. **Savatiano 2003**
   Magapanou (€4.50)
3. **Avantis Rhoditis 2003**
   Ktima Mountriha (€6.50)
4. **Xerolithia 2003**
   Creta Olympias (€5.80)
5. **Moschofilero 2003**
   Boutari (€4.90)
6. **Rapsani Epilegmenos Reserve 1998** Tsantali (€11.50)
7. **Samaropetra 2003**
   Ktima Kir Yanni (€7.30)
8. **Naoussa 2001**
   Ktima Founti (€6.50)
9. **Ktima Pavlidis White 2003**
   (€8.50)
10. **Avantis Syrah 2001**
    Ktima Mountriha (€11)

MOST EXCITING OR UNUSUAL FINDS

1. **Avaton 2002** Ktima Gerovassiliou (€11) *Warm fruit infused with herbs. Unique character. Despite being broader, it is reminiscent of Argentinian Malbec.*
2. **Pinot Noir 2001** Papaioanou (€9.50) *More sappy, earthy, rounded tannins; well oaked.*
3. **Petrino Kellari 1999** Megapanos (€16.50) *Full-bodied high-Nemea spicy Agiorgitiko, ageworthy structure.*
4. **Coma Verenices 2003** Ktima Mercouri (€11) *Made from 10-year-old Viognier vines. Striking apricot-stone fruit. Bottled three months after harvest.*
5. **Monemvasia Assyrtiko 2003** Ktima Moraiti (€9) *Two top Aegean-basin grapes. Floral, smoky, mineral-laden, tangy palate.*
6. **Lagorthi 2003** Oenoforos (€9.50) *Elegant, multilayered, aromatic nose, with grippy acidity. Lots of presence for only 11 per cent!*
7. **Plito 2003** Lyrarakis (€6.20) *A rare Cretan speciality in a super vintage. Citrus, juicy, truly fragrant. Concentrated.*
8. **Gentilini Rosé 2003** (€8.50) *Very ripe Moschofilero with a Muscat melon texture. Lime-chalky aftertaste. Dry.*
9. **Chardonnay 2003** Arvanitidi (€11.00) *Estate grown. Fresh with unflashy creamy richness. Refined.*
10. **Santorini Bareli 2002** Ktima Arghyrou (€10) *This comes from a tiny harvest. Compact, lime-honey, yeasty burgundian gloss.*

"The momentum is on and no one can stop it," declared one wine producer.

MICHAEL KARAM

"The Bordeaux and London fairs proved it, and the OIV [Office International de la Vigne et du Vin] congress in Beirut in 2005 will be our final test." Fighting talk indeed, reflecting the frustration, impatience, and ambition of a sector yearning to be recognized as a small, but serious, wine producer.

However, it was the same frustration, impatience, and ambition that finally persuaded Massaya to walk away from the UVL (Union Vinicole du Liban) in mid-January 2004. The producer, which played a major part in the renaissance of Lebanese wine, resigned after Lebanon's wine producers' association rejected an initiative to establish a wine-marketing board and launch a national advertising campaign.

Massaya maintained that action had to be taken to fight the growing domination of foreign wines on the local market, especially cheap Bulgarian varietals and high-end French labels. Massaya, which exports 70 per cent of its wine, predicted that, unless Lebanese wines were actively promoted at home, many producers would all but abandon the local market. The crunch will come when Lebanon honours its Euro-Med obligations in 2008, effectively making the country an open market for all European wines.

MICHAEL KARAM has lived in Lebanon since 1992. He is a business journalist and wine writer. His book *The Wines of Lebanon*, the first book ever written on the subject, will be published by Saqi Books in 2005.

This vote of no confidence in Massaya's proposal, and that company's subsequent resignation, is potentially damaging for such a small wine-producing country and deprives the UVL of one of its most effective ambassadors. Massaya will thrive with or without the UVL; its departure, on the other hand, devalues the credibility of the association and puts its president, Serge Hochar – who, it is said, fancies another try at the OIV presidency – in an awkward position, since Massaya will not now participate in the 2005 OIV congress.

- **Domaine des Tourelles,** one of the oldest names in Lebanese winemaking, has restarted commercial production after a hiatus of nearly 30 years. The winery, originally established by the French Brun family, enjoyed its heyday in the 1960s and early 1970s but turned its hand to making high-quality arak during the civil war. Current owner Elias Issa has invested $200,000 in new equipment from France and Italy and expects to produce 220,000 bottles from his 2004 harvest and one million bottles by 2009, with as much as 90 per cent earmarked for export to France, the US, and Canada.

- **Many Lebanese producers,** including newcomers Heritage and Chateau Fakra, have reported increased international demand for varietals, especially Cabernet Sauvignon and Syrah. This could prompt many of the smaller vineyards to tailor their production accordingly. However, such a 'New World' approach could blur an identity based on carefully blended wines and might lead to a two-tier wine sector: one boutique, one volume market. Domaine Wardy is Lebanon's biggest producer of varietals with five (Cabernet Sauvignon, Syrah, Merlot, Chardonnay, and Sauvignon Blanc) followed by Chateau Ksara (Cabernet Sauvignon and Chardonnay), Clos St Thomas (Chardonnay), and Chateau Fakra (Cabernet Sauvignon). Varietals currently make up 15 per cent of total Lebanese wine production.

- **Former *Decanter* Man of the Year** Serge Hochar, owner of Chateau Musar and president of the UVL, was unsuccessful in his bid for the presidency of the OIV. The old warrior, who is something of a hero in the wine world for his exploits of derring-do during the 15-year civil war, has said that he will not seek re-election. Industry insiders are not convinced. Watch this space.

- **Massaya continued to pioneer** the wine recreation/leisure trail by adding a series of sellout blues concerts in July and August 2003 to its already busy weekend itinerary of buffet lunches. The bug is contagious. Chateau Fakra is building what it calls a recreational wine-tasting centre at its winery in Kfardebian. Facilities will include a restaurant, conference rooms, minitheatre, wine shop, swimming pool, and gardens.

- **English oenologist Daniel Craker** has joined Massaya, the Franco-Lebanese collaboration between the Ghosn brothers and Hubert de Boüard de Laforest (coproprietor of Château Angélus), Dominique Hébrard (former coproprietor of Château Cheval Blanc), and Daniel and Frédéric Brunier (Domaine Le Vieux Télégraphe). Craker, who honed his skills in Jurançon, is not the first foreigner to make wine in the Bekaa, following as he is in the footsteps of the colourful Yves Mourad, who did much in the 1980s and 1990s to put Chateau Kefraya on the map.

Lebanese producers should improve viticulture methods, reduce yields, and utilize better-quality grapes. To do this, there will have to be significant replanting and restructuring of existing vineyards, the adoption of more up-to-date working methods, and the identification of new vineyards. This will mean further exploration of Lebanon's different regions and *terroir*, including a formal study of the various soil types and viticultural potential.

Bekaa Valley initiative

New vineyards have changed the lives of many of the Bekaa Valley's struggling farmers, who previously felt obliged to grow illegal hashish and opium, or fruit and vegetables that were severely undercut by those from neighbouring countries. Viticulture is changing the landscape of many towns as the demand for good *terroir* increases. There is no doubt that the current 1,500 hectares (ha) of vineyards could easily be expanded to 15,000. Producers talk of the Bekaa's 1,000-m (3,280-ft) plateau as a possible home to dozens of boutique wineries similar to those in the Napa Valley. In 1998, European experts pinpointed wine, olive oil, and honey as the most viable agro-industries. One wine producer told me that his biggest problem was producing enough wine to meet demand. "I could sell double," he shrugged. The government must put aside self-interest and blinkered dogma and launch an initiative that will create jobs, increase revenues, and raise the self-esteem of the country.

Identity crisis

The increased demand for varietals is worrying. Australia, Chile, and South Africa can get away with turning out correct but ultimately anonymous varietals because they have the production levels to fill the world's supermarket shelves; Lebanon doesn't. Its exports are nickel and dime by international standards, and if it ever produces 80 million bottles a year (it currently produces 6 million), it will still be only 1 per cent of French output. Lebanon needs to stick to producing wines with a distinct Lebanese identity (often expressed as the result of modern winemaking methods combined with the formidable Bekaa *terroir*) if it wants to compete in a niche market.

Buy Lebanese!

Although the export market is thriving, a national marketing campaign is essential. Any initiative should emphasize the quality of Lebanese wine, educate the drinker on the health benefits of drinking wine over, say, whisky or arak, and stress the economic importance of buying Lebanese. It should also target the tourist. Posters for Lebanese or Bekaa wine should be among the first images visitors see when they arrive at Beirut airport.

Getting the tourists back

Regional events, especially the 2003 invasion of Iraq, may have made Lebanon a haven for Arab visitors (the bulk of Lebanon's one million tourists come from Gulf Arab countries), but they have not helped Lebanon's fledgling wine-tourism sector, which targeted wealthy middle-aged Europeans in search of something a bit different. Since 9/11, the number of non-Arab tourists has dropped by 90 per cent. With a little imagination and vision, Lebanon's struggling wine route could be modified to include many of the country's cultural attractions. During the summer months, when Lebanon hosts its celebrated international music festivals, collaboration between the organizers and the UVL to tailor a mixed itinerary of music and wine could reap a lucrative harvest and promote Lebanon, its wine, and its festivals to a wider international audience.

Presenting well

Low volume is not necessarily a handicap. Lebanon can compete if positioned correctly. There are very small wineries in the New World with reputations that punch way above their weight and that sell limited quantities abroad. However, they have to look the part. Today's wine buyer is often as influenced by what's on the bottle as by what's inside it. Lebanese producers have to be educated in the importance of PR and have to be prepared to work (and spend) to create the right image and raise their profile. This message has filtered through to many, but not all, of Lebanon's wine producers. There are some stunning designs that would give the Californians and Australians a run for their money, but a lot of good wine is let down by poor and often garish labels. Lebanese wine is not cheap, and if Lebanese wine producers are to venture out of the restaurant sector and charge over £10 a bottle in the retail trade, they will have to improve their packaging. It is up to the UVL to encourage this.

No free publicity

Despite Lebanon's multisectarian make-up, religious tensions rarely arise when it comes to wine producing and grape growing. Since 1998 (the first year alcohol was officially served at the annual Baalbek Music Festival) there has been no overt hostility towards Lebanon's wine producers, and although Islamic MPs often abstain on parliamentary votes involving alcohol, they are nonetheless aware of the increasing economic benefits the wine sector offers their constituents. Despite this new climate of tolerance, sensitivities still persist. Visits from overseas heads of state provide perfect opportunities to promote Lebanon's best product, but they are never exploited. This is frustrating for the local producers, who feel that Lebanon's leaders should encourage their opposite numbers to sample Lebanese wine publicly. As one grower said, "If [Jacques] Chirac were seen drinking a glass of our wine, I would have no more wine to sell."

Grapevine

• **Beirut airport's** new duty-free shopping mall is selling more than 300 bottles of Lebanese wine each day. At an average price of $10 per bottle, annual revenues from that one outlet are over $1 million, making it Lebanese wine's best-performing retail outlet.

• **Chateau Kefraya** and Koroum Kefraya, which had been locked in dispute over the right to use the Kefraya name, have reached a settlement. Chateau Kefraya, the older of the two vineyards, retains the use of the name, while its rival will be known as Cave Koroum. The agreement paves the way for Cave Koroum to join the UVL.

• **Ksara** has invested $750,000 in its Bekaa winery and is committed to further corporate investment of $500,000 over the next three years as part of its final restructuring programme. It has also planted 7 ha of Syrah and Cabernet Franc vines. Elsewhere, Musar has leased another 50 ha of land in Amiq in the western Bekaa, while Kefraya has planted 43 ha of new grapes, including Chardonnay (3 ha), Viognier (5 ha), Syrah (15 ha), and Tempranillo (20 ha).

• **It has been a year of innovation** and increased production (25 per cent year-on-year growth in production) for Domaine Wardy. As well as producing Lebanon's first Christmas blend, owner Salim Wardy has produced a Premium Selection red and white with grapes from the highest vineyard in the Middle East (5,600 ft above sea level) and using the lowest yield (20–25 hl/ha). The reds are a blend of Syrah and Cabernet Sauvignon, while the whites are a blend of Viognier and Muscat.

• **Ex-Merrill Lynch investment banker** Naji Butros has adjusted his target and now expects to produce 130,000 bottles by 2008 at his recently established Chateau Belle-Vue in Bhamdoun, which is known more for its Gulf Arab tourists than its *terroir*. "The soil and the climate in Bhamdoun are perfect and we have great northeast-facing slopes," says Butros. He has planted Cabernet Sauvignon, Merlot, Syrah, Cabernet Franc, and Sauvignon Blanc vines purchased from France.

Advance report on the latest harvest

2003

Wine producers are reporting a unique harvest. The wettest winter in 15 years was followed by a 10-day heat wave in May, which contributed to a marvellous equilibrium between acidity and sugar content and an exceptional concentration of phenol compounds due to dry weather in September. The whites were aromatic with high acidity, producing vivid gunflint notes, finishing with a pleasant, mild, and unctuous taste, while the reds produced intense colour. They were more tannic than former vintages but with balanced, mellow tannins, supple and not astringent. All the different varietals are exceptionally fragrant and first indications are that the wines will be full-bodied and powerful with great length.

Updates on the previous five vintages

2002

Vintage rating: *90*

The year was full of surprises. After four successive years of drought, there was a long, cold, rainy winter, followed by a mild July and a hot August. The vines took longer to ripen their grapes and had high levels of sugar, acidity, and tannin. Grape maturity level varied from vineyard to vineyard, forcing growers to be selective in their picking. Fermentation went perfectly but, against all the odds, was very slow – therefore much longer – and the wines have turned out to be much bigger, riper, and fuller than expected.

2001

Vintage rating: *75*

According to Serge Hochar, 2001 was "a most bizarre year", with almost no rain and one of the earliest harvest dates in living memory. The crop was good, albeit 15 per cent down, with ripe fruits but without much tannin or acidity. Fermentation progressed well and the malolactic fermentation followed easily and naturally. The wines were easy and fruity, with good alcohol levels.

2000

Vintage rating: 75

The crop was healthy, although 15 per cent down, with grapes that were sweet yet tannic, and with good acidity. Alcohol levels were higher than usual – almost the same as 1999. It was an easy harvest and fermentation proceeded with hardly any problems. Malolactic fermentation followed its normal course. The wines were very well balanced, tannic, concentrated, and powerful.

1999

Vintage rating: 85

An exceptional year. The grapes reached maximum maturity with great all-round concentration, good acidity, and a high sugar level. These features were immediately apparent in the wine: very high alcohol, high acidity, and a lot of extract. The wines are highly concentrated; very rich, round, and full-bodied, with an exceptionally long finish. According to Serge Hochar, this was "really an exceptional year, perhaps the year of the millennium".

1998

Vintage rating: 70

For no apparent reason, some grapes were quite mature, while others could have waited two more weeks. The crop was typical, both in quality and quantity; grapes were in good shape with no problems or disease and good to eat. Fermentation went smoothly, but was quicker than usual. Results were good; 1998 was a very aromatic and fragrant year, but it lacked the body of 1997.

GREATEST WINE PRODUCERS

1. Chateau Musar
2. Chateau Kefraya
3. Chateau Ksara

FASTEST-IMPROVING PRODUCERS

1. Massaya
2. Domaine Wardy
3. Clos St Thomas
4. Chateau Ksara
5. Chateau Kefraya

NEW UP-AND-COMING PRODUCERS

1. Chateau Fakra
2. Heritage
3. Domaine des Tourelles
4. Clos de Cana
5. Cave Koroum

BEST-VALUE PRODUCERS

1. Chateau Ksara
2. Chateau Kefraya
3. Massaya
4. Domaine Wardy
5. Clos St Thomas
6. Chateau Fakra
7. Heritage
8. Vin Nakad

GREATEST-QUALITY WINES

1. Chateau Musar 1988 (LL 60,000)
2. Chateau Musar 1994 (LL 24,000)
3. Chateau Musar 1991 (LL 34,000)
4. Chateau Musar 1996 (LL 22,000)
5. Chateau Musar 1995 (LL 26,000)
6. Comte de M 1998 Chateau Kefraya (LL 46,000)
7. Comte de M 1999 Chateau Kefraya (LL 44,000)
8. Comte de M 2000 Chateau Kefraya (LL 42,000)
9. Chateau Ksara 1997 (LL 24,000)
10. Chateau Ksara 1998 (LL 21,000)

BEST BARGAINS

1. Chateau Kefraya 2001 (LL 20,000)
2. Blanc de Blanc 2003 Chateau Kefraya (LL 12,000)
3. Chateau Kefraya 2000 (LL 20,000)
4. Chateau Ksara 2000 (LL 15,000)
5. Hochar Père et Fils 2000 Chateau Musar (LL 14,000)

6. Réserve du Couvent 2003 Chateau Ksara (LL 10,000)
7. Classic Rosé 2003 Massaya (LL 8,000)
8. Syrah 2002 Domaine Wardy (LL 11,000)
9. Chardonnay 2002 Chateau Ksara (LL 18,000)
10. Les Emirs 2001 Clos St Thomas (LL12,000)

MOST EXCITING OR UNUSUAL FINDS

1. Selection 2002 Massaya (LL 13,000) *Big, juicy, and, lira for lira, the best red in town.*
2. Christmas Blend 2002 Domaine Wardy (LL 10,000) *A knockout! Exploding cinnamon and berries.*
3. Chateau Clos St Thomas 2000 (LL 20,000) *Unsung but packs a leathery punch of plums and tobacco.*
4. Cuvée de Printemps 2003 Chateau Ksara (LL 8,000) *A fabulous fruity summer red best served chilled.*
5. Reserve 2002 Massaya (LL 21,000) *Full-bodied and pulpy with notes of sandalwood and incense.*
6. Merlot 2002 Domaine Wardy (LL 11,000) *Great value. Spicy, plummy, and smoky.*
7. Chardonnay 2002 Clos St Thomas (LL 14,000) *Another unfancied runner that came in. Perfumed and wickedly flinty.*
8. Pinacle 2003 Chateau Fakra (LL 8,000) Vin de Table *that punches above its weight.*
9. Lacrima D'Oro 1995 Chateau Kefraya (LL 15,000) *Pudding wine with added eau de vie.*
10. Gris de Gris 2003 Chateau Ksara (LL 9,000) *Great value, full-bodied rosé.*

Israel

Daniel Rogov

Following an extended period in which the imagination of the wine-drinking public was captured by boutique wineries and *garagistes,* the last year might be regarded as the year of the major wineries.

DANIEL ROGOV

The Golan Heights Winery released the country's first varietal wines made from Sangiovese, Pinot Noir, and Gamay grapes, as well as the country's first oak-aged Syrah and first single-vineyard organically grown Chardonnay (which many hope will pave the way for future organic developments). Under its Yarden label, the winery also produced the country's first Semillon botrytis wine. Carmel, in its ongoing effort to woo more sophisticated wine drinkers, released a series of high-quality single-vineyard Cabernet Sauvignon, Syrah, and Chardonnay wines.

Not all of this is rosy, however, for after several years of what might be thought of as a mad rush by several wineries to plant as many grapes as possible, overplanting has led to a distinct grape glut. To that, one can add the distressing ongoing *Intifada* (uprising of the Palestinians) and a depressed economy, resulting in a consumer attitude that is largely motivated by value for money.

DANIEL ROGOV is the wine and restaurant critic for the Israeli daily newspaper *Haaretz* as well as for the Israeli version of the *International Herald Tribune.* He is the author of the recently released *Rogov's Guide to Israeli Wines* and is a regular contributor to *Hugh Johnson's Pocket Wine Book.* Rogov also publishes wine and gastronomic reviews and articles on his Internet site Rogov's Ramblings (www.stratsplace.com/rogov/home.html).

Ziv gets a grip

Now moving into his second year as CEO of Carmel, still the country's largest wine producer, it seems that David Ziv is exerting better control over the vineyards of the many independent growers affiliated with the winery. In these vineyards poor clones of Petite Sirah, Carignan, French Colombard, and Emerald Riesling are being replaced by Syrah, Zinfandel, Sangiovese, and Barbera. At the same time, to enhance quality, yields in vineyards producing Cabernet Sauvignon, Merlot, Chardonnay, and Sauvignon Blanc have been reduced dramatically.

Self-help

In what some perceive as a patriotic move to support the local wine industry, several prestigious restaurants have opted for all-Israeli wine lists, a chain of wine stores is considering opening branches that stock only local wines, and a new Internet site allows only Israeli wines as subjects for discussion. These initiatives have met with mixed reactions, some consumers responding enthusiastically and others regarding them as ethnocentric.

Downward trend?

The 90 boutique wineries and *garagistes* mentioned in last year's *Wine Report* have increased to more than 110, with another 15 on line to open in the near future. The numbers indicate that the popularity of such wineries may have peaked. Only a handful of these small wineries is included among the best producers in the country, and quite a few are now having problems selling their products. There is a chance that, within a year or two, their ranks will be reduced by anywhere from 30 to 50 per cent.

New wineries launched

Two new small- to medium-sized wineries are scheduled to release their first wines in the coming months – the independent Ella Vineyards, located on Kibbutz Netiv Halamed Hey in the Ella Valley (not far from the town of Beit Shemesh), and Yatir, a joint venture between Carmel and the cooperative village of Beit Yatir in the Judean Mountains. Advance and barrel tastings indicate that both wineries have high potential for releasing quality wines from Cabernet Sauvignon, Cabernet Franc, Merlot, Pinot Noir, Syrah, Petite Sirah, and Zinfandel. Both wineries are hoping to export at least 50 per cent of their production.

Since the country has no proper regulatory body and no valid appellation-control system, labelling and bottling procedures at some wineries are done in an unprofessional, even haphazard, manner. Wines continue to be bottled in batches – sometimes over a period of several months, sometimes over a period of a year or more – and there is no guarantee that even the same blend is used from batch to batch. In some cases, it is difficult to tell precisely what is in the bottle at all. A bottle labelled as Cabernet Sauvignon may at times have aromas and flavours that are remarkably similar to wines containing large amounts of Carignan or Argaman grapes.

Let's get professional

Good Israeli wines are already noted for their quality, but what is missing is a central body that will ensure orderly growth and increased sales, both locally and abroad. Perhaps the most important step would be to replace the obsolete and ineffective Wine Institute with a new institute that could function via fully fledged wine laws. The new institute should act both as a proper regulatory body (with control over defining a proper appellation system as well as regulating bottling and labelling) and as an industry representative. Such a body should also have a public-relations function, publishing and distributing educational, promotional, and statistical materials; marketing and promoting Israeli wines abroad; and representing the industry at wine fairs and seminars. The new institute should conduct serious research on determining which grapes are best suited to different subregions within the country and should encourage an atmosphere of cooperation among local wineries.

Never mind the quality, feel the price?

Until now, no winery has been brave enough to lower prices of the wines in their more prestigious series from one year to another to reflect shifts in quality. Considering the truly problematic 2002 vintage, the time for such a move may have come. As of this writing, only one winery, Amphorae, is considering making such a move. It is time for the wineries to fall more in line with international pricing policies that allow prices to rise or fall, depending on quality.

Advance report on the latest harvest
2003

A cold and wet winter with precipitation about one-third higher than normal was followed by unusually warm weather in May, leading to strong and rapid shoot growth and a hectic month of shoot positioning. Due to moderate and stable summer temperatures, the harvest stretched out to 17 weeks, concluding on 18 November. Overall, an excellent vintage year for both reds and whites.

Updates on the previous five vintages
2002

Vintage rating: *78*

In the north of the country, the warm weather in February and March, followed by a particularly cold spell in April and May, lengthened the ripening season and resulted in an extended 15-week harvest. May rains during blooming caused a 15 per cent reduction in yields. In the rest of the country, several prolonged hot spells caused some vineyards to lose as much as 80 per cent of their crop. Overall, only a few acceptable wines, and even fewer appropriate for long-term cellaring.

2001

Vintage rating: *85*

This was one of the earliest harvest years in recent history. Overall, a better year for reds than whites.

2000

Vintage rating: *89*

Fortunately the harvest was on schedule, since torrential rains hit the area just after picking. Had the crop been delayed, it would have been under the coldest and wettest conditions for the past quarter of a century. Whites and reds fared equally well during this good vintage.

1999

Vintage rating: 86

Early budbreak enabled the harvest to begin three weeks early, but cooler temperatures in mid-August, followed by a cold spell during September and October, prolonged the picking, which ended as late as mid-November. Good, long-lived reds and some excellent whites, especially from higher-altitude vineyards.

1998

Vintage rating: 85

Hot weather continued until early October, when a cold snap hit, extending the harvest well into November. A better year for reds than whites.

Grapevine

• **Argaman** is on its way out. The industry has largely acknowledged the fiasco of the Israeli-produced Argaman (a local Souzão–Carignan cross) and many vineyards are replacing it with far more noble varieties.

• **Local boutique wineries** are continuing to grow, but may have peaked in their local sales, and are now seeking to export their wines, with several consortia having been formed for this purpose. The most visible of these is a distribution organization under the wing of Carmel that will include the boutique wineries of Amphorae, Castel, Tzora, Bazelet ha Golan, Saslove, HaMasrek, Margalit, Flam, Yatir, and Orna Chillag.

• **Castel**, which has consistently made some of the best wines in the country, has switched entirely to kosher production with the output of the yet-to-be-released wines of 2002. Since the new kosher wines will not be *mevushal* (wines that have been 'cooked' or pasteurized), there is no fear that the quality will be affected.

• **At least two boutique wineries,** Saslove and Orna Chillag, have decided to produce kosher wines in addition to their regular non-kosher lines. Both will use the facilities of Carmel in order to do this, and both admit openly to hoping that this will be the way to reach foreign markets with their wines.

• **The battle over the control** of Recanati Wineries has now reached the courts. Both major partners, Lenny Recanati and the Ben-Ari brothers, are trying to gain control of the company. The whole affair has provided the popular press and gossip columns with plenty of material.

• **UDV Guinness,** the local arm of Coca-Cola International, has bought the medium-sized Tabor Winery and rumour has it that it is now negotiating a takeover of Barkan, the country's second-largest winery. Currently, local soft-drink producer Tempo is also reported to be negotiating the purchase of the medium-sized Tishbi winery.

• **Talk in the trade** has it that, with the change in name from Carmel-Mizrachi to Carmel, the winery is seeking to modernize its image further and consolidate changes in the company by appointing a new senior winemaker.

GREATEST WINE PRODUCERS

1. Golan Heights Winery (Yarden, Gamla, Golan)
2. Castel
3. Flam
4. Amphorae
5. Margalit
6. Dalton
7. Saslove
8. Galil Mountain
9. Tzora
10. Recanati

FASTEST-IMPROVING PRODUCERS

1. Carmel
2. Tishbi
3. Tabor
4. Sde Boker
5. Zauberman
6. Sea Horse Winery
7. Gush Etzion
8. Mayshar
9. Deux Paysans
10. Barkan

NEW UP-AND-COMING PRODUCERS

1. Har-El
2. Chateau Golan
3. Ella
4. Yatir
5. Alexander
6. Gustavo & Jo
7. Bazelet ha Golan
8. Orna Chillag
9. Zauberman
10. Bustan

BEST-VALUE PRODUCERS

1. Golan Heights Winery (Gamla, Golan)
2. Dalton
3. Galil Mountain
4. Flam
5. Amphorae
6. Recanati
7. Tishbi
8. Orna Chillag
9. Saslove
10. Barkan

GREATEST-QUALITY WINES

1. **Yarden Katzrin 2000** Golan Heights Winery (NIS 160)
2. **Yarden Katzrin Chardonnay 2000** Golan Heights Winery (NIS 85)
3. **Cabernet Sauvignon Special Reserve 2001** Margalit (NIS 160)
4. **Cabernet Sauvignon Reserve 2001** Flam (NIS 130)
5. **Grand Vin 2000** Domaine du Castel (NIS 160)
6. **"C" Blanc du Castel 2001** Castel (NIS 120)
7. **Cabernet Sauvignon 2001** Amphorae (NIS 130)
8. **Odem Organic Vineyard Chardonnay 2002** Golan Heights Winery (NIS 65)
9. **Yarden Cabernet Sauvignon 2000** Golan Heights Winery (NIS 95)
10. **Ramat Arad Cabernet Sauvignon 2000** Carmel (NIS 100)

BEST BARGAINS

1. **Classico 2002** Flam (NIS 65)
2. **Med.Red 2002** Amphorae (NIS 60)
3. **Merlot Aviv 2002** Saslove (NIS 58)
4. **Golan Cabernet Sauvignon 2002** Golan Heights Winery (NIS 48)
5. **Gamla Sangiovese 2001** Golan Heights Winery (NIS 64)
6. **Sauvignon Blanc Reserve 2002** Dalton (NIS 35)
7. **Sauvignon Blanc Reserve 2002** Barkan (NIS 35)
8. **Chardonnay 2002** Galil Mountain (NIS 37)
9. **Cabernet Sauvignon 2002** Galil Mountain (NIS 42)
10. **Chardonnay 2002** Dalton (NIS 34)

MOST EXCITING OR UNUSUAL FINDS

1. **Noble Semillon Botrytis 2001** Golan Heights Winery (NIS 80) *A bright, lively gold in colour, Israel's first botrytis Semillon combines unabashed honeyed sweetness with flavours and aromas of marmalade, pineapple, and ripe apricots.*
2. **Yarden Syrah 2000** Golan Heights Winery (NIS 95) *The first Syrah from this winery. Full-bodied, rich, and concentrated, with well-integrated tannins and generous oak balanced nicely by a bounty of red currant and berry fruits.*
3. **Ramat Arad Cabernet Sauvignon 2000** Carmel (NIS 100) *The best effort to date made from grapes grown entirely in the Negev Desert. This full-bodied red offers excellent balance between well-integrated tannins, hints of vanilla and smoke from the wood, and tempting aromas and flavours.*
4. **Cabernet Franc 2001** Margalit (NIS 150) *The first Cabernet Franc wine released in the country.* A blend of 90 per cent Cabernet Franc and 10 per cent Cabernet Sauvignon.
5. **Merlot Royal Reserve 2001** Chateau Golan (NIS 145) *This elegant and intense Merlot has deep, still-firm tannins, well balanced by raspberry, plum, and currant fruits on a complex background of dark chocolate and vanilla, all on a long, sweet finish.*
6. **Elul 2001** Sea Horse Winery (NIS 85) *From a still-young mini-boutique, this is a successful unfiltered blend of 70 per cent Cabernet Sauvignon, 28 per cent Merlot, and 2 per cent Syrah.*
7. **Clos de Gat Chardonnay 2002** Har-El (NIS 80) *The first release from this winery and a rousing success. Fermented and aged sur lie, with tempting ripe pear and pineapple aromas and flavours on the first attack yielding beautifully to citrus flowers, apple, and ripe apricots, all on a spicy background.*
8. **Merlot 2001** Zauberman (NIS 150) *The best Merlot ever by this boutique and one of the best ever made in Israel. Remarkably rich and full-bodied, this deep garnet/purple wine shows delicious plum, cherry, and currant fruits along with anise, vanilla, and spicy oak.*
9. **Yiron 2001** Galil Mountain (NIS 85) *Every bit as successful as the 2000 release, but this year a blend of 78 per cent Cabernet Sauvignon and 22 per cent Merlot, the grapes having been selected from two different vineyards.*
10. **Gamay Nouveau 2003** Golan Heights Winery (NIS 35) *The first wine ever made from Gamay grapes in Israel. Made by carbonic maceration, this wine is as fresh, young, and at least as rewarding as any Beaujolais Nouveau.*

Consternation and disbelief were among the responses to the publication, in late 2003, of rumours that unnamed Cape growers were adding flavourants to Sauvignon Blanc.

JOHN & ERICA PLATTER

And just when Sauvignon was winning international recognition as one of the best representatives of South African wine.

"The shadow of counterfeit wine production hangs over the Cape wine industry like a pall," charged wine writer Michael Fridjhon in a widely read column. "An increasing number of doubting Thomases, well-informed but strangely silent commentators, wonder at the precision, richness, and finesse of the country's top Sauvignons."

A difficulty for these top names was how to defend themselves; the Wine & Spirit Board, which certifies wines, revealed that it still lacked the scientific wherewithal to prove or disprove the addition of flavourants that are 'nature identical'.

According to South African scientists, methoxypyrazines, the natural compounds that account for the characteristic (grassy, herbaceous) high-flavour profiles of Sauvignon Blanc, are indistinguishable from pyrazine flavourants obtained from fruit and vegetables such as plums or capsicums

JOHN & ERICA PLATTER abandoned mainstream journalists' careers – he a foreign correspondent, she a news reporter-columnist – for a small vineyard in the Cape in 1978. Their writing has revolved around wine ever since. They launched the *John Platter South African Wine Guide*; now in its 25th annual edition, it has sold more than a million copies. Their *Africa Uncorked – Travels in Extreme Wine Territory* (Kyle Cathie, 2002) won the 2003 Glenfiddich Wine Book of the Year award. They are currently working on two new books. John Platter is the South African contributor to *Hugh Johnson's Pocket Wine Book* and a ministerial trustee of the body driving black economic empowerment in the winelands, the Wine Trust.

when using the gas chromatography techniques available to the Wine & Spirit Board. Pyrazines are not on the list of permitted additives/preservatives in winemaking and their use is strictly illegal. But they are freely available to the food-processing industry for use in jams, soups, and a host of other consumables.

The CEO of the recently formed wine industry coordinating body, the SA Wine & Brandy Company, Dr Johan van Rooyen, said that it was "a pity the Sauvignon flavourant allegations were unsubstantiated". But, in a tacit suggestion that all was not well, he said that the industry was "in the final phases of developing a detection system" and, as of the 2004 harvest, "any wineries suspected of producing wines with an unnatural flavour profile will be subjected to a stringent scientific and forensic audit. A producer whose wine shows evidence of tampering will be severely punished."

Since 2002, government scientists have been 'mapping' average regional pyrazine readings in wines to build up typical 'footprints' for specific areas in different vintages. Hot regions produce lower pyrazine levels than cooler ones. The idea was to enable officialdom to confront producers whose samples showed abnormally high pyrazine levels: wine certification could be withheld, explanations demanded, books – including the books of wine-industry suppliers? – inspected.

And a public inquiry and prosecutions? Not yet, apparently. But researchers say that Nuclear Magnetic Resonance (NMR) spectrometry, which uses isotopic analysis, could determine additions to wine; the same technology can be used to detect added alcohol or illegal chaptalization. So, why – after years of rumours and with so much at risk – weren't international labs and expertise used? Why weren't the forensic raids made? The industry and the government need to tighten up their audit and verification systems.

The hullabaloo was swiftly taken up by the international wine press. Jancis Robinson said: "If true, it would be unimaginably harmful to the industry and will affect the good guys as well as the bad [and] could potentially do as much damage to South African wine as 'antifreeze' did to Austria's wine reputation in 1985."

Pyrazine, while unlawful, is not a dangerous substance, which may account for the fairly swift easing of concern among big international buyers. Scores of growers signed affidavits confirming that their wines and wineries had nothing to do with wine flavourants. "It's been an expensive, time-consuming hassle. I don't know how many calls I've fielded," said one annoyed Sauvignon producer. "Of course we mustn't shoot the messengers, they're doing their jobs – rather corner the suspects; but what happened to the presumption of innocence until proven guilty?"

MEERLUST'S ITALIAN SHOES

In 1978, Giorgio Dalla Cia left the family wine and grappa business in Friuli to venture into Africa. Thrilled to discover *porcini* in the Stellenbosch forests, he and his fellow oenologist wife Simonetta put down permanent roots, becoming as devoted to Meerlust Estate as eighth-generation owner Hannes Myburgh. Now, after a distinguished quarter-century of bringing a classic European influence to bear on this quintessentially Cape property, he has retired. His going-away gifts included the Dalla Cia label (Chardonnay, Sauvignon Blanc) and the estate's grappa business (son George's baby); Giorgio continues to conduct tastings and play an *éminence grise* role. In 2004, young Chris Williams slipped into these capacious shoes – something of a homecoming. He understudied Dalla Cia here from 1995 to 2000 after abandoning a law degree to pursue viti-viniculture. He does not envisage 'a Rustenberg' (wholesale change), but the description of his brief indicates more than the mere passing of a baton: "Burnishing, tightening, freshening," he suggests. "The vineyards have never been better. I honestly believe we – it's a team thing – can make the best wines in South Africa." Part of the deal is that he can continue making The Foundry (see Most Exciting Finds list) wines on his own account at Meerlust. Meantime, Hannes Myburgh is preparing other new-generation ground: he has dispatched nephew George Myburgh Van Reenen to New York for 18 months to learn the US wine trade from Andre Shearer of Cape Classics, importer of Meerlust, Thelema, and other big SA names.

GOATS DO MARCH

French objections to Charles Back registering his Goats Do Roam label in the US (he is legal owner of the trademark in Europe) led to a protest march to the French Consulate in Cape Town that made front pages (*Le Figaro* included) and TV newscasts round the world. "The minute I told my staff what was going on, they started making up slogans (You Can't Get Our Goats!) and composing protest songs; we're thinking of cutting a CD." Back and the Fairview crew travelled into Cape Town, where they sang, chanted, and presented the French Trade Attaché with cheese and a magnum of wine, deciding ("he was a nice fellow") not to resort to their reserve weapon, vacuum-packed *bokdrolle* (goat droppings). "We tried to illustrate the ridiculousness of the objections," Back said. "The Goats are not trying to pass as French, they are very clearly labelled South African." He was "almost sure" that the objections would be withdrawn.

The newest addition to the Fairview range is a red blend, Goats Do Roam in Villages. This label refers to the 25 milking goats Fairview donated to an AIDS orphans' charity in the Caprivi strip. Surely no French quibbles here: "These Villages are definitely African," Back said.

BLACK GRADUATES

Coinciding with South Africa's first decade of democracy, 2004 saw the first 10 black graduates of the oenology faculty of Stellenbosch University. Fully grounded (if not yet seasoned) winemakers, these young pioneers have heavy role-model responsibilities to bear – the flip-side of being very much in demand. KWV got two minority groups in one person (black and female) when snaffling Nomonde Kubekha. Charles Back sponsored Busiswe Nokukhanya's studies and her chosen niche is in Fairview's lab. Mzokhona Mvemve and Allison Adams have been doing the business for Cape Classics: having studied on Indaba scholarships, they moved on to making the Indaba wines. Gyles Webb, recruiting for glamour winery Tokara, snapped up superbright Dumisani Mathonsi, 20 years old, who has put his Masters and PhD on hold.

WILD ABOUT WINE

The Kruger Park is South Africa's original Big Five game reserve, vying with the winelands as the country's most popular tourist destination. Soon, visitors pressed for time will be able to combine their WW (wine and wildlife) fixes. Having turned an old farmhouse into their Windmill wine shop, young food and wine entrepreneurs Thomas and Jacqui Bohm are now preparing the surrounding slopes for vineyards and excavating for a winery. Having consulted the experts, they have established it is not (all that) crazy to plant vines in the subtropics. In fact, their cool, breezy altitude on the panoramic Hazyview-Sabie route (mountain views to rival the Cape's) makes this a more likely spot than some on which Stellenbosch scientists are advising in Malaysia, India, and

other hotspots. These will be South Africa's most northerly vineyards and 'fizzophile' Jacqui intends making at least one bubbly. Which obviously would be misnamed Cap Classique.

NEW (US–CAPE) DEAL

Young Stellenbosch mover-shaker Mike Ratcliffe is the new Cape partner of US wine-and-vine eminences Zelma Long and Phil Freese. On his own account, quite separately from family farm Warwick, he has bought out Backsberg's Michael Back, the California couple's previous partner in their Paarl vineyard (planted 1998) and Simunye label. And he has brought in a New York-based wine importer as a fourth shareholder: Bartholomew Broadbent (son of Michael). Freese's consultancy commitments already see him in SA around three months a year; now he and Long have become even more frequent visitors. She is making the venture's wines herself, for the US market, at Tokara.

RIGHT ON AT KC

Adam Mason, previously SA production chief for high-flying winemaker Kym Milne's International Wine Services, has completed his first harvest at Klein Constantia. He has followed the 20-year-long class act of Ross Gower (busily building his own cellar on the farm Glen Stuart in Elgin), who must have wondered why locals kept lamenting the lack of a Cape icon wine. Surely Vin de Constance, his re-creation of the dessert wine that was an international icon in Napoleon's time, fitted that bill years ago? Most recent evidence of continuing French adoration for this wine came when KC was featured in a French-government-sponsored exhibition of Nine Mystical Vineyards. The company included Romanée-Conti, Mondavi-Rothschild, and d'Yquem. Perhaps its sweet dessert category – or perhaps its low-key marketing and pricing – accounts for Vin de Constance's relative obscurity. It pays homage to the classic Constantia desserts of the 1800s with superripe Muscat de Frontignan, which has consistently satin-textured, sumptuous, ripe apricot and marmalade qualities.

SURF'S UP

It is curious how many hot, inland vineyards lay claim to 'cool sea breezes'. But newly established (first vintage bottled in 2002) Fryer's Cove really is on the beach. Up the Cape West Coast, between Doringbaai and Strandfontein, it is so close to the frigid Atlantic breakers that overhead sprinklers have had to be installed to wash the salt off the Cabernet, Merlot, and Sauvignon Blanc vines. This is Stellenbosch (Lanzerac) winemaker Wynand Hamman's off-duty venture. His 2003 Sauvignon Blanc was especially striking.

WHAT A YEAR...

... for wining and dining best mates Ken Forrester and Martin Meinert, whose wines were served at South Africa's biggest birthday bash ever, Nelson Mandela's 85th. Unforgettably, they had a private meeting with the great man himself on the night. Then their vineyard 'canteen', 96 Winery Road, was judged one of SA's top 10 restaurants by the country's leading guide, Eat Out, and "original and visionary" Ken F received a special award for inspiring generations of restaurateurs and chefs. He has now built his own winery on the family farm, Scholtzenhof – previously Meinert did all the business at his Devon Crest winery – and this signalled a new chapter in their collaborations: Meinert is now devoting much more time to his own labels.

MISSIONARY POSITION

Grapes have always been grown – for sacramental purposes – around the Moravian mission at Elim, near Cape Agulhas, Africa's most southerly extremity, but this tiny, thatch-roofed village is becoming the Cape's coolest new wine hub. Joining Hein Koegelenberg of La Motte, already bottling from his Land's End vineyards, and Dave King (ditto from Quoin Rock) is a Johannesburg consortium headed by Carrie Adams (a partner in leading liquor store Norman Goodfellow's) and Nick Diemont (ex-Vergelegen and Bouchard Finlayson). Their 850-hectare (ha) Strandveld Vineyards feature 40 ha of newly planted Shiraz, Sauvignon Blanc, Pinot Noir, and Semillon, just a few kilometres from the beach. So far, all the action has come from the outside. Now the Elim community itself is becoming a player. Johan Laubser (ex-Winecorp) is advising on a project – still in blueprint stage – that will see Elim's villagers planting 225 ha of vines and building their own winery. "This magical place has", he predicts, "the potential to make all South Africa proud."

Black economic empowerment has been the official line in South Africa for the 10 years since the end of apartheid; in 2003 it became legislated policy through affirmative-action legislation. It is all taking place against the background of a lively national debate: is it to be 'broad-based' empowerment or 'enrichment of a few fat cats'?

Details of an industry charter were being mapped out during 2004, and the broad-stroke targets seem to be a 30–35 per cent black ownership of the wine industry by 2014 (that is 20 years after democratic rule). As land values in the winelands have become prohibitive, less costly investments in related downstream wine businesses will probably be the initial focus of government and private-sector partnership funding of black empowerment. But several big deals, involving land as well as businesses, are under discussion. In 2003, the first significant one was announced, the sale by Anglo-American Corporation of its scenic Boschendal Estate near Franschhoek (350,000 cases per year) for some $45 million to a foreign and local consortium, comprising a 30 per cent black stake.

The government seems committed to remaining consultative rather than prescriptive about black empowerment, urging industries to work out their own targets and timetables. But there is opposition in some conservative white business quarters, where the belief is that 'artificially stitched up' black partnerships and takeovers are impositions rather than real market-driven opportunities. And yet they still wonder, in this politically charged community, why South Africa's huge potential black wine-consuming market has never been penetrated in any serious way by the all-white-owned industry!

Update

Two more hardy annuals on the Cape (and other regions'?) 'fix it' list: (1) Viruses in the vineyards. Only painfully slow progress has been made in nailing/eliminating the vectors that spread the tenacious leafroll virus. It inhibits fruit ripening (worst in hot vintages) and curtails the viable life of vineyards but, because it doesn't kill quickly, its insidious effects on premium-wine quality and the economics of Cape wine induce a put-off-the-evil-day lethargy. The present remedy – to replant with great frequency – is too drastic and uneconomic in a competitive wine world.

(2) Higher and higher alcohols. Again, hardly a problem confined to South Africa. The ripe-fruit mantra means longer vine hang time, equals higher sugars, equals higher and higher alcohols; so do more efficient fermentation yeasts. Cape alcohol averaged around 12.5 per cent just 15–20 years ago (admittedly often in unripe, raw wines, with green tannins); now to find a 13.5 per cent wine is a treat; and 15.5–16 per cent monsters are hardly rarities. Wine science urgently needs to focus on vine physiology, to enable growers to achieve ripeness at lower sugar levels – and ferment with less efficient, aggressive, alcohol-booster yeasts.

Grapevine

• **As one of the Cape's** most experienced hands-on wine executives (viticulture his basic game). Gerrie Wagener has had a string of rather fine exes, including Boschendal, Vergelegen, and Wine Corp. Wagener has hit retirement age, but he is not ready to take it easy. He is to take over the management load from Italian textile magnate Giulio Bertrand at new super-league Morgenster, where Pierre Lurton is consultant winemaker, next door to Vergelegen.

• **Jabulani Ntshangase**, CEO of Thabani Wines and co-owner of Grand World of Wine, a suave wine and cigar shop in the hyper-cool Arabella Sheraton Hotel, near Cape Town's new Convention Centre, has won the BBQ (*Black Business Quarterly*) award for New Entrepreneur of the Year. His driving of the graduate winemakers' scheme (see Black Graduates) also won him the Ethekwini (Durban) Mayor's Achiever Award. Of the 25 students he's championed through the system, 60 per cent come from KwaZulu-Natal; 50 per cent have been female.

• **Vergelegen feels it has incubated** a candidate for iconhood: a dark, dense, opulently flavoured, blackcurrany

Cabernet stunner – working title: Vergelegen V. It is a 2001 due for release in 2004/5 and, though they are not specific yet, they are planning to price it somewhere in the Mondavi-Rothschild Opus One ballpark – $100 plus, with the emphasis on plus.

• **Super-golfer** Ernie Els's eponymous wine – a bordeaux-style blend made at Rust en Vrede – has pulled off a hole in 2001: a 5-star rating in South Africa's top wine guide. This follows the success of the first vintage, 2000, which picked up *Wine Spectator*'s highest-yet (93) score for a Cape wine. Also turning in a highly respectable card is another golf pro, David Frost, whose 25-ha Paarl vineyard is producing especially attractive Cabernets.

• **Who is Donald Hess** (of California's Hess Collection winery) eyeing now? Having sold his Swiss mineral water interests to Coca-Cola, his Hess Group has swallowed whole (he previously had a half-share) Paarl Winery Glen Carlou – the proverbial "offer we couldn't refuse". His non-negotiable: winemaker David Finlayson had to stay on. Hess's global portfolio now includes Peter Lehmann Wines in Australia, two Argentinian wineries, "and he's looking in Europe", says Finlayson.

Advance report on the latest harvest
2004

Despite slightly higher yields overall (by about 2 per cent) than in 2003, which was itself a bigger-than-average harvest, the latest vintage is reckoned to be among the best of the past 10 years. That makes it two outstanding, almost disease-free vintages in a row – in a 'turnaround' phase in Cape wine when vineyards and winemakers have never been in better export-honed shape. It was a relatively cool, much more drawn-out year, a couple of heat flashes just before harvest in January and February notwithstanding. Cabernet was being cut in late April, a good three or four weeks 'late'. Top red-wine producers around Stellenbosch and Paarl reported fine, concentrated flavours and deep colours from the longer hang time, with high extracts promising full, firm structures. The most expressive whites, in a pattern now repeating itself, came from the maritime-fringed regions of Constantia, Somerset West, Durbanville, Darling, and Walker Bay.

Updates on the previous five vintages
2003

Vintage rating: *90*

The vintage completed a run of six consecutive good to very good harvests. The crop, at 1.14 million tons, was about 5 per cent up on 2002, above average. Quality across the board was very good to outstanding. Generally a ripe, disease-free, dry, hot year with clean fruit – a typical Cape vintage. Many top growers reported unusually small berry size and thick, flavour-filled skins. There were some exceptional Cabernets.

2002

Vintage rating: *82*

Average-sized crop, but early attacks of mildew and later botrytis after a long heat wave made for patchy quality. More moderate alcohols were a plus. But, as usual, the survivors, from the top estates, seemed to produce fine top-end labels.

2001

Vintage rating: *85*

A lighter-than-average crop and a generally trouble-free, hot, and dry vintage. High alcohols and concentrated reds (the best sufficiently fruity to handle big tannins and alcohol). Should be a reasonably long-lived vintage.

2000

Vintage rating: *80*

Difficult, variable weather-wise, and with generally softer acids. An uneven, spottier vintage, but the lightish crop provided compensations in flavour intensity, where producers managed to gather before overripeness began flattening fruit profiles.

1999

Vintage rating: *75*

Large crop, very warm: big, juicy, accessible reds, mostly not for long cellaring (though some retained quite strident tannins). Typically a year when whites showed less excitement.

GREATEST WINE PRODUCERS

1. Vergelegen
2. Thelema
3. Charles Back (Fairview, Spice Route)
4. Boekenhoutskloof
5. Rustenberg
6. Steenberg
7. Jordan
8. Rust en Vrede
9. Kaapzicht
10. Neil Ellis

FASTEST-IMPROVING PRODUCERS

1. Hartenberg
2. Fleur du Cap (especially Unfiltered range)
3. Stellenbosch Vineyards (especially Genesis, Kumkani)
4. Nederburg
5. Zevenwacht
6. Blaauwklippen
7. Havana Hills
8. Bonfoi Estate
9. Kumala (especially Journey's End)
10. Eikendal

NEW UP-AND-COMING PRODUCERS

1. Rudera
2. Asara
3. Dornier
4. Remhoogte
5. Origin Wines
6. The Winery
   (Radford Dale, Vinum, New World)
7. Bellevue
8. Bilton
9. Avondale
10. Hillcrest Durbanville

BEST-VALUE PRODUCERS

1. Villiera
2. Kaapzicht
3. L'Avenir
4. Stellenbosch Vineyards
5. Newton Johnson
6. Zonnebloem
7. Goede Hoop
8. Kleine Zalze
9. Nitida
10. KWV

GREATEST-QUALITY WINES

1. **Cabernet Sauvignon V 2001**
   Vergelegen (not yet priced)
2. **Sauvignon Blanc Reserve 2003**
   Vergelegen (R135)
3. **Semillon-Sauvignon Blanc 2002** Vergelegen (R180)
4. **Cabernet Franc-Sauvignon 2000** Morgenster Estate (R260)
5. **Cabernet Sauvignon-Shiraz-Merlot 2000**
   Rust en Vrede (R250)
6. **Semillon 2003** Steenberg (R75)
7. **Vin de Constance 1999**
   Klein Constantia
   (R220 per 500-ml bottle)
8. **Galpin Peak Pinot Noir Tête de Cuvée 2001**
   Bouchard Finlayson (R380)
9. **Syrah 2001**
   Boekenhoutskloof (R140)
10. **Cabernet Sauvignon 2000**
    Thelema (R120)

BEST BARGAINS

1. **Chardonnay 2002**
   Vergelegen (R53.50)
2. **Merlot 2002** (R70) Cordoba
3. **Cabernet Sauvignon 2000**
   Tokara Zondernaam (R50)
4. **Chenin Blanc 2003** L'Avenir (R48)
5. **Cabernet Sauvignon 2000**
   Le Riche (R75)
6. **Keystone Cabernet-Merlot 2001** Kanu (R65)
7. **Golden Triangle Shiraz 2001**
   Stellenzicht (R60)
8. **Cabernet-Merlot-Cabernet Franc Mill Race Red 2001**
   Vergelegen (R45)
9. **Sauvignon Blanc 2003**
   Thelema (R45)
10. **Brut Natural Chardonnay 2001**
    Villiera (R54)

Grapevine

• **Coming over the Fairview horizon:** a red blend of Italian varieties (Nebbiolo, Sangiovese, Barbera, Primitivo), a first for the Cape as per usual for Charles Back, named after the Italian POW who taught him, years ago, to make both cheese and wine: Agostinelli. "A real character; looked like a skittle with braces," Back recalls.

MOST EXCITING OR UNUSUAL FINDS

1. **The Foundry Syrah 2001** Chris Williams (R145) *General acclaim on debut for own-label cracker made by Chris Williams, the youngster groomed to take estate grandee Meerlust into a new era.*

2. **The Chocolate Block 2002** Boekenhoutskloof (R100) *New-millennium, new-direction, new-combination red by foodie winemaker Marc Kent: Grenache, Shiraz, Cabernet, Cinsaut, Viognier.*

3. **Unfiltered White Blend: Viognier-Chardonnay-Semillon-Sauvignon Blanc 2002** Fleur du Cap (R85) *This venerable Cape range is bursting out of hibernation with some astonishing wines.*

4. **Mathilde Aszú 6 Puttonyos 2002** Signal Hill (R280) *So near and yet so far: a Cape Tokay made by French honorary South African Jean-Vincent Ridon; its origins (Furmint, Sauvignon from Stellenbosch, Swartland) have bamboozled all and sundry.*

5. **Dornatus 2003** Dornier (R65) *Chenin/Sauvignon Blanc/Semillon blend from artist Christoph Dornier's new Stellenbosch winery and vineyards. Watch this space.*

6. **Cabernet Franc 2001** Raats Family (R155) *Rarely stand-alone or even in the majority in the Cape (Cordoba and Warwick the notable exceptions), here showered with attention by Bruwer Raats.*

7. **Family Reserve T Noble Late Harvest 2001** Forrester (R115) *Brilliant new star in the Cape's botrytized dessert galaxy.*

8. **Ruby in the Dust 2003** Flagstone (R65) *What's the point of Ruby Cabernet? Here is modern creative force Bruce Jack's emphatic, unmitigated answer.*

9. **Steytler Vision 2000** Kaapzicht (R115) *Danie Steytler's arresting mix of Pinotage, Cabernet, and a dash of Merlot argues the case for making Pinotage an element of a Cape blend.*

10. **Brampton Viognier 2003** Rustenberg (R65) *Strapping screwcapped newcomer from the white variety of the moment: altogether something different from this classic old (established 1682) property long known (first bottling 1892) for its reds.*

Grapevine

- **Compared to Fairview's** volume business, cheese, its wines are, so to speak, small beer. At the 2003 World Cheese Championships in London, Fairview Roydon won the Camembert section, and La Beryl (named after his late mother) the washed-rind – "smelly socks", Back calls it – category.

- **Diversification** into cheese production is the new direction at many vineyards – Glen Carlou (Cap Salut), Anura (Forest Hill) – with olive groves the next most popular second string – Morgenster, Tokara (The Olive Shed), Devon Hill, Kloovenburg, Hildenbrand, Axe Hill, and L'Avenir.

- **Mme May Eliane de Lencquesaing** of Pichon-Longueville-Comtesse-de-Lalande has bought a spread in Stellenbosch, right next door to one of the Cape's most graceful estates, Rustenberg. Near neighbours include Thelema and Morgenhof, owned by fellow countrywoman Anne Huchon of the Cointreau family. The property will need extensive development.

The craze for $2 wine in California has created a whole new marketing approach for the majority of the state's wineries, one that calls for rethinking the pricing structure of lines of wines.

DAN BERGER

The famed Charles Shaw 'Two Buck Chuck', made by Bronco Wine Co, started the craze at Trader Joe's chain of stores, prompting many more companies into the niche with competing brands also selling for $2. As the fascination with these wines took hold, newspaper and television reports on the rush to buy the new bargain-basement wine rarely told of the impact on the former $5–7 price segment: it was in chaos, with discounts (and profit-margin declines) rampant. Moreover, the fascination with $2 wine added one element that was detrimental to all producers of $10–15 wine: it encouraged a good percentage of consumers to trade down to lower price points, creating a lot more competition at the lower end of the spectrum. So, although more people were drinking wine, profits were flat or declined.

Ultrapremium brand glut

In the ultrapremium category of wine, the most significant development in 2003 was the widening of the 'chic-boutique' niche. The established Napa cult wineries based on Cabernet of Screaming Eagle, Harlan, Colgin, and

DAN BERGER is an award-winning wine columnist syndicated by Creators Syndicate to newspapers around the world and is the author of *Dan Berger's Vintage Experiences*, a weekly newsletter on wine available by subscription. A speaker at wine symposiums, he is also a judge at national and international wine competitions and has written for *Decanter*, *Gourmet*, and numerous other publications.

others were joined by newcomers named T-Vine, Hundred Acre, and two dozen more. Sonoma County got even more of the new cults, many of them Pinot Noir producers in the Russian River Valley and the newly emerging Sonoma Coast. Then there were the additional Pinot producers from hot regions such as the Santa Lucia Highlands of Monterey and the Santa Rita Hills of Santa Barbara. With these inky-concentrated (and generally alcoholic) wines came prices to match: Chardonnays in the $50 range, Pinot Noirs in the $60 and above range, and even small amounts of Syrah commanding outrageous prices.

Consequently, the consumer was bombarded with dozens of new boutique producers. Since 2000, the number of California's bonded wineries has risen from about 850 to 1,340, most of the new ones tiny family-owned wineries, some owned by grape growers who had no home for their grapes and therefore started brands to make commercial use of their vineyards. The key question was: who would buy all these wines? The consolidation at the wholesale end of the market left the largest wholesalers with books so large that their sales people had a hard time carrying them, let alone fairly representing the wineries they carried.

Most of the new small wineries rely on direct sales to members of their wine clubs, using Internet sales and direct-marketing techniques to the other 25 states that allow reciprocal trade. Another 24 states do not permit wine sales into or out of their borders, which is why an imminent challenge of the states' rights to control their own destiny with regard to alcohol sales (supposedly granted to them by the 21st amendment to the US Constitution) is important to the destiny of these new chic-boutique wineries. Indeed, rulings in four major US District Courts said that shipping wine across state lines is permissible under the Commerce Clause of the US Constitution. Clearly, the conflict is one that must be adjudicated in the US Supreme Court – a challenge that may well come soon.

Grapevine

• **Many wine companies,** hoping to sell wine that is backlogged in the distribution system because of the California wine glut, have taken to discounting prior vintages in their tasting rooms. Among the companies that resorted to the tactic were Beringer Blass and Kendall-Jackson. Meanwhile, the larger companies created dozens of new labels – wines selling for $4–6 per bottle.

• **Bag-in-box wine,** long a staple in Australia, became a fully fledged up-market varietal category. Previous boxed wines were usually generic. The upscale version began with a $25 3-litre item called Black Box, a Napa Chardonnay. That was followed quickly by a $17 line of boxes called Hardy's Stamp from Australia; then another half-dozen US companies leaped into the arena with lines in the $15–20 range.

ALTERNATIVE WHITES TAKE CENTRE STAGE

Wine consumers continue to buy Chardonnay, still one of the nation's top-selling white wines, but increasingly over the last few years an ABC movement – anything but Chardonnay – has gained steam, leading to an interesting situation: Chardonnays with less malolactic fermentation and smaller amounts of noticeable oak. [*I suppose such wines are indeed anything but Chardonnay as far as most American Chardonnay consumers are concerned – Ed.*] However, many Chardonnays in the upper range of price (and reputed quality) are still being made with alcohol levels in the high 14 per cent range.

HOMELAND SECURITY ACT HURTS IMPORTS

California wineries and wholesalers are secretly chuckling over new US regulations that were sparked by the Homeland Security Act, which forces importers into a flurry of bureaucratic paperwork. Any importer who wishes to bring wine into the US must now file papers with the US Customs Service, giving details of the wine that are generally known only by the producer. This cuts at the heart of parallel importing (also known as the grey market). The new requirements also mandate that the exact date of arrival of shipments must be stated, and that if a shipment is early or late it will not be permitted to land. The regulations are an effort to thwart bioterrorism and involve three branches of the US government. They are forcing importers to spend a lot more time on paperwork, increasing the cost of importing. Some California wineries and wholesalers believe that the rules will eventually lead to smaller sales of some imports.

- **The California Wine Institute**, a trade organization, proposed that all vintaged wine be composed of 85 per cent wine from the named vintage, down from 95 per cent. The proposal would allow wineries to make a better wine in a difficult vintage, the Institute argued. But the membership declined to back the proposal, which will be reconsidered at a later date.

- **Robert Mondavi's joint venture** with Rosemount of Australia hit store shelves in 2003 with moderately priced lines called Kirralaa and Talomas. The former are Australian wines made by Tim Mondavi; the latter, California wines made by the team of winemakers at Rosemount. Both lines are priced under $20 per bottle.

- **The Napa Valley Vintners Association** is encouraging Napa Valley wineries to use the phrase "100 per cent Napa Valley" on all bottles that blend no other grapes into their wines. The idea is to imply a quality statement, as if blending in grapes from anywhere else would make an inferior wine.

- **The average price** for Napa Valley Cabernet Sauvignon grapes in 2002 was $4,016 per ton. Using the old formula that says a bottle of wine ought to cost 1 per cent of the price per ton, the average bottle of Napa Cabernet should be $40.

- **Santa Lucia Highlands** and Santa Rita Hills are emerging as the top challengers to Russian River Valley in terms of high-quality Pinot Noir production.

Prohibition remains a nasty spectre on the US cultural scene, best exemplified by the myriad groups trying to reinstitute a milder form of 'the great experiment' that failed. Groups purportedly campaigning for the public good – such as Mothers Against Drunk Driving, the Marin Institute, and the Robert Wood Johnson Foundation – have all targeted alcoholic beverages for government controls that seek to limit access to wine, beer, and spirits. One of the latest campaigns arose late in 2003, when a proposal for a uniform 'Alcohol Facts' label was submitted to the Alcohol and Tobacco Tax and Trade Bureau (TTB, formerly the BATF) by the National Consumers League (NCL), the Center for Science in the Public Interest (CSPI), and other righteous-sounding bodies.

The proposed label for alcoholic beverages "would give consumers clear information about alcohol content, serving sizes, calories, and ingredients," the groups said. It all sounds so benign…

The consumer groups say that the rules governing labelling on alcoholic beverages "suffer from jurisdictional gaps between the Food and Drug Administration (FDA) and the Treasury Department's Alcohol and Tobacco Tax and Trade Bureau". Under the guise of health, the organizations say that the new label is needed to allow consumers who are trying to maintain a healthy weight to get information about calories in the wine, beer, and spirits they are thinking of consuming.

The proposal would require details such as the alcohol content and number of 'standard servings' and would state the US Dietary Guidelines' definition of moderate drinking (one drink per day for women, two drinks per day for men). It would also have calorie information and a list of ingredients. For products that are usually sold in part on the design of their packaging, such as wine, such a huge label would declass wine, while the cost of establishing such detailed information would be especially burdensome to small family-owned wineries.

It should be noted that CSPI is the organization that, some years ago, attempted to require a government warning label to be placed in large red letters on the front of all alcoholic-beverage labels. The neo-Prohibition groups may genuinely believe they are doing society a favour by their actions, but they carefully ignore the health benefits of moderate consumption of wine, which is a detriment to the millions who could lead healthier and happier lives if they knew the truth.

In an effort to counteract this wave of opposition to alcoholic beverages, a group called Center for Consumer Freedom (CCF) established a website, www.neoProhibition.com, to alert consumers to the pressures to legislate against drinks.

Update

Higher alcohol levels continue to be seen in many of the state's best wines. It is hard to make a great Zinfandel with less than 14 per cent alcohol, but far too many Chardonnays and Cabernet Sauvignons get above 14 per cent, and some are above 15 per cent, leaving the palate gasping for a break.

Some winemakers now admit that full malolactic fermentation may not be appropriate for their wines, but they also say that a partial malolactic is not feasible for small lots of wine. Doing a partial ML requires that the wine be filtered, and they argue that such a procedure is impractical with small lots, since filters need a good quantity of wine to work properly.

One area of winemaking that seems to have improved is the use of oak as a flavouring element. A possible reason may be that the 2000 vintage lacked some fruit, and winemakers realized that, without sufficient fruit, they would be overoaking the wine. Also, the decline of the US dollar versus the euro (more than 35 per cent in the last two years) has raised the cost of French oak barrels from about $500 to $700, meaning that winemakers are far more careful about using newer barrels.

Grapevine

• **The parent company** of Geyser Peak Winery, Fortune Brands, marketer of Jim Beam, acquired one of the top wineries in California's Central Coast when it bought Wild Horse Winery. Owner-winemaker Ken Volk left the company after a brief consulting stint and will develop a new brand (as yet unnamed), to be released in 2006.

• **French importer** Jean-Claude Boisset acquired the assets of the bankrupt De Loach vineyards and winery for $17 million in a court-monitored auction late in 2003.

• **The Culinary Institute of America's** Napa Valley branch has opened a handsome and functional educational facility, the Rudd Center, to be used by students taking a culinary arts programme. The centre features an extensive tiered, terraced tasting facility.

• **Resveratrol is even better for you.** Research from a Harvard Medical School study indicates that wine is connected to longer life spans in laboratory animals and yeast. The chemical resveratrol is the key element. Resveratrol was previously identified as helping to protect the body from heart disease.

• **A boycott of French products** hurt sales of French wine early in 2003, but the impact was felt mainly on the east coast, where European imports typically have a stronger following. In California, the boycott manifested itself in slower restaurant sales of French wines, but by late in the year no one could see a real decline.

Advance report on the latest harvest
2003

The 2003 vintage in northern California (Napa, Sonoma, Mendocino) was marked by early rains and late heat spikes, contributing to lower overall yields. The result was a vintage of high quality, great colour concentration, and intensity of flavour. Heat in March led to shatter, reducing crop size. Then a cold May left the crop at least a month behind schedule. April rains affected Merlot most. Dramatic heat spikes in September moved the harvest forward a bit after many had felt that it would be a late year. There was a rush to get everything harvested, and much came in at the same time. Reds were expected to have high acid, high sugar, and low pH, which means that wines are hard to judge early on.

Updates on the previous five vintages
2002

Vintage rating: *91*

No prolonged summer heat, just many short heat spells late in the season, resulting in excessively high sugars in many varieties. The heat spells occurred after a relatively cool summer, so sugars rose quickly. Some awkward reds; whites survived better, since the slightly cooler summer left Chardonnay, Sauvignon Blanc, and Pinot Gris with good acids.

2001

Vintage rating: *93*

A warm summer followed by a cooling trend in September brought acids back up. Some fruit was harvested early, leading to better acidity structure. An excellent vintage with great potential for reds that will be aged.

2000

Vintage rating: *89*

An El Niño vintage. Flavours for most grapes were satisfactory, but many reds lacked body and richness unless harvested late, although the later flavours were a little contrived. Many reds appear to be ageing reasonably well. Choose carefully.

1999

Vintage rating: 99

The best reds were startlingly complex early, with bright fruit acids, and the wines had near-perfect structure. A better vintage than the vaunted 1997.

1998

Vintage rating: 90

Another El Niño vintage. Ripening was not bad, but early on the wines seemed to lack depth. Early reports were negative, but many winemakers made splendid blending decisions and the vintage turned out to be a lot better than expected. Many reds seem to be lighter, but ageing nicely.

GREATEST WINE PRODUCERS

1. Joseph Phelps
2. Stag's Leap Wine Cellars
3. Navarro
4. Gary Farrell
5. Au Bon Climat
6. Gloria Ferrer
7. Freemark Abbey
8. Robert Mondavi
9. Hess Collection
10. Gundlach Bundschu

NEW UP-AND-COMING PRODUCERS

1. Dutton Goldfield
2. Jeff Runquist
3. DuMol
4. Ortman
5. Terra Valentine
6. La Crema
7. Mayo Family
8. Casa Cassara
9. Clos Pepe
10. Carol Shelton

FASTEST-IMPROVING PRODUCERS

1. Morgan
2. Gallo of Sonoma
3. Trentadue
4. Firestone
5. Rodney Strong
6. Charles Krug
7. Louis Martini
8. Jekel
9. Rosenblum
10. Rancho Zabaco

BEST-VALUE PRODUCERS

1. Fetzer
2. Forest Glen
3. Sutter Home Vineyards
4. McManis
5. Bogle
6. Turning Leaf
7. Barefoot
8. Hess Select
9. Canyon Road
10. Delicato

GREATEST-QUALITY WINES

1. **Cabernet Sauvignon Bosché 1999** Freemark Abbey, Napa Valley ($65)
2. **Cabernet Sauvignon Cask 23 2000** Stag's Leap Wine Cellars, Napa Valley ($150)
3. **Pinot Noir 2000** Campion, Santa Lucia Highlands ($32)
4. **Petite Sirah 2000** Eos, Paso Robles ($45)
5. **Cabernet Sauvignon 2000** Chimney Rock, Stag's Leap District ($48)
6. **Dutton Ranch Syrah 2001** Sebastopol, Russian River Valley ($20)
7. **Backus Vineyard Cabernet Sauvignon 2000** Joseph Phelps, Napa Valley ($150)
8. **Syrah 2001** Foley, Santa Rita Hills ($30)
9. **Cabernet Sauvignon 1999** Tom Eddy, Napa Valley ($75)
10. **Cabernet Sauvignon 2000** Hartwell, Stag's Leap ($100)

BEST BARGAINS

1. **Syrah 2002** McManis, California ($10)
2. **Edelzwicker 2002** Navarro, Anderson Valley ($9.75)
3. **Shiraz 2001** Delicato, California ($7)
4. **Dancing Bull Zinfandel 2001** Rancho Zabaco, Sonoma ($9)
5. **Reds 2001** Laurel Glen Vineyards, California ($8.50)
6. **Sauvignon Blanc 2002** Canyon Road, California ($8)
7. **Petite Sirah 2001** Bogle, California ($10)
8. **Pinot Gris 2002** Sutter Home Vineyards, California ($7)
9. **Cabernet Sauvignon 2000** Hess Select, California ($11.50)
10. **A Thousand Flowers 2002** Hop Kiln, Russian River Valley ($9)

MOST EXCITING OR UNUSUAL FINDS

1. **Albariño 2002** Havens, Carneros ($24) *A rare example of a wine made from a grape far better known in Spain and Portugal.*
2. **Hildegard 2001** Au Bon Climat, Santa Maria Valley ($35) *An exotic effort by Jim Clendenen to re-create the original wine style of Corton-Charlemagne that was made from AD800 to 1759 from Pinot Blanc, Pinot Gris, and Aligoté.*
3. **Pinot Blanc 2002** Robert Sinskey, Napa Valley (half-bottles and magnums only; $18 per half-bottle) *A classic rendition of a grape that is out of favour in California.*
4. **Pinot Gris 2002** Navarro, Anderson Valley ($16) *Dramatic example of a grape that has become popular in a far simpler Italian form.*
5. **Petite Sirah 2000** Sable Ridge, Russian River Valley ($32) *Exciting rendition of an old California favourite, a very long-lived red wine.*
6. **Cabernet Franc 2000** Lang and Reed, Napa Valley ($32) *Rarely is there a Cabernet Franc with this graceful a structure and stylish fruit.*
7. **Sauvignon Blanc 2001** Voss, Napa Valley ($18) *A rare style for a California Sauvignon, paying homage to Marlborough, New Zealand.*
8. **Verdad 2001** Santa Ynez Valley ($20) *An alluring blend of Tempranillo, Syrah, and Grenache.*
9. **Muscat Canelli 2002** Eberle, Paso Robles ($12) *Classic Italian-style sweet wine.*
10. **Cabernet Franc 2000** Raymond Burr, Dry Creek Valley ($38) *A superb example of a bordeaux-style red wine, one of the top 'claretlike' wines in California.*

Pacific Northwest

Paul Gregutt

Long-simmering hostilities between the Washington State Liquor Control Board and the state's wholesalers and retailers have boiled over into what could lead to a revision of restrictions on wine sales and purchases.

PAUL GREGUTT

Costco Wholesale, a Seattle-based chain that owns and operates 410 warehouse clubs and is the single largest wine retailer in the US, has mounted a powerful legal challenge to the state's antiquated liquor laws. In a 38-page letter to the Washington state attorney general's office, Costco's lawyers state that current regulations "amount to and facilitate agreements to stabilize prices, allocate customers, restrict output and otherwise obstruct competition".

They further allege that many of the regulations, which together form the underpinnings of a "three-tier system" that places the state squarely in the middle of all alcohol sales from producers to vendors, violate federal antitrust statutes. Somewhat-similar legal challenges across the country are attempting to overturn draconian regulations restricting or forbidding interstate purchase and shipping of wine and spirits.

Such standard (in Washington state) practices as distributor price posting, minimum mark-ups, and prohibitions on credit and discounting are being challenged. Costco, whose wine sales total over $620 million annually, is making the case that consumers are the ultimate losers. Washington's complex regulations add significantly to the cost of a bottle of wine in-state; so much so that even wines produced in Washington

PAUL GREGUTT lives in Seattle and is the wine columnist for *The Seattle Times*, *Yakima Herald-Republic*, and *Walla Walla Union-Bulletin*. He is a contributing editor to *Wine Enthusiast* magazine and the author of *Northwest Wines* (Sasquatch Books, 1996).

may frequently be purchased at lower prices in California and elsewhere.

The issue is so complex that the Washington Beer & Wine Wholesalers Association, which generally finds itself at odds with the state over its dual role of regulating and selling wine and spirits (in state-run liquor stores), is expected to come out with a letter defending the state against Costco's allegations. This is certain to become the most important legal battle of the coming year.

Board games

Oregon has finally detached its moribund wine-marketing efforts from its state legislature, replacing the Oregon Wine Advisory Board with the new and (hopefully) far more independent Oregon Wine Board. The reinvented OWB will no longer be attached to the state Department of Agriculture and its new membership includes representatives from some of the state's most respected wineries.

Officially a semi-independent state agency, the new OWB retains a modest annual budget of roughly $800,000, derived from a wine tax of two cents per gallon and a grape-growers' tax of $25 per ton. A search for a full-time executive director is under way; meanwhile, long-time director Betty O'Brien will continue to head the office. Rumour has it that industry leaders have been trying to woo the Washington Wine Commission's highly regarded executive director, Steve Burns, but he has since returned to California to set up a consulting business.

Named to the OWB's nine-member board were winery and vineyard owners from eastern and southern Oregon, as well as from the heart of Pinot Noir country in the northern Willamette Valley. Eventually all board members will serve three-year terms, though six of the first nine appointees have shorter inaugural terms. The members are Ted Casteel of Bethel Heights Vineyard, Earl Jones of Abacela Vineyards and Winery, Harry Peterson-Nedry of Chehalem, David Adelsheim of Adelsheim Vineyard, Laura Lotspeich of Pheasant Hill Vineyard, Norm McKibben of Seven Hills Vineyard, Steve Girard of Benton-Lane, Scott Shull of Raptor Ridge Winery, and John Weisinger of Weisinger's of Ashland. McKibben, whose vineyard and winery are in the Walla Walla AVA that straddles the Washington/Oregon border, previously served as a member, and later chairman, of the Washington State Wine Commission.

Board members are hoping that the revamped organization will help Oregon's splintered vintner groups to find some common marketing ground. The first priority during the coming year should be hiring additional, more savvy marketing staff, who can be recruited freely, without the constraints of the state's hiring system.

HEATED DEBATE

At a conference held in Seattle last autumn, the Geological Society of America unveiled a study of the world's top 27 wine regions that predicted massive climatic changes over the next half-century. While noting that steadily rising temperatures have already impacted vintage quality (2003 in Europe, for example), the new study, developed by Greg Jones of Southern Oregon University, predicts that an average rise in temperature of 2°C during the coming years will improve viticulture in cool-climate growing regions. In parts of Germany, they are reaching back to 1540 to find a vintage as warm as 2003. But problems could arise in warmer regions, such as Chianti, where overripe fruit, water-stressed vines, and more active and resistant pests and diseases could become the norm. Jones, the son of Earl and Hilda Jones of Abacela Vineyards and Winery in central Oregon, believes that big changes are coming for many regions. Although some may prosper, at the very least wine styles will have to evolve; in more extreme situations traditional grapes may have to be replaced with varieties more suited to the new climate. Could England be the new Burgundy?

MUSICAL CHAIRS

Winemaker changes continue to rock the Pacific Northwest, as the explosion in the number of new wineries (now over 250 in Washington and 230 in Oregon)

Grapevine

• **Impressive new winery facilities** have opened for Stimson Lane's value Snoqualmie brand as well as its high-end Merlot specialist, Northstar. Also debuting recently was a new winery/tasting room for Desert Hills Winery, the Washington-based sister of Oregon's Duck Pond Cellars. Cañon de Sol Winery opened its new barrel room and tasting room in November 2003, and Basel Cellars moved into a massive, once-private mansion on the outskirts of Walla Walla. All these facilities, and many more being planned, point to an emerging focus on wine tourism in Washington wine country.

• **Two ambitious new projects** are being developed for the Woodinville area, the centre of wine tourism located just outside Seattle. In June 2003, Silver Lake Winery announced plans for a $20-million complex to include several wineries, two restaurants, and related retail businesses. Weeks later, an independent developer unveiled plans for a $12-million wine and culinary centre to be built on 1.6 hectares (ha) (4 acres) near the headquarters of Chateau Ste Michelle. When completed in early 2005, the project will be home to several wineries, tasting rooms, speciality food stores, and restaurants.

• **Long Shadows Vintners,** ex-Stimson Lane CEO Allen Shoup's ambitious consortium of six ultra-premium wineries, has added more winemakers to its all-star line-up. Joining Quintessa's Agustin Huneeus, Dunn Vineyard's Randy Dunn, and Michel Rolland of Le Bon Pasteur in Bordeaux are German producer Armin Diel and French vintner Philippe Melka. Gilles Nicault, formerly assistant winemaker for Woodward Canyon, has been named Long Shadows' resident winemaker.

heightens the competition for anyone with good winemaking credentials. Canoe Ridge Vineyard, part of the Chalone Wine Group, announced its second winemaker change in as many years, hiring Kendall Mix to replace Kevin Mott, who himself had replaced John Abbott. Mott has moved on to Woodward Canyon and Abbott has started his own winery, named Abeja. Previously, Mix was winemaker at Chateau Ste Michelle's Canoe Ridge Estate winery. New at Chateau Ste Michelle is Bob Bertheau, who replaces Eric Olsen, now winemaker at Sonoma's Clos du Bois winery. Bertheau will oversee the making of white wines for CSM.

In Oregon, Cheryl Francis, formerly with Chehalem, has left to start the Francis Tannahill winery with husband Sam Tannahill, ex-Archery Summit winemaker. Francis and Tannahill are also partners in the successful *négociant* brand A to Z with Bill and Deb Hatcher.

At Erath Vineyards, Gary Horner, most recently the winemaker for Benton-Lane, has been named head winemaker for the 40,000-case winery. Michael Beckley, who replaced long-time winemaker Rob Stuart two years ago, left by mutual agreement to concentrate on his own brand, named Quercus. Founder Dick Erath has come out of semi-retirement to become the director of wine. Completing the circle, Damian North takes over winemaking at Benton-Lane, after a stint at Tarra Warra Estate in Australia's Yarra Valley.

Grapevine

- **The grape glut,** though not nearly as endemic in the Pacific Northwest as in California, has created opportunities for a number of new *négociant* brands to enter the marketplace. The biggest is Precept Brands, founded in 2003 by former Corus Brands executives Andrew Browne and Dan Baty. Precept initially projected first-year sales of 70,000 cases split among four brands: Avery Lane, Barrelstone, Pavin & Riley, and Sockeye. With the purchase in autumn 2003 of existing 60,000-case Washington Hills Cellars, Precept doubled these projections, citing "growing consumer demand for high-quality, affordable premium wine". The purchase price was not disclosed. Winemaker Brian Carter will continue with Washington Hills, whose parent company will focus on its Apex and Bridgman labels.

- **After years of lobbying,** the Washington state legislature has agreed to invest $2.3 million every two years to fund new two-year and four-year degree programmes in viticulture and oenology at several state schools. With a new winery being opened every three weeks in Washington state, an estimated 4,700 additional winery jobs will need to be filled by 2006. The new programmes will be anchored by Walla Walla Community College's new $4.1-million Center for Enology and Viticulture. Laboratories, classrooms, and a fully functional winery are located in the facility, whose first student-made wines will be released under the College Cellars label late in 2004.

Washington vintners have employed a two-pronged strategy to promote their wines as serious contenders in terms of both price and quality. Relatively big corporate operations such as Columbia Crest, Hogue, and Covey Run have focused on making competitive wines in significant quantities and selling them at affordable price points. Washington Rieslings and Merlots have enjoyed particular success with this strategy. The leading boutiques — such as Quilceda Creek, Leonetti Cellar, and Andrew Will — have raised the quality bar ever higher and have consistently brought home big scores from the most influential critics and publications.

So far, the strategy has worked. But it may soon be a victim of its own success. The consumer, more than ever, wants cheap wine. With massive amounts of low-end Australian imports flooding the market and the rise of such novelties as Two Buck Chuck (a line of $2 wines exclusive to the Trader Joe's chain that has sold millions of cases), Washington's best budget bottles suddenly look expensive. With barely 12,000 ha (30,000 acres) of vineyard across the entire state, Washington will never produce the glut of grapes that allows wineries to compete with the giveaway prices coming out of California and Australia.

Still more threatening is the number of new, pricey boutique producers that has sprung up in the past few years. For every experienced, quality-driven winemaker such as Mike Januik (Januik Winery), who puts out excellent, limited-production wines at modest prices ($20 to $30), there are half a dozen wannabes whose first release comes with a $50 or $60 price tag. One new winery recently introduced a reserve Cabernet priced at $115 a bottle. The press release also touted the winery's "value-oriented Cabernet Sauvignon" priced at $26 and its "mid-range Cabernet Sauvignon" selling for $55. "We believe each of our wines offers a great value for the price," it went on to say.

No new Washington wineries should attempt such prices. There isn't another wine made in Washington priced at $115 and the few wineries who can legitimately lay claim to prices in the $50 and $60 range have earned that right by making truly great wines for a decade or more. They have shown consistent quality over many vintages and slowly established their pricing, based on what's in the bottle and what the consumer demands.

The game of pricing one-upmanship, which got so out of hand in the Napa Valley a few years ago, can only hurt the efforts of the many talented and dedicated winemakers and wineries, both large and small, who have worked to establish the image of quality at a fair price for Washington's wines. How must it feel to see the new winery on the block pushing its first or second vintage at prices double or triple those charged for wines that have proved themselves to be among the best made in America (and in some instances have bettered First-Growth Bordeaux in blind tastings)? New wineries need to take a long, hard look at the message they are sending when they let their egos run wild.

New AVAs run aground

Applications to create several new Oregon AVAs continue to crawl through the bureaucratic sludge. In the spring of 2002, a coalition of producers in the northern Willamette Valley – the heart of Oregon Pinot Noir country – first petitioned for six new proposed AVAs, to be called Chehalem Mountains, Eola Hills, McMinnville Foothills, Red Hills of Dundee, Ribbon Ridge, and Yamhill-Carlton District. Problems immediately arose. A Red Hills AVA was also being sought by a group in California, while in southern Oregon an application for a Red Hill AVA was in the works. Eola Hills ran into controversy relating to an existing Eola Hills winery that wanted to continue to source fruit from outside the proposed AVA. And the McMinnville Foothills application failed to produce the necessary historical documentation to support the name.

An updated list now includes proposals for a McMinnville AVA and a Dundee Hills AVA. Three other new AVAs – Eola Hills, Yamhill-Carlton District, and Chehalem Mountains – are being scrutinized by the TTB (the federal Alcohol and Tobacco Tax and Trade Bureau). Comments are also being accepted on a new application to create a Southern Oregon AVA encompassing the existing Applegate Valley, Umpqua Valley, and Rogue Valley AVAs. Wineries in the southern half of the state focus on different varieties from the Pinot Blanc/Gris/Noir wines made in the north. Though the new AVAs represent some sort of progress, all of this may be jumping ahead a bit too rapidly for out-of-state consumers, who barely recognize that Oregon is a wine-producing state and have no clue about how to pronounce Willamette, let alone where it is.

In Washington, the ongoing, slow-but-steady evolution of new AVAs is proceeding more smoothly and, quite frankly, makes more sense. A Horse Heaven Hills AVA is expected to be approved early in 2004 and applications are in process for several others, including a Columbia Gorge AVA that would be the third in the Pacific Northwest (along with Columbia Valley and Walla Walla Valley) to straddle the Oregon border. Currently there are two dozen growers and a dozen wineries in that region's proposed boundaries.

Advance report on the latest harvest
2003

Vintage rating: *87 (Washington: 90, Oregon: 84)*

Washington – A bone-dry, scorching-hot summer was saved by a brief but heavy early September rain that cooled things off during harvest. White wines are already quite ripe and fruity, with forward, precocious flavours and somewhat lower acid levels. The Merlot crop is reduced due to poor bloom and set, but on Red Mountain the grapes show superb colour, complexity, and balance. Look for dark, meaty, concentrated Cabernet Sauvignon, somewhat like the 1994s.

Oregon – A cold, wet April delayed budbreak, but a July heat wave brought seasonal heat totals close to record highs. In September, just as grapes were ripening, the same cold, wet weather that struck Washington vineyards hit northern Oregon, threatening botrytis. Then a late-season heat wave warmed things back up to the mid-30s °C (mid-90s °F). It's too soon to know which wineries prevailed against these odds, but look for a vintage of lower-than-normal acids, ripe to overripe fruit, and high levels of alcohol.

Updates on the previous five vintages
2002

Vintage rating: *92 (Washington: 94, Oregon: 90)*

Washington – For the fifth straight year Washington wine growers hit a viticultural home run. Weird spring weather brought 75 mm (3 in) of snow in early May; then a heat spike in mid-July fried some vines and badly stressed others, but all's well that ends well. Crop thinning and perfect autumn weather brought in a record crop that has high sugars, high acidity, and high extract, much like the splendid 1999s. The white wines are juicy and crisp and it looks to be another great year for Cabernet and Syrah.

Oregon – Touch and go from the beginning, as a cold, wet spring got things off to a slow start in the northern Willamette Valley. In southern Oregon a summer heat spike adversely affected some vineyards, while drought and isolated hail storms damaged others. Heavy rains hit the north as the harvest was getting under way; wineries patient enough to wait the rains out were greeted with warm, sunny weather throughout the rest of the month. Overall, 2002 wines show considerable variation, but winemakers who dodged the raindrops, heat spikes, and hailstones made concentrated wines with excellent balance.

2001

Vintage rating: *89 (Washington: 89, Oregon: 89)*
Washington – Extremely hot summer temperatures ripened cooler sites early and harvest began early, on 1 September. The hot weather finally backed off and picking extended well into November, making this both one of the earliest and latest harvests on record. Wines are lush, forward, and fruit-driven, though with more structure than the broadly fruity 2000s. Syrahs are the best of the reds, while the white wines are unusually ripe and tropical for Washington.
Oregon – Extensive green harvesting and exhaustive sorting at crush paid off for those who did the work, with wines showing clean brilliant fruit and great elegance. For too many wineries, however, the 2001s are soft, forward, and simple.

2000

Vintage rating: *89 (Washington: 87, Oregon: 91)*
Washington – A few Merlots and Cabernets from favoured sites are standouts, but the reds, though ripe enough, lack the structured concentration of the 1999s. The whites debuted fresh and pleasant, but should be consumed shortly.
Oregon – A magic vintage, the third in a row for Oregon. Ripening was so uniform that many wineries were buried in grapes as everything came in at once. The Pinots show loads of fruit, with lovely blackberry and cherry notes, as well as smooth, sweet tannins.

1999

Vintage rating: *95 (Washington: 96, Oregon: 94)*
Washington – Blue skies and warm daytime weather created virtually perfect conditions for ripening grapes with deep colours, intense flavours, and remarkable acid levels. The red wines show astonishing depth, power, muscle, and structure, making this a superb vintage for the cellar, and the best of the decade.

Oregon – A miracle vintage with exceptionally long hang time. Chardonnays are concentrated, even unctuous (particularly those from Dijon clones); the Pinots fine, ripe, and beautifully structured for ageing.

1998

Vintage rating: 91 (Washington: 90, Oregon: 93)

Washington – Notable for the spectacular, consistently warm summer weather. Both reds and whites came out loaded with ripe, lush flavours, though the whites and many reds are already past their prime. These jammy, ultra-ripe, California-style wines are not typical of Washington, nor do they reveal its particular strengths.

Oregon – Like Washington (and unlike northern California), this was an excellent, very ripe vintage for Oregon. Dramatically reduced yields and a dry harvest brought in good fruit, with lush, fat fruit flavours.

GREATEST WINE PRODUCERS

1. Quilceda Creek Vintners
2. Leonetti Cellar
3. Beaux Frères
4. DeLille Cellars
5. Ken Wright Cellars
6. Woodward Canyon
7. Andrew Will
8. Chateau Ste Michelle (single-vineyard wines)
9. The Eyrie Vineyards
10. Domaine Drouhin Oregon

NEW UP-AND-COMING PRODUCERS

1. Spring Valley Vineyard
2. Januik
3. Cadence
4. Forgeron Cellars
5. Penner-Ash Wine Cellars
6. Dunham Cellars
7. K Vintners
8. Syncline
9. Fidelitas
10. Cayuse Vineyards

FASTEST-IMPROVING PRODUCERS

1. Kiona Vineyards
2. Bookwalter
3. Sineann
4. Betz Family
5. Elk Cove
6. Three Rivers
7. Chehalem
8. Rex Hill
9. Matthews Cellars
10. Lemelson Vineyards

BEST-VALUE PRODUCERS

1. Columbia Crest
2. Waterbrook
3. Hedges Cellars
4. Covey Run
5. Avery Lane
6. Snoqualmie Vineyards
7. Columbia
8. Willamette Valley Vineyards
9. Erath Vineyards
10. Bridgeview Vineyards

GREATEST-QUALITY WINES

1. **Reserve 2000** Leonetti Cellar ($95)
2. **Muleskinner Merlot 2001** Spring Valley Vineyard ($30)
3. **Shea Vineyard Homer Cuvée Pinot Noir 2001** Shea Wine Cellars ($65)
4. **Cabernet Sauvignon 2000** Bookwalter ($28)
5. **Fries Vineyard Semillon 2001** L'Ecole No. 41 ($20)
6. **Champoux Vineyard Cabernet Sauvignon 2000** Soos Creek ($33)
7. **Ciel du Cheval Cabernet Sauvignon 2000** Waterbrook ($28)
8. **Ian's Reserve Chardonnay 2001** Chehalem ($28)
9. **Syrah 2001** Januik ($30)
10. **Eroica Riesling 2002** Chateau Ste Michelle/Dr Loosen ($20)

BEST BARGAINS

1. **Pinot Gris 2002** Elk Cove ($15)
2. **Semillon 2001** Columbia ($8)
3. **Amycas White 2002** Brooks ($12)
4. **Pinot Blanc 2002** Erath Vineyards ($13)
5. **Riesling 2002** Willamette Valley Vineyards ($8)
6. **Viognier 2002** Rulo ($18)
7. **Two Vines Chardonnay 2001** Columbia Crest ($9)
8. **Gewurztraminer 2002** Covey Run ($7)
9. **Merlot 2001** Cascade Cliffs ($15)
10. **Winemaker's Series Syrah 2001** Ste Chapelle ($10)

MOST EXCITING OR UNUSUAL FINDS

1. **Old Vine Zinfandel 2002** Sineann ($36) *Who knew Zinfandel this ripe and jammy could grow in the Pacific Northwest?*
2. **Cabernet Franc 2001** Walla Walla Vintners ($25) *Rarely bottled as a varietal, this fat, creamy, 100 per cent Cabernet Franc makes a persuasive case for more.*
3. **Clifton Vineyard Viognier 2002** Syncline ($19) *Wahluke slope fruit anchors a perfectly rendered Viognier as good as any in America.*
4. **Malbec 2001** Abacela ($20) *Abacela has pioneered Tempranillo, Dolcetto, and other unusual varieties in central Oregon, and this outstanding Malbec continues the streak of successes.*
5. **Pinot Blanc 2002** WillaKenzie Estate ($18) *This winery makes Pinot Blanc that is so fresh and bursting with tropical fruit that you will mistake it for a particularly fine Chardonnay.*
6. **Syrah 2001** Penner-Ash Wine Cellars ($30) *Syrah is all the rage in Washington, but Oregon can put out a powerful version of its own.*
7. **Barbera 2002** Cascade Cliffs ($18) *Though Nebbiolo has bombed in Washington, Barbera can be big and juicy and ripens well.*
8. **Dolcetto 2002** Woodward Canyon ($19) *Another very promising Italian grape being tested out with encouraging success in Washington.*
9. **Celilo Vineyard Lemberger 2002** Wind River ($30) *Lemberger (Blaufränkisch) rarely dazzles, but this glorious effort from a great vineyard shows its potential.*
10. **Winemaker's Series Syrah 2001** Ste Chapelle ($10) *This would be a fine effort by any standard, but the fact that it is from Idaho makes it even more remarkable.*

Legitimacy for an emerging wine region comes in small steps, but wineries in the Atlantic Northeast have picked up the pace, winning international competitions and taking their wines to national and international venues.

SANDRA SILFVEN

Virginia vintners showed off Merlots and Viogniers in Florence, Italy; the New York Wine & Grape Foundation held its annual competition at COPIA, The American Center for Wine, Food & the Arts, in Napa, California, with West Coast judges; and the 2002 Riesling from Standing Stone in New York became the first East Coast wine sold at COPIA. The New York City-based steakhouse chain Smith & Wollensky changed to selling American wines only and added a special section called 'Undiscovered Gems from the USA', which includes wines from Long Island, Virginia, New Jersey, and Ohio.

But it was sweeping honours for a Riesling from, of all places, Michigan, not the more likely New York Finger Lakes, that may have shifted this region into a new gear. The Semi Dry Riesling 2002 from Peninsula Cellars upstaged whites from around the world by not only winning the Riesling Cup in Corning, New York, but also Best White Wine at the International Eastern Wine Competition and Best White at the San Francisco International Wine Competition, where it shared the stage with Phelps Insignia and Dom Pérignon. On a similar level, the 2002 Estate Reserve Viognier (from only the second leafing) by Keswick Vineyards in Virginia was named Best White Wine in America at the Atlanta

SANDRA SILFVEN lives in Dearborn, Michigan, and has worked at *The Detroit News* for more than 30 years in many reporting and editing positions. She has written about wine for most of her career and produces the *Michigan Wine Report* for Detroit News Online at www.detroitnews.com/wine. She travelled widely in the Atlantic Northeast to produce this report.

International Wine Summit, where the Best Red was Cyrus from Alexander Valley Vineyards, California. While the Atlantic Northeast also has a sizable collection of best-of-class awards, it is significant that a Michigan Riesling and a Virginia Viognier were the best of the best because both states have a track record for these varieties.

New crop of wineries

The other big story in the region is growth. In the face of hurricanes, severe winters, cold springs, vine diseases, and an image problem, the number of new wineries is exploding. Ohio is approaching 80 wineries, from 63 in 2000. At 87 and counting, Pennsylvania surpassed Virginia with the second-highest number behind New York with 190, where Keuka Lake is the hot spot. New Jersey wineries have grown by almost 50 per cent to 24, Michigan is nearing 40, and the tiny Maryland industry is seeing young urban professionals buying and converting old tobacco farms.

Grapevine

- **Fourteen of Pennsylvania's** 80-plus wineries have formed the Pennsylvania Premium Wine Group to promote dry European-style wines. They have appointed a panel of experts to judge vinifera wines blind to decide which are qualified to wear a Pennsylvania Quality Assurance seal.

- **Taking the lead in the east,** Michigan's oldest and largest winery, St Julian, moved to Stelvin screwcaps for its mid-priced vinifera/hybrid blends and Native American wines. Owner David Braganini says it took his winery 30 years to get away from screwcaps and now his 19-year-old daughter thinks they're "way cool".

- **Louisa Thomas Hargrave** hides nothing in her personal account of how she and ex-husband Alex started the first commercial winery on Long Island 30 years ago. Her new book, *The Vineyard: The Pleasures and Perils of Creating an American Family Winery* (Viking Press), pours out sweet, poignant prose about the challenges facing a pair of Harvard grads who had never even planted a vegetable garden. They were the spark for a wine industry that would eventually garner wide acclaim and lure many wealthy investors, but ironically their decades of toil would end in divorce and the sale of the Hargrave Vineyard.

- **Martha Clara Vineyards,** named after the mother of owner Robert Entenmann (of Entenmann bakery fame), continues to evolve on Long Island. French-born Gilles Martin, former assistant winemaker at Roederer Estate in California, was named winemaker and a new 50-ft tasting counter has been opened.

- **Sparkling-wine producer** Larry Mawby of L Mawby Vineyards in Michigan could not believe his luck when he received official approval for his Sex label, but it has been flying off the shelf ever since. Sex is an inexpensive pink sparkling wine. Such has been the demand that Mawby will move the production of this wine, with his demi-sec Fizz, over to the *charmat* method, to create a new line of $10 sparklers under the M Lawrence label (using the initial of his surname and his full given name).

It takes only one weird wine to spoil a state's reputation in the mind of a savvy consumer. There are still too many bad wines in the Atlantic Northeast, either flawed by vineyard or cellar practices, or dumbed down to please the masses. It is even more pathetic when vintners think they are being clever and anoint them with so many hokey names. Above all, northeastern wines cry out for better clones, rootstocks, sites, and vineyard management, with attention to trellising, canopy management, and the dropping of fruit in the summer to make the vines stronger and the remaining clusters riper. There is too much use of American oak (it overwhelms the fruit); too much emphasis on Chardonnay (established wine regions do it better and price it more reasonably); too little knowledge of international styles, which may be why too many wineries mistakenly use the name Pinot Gris (think high-extract Alsace) for a lighter Pinot Grigio style; and there is too little emphasis and education on regional specialities. If it is Chambourcin that makes the best red wine, then leave the Cabernet Sauvignon to hotter regions and explain to vinifera drinkers what Chambourcin is all about. Also, I am traditional enough in loving true icewines to lament the dependence on cryoextraction – freezing late-harvest grapes – to make dessert wines, even though they are delicious. God bless Ohio, Michigan, Pennsylvania, and a few intrepid vintners in New York for making icewines the old-fashioned way.

Upping the quality

As for what the Atlantic Northeast should be doing, wineries need to look to Eric Miller at Chaddsford in Pennsylvania, who, as he described it, went kicking and screaming away from making what he perceived as classic European-style reds to a New World style. Based on trials to compare the analysis and flavours of grapes at the same Brix but with longer hang time, he decided that he preferred these fruit-forward reds to earthy types with harder tannins, which he had to fine and filter. To make the 2000 Merican – a blend of Cabernet Sauvignon, Merlot, and Cabernet Franc – he stopped looking at sugars for the earliest clean fruit and picking dates, and instead tasted the grapes for ripe grainy tannins and ripe fruit flavours. He let the grapes hang through three hurricanes in that vintage and lost most of his Chardonnay and Pinot Noir. However, he said that the season ended brilliantly for his late-ripeners, calling his Cab and Merlot blends the best he had made in the past 20 vintages, adding, "If only I had known." It is risky, but that is what the northeast should be doing.

Getting it right

In dealing with grape varieties that by themselves may need help in making a balanced wine, vintners have finally got creative by blending or cellar work. A few examples: Lamoreaux Landing (New York) produced T23, an unwooded Cabernet Franc bursting with fruit and spice; Breaux (Virginia) made Alexis, a late-harvest blend of Vidal, Sauvignon Blanc, and Semillon with a beguiling orange-peel twist; and Heron Hill (New York) debuted Eclipse White, a blend of Chardonnay, Pinot Gris, and Sauvignon Blanc that is reminiscent of Alsace wines. Blending and careful use of wood seem the way to go in a challenged region. Also, regional specialities are finally emerging and being promoted as such: Riesling in New York's Finger Lakes and Michigan; Merlot on New York's Long Island; Cabernet Franc and Viognier in Virginia.

• **Kinkead Ridge,** 60 miles east of Cincinnati, in the history-rich village of Ripley, has released its first reds, including the big Revelation 2001 ($18), an estate-grown Bordeaux-style blend, primarily Cabernet Sauvignon. Prior to establishing this 5-acre vineyard, owners Ron Barrett and Nancy Bentley operated a 40-acre Pinot Noir vineyard outside Portland, Oregon, which they sold to Tony Soter of Etude.

• **Delaware and New York** became the 25th and 26th states to allow Sunday sales at liquor stores. To placate New York liquor stores, which preferred being closed on Sundays, the state issued a controversial moratorium on new store licences, making existing licences more valuable. Rhode Island is also considering Sunday sales.

• **Kevin Zraly,** famed wine director of Windows on the World restaurant for 25 years, has joined Smith & Wollensky Restaurant Group as vice-president. He continues to teach a wine school in Manhattan.

• **Four small Long Island wineries** have banded together to open a single tasting room in Peconic, called The Tasting Room. They are Broadfields Wine Cellars, Sherwood House, Schneider Vineyards, and La Comtesse Thérèse.

• **Ladybugs dined on many vineyards** in the 2003 vintage, but the results were not as disastrous as in 2001. As one observer put it, "They came, they ate, they left." This time, wineries (and consumers) were well aware of the off flavours that could ensue if the bugs were crushed along with the grapes. More wineries used repellents safe for organic vines and bought sorting tables to pick out the undesirables.

• **Seneca Lake** became New York's newest American Viticultural Area (AVA), thanks to the work of Beverly Stamp of Lakewood Vineyards. Some wineries on Seneca's eastern shore are so sold on the regional character of their wines that they're talking of a subappellation for the vineyards south of Lodi.

Advance report on the latest harvest
2003

What a headache. First, in pockets of the Atlantic Northeast there were deadly cold temperatures in March. Then, across the region, the spring was long and cool, which delayed flowering. The summer was one of the rainiest in memory, with wet-weather predators rampant. It became critical to control early mildews by constant spraying and thinning of the shoots and leaves. Then came Hurricane Isabel in September, which turned out not as bad as billed, but prompted a few coastal wineries to pick early. A short burst of heat in October was the only saving grace for those who waited. Many growers picked well into November. Yields were down 40 to 50 per cent or more in most areas, with low sugars and diluted acids. Still, there were pockets of success. St Julian in southwest Michigan reports its biggest harvest ever and, in New England, Sharpe Hill and Sakonnet were able to control disease and reported a decent vintage.

Updates on the previous five vintages
2002

Vintage rating: *92 (Red: 90, White: 94)*
Most states, with the exception of Virginia and the Finger Lakes of New York, were thrilled with the quality of all the whites and, almost uniformly in the northeast, the reds. Rieslings especially showed well, along with Cabernet Francs and Pinot Noirs. Flavours were described as rich and intense for whites, concentrated with balanced acids for reds.

2001

Vintage rating: *93 (Red: 92, White: 94)*
Except for New Jersey, which was deluged with rain at harvest, this was a thrilling vintage for the quality of both reds and whites. Rieslings had high acids; Pinot Noirs showed spicy, upfront fruit. An invasion of ladybugs, however, tainted some wines in Ohio and nearby states when the bugs were scooped up by mechanical pickers and crushed with the grapes.

2000

Vintage rating: *78 (Red: 72, White: 84)*

Apart from New York, this was a difficult vintage for most states, with cool weather, rain, and hurricanes. Jim Law of Linden Vineyards in Virginia described it as "awful". Chardonnay and Riesling showed best; reds were underripe and diluted.

1999

Vintage rating: *90 (Red: 92, White: 88)*

Except for Connecticut, which was soaked by late rains, most states had a long, hot, dry season that led to exceptionally ripe, highly concentrated Cabernet Franc, Pinot Noir, and Merlot. Whites lacked some of their typical crispness and ageing ability.

1998

Vintage rating: *91 (Red: 95, White: 88)*

This El Niño vintage brought the northeast spring-like weather in February, which led to a long, hot season that produced wines with exceptional ripeness and unusual tropical notes. It was something new for most wineries, which went on to produce some pretty atypical wines: reds that were lush and concentrated; whites that were fuller, richer, and had less acidity. Rieslings lacked their usual crispness.

Grapevine

• **The state of Michigan** appealed to the US Supreme Court to protect its ban on interstate wine shipments to residents, which a lower court found unconstitutional.

• **Still for sale:** Sakonnet in Rhode Island and, once again, the property in New York now known as Galluccio Family Winery on the North Fork of Long Island. Only three years ago, the former Gristina Vineyards was purchased by Vincent Galluccio for $5.2 million. The asking price is now said to be $7.5 million.

• **Pindar winemaker** Mark Friszolowski left the Long Island winery to join the new start-up by NASCAR team owner Richard Childress in North Carolina. Pindar owner Dr Dan Damianos filled the post with his son Jason, who is winemaker at the family's other Long Island winery, Duck Walk.

• **Long Island winemaker Kip Bedell** of Bedell Cellars says that, from now on, their sister property, Corey Creek, will produce only white wines, and Bedell only reds. All the production will take place at Bedell, and Corey Creek wines will also be available at Bedell's tasting room.

GREATEST WINE PRODUCERS

1. Dr Konstantin Frank (New York)
2. Wölffer Estate (New York)
3. Lenz (New York)
4. Barboursville (Virginia)
5. Bedell Cellars (New York)
6. Markko (Ohio)
7. Sakonnet (Rhode Island)
8. Chaddsford (Pennsylvania)
9. Tomasello (New Jersey)
10. Huber (Indiana)

FASTEST-IMPROVING PRODUCERS

1. Heron Hill (New York)
2. Channing Daughters (New York)
3. Tabor Hill (Michigan)
4. St Julian (Michigan)
5. Anthony Road (New York)
6. Valley Vineyards (Ohio)
7. Fenn Valley (Michigan)
8. Ferrante (Ohio)
9. Clover Hill (Pennsylvania)
10. Chateau de Leelanau (Michigan)

NEW UP-AND-COMING PRODUCERS

1. Peninsula Cellars (Michigan)
2. Standing Stone (New York)
3. Winery at Black Star Farms (Michigan)
4. King Family/Michael Shaps (Virginia)
5. Martha Clara (New York)
6. Keswick Vineyards (Virginia)
7. Veritas (Virginia)
8. Raphael (New York)
9. Troutman (Ohio)
10. Turtle Run (Indiana)

BEST-VALUE PRODUCERS

1. Horton (Virginia)
2. Fox Run (New York)
3. Swedish Hill (New York)
4. Lakewood (New York)
5. Lamoreaux Landing (New York)
6. St Julian (Michigan)
7. Mount Nittany (Pennsylvania)
8. Oliver (Indiana)
9. Chalet Debonné (Ohio)
10. Winery at Wilcox (Pennsylvania)

GREATEST-QUALITY WINES

1. **Ingle Vineyard Johannisberg Riesling 2002** Heron Hill, New York ($16)
2. **Gewurztraminer Manigold Vineyard 2002** Peninsula Cellars, Michigan ($18)
3. **Dry Riesling 2002** Dr Konstantin Frank, New York ($14)
4. **Cabernet Franc 2001** Wölffer Estate, New York ($40)
5. **Old Vines Merlot 2000** Lenz, New York ($55)
6. **Octagon Fifth Edition 2001** Barboursville, Virginia ($30)
7. **Cuvee RJR 1998** Westport Rivers, Massachusetts ($20)
8. **Hardscrabble 2001** Linden, Virginia ($30)
9. **Merican 2000** Chaddsford, Pennsylvania ($35)
10. **Cadenza 1998** Allegro, Pennsylvania ($33)

BEST BARGAINS

1. **Chardonnay White Label 2001** Lenz, New York ($12)
2. **Bin 2000 Stonecastle Red NV** Horton, Virginia ($12)
3. **Chardonnay 2002** Fox Run, New York ($10)
4. **Main Road White NV** Bedell Cellars, New York ($10)
5. **Vidal Blanc 2002** Alba, New Jersey ($12)
6. **Seyval-Chardonnay 2002** Chateau LaFayette Reneau, New York ($9)
7. **Glaciers End Chardonnay 2002** Martha Clara, New York ($10)
8. **Rhode Island Red 2001** Sakonnet, Rhode Island ($11)
9. **Cabernet Franc 2002** Ferrante, Ohio ($13)
10. **Ballet of Angels NV** Sharpe Hill, Connecticut ($10)

MOST EXCITING OR UNUSUAL FINDS

1. **Tocai Friulano 2002** Channing Daughters, New York ($22) *Explosive pink grapefruit/pink peppercorn/floral aromas, while surprisingly soft and round on the palate.*
2. **Finger Lakes Riesling Reserve 2002** Heron Hill, New York ($25) *Bracing acidity supports an exciting abundance of lime, peach, nectarine, and mineral flavours.*
3. **Nebbiolo 2001** Breaux, Virginia ($40) *Full-bodied and elegant, like sticking your nose in a bowl of red raspberries, chocolate, and vanilla.*
4. **Cabernet Franc 2001** Michael Shaps (King Family), Virginia ($25) *Big, elegant wine with integrated ripe red fruit, acidity, and fine, silken tannins.*
5. **Solera Cream Sherry** St Julian, Michigan ($15) *Lush pecan, hazelnut, and butterscotch aromas develop into rich, full, creamy flavours on the palate. It is 100 per cent Niagara grapes.*
6. **Meritage 2001** Fox Run, New York ($35) *Layers of plums, cassis, cherries, and raspberry packed tight on the palate.*
7. **Sex NV** L Mawby, Michigan ($14) *Larry Mawby half-jokingly applied for permission to sell wine under the label Sex, and he could not believe his luck when it was accepted.*
8. **Brut NV** Martha Clara, New York ($19) *Crisp green apple/citrus aromas that tickle the nose, and refreshing fruit and acidity on the palate, with a delicious doughy note on the finish.*
9. **Gewurztraminer Dry 2002** Hermann J Wiemer, New York ($18) *A medley of peaches, rose petals, melons, and apples with a touch of citrus on the palate.*
10. **Chambourcin 2001** Tomasello, New Jersey ($16) *A velvet monster with Shiraz-like stewed blueberry and cranberry fruit, almost creamy on the palate.*

Grapevine

• **Seven wineries** in southern Chester County, Pennsylvania, near Philadelphia, have formed the Brandywine Valley Wine Trail, bringing the number of trails in the state to seven. Chaddsford is the major force in the bunch. Tiny Paradocx (it is owned by a 'pair of doctors') is the one to keep an eye on, with its Muscats and Viogniers.

Today's goal for the wineries of the rest of America is to create new traditions from new grapes, yet in established, familiar styles. History should help.

DOUG FROST MW

In the mid-19th century, vineyards around Cincinnati represented the most successful wine region in America, producing sparkling wines from Catawba. One hundred and sixty years ago, El Paso, Texas, was the site of the most important fortified wines in America. And about a hundred years ago, Missouri was the most significant wine-producing state in the country, with the equivalent of half a million cases of wine being shipped through the port of St Louis each year.

Despite these historical curiosities, the wine regions outside the US coasts must invent their own wine traditions, working with often-unknown grapes and reinventing styles.

In many ways, things are going swimmingly. The acreage, number of wineries, and volume of wine in the middle part of the country have roughly doubled in the past 10 years. Sales are commensurate. In states such as Missouri, sales of local wines represent nearly 7 per cent of all wine sold in the marketplace, a significant proportion considering the hegemony of the major national wine companies.

Only about 10 per cent of the wineries in these states have distribution outside their own areas. Depending largely on cellar-door traffic, most of these wineries have become adept at supporting and promoting their own wine tourism through festivals, grape-picking and grape-stomping parties, and through the local media.

DOUG FROST MW is the author of two wine books, including *On Wine* (Rizzoli International Publications, 2001). He is one of only three people in the world to hold the titles of both Master Sommelier and Master of Wine.

The drawback is that wineries selling large volumes of tourist-friendly wines become known only for their sweeter, softer styles, which affects sales of their drier wines. Local restaurants also become even more resistant to promoting local wines.

Restaurateurs are also often confused by the hybrid grapes used throughout the Midwest and Southeast. Most American customers know how a Chardonnay or Merlot likely to taste, but few have ever heard of Vignoles, Vidal Blanc, Norton, or Maréchal Foch, much less a dry Vignoles.

This reliance on hybrids, and even native varieties, is necessitated by the climate. As warm and humid as the summers can be, it is the winters in the Midwest that are most trying, having successfully ended the lives of almost all commercial vinifera vineyards in these states. In the Southeast US, endemic Pierce's disease is a guarantee that hybrids remain the primary choice for the foreseeable future.

And since the large wine-producing states of Texas, Virginia, and New York are abandoning hybrids (except when producing dessert wines), these states will have to go it alone in their efforts to explain these grapes to their customers. As if their marketing challenges were not great enough already.

We're from the government and we're here to help

The regulatory environment has improved since last year. For some states – such as Iowa, Missouri, Illinois, and Minnesota – newly funded efforts in viticulture offer the hope of a better understanding of existing grapes; new grapes are also in the offing.

In places such as Kansas, Nebraska, and Texas, growers are finding that their efforts are no longer bedevilled by state governments. Throughout the US, a great number of vineyards and wineries are shortening learning curves and multiplying opportunities for experimentation.

More importantly, the regulatory atmosphere has changed for wine sales, especially interstate wine sales via the Internet or telephone. States that have recently changed their shipping laws to allow consumers direct access to wines include South Dakota, South Carolina, and North Carolina. By most accounts, this loosening of regulations will continue, though perhaps not as rapidly as in 2003.

Grapevine

• Arizona has opened the door to direct shipment of wine, allowing consumers who have bought wine at a winery to have it shipped directly to their homes. Other wine shipments are still prohibited, but a court case is pending that may end the prohibition.

Although each area has its unique challenges and assets, producers can learn from each other. The success of Norton in Missouri, for instance, testifies to the need to seek the best conditions possible for each grape. So, rather than merely trying to compete with Missouri Norton, other regions have to find their own Nortons, as it were. Chambourcin may find one of its most suitable homes in southern Illinois, whereas Chardonel is more aromatic in cooler regions to the north.

In Washington state, Syrah is the most sought-after new grape. But, across the border in Idaho, Hell's Canyon's Stephen Robertson isn't ready to jump on to the Syrah bandwagon just yet. And while Sangiovese and Tempranillo are promising in Idaho, Robertson believes that they might perform far better in northwest Oregon. His view? "Viognier is a no-brainer in southwest Idaho."

Misguided enthusiasm for new or famous grapes isn't the only error being committed by many new wine regions; at times they make desperate efforts to emulate the styles of other regions. But why try to make a Chardonel that tastes like California Chardonnay instead of a uniquely styled wine? Tim Puchta of Adam Puchta Winery is intent on using Chardonel to make something crisp and citrous, like a New Zealand Chardonnay.

Puchta is one of a growing number of winemakers keenly aware of the larger marketplace who focus not merely on California or Australia but on all possible wine styles and origins. However, the trend is for ambitious wineries to make dry table wines with high alcohol and lashings of brand-new oak.

But there is great ferment. In Texas, the promise suggested a decade ago, long deferred, appears possible again. Idaho has quietly moved towards making wines that can stand alongside its partners in the Pacific Northwest. Missouri is setting the standard for French hybrids in America as well as for a native variety, Norton. America's best non-West-Coast sparkler is made in New Mexico. Colorado's output suggests that it has potential as great as any other state in this survey, though still unrealized. Wisconsin should be able to make wines that can stand alongside Michigan and eastern Canada, if not those from better-known areas.

And the rest of the states? Well, all of them make wine, some better than others. Judging from the quality that exists intermittently, only will and time (and perhaps money) stand in the way of delightful table wines throughout the US.

Selected highlights only. Vintage ratings would not be meaningful for such a vast and diverse area.

Advance report on the new harvest
2003

The theme for many of these areas is spring damage. Whether in central Texas, eastern Wisconsin, or Missouri, freeze and frost damage created very small crops, in some cases one-third of the normal size. But the wines that were made are sometimes very good. In Missouri, the reds are particularly worthwhile, but whites are in short supply. In Wisconsin, whites are among the best yet seen. Texas lost most of its white wines in the spring frost, and reds were significantly down as well. Colorado had a healthy crop, and Idaho saw another hot year, with great colour and aromatics.

Updates on the previous five vintages
2002

Idaho had another warm and sunny year, the harvest having finished before the second week of October. The whites are balanced, but reds are a bit high in alcohol. Though Missouri's white grapes were not as aromatic as in 2000, the reds are intense and concentrated. Georgia was a victim of the excessive rains that the rest of the Atlantic coast saw, including the Carolinas; the wines are a mixed bag. In the Southwest, it was yet again a drought year and wines show good concentration as a result, though some Arizona wines are rather high in alcohol. Colorado struggled, while Texas saw temperatures that were cooler than normal and precipitation that was higher than normal, with a very small crop.

2001

In Idaho, even ripening and a warm, quick year resulted in good quality overall. White wines are even crisper than usual and the reds show balance and length. Some lovely white wines were made in this vintage, but the Vignoles was difficult in Missouri. Some reds are a bit stingy, but some

Nortons are delightful. For New Mexico and Arizona, this was year four of the drought and forest fires raged throughout the area. The wines are as muscular as those in Texas.

2000

Idaho had a warm, ripe vintage but with very good acidity, resulting in wines of some longevity compared to 2001 and 1999. Missouri's wineries created wines as well balanced as any in the last four years and some Nortons are tops. It was another good year in New Mexico and Arizona, with cool conditions making for balanced wines.

1999

Idaho saw another sunny, warm year, but the crop was fairly small. What was there was really supple, rich, and elegant. Missouri experienced some challenges throughout the season and at harvest, yet offers wines with solid fruit and structure. It was a very good year for many in New Mexico, the second drought year in a row. Arizona had some hail, with a small, concentrated, tannic crop.

1998

Idaho's harvest was warm, easy, and clean, though the cycle began with cool weather. The resulting wines have pronounced acidity, but alcohols are sometimes quite high. Amazing rainstorms hammered many Missouri wineries, yet some of the reds are pretty, even charming, though they are the exceptions. It was a good year for some wines in New Mexico, Arizona, and Texas, but too short and hot for others, which are lacking in balance.

Grapevine

- **Typical of most of America's** new AVAs, North Carolina's Yadkin Valley, at 1.4 million acres, hardly suggests a selective sense of soil or climate. Still, NASCAR sports-car racing legend Richard Childress is opening a winery there under his own name in 2004, which will focus attention on the area.

- **Prices for some hybrids** are unrealistically high, as wineries faddishly seek out certain grapes. Should Chardonel or Traminette cost the same as Napa Valley Chardonnay? Hardly. Yet both grapes cost nearly the same as Chardonnay from Napa or Sonoma.

- **Lacrosse and Edelweiss** in the northern Plains are beginning to show good consistency in clean table wines and dessert wines. For reds, St Croix has seen some tasty bottlings in the last year or two.

GREATEST WINE PRODUCERS

1. Stone Hill (Missouri)
2. Gruet (New Mexico)
3. Montelle (Missouri)
4. Callaghan (Arizona)
5. Flat Creek (Texas)
6. Augusta (Missouri)
7. Vickers (Idaho)
8. Dry Comal Creek (Texas)
9. Becker Family (Texas)
10. Cap Rock (Texas)

FASTEST-IMPROVING PRODUCERS

1. Callaghan (Arizona)
2. HolyField (Kansas)
3. Becker Family (Texas)
4. Messina Hof (Texas)
5. Adam Puchta (Missouri)
6. Alto (Illinois)
7. Alamosa (Texas)
8. Hell's Canyon (Idaho)
9. Creekstone (from Habersham) (Georgia)
10. Chrisman Mills (Kentucky)

NEW UP-AND-COMING PRODUCERS

1. Alto (Illinois)
2. HolyField (Kansas)
3. Flat Creek (Texas)
4. Adam Puchta (Missouri)
5. La Cruz de Comal (Texas)
6. Dry Comal Creek (Texas)
7. Plum Creek (Colorado)
8. Milagro (New Mexico)
9. Hell's Canyon (Idaho)
10. Tiger Mountain (Georgia)

BEST-VALUE PRODUCERS

1. HolyField (Kansas)
2. St James (Missouri)
3. Cedar Creek (Wisconsin)
4. James Arthur (Nebraska)
5. Stone Bluff (Oklahoma)
6. Cuthills (Nebraska)
7. Messina Hof (Texas)
8. Chrisman Mills (Kentucky)
9. Wollersheim (Wisconsin)
10. Blue Mountain (Texas)

GREATEST-QUALITY WINES

1. **Chambourcin 2001** Alto, Illinois ($16)
2. **Syrah 2002** Callaghan, Arizona ($18)
3. **Blanc de Blanc 1999** Gruet, New Mexico ($22)
4. **Black Spanish 2002** Dry Comal Creek, Texas ($16)
5. **Travis Peak Select Moscato d'Arancio 2002** Flat Creek, Texas ($13 per 50-cl bottle)
6. **Late Harvest Vignoles 2002** Stone Hill, Missouri ($17)
7. **Signature Port NV** Adam Puchta, Missouri ($26)
8. **Chardonnay 2002** Vickers, Idaho ($15)
9. **Norton 2001** Stone Hill, Missouri ($18)
10. **Vidal Blanc 2002** Cedar Creek, Wisconsin ($11)

Grapevine

• **Utah continues to walk away** from the wine business, though neighbouring state Colorado is enjoying financial success, with nearly 50 wineries in business. In Utah, there are now only 30 acres of wine grapes left in the Four Corners area, once thought to offer the state's greatest promise. Utah made the shipment of wine into the state a felony this year.

BEST BARGAINS

1. **Chambourcin 2001** HolyField, Kansas ($16)
2. **Cream Sherry 2002** Stone Hill, Missouri ($15)
3. **Prairie Fumé (Seyval Blanc) 2002** Wollersheim, Wisconsin ($8)
4. **Cuthills de Chaunac 2002** Cuthills, Nebraska ($12)
5. **Schoolhouse White NV** St James, Missouri ($8)
6. **Cynthiana 2001** Heinrichshaus, Missouri ($13)
7. **Cynthiana 2002** Augusta, Missouri ($15)
8. **Vidal Blanc 2002** Alto, Illinois ($9)
9. **Cynthiana/Norton 2002** Stone Bluff, Oklahoma ($15)
10. **Chardonel 2002** St James, Missouri ($12)

MOST EXCITING OR UNUSUAL FINDS

1. **Grande Reserve 1997** Gruet, New Mexico ($26) *Very yeasty and leesy and very fun to drink.*
2. **Chardonel 2002** Augusta, Missouri ($10) *Delicious, crisp and clean, like apple and peach slices with citrus elements in the finish.*
3. **Syrah Three Vineyards 2002** Koenig, Idaho ($20) *Earthy, tannic, powerful — everything moderate-climate Syrah doesn't have to be, but it has a purpose all the same. It represents a distinct style of Syrah that means, at least for the moment, Idaho Syrah.*
4. **Malbec 2002** La Cruz de Comal, Texas ($15) *As mean and tannic a version of this often-simple grape as anything you'll get from France's Cahors region.*
5. **Cabernet Franc 1999** Tiger Mountain, Georgia ($23) *Fruity and aromatic, but as leafy as any Bourgeuil; fascinatingly close to some of Virginia's best work with the grape.*
6. **Vidal Blanc Blooming White 2002** Tabor Family, Iowa ($8) *Very pretty Vidal Blanc with lots of orange and mango notes to it.*
7. **Merlot 2000** Milagro, New Mexico ($18) *Brooding, leafy, tea-flavoured Merlot with lots of pretty cherry flavours to balance it nicely.*
8. **Syrah Deerslayer 2002** Hell's Canyon, Idaho ($20) *Very spicy, intense, and tannic style of Syrah.*
9. **Port 2001** Stone Hill, Missouri ($18) *This remains the standard against which all other non-vinifera ports should be judged.*
10. **Paulo Meritage 2001** Messina Hof, Texas ($30) *Delightful blue plum notes, powerful, intense middle, but with a lively, well-balanced finish.*

Grapevine

- **Two new grape varieties** have been introduced in the northern Plains. Frontenac is being planted and some growers are enthusiastic. A brand-new variety, Brianna, shows great promise with bright floral aromatics, pineapple fruit, and excellent cold-hardiness.

- **The Asian-ladybug problem** continues to pester, if not panic, Midwestern wine producers. This year saw ladybug problems in Nebraska, though fewer problems in Missouri and Illinois. The bug taints wines with the smell and taste of rancid peanut butter.

Canada

Tony Aspler

A long-standing dispute with the EU over wine and spirits was resolved when Canadian officials signed an agreement in September 2003.

TONY ASPLER

Under the terms of the agreement, Canadian wineries will no longer be able to use a range of generic names, such as chablis, chianti, mosel, port, sherry, and champagne, for locally made products. Following a phase-out period, provincial liquor boards will not list any wines so labelled unless they come from the geographical region that has produced them historically. The EU has also received assurances that the provincial liquor systems will take a more even-handed approach to imported products.

Following negotiations in 1989, Canada signed a bilateral wine and spirits agreement that permitted certain provincial policies favouring Canadian wineries to continue. But in the late 1990s the EU threatened to take Canada before the World Trade Organization unless Canada agreed to negotiate further. It has taken five years to hammer out the current agreement. Under its terms, Canada will maintain its current

TONY ASPLER is the most widely read wine writer in Canada. He was the wine columnist for *The Toronto Star* for 21 years and has authored 11 books on wine and food, including *Vintage Canada*, *The Wine Lover's Companion*, *The Wine Lover Cooks*, and *Travels with My Corkscrew*. Tony is writing *The Atlas of Canadian Wines*. He is a member of the North American advisory board for the Masters of Wine, creator of the annual Ontario Wine Awards competition, and a director of the Independent Wine & Spirit Trust. He is also a director of the Canadian Wine Library and serves on Air Canada's wine-selection committee. At the Niagara Grape & Wine Festival 2000, Tony was presented with the Royal Bank Business Citizen of the Year award. Tony also writes fiction, including a collection of wine murder mysteries featuring the itinerant wine writer-cum-detective Ezra Brant: *Blood Is Thicker than Beaujolais*, *The Beast of Barbaresco*, and *Death on the Douro*. He is currently working on *Nightmare in Napa Valley*. Tony Aspler's website can be found at www.tonyaspler.com

liquor-distribution system with its winery retail stores and Canadian wine stores. The agreement will also give Canadian products, including icewine, access to the European market, will accept Canadian winemaking practices, and will validate Canada's appellation system, Vintners Quality Alliance (VQA).

Fire destroys Okanagan winery

The forest fires that raged through British Columbia in August 2003 destroyed one Okanagan Valley winery and threatened at least three others.

St Hubertus Estate lost its administration office, wine shop, and production facility. The storage room that contained St Hubertus's bottles ready for shipping was undamaged, but 230 tons of grapes in vineyards surrounding the winery – about 3 per cent of the Okanagan Valley crop – were affected by heavy smoke.

St Hubertus looked like a little piece of Switzerland above the city of Kelowna on the shores of Lake Okanagan. Brothers Leo and Andy Gerbert named the property after their family lodge in Switzerland. They own two adjacent vineyards – St Hubertus and Oak Bay – which are among the oldest plantings in the Okanagan, dating back to the 1920s.

• **Igor Ryjenkov is the first Canadian** resident to become a Master of Wine. Born in Russia, Igor came to Canada in late 1992 from Moscow, where he received his degree in International Journalism and Foreign Languages. Ryjenkov is a product consultant for the Liquor Control Board of Ontario.

• **The scourge of the Asian ladybug** has once again hit the Bench area of the Niagara Peninsula. Wineries used hand-harvesting to shake the bunches before committing them to the hoppers. The more scrupulous producers employed agitating sorting tables to knock out the insects from the bunches or washed the grapes before crushing. They also resorted to vacuuming the bunches.

• **A direct-delivery wine club,** modelled on The (London) Sunday Times Wine Club, has been started by the Toronto Star, Canada's largest newspaper. Once a month, members can buy Ontario wines not available at the government-controlled Liquor Control Board of Ontario. They are seeking to extend to imported wines as well. The LCBO is not amused.

• **Inniskillin has been voted** New World Winery of the Year by the American magazine Wine Enthusiast. Cofounder Donald Ziraldo, an extreme skier, has announced that his winery will be an official sponsor of the Canadian Olympic Team. To commemorate the announcement, Inniskillin plans to produce a special Riesling icewine and has planted a parcel of vines for the project. First vintage is projected for 2010 – the year of the Vancouver Winter Olympics.

CANADIAN WINE SCREWED

Henry of Pelham, in Ontario's Niagara Peninsula, has become the first Canadian winery to have the courage to bottle a quality wine under screwcap. Proprietor Paul Speck took a gamble by packaging his 2002 Barrel Fermented Chardonnay, which retails at C$18.25, under screwcap, but he offset his odds by bottling only a quarter of the 1,000-case production under the new closure.

To set the mind of the apprehensive consumer at rest, Speck attached a neck label to the screwcap Chardonnay, which will be sold side by side on the shelves with the cork-closed bottles. The label explains that tradition, being a good idea that works, should be renewed: "Keeping with this new tradition, we are using screwcaps in our finest wines first."

REASONABLE STANDARDS

British Columbia has been a difficult place to find consensus on proposed National Wine Standards, but such an agreement has become a priority for BC Minister of Agriculture, Food & Fisheries John van Dongen. He has appointed a committee to meet the concerned parties: the BC Wine Institute, which represents wineries accounting for most of the wine production in BC, and the BC Winegrowers Association, which represents a majority of wineries, including many of the smaller operations. A prime objective of National Wine Standards will be to differentiate between true "grown in Canada" wines and imported wines, which, though only bottled in Canada, can still bear a "Canadian wine" identification. One proposal would identify such imports as "Cellared in Canada", the same designation as used in Ontario for offshore blends.

An agreement between the BC Wine Institute and the BC Winegrowers Association in such areas as appellation and accreditation practices would be a giant step towards unifying the BC grape and wine industry and making it more consumer-friendly and effective in both domestic and export marketing.

ICEWINE FAKES

The presence of significant quantities of fake icewine on liquor-store shelves in the Far East has prompted the Canadian government to fund research into the problem at a cost of C$1 million. Scientists at Brock University's Cool Climate Oenology and Viticulture Institute in Ontario have embarked on a four-year study to create models that will enable them to distinguish the genuine article from products made in basement freezers.

The severe winter of 2002/3 decimated the Ontario wine-grape crop. A late-winter freeze in early March virtually destroyed the Merlot and Sauvignon Blanc. The overall crop is estimated to be down 40–50 per cent. To help Ontario wineries to maintain their market position, a deal has been worked out between the Ontario wine industry, the local grape growers, the Liquor Control Board of Ontario, and the government of Ontario. To ensure that all wineries can remain viable through this difficult year, an amendment has been made to the Wine Content and Labelling Act that will allow Ontario wineries to blend up to 90 per cent of offshore wine into their domestic content. This change in the regulations will remain in force until 31 January 2005.

Under VQA regulations, all wines bearing Ontario appellations must be made from 100 per cent Ontario grapes. Ontario wines with offshore material blended in are labelled as "Cellared in Canada from imported and domestic grapes" and cannot use the VQA symbol. However, the LCBO will be placing these offshore blends on shelves next to VQA wines, which makes it confusing for the consumer, who must distinguish between a locally grown product and one that contains up to 90 per cent imported wine.

Wineries deserve help when faced with natural catastrophes, but it should not be at the expense of the truth in labelling.

Grapevine

- **Nine British Columbia wineries** picked their frozen grapes for icewine on 5 November – the earliest icewine harvest on record. The harvest was possible because the weather in the southern part of the Okanagan Valley enjoyed an unseasonably cold spell due to the presence of an arctic airflow. Temperatures dipped to −10°C (14°F).

- **The Canadian Vintners Association** has established the Canadian Vintners Association Scholarship. The C$1,000 award was created to acknowledge the potential of young winemakers and is dedicated to the memory of Frank Supernak. Winemaker Supernak was overcome by carbon dioxide fumes and died in November 2002 while attempting, in vain, to rescue Victor Manola, who had fallen into a fermentation tank while working in the cellar of Silver Sage Winery in Oliver, British Columbia.

- **A strip mall** houses the largest restaurant cellar in Canada, several miles from downtown Toronto. Via Allegro Ristorante boasts 47,000 bottles – Amarone is a speciality, with more than 100 selections – but its owner Phil Sabatino, who put the collection together, doesn't drink wine.

Advance report on the latest harvest

2003

Ontario – The Indian summer encouraged maximum ripeness, but it also woke up the ladybugs. The horrendously cold winter has reduced the tonnage of grapes to below 50 per cent of normal yields. Some varieties, such as Sauvignon Blanc and Merlot, are down to 25 per cent of last year's harvest, but the quality of the fruit is good because of Nature's draconian thinning.

British Columbia – A record grape crop following the hottest and sunniest year ever. The 2003 red wines are potentially even better than the highly lauded 2002s. Bill Dyer at Burrowing Owl will use extended maceration on his Cabernet Sauvignon for the first time – his usual practice in most years in California, but the first time with the Burrowing Owl Cabernet.

Updates on the previous five vintages

2002

Vintage rating:
Ontario: 86 (Red: 86, White: 85),
British Columbia: 94 (Red: 94, White: 94)

Ontario – Yields were slightly down from predicted levels, but the quality and concentration of fruit were excellent. Winemakers are predicting that 2002 will be one of the best vintages on record, particularly for red wines.

British Columbia – It is now likely that 2002 will go on record as being the best vintage yet, surpassing 1998 by having more moderate heat for further flavour development and allowing white wines to retain natural acid balance.

2001

Vintage rating:
Ontario: 84 (Red: 88, White: 83),
British Columbia: 92 (Red: 89, White: 94)

Ontario – A vintage compromised by the presence of ladybugs, which affected the flavour of some wines. Some Sauvignon Blanc was harvested almost two weeks earlier than usual. Rains in late September and October slowed down some of the mid-season harvesting, which helped the reds.

British Columbia – A high-end vintage for most whites. Red wines also did well, with excellent fruit ripeness and a softer-than-average tannin structure in all but the latest-ripening varieties.

2000

Vintage rating:
Ontario: 82 (Red: 80, White: 84),
British Columbia: 87 (Red: 85, White: 89)
Ontario – One of the worst years since 1987, but those who gambled and left fruit on the vine were rewarded with a late burst of sunny weather in October. Chardonnay and Riesling performed surprisingly well.
British Columbia – A cool early September opened up into a warm, sunny autumn, allowing crops to ripen fully, with higher sugar levels than 1999.

1999

Vintage rating:
Ontario: 84 (Red: 85, White: 84),
British Columbia: 87 (Red: 85, White: 90)
Ontario – Later-ripening varieties, especially red Bordeaux varieties, enjoyed the heat of an Indian summer. Riesling was the only noble variety that did not do well in the heat.
British Columbia – A challenging vintage until a very warm September and October allowed most varieties to ripen fully. Rated very good by growers who downsized their crop of red varieties for the cooler growing season.

1998

Vintage rating:
Ontario: 90 (Red: 93, White: 87),
British Columbia: 90 (Red: 93, White: 87)
Ontario – One of the longest, warmest, and driest years on record. Long hang time allowed red Bordeaux varieties and Pinot Noir to ripen fully with record sugar levels. The fruit came in clean and unspoiled. Reds showed best; whites tended to lack balancing acidity.
British Columbia – The best and hottest growing year on record, resulting in the best red wines BC has ever produced, remarkable for intensity, ripeness, and heft. White varieties, including Chardonnay, Sauvignon Blanc, and Riesling, showed almost California-like features, though the heat did decrease acid levels in earlier-ripening Germanic varieties such as Ehrenfelser.

GREATEST WINE PRODUCERS

1. Jackson-Triggs Vintners (British Columbia)
2. Blue Mountain Vineyards (British Columbia)
3. Henry of Pelham Family Estate (Ontario)
4. Mission Hill Family Estate (British Columbia)
5. Burrowing Owl (British Columbia)
6. Sumac Ridge Estate (British Columbia)
7. Cave Spring Cellars (Ontario)
8. Vineland Estates (Ontario)
9. Inniskillin Wines (Ontario)
10. Malivoire (Ontario)

FASTEST-IMPROVING PRODUCERS

1. Daniel Lenko Estate (Ontario)
2. Thornhaven Estate (British Columbia)
3. Hillside Estate Winery (British Columbia)
4. Thirty Bench Vineyard & Winery (Ontario)
5. Lake Breeze Vineyards (British Columbia)
6. Stag's Hollow Winery (British Columbia)
7. Peller Estates (Ontario)
8. Peninsula Ridge (Ontario)
9. Red Rooster Estate (British Columbia)
10. Lailey Vineyard (Ontario)

NEW UP-AND-COMING PRODUCERS

1. Southbrook Farm (Ontario)
2. Andora Estate (British Columbia)
3. Glenterra Vineyards (British Columbia)
4. 13th Street Wine Company (Ontario)
5. Niagara College Winery (Ontario)
6. Stratus (Ontario)
7. Legends Estate (Ontario)
8. Lake Breeze Vineyards (British Columbia)
9. Arrowleaf Cellars (British Columbia)
10. Petite Rivière Vineyards (Nova Scotia)

BEST-VALUE PRODUCERS

1. Colio Wines (Ontario)
2. Gehringer Brothers (British Columbia)
3. Jackson-Triggs Vintners (Ontario)
4. Lakeview Cellars (Ontario)
5. Golden Mile Cellars (British Columbia)
6. Jackson-Triggs Vintners (British Columbia)
7. Mission Hill Family Estate (British Columbia)
8. Hawthorne Mountain Vineyards (British Columbia)
9. Magnotta Wines (Ontario)
10. Inniskillin Wines (Ontario)

GREATEST-QUALITY WINES

1. **Vidal Icewine 1998** Palatine Hills Estate, Ontario (C$19.95 per 20-cl bottle)
2. **Okanagan Estate Meritage Proprietors' Grand Reserve 2001** Jackson-Triggs, British Columbia (C$24.99)
3. **Chardonnay Reserve 2002** Legends Estate, Ontario (C$27)
4. **Pinot Noir 2001 Reserve** 13th Street Wine Company, Ontario (C$32)
5. **Chardonnay 2002** Township 7 Vineyards, British Columbia (C$16.90)

6. **Meritage 2000** Thomas & Vaughan, Ontario (C$24.95)
7. **Totally Botrytis Affected Optima 2002** Quails' Gate Estate, British Columbia (C$29.99 per half-bottle)
8. **Pinot Gris 2002** Kettle Valley Winery, British Columbia (C$16)
9. **Gewurztraminer Limited Release 2002** Quails' Gate Estate, British Columbia (C$14.99)
10. **Okanagan Merlot Grand Reserve 2001** Jackson-Triggs, British Columbia (C$19.99)

BEST BARGAINS

1. **Niagara Riesling 2002** Inniskillin Wines, Ontario (C$11.25)
2. **Cabernet Merlot 2001** Sumac Ridge Estate, British Columbia (C$12.99)
3. **Pinot Noir Artists Series 2001** Calona Vineyards, British Columbia (C$9.95)
4. **Riesling 2002** Niagara College, Ontario (C$11.95)
5. **Select Late Harvest Vidal 2001** Birchwood, Ontario (C$11.95 per half-bottle)
6. **Chardonnay 2002** Hawthorne Mountain, British Columbia (C$11.99)
7. **President's Reserve Pinot Noir 2002** Gehringer Brothers, British Columbia (C$12.99)
8. **Merlot 2002** Magnotta Wines, Ontario (C$9.95)
9. **Late Harvest Vidal 2002** Colio Wines, Ontario (C$9.95 per half-bottle)

MOST EXCITING OR UNUSUAL FINDS

1. **Delaine Vineyard Chardonnay 2001** Jackson-Triggs, Ontario (C$16.95) *The 96-acre Delaine Vineyard is a combination of the names of Don Triggs and his wife Elaine. The first-fruit Chardonnay is impressive, as are Riesling and Pinot Noir.*
2. **Eagle Tree Muscat 2002** Jost, Nova Scotia (C$14.99) *A stylish, beautifully made New York Muscat.*
3. **Rock Oven Red 2001** Kettle Valley, British Columbia (C$28) *A 50/50 blend of Shiraz and Cabernet Sauvignon.*
4. **Pinotage 2001** Lake Breeze, British Columbia (C$25) *The only winery in Canada to produce this South African variety.*
5. **Malivoire Gewurztraminer 2002** Moira Vineyard, Ontario (C$28) *A rich and spicy Gewurz from the same vineyard that produces award-winning Chardonnay.*
6. **Syrah 2001** Burrowing Owl, British Columbia (C$25) *Amazing depth of colour and extract here, and a real sense of terroir.*
7. **Sandstone Gamay Reserve 2000** 13th Street Wine Company, Ontario (C$25) *A consistent gold-medal winner from 13th Street winery that has a heft and poise well beyond the profile of Gamay.*
8. **Malbec 2001** Sandhill, British Columbia (C$27.99) *The first home-grown Malbec in Canada.*
9. **Flame 2002** Silver Sage, British Columbia (C$19.95 per half-bottle) *A sweet Pinot Blanc with a red pepper in each bottle!*
10. **Chardonnay Reserve 2002** Legends Estates, Ontario (C$27) *This fruit winery has begun to turn out exemplary grape wines.*

Major producers in Chile are extending their areas by planting new vineyards, purchasing vineyards, or setting up long-term contracts with growers. This last route, however, can prove expensive.

CHRISTOPHER FIELDEN

Wildly optimistic forecasts for Chilean wine sales led to producers committing themselves to paying excessive prices for grapes. Merlot is an example: the contract price for the 2003 vintage in Curicó was US$0.43 per kilo at an average yield of 12–15 tons per hectare (tons/ha). At the time of the harvest, however, the spot price was only US$0.17 per kilo. In the Rapel Valley, the contract price for Pinot Noir grapes was US$0.30, but the spot price was just half this. This does not bode well for the independent grower without a contract. Even though he or she may have been supplying the same company for years, getting a contract is now unlikely and there will be downward pressure on the price offered.

Regional differences are beginning to play an important role in grape prices. While the spot price for Chardonnay from the Casablanca Valley was US$0.60 per kilo, it was US$0.28 in the Maipo Valley, US$0.25 in Curicó, and US$0.24 in the Rapel Valley. Pinot Noir from Casablanca sold for three times as much as elsewhere. The highest prices for Cabernet Sauvignon and Syrah were for grapes grown in the Maipo and Aconcagua valleys.

CHRISTOPHER FIELDEN has been in the wine trade for more than 40 years, during which time he has visited over 100 different countries. On his first trip to South America, he arrived in French Guiana by dugout canoe; he has been fascinated by the continent ever since. He is the author of 10 books on wine, including *The Wines of Argentina, Chile and Latin America* (Faber & Faber, 2001).

Chile: legend of the white horse

Each tank in a winery has a code showing the details of the wine it contains and the treatments it has received. On a recent visit to a vineyard in the Colchagua Valley, a casual enquiry as to what the letters CB stood for elicited the reply "Caballo Blanco" – white horse.

The long ripening season in Chile, three weeks or more than in Bordeaux, often results in grapes with an exceptionally high sugar content. This is particularly true of such varieties as Syrah and Zinfandel. Zinfandel bunches tend to ripen unevenly, with raisining in individual grapes. The result of this is that must can easily reach a potential alcohol of 18° or more. In these cases it is hard to ferment out all the sugar and the resultant wines would be unsaleable. This is when the white horse comes to the rescue.

"Caballo Blanco" is nothing less than a euphemism for water. If you have, for example, 1,000 litres of must with 18° of potential alcohol and add 500 litres of water, you have 50 per cent more 'wine' at an acceptable degree that will ferment out without a problem. While this process is illegal, it seems a logical solution to a difficult problem. Apparently the practice is not uncommon in California. Dare I suggest that another more natural, more acceptable, and more profitable solution would be to increase the yield?

Argentina: now you see it, now you don't!

A recent article in the Mendoza newspaper *Los Andes* announced that an agreement had been reached between the provincial governments of Mendoza and San Juan (responsible between them for 92 per cent of the country's wine production) and the wine producers that $15 million a year would be made available for promoting wines overseas. The sad state of Argentina's export trade is illustrated by the fact that Chile, which has half the area under vines of its neighbour, exports four times as much, while New Zealand, with just a ninth of the vineyards, earns an equal amount of hard currency from its wine sales. In fairness to the Argentinian producers, they are scarcely helped by the fact that they have 5 per cent tax on all wine sold abroad.

What is envisaged is the creation of COVIAR (Corporación Vitivinícola Argentina), comprising representatives of the two provincial governments and the trade, which will, no doubt, provide employment for many deserving people. It is only at the end of the article that you learn that the financial input of the two governments is precisely nothing – the whole project will be funded by three separate levies on the trade.

ARGENTINA: LA RIOJANA SPREADS ITS WINGS

The Chilecito-based cooperative cellar La Riojana, which has six *bodegas* in the province of La Rioja and is responsible for 80 per cent of the production of that province, has signed a 10-year agreement to take over control of Bodega Alfrán at Tupungato, in the Uco Valley, Mendoza province.

La Riojana, which has great ambitions for overseas sales, claims to have 40 per cent of the UK market for Argentinian wines and to have increased its exports during the past 12 months by the same percentage.

Alfrán was one of the first *bodegas* to be established in the Uco Valley, but it did not manage to keep pace with its competitors. With this deal, La Rioja hopes to be able to gain access to premium fruit, which will have to be vinified locally, since grapes cannot be transported across provincial boundaries. The cooperative will be able to broaden the range of wines that it can offer, given the much cooler climate of Tupungato.

ARGENTINA: WINE TOURISM MOVES AHEAD

Paradoxically, just as it auctioned off the contents of its award-winning Harvey's Wine Museum in Bristol, Allied-Domecq is investing considerable sums in creating a wine museum at its San Juan winery, Graffigna. This will also incorporate a chapel and a wine bar inside what used to be a large oak vat. These are expected to be major tourist attractions. Several San Juan wineries

are grouping together to create a wine route in the Tulum Valley, to the south of the city.

In Mendoza province, also on the tourist trail, the Salentein winery is doubling the size of its guest house and adding a swimming pool. It is also building a chapel and a conference centre.

The local tourism industry will also be helped by a new initiative: Winemap, a pack of six maps of the Mendoza wine region, gives details of wineries and places to stay.

ARGENTINA: RADIO-ACTIVE WINE

Despite the fact that Argentina has recently passed through a series of financial crises, the domestic wine scene appears to have strengthened. There has been a noticeable move away from cheap wine for everyday consumption to quality wine being drunk as a matter of course. Fine-wine boutiques are springing up not only all around Buenos Aires but also in provincial cities. Wine courses are being run for professionals and consumers. Indeed, such is the interest in wine that Mendoza radio station Red 101FM has two 30-minute programmes a day, presented by Mariana Di Leo.

ARGENTINA: GO SOUTH, YOUNG MAN

Thanks to an initiative of the provincial government of Neuquén, it looks as though Patagonia may become Argentina's vineyard region of the future. With substantial income from its oil and natural gas reserves, it has granted preferential credits for the establishment of vineyards. The main beneficiary of this is the Grupo La Inversora, which has planted 1,500 ha on barren slopes overlooking the Neuquén river, at San Patricio del Chañar, close to the state capital.

Some of the statistics are quite staggering. To irrigate the vines, 500 km (310 miles) of water pipes were installed, along with 6,000 km (3,728 miles) of piping for drip irrigation. The estate covers an area 18 km (11 miles) long by 2 km (1 mile) wide. In all, more than 2,000 people are supported by the project. The first vines were planted in 1999, and the first vintage was in 2002.

The company has kept a third of the vineyard area for its own winery, Bodega del Fin del Mundo. The rest is being sold off in 50-ha parcels at $21,000–23,000 per hectare. For this you get producing vines with drip irrigation installed. You also get a house for the vineyard manager, a tractor, and a shed to put it in. If you wish, for a small extra fee they will also build you a winery. If wine is not your scene, they are just as happy to plant cherry orchards for you.

Apart from the low set-up costs, the big attraction is the climate, which has a diurnal temperature difference of just over 20°C, which gives very concentrated fruit flavours. The main problem is wind, but windbreaks of poplars come as part of the package.

Next door is Finca María y Avelina, which has 107 ha of vines. Their Pinot Noir 2003, the first vintage, was chosen as the country's outstanding Pinot Noir of the year (though I must admit that it did not appeal much to me). A five-storey gravity-fed winery is under construction. When finished, it will incorporate a first-class restaurant and a tasting room. While digging out the latter, the skeleton of a dinosaur was discovered. The eventual name of the wine has not yet been announced, but punters in the know are betting on Bodega Saurus!

In the neighbouring, and notoriously corrupt, province of Río Negro, things are not moving so fast. Here production is dominated by Humberto Canale, which has long-standing irrigated vineyards on the north bank of the river. Catena Zapata had announced a major project for the barren southern bank, but this, at present, appears to be on hold.

Grapevine

- **Bodegas Chandon,** Argentina's dominant sparkling-wine producer, has changed production of its premium brand Baron B from bottle fermentation to tank fermentation. The producer insists that there is no deterioration in quality, but production costs are lower.

- **The owners** of the Don Cristobal winery, the only producer with commercial plantings of Verdelho in Argentina, now believe that their grape may have little to do with the Portuguese variety, but is rather the Verdejo from Spain.

Argentina has to give up using foreign wine names for its own wines, but while some companies seem quite prepared to do this, others are not. As Julio Nieto, export manager of Bodegas Chandon, says: "While we might have used words such as Champán and Champaña to describe our wines in the past, it is at least six years since we have done so." Another company to have roots in both France and Argentina, Allied Domecq, which produces Mumm and Pétigny sparkling wines in Argentina, no longer describes them as 'champagne' on their labels. However, on the product list inside the business card of the managing director of Allied Domecq Argentina, Mumm is described as a Champagne and Pétigny as a Champaña – old habits die hard!

Valentín Bianchi, a major producer of both still and sparkling wines in San Rafael, accepts that change will take place but thinks that the industry has up to 10 years to put changes into effect in South America. Not only does the company happily hand out baseball caps with the proud message "Champaña Bianchi", it also includes in its portfolio of still wines a Borgoña, a Chablis, and a Margaux. The defence? "We have been selling this last wine since long before the Bordeaux appellation Margaux existed."

The tradition of using wine names from France in Argentina is a long one. Indeed, another sparkling wine producer, Toso, claims that Argentina was granted the specific right to use the terms Champán and Champaña by the French during the 1930s.

Are such companies simply unprepared for an event that will have a significant effect on their marketing campaigns? Or could it be that they do not anticipate any new regulations will be applied? Whatever the case, Argentina must bite the bullet on the use of foreign names and ditch the practice now, if only for its international credibility.

Sauvignon Blanc – could the Chileans give a Sauvignonasse?

It has been generally known for more than 10 years that two of the grape varieties grown in Chile – Sauvignon Blanc and Sauvignonasse – are both indiscriminately labelled as Sauvignon Blanc, but regularizing the situation began only recently. However, this seems to have been done in a rather casual way, with mixed vineyards classified as 100 per cent of the dominant variety, and, in many cases, purely on the say-so of the grower.

Chileans like to claim that they are related varieties from within the Cabernet family, but this is something that is disputed by most ampelographers. The situation is further complicated by the fact that Chilean growers, among themselves, call the Sauvignon Blanc Sauvignon Americano and the Sauvignonasse Sauvignon Blanc. That they have distinctive characteristics is not disputed. Yet, despite these differences and the fact that Sauvignonasse is accepted to be a lesser grape, the prices paid for the two varieties at the 2003 vintage were exactly the same. This suggests that they are considered locally to be of equal standing and that they will continue to be blended and sold indiscriminately on international markets as Sauvignon Blanc.

• *Hormiga* is the Spanish word for 'ant', and one might well enquire as to the origins of the name of the Italian-owned, pure-Malbec winery Altos las Hormigas. When the vineyard was first planted, the young vines were totally consumed by black ants. Standing back in horror and admiration, the owners decided to name the wine, when it was finally produced, in their honour.

• **Aurelio Montes**, the high-flier from Chile, has now crossed the Andes and joined other compatriots such as Santa Rita and Concha y Toro in buying vineyards in Argentina. So far he does not have his own winery but is relying on that of Federico Benegas.

• **English importer Grape-2-Wine** was not amused to find that there had been an attempt to register its Chilean wine brand, Antu Mapu, in Chile. The culprits turned out to be the Cauquenes Cooperative, which had been supplying Grape-2-Wine with the wine. As a result, the co-op has lost a customer who was also acting as an agent for their wines in the UK. When last seen, they were seeking new importers.

• **Torrontés**, Argentina's flagship white grape, has always been considered Spanish, probably from Galicia. Genetic research shows that it is actually a cross of Muscat of Alexandria and Criolla Chica, a native of the Canary Islands. This suggests that its origins may go back to the earliest days of the conquistadors, who almost certainly brought both varieties with them.

• **It seems like a gesture of solidarity** that Austrian glass-maker Riedel should have given the sole distribution rights of its products in Argentina to Bodega Norton, which belongs to Austrian crystal manufacturer Swarovski.

Advance report on the latest harvest
2004

Chile – Crop set was below normal, and originally it was anticipated that the harvest would be approximately 25 per cent below average. However, favourable growing conditions during the summer have compensated for some of the potential shortfall, which may now be less than 10 per cent.

For the white varieties, the grapes have had high sugar levels, but also above-average acidity. In the Maule Valley, picking of white varieties, except for Semillon, finished by the beginning of March, and on 1 March it rained, with about 2.5 cm (1 in) falling. However, the Semillon and all the red grapes were healthy, and there has been no trace of botrytis or oidium.

The first half of March remained cool, with a resulting slowdown in the maturation of the red varieties. However, from the 18th, daytime temperatures went back over 30°C, giving concentrated fruit flavours and rich colours. The red-grape harvest is two to three weeks later than usual, but it is expected to produce outstanding wines once again.

In the upcoming region of the Leyda Valley, the harvest for Pinot Noir and Sauvignon Blanc began on 17 March, the same day as the previous year. There is optimism as to the quality of the wines.

Argentina – The summer began hot, with a continuing drought in January until the middle of the month, when there was a relieving rainfall and a drop in temperature. This slowed down the development of the red varieties, but they remain healthy and should provide excellent wines. The harvest of white varieties has begun, and the musts show great potential and strong varietal characteristics. The Sauvignon Blancs from 2004 promise to be outstanding.

Updates on the previous five vintages
2003

Vintage rating: 96 (Chile: 96, Argentina: 96)

Chile – This has turned out to be a very good year, though the crop was approximately 20 per cent less than normal. The summer was colder than usual, but the autumn provided excellent ripening conditions, with the result that the grapes reached optimum ripeness not only for sugars, but also for skins and pips. Those who restricted yields have made excellent wines, with concentrated fruit flavour. In some regions, such as Casablanca, quality has been rated as excellent, though the shortfall there was as much as 30 per cent.

Argentina – Each year a group of experts meets in Mendoza to evaluate the vintage. For the 2003 vintage, the official position is that the white wines are "very good" and the reds "outstanding".

Sherlock Holmes might have described this as a "barking dog" vintage, since there was a great deal of unfounded pessimism about the anticipated arrival of El Niño. Spring was cool, but the summer was the hottest on record, with rainfall well below average. The autumn was cooler, and grapes were picked in ideal conditions. Opinions are divided as to whether the wines will be as good as those from the excellent 2002 vintage, but there is undoubted optimism.

2002

Vintage rating: *95 (Chile: 92, Argentina: 97)*

Chile – What might have been an excellent vintage was marred by rain in southern regions during the harvest. It fell as far north as the Colchagua Valley, but did not affect such premium regions as Maipo, Casablanca, and Aconcagua. In the Casablanca Valley it was a very good vintage, with higher-than-average yields. Care must be taken in buying wines from the Colchagua Valley and further south.

Argentina – Considered in Mendoza to be the best vintage for 10 years or more. Abundant snowfall in the Andes assured plentiful water for irrigation. The ripening period was long, with cool, dry weather. This gave wines with concentrated fruit flavours. In Salta province, in the north, the vintage took place 10 days earlier than normal.

2001

Vintage rating: *94 (Chile: 96, Argentina: 91)*

Chile – This was an excellent vintage, with good wines being made throughout the country, particularly from Carmenère.

Argentina – Generally considered a good vintage, though the wines lack the concentration of flavours of the 2002s. Chardonnays are the most successful wines.

2000

Vintage rating: 92 *(Chile: 90, Argentina: 93)*

Chile – A large harvest of mixed quality, since there was some rain just before the vintage. The reds are considered better than the whites.

Argentina – High yields, but while the wines lack some concentration and structure, they are perceived to have good, classic varietal characteristics.

1999

Vintage rating: 97 *(Chile: 97, Argentina: 96)*

Chile – A difficult, drought-plagued year resulted in low yields of excellent quality. The red wines are firm and long-lasting, while the whites are lean and elegant. The best vintage for 15 years.

Argentina – The wines are similar in style to those of 2002, although the summer was hotter and drier, giving exceptionally healthy grapes.

GREATEST WINE PRODUCERS

1. Viña Montes (Chile)
2. Terrazas de los Andes (Argentina)
3. Viña Santa Rita (Chile)
4. Catena Zapata (Argentina)
5. Familia Zuccardi (Argentina)
6. Viña Errázuriz (Chile)
7. Casa Silva (Chile)
8. Bodega Norton (Argentina)
9. Casa Lapostolle (Chile)
10. Bodegas Trapiche (Argentina)

NEW UP-AND-COMING PRODUCERS

1. Dominio del Plata (Argentina)
2. Leyda (Chile)
3. Viña Haras de Pirque (Chile)
4. O Fournier (Argentina)
5. Medrano Estates (Argentina)
6. Val de Flores (Argentina)
7. Finca Sophenia (Argentina)
8. Bodega del Fin del Mundo (Argentina)
9. Dolium (Argentina)
10. Viña Botalcura (Chile)

FASTEST-IMPROVING PRODUCERS

1. Cono Sur (Chile)
2. Bodegas Salentein (Argentina)
3. Humberto Canale (Argentina)
4. Viña Los Vascos (Chile)
5. Nieto Senetiner (Argentina)
6. Santiago Graffigna (Argentina)
7. Michel Torino, Bodega La Rosa (Argentina)
8. Viña Valdivieso (Chile)
9. Roca (Argentina)
10. Santa Helena (Chile)

BEST-VALUE PRODUCERS

1. Viña Casablanca (Chile)
2. Trivento Bodegas y Viñedos (Argentina)
3. Viña San Pedro (Chile)
4. Bodega Norton (Argentina)
5. Concha y Toro (Chile)
6. Medrano Estates (Argentina)
7. La Riojana (Argentina)
8. Viña Montes (Chile)
9. Familia Zuccardi (Argentina)
10. Casa Silva (Chile)

GREATEST-QUALITY WINES

1. **Montes Alpha 'M' 2000** Montes, Colchagua Valley, Chile (CLP 45,000)
2. **Gran Malbec 1999** Terrazas de los Andes, Argentina (AP 100)
3. **Don Maximiano Founder's Reserve 2000** Viña Errázuriz, Aconcagua Valley, Chile (CLP 39,900)
4. **Angelica Zapata Chardonnay Alta 1999** Catena Zapata, Argentina (AP 35)
5. **Casa Real Cabernet Sauvignon Etiqueta Exportación 1999** Viña Santa Rita, Chile (CLP 28,000)
6. **Trapiche Late Harvest Chardonnay 2003** Argentina (AP 85 per half-bottle)
7. **Floresta Cabernet Sauvignon 1999** Viña Santa Rita, Chile (CLP 18,000)
8. **Marqués de Casa Concha Cabernet Sauvignon 2001** Concha y Toro, Puente Alto, Chile (CLP 18,000)
9. **Paisaje de Tupungato 2001** Finca Flichman, Argentina (AP 50)
10. **Norton Perdriel Single Vineyard 2000** Argentina (AP 160)

BEST BARGAINS

1. **Viognier 2003** Trivento, Argentina (AP 8)
2. **Reserve Merlot 2002** Montes, Chile (CLP 3,700)
3. **Pinot Gris 2003** Lurton, Argentina (AP 10)
4. **Syrah 2001** Ventisquero, Chile (CLP 2,300)
5. **Pircas Negras Organic Barbera 2003** La Riojana, Argentina (AP 8)

6. **Casablanca Sauvignon Blanc 2002** Santa Isabel Estate, Chile (CLP 5,500)
7. **Caballero de la Cepa Merlot 2001** Finca Flichman, Argentina (AP 12)
8. **Caladoc 2002** Familia Zuccardi, Argentina (AP 10)
9. **Gato Negro Cabernet Sauvignon 2002** Viña San Pedro, Chile (CLP 1,400)
10. **Pionero Carmenère 2002** Morandé, Chile (CLP 1,800)

MOST EXCITING OR UNUSUAL FINDS

1. **Ancellotta 2002** Familia Zuccardi, Argentina (AP 10) *Sr Zuccardi must have discovered this Italian grape, which is used primarily for Lambrusco, during his holidays in Emilia-Romagna – it is certainly a novelty in Argentina!*
2. **Malamado 2001** Familia Zuccardi, Argentina (AP 32) *A late-harvest fortified Malbec, à la mode de Porto.*
3. **Miscelánea 1997** Weinert, Argentina (AP 28) *The company dustbin in which the remnants of other bottlings are put. There are 17 different varieties in this blend, including Malbec and Moscatel de Alejandría.*

Despite its subtropical climate, Cuba appears keen to establish a reputation for itself as a wine-producing country.

CHRISTOPHER FIELDEN

Some years ago, the first winery, a joint venture between the Cuban government and Italian wine producer Fantinel, began to make wine from grapes grown in the western province of Pinar del Río. Now Bodegas del Caribe, a joint venture between the Cubans and Spanish winery Palacio de Arganza, has planted 20 hectares (ha) of vines on three separate sites to the east of Havana. A winery has also been built at Ceiba del Agua, close to the capital. The initial investment is in the region of US$2.5 million. The first wines, named Castillo de Wajay, have recently appeared on the domestic market.

Trials have been carried out with some 20 different grape varieties, for both wine production and table grapes. While several international varieties – such as Cabernet, Chardonnay, Pinot Noir, and Syrah – have been planted, emphasis has been placed on traditional Spanish varieties, including Tempranillo, Albariño, Monastrell, Viura, Mencía, and Godello. In the initial stages, must will also be imported from Spain. Daniel Vuelta Fernández, the president of Bodegas del Caribe and Palacio de Arganza, is optimistic that world-quality wines will be produced. The first fruits from the vineyards, he claims, are comparable to Spanish wines.

Some years ago, Bodegas Fantinel promised to flood the European market with Cuban wines. So far this has not happened; let's see what

CHRISTOPHER FIELDEN has been in the wine trade for more than 40 years, during which time he has visited over 100 different countries. On his first trip to South America, he arrived in French Guiana by dugout canoe; he has been fascinated by the continent ever since. He is the author of 10 books on wine, including *The Wines of Argentina, Chile and Latin America* (Faber & Faber, 2001).

the new opposition can do. With two vintages a year, in December and July, quantity should not be a problem, but disease, especially rot in the humid climate, may well pose a serious problem.

Miolo extends subtropical plantings in Brazil

For some years, Brazil's leading premium winery, Miolo, has sold wines from grapes grown in the subtropical São Francisco Valley under the brand name Terranova. Now, in a joint venture with the Lovara Corporation, Miolo is extending plantings on the Ouro Verde estate near Casa Nova in Bahía state.

A total of 50 ha of drip-irrigated Syrah, Cabernet Sauvignon, and Muscadel (sic) has been added to the original 80 ha of Muscat. Further plantings of up to 350 ha are a possibility. Lying at an altitude of 350 m (1,150 ft) above sea level, just 9° south of the equator, the vineyards have a dry climate, with water available for irrigation. Despite their subtropical location, the lack of humidity makes this the most suitable land in Brazil for planting vines.

• **In a bid to support** local domestic producers, Brazil and Uruguay have forbidden the import of wine packaged in containers of more than 1 litre. In both markets, most wine is purchased by consumers in demijohns of 3, 5, or 10 litres. Without this protection, the market would be flooded with cheap wine from Argentina, which already has a solid presence on the 1-litre tetrabrick market. So far, this restriction on trade has been accepted as necessary by Mercosur.

• **Distillation has long been** a government monopoly in Uruguay. However, wine producers can now distil their own residues from the presses. This has led to wine museums being raided to put antique stills back into service; other producers are trying to buy second-hand stills overseas. One problem is that wine production in the country is still assessed through the residual *marc*. This means that INAVI (Instituto Nacional de Vitivinicultura) inspectors have to carry out their calculations at each winery before the *marcs* can be released for distillation. The local custom is to drink Uruguayan grappa blended with honey, which certainly softens its innate combativeness.

• **It was not only California** that suffered from bad advice from Davis about phylloxera-resistant rootstock. The Casa Madero winery in the Parras Valley in Mexico planted on AXR1 and progressively lost its whole vineyard to the pest. New vines were planted at the rate of 40 ha a year to reach full production again, but they came under attack from Pierce's disease. Fortunately, Casa Madero has been able to keep this under tight control. The opportunity to replant the vineyard has led to better wine, as a result of denser vine planting, vertical trellis management, and more controlled irrigation. Night harvesting has also been introduced for all the white fruit and some of the red.

As you enter the Brazilian Serra Gaucha town of Garibaldi, a large sign announces it as the champagne capital of Brazil. The website of local company Peterlongo states that it is the official site of Brazilian champagne, and another company, Champagnes Georges Aubert, claims that it is the first Brazilian sparkling-wine company to be established by a "French champagne producer", despite the fact that the eponymous M Aubert came from Die, in the Rhône Valley.

There is no doubt that champagne is well established in Brazil as a generic term for sparkling wine. Indeed, it is enshrined in the wine laws.

Perhaps it is not surprising that the term Asti is in general use, since most of the local growers are of Italian extraction and the first Moscato sparkling wine was made by Emanuele Peterlongo, a native of Piemonte, as long ago as 1913. What is surprising, however, is that the Brazilians have been able to fight off the authorities in Champagne, France, and the European Union over their use of the champagne name for so long.

The one French champagne company to produce sparkling wines in Garibaldi, Moët & Chandon (Chandon do Brasil), used to describe their tank-fermented wines as *champanhas*. Now they are more circumspect, describing them as *espumante*, possibly to differentiate them from genuine champagne imported from their parent company in Epernay, or perhaps to justify their higher price compared to other domestic wines.

If the Brazilians want to develop their export trade to Europe, they need to adopt a less cavalier attitude to the use of European wine names, though most producers seem keener on mining the enormous potential of their domestic market, rather than looking overseas for expanding sales.

Team effort needed in Uruguay

Sadly, Uruguay, one of the smallest players in the highly competitive world of wine exports, is having difficulty in presenting a united front. On one side is the long-standing Centro de Bodegueros, and on the other the more recently formed (1999) Asociación de Bodegas Exportadoras. To make things more complicated, the latter organization calls its website winesofuruguay.com. In the middle of this is INAVI, the official parastatal body, which looks after the promotion of Uruguayan wines at home and abroad. With the limited resources available, it seems crazy that the bodies cannot amalgamate and present a solid front.

Advance report on the latest harvest
2004

Brazil – The Serra Gaucha, where most of Brazil's quality wine is produced, reports an outstanding vintage after a dry summer. While the quality is in part due to favourable climatic conditions, much also comes from improved techniques, both in the vineyards and the wineries. The 2004 vintage is considered to be one of the best in Brazil's winemaking history.

Uruguay – The summer has been very cool, but dry and sunny. The harvest began up to two weeks later than usual. Where yields have been restricted, this has meant great concentration of fruit flavours, high natural sugar content, and ripe tannins. The general opinion is that this is an excellent vintage.

Updates on the previous five vintages
2003

Bolivia – In a market that does not set much store by vintages, this was perceived to be a good year.

Brazil – Generally thought to be a better year for the wines from the subtropical São Francisco Valley. In the Serra Gaucha, rain caused some problems, but there are some outstanding wines.

Mexico – In Baja California, it was a very hot summer. Generally this gave excellent red wines, particularly Cabernet Sauvignons from the Guadalupe Valley. White wines from San Antonio de las Minas were also first-class, but there was some burning of grapes from the valleys of Santo Tomâs and San Vicente. This is thought to be largely due to salination problems. In Parras, 2003 is rated as the best vintage ever; the red wines are outstanding.

Uruguay – Problems at the time of flowering led to a small crop, perhaps 50 per cent below average. The summer was very hot, with the vintage beginning two weeks earlier than normal. The quality is perceived to be good to very good.

2002

Bolivia – A poor, rain-affected vintage.
Brazil – Excellent, particularly for Pinot Noir and Chardonnay. There were low yields due to poor weather at flowering, but it was a fine, warm summer.
Mexico – The main vineyards of Baja California had a small crop of good wines. Low winter rainfall was a problem. The Parras Valley had similar problems but made good wines.
Uruguay – Generally considered to be a very good vintage, since the grapes were slow to ripen, but ultimately had fine concentration. Particularly good for Uruguay's speciality grape, Tannat.

2001

Bolivia – Very good wines, with the reds showing particularly well.
Brazil – Heavy rains at the time of picking in the Serra Gaucha diluted what would have been excellent wines.
Mexico – Very good, full, fruity red wines from Baja California. The Parras Valley had firm, concentrated wines, but low production figures due to replanted vineyards coming back onstream.
Uruguay – Again, rain at picking resulted in very good, rather than excellent, wines.

2000

Bolivia – An excellent vintage, whose wines now need to be drunk.
Brazil – No more than average in quality and quantity.
Mexico – Big, full-bodied, tannic wines. The reds are showing well.
Uruguay – An excellent vintage of ripe, well-balanced wines.

1999

Bolivia – No more than average wines, which should now be consigned to history.
Brazil – A good year, with the best reds still showing well.
Mexico – This was perceived to be a good average vintage.
Uruguay – Sound but undistinguished wines.

GREATEST WINE PRODUCERS

1. LA Cetto (Mexico)
2. Bodegas Carrau (Uruguay)
3. Vinícola Miolo (Brazil)
4. Monte Xanic (Mexico)
5. Cesar Pisano e Hijos (Uruguay)
6. Angheben Adega de Vinhos Finos (Brazil)
7. Château Camou (Mexico)
8. De Lucca (Uruguay)
9. Establecimiento Juanicó (Uruguay)
10. Bodegas y Viñedos de la Concepción (Bolivia)

FASTEST-IMPROVING PRODUCERS

1. Angheben Adega de Vinhos Finos (Brazil)
2. Bodega Carlos Pizzorno (Uruguay)
3. Campos de Solano (Bolivia)
4. Dante Irurtia (Uruguay)
5. Casa Madero (Mexico)

NEW UP-AND-COMING PRODUCERS

1. Angheben Adega de Vinhos Finos (Brazil)
2. Campos de Solano (Bolivia)
3. Traversa Hermanos (Uruguay)

BEST-VALUE PRODUCERS

1. LA Cetto (Mexico)
2. Dante Irurtia (Uruguay)
3. Cooperativa Vinícola Aurora (Brazil)
4. Establecimiento Juanicó (Uruguay)
5. Bodegas de Santo Tomás (Mexico)

GREATEST-QUALITY WINES

1. **Merlot 1999** Monte Xanic, Mexico (MP 400)
2. **Gran Tradición 2000** J Carrau Pujol, Uruguay (UP 350)
3. **Cabernet Sauvignon Reserva Privada 1996** LA Cetto, Mexico (MP 550)
4. **Gran Casa Magrez 2000** Château Pape-Clément/ Establecimiento Juanicó, Uruguay (UP 700)
5. **Cabernet Sauvignon NV** Angheben Adega de Vinhos Finos, Brazil (BR 90)
6. **Arretxea Grande Reserve 2002** Cesar Pisano e Hijos, Uruguay (UP 800)
7. **Adagio Cantabile Chardonnay 2002** Toscanini Hermanos, Uruguay (UP 400)
8. **Amat Tannat 2000** Bodegas Carrau, Uruguay (UP 500)
9. **Sauvignon Blanc-Semillon-Viognier 2002** Viña Tacama, Peru (PP 1,400)
10. **Reserva Chardonnay 2002** Vinícola Miolo, Brazil (BR 40)

BEST BARGAINS

1. **Botrytis Gewurztraminer 2002** Dante Irurtia, Uruguay (UP 300)
2. **Petit Syrah 2001** LA Cetto, Mexico (MP 45)
3. **Sauvignon Blanc 2003** Bodega Carlos Pizzorno, Uruguay (UP 95)
4. **Don Pascual Tannat Reserva 2000** Establecimiento Juanicó, Uruguay (UP 110)
5. **Terranova Cabernet Sauvignon-Syrah 2001** Vinícola Miolo, Brazil (BR 16)

MOST EXCITING OR UNUSUAL FINDS

① **Florencia Marsanne 2002** De Lucca, Uruguay (UP 350) *A late-harvest wine with wonderful complex flavours.*

② **Petit Verdot 2000** Bodegas Pomar, Venezuela (VP 10) *The most successful wine from Venezuela's subtropical, two-vintages-a-year vineyards.*

③ **Vilamar Nebbiolo 1999** Bodegas Carrau, Uruguay (UP 1300) *An excellent wine from very old vines. Probably the country's sole straight Nebbiolo.*

④ **Gewurztraminer Orgánico 2001** Velho Museu, Atelier do Vinho, Juan Carrau, Brazil (BR 30) *The country's first commercial organic wine, grown down on the southern border with Uruguay.*

⑤ **Zinfandel 2002** LA Cetto, Mexico (MP 80) *Made from 100-year-old dry-farmed vines on the border with California.*

Grapevine

• **Oregonian winemaker Bill Swain** has left the Bodegas Pomar winery in Carora, Venezuela. His replacement is Guillermo Vargas, assisted by Frenchman Michel Salgues. As a result of competition from Chilean wines at the bottom end of the market, Pomar has sought to move up-market with a range of straight varietal wines, including a Syrah, a Tempranillo, and a Petit Verdot.

• **Vinhos Salton,** Brazil's third-largest producer of sparkling wines, has transferred its production facility from a cramped site in the centre of Bento Gonçalves to Tuiuti, some 8 km (5 miles) out of town, where it has its 50-ha estate. The new winery and cellars will enable it to double production. Tourists are being encouraged to visit a new mini wine theme park.

• **Viña Tacama,** the oldest winery in the southern hemisphere, has just launched Peru's first wine to be aged in French *barriques*, a Tannat Reserva 2000. The agrarian revolution, terrorism, and political uncertainty have meant that there has been little hard currency with which to invest in equipment, so progress has been slow. Is this the beginning of a renaissance in Peru's wine industry?

• **A basket of basic prices** for calculating the cost of living in Peru was created in 1933, but, for the first time, the cost of a bottle of wine has now been included.

• **There is an opportunity** for developing a domestic market for screwcapped wines in Brazil, since less than 30 per cent of families own a corkscrew. Or maybe there is an opportunity for a corkscrew company?

Drought was the most pressing issue over the past year. It caused the first decline in Australia's grape harvest in seven years of otherwise bullish growth.

HUON HOOKE

The 2003 harvest was 1.36 million tons, 10 per cent lower than 2002 despite a 6 per cent increase in the area of bearing vines. As I write, the drought has broken in Western Australia, South Australia, and much of Victoria, although more than 80 per cent of New South Wales is still drought-declared. NSW is the third-largest wine-growing state. At the same time, new plantings have slowed right down over the past three years and there are forecasts that Australia will soon have a serious shortage of grapes. At the moment, this is hard to imagine, since reports surface that Western Australia, whose industry is strongly premium (read 'high-price') focused, has to quickly find a home for 5 million litres of unsold red wine to make room for the next vintage. However, white fruit, especially Chardonnay for the low- to mid-priced bottle (A$8–15) market, is already scarce across the country.

The second worry, at least for the big exporters (mainly the largest 20 or 30 wineries) is currency-related. The Aussie dollar's value against

HUON HOOKE is coauthor of *The Penguin Good Australian Wine Guide*, the country's most respected buyer's guide. He is a wine-marketing and production graduate of Roseworthy Agricultural College and has been a weekly columnist for the John Fairfax Group of newspapers since 1983. Huon writes columns in the Good Living section of the *Sydney Morning Herald* and the *Good Weekend* magazine of the *Herald* and Melbourne's *Age*. He is also contributing editor of Australian *Gourmet Traveller WINE* magazine and writes for various other publications, such as *Decanter* and *Slow Wine*. He has been judging in wine competitions since 1987 and judges eight to 10 shows a year in Australia and abroad. Huon has judged in New Zealand, South Africa, Chile, Belgium, Slovenia, Canada, and the US. He currently chairs several Australian competitions and is senior judge at Adelaide and Sydney.

the US greenback has soared by about 50 per cent during 2003, from around 50 cents to almost 75. If this holds in the long term, it will have devastating implications for wine exporters already facing tight margins and the stiffest competition they've ever seen. At the time of writing, exports are still booming along in volume terms, but value has predictably slid backwards.

David routs Goliath

Winery buy-ups by multinational drinks corporations have become the bane of the wine industry, so when Barossa Valley hero Peter Lehmann fought off the unwelcome advances of Allied Domecq, he became even more of a *cause célèbre*. The company he founded in 1978 is one of Australia's largest wineries, crushing more than 9,000 tons of Barossa fruit annually and selling 7 million bottles around the world. In mid-2003, Allied Domecq made a takeover bid for Lehmann and Swiss company Hess made a counteroffer. Lehmann, who has the interests of employees, grape growers, and the local community at heart more than most bosses, had checked out both suitors and recommended Hess. Since he was no longer a director, he was within his rights – although controversial – giving advice to shareholders. Big corporations are a two-edged sword: they provide funds to enable expansion, but they're ultimately interested only in profits and seldom take a long-term view. But profits from wine can be inconsistent and short-term decision-making is incompatible with making quality wine and building a solid market. The same week Allied gave in, Peter Lehmann Wines won the Robert Mondavi Trophy for Winemaker of the Year at the International Wine and Spirit Competition. The odd bottle was opened….

Grapevine

• **The Reynolds Wine Company,** which flowered briefly before crashing spectacularly, looks certain to go to investment bank Babcock & Brown. B&B withdrew its A$30-million offer, but talks are continuing. Reynolds was floated in 1999; about 900 hectares (ha) of vines were planted and a 20,000-tonne winery was built near Orange. A US distribution agreement was struck with Trinchero Family Estates, owner of Sutter Home. Wine was sold under the Reynolds, Hand Picked, and Little Boomey brands before it all fell apart, when the Taxation Office ruled that Reynolds had to pay A$19 million, forcing it into receivership.

• **Dromana Estate founder** Garry Crittenden will launch his new Crittenden at Dromana label in 2004. Crittenden is no longer involved with the public company he founded, Dromana Estate, although his son Rollo is chief winemaker. Garry Crittenden still owns the original vineyard, winery, and restaurant.

SMOKE GETS IN YOUR WINE

The controversial reverse osmosis (RO) technique has been put to good use, salvaging millions of litres of smoke-tainted wine from the alpine regions of northeastern Victoria. Vineyards in the Ovens, Kiewa, King, and Buffalo valleys were shrouded in smoke for weeks during the bushfire crisis in early 2003. It wasn't until the grapes were picked, crushed, and fermented that the taint was discovered. An estimated 7,000 tons of grapes were affected, with losses of A$5 million due to grapes being downgraded or rejected by wineries. But Melbourne winemaking consultancy Wine Network found an answer: it adapted its RO equipment, normally used to remove water or volatile acidity, to filter out the tainting compound, 4-methyl guaiacol. In the worst cases, the taint rendered wine unpalatable. Red wines were more affected than whites, since the smoke residue is trapped on the skin of the grape, and red wine is fermented with skins.

SWEETNESS IN YELLOW TAIL'S STRENGTH

The spectacular success of Yellow Tail in America has polarized the wine business. While there is widespread admiration for Casella, the family-owned Riverina winery that has the tiger by the tail, expecting to sell 5 million cases in 2003, the wines' sweetness bothers the purists. Many accuse Yellow Tail of pandering to the lowest common denominator, because all its wines – Chardonnay, Shiraz, Cabernet Sauvignon, Shiraz Cabernet, and Merlot – have very obvious levels of residual sugar. In 2003, Yellow Tail Shiraz became the top-selling 750-ml-bottle red in the US and the brand was the fastest-growing in the US, with a 446 per cent growth rate over 12 months. Yellow Tail's defenders say it is only doing what Orlando Barossa Pearl and Lindemans Ben Ean did in the 1960s and 1970s: introducing new drinkers to the pleasure of a glass of wine.

Grapevine

- **Pipers Brook Vineyard** founder Dr Andrew Pirie has bought back the right to use his own name on a range of wines. Pirie and PBV's new owner, Belgium-based Kreglinger Wine Estates, reached agreement for Pirie to release a range of Pirie Tasmanian wines starting with the 2004 vintage. The eponymous Pirie sparkling wine will be renamed. Dr Pirie will make his wines at Rosevears Estate in the West Tamar region, where he has been retained as winemaker. He also consults to Parker Coonawarra Estate and Tasmania's Dalrymple.

- **McGuigan Simeon's acquisition** of Riverina family company Miranda Wines for A$25.5 million makes McGuigan the third-biggest wine producer and second-biggest grape grower. Miranda's business complements McGuigan's portfolio, especially by the addition of a major slice of the cask market, where McGuigan did not previously have a presence. Forty-five per cent of the Australian wine sold in Australia is still sold in casks, affectionately known as "bladder packs".

SCREWCAPS NOT A PANACEA AFTER ALL?

Screwcaps have taken hold in Australia like nowhere else (except perhaps New Zealand), but it is not all plain sailing. Sulphidic or reductive aromas are a worrying side issue in delicate white wines under screwcaps. This off note is especially evident in Riesling, Semillon, Sauvignon Blanc, and 'Sem/Sav' blends. While winemakers publicly deny it is a serious problem, saying they would much prefer a little 'reduction' in some wines than around 6 per cent of bottles ruined by cork taint and random oxidation, many of them admit they are concerned but mystified about the cause. However, winemakers who routinely add copper sulphate to their Rieslings immediately after fermentation and before protein stabilization never have the problem.

ALL CHANGE AT HARDY

Winemaker burnout hit the Hardy Wine Company hard in 2003. Chief red winemaker Stephen Pannell resigned in November, following earlier losses of Larry Cherubino, chief winemaker at Houghton, Steve Flamsteed from Yarra Burn, Anna Flowerday from Leasingham, and, some months before them, chief white winemaker Glenn James. Pannell, Cherubino, and Flowerday quit to "do their own thing". But at least with the more senior winemakers, the high pressure of their jobs and the demands of a four- or five-month-long vintage exhaust even the most passionate. The uncertainty posed by the new owner, US-based Constellation Brands, may also be a factor. Experienced Western Australian winemaker Rob Bowen has taken over the Houghton job.

Grapevine

• **Australia's globe-trotting viticulturist** Dr Richard Smart has moved to Tasmania in order to direct the biggest single vine-planting venture the island state has seen. Gunns, Tasmania's biggest private forestry and timber company, will plant up to 200 ha of new vineyards. Gunns has leapt into the wine industry, boots and all, buying Tamar Ridge for a reported A$14.8 million. Smart, who consults to around 20 clients in Australia and all over the world, will live in Launceston and conduct his business from there.

• **Deen De Bortoli's sudden death** in November 2003 shocked the wine community. The patriarch of the wine company of the same name was 67. Deen steered the family-owned business through a period of remarkable growth

from a 2,000-ton to a 70,000-ton annual crush. In 2003, the Riverina-based company celebrated its 75th anniversary. In his 50-year career, De Bortoli launched its Noble One Botrytis Semillon, which became an icon, and developed a second winery in the Yarra Valley.

• **Dr Tony Jordan**, the man who has guided Domaine Chandon Australia since its establishment in 1986, has been promoted to manage all the French-owned LVMH (Louis Vuitton Moët Hennessy) group's wine interests in Australia and New Zealand. These include Cape Mentelle, Cloudy Bay, and Mountadam, as well as Chandon itself. At Cape Mentelle and Cloudy Bay he replaces founder David Hohnen, who has retired to develop his own vineyard and farm in the south of Margaret River.

Australia's minimum varietal- and regional-labelling requirements are tighter than some countries but could be tightened further. Producers can blend up to 15 per cent of wine from another variety and region and still use the regional and varietal names. A Coonawarra Cabernet could be, say, 15 per cent Coonawarra Malbec and 15 per cent Riverland Cabernet, in other words only 70 per cent Coonawarra Cabernet.

Water into wine

Alcohol levels need to be reined in. Alcohol strength in many wines is now out of control. 'Parkerization' is often blamed: there is widespread debate over whether red wines ought to be made bigger, with higher alcohol, to suit the palate of leading US critic Robert Parker. There are several Aussie reds made exclusively for the US market, where Parker has such clout. But this style is not always what winemakers – even in the warm-climate regions – or the public prefer.

Some of the great Australian red wines of the 1940s and 1950s were made from superripe grapes diluted with water. Although illegal now, technology has accidentally found a way around the law. Legal modern techniques to concentrate must or wine, such as reverse osmosis and freeze concentration, yield grape-derived water as a by-product. Canny winemakers do not waste it: they use it in other wines that need dilution to cut back excessive alcohol.

There is no shortage of theories, including the overefficiency of new yeast strains, but no one seems to have the answer. Of course, the best way to achieve the right balance in any wine is on the vine, with correct viticulture. However, anecdotal evidence suggests that mature vines, planted in good sites, not overcropped, overwatered, or fertilized, tend to ripen their fruit at acceptable alcohol levels. There is a lesson there.

Update

There have been no changes to any of the issues raised here in the last edition of *Wine Report*: grape-juice concentrate is still permitted as an additive; barrel samples are still permitted as entries in some major wine shows; wine continues to be overoaked, though there is a gradual improvement in oak balance; and medal stickers are still used for wines coming from batches that did not win the award.

Advance report on the latest harvest
2004

This year is a mixed bag. Original estimates for a massive crop were trimmed after a combination of severe mid-February heat, especially in South Australia, and crop thinning. Still expecting 1.7 million tonnes: 22 per cent higher than 2003's short one. It was a stop-start harvest due to alternating periods of heat and cool. The southern parts of Victoria had high yields and avoided extremes of heat and cold. Coonawarra has big crops and, while quality is mostly good, those who overcropped will have a nail-biting finish. Clare suffered in the February heat, while McLaren Vale and Barossa have made excellent Shiraz, and Adelaide Hills looks very good overall. Very dry conditions continue in most regions, despite promising rains early in the summer. The Yarra Valley quality is good despite a wet end to the harvest: lower yields would have made it a great year. The Hunter made very good Semillon and Chardonnay but reds are light.

Updates on the previous five vintages
2003

Vintage rating: 86

Universally, 2003 was a year of reduced yields caused by general drought, with small bunches of small berries. Rain close to harvest resulted in berry split, further cutting yields in several regions, stretching from Tasmania to central Victoria to McLaren Vale. Smoke taint from the disastrous January bushfires in the Alpine valleys of northeastern Victoria added insult to injury. The total harvest was down 15–20 per cent on forecasts, but, despite the hardships, quality was reported to be very good in most areas. Some noted 'big red' regions such as Heathcote, Barossa, and McLaren Vale struggled to attain flavour ripeness despite very high alcohols, because a hot summer abruptly turned into a cool late summer and autumn. Some reds have unripe tannins. The best wines are Shiraz and Chardonnay, with patches of excitement created by Adelaide Hills Sauvignon Blanc, Clare and Eden Valley Riesling, Coonawarra Cabernet and Merlot, and Yarra Valley Pinot Noir. Southern Victoria had a very good vintage. Late rain spoiled the Tasmanian vintage and to a lesser degree the Great Southern in Western Australia. Margaret River was just fair, and quite variable. Hot, dry summers and low yields tend to favour reds rather than whites, although it is remarkable how good the better-made 2003 whites are looking in their youth.

2002

Vintage rating: 93

Record cool temperatures during the summer brought South Australia an outstanding vintage, especially for white wines in Clare and the Barossa – and even McLaren Vale, not noted for fine dry whites. The Riverland had a great year with some fine whites and reds showing superb colour and varietal flavour. There is a slight question mark over flavour ripeness for reds in cooler areas like Eden Valley. The Hunter Valley, Mudgee, Orange, Hilltops, and Riverina all had an excellent vintage, while southerly regions like Tasmania and southern Victoria were able to ripen their grapes fully despite a very late harvest, thanks to a long, dry Indian summer. Unhappily, yields were miserly, especially in cool regions such as Tasmania, Yarra, Mornington, and Geelong. Western Australia was less favoured, although whites are good.

2001

Vintage rating: 85

In contrast to 2002, this year had one of the hottest summers on record in South Australia, bringing an early harvest of good, rich, ultraripe reds. The whites were also remarkably decent, because the heat wave preceded *veraison*. A good Hunter Semillon year, although it was a wet harvest for the Hunter, Mudgee, Cowra, and Orange. It was a very good year for southern Victoria and Tasmania – especially for Pinot Noir. It was a special year for Western Australia reds, especially Margaret River Cabernets. Other highlights are in Eden Valley, the Adelaide Hills, and – for big reds – the Pyrenees.

2000

Vintage rating: 75

A great vintage for Hunter Shiraz wines, which are opulent and will be long-lived. Pinot Noir in southern Victoria and, especially, Tasmania are sensational. The Tassie Pinots are like the 1994s: dark, opulent, powerful, and long-lived. The big disappointment was in South Australia – all regions had a very ordinary start to the new millennium, except Coonawarra, which had a much better vintage and made excellent reds, thanks to its being spared the vintage rain. Central Victoria had a very good vintage of concentrated reds. Mudgee, Cowra, and Orange all had an unusually wet vintage and made dilute wines.

1999

Vintage rating: *85*

The quality of reds, especially in the Barossa and McLaren Vale, turned out to be remarkably high, certainly higher than expected. Coonawarra again was very good. In southern Victoria, it was a fairly ordinary year, although Bendigo-Heathcote and Rutherglen made good wines. Tasmania was fairly disappointing. The Hunter had a good year, especially for Semillon. Margaret River reds are really outstanding and for long keeping.

• **Just what the world needs** – more wine brands! Both the ex-Southcorp group chief winemaker Philip Shaw and former Penfolds chief winemaker John Duval will soon launch their own wines. Shaw retired from Southcorp in November, and Duval left the company a year earlier. Shaw was the linchpin behind Rosemount's rise to global success between 1982 and its merger with Southcorp in 2000. He will start producing his own wines from the 50-ha vineyard he established in Orange in 1988, which has supplied the grapes for the Rosemount range of Orange regional wines. Duval, who still consults to Penfolds, has made 2003-vintage reds in the Barossa and McLaren Vale to release in 2005.

• **An Australian invention** may yet be the saviour of the beleaguered wine-cork industry. Procork is a series of membranes applied to both ends of a normal one-piece wine cork. Procork's Dr Gregor Christie says that testing at the Australian Wine Research Institute has given it the thumbs up. Other independent testing commissioned by the company showed that Procork outperformed all closures, including screwcaps, in the areas of freshness, flavour, consistency, and sulphide taint. The first Procorks have hit the market in the bottles of Pyrenees winery Mount Avoca.

• **About 200 million bottles** of Australian wine will be sealed with screwcaps in the calendar year 2004, according to Clare winemaker and screwcap advocate Jeffrey Grosset. This compares with about 200,000 in the year 2000, which is a thousandfold increase in four years, and gives an idea of just how quickly screwcaps have been adopted by our winemakers and ultimately by drinkers. Grosset says his figures are very approximate and were arrived at by speaking to the main suppliers of screwcaps.

GREATEST WINE PRODUCERS

1. Southcorp (Penfolds, Seppelt, Wynns, Rosemount, Coldstream Hills, Devil's Lair)
2. Cullen
3. Petaluma
4. Henschke
5. Grosset
6. BRL Hardy (Hardys, Houghton, Yarra Burn, Brookland Valley)
7. Cape Mentelle
8. McWilliam's (Mount Pleasant, Brand's, Lillydale)
9. Giaconda
10. Tyrrells

FASTEST-IMPROVING PRODUCERS

1. Brand's
2. Beringer Blass (Wolf Blass, Jamiesons Run, Maglieri)
3. Hungerford Hill
4. Howard Park
5. Fox Creek
6. Willow Creek
7. D'Arenberg
8. Nepenthe
9. Voyager Estate
10. Balnaves

NEW UP-AND-COMING PRODUCERS

1. Bindi
2. Murdock
3. Higher Plane
4. Curly Flat
5. Kilikanoon
6. Mitolo
7. Shadowfax
8. Ferngrove
9. Cardinham Estate
10. Serafino

BEST-VALUE PRODUCERS

1. BRL Hardy (Stepping Stone, Leasingham, Bastion, Banrock Station)
2. Beringer Blass (Jamiesons Run, Saltram, Annie's Lane, Ingoldby)
3. De Bortoli (Windy Peak, Deen De Bortoli, Sacred Hill)
4. McWilliams
5. Trentham Estate
6. Zilzie
7. Orlando Wyndham (Jacob's Creek, Jacob's Creek Reserve, Richmond Grove)
8. Southcorp (Wynns, Seppelt, Leo Buring, Lindemans bin range)
9. Taylors (Wakefield Estate in Europe)
10. Kirrihill Companions

GREATEST-QUALITY WINES

1. **Diana Madeline Cabernet Sauvignon Merlot 2001** Cullen (A$85)
2. **Belford Semillon 1997** Tyrrells (A$28)
3. **The Contours Riesling 1998** Pewsey Vale (A$28)
4. **Watervale Riesling 2003** Grosset (A$33)
5. **Grange 1999** Penfolds (A$350+)
6. **Arras Pinot Noir Chardonnay Brut 1998** Hardys (A$60)
7. **RSW Shiraz 2001** Wirra Wirra (A$48)
8. **Descendant Shiraz Viognier 2001** Torbreck (A$125)
9. **Eileen Hardy Chardonnay 2001** Hardys (A$40)
10. **Johann's Garden (Grenache Mourvèdre Shiraz) 2002** Henschke (A$31)

BEST BARGAINS

1. **Koonunga Hill Shiraz Cabernet 2002** Penfolds (A$15)
2. **Black Creek Chardonnay 2003** De Bortoli (A$15)
3. **Orange Chardonnay 2001** Templer's Mill (A$17)
4. **Viognier 2003** Trentham Estate (A$19)
5. **Cella Rage Cabernet Merlot 2002** Carbunup Crest (A$12)
6. **Pinot Noir 2002** Coldstream Hills (A$28)
7. **Bastion Riesling 2003** Leasingham (A$15)
8. **Chardonnay 2003** Wolf Blass (A$12)
9. **Georgiana Sauvignon Blanc Semillon Chenin Blanc 2003** Cape Mentelle (A$16)
10. **Oomoo McLaren Vale Shiraz 2001** Hardys (A$14)

MOST EXCITING OR UNUSUAL FINDS

1. **Maglieri's new 2002 Italian trio – Sangiovese, Barbera, and Nebbiolo** (all A$24) *Seldom does a winery burst on to the market with one, let alone three, excellent new examples of these difficult Italian varieties. They are all quite different and faithfully represent the grape varieties.*
2. **Dalliance Sparkling Chardonnay 2000** (A$23) and **Reserve Dalliance Sparkling Chardonnay 1998** (A$26) both Hungerford Hill *A reborn wine company unexpectedly fields two remarkable, fine, complex, cold-climate Tumbarumba blanc de blancs, presumably sourced from its former owner, Southcorp.*
3. **Saperavi 2002** Symphonia (A$29) *This rare-in-Australia but common-in-Russia red grape has a deeply coloured, tannic but powerful expression in the hands of Symphonia's Peter Read.*
4. **Innes Vineyard Littlehampton Pinot Gris 2002** Henschke (A$29) *Australian Pinot Gris is mostly weak and uninspiring, but this Adelaide Hills example is excitingly rich, smooth, and packed with exotic flavours.*
5. **The Baroness Merlot Cabernet Franc Cabernet Sauvignon Blend 1998/2000/2001** Irvine (A$45) *An innovative, rule-bending blend of varieties and vintages, silky-textured and marvellously nuanced.*
6. **Skilly Ridge Tempranillo 2002** Ingham's (A$28) *Surprisingly Rioja-like for its concentration, coconutty American oak and lively acid/tannin combination.*
7. **Reserve Shiraz Viognier 2002** Yering Station (A$58) *Blending Shiraz and Viognier is a recent Australian fascination and this maker is one of the leaders, with cool-grown Yarra Valley grapes.*
8. **Henry's Seven Shiraz Grenache Viognier 2002** Henschke (A$28) *2002 was a fine year for southern-Rhône-style blends, and this new concept from Henschke has a beguiling array of spice and berry flavours.*
9. **Adelaide Hills Viognier 2003** Shadowfax (A$21) *Viognier is one of the new playthings, and Shadowfax's Matt Harrop extends his prodigious talents. It has length and spicy complexity coupled with fine texture and balance, avoiding the usual pitfalls of excessive phenolics and alcohol heat.*
10. **Buloke Reserve Tempranillo 2003** Zilzie (A$9) *Aussie Tempranillo is a rare enough item, but to produce a worthy example at such a giveaway price is a first.*

New Zealand

Bob Campbell MW

The premium image of New Zealand Sauvignon Blanc is under threat.

BOB CAMPBELL MW

The prospect of a large 2004 vintage, a growing subclass of indifferent wines, and increased competition from other countries are putting pressure on the fragile premium that New Zealand Sauvignon Blanc currently commands.

Quality-conscious Sauvignon Blanc producers will certainly reduce their crop levels by thinning bunches at *veraison*, but there is some concern that the majority of growers will leave their vines untouched. Ironically this short-term pursuit of quantity rather than quality is likely to reduce the price of Sauvignon Blanc, ultimately depriving growers of income.

Marlborough is New Zealand's Sauvignon Blanc capital. This booming region has 86 per cent of the country's Sauvignon Blanc vines, with well over half its own vineyard area devoted to Sauvignon Blanc. The international success of Sauvignon Blanc has encouraged a steady inflow of new growers seeking a rapid and handsome return on their investment, but with less interest in developing a long-term brand. The wine has become a commodity that is regularly traded in bulk and unlabelled bottle.

While New Zealand's Sauvignon Blanc makers have yet to feel any serious competition from the wines of other countries, there is no doubt that the gap is closing both in quality and style. Jancis Robinson recently

BOB CAMPBELL lives in Auckland, where he is the wine editor for *Cuisine* magazine and coauthor of *Cuisine Wine Country*, a comprehensive annual guide to New Zealand's wineries. He writes for publications in seven countries and has judged at wine competitions in seven countries. Bob established his own wine school in 1986, and 18,000 people have graduated from his wine diploma course.

praised a number of Australian Sauvignon Blancs and suggested that New Zealand producers should not be complacent.

Sauvignon Blanc has helped establish New Zealand internationally as a serious producer of quality wine. If the quality of Sauvignon Blanc suffers, New Zealand's reputation is likely to be similarly tarnished.

Getting our act together

The New Zealand government has introduced legislation that will allow the wine industry to develop and enforce specific wine standards. From 1 January 2004, all winemakers must develop, register, and maintain wine-standards management plans that document all winemaking processes and establish audit trails.

The legislation was at least partly prompted by labelling scandals that rocked the industry six or seven years ago. Although the legislation was developed in consultation with the wine industry body, New Zealand Winegrowers, it has been criticized for being overly restrictive and expensive to maintain.

Come what May

Peter Hubscher, managing director of Montana, will retire from his position in May 2004. His replacement is Brian Johnston, previously operations director for Montana's owner, Allied Domecq. This move has resulted in some unease in the wine industry. Although well known as a tough negotiator with grape growers and other suppliers, Hubscher has earned considerable respect for his contribution to the industry as chairman of New Zealand Winegrowers. Montana produces about half of New Zealand's wine. By his actions, Hubscher, who joined Montana as winemaker in 1973, clearly recognized that what was good for the wine industry was good for Montana. He becomes non-executive chairman of Montana when the present chairman retires in May.

Work shy

A shortage of vineyard workers is causing problems in expanding wine regions such as Marlborough and Central Otago. Shortages have meant a drop in the quality of vineyard labour and in some cases have forced mechanization, such as machine-harvesting, to replace more labour-intensive methods. Although labour shortages are causing serious problems now, they are expected to reach critical levels as vineyard areas expand further in the years ahead.

The French use *grand cru* classifications or the cosiness of a *grande marque* club to show a quality pecking order. In the absence of an *appellation contrôlée* system, how can New Zealand winemakers let the public know that all Marlborough Sauvignon Blanc and Central Otago Pinot Noir labels are not equal?

Perhaps we should follow the Australian lead and produce a classification of wines based on auction price, although the secondary market in New Zealand is not yet active enough to be a reliable indicator.

In the end, the market will figure out its own pecking order, but there is a need for a quasi-official guide to fast-track the process.

Irrigation irritation

During a predawn morning jog in Marlborough, I was serenaded by waking birds and the sound of irrigation drippers watering verdant vines. Sadly, it was raining. While increasing water shortages in some regions will, to some extent, remedy the problem, irrigation abuse is a widespread problem in New Zealand vineyards. If growers turn down the tap, New Zealand's wine quality will instantly improve.

Harvesting headaches

Wine quality is greatly influenced by the date on which the grapes are picked. For many vineyards, the grape-picking date is determined not by weather but by their advance booking for the shared mechanical harvester. Control over picking date should be a necessity, not a luxury.

Opinion update

A short vintage in 2003 seems likely to escalate the practice, noted in last year's *Wine Report*, of importing bulk wine from other countries and exporting it as bottled wine. Last year I was critical of wines that showed excessive oak character. I am pleased to report that the latest batch of newly released wines does seem to show less oak influence. Despite my protestation, there are no moves to stifle false claims of organic status, to retain extra wine-show samples, or to offer any indication that a wine is made from grapes grown in the winemaker's own vineyard.

Advance report on the latest harvest
2004

Crop estimates after a generally good fruit-set suggested that the New Zealand harvest would total around 170,000 tonnes – more than double the previous frost-affected vintage and a new record by a large margin.

Torrential rain throughout most of the country in February, and well before the beginning of what was shaping up to be late vintage, caused considerable anxiety. Central Otago was badly affected by a spring frost, with the official loss estimated at 30 per cent.

An Indian summer saved the day. Relatively cool but fine weather after February helped to dry out any botrytis from the rain. Winemakers throughout the country are enthusiastic about the quality of their wines. Many high-quality wines will be made, although heavy-cropping vineyards in some regions failed to produce fully ripe grapes. Central Otago was again hit by frost late in the season, adding to the woes of a region that had, until now, enjoyed a string of excellent vintages.

Updates on the previous five vintages
2003

Vintage rating: North Island 63 (Red: 60, White: 65), South Island 78 (Red: 75, White: 80)

All regions except Central Otago and Nelson suffered frost damage, ranging from minor in Auckland to severe in Hawke's Bay. As a result, the harvest was down 36 per cent on the previous year, despite a 12 per cent increase in vineyard area. Only Nelson and Central Otago showed an increase in grape tonnage on the 2002 harvest. The North Island suffered from generally wet conditions, while the South Island was relatively dry with drought conditions in some areas. Many grape growers in frost-affected areas tried to recover some production by harvesting later-ripening grapes from 'second set', but this often resulted in unsatisfactory wines with varying ripeness levels. The crop of Marlborough Sauvignon Blanc was significantly reduced by frost, although the damage was such that little second set occurred, and the quality was good with some outstanding wines made.

2002

Vintage rating: *North Island 84 (Red: 83, White: 85), South Island 88 (Red: 88, White: 88)*

A long, hot, dry spell of autumn weather resulted in a miracle vintage with many outstanding wines. Gisborne enjoyed a vintage that several winemakers described as the best ever. Hawke's Bay produced many good wines, both white and red. Fears that a high crop of Sauvignon Blanc in Marlborough resulted in wide variation in quality were not entirely unfounded, although the best wines were exceptional. Canterbury had a cool, late vintage with average to above-average wines, while Central Otago boasted some of the region's best-ever reds amid fears that some grapes may have been allowed to overripen.

2001

Vintage rating: *North Island 68 (Red: 65, White: 70), South Island 85 (Red: 83, White: 88)*

Almost every malady imaginable seemed to afflict this vintage, including fire, frost, hail, rain, and drought. Grape growers would not have been surprised had a plague of locusts descended. It is officially described as a "typical New Zealand vintage, in that there has been a lot of regional variation", although the wines of the South Island are significantly superior, while an Indian summer favoured later-ripening varieties in the North Island.

2000

Vintage rating: *North Island 82 (Red: 78, White: 85), South Island 83 (Red: 83, White: 82)*

Quality was high in the South Island but more variable in the North Island, although Chardonnay performed well in all regions except Gisborne. Vineyards planted on marginal sites and those carrying excessive crop levels may have failed to produce fully ripe grapes.

1999

Vintage rating: *North Island 78 (Red: 78, White: 78), South Island 79 (Red: 80, White: 78)*

The wines of this vintage are of variable quality. The South Island regions fared a little better than those in the North Island.

GREATEST WINE PRODUCERS

1. Dry River
2. Felton Road
3. Cloudy Bay
4. Ata Rangi
5. Fromm
6. Te Mata Estate
7. Craggy Range
8. Neudorf
9. Villa Maria
10. Pegasus Bay

NEW UP-AND-COMING PRODUCERS

1. Spy Valley
2. Waipara Hills Wine Estate
3. Herzog
4. Kingsley Estate
5. Muddy Water
6. Escarpment
7. Akarua
8. Unison
9. Bilancia
10. Mountford

FASTEST-IMPROVING PRODUCERS

1. Saint Clair
2. Trinity Hill
3. Pegasus Bay
4. Peregrine
5. Mount Riley
6. Mills Reef
7. Greenhough
8. Two Paddocks
9. Mission Estate Winery
10. Palliser Estate

BEST-VALUE PRODUCERS

1. Montana Wines
2. Spy Valley
3. Saint Clair
4. Framingham
5. Drylands
6. Coopers Creek
7. Villa Maria Estate
8. Mission Estate Winery
9. Hunter's
10. Babich

Grapevine

• **New Zealand's** hot, dry 1998 vintage is credited with producing many great red wines, particularly from Bordeaux varieties. At the time, Te Mata owner John Buck cautioned that nearly half of New Zealand's wineries had experienced a drought vintage and would be likely to harvest their grapes too late. Buck's prophecy now appears to have been correct. Many 1998 reds are now at or slightly past their best, despite predictions that the best would age for a decade or more.

• **David Hohnen,** founder of Cloudy Bay, has left the 18-year-old winery to pursue his own interests on farming properties he owns in Margaret River,

Western Australia. Hohnen had relinquished his shares in the company to Veuve Clicquot Ponsardin some time ago. His place has been taken by Dr Tony Jordan, who will retain his current position as CEO of Domaine Chandon. Domaine Chandon and Veuve Clicquot are both owned by the Louis Vuitton Moët Hennessy group (LVMH).

• **Having been purchased** by Australia's BRL Hardy as recently as 2000, New Zealand's second-largest wine producer, the Nobilo Wine Group, discovered it had a new corporate owner in 2003, when BRL itself was taken over by US drinks giant Constellation Brands, the world's largest wine business.

GREATEST-QUALITY WINES

1. **Block 5 Pinot Noir 2002** Felton Road (NZ$60)
2. **The Quarry 2002** Craggy Range (NZ$60)
3. **Homage 2002** Trinity Hill (NZ$100)
4. **Craighall Riesling 2003** Dry River (NZ$32)
5. **Gewurztraminer 2003** Dry River (NZ$36)
6. **Sauvignon Blanc 2003** Palliser Estate (NZ$23)
7. **Taylor's Pass Vineyard Sauvignon Blanc 2003** Villa Maria (NZ$25)
8. **Late Harvest Riesling 2003** Martinborough Vineyard (NZ$35 per half-bottle)
9. **Lismore Pinot Gris 2003** Ata Rangi (NZ$26)
10. **Gimblett Gravels Merlot 2002** Craggy Range (NZ$26)

BEST BARGAINS

1. **The Stones Sauvignon Blanc 2003** Cairnbrae (NZ$17)
2. **Pinot Noir 2002** Dry Gully (NZ$29)
3. **The Underarm Syrah 2002** Red Rock (NZ$25)
4. **Dry Riesling 2003** Felton Road (NZ$25)
5. **Chardonnay 2002** Mount Riley (NZ$18)
6. **Gewurztraminer 2003** Spy Valley (NZ$20)
7. **Pinot Gris 2003** Spy Valley (NZ$20)
8. **Pinot Gris 2002** Morton Estate (NZ$17)
9. **Riesling Canterbury/Marlborough 2003** Waipara Hills Wine Estate (NZ$20)
10. **Classic Riesling 2003** Framingham (NZ$19)

MOST EXCITING OR UNUSUAL FINDS

1. **Gimblett Gravels Syrah 2001** Kingsley Estate (NZ$42) *Voted top wine in the Tri-Nations Wine Challenge, a Sydney-based competition that compares the best from Australia, New Zealand, and South Africa.*
2. **Montepulciano 2001** Herzog (NZ$59) *A modest number of New Zealand wineries is experimenting with Italian grape varieties, and most are learning that what works in Tuscany does not necessarily work in Hawke's Bay or Marlborough. This is the spectacular exception. A product of fanatical attention to detail in both vineyard and winery.*
3. **Vin Gris 2003** Felton Road (NZ$22) *Both unusual and a relative bargain, this whiteish wine is made by draining some of the juice from Pinot Noir grapes before fermentation. It is made only in vintages where Pinot Noir might otherwise lack sufficient colour and possibly flavour.*
4. **Aria Late-Picked Riesling 2002** Pegasus Bay (NZ$32) *Voted top sweet wine at the Tri-Nations Wine Challenge. Moderately sweet wine with some botrytis influence, but retaining plenty of varietal character.*
5. **Sauvignon Blanc 2003** Gravitas (NZ$29) *The second vintage from an uncompromising new Marlborough producer determined to make high-quality Sauvignon. The grapes are (unusually) hand-picked from low-yielding vines and whole-bunch pressed to produce a gentle yet powerful expression of Marlborough Sauvignon Blanc.*

6 Canterbury/Marlborough Riesling 2003 Waipara Hills (NZ$19.95) *This new winery upset several local producers when, despite bearing the Waipara name, it began making wines from Marlborough as well as Waipara. However, while this regional blend raised a few eyebrows, critics have been partly silenced by its stunning quality and exquisite balance.*

7 Chardonnay 2003 Felton Road (NZ$22) *Felton Road makes two Chardonnays. This is the unoaked version. The low-yield, extended-lees-contact wine shines like a beacon, although the many other winemakers that make thin, simple, and generally unappealing unoaked Chardonnay refuse to be guided by it.*

8 AD Semillon 2000 Alpha Domus (NZ$28) *Most New Zealand Semillon is thin and grassy, thanks to the widespread use of a poor clone of the variety. This wine is the exception. It is rich, ripe, oily, and very Australian-like. In fact, it gave a good account of itself in hand-to-hand combat against a number of excellent Australian Semillons.*

9 Elspeth Malbec 2002 Mills Reef (NZ$40) *This wine has extraordinary intensity and, I think, longevity. Pure Malbec was responsible for the 'black wine of Cahors' in 19th-century France, but in 21st-century New Zealand it is a rarity, with most of the country's small production lost in Bordeaux-type blends.*

10 Gewurztraminer 2003 Lawson's Dry Hills (NZ$22) *It took a six-wine vertical tasting to make me aware of this wine's true potential. Dead dry with high (14 per cent) alcohol and an exquisite purity of Turkish delight and rose-petal flavours. Worth waiting for.*

• **Marlborough winery owner** Jane Hunter was presented with an award for her contribution to quality wine production at the International Wine and Spirit Competition awards in London. Jane Hunter has devoted 20 years to building a very successful company and promoting Marlborough's profile as a premium wine area.

• **Kim Crawford Wines** joined a growing list of wine producers sold to offshore companies when it was purchased by Canadian wine producer, marketer, and distributor Vincor International for a reported NZ$14.8 million.

• **A new NZ$2.3-million** Wine Research Centre of Excellence was completed in Marlborough in December 2003. The centre will provide tertiary facilities for students of viticulture and oenology, as well as housing eight scientists from HortResearch who will conduct viticultural research.

• **The New Zealand dollar** reached a five-year high against the US dollar in July and has since continued its climb, putting pressure on wine exporters who had not bought US dollars in advance.

The Asian wine phenomenon continues to gather pace, spurred on by strong consumption growth in the big markets of the region and, increasingly, by export opportunities for the better and larger Asian producers.

DENIS GASTIN

Wine emulating contemporary western styles is now made using modern winemaking facilities in 10 countries in Asia. At the last count (there are no official statistics), there were at least 700 wineries throughout Asia principally or exclusively producing grape wine, many at the higher end of quality expectations. Half of them are in China, in 26 provinces, and more than a quarter in Japan, in a trail from Miyazaki, in the subtropical south, to Hokkaido, in the almost sub-Arctic north, but concentrated principally in Yamanashi, Nagano, and Hokkaido. The remainder is spread sparsely over the continent, from India to Indonesia – including Thailand, Korea, and Vietnam. Fledgling operations can even be found in Taiwan, Sri Lanka, and Bhutan.

DENIS GASTIN grew up in Australia's northeast Victorian wine regions and has had a lifelong interest in wine. Assignments as an Australian trade official in China and Japan opened up new wine vistas for him and, after leaving the government, he has written extensively about the Asian industry. His particular interests are the more unusual aspects of winemaking, the more remote and least understood regions of the wine world, and the groundbreaking work that some of the industry champions have been doing with exotic grape varieties and new wine styles. Denis is a feature writer and Australian correspondent for Japan's liquor-industry newspaper, The Shuhan News. He has contributed to various other journals and wine reference books, including The Oxford Companion to Wine, The World Atlas of Wine, and Hugh Johnson's Wine Companion and Pocket Wine Book (Mitchell Beazley).

China: superpremium wines arrive

A superpremium category is emerging for domestically produced wines as wineries target the small but lucrative market segment currently dominated by imports. The benchmark of around Rmb 100 per bottle was set some time ago by industry leader Changyu. Though higher than the average domestic price of Rmb 38, this is still much lower than the price of imports, which average Rmb 357. Changyu's price was vaulted over spectacularly when established quality producer Dragon Seal put out a limited-release Syrah in 2003 that sold quickly at Rmb 300 per bottle – followed by a limited-release premium Cabernet Sauvignon in 2004 at the same price. Newcomer Rongchen Diamond (Huailai, Hebei province) went way beyond this with a Cabernet/Merlot priced at Rmb 800, which it insists is selling well. Changyu is now fighting back with the release of a 'Château' range at around Rmb 300 and with a very imaginative strategy of offering 600 whole barrels for private sale – at Rmb 80,000 each!

Grapevine

- **Suntime (Xintian),** which has come a long way since its launch in 1998, is starting to rival the output of traditional industry leaders Great Wall, Changyu, and Dynasty. Suntime has 10,000 hectares (ha) of vines in Xinjiang, consisting mostly of classic European varieties. From a crush of just 5,000 tons in 2000, it declares that it will achieve its full 100,000-ton production capacity in 2004/5. Suntime is targeting younger, fashion-conscious consumers with elaborate promotional campaigns featuring media stars and pop icons and is using unconventional packaging to stand out and to broaden its market base. It now has tetra packs in a variety of styles and sizes, from 15 ml to 1.5 litres. It is also relying on its scale economies and operational flexibility as a newcomer to put wine into the market at prices that its competitors cannot hope to match profitably.

- **At Japan's first national wine show,** held in Yamanashi in July 2003, a panel of local and international judges awarded only two gold medals, but 20 silver and 100 bronze. The gold medals were awarded to Domaine Sogga, for its Chardonnay 2002, and to Sapporo, for its Grande Polaire Hokkaido Yoichi Kifu (Botrytis) Kerner 1994.

- **China's white-grape shortage** continues and, although prices paid to growers dipped slightly in 2003 due to a general oversupply of grapes, prices are still higher for white grapes than for red. Reversing the trend of the 1990s, some red-grape vineyards are being replaced with white varieties, and there have been extensive new plantings of Chardonnay, Italian Riesling, and German Riesling. White wines have made a strong return to favour with consumers and have grown to around 30 per cent of domestic sales, despite rising retail prices.

- **China's regional authenticity system** is expanding. Changli county in Hebei province and Yantai in Shandong province were the first two designated regions, promulgated by China's National Quality Supervision and Inspection Bureau in 2002. Two more regions were added in 2003 – Shacheng in Hebei province (the home of industry giant Great Wall) and Helanshan Dongli in Ningxia province, the first designated region in western China.

Lobbying helps Japanese producers

While there are now 360 companies licensed to make wine in Japan, the number of active wineries is around 170. One factor limiting development has been the nation's Agricultural Land Law, which prevents companies from renting or buying farmland. There is an exemption for specially constituted 'agricultural corporations', but strict eligibility criteria make such entities difficult to establish and complicated to operate. However, a recent breakthrough has come in response to intensive lobbying by prefectures where wine is important to the economy. Several exempt zones have now been declared in which corporate ownership or rental of farming land will be permitted – notably in Yamanashi and Nagano prefectures, where most of the bigger wine companies have their headquarters. This presents the Japanese industry with an opportunity to compete in the local-market mid-price range, now dominated by imports, with quality wines of 100 per cent local origin. Wineries should now have greater scope to practise and showcase (to contract growers) the viticultural practices essential to produce quality wines as well as to utilize economies of scale to lower prices.

- **An excellent Kainoir** (Black Queen × Cabernet Sauvignon cross) released by Yamanashi winery Asahi Yoshu gives real substance to the winery's declared medium-term goal of producing challenging red wines. The 80-year-old former cooperative is being revitalized and repositioned by new owners, young husband-and-wife winemaking team Tsuyoshi and Junko Suzuki. Their new Koshu releases also justify their fresh and innovative approach to their first priority, which is getting the traditional (white) styles right.

- **Kerner may be** an underappreciated variety in Germany, but it is rapidly assuming the status of 'signature' variety for the fast-developing wine industry in Hokkaido, Japan's northernmost island. It is flourishing in the austere conditions and producing wines of substance and power, particularly, though not exclusively, as a dessert wine. Sapporo's Grande Polaire Hokkaido Yoichi Kifu (Botrytis) Kerner 1994 took the top award (Superior Gold Medal) at the inaugural Japan Wine Competition in 2003 – and, yes, it is a current release, though of extremely limited availability. Sapporo's Petite Grande Polaire Hokkaido Yoichi Osozumi (Late Harvest) Kerner 2002 is almost as good. Yamazaki Winery's Kerner Dry 2002, the first vintage from this impressive new winery, shows how well it can be done as a dry wine, though they also included a classy sweet version in the inaugural line-up.

- **Château Mercian** is one of several Yamanashi wineries doing a rethink on the region's staple variety, Koshu, Japan's own *Vitis vinifera*. It has released two new styles: Koshu Gris de Gris is a fresh, minimal-intervention style, and Koshiki Jikomi Koshu attempts a reinvention of the more traditional style, using a whole-bunch press technique. Other notable experiments with new Koshu styles are in the works at Chuo Budoshu (Grace), Manns Wine, Katsunuma Jozo, and newcomer Asahi Yoshu.

WINE BOARD FOR INDIA

It is a significant breakthrough for the wine industry that in India, a country with widespread alcohol prohibition, a Wine Board has been established in Maharashtra state, India's largest wine-producing region. The chairman is Dr Ashok Ganguly, ex-chairman of Hindustan Lever, India's largest consumer-goods company. Prominent wine entrepreneur Rajeev Samant, founder of Sula Wines, one of India's newest and most prominent wineries, has also been coopted.

The board's charter is to promote grape growing, wine production, wine consumption, and wine marketing. An immediate priority is to set up a wine institute to promote and nurture modern viticultural and oenological skills in a public/private-sector partnership.

WINERY EXPANSION IN INDIA

Wine consumption in India has trebled in the last five years, albeit from a very small base, and continues growing at around 20 per cent per year. India's internationalized professional fraternity is the driving force, and existing wineries are responding to increased demand by expanding their capacity and establishing a surprising number of new wine ventures in the states of Maharashtra and, to a lesser extent, Karnataka. India's three largest established wineries (Indage, Grover, and Sula) produce around 2 million bottles between them — still only a drop in the bucket in this vast and populous land — and each has an established export market. In Maharashtra alone, 10 new wineries have been licensed to open in 2004.

BALI HIGH

Bali wine pioneer Hatten Wines will reach a significant milestone in 2005: the 150th vintage for its mainstay product, Hatten Rosé. A long history in winemaking? Not really. The milestone will coincide with its 10th year in wine. Aided by a year-round supply of Alphonse Lavallée (red) grapes from Singaraja in the island's north, just 2° from the equator, Hatten has made at least 12 'vintages' each year. The growers are now being synchronized to achieve monthly 'vintage' cycles.

Another major milestone for this innovative winery was winning Bronze at the 2003 London International Wine and Spirit Competition for its semi-sweet Alexandria, made from Belgia (Muscat family) grapes grown in the winery's own vineyards. Hatten's sparkling wines — Tanjung, a white méthode champenoise made from a mysterious local grape called Probolingo Putih, and a blush version, Jepun, based on the Alphonse Lavallée — have won a staunch following locally.

THAILAND AT THE SUMMIT

The Asia-Pacific Economic Cooperation (APEC) Heads of State Summit held in Bangkok in 2003 was an opportunity for the Thai hosts to showcase some local wines to visiting dignitaries. Wines from two of the country's newest wineries, Khao Yai and Siam Winery, were served during the gala dinner. Each was a statement showing the enormous progress in the local wine industry in recent years.

Khao Yai, a 40,000-case winery founded by Piya Bhirombhakdi, a major stakeholder in the giant Boon Rawd brewery (maker of Singha beer), emphasizes traditional western wine styles. It draws principally from Shiraz, Tempranillo, Chenin Blanc, and Colombard vines in its 80-ha vineyard in an elevated valley in the foothills around the Khao Yai National Park, about 200 km north of Bangkok.

Siam Winery, now Thailand's biggest, is best known for its Spy Wine Cooler and is owned by the Yoovidhya family, which made a fortune building the Red Bull energy drink into a global brand but also produces wine under the Châtemp and (appropriately named) Monsoon labels. These brands encompass a range of styles based principally on Malaga Blanc and Pok Dum (possibly a local mutation of the hybrid Black Queen), supplemented by small quantities of Shiraz, Black Muscat, and Colombard. Most of the grapes are grown on 'floating vineyards' (strips of land separated by canals, tended and harvested by boat) in the Chao Phraya delta, 40 km from Bangkok.

Both Khao Yai and Siam have put considerable new creative momentum and substance behind the solid start to the Thai wine industry, which was forged a decade ago by the pioneering Château de Loei, in the north of the country, near the border with Laos.

TRADEMARKING CABERNET IN CHINA

An audacious attempt to trademark 'Cabernet' in China has been made by one of the nation's oldest and most respected wineries, Changyu. The winery claims that it first created Cabernet (or, more specifically, the Chinese transliteration Jie-bai-na) as a brand in the 1930s and has released wines continuously under this 'brand' for more than 70 years. The State Trademark Administration awarded a certificate of registration to Changyu in May 2002, but the case is now in formal arbitration, having been strongly contested by other leading producers, including Great Wall, Dynasty, and Weilong. Unsurprisingly, they see a varietal descriptor as a right to be shared by the industry at large, whatever the history, rather than the property of one single producer.

Grapevine

● **Great Wall wineries'** main priority was consolidation during 2003 and 2004 – even though this meant lower sales and reduced production. Following the acquisition by COFCO Wines & Spirits of equity from local farmers and local governments, the three Great Wall operations – at Shacheng, Huaxia, and Yantai – no longer operate as separate enterprises. They now come under central sales and marketing control with the objective of slashing production and management costs and to improve returns. Henceforth, the three Great Wall wineries will feature only as a place of origin on labels.

The biggest constraint to producing good wine in Asia is the lack of a genuinely wine-focused viticultural tradition. Most of the vineyard area produces grapes for the table or for drying, although much of the recent expansion has been in wine-grape varieties. Traditional grape growers are not yet confident enough to make the commitment to the different viticultural practices that are required for good wine, and wineries are limited (by land-ownership laws, among other things) in the extent to which they can do this themselves. With heavy investment in modern winery equipment now behind them, the next challenge for most Asian winemakers lies in the vineyards, with yield management and ripeness the priority targets.

The principal challenge is to deal with growers' natural tendencies to go for volume, on the one hand, and to pick early to avoid fungal and other endemic diseases, on the other. The ripening issue has been exacerbated by the absence of regulations setting standards for the addition of sugar. It is all too easy to get a required level of alcohol, but this is almost always at the expense of flavour and character.

Strength in accuracy

In Japan, there is a widespread practice of declaring on labels an alcohol level of "less than 15 per cent". In China, one leading company declares almost its total range at 12 per cent: an amazing feat of consistency if it were correct, but one suspects that it is, rather, a 'default' setting. There should be a labelling law in these countries to ensure a certain minimum accuracy of alcoholic strengths. Better regulations are also required to stop inaccurate or misleading declarations on the origin of grapes, the year of vintage, and grape varieties.

Grapevine

• **China's Dragon Seal** continues on its trend-setting way, expanding an already impressive varietal range by adding a Pinot Noir (China's first) and a Sauvignon Blanc (still very rare in China) in 2004. The Pinot Noir is from grapes grown in Hebei; the Sauvignon Blanc is from new vineyards in Gansu province, in the fast-developing western region of China. A Vin Nouveau, using Gamay grapes and a semi-carbonic-maceration technique, has also been released in very limited quantities – another first for China. But, after a brief return for the 2002 vintage, Rhine Riesling will miss a year due to a poor crop in 2003.

Advance report on the latest harvest
2003

China – Very wet conditions in the eastern provinces (Hebei and Shandong) produced big berries with low sugar and acid levels in most white varieties, though late-maturing reds were generally of good quality and some better than average. Rainfall during harvest caused widespread fungal disease in most regions and was particularly devastating in parts of Shanxi province in central China. Even in the west, where conditions are generally more amenable, colder and wetter weather than usual impacted adversely on quality. Overall, 2003 was not a good year.

Japan – Extensive summer rainfall severely dented yields and kept sugar levels low in all the major regions. A few of the later-picked varieties saw some recovery when rains eased late in the harvest in some locations – late-picked reds in some vineyards in Yamanashi and the Komoro district of Nagano, for example. But, overall, it was a poor year and the wines generally suffer from suppressed natural flavours and colours.

India – Vintage was over early in Maharashtra. Warmer weather throughout the ripening period and a weaker monsoon season saw fruit ripening early, relatively free of disease problems. Sauvignon Blanc and more aromatic wines will not be as intense as in some previous years, but the reds matured perfectly and generally were picked at high sugar levels, so there will be lots of flavour and colour. In Bangalore, conditions were close to ideal. The weaker monsoon and drier conditions permitted grapes to be left on the vine to reach full maturity.

Updates on the previous five vintages
2002

China – Grapes were very late to ripen in China's Hebei province, but wineries that could delay picking produced wines with good flavour and colour. Grape growers in Shandong province, which is further south and coastal, made even better use of the cooler and drier conditions, achieving desired sugar levels and robust colouring, with very little rot.

Japan – Conditions were very good in Japan's main regions, Yamanashi and Nagano. There were a few typhoons in the early summer, but no damage to vines or fruit. With sustained sunshine and little rain late in the season, the vineyards enjoyed much lower levels of rot, encouraging growers to wait for optimal ripeness before picking. Nagano Merlot looks promising.

India – A weaker-than-usual monsoon season delivered drier-than-normal conditions, which favoured even ripening patterns and made rot more manageable. The white varieties came off well in Bangalore, as did most of the reds, though some red varieties did suffer insect and fungal attacks. In Maharashtra, it was an excellent year, with good diurnal variations at the critical points, and slow, even ripening.

2001

China – Vintage conditions were generally very good in China. Extended dry spells during a late ripening period in Hebei permitted fruit to develop good sugar levels and colour, although some vineyards sustained hail damage. Part of Shandong suffered both late spring frosts and summer hailstorms, so yields were reduced. Shandong also had fungal disease problems brought on by late rains.

Japan – Both Yamanashi and Nagano had an excellent vintage. The wines are generally softer and more fully flavoured than usual.

India – A very good year, with slow, even ripening conditions and a relatively dry harvest period.

2000

China – In Hebei and Shandong, long dry periods during ripening and harvest provided welcome relief for most growers from the usual fungal disease problems.

Japan – Yamanashi and Nagano had a good year, though it was better in the former than the latter. Nagano's Kikyogahara district, renowned for its Merlot and Cabernet, had an average year.

India – An excellent year in Bangalore, where light rains in the late ripening period brought temperatures down and assisted flavour concentration.

1999

China – It was a drier year than usual in Hebei and Shandong, resulting in good sugar content and colour achieved by most growers. Shandong, however, did not avoid the usual fungal problems.

Japan – Nagano and Kikyogahara had an excellent year, with regular weather conditions through the vintage. Yamanashi did not fare so well.

India – It was a very good year in both Bangalore and Maharashtra, although some of the Bangalore reds lacked concentration.

1998

China – Hebei and Shandong had an average vintage. Although it was reasonably dry during the late ripening season, growers still had to battle the usual fungal problems caused by occasional rains, especially in Shandong, encouraging many contract growers to take the fruit early. For those who waited, average ripeness was achieved.

Japan – For most producers in Yamanashi and Nagano it was a difficult vintage. In Yamanashi, there was heavy snow in the winter months, followed by a wetter-than-average 'wet' season that continued on well into August. Nagano also had a very wet year, with the Kikyogahara district heavily affected. Underripened grapes and fungal disease were common problems in both prefectures. Surprisingly, however, Nagano's Hokushin district avoided much of the rain and enjoyed one of its best vintages.

India – It was a very good year in Maharashtra, but rains during harvest created fungal problems for some red varieties in Bangalore, where, otherwise, it was a good year.

• **A new chapter in the Koshu story** is unfolding in Yamagata prefecture in the north of Japan's main island, Honshu. Koshu vines were taken to Yamagata some time in the Edo Era (1603–1867) by migrants from Yamanashi, the recognized home of Koshu and, indeed, of the Japanese wine industry. Yamagata Koshu vines are said to be quite primitive compared with present-day Yamanashi Koshu and they grow in more mountainous country. Previously, Yamagata Koshu had disappeared into nondescript blends but, lately, some local wineries have produced straight Koshu wines. The quality of the first release, Oura Koshu, made in the Oura family winery near the city of Nanyo by Hiroo Oura, a recent graduate of Yamanashi University, will freshly challenge the complacency that has characterized the industry's approach to this vine.

• **Rajeev Samant's Sula Wines,** which successfully introduced Sauvignon Blanc and Chenin Blanc vines to India in the mid-1990s and released the first wines from these varieties in 2000, has now launched a Shiraz 2003. This follows the market's endorsement of a Cabernet/Shiraz blend – Sula's first red-wine release and the blend another first for India. The Shiraz vines came from Australia, and the wine is made under the direction of California winemaker Kerry Damskey. In addition to burgeoning domestic-market success, Sula is now exporting to the US, France, and Italy. Exports already account for 7,000 of its 40,000-case annual output. All this in six vintages!

GREATEST WINE PRODUCERS

1. Château Mercian (Japan)
2. Suntory (Japan)
3. Dragon Seal (China)
4. Grace Winery (Japan)
5. Marufuji Rubaiyat (Japan)
6. Changyu (China)
7. Great Wall (China)
8. Manns (Japan)
9. Hua Dong (China)
10. Indage (India)

FASTEST-IMPROVING PRODUCERS

1. Hayashi Noen (Japan)
2. Lou Lan (China)
3. Izutsu (Japan)
4. Dynasty (China)
5. Katsunuma Jozo (Japan)
6. Grover Vineyards (India)
7. Okuizumo (Japan)
8. Takeda (Japan)
9. Weilong (China)
10. Hatten (Bali, Indonesia)

NEW UP-AND-COMING PRODUCERS

1. Suntime (China)
2. Domaine Sogga (Japan)
3. Tsuno Wines (Japan)
4. Sula (India)
5. Yamazaki (Japan)
6. Shanxi Grace (China)
7. Mogao (China)
8. Khao Yai (Thailand)
9. Asahi Yoshu (Japan)
10. Guizhou Moutai (China)

BEST-VALUE PRODUCERS

1. Dragon Seal (China)
2. Tsuno Wines (Japan)
3. Grace Winery (Japan)
4. Marufuji Rubaiyat (Japan)
5. Hayashi Noen (Japan)
6. Grover Vineyards (India)
7. Izutsu (Japan)
8. Kitanoro Jozo (Japan)
9. Weilong (China)
10. Great Wall (China)

GREATEST-QUALITY WINES

1. **Private Reserve Hokushin Chardonnay 2001** Château Mercian, Japan (¥6,000)
2. **Tomi no Oka Cabernet/Merlot 1997** Suntory, Japan (¥10,000)
3. **Private Reserve Koshu Toriibira 1999** Château Mercian, Japan (¥3,500)
4. **Cru de Huailai Cabernet 2002** Dragon Seal, China (Rmb 300)
5. **Private Reserve Jyonohira Cabernet 1999** Château Mercian, Japan (¥10,000)
6. **Cuvée Misawa Private Reserve Chardonnay 2002** Grace Winery, Japan (¥8,000)
7. **Cabernet Sauvignon/Merlot/Petit Verdot 2001** Marufuji Rubaiyat, Japan (¥4,500)
8. **Chardonnay Unfiltered 2002** Domaine Sogga, Hideo Vineyard, Obuse Winery, Japan (¥5,000)
9. **Cuvée Misawa Private Reserve Cabernet/Merlot 2002** Grace Winery, Japan (¥10,000)
10. **Méthode Traditionnelle Sparkling NV** Marquise de Pompadour, India (Rp 720)

BEST BARGAINS

1. **Campbell Early Rosé 2002** Tsuno Wines, Japan (¥1,200)
2. **Toriibira Koshu 2002** Grace Winery, Japan (¥2,000)
3. **Rosé 2002** Dragon Seal, China (Rmb 25)
4. **Petite Grande Polaire Hokkaido Yoichi Osozumi (Late Harvest) Kerner 2002** Sapporo, Japan (¥1,510)
5. **Huailai Reserve Cabernet Sauvignon 2002** Dragon Seal, China (Rmb 120)
6. **Chardonnay (Estate Grown) 2002** Shanxi Grace, China (Rmb 68)
7. **Sauvignon Blanc NV** Sula, India (Rp 450)
8. **Cabernet-Shiraz NV** Grover Vineyards, India (Rp 450)
9. **Chardonnay Estate 2003** Tsuno Wines, Japan (¥2,600)
10. **Dry White (Longyan) NV** Great Wall, China (Rmb 35)

MOST EXCITING OR UNUSUAL FINDS

1. **Cru du Huailai Syrah 2002** Dragon Seal, China (Rmb 300) *Second vintage of China's pioneer Syrah, from very young vines grown from imported French cuttings. Dragon Seal has invested heavily in viticultural improvement, and it shows.*
2. **Chardonnay Unfiltered 2002** Domaine Sogga, Hideo Vineyard, Obuse Winery, Japan (¥5,000) *Like most of the wines from this young winemaker bent on experimentation, this wine is a unique style interpretation – not burgundian, not New World. All his own work.*
3. **Koshu 2001** Oura Budoshu, Japan (¥3,000) *This first-release Koshu from a small Yamagata prefecture winery sets a new quality benchmark for this unique Japanese variety rarely seen outside its traditional Yamanashi home. From very old vines in elevated vineyards.*
4. **Empery Cupid Wild Grapes Wine 2000** East of Eden, South Korea (Won 25,000) *A sweet red wine made from wild amurensis grapes, the only variety grown by this maker. This is the only wine of its kind in Korea. Virtually organic.*
5. **Kerner Dry 2002** Yamazaki Winery, Japan (¥2,000) *An undervalued variety in Europe but emerging as a signature variety in Hokkaido in both sweet and dry styles. Best dry version to emerge so far. One to put down.*
6. **Méthode Française Cabernet Sauvignon/Chardonnay Free Run 2002** Dragon Seal, China (Rmb 70) *Unusual blend that works well in this lively sparkling format. Good fruit, good winemaking.*
7. **Shanxi Rosé NV** Shanxi Grace, China (Rmb 70) *An unusual blend for rosé – Cabernet Sauvignon, Cabernet Franc, and Merlot – from the emerging Shanxi region in China's central west. Bordeaux without colour.*
8. **Kainoir 2002** Asahi Yoshu, Japan (¥2,000) *An obscure local variety (Black Queen x Cabernet Sauvignon cross) that rarely shines, but this is a noteworthy exception, showing uncharacteristic depth and substance.*
9. **Pinot Noir 2002** Yamazaki Winery, Japan (¥2,600) *A most unexpected achievement, given the bitterly cold conditions of Hokkaido and very new vines. First vintage and one of only four Pinots in Japan.*
10. **Vin Nouveau Gamay 2003** Dragon Seal, China (Rmb 66) *First Gamay and first use of semi-carbonic-maceration technique in China. From established but always pioneering winery.*

The event of the year occurred during, but not at, VinExpo 2003 in Bordeaux, with the largest-ever conference of biodynamic and biodynamically inclined producers at Hangar 14, just off the Quai des Chartrons.

MONTY WALDIN

The conference was called La Renaissance des Appellations ('the rebirth of the concept of controlled regions of origin') and was organized by Loire producer Nicolas Joly of the *monopole* Coulée de Serrant in Savennières. Joly travels the world arguing that a wine must be true to its origin before it can be considered good. His argument, in its simplest form, is that industrialized viticulture nullifies the nuance of *terroir*. For instance, wines made from vines fed by chemical fertilizers rather than the soil will taste banal. In Joly's eyes, a chemically maintained soil will produce similar wines whether the vines are located in the Maipo Valley or the Médoc. Other techniques that result in standardized wines include reverse osmosis and single-strain cultured yeasts. Critics of Joly argue that using organic or biodynamic methods does not necessarily make a wine good, even though it may be true to its *terroir*.

MONTY WALDIN While working on a conventionally farmed wine domaine in Bordeaux as a teenager, Monty Waldin realized that the more chemicals were applied to a vineyard, the more corrective treatments became necessary in the winery. When the opportunity arose to write about wines, he specialized in green issues and now writes a regular column on environmental matters for *Harpers*, the weekly journal of the wine and spirit trade in the UK. His first book, *The Organic Wine Guide* (Thorsons, 1999), is soon to be joined by a guide dedicated to biodynamic producers. Monty's interest in biodynamics was stimulated in 1999 by six months working on a family-owned biodynamic vineyard in California's Mendocino County. Previous winemaking experience in Chile contributed to his latest book, *Wines of South America* (Mitchell Beazley, 2003). Monty's next book will be *Biodynamic Wines* (Mitchell Beazley Classic Wine Library, 2004).

Attending Joly's Renaissance des Appellations conference were more than 70 organic and biodynamic producers from Australia, Austria, Chile, France, Germany, Italy, New Zealand, Slovenia, South Africa, Switzerland, and the US. Heavy hitters included Madame Lalou Bize-Leroy of Domaine Leroy and Domaine d'Auvenay in Burgundy, Anne-Claude Leflaive of the eponymous Puligny-Montrachet domaine, Jean-Michel Deiss from Alsace, Gérard Gauby from Roussillon, Mike Benziger from California, Michel Chapoutier from the Rhône, Alvaro Espinoza from Chile, and Guy Bossard of Domaine de l'Ecu in Muscadet.

The interest in M Joly's conference reflects a growing worldwide interest in biodynamics. The area under certified biodynamic management is rising significantly worldwide, especially in the New World. In Europe, France leads the way. It is estimated that at least one in ten French producers with organic certification is either also certified biodynamic or trialling biodynamics on a significant scale. This means making use of three things:

• Biodynamic compost ('normal compost' to which the solid biodynamic preparations of composted oak bark, camomile, dandelion, horsetail, yarrow, and nettle have been added, with the biodynamic valerian tea sprayed over the pile);

• Regular applications of the Horn Manure 500 spray preparation to stimulate the life of the soil and the vine roots within it;

• Regular applications of the Horn Silica 501 spray preparation, which stimulates the vine's relationship with the sun in particular and the cosmos in general.

Cynics might justifiably complain that biodynamics has become something of a fashion, if not yet in mainstream agriculture, but there appears to be increasing evidence of the acceptance of the benefits of biodynamics.

Grapevine

• **Santa Emiliana's VOE** in Chile's Colchagua Valley, the most exciting biodynamic project in the southern hemisphere, produced the top wine, Coyam 2001, at the first Wines of Chile wine competition. The wines were judged blind by tasters including Robert Joseph, Anthony Rose, and MWs Tim Atkin and Jancis Robinson in December 2003 in Santiago.

• **The UK Soil Association's** Red Wine of the Year 2003 was Richmond Plains Pinot Noir Reserve 2001 from New Zealand; the White Wine of the Year was Domaine Huet Vouvray Le Mont Sec 2001 from the Loire.

• **Fabril Alto Verde** in San Juan, Argentina, harvested its first organic Cabernet Sauvignon in 2003, and bottled it just before the end of the year. The estate was also the only organic wine producer featured in *Wines of Argentina*, a guide to Argentinian wine written for the French and South American markets by Michel Rolland and Enrique Chrabolowsky.

BIO-WHAT?

California superpremium-red producer Quintessa is part of Constellation Wines. Neither of Constellation Wines' halves, Canandaigua in the US or BRL Hardy in Australia, has previously shown much interest in organics, but biodynamic consultant Jeff Dawson was hired by Quintessa in 2000. "We worked on 40 acres of the 125-acre Quintessa vineyard," he says. "By 2003 these blocks were making the blend, whereas before they were not. I take this to be a direct result of the positive effect biodynamics has had here."

Quintessa's owners, the Huneeus family, seem equally impressed by the effect of biodynamics and, most growers agree, once you have put the chemical toolbox in the garage, it makes no sense to get it out again.

The missing link for biodynamics in the US and elsewhere is that it lacks market presence. One critic of the official biodynamic rule-setting agency in the US, Demeter USA, is independent consultant Greg Willis of Agri-Synthesis. "Demeter has been in business for over 50 years, yet only a minuscule percentage of American farmland is biodynamic."

California wine producer Everett Ridge in Healdsburg dropped out of official Demeter biodynamic certification in 2002 because, as owner Jack Air says, "We found there was not enough connection between biodynamics and US consumers."

Grapevine

• **Will de Castella** released his first Cabernet Sauvignon from organic grapes from his Jean Pauls Vineyard in Yea, Victoria, in 2003 (from the 2002 vintage). The first biodynamic trials began in 2003.

• **Organic Vignerons Australia,** a South Australian organic estate winery and merchant, launched its first wines in 2003, sourced from Brett Munchenberg in Loxton, Terry Markou in Adelaide Plains, and Temple Bruer vineyards in Langhorne Creek, as well as its own Lone Pine vineyard.

• **Nikolaihof,** Austria's leading biodynamic domaine, reported that its Riesling Federspiel has been deemed the healthiest wine in the world of all those that have been tested by the German Society for Environmental and Human Toxicology (DGUHT). This body claims to demonstrate the stress level of a wine within the parameters of pH value, redox potential, and conductivity.

• **Bonterra has launched** two new organic tri-varietal wines to complement its existing single-varietal organic range. This is the first time that Bonterra has produced a tri-varietal blend. The new wines, one red (Shiraz, Carignan, and Sangiovese) and one white (Chardonnay, Sauvignon Blanc, and Muscat), retail in the UK at £6.99.

• **Fetzer Vineyards'** Paul Dolan reaffirmed his company's commitment to have all estate and purchased grapes certified organic or biodynamic by 2010.

• **Viña Santa Ines** harvested its first organic Carmenère and Sangiovese in 2003. The whole of its 250-hectare (ha) Isla de Maipo estate vineyard is now certified organic.

GETTING THE FACTS RIGHT

Data on Europe's organic farming sector are, from a wine perspective, hit and miss. Statistics from Spain never differentiate between vines in first- and second-year conversion and those that are fully organic. Italy does not coordinate statistics on organics at a national level in any meaningful way, and local certifiers do not distinguish between vines grown for wine and those produced for table grapes or raisins. Since Italian vineyards tend to be the most polycultural in the world, with olives and vines growing together in the same plot (ideally something we should see much more of in a perfect and more polycultural, sustainable world), it is anyone's guess how figures for the surface area for each crop are calculated.

Help may be at hand. The EU and the Swiss Federal Office for Education and Science are funding a project called EISfOM (European Information System for Organic Markets) to develop proposals for improving access to production and market data throughout Europe's organic farming sector. FiBL, the Swiss Research Institute of Organic Agriculture, is a major partner in the project. It is responsible for coordinating specific elements of the work, as well as all project tasks that may be allocated to Switzerland, which is not part of the EU but has the toughest organic and environmental standards in the world.

The international project team, which includes partners from Denmark, Germany, Italy, the Netherlands, Austria, Poland, and Switzerland, will be led by Dr Nic Lampkin of the Institute of Rural Studies at the University of Wales in Aberystwyth.

By coordinating regional, national, and European authorities engaged in data collection, the process of data gathering and processing will be streamlined.

Grapevine

- **Joseph Phelps Vineyards** in St Helena began working with biodynamic consultant Andrew Lorand in January 2004. He will convert its 40-acre Las Rocas Vineyard in Stag's Leap to biodynamics and will oversee the 20-acre Backus Vineyard, which has been farmed biodynamically since 2000. Phelps aims to convert its eight-ranch, 300-acre portfolio to biodynamics in the future.

- **Villa Maria's Vidal Estate** entered its 50-ha Joseph Soler vineyard in Hawkes Bay into organic certification in 2004.

- **Casa Lapostolle** is continuing its piecemeal conversion to organics, with its Requinoa vineyard due full certification in the 2004 harvest for its 75 ha of red grapes, with the 40 ha of white to follow in 2005. Biodynamic trials are running in all Casa Lapostolle's major vineyard sites (Requinoa, Casablanca, and Apalta Valley).

GLOBAL ORGANIC VINEYARD PLANTINGS

CURRENT STATUS OF CERTIFIED ORGANIC VINEYARDS

Country or region	Hectares certified organic	Percentage of vineyards	Year	Comments
Europe	60,000	1.6	2000	No official statistics exist, but this Swiss-based estimate appears in the paper Organic Viticulture in Europe (FiBL). The figure is questionable, since it seems to be based on Italy having 30,000 ha and Spain 20,000 ha.
Argentina	<1,000	<1.0	2003	Based on 100,000 ha of fine-wine vineyards, whereas Argentina has around 200,000 ha of vines in total.
Australia	<1,100	<1.0	2002	No official figures exist, but unofficial estimates put the total at 0.5–0.75% of Australia's vineyards.
Austria	1,066	1.8	2004	In 2004, Austria had 1,066 ha of certified organic and Demeter-certified biodynamic vineyards, a rise of 59% from 1998, when there were 631 ha. There are around 300 producers, the vast majority of whom sell grapes to cooperatives or at the farm gate. Only four producers were biodynamic (three fully certified plus one in conversion).
Bulgaria	0	0	2004	Bulgaria still has no vineyards certified organic to EU norms. The aim is to get an organic programme started before Bulgaria's entry into the EU in 2007.
California	2,900	1.3	2004	California Certified Organic Farmers (CCOF), the state's largest certification body, reported that 2,900 ha of wine vineyards were certified organic in December 2003, a 31% rise on the 2001 figure of 2,200 ha. By 2006, California will have nearly 300 ha of Demeter-certified biodynamic vineyards if current conversion rates are maintained.
Canada	125	1.5	2003	Only two of Canada's wine-producing provinces have organic vineyards: British Columbia (45 ha) and Ontario (80 ha). There is one Demeter-certified biodynamic vineyard, Feast of Fields, in Ontario.
Chile	<1,600	1.5	2003	A steep rise since 2000, when the figure was around 0.1%.
England	31	<1.0	2003	All nine of the UK's organic sites are located in England. Only two wineries, Davenport and Sedlescombe Organic Vineyard, ferment and bottle their own wines, although both custom crush for and buy in grapes from other organic producers.
France	15,002	1.7	2004	Greatest concentrations of organic vineyards are found in Languedoc-Roussillon (4,486 ha, 323 producers), Provence (3,607 ha, 258 producers), and Corsica (3,795 ha, 270 producers). Around 10–15% of all organic vineyards are using the main biodynamic methods in whole or in part.
Germany	2,024	2.0	2003	The bulk of growers are divided between the following organic bodies: Ecovin (289 members with nearly 1,000 ha), Naturland Fachverband Wein (20 members with 148 ha), and Bioland (130 members with 300 ha).

Country or region	Hectares certified organic	Percentage of vineyards	Year	Comments
Greece	850	<5.0	2002	*Greece's organic vineyards represent 11% of its organic farm area, the highest in the EU.*
Italy	31,000	3.4	2002	*Italy does not publish national statistics for its organic vineyards, although the country has more than 1.2 million ha of organic farmland (all crops), which accounts for more than 25% of EU farmland (all crops). Roberto Pinton (Professor of Crop Science and Agricultural Engineering, University of Udine) estimates Italy's organic vineyards at 31,000 ha, producing 1.3 million hectolitres (hl) of wine annually, of which 20% is sold in bulk, 30% sold in Italy, and 50% exported.*
New Zealand	180	<1.0	2004	*This represents around 3% of the NZ wine industry's 400-odd wine producers.*
Portugal	700	<0.3	2004	*Portugal's organic statistics also include a proportion of non-wine grapes. Portugal has just under 100 organic wine-grape growers, but only 10 make wine commercially.*
Spain	16,037	<1.3	2002	*These figures do not differentiate between growers in first-year, second-year, or full organic conversion. La Mancha, Rioja, and Penedès are driving Spain's organic wine scene, which, like Spain's organic food sector, is entirely geared to exports.*
Uruguay	16.5	<0.2	2004	*Of Uruguay's 3,000 ha of fine-wine vineyards, only 16.5 ha were certified organic in 2004. They belong to Vinos de La Cruz, Uruguay's first certified organic-wine producer.*

- **De Martino** in Isla de Maipo saw all 300 ha of the family estate become 100 per cent certified organic in 2003. The quality of its organic Nuevo Mundo wines will improve because, from 2003, the best plots, from which the De Martino top Family Reserve line of Carmenère and Cabernet Sauvignon are sourced, will have organic status. Organic Sauvignon Blanc, Merlot, Chardonnay, and Sangiovese will come on stream to add to the original Malbec and Cabernet Sauvignon.

- **TerraMater** in Chile has temporarily shelved the idea of making organic wines, being unable, it says, to find a reliable source of good-quality organic grapes. TerraMater has no plans to convert any of its own vineyards at this stage.

- **Viña Los Vascos** in Chile has entered 70 ha of its 220-ha Peralillo vineyard to certified organic management. This will be the first official foray into organics by Domaines Barons de Rothschild (Lafite).

- **Errázuriz** will bottle its first certified organic Cabernet Sauvignon from the Don Maximiano (Max I and Max III) Aconcagua vineyards in 2004.

- Both **Will Davenport's** eponymously named vineyard in East Sussex and his Horsmonden Vineyard in Kent gained full organic certification in 2003 with the release of the Limney Estate Dry Fumé White and the Horsmonden Dry White wines. Davenport's push towards biodynamic management continues.

Wines made from fungal-resistant hybrid crossings with the same 'unfoxy' quality characteristics as *Vitis vinifera*, such as those developed in Germany, should be officially recognized across the EU as being eligible for quality-wine status. So far, only the Bundesortenamt (Federal Plant Patent Office) in Germany has officially given Regent, Solaris, and Johanniter such status. These vines offer one solution to the use of copper in the vineyard, for which no effective alternative has been found, or indeed sanctioned, by Europe's organic rule-makers. According quality-wine status to Regent, for example, would encourage growers in the New World, whose organic wines are targeted at the European market. Regent might prove very effective in South Africa, for instance, where mildew pressure in the more humid coastal regions is seen as a real obstacle by would-be organic producers.

Global standards required

A globally recognized and agreed organic grape-growing standard is desirable for those who believe that there are too many contradictions and anomalies in the way certification bodies operate: for instance, tolerance of parallel production (when only part of a vineyard is farmed organically) and the use of organic raw materials in compost (manure from animals fed only on organic material rather than on 'organic materials where available').

Swiss certification bodies like IMO (Institut für Marktökologie, which certifies the VOE vineyard in Chile, for example) are much stricter over the issue of parallel production than other European certification bodies, setting wider 'buffer zones' between organic and conventionally farmed parcels. Sadly, a world organic grape-growing standard is unlikely to appear while growers in European countries continue to argue over, for example, exactly how many kilos of copper per hectare per year may be used to counter downy mildew.

As for a global winemaking standard, this seems even further away, especially in the EU, where no organic winemaking standard exists, meaning that wines must be described as "made from organically grown grapes" and not as "organic wine". Perhaps the EU could adopt the winemaking rules featured in America's National Organic Program, which do permit use of the term 'organic wine' if, for example, no sulphur dioxide is used during winemaking.

Transparent labelling

The listing of aids, agents, and additives should be mandatory on wine labels. This would expose some of the spuriously marketed 'natural' wines made by conventional producers, and would indirectly promote the work of the best organic growers, who manage to bottle without fining or filtering wines that remain stable in bottle until consumed.

Grapevine

• **In Alsace,** the only major official conversion to full biodynamic status in 2003 was JosMeyer.

• **St-Emilion's Château La Tour Figeac** may abandon biodynamic practices for the 2004 campaign if persistent problems with grey rot are not solved. The owner accepts that excessive ploughing rather than biodynamics may be the cause of fungal pressure (ploughing releases moisture on to the grape skins and liberates soil nitrogen, which increases vine vigour).

• **Corsican vineyard** Domaine Comte Abbatucci gained Demeter biodynamic certification for its 24-ha Ajaccio vineyard in 2003. Domaine Pero-Longo in Sartène achieved full organic certification for its 22-ha vineyard, and has entered the Demeter biodynamic certification programme.

• **Le Soula,** the collaboration in the Coteaux de Fenouillèdes between UK wine merchants Richards Walford and Gérard Gauby in Roussillon, is applying for organic certification at Richards Walford's insistence. Gauby's own vines, although farmed biodynamically, will remain uncertified. "Gauby is not the kind of chap to sign up to clubs," said Roy Richards.

• **Two of Germany's** leading organic growers, the Graf von Kanitz (Rheingau) and the president of the VDP, Michael Prinz zu Salm-Salm (Nahe), greeted the exceptionally hot 2003 vintage with a degree of caution, and both asked that the quality of the vintage be defined only when the wines were bottled.

• **Weingut Wilhelm Zähringer** in Baden sold out of its debut 2003 vintage of the white hybrid Johanniter in eight weeks; its 1999er Zaehringer Edition Nr 24 Pinot Noir Spätburgunder Auslese was the first German red wine to win gold at the annual International Competition of Organic Wines at Biofach, the world's largest organic fair, which was held in Nuremberg.

• **Generous subsidies** (of around €350 per hectare per year) have encouraged larger Greek producers like Château Carras and some small cooperative growers, especially on islands like Santorini and Samos, to convert to official organic certification. In contrast, estate wineries such as Biblia Chora in the northern Greek region of Pangeon, which adopted organics from scratch as a way into export markets, are producing the best Greek organic wines. Being subsidy-driven is one thing; being quality-driven is quite another.

• **Kawarau Estate** in Central Otago harvested and released its first Pinot Gris from certified organic vines in 2003 and is developing a 5-ha block on its existing 16-ha vineyard.

• **Cooper Mountain,** the only certified biodynamic vineyard in Oregon, released its first wine to be labelled under the new USDA organic rules as "certified organic". The wine, a 2002 Pinot Noir, can be labelled "organic wine" rather than merely "wine from organically grown grapes", since no sulphites were added during winemaking. It is blended from 100 per cent certified organic and biodynamic fruit.

GREATEST WINE PRODUCERS

1. Domaine Leroy (Burgundy, France)
2. Domaine Marcel Deiss (Alsace, France)
3. Nikolaihof (Wachau, Austria)
4. Domaine Zind Humbrecht (Alsace, France)
5. Domaine Leflaive (Burgundy, France)
6. Domaine Huet (Loire, France)
7. Domaine Pierre Morey (Burgundy, France)
8. Cascina degli Ulivi (Piemonte, Italy)
9. Antiyal (Maipo Valley, Chile)
10. Weingut Wittmann (Rheinhessen, Germany)

FASTEST-IMPROVING PRODUCERS

1. Jean-Pierre Fleury (Champagne, France)
2. Domaine Montirius (Rhône, France)
3. Holmes Brothers/Richmond Plains (Nelson, New Zealand)
4. Weingut Schonburger (Burgenland, Austria)
5. Duval-Leroy (Champagne, France)
6. Larmandier-Bernier (Champagne, France)
7. David Leclapart (Champagne, France)
8. Domaine Zusslin (Alsace, France)
9. Fabril Alto Verde (San Juan, Argentina)
10. Sedlescombe Organic Vineyard (East Sussex, UK)

NEW UP-AND-COMING PRODUCERS

1. Domaine Lafarge (Volnay, Burgundy)
2. Domaine Lafon (Mâcon, Burgundy)
3. Le Soula (Roussillon, France)
4. Domaine Les Bastides (Provence, France)
5. Domaine Les Côtes de la Molière (Beaujolais, France)
6. Clos de Morta Maio (Corsica, France)
7. Domaine Trapet Père et Fils (Burgundy, France)
8. Araujo Estate (Napa Valley, California)
9. Biblia Chora Estate (Pangeon, Greece)
10. Kumala (South Africa)

BEST-VALUE PRODUCERS

1. Domaine de la Grande Bellane (Rhône, France)
2. Fabril Alto Verde (San Juan, Argentina)
3. Domaine de Brau (Cabardès, France)
4. La Riojana Cooperative (La Rioja, Argentina)
5. Kumala (South Africa)
6. Domaine Huet (Loire, France)
7. Fasoli Gino (Soave, Italy)
8. VOE (Chile)
9. Kendermanns Organic (Germany)
10. Bonterra (new tri-varietal range) (California)

GREATEST-QUALITY WINES

1. **Clos de la Roche 1999** Domaine Leroy, Burgundy, France (€530)
2. **Grasberg 1999** Domaine Marcel Deiss, Alsace, France (€31)
3. **Coyam Red 2001** VOE, Colchagua Valley, Chile (export only; £8.95 in UK)
4. **Riesling Steiner Hund Reserve 2001** Nikolaihof, Wachau, Austria (€25)
5. **Vouvray Cuvée Constance 2002** Domaine Huet, Loire, France (€70 per 50-cl bottle)
6. **Bienvenues-Bâtard-Montrachet 2000** Domaine Leflaive, Burgundy, France (€92)
7. **Gewurztraminer Grand Cru Rangen de Thann Clos St Urbain Vendange Tardive 2001** Zind Humbrecht, Alsace, France (€75)

8 **Cuvée des Monstres 2000** Domaine de Grande Maison, Monbazillac, France (€50 per half-bottle)

9 **Syrah Col.leccio 2000** Albet i Noya, Penedès, Spain (€11.50)

10 **Cuvée Valeria 2001** Domaine Les Bastides, Provence, France (€10.50)

BEST BARGAINS

1 **Torrontés 2003** La Riojana, Argentina (export only; £4.49 in UK)

2 **Novas Cabernet Sauvignon 2001** VOE, Maipo Valley, Chile (export only; £5.95 in UK)

3 **Chardonnay 2001** Organic Vineyards of California (export only; £3.99 in UK)

4 **Côtes du Rhône Valréas 2001** Domaine de la Grande Bellane, Rhône, France (€3.85)

5 **Organic White 2002** Kendermanns, Germany (export only; £4.49 in UK)

6 **Organic Colombard/ Chardonnay 2002** Kumala, South Africa (export only; £4.49 in UK)

7 **Red (Shiraz/Carignan/ Sangiovese) 2000** Bonterra, California (export only; £6.99 in UK)

8 **Touchstone Syrah 2002** Fabril Alto Verde, San Juan, Argentina (export only; £5.50 in UK)

9 **Cuvée Gabriel Merlot 2003** Domaine de Brau, Vin de Pays d'Oc, France (export only; £4.35 in UK)

10 **Eden Collection Shiraz Cabernet 2002** Australia (export only; £5.49 in UK)

MOST EXCITING OR UNUSUAL FINDS

1 **Verdelho 2003** Wilkie Estate, Australia (A$16–18) *Unusual to see Australia's organic producers working with something other than Chardonnay or Sauvignon Blanc.*

2 **Davenport Dry White 2001** Horsmonden, England (£5.99 ex cellar) *An English winemaker crafts a ripe-tasting English wine without recourse to excess chaptalization or residual sugar.*

3 **Sangiovese 2001** Boirà, Italy (export only; £5.49 in UK) *Rare to find a Marche producer with the confidence to barrel-age Sangiovese without drowning it in oak.*

4 **Porfyros 2000** Domaine Spiropoulos, Greece (€12.50) *Unusual combination of Cabernet Sauvignon and the Greek St George grape.*

5 **Syrah 2000** Domaine Lattard, Vin de Pays de la Drôme, Languedoc-Roussillon, France (€3.35 ex cellar) *A warm-climate Syrah but no reduction on the nose – the benefit of healthy soil and the absence of chemical, N-rich fertilizers, perhaps?*

6 **Via Agusta Monastrell 2002** Los Frailes, Valencia, Spain (export only; £3.99 in UK) *Unusual for being a subtle wine made from a DO known for chucky monsters.*

7 **Lahrer Schutterlindenberg BACAT 2002** Weingut Stadt Lahr, Baden, Germany (€5.60) *A deliciously crisp, clean white based on the hybrid Johanniter.*

8 **Regent QbA Trocken 2000** Weingut Geier, Baden, Germany (€4 per litre bottle) *Good example of how a hybrid red variety like Regent can make quaffing reds with ripeness, softness, and colour.*

9 **Ovilos 2002** Biblia Chora Estate, Pangeon, Greece (€4.50 ex cellar) *Stunning barrel-fermented Greek white blend of Sauvignon Blanc and Assyrtiko which has incredible freshness (from the Assyrtiko).*

10 **Château Doisy-Dubroca 2001** Louis Lurton, Sauternes, France (€23) *Unusual for being the first organic Sauternes to show purity of fruit and 'noble' noble-rot flavours.*

The study of wine's health effects continues apace. The benefits of light drinking and the harm of heavy drinking (the principle of the J-curve) continue to be highlighted for a range of medical conditions.

BEVERLEY BLANNING MW

It is good to see more research focusing on wine in particular, rather than alcoholic drinks in general. This means that wine's specific and unique properties compared to other drinks should be better understood. Unfortunately, there is bad news as well. Binge drinking, particularly among the young, shows no sign of abating. There is also more research indicating the additional risks to women drinkers, even at comparatively low levels of consumption.

Medical profession supports light drinking

A recent article in *Australian Family Physician* points out the strong evidence from population studies associating cardiovascular benefit with light to moderate alcohol consumption. The authors state that "blanket discouragement of all levels of alcohol consumption can no longer be justified" and suggest that the role of the general practitioner should be to tailor advice "to minimize harm and maximize benefit". A suggestion of change in the US medical profession's attitude to alcohol may also be surmised from an editorial in the *New England Journal of Medicine*. The journal suggests the need for a study to evaluate explicitly the efficiency of alcohol in lowering the risk of a heart attack in patients already suffering from

BEVERLEY BLANNING MW left a career in advertising to pursue her interest in wine, which she combined with her love of travelling, taking tourists on wine tours across the world. Based in London, she writes for a number of publications, gives lectures, and organizes tasting events. Beverley became a Master of Wine in 2001, specializing for her dissertation on the effects of wine on health.

cardiovascular disease. The editorial states that, if alcohol were deemed to be a safe and effective measure, "one could advise patients with cardiovascular disease on the use of alcoholic beverages as medical therapy".

US research focuses on wine

Until now, the additional advantages conferred by wine consumption have been shown only by European and Scandinavian research. Now data from the US have been published that confirm the conclusions of other studies in showing wine's benefits compared to other beverages. The results are part of the ongoing Kaiser Permanente study. Leading researcher Arthur Klatsky states: "Independent of total alcohol intake, wine-drinking frequency was associated with lower risk of mortality… Drinkers of any type of wine have a lower mortality risk than do beer or liquor drinkers, but it remains unclear whether this reduced risk is due to nonalcoholic wine ingredients, drinking pattern, or associated traits."

Another step forward in understanding wine's effects is the unprecedented decision of the US federal government to commit the sum of $7.6 million to the scientific exploration of the link between moderate wine consumption and reduced risk of heart disease. François Booyse PhD, who will lead the research at the School of Medicine at the University of Alabama, described the grant as "a major milestone". He said that the research programme "represents the first major consensus by both the scientific and health professionals of the emerging importance of the scientific implications, issues, and unanswered questions remaining in the rapidly evolving area of wine and cardiovascular health".

Resveratrol: further benefits identified

Recent research has shown that the antioxidant resveratrol may help to fight chronic bronchitis and emphysema. A study showed that resveratrol could reduce the amount of harmful chemicals in the lungs that cause these diseases. Dr John Harvey of the British Thoracic Society said, "It seems that drinking red wine in moderation as part of a healthy, balanced diet can reduce lung inflammation." Although there is probably not enough resveratrol in a glass of red wine for regular drinkers to stop chronic lung disease, it is thought that the antioxidant could be administered directly to sufferers via an inhaler.

Another recent study suggests that resveratrol may increase cell survival, directly contributing to increased life expectancy. It appears that resveratrol may mimic the life-extending effects of calorie restriction by directly stimulating the activity of an enzyme known as SIRTI, which promotes cell survival. It is hoped that the discovery may help to develop a drug to lengthen life and prevent or treat age-related diseases. The researchers found that resveratrol prolonged life in yeast, and ongoing study suggests similar protection in multicellular organisms. However, further research is needed before definite conclusions can be drawn regarding use in humans.

Rise in at-risk drinkers in the UK

The long-awaited UK government strategy on alcohol misuse was published in March 2004. It estimated the annual cost of alcohol misuse to be around £20 billion. Two patterns of drinking were identified as particularly harmful: binge drinking and chronic drinking. Binge drinkers tend to be under 25 and are most at risk of accidents and alcohol poisoning. Chronic drinkers are older – usually over 30 – and at risk of a greater variety of health problems, including cirrhosis, cancer, haemorrhagic stroke, and suicide.

Recommended 'sensible drinking limits' remain unchanged, but the government plans to make communication of these limits clearer – for example, by including more information on products and at point of sale. This is a development to be welcomed, and one that is already practised by a number of retailers. There are also plans for greater education to change attitudes and behaviour among the young. Involvement of the alcohol industry is voluntary at present, so it remains to be seen exactly what impact, if any, the strategy will have. Although the strategy at first sight appears to lack teeth, it is perhaps realistic to acknowledge that changing attitudes and behaviour towards alcohol is a long-term problem that is not easily resolved. The shame is that it took quite so long for the strategy to appear in the first place.

Binge drinking – the harm revealed

We may have believed that too much alcohol causes loss of memory from the night before, but new Dutch research shows that hangovers clearly reduce memory the day after. The researchers concluded that an alcohol-induced hangover (from a dose of 8–9 standard drinks) interferes with the body's capacity to retrieve memories.

In Finland, researchers have revealed that men who habitually take more than six drinks in one session are more likely to die in the following years, compared to those who do not. The mortality rate of heavy drinkers was 50 per cent higher, with significantly higher death rates from coronary heart disease, cirrhosis, and accidents. Although there were considerably more spirits drinkers than wine and beer drinkers in the sample, there was no evidence that the type of beverage made any difference to the results.

BINGE DRINKING IN IRELAND HIGHEST IN EUROPE

A survey conducted for Ireland's Department of Health on drinking habits in Europe showed that 58 per cent of male drinking in the country is binge drinking. This is the highest rate in Europe. It was further revealed that 48 per cent of men and 16 per cent of women binge at least once a week and that Ireland has more alcohol-related problems than any other European country.

DANGERS FOR WOMEN DRINKERS

Two recent reports highlight the current and growing dangers for women drinkers. The Mayo Clinic Women's HealthSource suggests that alcohol consumption could increase health risks for women at a greater rate than for men. The report says that women may develop alcohol-related diseases in less time and at lower levels of consumption than men. It has long been known that women are less well equipped to metabolize alcohol than men, and growing levels of consumption, especially among young women, give cause for concern.

FURTHER RESEARCH ON BREAST CANCER

Following last year's report on the link between alcohol consumption and breast-cancer incidence, even at low levels of consumption, a recent piece of research found that older women with a history of alcohol use – defined as two drinks a day or more – had an 80 per cent higher risk of contracting hormonally sensitive (the most common) forms of breast cancer compared to non-drinkers. As with most research concerning alcohol and health, no distinction was made between different types of drink, so it is not possible to isolate the effects of wine on breast-cancer incidence. This would be beneficial, especially since scientists in Los Angeles recently found that phytochemicals found in grape skins and seeds reduced breast-cancer tumours in mice.

DEMENTIA

The Copenhagen City Heart Study has shown an association between moderate wine consumption and reduced risk of dementia. Moderate consumption of beer or spirits did not have this effect. In fact, beer consumption was associated with a significantly higher likelihood of dementia. Contrary results from a prospective study in the US found that, for adults over 65, moderate consumption of any alcohol was associated with lower risk of dementia. Participants consuming one to six drinks a week had a 54 per cent lower risk of developing various dementias, including Alzheimer's disease, than abstainers. Those drinking up to 13 drinks a week also benefited from reduced risk, but those consuming more than 14 drinks a week increased their risk by 22 per cent.

BAD NEWS FOR TEETH

Professional wine tasters have always known that continuous slurping of acidic wine causes damage to tooth enamel. But now it seems that any alcohol consumption may increase the likelihood of gum disease. A new American study, which monitored 40,000 health professionals, concluded that alcohol was a risk factor for developing periodontitis, a disease affecting the gums and nearby tissues. It was not clear whether any one type of drink was more closely linked to the disease than others, although a high intake of red wine did appear to raise the risk slightly more than other drinks.

WINE DRINKERS GET PREGNANT FASTER

A Danish study has shown that women trying to conceive are likely to do so more rapidly if they drink wine in moderation. Previous research has indicated that excessive drinking has a negative impact on conception. The researchers found that beer drinking had no impact on the waiting time to pregnancy, but moderate wine drinkers experienced significantly shorter waiting times compared to women who said they drank no wine at all.

ALCOHOL AND STRESS

Researchers in Canada have found that moderate alcohol consumption reduces psychological stress at work. Respondents were classified as abstainers, low-risk drinkers (less than 10 drinks for women or 15 for men in the last seven days), and high-risk drinkers (who drank more than these amounts). Compared to low-risk drinkers, abstainers were 25 per cent more likely to report stress. For high-risk drinkers, the figure rose to 75 per cent. This is in line with other studies that show the beneficial psychological effects of moderate drinking.

DRINKING AND STROKE

It has previously been reported that moderate drinking seems to have a protective effect against ischaemic stroke (caused by a blood clot in the brain) and that heavy drinking has an adverse effect on haemorrhagic stroke (caused by bleeding in the brain). A new study has analysed previous research on the impact of drinking on stroke. One of the main findings was a significant increase in the risk of both types of stroke among heavy drinkers (those consuming more than 7.5 UK units per day), compared with abstainers. In contrast, there was a 28 per cent reduction in the risk of ischaemic stroke in those consuming 1.5 to 3 units per day. Another piece of research, conducted on male physicians in the US, shows that light and moderate drinking after a first stroke reduces risk of death in subsequent years. The risk of dying was 33 per cent lower in those consuming one to six drinks per week.

BENEFITS FOR SENIORS

In a population of Caucasian and Japanese Americans over 65 years old, tests have shown a positive relationship between alcohol consumption and cognition. The tests covered attention span, short- and long-term memory, mental manipulation, abstract thinking, and reaction times. Current drinkers (defined as consuming five or more drinks in the past year) produced higher cognition scores than abstainers. This superiority was especially pronounced among the women in the sample, and the Caucasians fared better than the Japanese. The latter finding may be attributed to the known absence of the enzyme aldehyde dehydrogenase in about half of all Japanese and Chinese individuals. This enzyme enables the body to metabolize alcohol more rapidly and dramatically affects the body's response to alcohol.

Another study on the elderly in Australia found that abstainers were twice as likely to enter a nursing home as people who were moderate drinkers. In this instance, the protective effect was found equally for men and women. Leading investigator John McCallum of the University of Western Sydney said, "Moderate alcohol consumption is associated with lesser risk of dementia, a leading reason people have to go to a nursing home." The study also found that drinkers spent less time in hospital and fewer died during the 14-year research period.

LABELLING AND HEALTH MESSAGES: THE DEBATE GOES ON

Any message appearing on a wine bottle regarding health is more likely to be a warning than a message about beneficial effects. In December 2003, a proposal for an Alcohol Facts Label was submitted to the US Alcohol and Tobacco Tax and Trade Bureau by, among others, the National Consumers League and the Center for Science in the Public Interest. These groups argue that clearer labelling would enable the buying public to make informed decisions about the products they consume. The proposed labelling would disclose alcohol content, standard servings, calorie information, and ingredients. In the UK, the Wine and Spirit Association has also suggested that unit labelling on drinks could be useful. This issue was highlighted in *Wine Report 2004* and is particularly appropriate given the recent news that the majority of the adult population does not know the definition of a standard drink or how much alcohol can safely be consumed in a day.

In summer 2003, Britain's leading liver specialists called on the government to introduce official health warnings on all alcoholic drinks. This is in response to the dramatic increase in cirrhosis deaths among men and women, especially in the 35–44 age group. A petition, signed by 500 senior doctors, requested that the "sensible drinking limits" should be explained, proposing the following wording: "HM Government Health Warning. This product contains x units of alcohol. Consumption of more than 21 units/week for men and 14 units/week for women can damage your health."

- Widespread Anglo-Saxon cultural acceptance of binge-drinking practices, which are injurious to health and undermine attempts to communicate the real benefits of moderate consumption of wine and other alcoholic beverages. Binge drinking is on the increase in the UK and the US.
- Restrictive laws prohibiting labelling of proven health claims about wine.
- Current ban on ingredient labelling. Given the rise in consumer interest in organic wine and naturally produced food, it would be of interest to many to know which ingredients were used in the production of the wine (even if those ingredients are no longer present).
- In the US, the legal requirement for health warnings on every bottle of wine.
- Sensationalist media reporting (both positive and negative) of issues relating to wine and health.

Things that should be happening

- Accurate, up-to-date dissemination of widely accepted information relating to the health benefits of moderate consumption, supported by government and the medical profession. Slowly but surely, this is starting to happen, as research results become consistent and established.
- The possibility of producers being able to include proven, specific, health-related information about wine on their bottles.
- International standardization of the definitions of a unit of alcohol and moderate consumption. Both vary enormously from country to country, causing consumer confusion regarding safe or desirable consumption levels.
- Unit labelling on bottles to indicate the number of units per bottle – already practised by many large retailers in the UK.
- Increased research into the benefits of white wine versus red wine.
- Increased research distinguishing between the health effects of wine versus beer and spirits, especially in vivo research to establish the effects of antioxidants on the body.
- Policies designed to promote sensible, responsible drinking – for example, longer licensing hours and acceptance of minors in drinking environments to discourage antisocial behaviour.

TOP WINE HEALTH BENEFITS

1. Increased longevity from moderate alcohol consumption.
2. Significant protection against cardiovascular diseases, specifically coronary heart disease (the number-one killer in the Western world) and ischaemic stroke, from moderate consumption.
3. Drinkers, especially wine drinkers, have lower risk of many other diseases, including stress-related illnesses and the common cold.

TOP WINE HEALTH HYPES

1. Drinking is good for you – it always depends on individual circumstances.
2. The benefits of consumption are accrued equally by young and old – most of the proven benefits are to men over 45 and post-menopausal women.
3. Red wine is better than white in providing health-related benefits – in fact, the biological effects of white wines appear to be disproportionately high relative to their total polyphenol content.
4. Wine is necessarily a better option than beer or spirits – although some research does suggest this to be true, other studies show that it is alcohol that confers the major health benefit. Moreover, lifestyle factors may explain wine's apparent superiority over other forms of alcoholic drink.
5. Resveratrol is the most important beneficial agent in wine.
6. The idea that regular, moderate consumption of wine is an acceptable substitute for improving health outcome in place of changing diet and other lifestyle factors, such as regular exercise.

TOP WINE HEALTH DANGERS

1. Most dangers stem from excessive alcohol consumption – both binge drinking and prolonged, heavy use. Risks of misuse of alcohol include:
   - alcoholism;
   - risk of accidents (especially among the young);
   - violent crime;
   - domestic violence and child abuse;
   - suicide and depression;
   - severe damage to every major system in the body, including the heart, and increased susceptibility to many different diseases;
   - foetal alcohol syndrome (FAS) in babies born to women who drink heavily during pregnancy.
2. Increased risk of breast cancer, even at low levels of consumption. This risk has been shown for women of all ages but is of most significance to young women, who have less to gain from the protective effects of alcohol against cardiovascular disease.
3. Increased risk of health problems for women drinkers at relatively low consumption levels.
4. Ignorance of sensible drinking limits, including misunderstanding of what constitutes a binge (approximately six standard drinks). (For up-to-date information, visit www.drinkingandyou.com)

TOP WINE DANGER MYTHS

1. Drinking of any kind is bad for you.
2. Drinking any alcohol while pregnant significantly increases the risk of FAS. Nearly all known cases of FAS involve mothers with chronic alcohol problems. However, controversy continues over whether there is a safe limit of consumption for pregnant women.

At last we have an explanation for naturally occurring clones, including colour mutations – chimerism.

DR FRANÇOIS LEFORT

Chimerism describes the situation in which genetically different cells coexist in one plant where, theoretically, only one genetic background should exist. It was first discovered in 2002 in Pinot Meunier and Primitivo di Gioia, then later detected in Chardonnay and Pinot Noir clones.

To give a famous example, Pinot was described as a French native variety by Columella in the 1st century AD; therefore, it is at least 2,000 years old. Over this long period, naturally occurring mutations have accumulated in one of the cell layers, leading to the creation of many different Pinot clones (somatic mutations). They are all Pinot varieties but with slight differences, since the mutations affect the phenotype (the visible characteristics of the plant). The most obvious visible characteristic is colour, the colour mutants of Pinot Noir being Pinot Meunier, Pinot Gris, and Pinot Blanc.

Somatic mutations have thus been a positive factor in the creation of an abundance of grape varieties. French varieties alone include several hundred such mutations. These somatic mutations contribute to the characteristics of a specific clone, making it different from another clone of the same variety. Although these mutations are passed along when the plants are propagated through traditional cuttings, they are not always transferred through crosses involving fertilization, resulting in a loss of information that can affect the phenotype of the offspring. Chimerism is, however, of much greater concern in genetic engineering, since a plant

DR FRANÇOIS LEFORT is a professor at the University of Applied Sciences of Lullier in Geneva. He specializes in the diversity of grapevine varieties and was the creator of the Greek Vitis database. He is involved in building similar databases in Bulgaria, Russia, and the Ukraine.

propagated by in vitro regeneration could carry mutations, resulting in a variety phenotypically and genetically different from the parent. But not all varieties include chimeric clones, and some seem to be more prone to accumulating somatic mutations than others.

Wild vines have more sex

There is a far wider range of grapevine varieties in the Old World than the New. Turkey and the CIS (Commonwealth of Independent States) countries have huge numbers of as-yet-unnamed varieties. Turkey alone has more than 3,000 unidentified varieties. These regions are very interesting to Western geneticists and breeders, not only because they may be the sites of the first domesticated vines, but also because the wild subspecies *Vitis vinifera silvestris* grows in abundance. Unlike the domesticated *Vitis vinifera vinifera*, which is mainly hermaphrodite, the *silvestris* subspecies has male, female, and hermaphrodite forms.

Hermaphrodite wild vines are thought to account for 5–7 per cent of the wild population and could have been the source material for domestication. Wild vines are, however, almost extinct in the rest of Europe due to phylloxera, so these Turkish and Caucasian sources could be an important addition to the gene pool. Domesticated female varieties are becoming very rare, since they need to have hermaphrodite varieties cultivated in their vicinity as pollen donors for pollination and berry development. The trend towards homogeneous vineyards has resulted in the reduction of the use of uniquely female varieties, although they can still be found, for example, in Albania.

The main Western collections (INRA [Institut National de la Recherche Agronomique] in Montpellier and Davis in California) contain several dozen varieties from Turkey and the CIS states, but they are far from complete. Unknown in the West, however, does not mean totally unknown, since Soviet scientists such as Negrul and Vavilov have done important work on grapevine diversity. The Soviet collections are particularly interesting in the areas of resistance to salinity and drought. Sixty years of breeding programmes have resulted in large numbers of hybrids, some of which are still being evaluated. Western and CIS scientists work together on different programmes and communicate via informal networks. One important result will be the release in 2004 of the first issue of the Bulgarian database, which will be followed by the Russian and Ukrainian Vitis database.

Bulgaria has a long tradition of working in classic vine genetics, its breeders having produced a number of hybrids in the last 50 years, mainly through crossing famous French varieties and native Bulgarian varieties. The most promising are only now being planted.

HYBRIDS VERSUS GMOs

Hybrid vines are created by crossing different *Vitis* species. The new vine will have resistant traits selected from other *Vitis* species, mainly from North America. Although hybrid vines have been developed since the 19th century, mainly in the US and France in response to phylloxera, cultivation of most of these hybrids was abandoned in France, although some met with more success in the US. Breeding programmes from the past 30 years, using some of the old hybrids as parents, are now beginning to show really interesting results: some commercial planting has started in Germany and an evaluation programme has begun in France, Switzerland, and the US of a dozen new hybrids with strong resistance to both oidium and downy mildew. It can take up to 30 years of research before breeding programmes produce results.

However, new hybrids with useful traits for the grower will change European vineyards only if regulations – for example, AOC legislation in France – can be adapted to permit them for quality wines. Where constraints are fewer, as in the New World or Germany, new varieties could be introduced rapidly.

Hybrids with natural resistance to oidium and downy mildew are particularly welcomed by organic growers in regions with humid conditions in autumn, since they make organic viticulture much more practicable. On the other hand, there is a strong trend towards working with genetically engineered grape varieties and less interest in classic improvement, or even genetic engineering, of rootstock. This trend is due to the involvement of more and more molecular biologists, who have gradually replaced classic geneticists, mainly because of better commercial returns in GMO research. These two contrasting disciplines will pose a challenge to restrictive legislation in countries such as France, Spain, Italy, and Greece. In countries without a moratorium on GMOs (that is, almost everywhere outside the EU), genetically modified plants, including vines, could well become widespread.

Although public concern about GMOs led to large French wine companies pulling out of GMO research, there is no opposition in New World countries, where wine is considered more as a commercial product than a cultural entity. EU producers quite reasonably fear genetically modified Cabernet Sauvignon, Merlot, Chardonnay, and so on from New World countries emerging on the world market.

Another challenge faced by genetic engineering is chimerism (see lead story). The discovery of the chimeric nature of many old and famous wine varieties places a question mark over the practicality of creating genetically engineered vines. In addition, public concern about wine made from genetically engineered vines does not seem to be diminishing in Europe, where GMOs are regarded with deep suspicion.

ARE HYBRIDS SHAKING OFF THEIR MONGREL IMAGE?

Generally speaking, hybrids created from non-vinifera vines are not permitted in quality wines in many countries in the EU. They are, however, grown and vinified successfully in other parts of the world, notably the US and Canada.

Many hybrids were created in France at the turn of the 20th century: Soleil Blanc, Leon Millot, Maréchal Foch, Landal, Chambourcin, Chancellor, Seyval Blanc, and Vidal Blanc. Others, such as Johanniter, Solaris, Bronner, Helios, Saphira, and Regent, were created mainly in Germany over the past 30 years. About 30 more hybrids are presently available for wine and table grapes, some of them with names recalling a famous parent – for example, Chardonel, Cabernet Carbon, and Muscat Bleu. Organic growers are using more and more of these hybrids because they are well adapted to the cooler, wetter climate of northern Europe and therefore have fewer problems with disease. Planting authorization is on the way for many of these varieties, but acceptance by wine consumers will take much longer.

In the US, the most widely planted hybrids for wine production are Seyval Blanc, Vidal Blanc, Chancellor, Baco Noir, Chelois, and Maréchal Foch – all old French hybrids created at the turn of the 20th century.

NEW PARENTAGE DISCOVERIES

• Cabernet Sauvignon was shown to be the progeny of Cabernet Franc and Sauvignon Blanc.

• Silvaner was discovered to be the offspring of Österreichisch Weiss and Traminer.

• Traminer crossed with Roter Veltliner gave birth to Rotgipfler.

• Two separate crosses involving Roter Veltliner and Silvaner resulted in Neuburger and Frühroter Veltliner.

• Frühroter Veltliner was itself found to be involved in a cross with Grauer Portugieser, which gave Jubiläumsrebe.

• Petite Sirah (also known as Durif) was shown to originate from a cross between Syrah and Peloursin, both French varieties.

• Syrah's origins are finally revealed as the result of two minor French varieties – Mondeuse Blanche from Savoie and Dureza from the Ardèche – putting an end to the more romantic theories of Iranian or Palestinian origin.

• In Portugal, Boal Ratinho was discovered to be a cross of Malvasia Fina and Siria.

• Castelo Blanco was found to be a cross between Fernão Pires and Diagalves.

• In Switzerland, Cornalin du Valais originated from a cross between Mayolet and Petit Rouge (which came from the neighbouring Italian region of Val d'Aosta, suggesting that it had been brought to Valais when it was no longer cultivated in Val d'Aosta).

CROSSES BEAR FRUIT

INRA in Montpellier has produced some exciting new varieties from crosses between *Vitis vinifera* varieties. Aranel, Chasan, Caladoc, Marselan, and Portan are all performing well in the south of France.

Marselan, a red variety created from a cross between Cabernet Sauvignon and Grenache Noir in 1961, was found again and registered by Dr Alain Bouquet as an official variety in 1990. Despite the fact that it can be used only for *vin de pays* wines, new plantings of Marselan are spreading in the south of France, due to the fine quality of the wine it produces.

Still in the shadows is Aranel, a white variety recommended for the south of France. It was created from a 1961 cross between Grenache Noir and St-Pierre Doré, a famous old variety that was grown in St-Pourçain. More will be heard about this variety.

Gamaret and Garanoir, both with the same parentage (Gamay Noir x Reichensteiner, 1970), are two very promising crosses that have been spreading in Switzerland, especially the south, over the past few years.

Such work on clones is now carried out with different multiloci markers and should provide unique identities for the hundreds of clones of French varieties such as Pinot, Chardonnay, Cabernet Sauvignon, Gamay, et al.

FIRST POLYPLOID GRAPEVINE FOUND

Grapevines are diploid organisms, which means they have two sets of chromosomes (one from the mother plant, the other from the father). But in the last half of the 20th century, triploids (three sets of chromosomes) or tetraploids (four sets of chromosomes) have been artificially produced by in vitro embryo culture or other biotechnological methods in a search for better characteristics, such as larger berries or seedlessness (triploids are sterile, thus produce no seeds). So far, these new triploid or tetraploid varieties have been created in Japan from hybrids of local *Vitis amurensis* or *Vitis coignetiae* and American *Vitis labrusca* and European *Vitis vinifera*, but the first-ever natural triploid variety has been found. Called Sinambel or Toska, this triploid vine was discovered in Albania by Emmanuel Ladoukakis, who was involved in a genetic-profiling study. It is the first discovery, even though about 1,000 varieties have been subjected to genetic identification all over Europe.

Grapevine

- **Not all Sangiovese is Sangiovese.** Molecular genetics has helped resolve the identities of 25 Tuscan grape varieties that were believed to be Sangiovese. Three of these were not Sangiovese, although they were genetically related to the famous variety. Refining the analysis, it was possible to identify the remaining 22 true Sangiovese as different clones.

- **A pair of French varieties** — the minor, abandoned Gouais Blanc (known in Austria as Heunisch Weiss) and Pinot — has been shown to be the parents of up to 16 French grapes: Aligoté, Aubin Vert, Auxerrois, Bachet Noir, Beaunoir, Franc Noir de la Haute Saône, Chardonnay, Dameron, Gamay Blanc Gloriod, Gamay Noir, Knipperlé, Melon (aka Muscadet), Peurion, Romorantin, Roublot, and Sacy.

Widest-cultivated white-grape varieties

Global, wine grapes only.

Grape variety	Hectares in 2002*	Main countries
1. Airén	578,200	Spain
2. Chardonnay	411,100	USA, France, Italy
3. Ugni Blanc	337,800	France, Italy, Argentina
4. Rkatsiteli	277,200	Ukraine, Georgia, Moldova
5. Sauvignon Blanc	178,000	France, Moldova, USA
6. Riesling	136,900	Germany, Ukraine, China
7. Muscat of Alexandria	128,000	Spain, Chile, Algeria
8. Catarratto	125,500	Italy
9. Malvasia Bianca	122,000	Italy, Spain, Croatia
10. Chenin Blanc	107,100	South Africa, France, USA

*Estimated. Source: Patrick W Fegan, *The Vineyard Handbook* (Chicago Wine School, 2003).

Widest-cultivated black-grape varieties

Global, wine grapes only.

Grape variety	Hectares in 2002*	Main countries
1. Cabernet Sauvignon	614,800	France, Chile, USA
2. Merlot	598,000	France, Italy, USA
3. Grenache	572,800	Spain, France, Italy
4. Syrah	309,700	France, Australia
5. Carignan	290,400	France, China, Tunisia
6. Bobal	230,400	Spain
7. Tempranillo	216,200	Spain, Argentina, Portugal
8. Pinot Noir	207,300	France, USA, Germany
9. Sangiovese	190,200	Italy, Argentina, USA
10. Monastrell/Mourvèdre	175,400	Spain, France, Australia

*Estimated. Source: Fegan, *The Vineyard Handbook*.

Widest-cultivated grey/*rosé*-grape varieties

Global, wine grapes only.

Grape variety	Hectares in 2002*	Main countries
1. Pinot Gris	47,900	Italy, Germany, USA
2. Gewürztraminer	33,100	Moldova, France, Ukraine

*Estimated. Source: Fegan, *The Vineyard Handbook*.

Fastest-growing white-grape varieties

The greatest global increase in recent plantings of white (wine only) grape varieties.

Grape variety	Hectares in 2002*	Hectares in 1990*	Increase
1. Welschriesling	139,800	47,900	192%
2. Chardonnay	411,100	171,200	140%
3. Moscato Bianco	101,900	44,000	132%
4. Sauvignon Blanc	178,000	110,400	61%
5. Isabella	76,900	51,900	48%
6. Fetească Albă	65,200	45,400	44%
7. Grüner Veltliner	60,700	51,300	18%
8. Malvasia Bianca	122,000	105,400	16%
9. Macabeo	117,500	107,500	9%
10. Riesling	136,900	128,900	6%

*Estimated. Source: Fegan, *The Vineyard Handbook*.

Fastest-growing black-grape varieties

The greatest global increase in recent plantings of black (wine only) grape varieties.

Grape variety	Hectares in 2002*	Hectares in 1990*	Increase
1. Syrah	309,700	86,700	257%
2. Pinot Noir	207,300	102,200	103%
3. Cabernet Sauvignon	614,800	315,500	95%
4. Tempranillo	216,200	117,200	84%
5. Merlot	598,000	382,400	56%
6. Malbec	62,800	42,000	50%
7. Cabernet Franc	129,200	97,900	32%
8. Alicante Bouschet	60,700	48,400	25%
9. Gamay Noir à Jus Blanc	94,900	86,500	10%

*Estimated. Source: Fegan, *The Vineyard Handbook*.

Grapevine

• **The most important finding** presented at an international collaboration on genotyping wild and cultivated vines in Madeira in October 2003 was that native varieties are more related to local vines, whatever the region, with the single exception of Greece, which appears to be the main donor region. This discovery allows researchers to trace movements of plants between regions. Simply stated, if some French varieties have something Greek-looking in their chloroplast (see opposite) that cannot be found in their wild French relatives, it is probably because some Greek shoots were brought to Gaul.

BEST WINES FROM NEW VARIETIES OR NEW CLONES

① **Marselan 2002** Christophe Clipet, Domaine du Chapitre, INRA, Villeneuve-lès-Maguelonne, Hérault, France (€6) *Red wine from Marselan (Cabernet Sauvignon x Grenache Noir, 1961).*

② **Solaris Passerillé 2002** Jean-Laurent Spring, Station Fédérale de Recherches de Changins, Nyon, Switzerland (not available commercially) *White wine made by passerillage from the hybrid Solaris (Merzling x [Saperavi severnyi x Muscat Ottonel]), 1975.*

③ **Gamaret et Garanoir 2002** Alexandre de Montmollin, Station de Viticulture de l'Etat de Genève, Geneva, Switzerland (SF 16) *Blended red wine from Gamaret (Gamay Noir x Reichensteiner, 1970) and Garanoir (Gamay Noir x Reichensteiner, 1970) matured in oak casks.*

④ **Caladoc Rosé 2002** Christophe Clipet, Domaine du Chapitre, INRA, Villeneuve-lès-Maguelonne, Hérault, France (€6) *Rosé wine from the cross Caladoc (Grenache Noir x Malbec, 1958).*

⑤ **Aranel 2002** Christophe Clipet, Domaine du Chapitre, INRA, Villeneuve-lès-Maguelonne, Hérault, France (€6) *White wine from the cross Aranel (Grenache Noir x St-Pierre Doré, 1961).*

⑥ **Johanniter 2003** Eric Levraz, Levraz and Stevens, Pessy, Geneva, Switzerland (SF 10) *Organic white wine from the hybrid Johanniter (Riesling x [SV 12.481 x (Pinot Gris x Chasselas)]).*

⑦ **Wygarte 2002** Hallauer, Rimuss und Wein Kellerei, Haller, Schaffhausen, Switzerland (SF 12) *Organic red wine from the hybrid Regent (Diana x Chambourcin).*

⑧ **Chasan 2000** Vin de Pays, Mas de Rey, Arles, Bouches du Rhône, France (€6.60) *From the cross Chasan (Chardonnay x Listan, 1958).*

⑨ **Lizerger Regent 2002** Monika and Bruno Martin, Lizerg, Switzerland (SF 12.50 per 50-cl bottle) *From the hybrid Regent (Diana x Chambourcin).*

⑩ **Diolinoir 2002** Antoine and Christophe Bétrisey, St-Léonard, Valais, Switzerland (SF 21) *Matured in oak casks. Diolinoir is a 1970 cross between Pinot Noir and Rouge de Diolly, which was recently identified by molecular markers as being Robin Noir, a French variety from the Drôme region, now maintained only in ampelographic collections.*

Grapevine

• **Photosynthesis** and nitrogen metabolism are affected by the vine's chloroplast, which Rosa Arroyo and colleagues have recently discovered to be maternally inherited (given by the mother plant, not by pollen of the father plant). Efforts will now be made to try to identify advantageous chloroplast genomes.

• **Chilean Cabernet Sauvignon** comes from the French collection in Colmar. This was discovered during a study of Cabernet Sauvignon clones with genetic markers by P Hinrichsen of the National Institute of Agronomy in Chile. Further research showed that a similar clone was introduced into Australia in 1840.

BEST WINES FROM UNUSUAL, OBSCURE, OR REDISCOVERED VARIETIES

1. **Shesh I Zi 2000** Dr Vangjel Zigori, oenologist, produced only for the Marikaj restaurant at Marikaj, Tirana, Albania (not commercially available) *Traditional sweet red wine from Shesh I Zi, a native Albanian grape from Tirana.*

2. **Shesh I Bardhe 2000** Dr Vangjel Zigori, uniquely produced for the Marikaj restaurant at Marikaj, Tirana, Albania (not commercially available) *Dry white wine from Shesh I Bardhe, a native Albanian white grape from the plain of Tirana.*

3. **Kotsifali Blanc de Noir 2002** Nikos and Takis Miliarakis, Minos Kritis Wines, Peza Pediados, Heraklion, Crete, Greece (€6) *Dry white wine from red Kotsifali grapes, a very old Cretan variety.*

4. **St-Pourçain 2002** Union des Vignerons de St-Pourçain, St-Pourçain, Allier, France (€4) *Dry white wine from a blend of Chardonnay, Sauvignon Blanc, and Tressallier, an old native Bourbonnais variety.*

5. **Côtes d'Auvergne 2002** Annie Sauvat, Boudes, Puy de Dôme, France (€4.50) *A blend of Gamay Rouge and Pinot Noir. Côtes d'Auvergne is a very old French vineyard.*

6. **Mondeuse Rouge 2002** Savoie, Christophe Bouvet, St-Pierre d'Albigny, Savoie, France (€5.50) *From Mondeuse, an old native variety cultivated in Savoie and Bugey vineyards.*

7. **Roussette de Savoie Cru Chautagne 2002** Maison de Chautagne, Ruffieux, Savoie, France (€5.70) *White wine from the variety Altesse. Legend has it that Altesse was brought back from Cyprus, but it is just a legend.*

8. **Mondeuse Blanche 2002** Savoie, Philippe Grisard, Freterive, Savoie, France (€6) *Old native variety from Savoie. Mondeuse Blanche is one of the parents of Syrah.*

9. **Bugey Brut 2002** Caveau Domaine Monin, Vongnes, Ain, France (€5.67) *A sparkling wine made with a blend of old native white varieties, including Molette, Altesse, and Jacquère.*

10. **Jacquère 2002** Savoie, Christophe Bouvet, St-Pierre d'Albigny, Savoie, France (€3.86) *From Jacquère, an old native variety cultivated in Savoie and Bugey vineyards.*

Grapevine

• The DNA of 2,700-year-old grape pips has been extracted and amplified for the first time by Rosa Arroyo and this author. The pips were discovered in Pieria in Macedonia by archaeobotanist Evi Margaritis. In 2003, Jean-François Manen managed to amplify nuclear genome sequences from ancient French and Hungarian grape pips and showed that some of the Hungarian pips could be related to modern Italian/Croatian vines and some of the French ones to French/Austrian varieties.

• If you plan to establish a vineyard based on French varieties, everything you need to know about registered clones is available from the professional section of the website of Onivins (Organisme National Interprofessionnel des Vins). The 667 clones registered for 109 wine varieties, 66 clones registered for 12 table-grape varieties, and 157 clones registered for 24 rootstock varieties are all listed. The website address is www.onivins.fr/Plan.asp

I am not a natural list-maker, but this is fun! I am enormously fortunate in tasting, and drinking, a staggering amount of fabulous wine every year.

SERENA SUTCLIFFE MW

This happens at my own table, with generous friends and clients, at comprehensive tastings put on by producers, at Sotheby's lunches, dinners, and pre-sale tastings, with wine merchants, and while leading major verticals and horizontals round the world. Crystallizing this into three small lists is, of course, a hedonistic lucky dip, but I have tried to choose wines that really made their mark and demanded attention. The Greatest-Quality list tends to attract jealousy, but there we are – those were my orders. The Most Exciting or Unusual Auction Finds are the nuggets, where it pays to be adventurous – fine wine is phenomenally resilient. And the Best Auction Bargains are an act of kindness to you, the reader, like giving away the name of a favourite, unknown restaurant. Auctions are full of these gems, especially today, when the market is polarized on comparatively few wines. There is a lot of stunning wine out there. In the two great single-owner sales in New York in autumn 2003, one was rich in mature California wines, which proved that they do age well when properly stored, and the other was the dream cellar of all time, a roll call of most of the best wines that France has ever made. This is why I am in the auction business.

SERENA SUTCLIFFE MW is the head of Sotheby's International Wine Department, with auctions in London and New York. Fluent in several major European languages, she became interested in wine while translating for the UN in France in the 1960s. In 1976 she became the second woman to qualify as a Master of Wine. Serena later served as chairman of the Institute of Masters of Wine. She is a regular lecturer and broadcaster in Europe, the United States, and Asia, the author of several books on wine, and she regularly writes for publications all over the world. Serena is married to fellow MW David Peppercorn.

PEAKING VINTAGES

BORDEAUX

1997 Provides lovely drinking from now.

1994 Peaking.

1993 Peaked.

1992 Peaked, if you bothered to get them at all!

1987 Peaked.

1985 Peaked except for First Growths and top Seconds.

1984 Mostly unpleasant as well as past their best.

1983 Mostly at their peak, except for gems like Margaux, Palmer, Pichon Lalande, and Cheval Blanc.

1982 Many have peaked, except for First Growths, Super Seconds, top St-Emilions, and Pomerols.

1981 Drink now for optimum pleasure.

1980 Too old.

1979 Peaked, but top wines still drinking well. Try Haut-Brion!

1978 Peaked, but top wines still drinking well.

1977 Forget it.

1976 Peaked. Lafite and Ausone still looking good.

1975 Mostly peaked. Exceptions include Pétrus, Latour, La Mission Haut-Brion, Pichon Lalande, Cheval Blanc.

1974 Enough said.

1973 Ditto.

1972 Ditto.

1971 Peaked. Top Pomerols still glorious, viz the heavenly, 'roasted' Pétrus. La Mission Haut-Brion is excellent.

1970 Mostly peaked. Exceptions include Pétrus, Latour, La Mission Haut-Brion, Trotanoy, La Conseillante, Pichon Lalande, Ducru-Beaucaillou, Palmer, Giscours, Beychevelle.

1969 Don't even think about it.

1968 Ditto.

1967 Peaked a long time ago. Pétrus is still good.

1966 Mostly peaked. Exceptions include Latour, Cheval Blanc, Pétrus, Haut-Brion, La Mission Haut-Brion.

1964 Mostly peaked. Exceptions include Pétrus, Latour, Haut-Brion, La Mission Haut-Brion.

1962 Peaked, although the First Growths are still good.

1961 Most wines are still wonderful. That small crop gave the vital concentration.

1959 The top wines are still magic.

RED BURGUNDY

1997 Delicious drinking from now.

1994 Drink now, since that dry finish will intensify.

1992 Delicious now.

1990 *Grands crus* have further to go.

1989 As above.

1988 The top wines mostly have further to go.

1987 Should have been drunk.

1986 As above. Even Jayer is at its best.

1985 Mostly at, or over, its peak, except for top *grands crus*, such as Drouhin's Bonnes Mares.

1984 Don't go there.

1983 A very few are hanging on.

1982 As above, for different reasons.

1981 Peaked.

1980 Past their peak. Even those brilliant Jayers should be drunk. La Tâche is still amazing, though.

1979 Peaked.

1978 There are still some wonders at the top. They have a signature gaminess.

1977 Treat them as if they were never there.

1976 Peaked a long time ago, with the odd, rare exception.

1975 Should not be mentioned in polite society.
1974 Unpleasant and old.
1973 Peaked a long time ago.
1972 One or two survivors, viz de Vogüé's Musigny Vieilles Vignes.
1971 Stay with DRC or similar here.
1970 It is pretty well all over.
1969 Some survivors at *grand cru* level, with scent and finesse.
1966 A few still live gloriously on; Romanée-Conti is mind-blowing.
1964 A few terrific wines at *grand cru* level.
1962 A few top wines are still magnificent.
1961 As above.
1959 As above.

WHITE BURGUNDY

1997 Very nice drinking now.
1994 Mostly at their peak.
1993 As above.
1992 As above; they matured faster than many expected.
1991 Mostly at their peak.
1990 Some top wines still have a bit to go, others are glowing right now.
1989 As above.
1988 Mostly at their peak or over it.
1987 Peaked.
1986 Mostly peaked. Some *grands crus* are lovely right now.
1985 Many of the top wines are so fat and full that they will stay around for ages, such as the Bâtards of Ramonet and Niellon.
1984 Peaked a very long time ago.
1983 Some tremendous wines at the top. They seemed alcoholic and heavy when young, but boy, are they marvellous now. Some of the greatest white burgundies of my life come from this vintage, such as Corton-Charlemagne from Latour and Bonneau de Martray.
1982 Virtually all peaked a long time ago.

1981 Peaked a long time ago.
1980 As above.
1979 Virtually all peaked some time ago.
1978 As above, but some gems live on, viz Chablis Les Clos from Drouhin, which now looks like a Côte d'Or wine.
1976 Peaked, but there are some stunners still about at *grand cru* level.
1973 Peaked, with the odd surprise at *grand cru* level.
1971 Peaked, with some stunners left.
1970 As above.
1969 As above.
1967 It starts getting esoteric from here, but the odd surprise.
1966 Mostly history, but DRC's Montrachet makes history.
1964 Peaked a long time ago, with a few exceptions hanging on.
1962 Peaked, of course, with a few marvellous exceptions.
1961 As above.

RED RHONE

1997 Drink from now.
1994 Start drinking up.
1993 Peaked.
1992 Peaked.
1991 Peaked for the south, fine for the north.
1990 Excellent, the best will keep.
1989 As above.
1988 As above.
1987 Peaked, so drink now.
1986 As above.
1985 At peak, although the best will keep.
1984 Peaked.
1983 Peaked for the south, but the top wines from the north still have life.
1982 Peaked everywhere, although the north is better.
1981 Peaked for the north, a few good ones left in the south.

1980 Peaked.
1979 Peaked, but the best are still drinking well.
1978 Mostly at its peak, but with some amazing wines.
1976 Peaked some time ago, but Hermitage La Chapelle lives on to delight.
1972 Peaked.
1971 As above, but glorious Hermitage from Rayas and Chave.
1970 Peaked, but great Hermitage La Chapelle.
1969 Peaked, but glorious La Chapelle, with Chave and Rayas still there.
1967 Peaked, but tremendous La Chapelle.
1966 As above.
1964 As above.
1962 As above.
1961 The top wines are still out of this world (La Chapelle et al).
1959 As above.

PORT

1997 Don't touch.
1994 As above.
1992 As above.
1991 As above.
1985 Start drinking but will keep.
1983 As above.
1982 Drinking well now and over the next few years.
1980 As above.
1977 Drinking very well now, but will obviously keep.
1975 Drink up fast.
1970 Fabulous vintage; glorious now, but will stay that way for ages.
1966 Excellent wines right now, but will keep, of course. The fruit in them is quite beautiful.

1963 Huge, powerful wines, for drinking or keeping.
1960 Beautiful now.

1958 Mostly peaked, but don't say that to Noval Nacional! Extraordinary wine.
1955 Superb now and not about to fall off the perch.
1950 Drink up, but the Nacional is eternal.
1948 Great now.
1947 Drink now.
1945 Still there, after all these years. Mammoth.

GERMANY

1996 Broach and enjoy.
1995 As above.
1994 Peaked.
1993 Approaching peak, but the best will mature in splendid fashion.
1992 Peaked.
1991 Peaked.
1990 Excellent and the best will age beautifully.
1989 As above.
1988 As above.
1987 Peaked.
1986 Mostly peaked.
1985 Mostly at peak.
1984 Dreadful vintage.
1983 Mostly peaked, but some wines beautifully present.
1982 Peaked a long time ago.
1981 As above.
1980 Forget it.
1979 A very few survivors.
1976 Tremendous, with a plethora of fantastic wines still vying for top honours.
1975 As above.
1971 The tops and still magnificent in the upper echelons.
1967 Peaked some time ago, but a few stunning survivors at TBA level.
1959 At peak, and glorious with it.
1953 Peaked, with a few beauties left.

GREATEST-QUALITY AUCTION WINES

1. **Château Laville Haut-Brion 1961** Pessac-Léognan With lunch at the property. Riveting, ultrarich nose, ginger and lime taste, absolutely ageless. One of the most memorable wines of my life.

2. **Château d'Yquem 1929** Sauternes At an unrepeatable tasting at the château, to mark the retirement of Alexandre de Lur-Saluces. Extraordinary opulence – a record 150 g of sugar and a rum-and-raisin taste.

3. **Château La Mission Haut-Brion 1975** Pessac-Léognan At a formidable tasting at the château, to mark the retirement of Jean-Bernard Delmas. Intellectual and sensual, a wondrous wine and a chef d'oeuvre of ripe plums and great Havanas.

4. **Montrachet 1989** Domaine Ramonet At a private dinner. Pure breed, intensity, immense glycerol. The most complete white burgundy imaginable. Magic.

5. **Krug 1979** At the home of a fellow 'Krugiste'. Classic Krug greengages on the nose. So long, toasty, and full of candied fruit, vanillin, and apricots. Stunning.

6. **Hermitage 1989** Chave At a friend's chalet in Zermatt. Maybe it was the altitude, or the white truffles, but it was gloriously exotic and concentrated, with so much wild depth and glycerol. A masterpiece.

7. **Penfolds Grange 1982** South Australia At the Harter family cellar presale tasting in New York. Stood out among all the gems for its glorious sweet and spicy qualities. Just so complex and full of leather and liquorice.

8. **Robert Mondavi Cabernet Sauvignon Reserve 1974** From an imperial tasted at a Sotheby's seminar in New York before the sale of the Robert Paul collection. Smoky cassis nose and a rich, melting taste of coffee and currants – so showy and lush.

9. **Echézeaux 1985** Henri Jayer Drunk with roast woodcock at home. It combines roses, raspberries, and game on the nose, with added redcurrants on the palate. At its melting best.

10. **Château Coutet 1908** Barsac Ended a dinner party at home. Dark molasses colour, carrying on to the taste. Its exotic richness stopped everyone in their tracks.

MOST EXCITING OR UNUSUAL AUCTION FINDS

1. **La Tâche 1980** DRC In New York, in the afternoon. Much better than tea! Exciting because it is still so good. Damp earth, black truffles, with all the persistence and sublime intensity of the climat.

2. **Cuvée L Chardonnay 1981** Sonoma, Kalin Cellars At a home dinner party. The brilliant Terrance Leighton's oeuvre, with just so much class, nutmeg, and lime. Seamless and without age.

3. = **Château La Louvière Blanc 1967** and **Château Couhins Blanc 1967** Pessac-Léognan At home, among adventurous friends. Who could believe that white bordeaux from a modest year could last so beautifully. But they can!

5. **Cabernet Sauvignon Cask 23 1984** Napa, Stag's Leap Wine Cellars Tasted at the winery and a homage to vineyard selection. Minty, with huge layers of mature fruit.

6. **Château La Mission Haut-Brion 1971** Pessac-Léognan Tasted at the château. Superb, cigary opulence, ripeness, balance, and depth.

Simply wonderful – it is time this wine came out of the closet!

⑦ Roussanne Vieilles Vignes 2001 Château de Beaucastel *At a Wine Society tasting. Tiny yields, 80-year-old vines, like a heavenly Chignin-Bergeron. Wild herbs, lemon zest – intoxicating.*

⑧ Red Rock Terrace Cabernet Sauvignon 1978 Napa, Diamond Creek *At the Robert Paul collection presale tasting, New York. Spicy, vanillin, and really impressive.*

⑨ Muskat Ottonel Weisser Schilfwein 2001 Weingut Willi Opitz, Neusiedlersee, Austria *At a Masters of Wine sweet-wine tasting. Minute quantities are made. Unusual since it is so well bred for a Muskat. Extraordinary concentration, soft and mouth-coating, with the acidity totally integrated in the super sugar.*

⑩ Substance Grand Cru Blanc de Blancs disgorged 17 October 2002 Jacques Selosse *Drunk at home, greedily, à deux. Pure Avize and pure bliss. There may be more about, but I have come across it only once.*

BEST AUCTION BARGAINS *(hammer price)*

① Brunello di Montalcino 1995 Biondi-Santi; at the New York May 2003 sale (12 bottles: $400) *A complete aberration: lucky for some!*

② Graham's Vintage Port 1985; at the London June 2003 sale (11 bottles: £250) *And 12 bottles went for £380! As they say, do the maths. Splendid port, too.*

③ Clos Vougeot Musigni 1998 Gros Frère et Soeur; at the London June 2003 sale (12 bottles: £180) *A blueberry, burgundy bargain with real grand cru quality at a miniature price.*

④ Cyril Henschke Cabernet Sauvignon 1989 Henschke; at the New York October 2003 sale (12 bottles: $350) *The proof that, even in a meteoric single-owner sale (the Robert Paul collection), there are bargains to be had, especially coming from one of Australia's best producers.*

⑤ Bollinger RD 1975; at the London November 2003 sale (12 bottles: £400) *An insane price for one of the best champagnes ever, in pristine condition and original cases. Someone must have had a good Christmas!*

⑥ Chassagne-Montrachet Caillerets (Blanc) 1999 Jean-Noël Gagnard; at the London September 2003 sale (12 bottles: £220) *A superb producer in a highly regarded year, emphasizing again that the auction room is a great hunting ground for white burgundy.*

⑦ Meursault Tessons 1996 Michel Bouzereau; at the London September 2003 sale (12 bottles: £160) *Bringing it home once more – another snip for a good grower in a very good year.*

⑧ Château de Fargues 1986 Sauternes; at the New York September 2003 sale (six bottles: $325) *A wonderful bonne bouche, Alexandre de Lur-Saluces' own great Sauternes, made with Yquem methods, in a classic year.*

⑨ Château Margaux 1978; at the New York May 2003 sale (seven bottles: $800) *Amazing value for a First Growth that is both marvellous and ready to drink.*

⑩ Dutton Ranch Chardonnay 1998 Kistler; at the New York September 2003 sale (12 bottles: $450) *Normally Kistler Chardonnays are snapped up aggressively, but this one sneaked in under the wire.*

For the first quarter of 2003, external economic forces in the shape of the looming Iraq war and the depressed stock market continued to have a dampening effect both inside and outside the salesroom.

ANTHONY ROSE

As winter deadlock was replaced by spring thaw, and the Iraq war came and went, a postwar feel-good factor drifted hopefully into the salesroom amid cautious, albeit misplaced, optimism that the troubles were over.

A renewal of confidence in global financial markets was mirrored in the wine market in general and bordeaux in particular. As the 2002 campaign began without really taking off except at First Growth level, the American critic Robert Parker gave a fillip to the 2000 vintage by confirming the likes of Lafleur, Pavie, Lafite, Margaux, and Pétrus as 100-point scores. And as bordeaux divided like parents and children into older and younger groups, the much-hyped 2000 vintage, as predicted last year, became the precocious genius, outshining its siblings by some margin.

Throughout 2003, the market for younger wines generally was, in the discreet language of the auctioneer, "selective". Vintages 1995 and 1996 remain the only two in the decade spanning 1990 to 2000 with convincing long-term ageing potential, yet in the first half of the year First Growths were dropping back. After a mini-surge in the middle of the year

ANTHONY ROSE is the award-winning wine correspondent for *The Independent* and writes for a number of other publications, including *Wine International*, *BBC Good Food Magazine*, *Harpers*, and *PLC Director*. He specializes in the auction scene, writing a monthly column on the subject for *Decanter* and contributing to *The Oxford Companion to Wine* on auction and investment. Anthony is married to an Australian wine photographer and lives in London.

and early autumn, none had yet breached the £2,000 high-water mark by the year's end. The highlight of 2003 was at Christie's early summer sale in London, where an astonishing £34,098 was paid for a case of the 1961 on a presale estimate of £13,000–18,000, while the legendary 1929 and 1928 both sold for £27,500 on an estimate of £17,000–22,000. But after the heady days of record prices set by Christie's and, two weeks later, Sotheby's First Growth sales, the air seeped out of the end-of-season balloon. Younger clarets were again soft, with multiple lots of 1995 Mouton, 1998 Léoville-Las-Cases, Ausone, and Mondotte, and 1999 Pavie and Quinault L'Enclos all failing to reach their reserves. The 2000 vintage ports also fared poorly, making a brief first appearance at auction before sinking without trace, with the sole exception of Warre's 2000, which sold for £264 a case.

Unstoppable 2000s?

Although too young to drink, 2000 bordeaux has been the subject of feverish trading activity throughout the year, constituting 25 per cent of the London International Vintners Exchange's (Liv-ex) business. According to Liv-ex's bordeaux index chart, 2000 rose from a base of 100 in August 2001 to 115 by the beginning of 2003, surging to over 140 by the end of 2003. The excitement over 2000 was highlighted by end-of-year sales by both Sotheby's and Christie's, which saw increased prices for many 2000s confirmed.

At Sotheby's, Cheval Blanc sold for £4,600, while top of the 2000 Médoc First Growth section was Margaux with £3,910, followed by Latour at £3,450, Lafite at £3,220, with Mouton bringing up the rear at £2,990. Although Christie's prices were a little lower, the top wines all exceeded their high estimates. How long can the 2000s keep rising? Indeed, if the 2000s outclass the 1982s, as seems possible, there may be no stopping them. On the other hand, it may be that the market for 2000s is temporarily saturated, given that supply is likely to remain constant for the foreseeable future. However, other factors are involved, such as the declining dollar at the end of 2003, which helped to dampen American enthusiasm for a vintage that they bought heavily into *en primeur*. A strengthening of the market in 2004 could change that. The most likely brake on growth of the 2000s, and the rest of the market for that matter, would be from the *deus ex machina* of external forces, which no one, whether Gordon Brown, Robert Parker, or George Soros, can predict.

IS BURGUNDY THE NEW BORDEAUX?

This was the big question in 2003, when a number of burgundian names achieved fabulous prices. Yet burgundy is a more specialist market than bordeaux for a variety of reasons. Not only does it deal in much smaller quantities, but there are no classifications to make life easy for investors. Vintages are also far less easy to get a handle on, so, while bordeaux has its signposts, burgundy has very few outside the great names. For this reason, burgundy requires a certain degree of inside knowledge of the great names and how they have performed in great vintages. The Domaine de la Romanée-Conti is the only constant blue chip, the premier *grand cru* if you like, but there's another division of key names jostling for attention, and that division is now providing real interest and excitement.

This year's superstar has been Henri Jayer, especially for his Cros Parantoux, which has now reached the equivalent of *grand cru* status. On 22 November 2003, at Sotheby's New York, six bottles of Jayer's 1985 Richebourg made the fifth-highest sale price of the year with $35,250. At Sotheby's London on 19 November, Henri Jayer was also the star performer with six magnums of his 1988 Vosne-Romanée Cros Parantoux fetching £9,200 and six magnums of 1976 Echézeaux £5,750. The 1978 Vosne-Romanée went for £5,290 and £5,520 was paid for three magnums of 1976 Richebourg.

Other notable performances throughout the year have come from a growing band of sought-after names, including Dujac, Jean Gros, Rousseau, Leflaive, Lafon, Ramonet, Roumier, and Rouget.

BEST CELLARS

Two exceptional American cellars came to auction in 2003. First, the Aulden Cellars/Sotheby's New York sale of the Robert Paul collection on 4 October brought a total of $2.2 million, well over the high estimate of $1.7 million. Among the highlights, 12 bottles of 1945 Château Mouton-Rothschild brought $76,375, two offerings of 1961 Château Mouton-Rothschild in magnum sold for $23,500, and 12 bottles of 1961 Château Haut-Brion for $18,212. A case of 1982 Le Pin achieved $45,825 and 1982 Pétrus $27,025. Burgundy, Rhône, and Italian wines also featured prominently. Six bottles of 1985 Henri Jayer Echézeaux brought an impressive $11,750 over a high estimate of $6,000, a case of 1990 Châteauneuf-du-Pape Hommage à Jacques Perrin Beaucastel achieved $4,993, and 14 bottles of Barolo Monfortino Riserva from Giacomo Conterno, 1952, 1961, 1964, and 1967, sold for $9,400.

The following month, on 22 November, Aulden Cellars/Sotheby's surpassed the Paul collection with a sale of the Harter family cellar. The sale brought an impressive $3.08 million, soaring above the expected $1.8–2.4 million, setting world records for 1945 Mouton-Rothschild at $70,500 and 1961 Lafleur at $73,437. Classic red bordeaux wines sold well generally, with La Mission Haut-Brion taking a starring role. A case of the 1947 sold for $16,450, of 1961 for $19,387, and three magnums from 1949 for $13,512. From Burgundy, a magnum of the outstanding 1985 DRC Romanée-Conti brought $12,337 and a case of 1990 Leroy Chambertin $11,162. The legendary Henri Jayer was represented by six bottles of 1985 Richebourg that soared above estimate to sell for $35,250.

OZ BARRELS MAKE A MILLION

Could the Australian barrel auction be taking over from the barbie? Attracting 350-odd wine lovers from Queensland, New South Wales, and Victoria to a pre-auction brunch on Sunday 19 October, the 2003 Coonawarra Barrel Series Auction raised its millionth dollar in proceeds, generating the highest-ever average barrel price of A$19,491. Katnook Estate and Punters Corner Wines set the benchmark with A$27,240 (including 13.5 per cent buyer's premium) for each barrel, with approximately $18,000 heading to the South Australian Autism Association. Sotheby's auctioneer Richard O'Mahoney was the man with the hammer, knocking down each barrel in five-case lots.

The Coonawarra auction was followed by Langton's Great Wine Estates Auction, held on the lawns of the Cape Mentelle Winery in Margaret River. More than A$30,000 was raised for the Busselton Population Research Foundation founded by the late Kevin Cullen, with top lots A$22,750 for the 2002 Howard Park Cabernet and the same for the 2003 Moss Wood Cabernet Sauvignon, while the barrel of Cullen's Diana Madeline Cabernet Merlot made A$20,475.

MUSEUM PIECES GO UNDER THE HAMMER

Bonham's wine department recorded turnover in excess of £1.2 million for 2003, up 23 per cent on 2002. The sale of the contents of Harvey's Wine Museum on 30 September raised a total of £781,861, with £2,695 paid for six magnums of 1970 Latour and £1,595 for six bottles of 1961 La Mission Haut-Brion. The most significant sums were for the more fabulous mementoes of the museum itself, such as rare bottle stands, silver-gilt wine labels, antique drinking glasses and delft, along with books, prints, bottle tickets, and corkscrews. The highest price paid was for a pair of George IV silver-gilt coaster trolleys by Benjamin Smith (1828), which sold for £85,580. Highlights of the year included six magnums of 1961 Latour selling for £15,950 and six magnums of 1970 Pétrus for £7,700, while a dozen bottles of 1985 Jayer Echézeaux made £4,730.

GUESSTIMATES?

Both auctioneer and seller are pleased when bids leave the estimate standing, as the following 2003 prices illustrate, but are they a case of underestimating or overperforming? Only time will tell.

• Christie's 20 March: £1,760 for 1979 Louis Latour Corton-Charlemagne (estimate £500);
• Sotheby's 30 April: £1,035 for Robert Arnoux 1971 Vosne-Romanée Les Suchots (estimate £150);
• Christie's 22 May: £34,098 for a case of 1961 Château Latour (estimate £18,000);
• Sotheby's 18 June: £4,370 for six bottles of 1959 Hermitage La Chapelle (estimate £800);
• Sotheby's 16/17 September: £1,127 for 36 bottles of 1990 Brunello di Montalcino, Castelgiocondo, Frescobaldi (estimate £480);
• Christie's 18 September: £1,980 for a jeroboam of 1957 DRC La Tâche *grand cru* (estimate £420);
• Sotheby's 22 October: £943 for 11 bottles of M Dugat 1982 Griotte-Chambertin (estimate £160);
• Christie's 13 November: £2,640 for a jeroboam of Dujac 1978 Clos de la Roche *grand cru* (estimate £600);
• Sotheby's 10 December: £2,530 for two bottles of Armand Rousseau 1949 Chambertin (estimate £400);
• Sotheby's 10 December: £7,475 for 12 bottles of Henri Jayer 1988 Echézeaux (estimate £2,600).

• **World-record prices** were achieved at Christie's Latour sale in London for almost every one of the 64 estate-sourced vintages between 1863 and 1996 that were offered. The 180-lot collection more than tripled presale estimates.

• **Free fine-wine tracker** www.decanter.com provides historic monthly prices for some 2,500 wines going back to 1976.

• **Another free service** is www.vines.org/servlet/VinesAuctionCall, which lets you make a general search for, say, 1996 Château Margaux, focusing on each individual lot as it appears in the catalogue with estimate and price. Or you can choose from a category such as bordeaux over a period of vintages, and this will furnish you with a chart of lowest to highest prices at auction in each vintage.

• **The benefit of** www.wine-searcher.com lies in its speed and simplicity. It is free for limited access to wines from sponsors' stores. For £16.50 a year, the subscription Pro Version helps you locate prices and stockists and includes extra services such as searches for specific bottle sizes and prices over previous years.

• **You can subscribe** to www.Liv-ex.co.uk or www.Liv-ex.com for £39.95 plus VAT. This is an electronic trading and auction platform offering detailed price and market information to private collectors and the wine industry.

Exceptional growth 1999–2003

Position 2004	2003	Vintage	Wine	1999	2002	2003	% growth [1]	% growth annualized [2]
1	–	1961	Latour	7,920	8,580	34,098	331	44
2	1	1978	La Tâche	5,136	15,630	14,330	179	29
3	2	1991	Chave Cuvée Cathelin	2,400	6,996	6,500	171	28
4	–	1998	Le Pin	2,900	6,540	7,590	162	27
5	–	1982	Le Pin	11,550	15,950	27,495	138	24
6	7	1978	Guigal Côte Rôtie La Landonne	2,736	6,744	6,000	119	22
7	5	1982	Pétrus	7,800	19,550	16,215	108	20
8	9	1989	Pétrus	6,156	14,832	11,500	87	17
9	10	1990	Le Pin	4,944	11,808	9,200	86	17
10	3	1982	Lafleur	5,532	15,756	9,825	78	15
*		N/A	PetroKazakhstan	0.41	9.35	12.47	2,971	134.84

Prices in GBP per case of 12 bottles (best hammer price achieved in year indicated). **Source:** Christie's, Sotheby's, and Morrell's.

[1] Percentage growth between 1 July 1999 and 30 June 2003. [2] Annualized growth between 1 July 1999 and 30 June 2003. *Highest stocks and shares growth over 1 July 1999 to 30 June 2003, courtesy of Jeff Fischer and Tom Jacobs of Complete Growth Investor LLC (www.completegrowth.com).

Since it would be impossible to track every wine auction price, the examples above should be regarded as 10 of the wines that have shown exceptional growth, rather than the 10 most exceptional. An obscure wine in an obscure auction might have done much better, but the data would be of no practical value, since the idea is to illustrate the sort of gains that the lucky owners of the above wines might reasonably be expected to enjoy if the wines had been sold at a major auction house in 2003.

Grapevine

• **The 1982 vintage** started the year as it meant to go on – with a good performance despite the general gloom. This solid blue-chip vintage held up well throughout the year, with increases over late summer prices in all First Growths. Cheval Blanc reached £4,370 a dozen, Lafite and Mouton £3,680, while six bottles of Lafleur fetched £3,335. In the autumn, the 1982s rose again with Cheval Blanc reaching £4,620 and Latour £4,180. By the end of the year, the best results were the £27,495 paid for Le Pin, £16,215 for Pétrus, £5,750 for Cheval Blanc, and £5,374 for Latour, with Trotanoy reaching £2,300 and Pichon-Lalande £2,145.

Blue-chip growth: 1998 vintage

Position 2004	2003	Wine	1999 [1]	2002 [2]	2003 [2]	% growth [3]	% growth annualized [4]
1	1	Le Pin	2,900	6,540	7,590	162	27
2	2	Trotanoy	800	1,740	1,550	94	18
3	3	Pétrus	3,800	7,520	6,460	70	14
4	4	Cheval Blanc	1,150	2,110	1,840	60	12
5	7	Ausone	1,150	1,420	1,725	50	11
6	6	Haut-Brion	875	1,090	1,230	41	9
7	5	Lafite	800	1,150	1,035	29	7
8	9	Margaux	780	830	860	10	2
9	8	Mouton	780	910	800	3	1
10	10	Latour	780	780	710	–9	–2
*		3M**	35.94	58.27	63.63	77	15.35
*		Dow Jones**	100.32	89.50	88.90	–11	–2.98
*		S&P 500**	129.51	96.48	96.82	–25	–7.01
*		FTSE100	6,318.50	4,656.40	4,031.20	–36	–10.63
*		NASDAQ	2,686.12	1,463.21	1,622.80	–40	–11.84

Prices in GBP per case of 12 bottles. **Sources:** *En primeur* prices Wine Society in bond, excluding VAT.

[1] *En primeur* price 1 July 1999. [2] Best auction price in year indicated.
[3] Percentage growth over 1 July 1999 to 30 June 2003. [4] Annualized growth over 1 July 1999 to 30 June 2003. * Stocks and shares performance over the same period, courtesy of Jeff Fischer and Tom Jacobs of Complete Growth Investor LLC (www.completegrowth.com). ** Dividends included. Price on reference date adjusted for dividends. Exchange-traded funds used for Dow Jones Industrial Average and S&P 500.

Grapevine

• **London was bullish for burgundy** in 2003. At Christie's, Dujac 1985 and 1990 Clos de la Roche both fetched £4,384 a case, while its 1990 Echézeaux fetched £2,090 and 1989 Clos de le Roche £1,650. Meanwhile, at Sotheby's, £2,185 was paid for a case of Emmanuel Rouget's 1989 Vosne-Romanée Cros Parantoux (on a high estimate of £900), while a case of the 1992 Domaine Leflaive Bâtard-Montrachet made £2,990, and six magnums of Ramonet's 1986 Chassagne-Montrachet Les Ruchottes brought £1,840. The year ended strongly at Sotheby's, where in November a case of 1985 Chambertin from Armand Rousseau sold for £4,370 on an estimate of £1,200–1,800.

Blue-chip growth: 1999 vintage

Position	Wine	2000 [1]	2003 [2]	% growth [3]	% growth annualized [4]
1	Haut-Brion	775	1,476	91	17.46
2	Lafite	775	1,092	41	8.94
3	Pétrus	3,650	5,076	39	8.59
4	Mouton	775	936	21	4.83
5	Margaux	775	912	18	4.15
6	Latour	775	900	16	3.8
7	Cheval Blanc	1,146	1,272	11	2.64
8	Ausone	1,146	1,044	–9	–2.3
9	Trotanoy	550	408	–26	–7.19
10	Le Pin	3,300	N/A	N/A	N/A
*	Altria Group**	22.18	44.14	99	25.78
*	Dow Jones**	98.73	88.90	–10	–3.45
*	S&P 500**	138.72	96.82	–30	–11.30
*	FTSE100	6,312.70	4,031.20	–36	–13.89
*	NASDAQ	3,966.11	1,622.80	–59	–25.67

Prices in GBP per case of 12 bottles. **Sources:** *En primeur* prices Wine Society in bond, excluding VAT.

[1] *En primeur* price 1 July 2000. [2] Best auction price in year indicated.
[3] Percentage growth over 1 July 2000 to 30 June 2003. [4] Annualized growth over 1 July 2000 to 30 June 2003. * Stocks and shares performance over the same period, courtesy of Jeff Fischer and Tom Jacobs of Complete Growth Investor LLC (www.completegrowth.com). ** Dividends included. Price on reference date adjusted for dividends. Exchange-traded funds used for Dow Jones Industrial Average and S&P 500.

Grapevine

• **Sotheby's New York sale** in December saw six magnums of 1990 Bonnes Mares from Georges Roumier go for $8,225 and 12 bottles of 1995 Chevalier-Montrachet from Domaine Leflaive for $8,225. A single bottle of the 1906 La Romanée, Domaine du Château du Vosne-Romanée from Bouchard Père sold for a spectacular £3,518.70 and just one bottle of 1864 Bouchard Père Le Montrachet made £3,298.70.

• **Provenance is everything,** as Christie's grand Latour sale in London demonstrated in May 2003, with a case of 12 bottles of 1955 Latour achieving £10,104, while later in the day a case of the same wine that did not come direct from Latour's cellars sold for just £1,705.

BEST AUCTION BARGAINS FOR CURRENT DRINKING

Prices are in GBP per case of 12 bottles rounded to the nearest £10.

1. **Martinez Vintage Port 1985** (£175) *Undervalued vintage port with excellent depth of ripe, plummy fruit and good balance between power and finesse.*

2. **Château Talbot 1986** St-Julien (£460) *This graceful example of Talbot, with its evolved, richly concentrated, leathery ripe fruit, is only now reaching its drinking window. It is surely a great buy at this price.*

3. **Château Rausan-Ségla 1990** Margaux (£560) *Just starting to come into its own now, this is a fine vintage for Rausan-Ségla, a wine full of spice, fruit, and richness with time to go.*

4. **Château Léoville-Barton 1994** St-Julien (£210) *Some off-vintages represent the best value and 1994 is no exception in the case of Léoville-Barton, whose traditional style is ready now but will keep a few years yet.*

5. **Château La Mission Haut-Brion 1995** Graves (£630) *It would be hard to deny that this rich, classic, concentratedly minerally quintessence of Pessac-Léognan is one of the wines of the vintage.*

6. **Réserve de la Comtesse, Pichon-Lalande 1996** Pauillac (£240) *A chip off the Pichon-Lalande block, which itself was a sensational wine in 1996, Mme de Lencquesaing's classy, opulent second wine is worthy of the grand vin.*

7. **Château Grand-Puy-Lacoste 1996** Pauillac (£390) *Still a great price for this dense, concentrated, and complex Pauillac – even cheaper now than last year!*

8. **Clos Mogador 1998** Priorat (£140) *Supertarry and liquoricey, almost Shiraz-like richness and concentration with minty freshness from pioneering Priorat producer René Barbier.*

9. **Cuvée Réservée 2000** Domaine du Pégaü, Châteauneuf-du-Pape (£180) *Aromatically spicy, seductively rich, and powerfully peppery southern Rhône beauty based on late-harvest Grenache. This is drinking now but will age superbly for 10 years.*

10. **Château de Beaucastel 2000** Châteauneuf-du-Pape (£240) *Some like it young and, while it is still early days for this brooding, sumptuously rich, spicy, blackberryish red, buy a case, try a bottle, and hold – if you can.*

rd Smart & Caroline Gilby MW

European vintners are turning to space-age technology in an attempt to gain a better understanding of factors affecting wine quality.

DR RICHARD SMART   DR CAROLINE GILBY

The EU-backed project, using the European Space Agency (ESA), is called Bacchus. The aim is to make images of the continent's vineyards in unprecedented detail, which will help to improve production management and grape quality. The Bacchus consortium includes some 14 public and private institutions from Italy, France, Spain, and Portugal.

The project will use multispectral satellite images of a remarkably high resolution along with higher-resolution aerial photography. Conditions of vine health and stress are more evident in such multispectral images than they are to the eye. Researchers will then be able to compare the images with the volume and quality of wine from each vineyard. A less lofty but equally important task will be to develop standardized methods to register vineyard area and wine production. The French Research Institute CEMAGREF has the demanding role of developing technology for

DR RICHARD SMART, 'the flying vine doctor', is an Australian vineyard consultant with clients in 20 countries. He began his career in viticultural research in Australia, spanning to Israel, the USA, France, and New Zealand. Richard is coauthor of the seminal work *Sunlight into Wine* (Winetitles, 1991) and is considered an authority on canopy management of grapevines. He has a regular column, Smart Viticulture, in *The Australian & New Zealand Wine Trade Journal*, is widely published in scientific and other journals, and is the viticulture editor for *The Oxford Companion to Wine*.

DR CAROLINE GILBY MW started her career as a research scientist working on plant tissue culture, but she left to join the wine trade. She became senior wine buyer for a major UK retail chain, covering Eastern Europe. She is now a freelance writer and independent consultant to the wine trade, and served four years on the Wine Standards Board. Caroline also lectures WSET Diploma students on tasting technique, vinification, and wine handling, and judges at international wine shows.

automatic recognition of vineyards from the images. The 30-month Bacchus project began in 2003 with a survey of pilot sites, including Bordeaux and Italy's Frascati vineyards.

Hot stuff?

Europe and North America experienced warmer-than-normal summer temperatures in the 2003 season. Warm temperatures normally produce an earlier harvest with higher sugar levels. Grapes ripen quickly and higher temperatures can, in fact, be too high for optimal flavour and aroma development. There are strong beliefs that growing grapes in hot climates leads to lack of fruit flavour in many varieties.

European vintners are optimistic, with some suggesting that the vintage may produce as good a quality as the classic 1947. Temperatures in some regions have been the highest for more than 50 years. German growers have seen the harvest date brought forward by three weeks – a direct effect of higher temperatures. Earlier ripening can also cause lower-than-normal yields. The French industry association Onivins has sounded a note of caution about high temperatures always producing higher quality, however, declaring that "fragrance may leave something to be desired".

Château Haut-Brion of Bordeaux had its earliest harvest ever, on 13 August. The next earliest was in 1893, which started on 15 August. The 2003 vintage started with Sauvignon Blanc at 14 per cent potential alcohol. Delaying the harvest any longer would have led to a further loss of acidity.

There were other implications of the hot northern summer. With higher temperatures, vine water stress is more likely. In Italy's Barolo region, there was debate about whether emergency drip irrigation should be allowed, with strong arguments for and against.

Regions that traditionally have been seen as too cold for commercial viticulture, of course, benefit from warmer seasons. English vintners were overjoyed with no frost problems, well-timed rains, and the heat wave. Grapes were much riper than normal, and yields were better.

Some observers claim that this hot summer was not just a fluke of nature but more a sign of things to come, due to global warming. There have been recent patterns of good vintages in some regions, such as Piedmont. Dr Gregory Jones of Southern Oregon University studied Sotheby's vintage rating (a 100-point scale) and weather data for 27 top wine-producing regions for the last 50 years. Overall, he found that an average temperature increase of 2°C was associated with higher vintage ratings. He also predicted the outcome of a further 2°C rise over the next 50 years. It is likely that varietal preferences in some regions might change and that other new wine regions might develop – for example, southern England.

NELSON GETS THE BUG

New Zealand was similar to Australia in that not all vineyard regions were infested with phylloxera, the aphid that destroys grapevine roots. While it has been found in the neighbouring Marlborough region for more than two decades, it has only recently been found in Nelson. Many growers had anticipated the arrival of the pest and had planted on rootstocks, but around 170 hectares (ha) will have to be replanted at a cost of NZ$2.2 million. The upside is that the Nelson region will benefit from having the newest clones and varieties planted.

SMART SPRAYING

Sprayer technology is helping vine growers to use pesticides more effectively. The newly available WeedSeeker is one such example. Previously, growers would apply a blanket covering of herbicide spray to the ground, irrespective of the density and presence of weeds. The new technology detects the presence of weeds and triggers a release of precisely directed herbicide. While the equipment has been available since 1995, it is only now beginning to be widely used in vineyards in the US and Europe.

BLACK GOO IN NURSERIES?

California consultant James Stamp tested planting material from nurseries for major vine diseases. He found that a high proportion of cuttings were discoloured internally, which was linked to the presence of 'black goo', a combination of fungi that causes poor vine growth. Even more alarming was the finding that some of the material tested positive for important viruses, even though it is "certified material". Such results are not limited to California, having also been reported in Australia, New Zealand, and Europe.

Grapevine

• **The tiny vine mealybug** is being discovered in more and more of California's Central Coast vineyards. During the 2003 season, efforts were made to monitor pest infestations and prevent further spread. This requires that harvesters be washed down before entering new vineyards and that labourers wash down footwear and preferably change their clothes. For the moment no effective control of the pest has been found acceptable.

• **Icewine has been defined** by the international wine-regulating body OIV (Office International de la Vigne et du Vin). The minimum harvest temperature is −7°C and grapes must be frozen at harvest and pressed in this state. This will prevent wines made from artificially frozen grapes being sold as icewine.

• **One of Japan's oldest vineyards** was at Inamicho, in southern Hyogo prefecture. The 30-ha Banshu vineyard had 60 grape varieties and was run by the central government in the Meiji era (1868–1912). Now a young wine enthusiast, Ritsuo Sato, has replanted part of the same land to Cabernet Sauvignon in an effort to re-establish winemaking in the region.

LIVING VINE MUSEUM IN SWITZERLAND

Staff at the Swiss research centre of Wadenswil have begun to explore technologies of the past as well as those of the future. Retired director Werner Koblet has been collecting old varieties that have fallen from favour. The long-forgotten varieties were 'discovered' growing around local farmhouses. One variety, Elbling, was thought to have been brought by the Romans. Using old winemaking methods, the museum has made wine from the varieties, but the resulting wines do not taste very good.

NAPA GOES GREEN

Tensions exist between ecology conservation groups and farmers all over the world. Growers in California's Napa Valley are proactive in trying to demonstrate good intentions in their vineyards to conserve the environment. These initiatives include working with the conservation movement and other industry groups to encourage growers to adopt Napa Green, a voluntary protocol launched in 2002 to protect the environment. Of particular concern are local watershed stewardship efforts. About 90 per cent of the Napa River watershed is privately owned, making this work all the more important.

CHUCK BUCKS RULES, OK!

Due to the grape surplus of 2003, so many acres of vineyards were removed and burnt in California's Central Valley that local officials had to modify rules on agricultural burning. To add insult to injury, the old grape stakes cannot be burnt because they have been chemically treated, so some 50 million have been taken to landfills.

The best grape prices that growers were able to achieve were below the cost of production, so removal was their only option. Stocks of surplus wine have been mopped up by 'super-value' wines, led by the notorious 'Two Buck Chuck'. Such booming sales have, however, put pressure on small, premium-wine producers of Napa and Sonoma, who are finding it increasingly hard to sell expensive wines in a price-conscious market.

SICK SYRAH

In 2003, there were widespread reports of Syrah vines showing early-season red foliage and delayed maturity around Paso Robles on the Central Coast. This disorder has been observed in several vineyards before, and tests show that wine quality is greatly damaged. While the symptoms appear to come and go, vines can be killed by the problem. Some specialists believe that a virus or related organism may be responsible.

The *Wine Spectator* claims that Syrah will be the next big variety, not only for California. This may be the case, but the problems of vine health need to be sorted out. Fortunately, this problem is not evident in Australia, but there are reports from France and South Africa of what may be a similar disorder.

POMPEIIAN VARIETIES REVIVED

Glenn McGourty, Farm Adviser for Mendocino and Lake counties of California, is thinking outside the square. He is experimenting with ancient Roman grape varieties, some of which were grown in Pompeii, buried by ash from Mount Vesuvius in AD79. The varieties include Aglianico, Fiano, Greco, Dolcetto, Freisa, and Corvina. Some of the vines were imported from Italy and are now undergoing 'sanitization' (virus elimination). Following eight years of evaluation, some of the varieties were found well adapted to the local climate, producing good wine.

BAND ASKED TO SLOW DOWN

The antelope brush ecosystem indicates good soil drainage in the Okanagan Valley. And vineyards like good soil drainage; it is important for quality. No wonder conservationists are alarmed at vineyard expansion, which is now threatening the very survival of these ecosystems. The local vineyard area is expected to double over the next few years. This ecosystem is among the four most threatened habitats in Canada and is home to 88 species of plants, insects, and animals considered at risk by the British Columbia government.

Grapevine

- **No glassy winged sharpshooter eggs** were found on imported nursery plants in Sonoma County in 2003. Since eggs had been discovered in previous years, this indicates that quarantine procedures are working. The insect can spread Pierce's disease, a scourge capable of killing vines.

- **China's Agricultural University** has set up a research centre at Changli in north China's Hebei province. The aim is to teach grape and wine production; courses will be offered up to PhD level.

- **Syrah sudden death** is worrying growers in Languedoc-Roussillon. Reportedly affecting as much as 20 per cent of vines in some areas, the problem seems to be worst around the Mediterranean basin and is believed to be caused by blockages at the graft union. Research is going on into the cause, as yet unknown, although links with specific clones and rootstocks or poor-quality material from the Syrah boom 20 years ago have been ruled out.

- **A new database project** called Phénoclim has been set up by INRA (Institut National de Recherches Agronomiques) researchers to look at the effect of global warming on flowering time and the risk of frost damage in different fruit varieties, including grapevines. The project aims to enable growers to receive guidance on pruning times and frost-protection measures. Early analyses show a trend towards earlier flowering time, especially in the 1990s, as well as an advance in harvest dates. For example, in the Médoc the harvest now starts around 20 days earlier than in 1954.

Much of the land being converted to vineyards is on reserve land. The Osoyoos band has recently planted 500 ha of vineyards as part of their mandate to become economically self-sufficient by 2005. The band is being asked to limit future plantings but is seeking compensation for income foregone.

SCARY BIRD-SCARER

An Ottawa company has developed a new method of protecting vineyards from birds. Bird-control costs can be a major financial burden for growers all over the world, but losses without protection can be as high as 60 per cent. iScarecrow uses a camera mounted in the centre of the vineyard to detect incoming birds, and a network of wires above the vineyard allows Scarebots to be sent to intercept them. The devices travel at up to 34 km/h (21 mph) and screech bird-distress calls. For the moment the system costs more than netting, but its continued use would make it more cost-effective.

GRAPE GLUT CAUSING LOWER LAND PRICES

Growers in California have witnessed a significant decline in grape prices due to overplanting over the last few years. Oversupply is now affecting real-estate values around Paso Robles in the Central Coast. In the 10 years since 1992, wine-grape plantings have more than tripled to over 10,000 ha. Prices have fallen more than 6 per cent, and some growers were forced to sell to Central Valley wineries at the lower Central Valley prices. One grower, Jim Smoot, reported a $50,000 loss from his 40 acres of vineyard due to falling prices. Some new entrants to the industry are having problems financing loans, and as a result there are more vineyards on the market. While premium vineyards might still sell for $75,000 per acre, recent sales have seen prices in less desirable locations fall to $30,000 per acre. Further south in Santa Maria, former vineyard land is being sold at reduced prices to strawberry growers.

ALSACE GMO TRIALS OPPOSED

Hundreds of French winemakers are protesting against field trials of genetically modified vines planned for Alsace by government research agency INRA. The rootstock vines have been developed with resistance to fan-leaf virus. The protest is being spearheaded by Terre et Vin du Monde, an organization set up in 1998 to press for a moratorium on GMO vine and wine marketing and transparency in research. The group includes some 400 French producers and 200 from Germany, along with others in the US, Italy, and Spain. The group has written to the authorities with a request to discontinue the trials, citing dangers to the local population and economy.

AUTOMATIC RESPONSE TO THAT SINKING FEELING

A prototype automatic grape sorter invented by Philippe Bardet of Château Val d'Or in St-Emilion has proved its worth in 2003. It sorts machine-harvested grapes and is reckoned by the designer to produce better results than hand selection, since the naked eye cannot spot pigmented but underripe berries. First it pours the grapes on to a vibrating grid to remove undeveloped berries, then a rotating drum picks up damaged and rotten fruit, while whole grapes bounce off into a flotation tank. Here they are separated on the basis of density – ripe fruit sinks and unripe fruit floats. In 2003, Bardet reckons to have selected out 10 per cent rotten fruit and 5 per cent underripe berries. Other advantages include labour saving – only five people are required to pick an area that would need 120 to hand-harvest. Being confident of the ability to select fruit so effectively also allows growers the freedom to wait for full ripeness.

GUYOT MARCHES ACROSS VALPOLICELLA

Guyot training is becoming more widespread in Valpolicella and is expected to be a requirement of the anticipated DOCG status for the area, currently due in 2005. Local opinion is split over the suitability of Guyot training for the vigorous Corvina (the most important grape in the area, accounting for around 80 per cent of all vines). It suffers from basal bud infertility, requiring long canes and a lot of canopy management, which can be expensive on sloping sites. Ripening is about 10 days earlier on Guyot than on a traditional Pergola Veronese system, though this can mean sugar ripeness ahead of

phenolic ripeness. The vine is also inclined to produce more compact, yet bigger, bunches with larger berries on Guyot, as well as being more prone to rot. Trials with growth regulators like Gibberellic acid to open up bunches and application of copper-based compounds at flowering to reduce fruit set have proved inconclusive, according to local agronomist Claudio Oliboni.

OLD VINES VERSUS YOUNG VINES

Hans Schultz at Geisenheim is running trials to try to determine the real influence of age on fruit quality. Part of an old Riesling plot has been replanted with the same Riesling clone on the same rootstock. One of the problems with this type of comparison is the effect of comparing high-yielding young vines with older, less productive plants. A French technique called échelle de taille is being used to prune the vines to give the same yield in both young and old plants. Schultz reports no consistent difference in wine quality as yet, but this is a long-term project. A vine-density trial with Riesling took 15 years to give reliable results, which showed that high-density plantings give more aroma precursors and better amino acid levels in dry years, reducing the risk of stuck ferments and avoiding 'off' flavours.

MEASURING SOIL WATER WITH RADAR

Researchers Yoram Rubin and Susan Hubbard at UC Berkeley have announced details of their ground-penetrating radar (GPR) unit, which monitors vineyard soil water. The technology has the potential to improve wine quality by allowing viticulturists to refine their irrigation strategies and reduce water wastage. The device, a vacuum-sized machine, is dragged through the vineyard, where it skims the soil surface, sending electromagnetic pulses into the first few metres of soil. The speed of transmitted and reflected signals is slower in wet soil, so the signals can be analysed to determine moisture levels.

Gyles Webb at Tokara, Stellenbosch, uses another system, EM38 soil survey, to achieve similar results. It sends electromagnetic pulses into the ground to measure soil conductivity and can be linked to GPS to generate an accurate 3-D map of the site.

SPY IN THE SKY

Infrared aerial photography is being used by Gyles Webb of Tokara Winery in Stellenbosch to provide data on the state of vegetative development in his vineyard. This allows him to pick out differences that cannot be spotted by eye and to take corrective action. It also allows him to demarcate plots for picking and vinifying separately. He reports major differences between wines, though his holy grail is to get all his fruit evenly ripe. He has also conducted berry-sampling trials for the past two vintages to assess ripening. A similar approach is being used in Chile at Viñedo Chadwick, where infrared aerial photography was introduced in 2003 to interpret vigour within the vineyard and to confirm picking lots.

Grapevine

• **Marselan,** a cross between Cabernet Sauvignon and Grenache Noir, was developed by researchers at INRA in France in 1961. Their aim was a high-yielding, large-berried vine, but the result was a vine with tiny berries weighing just 1.3 g (0.05 oz), deemed valueless at the time. Today, with increasing emphasis on quality, Marselan has been rediscovered and, after several years of trials, is now going into commercial production. The Anglo-French wine company Adel vinified around 2,000 hectolitres (hl) in 2003 under the Devereux label and believes that Marselan shows real potential as a distinctive and potentially high-quality grape.

• **A trial assessing the impact** of leaf-surface area on Cabernet Sauvignon has been carried out by Pedro Izquierdo,

viticulturist at Viña Errázuriz, as part of an ongoing research programme into fine-tuning viticultural practice in Chile. Entire rows were trimmed to three levels of canopy, with 8, 12, and 16 leaves per shoot. Results showed higher alcohol and acidity, along with increased levels of polyphenols and colour intensity, in the 16-leaf shoots.

• **The minimal pruning trials** mentioned in *Wine Report 2004* are showing promising results, with Riesling harvested at potential alcohol levels of 13.6 to 14.7 per cent, Pinot Noir at 12.7 per cent, and Cabernet Franc at 13.3 per cent. Schultz admits that 2003 was an exceptional year, but minimal pruning appears to work well in cool climates, and well-known estates such as Basserman-Jordan in the Pfalz are now trying it.

Wine consumers are bombarded with ideas about factors affecting wine quality: climate, soil, geology, clones, rootstocks…. The list is endless, and let us not forget the age of the vine – all those myths about older vines making better wine! Bona fide factors that really do affect the quality of wine have been an active area of my research for more than 30 years. The three most important are climate, grape variety, and soil. I often use the analogy of a three-legged stool. If you do not have all three legs the same length, the stool is unstable and topples. And so does wine quality if equal attention is not paid to all three factors. As to other factors that are supposed to affect quality, there are at least two that should be scientifically investigated. I would like to see serious research into:

• Yield control – how much is quality really improved by pruning for reduced yield, green-harvesting, or crop thinning? While these practices, particularly the last two, are almost universally endorsed by winemakers, there are few studies to show benefits, given the large number of varieties and regions that need to be explored.

• Old vines make better wine – this subject is now being investigated for cool-climate white varieties by Hans Schultz at Geisenheim, and we await the results with interest. It is difficult to predict how this might apply to other varieties in warmer climates, however.

Vine mealybug control needed

This pest must be controlled and its spread halted. Research must be conducted into how nursery material can be sterilized, the control of ants, and non-insecticide treatments.

Grapevine

• **White grape varieties** can be planted in Rioja once again. The *consejo regulador* has lifted the 1992 region-wide ban on planting.

• **Transmission of leaf-roll virus** by vine mealybug is still a major concern in South Africa. Growers can now gain access to an online service estimating degree days for the six main viticultural areas. Once the value approaches 235 degree days, a possible outbreak of vine mealybug is indicated. Growers can use this information to take preventive measures with pheromone traps and physical monitoring.

Screwcaps come under scrutiny, following claims of off-odours.

DR RON JACKSON

A few years ago, the Australian Wine Research Institute (AWRI) carried out a comprehensive study on wine closures, including cork, cork substitutes, and screwcaps. Of the many findings, data from the screwcap studies have attracted the most attention. Screwcapped wines retained their fruity/floral character and showed no oxidation or corky off-odours. Independent studies on screwcaps have demonstrated that Riesling wines can retain their fruity character for upwards of 30 years. However, a few samples in the AWRI study showed rubbery or other sulphide off-odours. This finding has sparked much debate. Those favouring cork closures argue that limited oxygen uptake (associated with cork use) neutralizes hydrogen sulphide and other reduced-sulphur compounds. Such compounds could exist in the wine before bottling (where they may be masked by other flavourants or by bonding with non-volatile compounds) or could occur subsequent to bottling. Others counter that the presence of reduced-sulphur odours indicates inadequate preparation before bottling and that the problem is not related to the type of closure. Reduced-sulphur odours can occur in wines sealed with any type of bottle closure.

The closure issue has highlighted one of the controversial issues in winemaking – does the limited uptake of oxygen in cork-sealed bottles

DR RON JACKSON is the author of *Wine Science* (Academic Press, 2000) and *Wine Tasting* (Academic Press, 2002), as well as contributing several chapters to other texts and encyclopedias. Although retired, he maintains an association with the Cool Climate Oenology and Viticulture Institute of Brock University in Ontario, Canada, and has held professor and chair positions at the botany department of Brandon University in Manitoba, Canada.

have benefits? For the majority of white wines, there is general agreement that any post-bottling oxidation is detrimental. However, anecdotal evidence suggests that for some wines, such as Sauvignon Blanc and Shiraz, slight in-bottle oxidation may be beneficial. There is no doubt that oxygen can deactivate the rotten-egg smell of hydrogen sulphide, and circumstantial evidence indicates that oxygen slowly negates the burnt-rubber smell of 2-mercaptoethanol. Whether slow or intermittent oxygen ingress aids, or is essential to, the formation of a desirable aged character in older red wines is unknown from a purely scientific perspective. Although limited oxygen uptake is associated with cork closures, its occurrence is variable and unpredictable. The same is true for synthetic corks. Any potential benefit from marginal oxygen uptake cannot therefore be guaranteed.

Of one thing we can be certain – the controversy over the 'best' sealant for wine is going to continue. However, from the rate at which wineries are adopting screwcap closures, we will soon be able to make our own decisions on the relative merits of screwcaps. The retention of the fresh, fruity character of young wines will undoubtedly please most consumers. Concerns about how to lay down wines in a cellar will be gone – upright will be as good as horizontal. Whether screwcaps will retard the development of an aged (oxidized?) character of 'fine' wines is a moot point. This may not be known for years.

Grapevine

• ProCork® is offering corks coated with a membrane that possesses specified oxygen permeability. Membranes impervious to TCA are apparently also available.

• Screwcap producers are working on different polymers for their inner-cap sealant, which will possess specified oxygen permeability.

• Barrelmate® is a device designed to promote 'desirable' microoxidation of wines matured in barrels. It purportedly eliminates the need for manual racking to obtain the oxygen exposure that its proponents say produce better flavour, milder tannins, and improved wine structure. Scientists who have instituted studies on the effects of microoxidation on wine phenolics and its sensory effects may answer this thorny issue.

• Wine, like any food or beverage, can become contaminated with natural toxins. Although wine does not contain serious bacterial toxins, it may show trace amounts of fungal toxins (mycotoxins), generally produced by spoilage fungi that can grow on grapes before or after harvest. The latest to attract interest, ochratoxin A, is under active investigation in many wine regions. Although more common in red wines than in whites, and in wines from warmer regions, current data suggest that ochratoxin A does not constitute a health risk in wine. So, after a flurry of attention, it too may fade from consumer consciousness, as have aflatoxin and trichothecins.

TCA NOT THE ONLY CULPRIT IN THE DOCK

Ever since Dr Tanner first identified TCA (2,4,6-trichloroanisole) as an important source of mouldy (corky) odours in wine, it has been generally viewed as the principal causal agent of such odours. Recently, though, questions as to its importance have arisen. In last year's *Wine Report*, I noted research conducted by Dr Soleas on some 2,400 wines. TCA was present in sensory-significant levels in only about half of the wines identified with a corky taint. This clearly indicated that some other compound(s) were involved. To this end, Dr Chatonnet has provided an additional known musty-smelling compound to the long list of corky off-odours found in wine. The compound is a variant of TCA, with bromine atoms replacing the chlorine atoms on the anisole molecule – producing 2,4,6-tribromoanisole (TBA). It presumably is recognized by odour receptors in the nose as if it were TCA, consequently producing a similar smell. TBA can be derived from microbial methylation of the common flame retardant tribromophenol, which is found as a contaminant in some wooden, plastic, and cement structures.

Other compounds known to generate mouldy odours in wine include TeCA (another variant of TCA, with an extra chlorine atom), pentachloronitrobenzene (PCNB, a related compound used as a pesticide), and chloropyrazines, plus chemically unrelated compounds such as quaiacol, 3-methyl-1-butanol, and 1-octanol (largely products of fungal growth), as well as sesquiterpenes such as geosmin and 2-methylisoborneol (produced by bacteria). With such a diversity in compounds producing mouldy odours, what is (are) the principal cause(s) of corky odours?

There are numerous critical problems in answering this question. What do people exactly mean when they say, "The wine smells corky"? Even most professional tasters are not trained to distinguish among the different chemicals known to generate 'corky' odours in wine. They are also unlikely to all have similar threshold levels for detection. Even if they do, my own training sessions with the Manitoba Liquor Control Commission clearly demonstrate that asking tasters to look for faults dramatically increases the number detected. It may be only when electronic noses (instruments that simulate the action of the nose) are used in such studies that we will finally begin to determine the relative importance of these compounds to corky odour production in wine. Then, hopefully, we can begin effectively to eliminate their presence in wine.

SEEING IS BELIEVING

In *Wine Report 2004*, I commented on the disconcerting evidence that what tasters see often markedly biases what they detect. This conflicts with the general view that experts sample wines objectively. The level to which visual information biases perception seems to depend on the apparent veracity of the information available (for example the wine's colour or label) and the degree of conflict with the wine's taste and smell.

In recent studies conducted by Parr in New Zealand, wine experts' opinions were less influenced than those of novice tasters by adjusted sample colour. The wines' odour and taste characteristics clashed strikingly with clues given by their adjusted colour, at least for the experts.

In a separate study by Delwiche in the US, novice tasters were asked to taste and describe three samples of white wine, two of which had been doctored to appear as a rosé or red wine. The comments on the samples corresponded with the general impressions people have about the taste and flavour characteristics of white, rosé, and red wines, which indicates that established connections between colour and flavour expectations easily override sensory perception.

The moral of the story is that, if one wants an unbiased assessment, it is essential that tasters really taste blind – they must not see the wine's colour. In addition, no information about the wine's origin or type should be available. In this way, only the wine's flavour can affect judgment.

YELLOW-ORANGE, THE NEW RED?

Researchers have always felt uneasy about the explanation given for the colour of red wine. The methods used have required assumptions that often were not verifiable. Recent studies have shown that this disquiet is partially justified. Not that anyone is claiming final victory, but we now understand wine colour a little more clearly.

Tannin-like compounds, called anthocyanins, have long been known to be the principal pigments in young red wine. As a wine ages, free anthocyanins oxidize or combine with themselves and other compounds to form the stable tawny pigments that characterize aged red wines. One of the benefits

Grapevine

• **Fraud is rarely detected** as a result of consumer complaint. Thankfully, chemists are continuing to add to their arsenal of authentication techniques. These analytical procedures can ferret out almost any form of fraudulent activity that could jeopardize wine quality or trueness of character. In a recent study of sparkling wines, Francioli and co-workers discovered chemical indicators of age (vitispirane, TDN, and diethyl succinate), making it possible to verify chemically whether higher-priced champagnes have indeed been aged on yeast as long as stipulated.

• **Eglinton and Henschke** have demonstrated that Saccharomyces bayanus may be better suited to producing flavourful wines than Saccharomyces cerevisiae (traditional wine yeast). The researchers found that the colour intensity of Shiraz and Cabernet wines improved with the use of Saccharomyces bayanus. The wines also showed more orange-peel, apricot, honey, and nutty flavours and were less estery in character than versions made with Saccharomyces cerevisiae.

of slight oxidation during in-barrel ageing is the production of a certain amount of acetaldehyde, which activates stabilization of the wine's colour. Most stable anthocyanin complexes have been thought to form in association with tannins. Not only do these complexes protect the anthocyanin chromophore (part of the anthocyanin molecule that generates colour), but they also increase colour depth and reduce colour loss – by enhancing solubility, precipitation is limited. Because anthocyanin-tannin complexes are known to possess yellowish, orange, reddish-brown to tawny colours, they were assumed to be largely instrumental in generating the aged colour of red wines. Most of these complexes are large polymers. It was surprising, therefore, to learn that a new set of modified anthocyanins, of small molecular size, may significantly contribute to the colour shift in red wines. These are yellow-orange xanthylium compounds. Their study may shed new and practical information on the nature of red-wine colour.

ARE YOUR GLASSES IN GOOD SHAPE?

The effect of glass shape on perception has spawned the production of wine glasses in a cornucopia of shapes – some supposedly accentuating the properties of a particular wine type. Scientists such as Delwiche and Cliff have been investigating the significance of glass shape to a wine's characteristics. This has

• **Screwcaps might be the only way** to keep rosé wines in the pink. A new role for anthocyanins has been discovered in rosé wines made from Cabernet Sauvignon. Like all rosés, they do not age well, losing colour and fragrance within a few years. Tominaga and co-workers in Bordeaux have found that anthocyanins limit the loss of an important aroma compound, 3-mercaptohexan-1-ol, which is critical to the fruity character of the wine. The protection provided by anthocyanins is suspected to result from their antioxidant properties. Regrettably, though, this oxygen-absorbing action also results in the early loss of the rosé colour – turning the wines orange. Since rosé wines do not contain sufficient other oxidizable phenolics to protect anthocyanins from oxidative browning, the obvious solution would be the use of screwcaps.

• **Always the poor cousin**, rosé has been viewed as possessing few of the qualities of red or white wine, yet exhibiting the failings of both. These deficiencies could be rectified, according to new research being conducted by Salinas and co-workers in Spain. Leaving the juice on the seeds and skins under cool conditions prior to fermentation increases fruit flavours and varietal aroma. In addition, supplying pectolytic enzymes to the juice–seed–skin mixture enhances colour stability – a major problem with all rosés. Enzyme treatment also improves the fresh, fruity character of the wine. Such techniques may herald a new era for rosés.

required devising means of ensuring that tasters neither see nor feel the glasses involved.

As you might expect, shape does affect the intensity of the wine's fragrance – those possessing a wide base and narrow neck enhance the perception of the wine's aroma. However, the differences detected from a variation of shapes on the wide–narrow theme were marginal. Published evidence does not support the view that particular shapes uniquely enhance the character of specific wines. The one exception may involve flutes for sparkling wines, which facilitate observation of the bubbles. Whether they enhance flavour detection has not been studied. Incidentally, the ISO wine-tasting glass proved fully adequate to tasting both red and white wines. The ISO glass also enhanced colour perception by maximizing wine depth relative to wine volume.

That particular shapes are not uniquely suited for tasting particular wines does not mean that they do not affect perception or, indeed, aesthetic pleasure. Science has amply confirmed that visual and psychological influences often have a greater effect on what we perceive than the more subtle sensory data provided by taste and smell.

STABLE PROTEINS ENHANCE WINE TEXTURE

Many wines, especially reds, are rough in their youth. During maturation, they can lose their harshness and taste smoother. This has usually been explained as the progressive association of smaller, more bitter-tasting tannins into large complexes. These tend to be less bitter and eventually may precipitate (forming sediment in the bottle), leaving the wine with a refined mouth-feel sensation.

New factors in this ageing process may be the ill-studied, stable, soluble proteins in wine. Most of these proteins come from the juice of crushed grapes. Fukui in Japan believes that their reaction with tannins and tannin-polysaccharide complexes decreases their ability to react with taste receptors in the mouth. If this role is confirmed, the stable proteins in wine (that is, those not involved with haze production) may provide winemakers with a new measure of how well a wine will age. It may also supply an additional means of regulating wine quality.

ICEWINE INVESTIGATION

The scientific understanding of icewine production is still in its infancy. One of its fascinating aspects relates to how yeasts survive and ferment in the viscous, syrupy juice extracted from frozen grapes. Inglis and co-workers have started to unravel the mystery. The yeast increases its production of enzymes that convert acetaldehyde (produced during sugar fermentation) to acetic acid, rather than the more frequent change into alcohol. In the process, energy is generated that can be used to increase the production of glycerol. Glycerol helps limit water loss from yeast cytoplasm (essential for growth and metabolism) in the highly osmotic juice. Inglis is also investigating how best to inoculate the juice with yeasts to achieve adequate alcohol production. Reaching the desired 12 to 14 per cent alcohol content is a frequent problem for producers.

STICKING POINTS

In an ideal world, the sugars from crushed grapes would ferment easily. In the real world, fermentation may occur slowly or stop altogether before completing the conversion of grape sugars into alcohol. Many researchers have looked into fermentative failure and have discovered a number of causes: fermentation temperatures being too high or too low; insufficient nitrogen; osmotic effects of high sugar content; insufficient oxygen to produce essential cellular components; toxic fermentation byproducts; and 'killer' factors that destroy yeast cells.

Sablayrolle in France is approaching the problem in a different way. He has started to divide incomplete fermentations into separable and definable categories, each characterized by its own dynamics. Two categories have been differentiated so far – vinifications with slow fermentation rates and fermentations coming quickly to a premature stop. Separating incomplete fermentations into distinguishable groups may facilitate the development of strategies to reverse their damaging effects.

RED WINES LIKE IT COLD

Maceration, the technique of leaving juice in contact with seeds and skins after grape crushing, has become standard practice in the production of many white wines. It usually lasts 6–24 hours at cool temperatures and is followed by pressing, which liberates the juice, then by fermentation. With red wines, maceration normally occurs simultaneously with fermentation, lasting several days to weeks. However, a cold, pre-fermentative maceration period for red wines is almost unheard of. If it occurred, it was unintentional and the result of delayed barrel fermentation in cold, unheated cellars.

Recently, however, several researchers have shown the benefits of cold maceration for some red wines. Its utility was first demonstrated for the delicate variety Pinot Noir, where it improved colour and flavour extraction. Nevertheless, cold maceration can also benefit more flavourful and fully coloured varieties, such as Shiraz and Cabernet. Marais has now extended these findings to Pinotage. Whether this heralds a new trend in red winemaking, where cool pre-fermentative maceration becomes a norm, is too soon to tell. In the increasingly competitive world of wine, any practice that promises to distinguish a wine from its competitors will soon be extensively tested worldwide.

HEAT ZAPS HAZE

Consumers take wine clarity for granted. This is not the case for winemakers, who spend time and money producing crystal-clear wines. Unavoidably, a lot of wine is lost in the process. It is estimated that protecting wine from protein-induced haze results in the loss of A\$50 million worth of wine in Australia alone, as wine is discarded with the bentonite used to remove haze-producing proteins. On a world scale, the economic losses associated with attaining wine clarity are staggering. Any procedure that could reduce this wastage would indeed be welcome. Such a solution may be on the horizon.

Waters and co-workers in Australia have demonstrated the economic value of the combined action of a very short high-temperature treatment with protein-degrading enzymes. The heat favours the rapid degradative action of the enzymes. By destroying haze-generating proteins, the amount of bentonite (or other fining agents) needed to achieve protein stability is greatly reduced. Correspondingly, much wine can be saved. The process has no adverse sensory effect on the wine.

HOW TO AVOID FERMENTING TROUBLE

Different species and strains of yeast and lactic acid bacteria can give wine a distinctive 'signature'. Strain selection is a powerful tool when making wines with a distinctive character, and the number of strains now available is bewildering. However, some yeast strains may selectively inhibit the action of particular bacterial strains used to induce malolactic, and this may not always be desirable. Henschke and co-workers have simplified the choice by developing a standardized laboratory method for testing compatibility between yeast and bacterial strains. Once a winemaker has made his or her selection of a strain or strains of yeast, the test should indicate whether the chosen bacterial strain can successfully complete malolactic fermentation.

TRUFFLE AROMAS ARE SULPHUR FAULTS

Most reduced-sulphur compounds possess repulsive, putrid odours, with apt descriptive terms that include "rotten eggs", "barnyardy", and "skunky". However, recent studies show that certain assumed varietal aromas are due to related compounds, and this has raised eyebrows. The latest in the salvo of findings comes from the lab of Tominaga in Bordeaux. He has highlighted the importance of benzenemethanethiol to the aroma of Sauvignon Blanc, Semillon, and Chardonnay wines and has also discovered its significance in the aged character of champagne. The compound donates a smoky (toasty?) empyreumatic fragrance. Another significant sulphide is dimethyl sulphide. De Pinho has associated an increasing presence of this compound with the aged character (for example, quince and truffle) of ports.

GOÛT DE LUMIÈRE

Several years ago, Maujean spearheaded research on champagne off-odours induced by exposure to light. Several reduced-sulphur compounds were identified as the causal agents of what they called *goût de lumière*. The issue has recently been reinvestigated by D'Auria and co-workers in Italy. Surprisingly, they have not confirmed the presence of the compounds found by Maujean, such as hydrogen sulphide, methyl mercaptan, and dimethyl sulphide. Instead, they detected an increased presence of 2-methylpropanol (higher alcohol) and a significant modification as well as reduction in the presence of many fruit esters. This raises the question of whether the light-induced off-odours in champagne identified by these respective researchers are identical or not (despite a common name).

Spotting the trends that made most impact in the world of online wine since the publication of *Wine Report 2004* has been pretty easy.

TOM CANNAVAN

Three of them spring to mind. First, the very fabric of the Internet has continued to consolidate – from the increasing availability of broadband connections, to the maturing depth and professionalism of websites. Second, after the meltdown of confidence that greeted the turn of the millennium, there is suddenly a mass of activity in online wine selling and a plethora of new online merchants. Third, and easily the most depressing of the trends, is the increasing menace of spam (junk e-mail) and computer viruses.

Getting technical

Broadband? Wi-fi? 3G? Wi-Max? Don't worry, we will keep the confusion of computer jargon to a minimum, but it's important to point out that Web accessibility – the ease with which we can communicate and access online information – is moving forward more quickly than ever.

According to figures issued by the Office for National Statistics, more than 12 million households in the UK had access to the Internet by the end of 2003; that is almost half of all British homes. In the US, the

TOM CANNAVAN has published wine-pages.com since 1995, making it one of the world's longest-established online wine magazines, as well as one of the most popular. Updated daily, wine-pages.com contains more than 9,000 pages of content, including over 12,000 tasting notes and the world's biggest BYO directory. In 2003 Tom was short-listed for the Prix du Champagne Lanson award for his work on wine-pages. According to Jancis Robinson MW, "wine-pages.com should be of interest to any wine lover seeking independent advice" (*Financial Times*). Robert Parker finds this "all-inclusive ... superb site ... friendly, easily navigated, with plenty of bells and whistles" (*The Wine Buyer's Guide*).

50 per cent barrier was breached way back in 2001, and latest figures suggest that around 70 million US homes are wired for the Internet.

A couple of years ago, surfing to content-rich websites was painfully slow, thus limiting some applications. But new broadband connections (broadband is about 10 times faster than a dial-up modem) are currently running at more than 35,000 per week in the UK alone.

Add to this the growing sophistication of mobile computing devices (phones and PDAs) and the growth of wireless Internet access, and there seems little doubt that more and more of our leisure and business needs will be served online. For wine, as for almost any other sector, the usefulness of the Internet is absolutely proven: for many people it is not an alternative method of communicating or finding information, but an easy first choice.

The professionals

Some of us were early adopters of the Internet as a mechanism to feed our passion for wine. There was something liberating and exciting about this new medium. While small, quirky, mostly amateur websites proliferated through the mid-1990s, we celebrated whenever a 'professional' wine business took its first tentative steps to join us. Now the Web is a much more serious place, and professionally maintained sites from the likes of Google and Amazon have become household names. Just about every wine business now has a Web presence and, with a few regrettable exceptions, quality is at an all-time high.

E-commerce fights back

The landscape of high-street wine has been transformed over the past decade or so. Where once independent merchants served a specialist market, now overcrowded conurbations are full of supermarkets, chains, convenience stores, and garage forecourts stacked high with big-selling wine brands. In the boom days of e-commerce, big players like Madaboutwine, Wineplanet, and Chateauonline tried to compete in this arena, slugging it out on price.

Gradually, most of these businesses went to the wall, the costs of acquiring customers and the difficulties of delivering masses of cheap wine proving unsustainable. Many people began to question the whole viability of selling wine online. But, suddenly, it is mini-boom-time again. Since *Wine Report 2004* there has been more start-up activity than I can remember since the late 1990s. However, the picture has also changed significantly: instead of venture-capital-backed mega-retailers, it is the independent wine sector that is all the rage. The best local merchants, plus a new army of Web-only independents, have realized that not only does the Web offer them a shop window to the nation but, crucially, it affords them the opportunity to plug a valuable gap in the market; that gap is called diversity.

For all wine's easy availability, you will scan your local superstore's wine aisles in vain for a choice of fine Mosel Rieslings or Loire reds. But now the Internet is delivering genuine alternatives to the high street, with personalized service and wines that are just a bit different. This smaller, more tightly focused approach is a whole different ball game from the big-money start-ups of the late 1990s. Let's hope that this is not the start of a boom-and-bust cycle, but a more realistic and sustainable second attempt at getting it right.

Making it easy

There are still many awkward aspects to selling wine online. Limiting sales to unmixed whole cases is still a huge turn-off for most consumers, no matter how much easier it makes stock control and supply. Ideally, consumers want total flexibility to create their own mixed cases and to order odd numbers of bottles if that is what they require. Problems with deliveries also continue to dog direct selling: the frustration and inconvenience caused by broken bottles or incorrect orders guarantee that online customers will not do repeat business.

The ease with which we can complete transactions is still an issue too. It can be a pain to shop for the first time with an online store, with the need to fill in forms, type complicated numbers, and enter lengthy delivery details. We still need a viable Internet currency that can be topped up online and spent in a one-click process by entering a PIN number.

Salvation might come from an unlikely quarter: music downloads. Downloading music from the Web is a huge growth area, and all sorts of mechanisms are being refined to let young people – many without credit cards – pay small amounts of money with minimum hassle. This could open up a whole new world: not just for buying wine, but also for purchasing key information or reading pay-per-view wine content.

Grapevine

• **US readers** are still faced with a bureaucratic quagmire in the shape of the 'three-tier' system. This system, a hangover from the days of Prohibition, seeks to emasculate the wine trade by breaking down the shipping, wholesaling, and retailing of wine into discrete business areas, which makes interstate direct selling of wine a complex and, in some states, illegal practice. Take a look at two grassroots movements fighting for change: freethegrapes.org and coalitionforfreetrade.org

ALL THE NEWS THAT'S FIT TO CLICK

Whatever your favourite wine region or producer, they will almost certainly have a website – from the smallest *garagiste*, to the largest Australian corporation. Take a site like that of Burgundy *négociant* Nicolas Potel (nicolas-potel.fr) as just one example. Multilingual versions are available (French, English, German, Spanish, and Japanese), along with an easy-to-use collection of information, including the history of the domaine, details of its wines, the latest news from the vineyards, a photo gallery, and more. There is a now a fantastically rich collection of wine information and resources on the Internet, reachable at the click of a button. Everyone from professionals in the wine trade to curious consumers will find that data on producers, wines, and regions have never been easier to access.

In terms of independent commentary and opinion, again the choice is ever increasing. One example is vines.org, which was launched just as the last edition of *Wine Report* went to press. It has matured into a very useful cross-referenced database of wine producers (8,000 of them), appellations, grape varieties, and auction prices (on 75,000 lots).

New independent voices are piping up too, like Bill Nanson's promising burgundy-report.com, Neal Martin's tasting notes collection at wine-journal.com, British writer Richard Ross's wine-lines.com, and Canadian writer Natalie MacLean's natdecants.com. All are offering their thoughts and opinions free of charge.

The market for subscription-based wine sites must be nearing saturation point. From giants like erobertparker.com and winespectator.com to individuals like jancisrobinson.com, there are numerous online pundits and resources that require payment for access. Burgundy aficionados swear by Allen Meadows and his burghound.com (US$110 per year), while some follow American guru Stephen Tanzer at wineaccess.com/expert/tanzer (US$80 per year). In the UK, wine columnist Matthew Jukes asks £30 for annual access to his expertwine.com. With getting on for 20 such sites already competing for the browsing dollar, there can be little scope for more sites following the subscription model. Look out for casualties too, with some subscription services failing to cover their costs.

TAKING HI-TECH A STEP TOO FAR

Not all websites are models of the new professional thinking that exemplifies the Web in 2005. Some companies seem happy to allow their corporate websites to be riddled with bad practice, most notably a tendency to overdesign. When will companies realize that the Web is the absolutely key medium in the 21st century for research and information? Glossy brochures and corporate videos are all very well, but, these days, a company's Web presence is the most crucial bit of presentation to get right.

… and viruses, of course. The deluge of unsolicited junk mail that pours through every innocent's inbox day after day is already deeply frustrating and could threaten the development of the Internet for all users – surfers and website operators alike. The fact that some contain viruses so nasty that they can paralyse the Internet for 24 hours is another menace.

"But what does this have to do with wine?" I hear you ask. Well, online wine buffs, e-commerce wine shops, and wine-related resource sites should all be deeply concerned. Already over 50 per cent of all e-mail is unsolicited junk. It costs the US economy alone some $9 billion a year just to deal with spam, and estimates put the figure for Europe around €3 billion. Internet research company Jupiter Media Metrix predicts that consumers will receive about 206 billion junk e-mails by 2006 – an average of 1,400 per person. With every piece of spam said to cost $1 in lost productivity, each of us is bearing a small proportion of the cost.

There needs to be a three-pronged approach to defeating spam, whether malicious or merely annoying:

1. Legislation National governments and agencies like the Advertising Standards Authority in the UK have wheeled out some totally toothless measures over the past year or two that will do nothing to stem the tide of junk mail, much of it from the Florida city of Boca Raton and various Far East destinations. US, British, and other governments need to take a much more active and 'joined-up' approach to outlawing spammers and prosecuting the guilty.

2. Technology Big Internet service providers like AOL must get their act together and put spam-catching software in place on a compulsory basis. Sure, a few businesses might bleat that they are barred from sending 'legitimate' unsolicited bulk mail (spam, to my way of thinking), but the problem is too real and too severe not to take drastic action. At a personal level, make sure that your virus software is up to date and consider a personal spam-busting program like the excellent and free mailwasher.net

3. Behaviour Think carefully before typing your e-mail address into open forums on the Web, or before subscribing to sites unless you know and really trust them. There are plenty of people out there who will sell you a 'scavenging' program: point it at any website or group of sites and it will harvest every e-mail address, from every page, and return them for you to begin spamming.

With its endless complexity and ever-changing nature, wine is a topic that is fantastically well suited to discussion, research, and communication on the Web. Let's all do our bit to make sure spam and viruses do not spoil that.

Best Internet wine sites

All sites in the first four 'best' lists are free-to-access, English-language sites unless qualified by the following codes. These codes also apply to the Best Regional Wine Sites, although the primary language for many of these will be the appropriate native tongue.

[S] = paid subscription required for some/all content;
[R] = no paid subscription, but registration required for some/all content;
[E] = non-English-language site, but with English-language version.

Editor's note: I asked Tom not to include his own site, wine-pages.com, in any of his lists because, inevitably, he would either be accused of self-promotion or (more in line with his character) he would not rate his site highly enough. I declare an interest in that I have a small corner at wine-pages.com, however, I would place wine-pages.com at number two under Best Wine Sites and number one under Best Wine Forums. TS

Alexa.com – the world's most popular wine sites

I retain a healthy dose of scepticism when it comes to online polls and Top 100s because, too often, there is a strong whiff of vote-rigging about them. (It is usually not too difficult on the Net with a little technical knowledge.) The Top 50 list is compiled by alexa.com, a partner of the Google search engine. Alexa ranks sites according to various criteria, including how often surfers search for them. Though I very much doubt the validity of some of the sites making it onto this list, it is nevertheless a recent snapshot of Alexa's Top 50.

WORLD'S MOST POPULAR WINE SITES

Sites are either Retail [Ret], Information [Inf], or Other [Oth].

1. www.winespectator.com [Inf]
2. www.wine-searcher.com [Oth]
3. www.wine.com [Ret]
4. www.winecommune.com [Oth]
5. www.bbr.com [Ret]
6. www.erobertparker.com [Inf]
7. www.bevmo.com [Ret]
8. www.wineaccess.com [Oth]
9. www.vitisphere.com [Inf]
10. www.verema.com [Inf]
11. www.winenara.com [Ret]
12. www.wine-pages.com [Inf]
13. www.virginwines.com [Ret]
14. www.reservaycata.com [Ret]
15. www.napavalley.com [Inf]
16. www.wineloverspage.com [Inf]
17. www.localwineevents.com [Inf]
18. www.winebusiness.com [Inf]
19. www.westcoastwine.net [Inf]
20. www.napacabs.com [Ret]
21. www.decanter.com [Inf]
22. www.lavinia.es [Ret]
23. www.iwawine.com [Ret]
24. www.chateauonline.com [Ret]
25. www.winebid.com [Oth]
26. www.lastorders.com [Ret]
27. www.todovino.com [Ret]
28. www.winecountry.com [Inf]
29. www.majestic.co.uk [Ret]
30. www.klwines.com [Ret]
31. www.wines.com [Oth]
32. www.oddbins.com [Ret]
33. www.zachys.com [Ret]
34. www.alko.fi [Ret]
35. www.sams-wine.com [Ret]
36. www.wine.co.kr [Ret]
37. www.brentwoodwine.com [Oth]
38. www.wine21.ne.jp [Ret]
39. www.wine-tasting-party.com [Ret]
40. www.winex.com [Ret]
41. www.winelibrary.com [Ret]
42. www.tizwine.com [Inf]
43. www.primewines.com [Ret]
44. www.laithwaites.co.uk [Ret]
45. www.1855.com [Ret]
46. www.vinote.com [Inf]
47. www.geerwade.com [Ret]
48. www.bacchuscellars.com [Ret]
49. www.filewine.es [Ret]
50. www.mywineauction.com [Oth]

BEST NEW WINE SITES

1. www.burgundy-report.com
2. www.wine-journal.com
3. www.natdecants.com
4. www.bluewine.com
5. www.winebusiness.com

BEST WINE SITES

1. www.wine-searcher.com [S]
2. www.erobertparker.com [S]
3. www.winespectator.com [S]
4. www.bbr.com
5. www.decanter.com [R]
6. www.jancisrobinson.com [S]
7. www.epicurious.com/run/winedictionary/home
8. www.wineloverspage.com
9. www.vines.org
10. www.wineanorak.com

BEST WINE FORUMS

1. www.erobertparker.com [R]
2. www.ukwineforum.com
3. www.wldg.com
4. www.auswine.com.au/forum
5. www.westcoastwine.net
6. groups.msn.com/BordeauxWineEnthusiasts
7. www.enemyvessel.com/forum
8. forums.egullet.com [R]
9. news:alt.food.wine
10. www.superplonk.com/forum [R]

BEST WINE RETAILERS ON THE WEB

1. www.bbr.com [UK]
2. www.oddbins.com [UK]
3. www.wine.com [US]
4. www.majestic.co.uk [UK]
5. www.bevmo.com [US]
6. www.uvine.com [UK]
7. www.wineaccess.com [US]
8. www.auswine.com.au [AUS]
9. www.winecommune.com [US]
10. www.wineshop.it [IT] [E]

BEST REGIONAL WINE SITES

Sites are in national languages. Those with an English-language version are marked [E].

Argentina
www.winesofargentina.com [E]
www.argentinewines.com/ing [E]

Australia
www.winestate.com.au
www.wineaustralia.com

Austria
www.austrian.wine.co.at [E]
www.weinserver.at

Belgium
www.boschberg.be

Brazil
www.academiadovinho.com.br

Bulgaria
www.winebg.com [E]

Canada
www.canwine.com [E]

   British Columbia
   www.bcwine.com

   Ontario
   www.winesofontario.org

Chile
www.chilevinos.com

China
www.wineeducation.org/chinadet.html

Croatia
www.hr/wine [E]

Cyprus
www.cyprus-wine.com [E]

Czech Republic
www.znovin.cz [E]

Denmark
www.vinavl.dk
www.vinbladet.dk/uk/ [E]

Estonia
www.veiniklubi.com

France
www.frenchwinesfood.com [E]
www.abrege.com/lpv

   Alsace
   www.alsacewine.com [E]
   www.alsace-route-des-vins.com [E]

   Bordeaux
   www.bordeaux.com [E]
   www.medoc.org [E]
   www.sauternes.com

   Burgundy
   www.bivb.com [E]
   www.burghound.com

   Champagne
   www.champagnemagic.com [E]
   www.champagne.fr [E]

   Corsica
   www.corsicanwines.com [E]

   Jura
   www.jura-vins.com [E]

   Languedoc
   www.languedoc-wines.com [E]

   Loire
   www.interloire.com
   www.loirevalleywine.com [E]

   Provence
   www.provenceweb.fr/e/mag/
    terroir/vin [E]

   Rhône
   www.vins-rhone.com [E]

   Southwest of France
   www.vins-gaillac.com [E]

Georgia
www.sanet.ge/wine [E]

Germany
www.winepage.de [E]
www.germanwine.de/english [E]

Greece
www.greekwine.gr [E]
www.greekwinemakers.com [E]

Hungary
www.winesofhungary.com [E]

Indonesia
www.hattenwines.com [E]
Israel
www.israelwines.co.il [E]
Italy
www.agriline.it/wol/wol_eng/
    Default.htm [E]
www.italianwineguide.com [E]
> **Piedmont**
> www.piedmontwines.net [E]
> www.langhe.com [E]
> **Tuscany**
> www.chianticlassico.com [E]
> www.wine-toscana.com [E]

Japan
www.kizan.co.jp/eng/
    japanwine_e.html [E]
Latvia
www.doynabeer.com/wine [E]
Lebanon
www.chateaumusar.com.lb [E]
www.chateau-kefraya.com [E]
Luxembourg
www.luxvin.lu [E]
Macedonia
www.macedonian-heritage.gr/Wine [E]
Malta
www.vomradio.com/website/features/
    jan03/wine_feature [E]
www.marsovinwinery.com [E]
Mexico
www.mexicanwines.homestead.com [E]
www.montexanic.com.mx [E]
Moldova
www.turism.md/eng [E]
Morocco
www.harpers-wine.com/winereports/
    morocco.cfm
New Zealand
www.nzwine.com
www.tizwine.com
Peru
www.barricas.com
Portugal
www.vinhos.online.pt
www.winesfromportugal.co.uk
> **Madeira**
> www.madeirawine.com/html/
>   nindex.html [E]

Port
www.ivp.pt [E]
www.portwine.com [E]
Romania
www.aromawine.com/wines.htm [E]
Russia
www.russiawines.com [E]
www.massandra.crimea.com [E]
Slovenia
www.matkurja.com/projects/wine [E]
South Africa
www.wosa.co.za
www.wine.co.za
Spain
www.filewine.es [E]
> **Ribera del Duero**
> www.winesfromribera
>   delduero.com [E]
> **Rioja**
> www.riojawine.com [E]
> **Sherry**
> www.sherry.org [E]

Switzerland
www.wine.ch [E]
Tunisia
www.tourismtunisia.com/
    eatingout/wines.html [E]
United Kingdom
www.englishwineproducers.com
www.english-wine.com
United States
www.allamericanwineries.com
> **California**
> www.napavintners.com
> www.wineinstitute.org
> **New York**
> www.fingerlakeswinecountry.com
> **Oregon**
> www.oregon-wine.com
> **Texas**
> www.texaswinetrails.com
> **Washington**
> www.washingtonwine.org
> www.columbiavalleywine.com

Uruguay
www.travelenvoy.com/wine/
    uruguay.htm [E]

BEST WINE-SITE LINKS

These are sites with links to other wine sites:
www.vine2wine.com
www.bboxbbs.ch/home/tbm
www.wineweb.com

BEST VINTAGE-CHART SITES

www.winetech.com/html/vintchrt.html
www.bordeaux-vintage-charts.com
www.burgundy-vintage-charts.co.uk
www.port-vintage-charts.co.uk
www.champagne-vintage-charts.com

BEST TASTING-NOTE SITES

www.erobertparker.com [S]
www.tastings.com
www.finewinediary.com
www.winemega.com [E]
www.stratsplace.com/rogov
www.yakshaya.com
www.wine-journal.com
www.thewinedoctor.com

BEST WINE-EDUCATION SITES

www.wset.co.uk
www.wineeducation.org
www.thenoseofwine.com
www.wineeducators.com
www.wine.gurus.com

BEST VITICULTURE SITES

www.grapeseek.com
http://students.sivan.co.il/michaels/Grap
Pede.html

BEST OENOLOGY SITES

home.att.net/~lumeisenman/
contents.html

BEST SITE FOR GRAPE VARIETIES

www.wine-lovers-page.com/
wineguest/wgg.html

BEST SITES FOR FOOD-AND-WINE PAIRING

www.foodandwinematching.co.uk
www.stratsplace.com/winefood.html

THE FAR SIDE OF WINE

www.winespirit.org
www.winelabels.org
www.thomasarvid.com
www.howstuffworks.com/
question603.htm
www.liquidasset.com

A number of these wines will be available on certain markets, but many are so new, restricted in production, or downright obscure that the only way to get hold of them would be to visit the producer – if he has not already sold out.

The entire *raison d'être* of this section is to bring to the attention of serious wine enthusiasts the different and most surprising wines being developed in classic areas, the best wines from emerging regions, and other cutting-edge stuff. The prices are retail per bottle in the local currency of the country of origin (see About This Guide, p.9). My tasting note follows the contributor's own note, for comparison or contrast, or simply a different take.

Zeltinger Sonnenuhr Riesling Eiswein 1998 Markus Molitor (Germany, €62.90 per half-bottle) *Touches of honey, toffee apple, and butterscotch. Luscious and opulent style of eiswein.* Michael Schmidt *The honey is unmistakable, but it is youthful honeyed lemon, with a plethora of candied fruits starting to build. The acidity is to die for, and the wine is to kill for!* Tom Stevenson

Gold Label 1996 Lanson (Champagne, €27.50) *At my Christie's Champagne Masterclass in November 2003, I said that tasting Lanson 1996 is "like gargling with razor blades", and I meant that as a compliment, since it is a yardstick 1996. At €27.50, it is also the best-value, greatest-quality 1996 on the market.* Tom Stevenson

Palo Cortado P-D-P Osborne (Sherry, €95) *Although not age-certified, this wine is certainly very old indeed, which shows in its penetrating nose as well as in its great complexity and length. It is sweetened but cannot be called sweet: a beautiful wine with which to end a meal.* Julian Jeffs QC *I totally agree, Julian. Its finish is super-intense and razor-sharp, but not what anyone would describe as sweet. An ideal pick-me-up for young parents, after a long Christmas day, with roasted chestnuts by the fire.* Tom Stevenson

Vin Santo Recinaio 1998 Sangervasio, Tuscany (Central & Southern Italy, €50) *Light, quite luminous tawny-brown hue. Blast of sweets and fruits on the nose – toffee, caramel, vanilla fudge, also some spice and herb. Silky mouthfeel, sumptuously sweet palate balanced by reasonable acidity, rich and candied but not cloying on the finish. Sheer indulgence.* Nicolas Belfrage MW

Not a vin santo fan really, but this is knockout stuff! But for the fabulous acidity, the sweetness and viscosity would be cloying. Tom Stevenson

Barbeito Boal Colheita Cask 81a 1995 (Port & Madeira, €25 per 50-cl bottle) *Pale amber colour; refined aromas reminiscent of flowers and candied peel; fine and delicate, yet pronounced with glacé fruit and chestnuts on the palate and characteristic nervy acidity on the finish. Elegant. Delicious.* Richard Mayson
I just love the acidity, and nervy it is, too. Tom Stevenson

Apóstoles Very Old Palo Cortado
González Byass (Sherry, €33) *Deep, old mahogany colour. Dry, elegant, very long and complex – the perfect apéritif for a cold winter's day.* Julian Jeffs QC
So deep, long, and powerful for such a lightly balanced Palo Cortado, this is a great sherry with a warming off-dry finish. Tom Stevenson

Grüner Veltliner Loam 2002 Kurt Angerer (Austria, €12.80) *Fine citrus and stone fruit aromas on the nose; on the palate, mandarin and a hint of residual sugar supported by perfectly ripe acidity. Persistent length.*
Dr Philipp Blom
I find your notes eerily precise, Philipp: citrus and stone fruits can indeed be found on the nose, but mandarins are even more evident on the palate and finish. Tom Stevenson

Verdad 2001 Santa Ynez Valley (California, $20) *A blend of Tempranillo, Syrah, and Grenache, with an alluring fruit aroma of cranberry, tobacco leaves, and a trace of some mysterious spice. Leans on fruit rather than oak, and finishes lean enough to work with a wide array of foods.*
Dan Berger
Lovely sappiness of fruit, very smooth, with oak that is present, but more in a tactile than an aromatic sense, and definitely understated. A beautiful wine, Dan – thanks for submitting it. Tom Stevenson

Oloroso Sibarita Aged 30 Years
Domecq (Sherry, €48) *A deep, dark, dessert oloroso with a real 30-year-old nose, softened with Pedro Ximénez but to a remarkably restrained degree, producing a multilayered flavour and enormous length. A superb wine to end a meal with, especially if the last course is Stilton cheese.* Julian Jeffs QC
Softened but not really sweetened by Pedro Ximénez, this wine has such a powerful finish. Tom Stevenson

Gewurztraminer Manigold Vineyard 2002 Peninsula Cellars, Michigan (Atlantic Northeast, $18) *A rich, glycerol-packed, low-acid, high-pH palate with high alcohol that gives the impression of a round, oily wine, but the spicy phenols from the ripe skins leave a dry, zesty finish.*
Sandra Silfven
The first world-class dry Gewurztraminer produced outside Alsace. Tom Stevenson

Muscat VT 2001 Jean-Marc & Frédéric Bernhard (Alsace, €18) *Beautifully sweet and succulent, elegant, botrytized Muscat fruit of great finesse. Drink as young as possible.* Tom Stevenson

Riesling SGN 1989 Fernand Engel (Alsace, €20) *Complex, petrolly, honeyed, mature Riesling aromas, with exceptionally fresh fruit on the palate. Its mature, not overly sweet fruit makes this Riesling an ideal accompaniment to a dish like Emil Jung's foie de canard poêlé aux pommes.* Tom Stevenson

Millésime 1996 Collard-Chardelle (Champagne, €17.10) *Extraordinarily rich, with huge flavours and massive acid. Amazing considering it is 50 per cent Meunier (plus 25/25 Chardonnay/Pinot Noir). Already has*

focus and finesse well above its station and promises great complexity, too. Tom Stevenson

Château Lezongars L'Enclos 2000
(Bordeaux, €8.75) *A wonderfully seductive, modern claret.*
David Peppercorn MW
This was a delightful island of class amid a sea of wannabes from bizarre places. Pure elegance, David.
Tom Stevenson

Côtes du Rhône Dimanche d'Octobre en Famille 1999
Domaine de la Présidente (Rhône Valley, €50) *A 100 per cent Viognier. Very rich and deep, unctuously textured, and beautifully balanced with notes of flowers, honey, and minerals.* Olivier Poels
I am not an avid fan of Condrieu, but if most overrated Condrieu were closer in style to this modest Côtes du Rhône, I might be! The oak here is fairly dominant, but "flowers, honey", and "unctuously textured" say it all, Olivier. Tom Stevenson

San Martino IGT Toscana 2000
Villa Cafaggio, Tuscany (Central & Southern Italy, €40) *Deep ruby. Some spice and tea on nose. Quite rich cherry-juice fruit on the palate, sour cherry to be precise, but without the sour. Tannins firm but unobtrusive, pleasantly chewy, red fruits including morello cherry and cranberry, slightly herbaceous, hints of coffee and tobacco at back, and long sweet fruit on the finish.* Nicolas Belfrage MW
Incredibly deep, well structured, and classy, with concentrated morello cherry fruit perfectly balanced by grippy tannins. Tom Stevenson

Antique Oloroso Fernando de Castilla (Sherry, €24) *The colour of light mahogany, dry to the palate, it is long and complex. It has not had any of the modern treatments, such as ultracooling, to prevent its throwing a*

deposit if kept for a year or two, so it might throw one. But who would not drink it right away?* Julian Jeffs QC
A bone-dry oloroso that makes a brilliant apéritif. Tom Stevenson

Fonseca Quinta do Panascal 1991
(Port & Madeira, €35) *Opaque colour, youthful purple rim; closed, dense, and intense, needing time to open up; rich and fleshy, backed by big, tight, ripe tannins. Massive wine. Great length and depth.* Richard Mayson
Huge, but beautifully balanced, with voluptuous fruit. Tom Stevenson

Viognier 2002 Graf Hardegg (Austria, €33) *Beeswax and exotic fruit on the nose; on the palate, surprisingly elegant and well defined. Wood still prominent on the finish, marrying with beautiful varietal fruit.* Dr Philipp Blom
One of the most elegant and gracefully poised renditions of this grape I have ever tasted. Drink now to 2006. Tom Stevenson

The Foundry Syrah 2001 Chris Williams (South Africa, R145)
A fruit-and-spices-packed (black cherries, liquorice, cloves) Syrah, with exceptional, filled-out complexity and length. Needs a year or two cellaring. John & Erica Platter
And great acidity, too. Drink 2005 to 2008. Tom Stevenson

The Chocolate Block 2002
Boekenhoutskloof (South Africa, R100) *A 1997 from Marc Kent announced that South Africans could look forward to proper import-substitution Syrah. Now he has flayed followers with a chocolaty Grenache/Syrah/Cabernet Sauvignon combo spiced with a shot of Viognier: juicy, limpid, savoury-sweet, and forthright.* John & Erica Platter
Varietally seamless, with toasty-chocolaty oak. Very classy. Tom Stevenson

Solera Cream Sherry St Julian, Michigan (Atlantic Northeast, $15)
This is Michigan's most-awarded wine

and winner of the Jefferson Cup in 2002, a competition run by Doug Frost for all the winners of other American contests. It has a deep-amber hue, with concentrated butterscotch, pecan, and hazelnut aromas, leading to full, rich flavours on the palate. The solera system was developed in 1975 and yields 1,200 cases per year. It is 100 per cent Niagara. Sandra Silfven

The more times I taste this wine, the more impressed I am with its quality, and the more amazed I am that this is a pure Niagara, yet has no foxiness. To mimic so cleverly the style of a wine made an ocean away is amazing enough, but to do it with Niagara has more to do with alchemy than oenology. Inevitably it was outclassed in the company of authentic sherry of the superpremium ilk of Fernando de Castilla Antique Oloroso, Gonzáles Byass Apóstoles Very Old Palo Cortado, Domecq Oloroso Sibarita Aged 30 Years, and Osborne Palo Cortado P-D-P, but St Julian's hallmark long, sweet, toasty finish was not made to look silly. Tom Stevenson

Barolo Bussia Dardi le Rose 1999

Poderi Colla, Piemonte (Northern Italy, €35) Nothing flash about this yardstick Barolo from one of the finest sites in Monforte and made in the traditional manner. Typical medium-depth colour with brick-oranging towards the rim; ethereal rose and violet on the nose, with hints of goudron, leather, and spice. Firm but not excessive tannic structure, mainly grape tannins (no new small oak employed) overlaid by sweet, almost porty fruit that carries through and lasts. Nicolas Belfrage MW

I get the alcohol in the fruit, Nick (even though it is 'only' 13.5 per cent), but not the porty character. Perhaps it is a combination of the alcohol and puckering tannins? The leather is there, too. How long does it need? A good seven years, perhaps? Tom Stevenson

Cuvée Merret Fitzrovia Rosé 2000

RidgeView Estate (Great Britain, £18.95) Delicious balance of all the elements — fruit, acidity, and flavour — bound up in a gentle mouth-filling mousse. Sparkling wine for enjoying! Stephen Skelton MW

Totally agree, Stephen, but it is not only for enjoying now — it has the capacity to retain its freshness for at least 18–24 months, during which it will get silkier and silkier. Tom Stevenson

Château de Roques Sauvignon Blanc 2002 (Bordeaux, €6) Fruity and full in the mouth without any 'cattiness'. Beautifully made.
David Peppercorn MW

Could not agree more, David. Absolutely delicious. Tom Stevenson

Château Palvié 2001 Gaillac
(Southwest France, €8) Translucent garnet appearance. Spicy nose (Syrah), redcurrants and blackcurrants (from the Braucol or Fer Servadou) carrying through to the palate. A nice medium-weight wine to accompany grills or roast fowl. Paul Strang

Absolutely right: blackberries and fresh ground black pepper — wonderful! Tom Stevenson

Yarden Katzrin 2000 Golan Heights
Winery (Israel, NIS 160) Ripe, bold, and concentrated, with still-tight tannins reflecting its youth, but with the kind of balance and structure that bode very well for the future. A blend of 88 per cent Cabernet Sauvignon, 9 per cent Merlot, and 3 per cent Cabernet Franc, this remarkably full-bodied wine shows currants, black cherries, and purple plums along with spices and smoky wood, all distinctive and well crafted. Approachable now but needs time to reveal its elegance. Best 2005–12, perhaps longer. Daniel Rogov

A class act, Rogov, but the wine needs time for the oak to give way to the fruit (of which there is plenty). Truly outstanding. Tom Stevenson

Côtes du Rhône Rasteau 2001

Domaine Gourt de Mautens (Rhône Valley, €25) *Made from very low yields, this Rasteau possesses extraordinary intensity and concentration. Jérôme Bressy has improved, with this vintage, the finesse of his wine. The result is fantastic, with a perfect balance between fruit, acidity, and oak. Medium- to full-bodied, the wine shows a velvety texture, finishing very long and pure.* Olivier Poels
One of those rare combinations of intensity and finesse that occasionally occurs in a modest appellation. Tom Stevenson

La Chapelle San Roch Blanc 2002

La Préceptorie de Centernach, Vin de Pays du Val d'Agly (Languedoc-Roussillon, €8) *Tactful oaking gives a New World character. Lemony nose with spring flowers. Plenty of grass on the palate, with good acidity. Long finish. Would suit spicy fish dishes.* Paul Strang
Would have preferred less noticeable oak, but there is no denying this is a standout. Tom Stevenson

Marselan 2002 Devereux, Vin de Pays de l'Aude (Vins de Pays & Vins de Table, €4.50) *Quite deep colour; soft, ripe, plummy fruit on nose and palate, with a touch of spice. Undemanding, soft tannins; easy to drink.* Rosemary George MW
More winey, more acidity, and more raspberry than the Domaine du Chapître (the other wine made from this new cross), this leans closer to Grenache than Cabernet, yet is reminiscent of neither. Tom Stevenson

Premium 2000 Quinta de Pancas, Estremadura (Portugal, €45) *Deep, dark centre, thin purple rim; dense peppery-spicy nose if still a little closed and surly at this stage; rich, superripe and impressively well structured on the palate. Fine and well-focused blend of Touriga Nacional and Syrah.* Richard Mayson

Surly, Richard, I like it! Although it does not know whether it is supposed to show its fruit or oak at the moment. Like a teenager will have the confidence to be his own person after a few years, so will this. And in 5–10 years, it will be a classic. Tom Stevenson

Aurum Grüner Veltliner 2002 Josef Ehmoser (Austria, €14) *Experiments with barrique-fermented Grüner Veltliner have variable results, but, with its buttery richness and depth and its lovely toasty length, this example shows that Grüner Veltliner and wood can marry beautifully.* Dr Philipp Blom
I think the wood has tamed rather than married the Grüner Veltliner, Philipp, but it is a very voluptuous wine. Although the Grüner Veltliner ages very well, this wine deserves to be drunk as youthful as possible. Tom Stevenson

Cabernet Sauvignon 2000

Bookwalter (Pacific Northwest, $28) *In 2000 Bookwalter has made its best Cabernet to date. It is dense, dark, and packed with powerful fruit, muscled around carefully balanced oak, and buttressed with spicy acid.* Paul Gregutt
Phew! Pretty good, Paul. Does not hit all at once (as so many New World wines do); it seems almost "so what?", then flavours creep up, and that excellent acid provides a very long finish. Drink 3–5 years. Tom Stevenson

Koonunga Hill Shiraz Cabernet 2002 Penfolds (Australia, A$15) *A top vintage for this consistent-value red, a junior model of the Penfold red-wine style. Deep colour; sweet berry/plum and light herb/spice aromas; fruit-driven and with excellent depth of flavour for the price. And it will live happily for 15+ years.* Huon Hooke
I am sure it will last 15-odd years, but the complexity it will gain would not outweigh its current freshness and creaminess of youthful fruit. I love this wine now and would drink it over the next 2–3 years. Tom Stevenson

Black Creek Chardonnay 2003 De Bortoli (Australia, A$15) *Cool-climate Tumbarumba and warmer-grown Hunter grapes are blended here. Lively acidity lifts this modestly priced Chardonnay to greater heights. The aromas of stone fruits, citrus, and herb show some lees complexities and it is fresh, zippy, firm, and very drinkable.* Huon Hooke
So nice to drink such a fresh and lively, unassuming Australian Chardonnay. Good acids are highlighted by a touch of residual CO_2, to provide the finishing touch. Tom Stevenson

Lirac Cuvée de la Reine des Bois 2001 Domaine de la Mordorée (Rhône Valley, €20) *Notice the appellation. This 2001 Lirac is an incredible lesson for other proprietors. It offers a deep, opaque ruby colour and a fantastic nose of black fruits, herbs, and oak flavours. Full-bodied, with excellent fruit depth, it should have 10 or more years of life.* Olivier Poels
This is definitely a Lirac to age. It reminds me of the good old days of Castel Oualou. Like the 1978, which was still drinking beautifully the last time I tried it. A great selection, Olivier. Tom Stevenson

Curious Grape Pinot Blanc 2001 New Wave Wines (Great Britain, £6.99) *Although only 10.5 per cent alcohol, this has the mouthfeel of a 12–13 per cent wine. Just off-dry with a really long persistent finish.* Stephen Skelton MW
It is the acidity that gives away the fact that this is not a 12–13 per cent wine, and it is the acidity that is the making of this wine. Lovely, mouth-watering – not Curious at all! Tom Stevenson

Fries Vineyard Semillon 2001 L'Ecole No. 41 (Pacific Northwest, $20) *Fries has traditionally provided grapes for L'Ecole's best Semillon (of three that they make). The wine is so big and bursting with ripe and delicious fruit that it makes you wonder why so few wineries bother with Semillon.* Paul Gregutt
I am not sure what is bigger, the oak or the fruit, but Marty (owner-winemaker) never uses a matchstick when a club will do. Tom Stevenson

Syrah 2001 Januik (Pacific Northwest, $30) *A stunning wine, displaying immense purple/black density, scents of mint, sweet berry, and a smooth, ripe, voluptuous mouthfeel.* Paul Gregutt
You missed the coffee! Washington might have wiped the floor with Bordeaux (Wine Report 2004), but if you try this side by side with Craggy Range 2001 Le Sol Syrah, New Zealand would blitz Washington. That is not to say the Januik is not a tremendous wine, because it is. And vive la différence! Tom Stevenson

Tocai Friulano 2002 Channing Daughters, New York (Atlantic Northeast, $22) *Totally unique in the northeast. Explosive pink grapefruit/pink peppercorn/floral aromas, while surprisingly soft and round on the palate. It is the wine other winemakers talk about.* Sandra Silfven
Spot on, Sandy, and by the time I tasted it, intense grapefruit flavours were searing through the palate, too. I have never tasted a Tocai Friulano (Sauvignonasse) quite like it at any level of ripeness, which makes me wonder if the vines planted here are, in fact, Tocai Friulano. Whatever the variety is, this is one heck of a distinctive wine. Tom Stevenson

Pinot Blanc 2002 Robert Sinskey, Napa Valley (California, $18 per half-bottle) *Delicate white wine with bright melon-pear and citrus fruit, with a crisp finish. Made only in half-bottles and magnums.* Dan Berger
Wonderfully fresh, Dan. Tom Stevenson

Syrah 2001 Burrowing Owl (Canada, C$25) *Winemaker Bill Dyer brings a Napa perspective to this wine grown in a cooler climate. Deep purple-black colour with a nose of blackberries and blackcurrants; bitter chocolate and spicy blackberry on the palate; mouth-filling and rounded with a tannic lift on the finish.* Tony Aspler
I cannot argue with that, Tony, this British Columbia Syrah does indeed have a Napa perspective. A bit riper and more intense, and it could even have been grown in Washington. But it is delightful as it is. Tom Stevenson

Château de Cruzeau Blanc 2001 (Bordeaux, €9) *This wine has all the intensity of the vintage, with lovely crisp, spicy acidity. A delicious wine at a fraction of the price of the major classified areas.* David Peppercorn MW
Heady Sauvignon Blanc aromas followed by crisp, pungent, passion-fruit flavours. Tom Stevenson

Mâcon La Roche Vineuse Vieilles Vignes 2001 Domaine Olivier Merlin (Burgundy, €8.40) *Clean as a whistle, fresh, and flowery, this 2001 may turn out to have more staying power than the lusher 2002. Meanwhile, it is delicious now.* Clive Coates MW
Serious Mâcon. Keep 2–3 years. Tom Stevenson

Clos Saint-Jean 2000 Cahors (Southwest France, €20) *Brilliant ruby colour. A bouquet of cherries and damsons. Splendid attack with an avalanche of red fruits. Almonds too. Nice acidity and tannins already well integrated. No detectable oak. The finish needs time to develop.* Paul Strang
Needs 3–4 years, but should be splendid. Tom Stevenson

Collio Bianco Vigne 2002 Zuani, Friuli (Northern Italy, €17) *The oak-fermented version of this wine may have more going on, but it is the purity of the fruit character of this Friulian blend that seduces. A cocktail of fruity aromas greets the nose, both common (apple, pear) and more exotic (pineapple, mango). The palate repeats the experience with a dry sweetness and light viscosity that further entice. Delicious and moreish.* Nicolas Belfrage MW
Tastes like Sauvignon Blanc to me, Nick, and pretty good in an assertive, not-too-obvious way. Tom Stevenson

Moric 2001 Velich (Austria, €37) *On the nose, smoky and concentrated, ripe tannins, and density reminiscent of a Côte Rôtie, with notes of dark berries and roasted meat. Extract sweetness on the length.* Dr Philipp Blom
High acids accentuate the fruit, particularly on the finish. Some pepperiness, but this should disappear. Excellent, and I hear the 2002 is even better. Tom Stevenson

Rapsani Epilegmenos Reserve 1998 Tsantali (Greece, €11.50) *Rich and spicy, with sweet, warm fruit. Still showing youth on the chunky tannic backbone. Generously oaked with toasty age-worthy character.* Nico Manessis
Lovely, fresh, clean, sweet fruit. It would be interesting to follow the development of this wine over the next three years, as its tannins are refined and the fruit takes on more finesse. Tom Stevenson

Grand Vin 2000 Domaine du Castel (Israel, NIS 160) *Still muscular and with firm tannins due to its youth, but already showing the promise of elegance, this intense wine offers multiple layers of black fruits along with an appealing earthy herbal note and a long, spicy finish. The wine is approachable now but will be best between 2005 and 2012.* Daniel Rogov
I would not want to drink this before 2005, but I am not so sure about it being at its best towards the end of your potential longevity window, Rogov. From the tannin alone, it will certainly

be alive and well in the year 2012, but will it still have enough fruit? Whatever, this is an excellent wine, and curiously not unlike the big, thick, tannic wines of southwest France. Tom Stevenson

Albariño 2002 Havens, Carneros (California, $24) *Exotic peach, herb, and lime aroma, with pear and spice notes. Lower-alcohol and perfectly balanced dry white wine from a grape better known in Spain and Portugal.* Dan Berger

It does not have the extraordinary mélange of simplicity and finesse that a top Albariño from Rías Baixas has, but it can be compared favourably with some of the Alvarinho (the Portuguese name) wines from Vinho Verde. And it is refreshing to see the pursuit of varietal purity without the quest for high sugar levels getting in the way. Tom Stevenson

Pinot Gris 2002 Navarro, Anderson Valley (California, $16) *Dramatic fruit.* Dan Berger

A delicious, fresh purity of fruit, with 100 per cent natural structure. Tom Stevenson

Eagle Tree Muscat 2002 Jost (Canada, C$14.99) *Jost produces a bewildering 37 labels, but this is its triumph. Spicy and aromatic, it has a lovely lifted nose and an evenly balanced flavour of orange and carnations; very dry in an Alsace style.* Tony Aspler

You are right about the equal balance of orange and carnations, Tony, and I do like it, but I think it would be even better if it had more orange and fewer carnations! Tom Stevenson

Marqués de Casa Concha Cabernet Sauvignon 2001 Concha y Toro, Chile (Chile & Argentina, CLP 18,000) *Very deep in colour, with an intense, introverted nose of tobacco, cedarwood, and classic blackcurrant. On the palate, big tannins mask intense,* deep, ripe plum fruit, but with the necessary balancing acidity. Rather an old-fashioned style, but a great wine that will last well. Christopher Fielden

Call me old-fashioned, but I much prefer this understated richness to the exaggerated cassis that some Chilean wines have. I like the acidity — a quality often overlooked in red wines — and can see this evolving gracefully over the next five years or so. Tom Stevenson

Sangiovese 2002 Maglieri (Australia, A$24) *This Sangiovese has a rich red-purple hue and a vibrant black-cherry, sweet-plum aroma with a hint of coconut. It has good depth of properly ripe flavour balanced by supple tannins on a clean and quite stylish finish. I like its intensity and balance.* Huon Hooke

And I like the ratio of acidity to tannin, which gives this very youthful wine a crispness and length. Tom Stevenson

Marselan 2002 Christophe Clipet, Domaine du Chapitre, Institut National de la Recherche Agronomique, Villeneuve-lès-Maguelonne, France (Grape Varieties, €6) *Intense black ruby colour, very attractive. Aromas of pepper and very ripe fruits — plum, fruit brandy (kirsch and raspberry), and cocoa. Fruity and spicy on the palate, with developing flavours of cocoa and pear brandy. A rounded and silky wine.* Dr François Lefort

Deep colour, floral and soft-fruit aromas, full raspberry-blackcurranty fruit on the palate, a touch smoky, and reminiscent, in parts, of Carmenère. A straightforward yet substantial wine, and amazing value. Tom Stevenson

Hildegard 2001 Au Bon Climat, Santa Maria Valley (California, $35) *Ripe peach/apricot notes with a rich, layered entry and a creamy texture, yet with lower alcohol and good acid. This blend of Pinot Blanc, Pinot Gris, and Aligoté*

is an effort by Jim Clendenen to re-create the original wine style of Corton-Charlemagne that was made from AD 800 to 1759, using grapes picked at lower sugars, a wine with "the unctuous character that Chardonnay cannot achieve". Dan Berger

Sorry, but Corton-Charlemagne it ain't – not even close. I do not see how "grapes picked at lower sugars" can produce a 13.5 per cent wine. It is much too hefty, it lacks acidity, and the fruit should always dominate the oak, not the other way around. I am surprised that you rate such an alcoholic bruiser so highly, Dan, but the project is interesting, hence its inclusion as one of this year's more unusual wines. Tom Stevenson

Solaris Passerillé 2002 Jean-Laurent Spring, Station Fédérale de Recherches de Changins, Nyon, Switzerland (Grape Varieties, not available commercially) *Beautiful greenish golden colour. Honey and dry fruits, well balanced, and sweet with a long finish.* Dr François Lefort

More fascinating than spectacular. Lacking botrytis character, the nose needs some bottle-age development, and the honeyed fruit-salad sweetness tends to cloy at the moment, but this should settle down and assume some complexity over the next couple of years. Tom Stevenson

Château de Pez 1999 (Bordeaux, €26) *This newly promoted cru exceptionnelle, owned by Roederer, shows lovely dense mature fruit and harmony and is full-bodied for 1999, beginning to drink well.* David Peppercorn MW

I bought the 2000 Château de Pez in preference to the 1999, but this is a toasty-cedary delight, with more than enough tannins to keep it going. Tom Stevenson

Domaine de Merchien 2001 Coteaux du Quercy (Southwest France, €6) *Bright ruby, with a powerful nose*

of crushed fruits. The high Cabernet Franc content provides rich curranty flavours backed by the power of Malbec and Tannat. A big wine at a little price. Paul Strang

Fruity-floral with a persistence that can only be Tannat. Tom Stevenson

Tinto Lerma Crianza 2000 Bodegas La Colegiada, Ribera del Arlanza (Spain, €5.50) *Slightly closed nose, but lovely deep, dark fruit apparent, with a tender, almost chewy-fruit texture and hints of nutmeg on the nose. Firm tannins softening as the wine develops in the glass to a long finish. This is Ribera del Duero quality at a country-wine price.* John Radford

More warm and spicy than fine, but I would not argue over the value! Tom Stevenson

Conde de Vimioso 2001 Falua, Vinho Regional Ribatejano (Portugal, €4) *Black-cherry fruit with a touch of vanilla and spice. A wine that tastes much more expensive than it is.* Richard Mayson

Paradoxically chunky-chic with a touch of floral finesse. Tom Stevenson

Duet Riserva 2000 Edi Simčič, Slovenia (Eastern & Southeastern Europe, SIT 8,500) *Still a baby of a wine, but so impressive. It is packed with rich, ripe black cherry and cassis fruit. Beautifully structured with a fine-grained tannin backbone and balanced acidity. Lots of vanilla oak at present but this will settle.* Dr Caroline Gilby MW

Black cherry, yes, but more (fresh fruit) blackberry than (concentrated) cassis for me, although there is a little of that, too. Definitely needs a year or three. Tom Stevenson

Cuvée Los Abuelos 2001 La Terre Inconnue, Vin de Table (Languedoc-Roussillon, €26) *Deepest garnet, but brilliant and translucent. Romanesque legs, massive fruit and herbs on the nose, carrying through to a powerful*

and very complex palate. *Persistent, long finish. A blockbuster equally easy to love or hate.* Paul Strang
Seems like a beautiful wine in a tasting line-up, Paul, but it really cloys if you try to drink it, and, let's be honest, it is not surprising considering the sweetness of this red wine. There is at least 15 g of residual sugar per litre here – I know, I tested it! Tom Stevenson

Ktima Alpha White 2003 Alpha Estate (Greece, €12) *Sauvignon Blanc with fully ripe fruit and depth on the palate balanced by brisk acidity. Terrific length and broad grapey character. An impressive newcomer.* Nico Manessis
High alcohol (14.4 per cent), crisp Sauvignon, with broad but deep finish. Weird or not? Tom Stevenson

Chateau Kefraya 2001 (Lebanon, LL 20,000) *From the makers of Comte de M comes a pleasing blend of Cabernet Sauvignon, Mourvèdre, Carignan, and Grenache. Medium-bodied, it has impressive length with bashful, layered notes of raspberries, pepper, and thyme. Great value.* Michael Karam
The oak is not bashful either, Michael, but there is plenty of deliciously clean, really quite classy fruit backing it up. Excellent. Tom Stevenson

Viognier 2003 Trivento, Argentina (Chile & Argentina, AP 8) *Subtle blend of ripe apricots and grapefruit. Good easy drinking, an excellent example of the variety for the price.* Christopher Fielden
The nose is still showing cool fermentation aromas, but these will be subsumed before this book gets to print, and there is plenty of ripe peach flesh waiting to show through, particularly on the finish. Tom Stevenson

Sauvignon Blanc 2003 Gravitas (New Zealand, NZ$29) *A gentle yet powerful expression of Marlborough Sauvignon Blanc.* Bob Campbell MW
Not so gentle when tasted after the Château de Roques, Bob, and this has all the 'cattiness' that David Peppercorn delights in the absence of in that wine, but it is an attractive cattiness. Tom Stevenson

Domaine du Clos Perche 2001 Coteaux du Languedoc St-Christol (Languedoc-Roussillon, €3) *Pale-ish pink on the rim, nicely translucent; absence of legs suggests short maceration; plenty of crushed fruit and perfumes of the garrigue on the nose; smoky and spicy in the mouth, light Mourvèdre character; easy-drinking, outdoor style of wine.* Paul Strang
Well, there were legs on mine! Not a great wine, but only an idiot would expect class at €3 a bottle, which is amazing value. Tom Stevenson

Spätburgunder R Auslese Trocken 1999 Bernhart (Germany, €33.50) *Full-bodied and powerful burgundy-type Spätburgunder, with great mineral extract and an aroma of black berries. Aged in 100 per cent new barriques.* Michael Schmidt
Just a tad of VA-lift I would have preferred not to notice, but undeniably charming all the same. Tom Stevenson

Laumersheimer Kirschgarten Dornfelder Trocken Barrique 1999 Knipser (Germany, €15.50) *Great intensity of cherry fruit with herbs and spices; slightly smoky. Velvety texture, elegant, long finish.* Michael Schmidt
As dark as night, with floral fruit. Almost Malbec in its floral-violety aromas, although a completely different, much lighter structure. And yes, it is indeed velvety, elegant, and long. Tom Stevenson

Recioto della Valpolicella Classico TB 2000 Tommaso Bussola, Veneto (Northern Italy, €50) *This wine, from grapes dried for five months, in the process losing over half of their weight and much liquid, hits the nose with a*

blast of morello cherry fruit, cherries under alcohol. Very rich on the palate but with a gentle bitterness at the back that cuts through the sweetness and prevents cloying. Notes of herbs and spices intermingle with fruit and alcohol to effect a delicious headiness. No wonder it consistently scores in the high 90s with Parker and other pundits. Nicolas Belfrage MW
Port on toast! Tom Stevenson

Roncùs Bianco Vecchie Vigne 1999

Roncùs, Friuli (Northern Italy, €24) *A great blend, for its innate class and its uncommon elegance, for its complexity without loss of freshness, because it succeeds in being profoundly, intimately, proudly Friulian – indeed, of the Collio. Decisive attack, dry, clean, which, though subtle, immediately states its case and reveals the solid and determined character of the wine.* Franco Ziliani
I like this wine, Franco, but not quite as much as you. It is very big for Friuli, but it does not quite have the structure to support the alcohol. However, it does make a statement you cannot ignore. Tom Stevenson

Sangiovese 2001 Boirà, Italy (Organic & Biodynamic Wines; export only, £5.49)

A Marche producer with the confidence to barrel-age Sangiovese without drowning it in oak. Monty Waldin
Sweet, simple, and tasty. And if you had not said the contrary, I would have thought this had been made with more than a handful of medium-toasted oak chips! Tom Stevenson

Monte Ducay Cariñena Crianza 2000 Bodegas Gran Ducay (Spain, €2.50)

Ruby-red colour with musky soft fruit on the nose and a delicious sweet-fruit definition on the palate – simply delicious. John Radford
Fuller and heavier than my definition of "simply delicious", John, but it is a bloody good food wine at a ridiculously cheap price. Tom Stevenson

Cabernet Sauvignon Reserve 2001

Flam (Israel, NIS 130) *Deep royal purple/garnet, with excellent extraction but still showing a remarkable softness, this is going to be another conquest for the Flam brothers. With excellent balance between wood, tannins, and fruit, the wine is distinctly Mediterranean, showing traditional Cabernet blackcurrants as its dominating flavour, but this is well set off by black cherries, spices, and generous hints of black olives and leather. Drink now to 2009.* Daniel Rogov
Not a great wine but a very nice one, with clean fruit and fine, grippy tannins. Already nicely together. Tom Stevenson

Syrah 2002 Callaghan, Arizona (Other US States, $18)

With enough black pepper to taste like a peppermill, this tannic wine could be off-putting, but it is also dense and almost seductive. Doug Frost MW
And just enough sweetness on the finish to balance all of that, Doug. For Arizona, it is mind-bogglingly good! Tom Stevenson

Norton 2001 Stone Hill, Missouri (Other US States, $18)

Norton's glass-staining ability is in full view, alongside the black plum and cherry notes and slightly meaty aromas. The mouth is extravagantly juicy, fairly tannic and tart at the end, with bittersweet chocolate hints. Doug Frost MW
Fuller, fatter, and softer than the 2000, with so much colour that it appears to stain the glass when swirling the wine around. Stone Hill Norton definitely rates as the most consistent, internationally acceptable quality from a native grape. Tom Stevenson

The Underarm Syrah 2002 Red Rock (New Zealand, NZ$25)

Christened after an infamous underarm bowling incident when

Australia beat New Zealand at cricket in an unsporting manner, this wine promises to raise a few Aussie eyebrows, although its cool-climate and rather peppery characters nod more in the direction of the Rhône than the Barossa. A second label of Craggy Range, a new winery that is making waves with its often-spectacular wines. Bob Campbell MW
Although this tastes like all the rough edges that were rejected to make Craggy Range Le Sol Syrah so smooth, there is nothing green or unpleasant. In fact, the more you taste it, the smoother it becomes. Tom Stevenson

Gewurztraminer 2003 Lawson's Dry Hills (New Zealand, NZ$22) *Dead dry with high (14 per cent) alcohol and an exquisite purity of Turkish delight and rose-petal flavours. Worth waiting for.* Bob Campbell MW
A very nice, elegant Gewurztraminer, this is definitely one of the best New World examples of this grape, but it has been made in too much of a pretty-pretty style. However, having taken this step, hopefully the winemaker, Mike Just, lives up to his name, and goes the extra mile to produce a totally natural Gewurztraminer, with no adjustments and completely dry. If he needs any encouragement, he should taste Gewurztraminer Manigold Vineyard 2002 Peninsula Cellars or, at the very least, speak to its winemaker, Bryan Ulrich, who has gone that extra mile (and could do with some company!). Tom Stevenson

Crémant du Jura Brut NV Richard Delay (Jura & Savoie, €5.50) *Greenish with a fine mousse, the nose has appley Chardonnay notes together with great autolytic character. Lovely bubble texture on the palate, spicy apples, and toasty, with a nice acid structure and great length. An example of the most normal wine* style to emerge from the Jura, it offers stunning value.* Wink Lorch
Are we tasting the same wine? I am not questioning your palate, Wink, but I am questioning whether our bottles were disgorged at the same time, because there is no toastiness on my wine. Mind you, I cannot disagree with your conclusion: it does offer stunning value. It is not a great sparkling wine, nor is it pretending to be champagne. My bottle is very fresh, the mousse far more assertive than your "lovely bubble texture" would suggest, with the appley notes you mention, and very clean, but the finish merely shows reasonable, rather than great, length. But give it another nine months post-disgorgement ageing, and we could be tasting the same thing! Tom Stevenson

Pago de Campean Barrica 2001 Co-op El Soto, Tierra del Vino de Zamora (Spain, €2.80) *Big, bright, ripe fruit on the nose, replicated on the palate with an enormous structure, tannins, and extraction. The concentration and development belie this ridiculous low price.* John Radford
Pure rusticana, but absolutely clean. Big, thick, and soupy in an immensely drinkable way. Tom Stevenson

Finca Sanguijuela Acinipo 2001 Bodega Friedrich Schatz (Spain, €30) *Like many north Europeans on holiday in Spain, the Lemberger reveals assets it never displays at home in Württemberg – a lovely spicy warmth with some dark, concentrated fruit, quite high extract. The musky fruit finishes it off with style.* John Radford
You are absolutely right about the musky fruit on the finish. When I picked it up on the nose, I thought it was an oxidative characteristic, but the same aroma on the finish was definitely musky. In fact, I would say that there is either the odd Muscat vine in their vineyard, and they do not

realize it, or they have deliberately cut the wine with some Muscat for effect. Tom Stevenson

Chardonnay Riserva 2000 Marjan Simčič, Slovenia (Eastern & Southeastern Europe, SIT 2,640) *Former rock star Marjan Simčič describes this as "a Tyson white wine", and it is certainly not shy. Full toast and sesame aromas, with nutty complexity and plenty of weighty fruit and creamy texture.* Dr Caroline Gilby MW *Exclusively for lovers of fat, toasty Chardonnay.* Tom Stevenson

Selection 2002 Massaya (Lebanon, LL 13,000) *Poised to set new standards for Lebanese wines in this class, this blend of Cinsault, Syrah, Cabernet Sauvignon, and Grenache produces notes of plums, berries, pepper, and chocolate with impressive length. It is a joy at the price and bettered only by the 1999 (if you can find any).* Michael Karam *Definitely plums on the nose, Michael, and if you ignore the psychological influence of colour association, there is apple purée, too. The Syrah seems dominant at the moment, and I can see it developing into cassis and coffee with time.* Tom Stevenson

Pinot Gris 2003 Lurton, Argentina (Chile & Argentina, AP 10) *A Dolly Parton of a wine, with a lot up front. Full nose of melons and guavas, on the palate a tropical fruit salad. Not a wine to tangle with for long.* Christopher Fielden *This might be top-heavy, but it is too fat and weighty for Dolly Parton. Nearer Pinot Gris than Pinot Grigio, and the 13.5 per cent alcohol adds to the illusion of spice on the palate. Definitely a food wine.* Tom Stevenson

Huailai Reserve Cabernet Sauvignon 2002 Dragon Seal, China (Asia, Rmb 120) *Innovative winery consistently showing, through carefully managed viticultural and winemaking practices, just what can be achieved with the classic varieties in this part of the world. Good structure and good varietal definition.* Denis Gastin *Soft, smoky, fruit-bush fruit.* Tom Stevenson

Idylle Vin de Savoie Arbin Mondeuse Prestige 2002 Domaine de l'Idylle (Jura & Savoie, €8) *A deep and youthful ruby colour of medium-full intensity. The nose shows a rich fruit-cake character with plenty of spice. Tannins are fairly obvious but have been handled well and are balanced out by creamy-textured rich fruit. It can age for a couple of years and is a good example of modern-style Mondeuse that allows the Syrah-like fruit to sing through.* Wink Lorch *A lot of words for a decent Mondeuse that should not be broached for at least two years, but it will be worth the wait.* Tom Stevenson

Gran Malbec 1999 Terrazas de los Andes, Argentina (Chile & Argentina, AP 100) *A really great Malbec, with tobacco and liquorice on the nose. On the palate, ripe blackberries, with their seeds, soft Morocco leather, and black pepper.* Christopher Fielden *Too much oak, but very good fruit underneath.* Tom Stevenson

Yarden Katzrin Chardonnay 2000 Golan Heights Winery (Israel, NIS 85) *One of the very best Chardonnays produced in Israel. Aged for 10 months sur lie and unfiltered, this full-bodied, deep-gold wine has layers of aromas and flavours that include poached pears, apples, and passion fruit, all nicely reflecting the influence of the oak. Intense and concentrated, the wine also shows tantalizing hints of spices and vanilla, with a long finish yielding a gentle hint of tobacco smoke. Drink now to 2010.* Daniel Rogov *I would be going wild about a quality such as this from Israel 15 years ago,* but the wine world has moved on and I find it rather simple – lifted Chardonnay fruit with far too much oak, although it is better than a couple of Chardonnays that deserve a place in the Top 100 because of their origin, so it might just make it. Tom Stevenson

Chardonnay Goud 1999 Wijnkasteel Genoels-Elderen, Belgium (Belgium, Netherlands & Scandinavia, €21) *The prestige wine of the estate. Nearly exotic, with 13.5 per cent alcohol and 100 per cent vinification in wood. Deep gold-yellow, intense nose of ripe apple, citrus, and some smoke from the toasted barrels. Rich and at the same time subtle on the palate, with the sweetness of the fruit, acidity, and minerals. Very harmonious. The wood is well integrated. Good length. Still young, needs some bottle maturation. Reminiscent of a Meursault or a Puligny.* Gert Crum
Definitely superior to Genoels-Elderen's Chardonnay Blauw, but very oaky, very international – although that in itself is a compliment for a Belgian wine. Tom Stevenson

Swallowtail Fetească Neagră Gran Riserva 2001 Vinarte, Romania (Eastern & Southeastern Europe, 380,000 lei) *The Romanians have great hopes for Fetească Neagră as their signature grape, and this is the best so far, produced from high-density plantings way above the norm for Romania. Dense dried black-cherry fruit and a touch of coffee and leather, backed by powerful tannins and firm acidity. Built to keep.* Dr Caroline Gilby MW
Could do with a higher ratio of acidity to tannin, but it is the best example of this grape I have tasted to date, and it does give hope about the sort of quality that might be achieved two or three vintages down the line. Tom Stevenson

Chateau Ksara 2000 (Lebanon, LL 15,000) *Cabernet Sauvignon, Merlot, and Petit Verdot. A youngish but correct wine, it is surprisingly long, medium-bodied with discreet yet heady notes of fruit, especially blackcurrants with hints of spice. Not overwhelming. Sweet and tannic with good acidity.* Michael Karam
Pure blackcurrants on the nose. A bit simplistic, but clean and very fresh, with enough grippy tannins to accompany food. Tom Stevenson

Finger Lakes Riesling Reserve 2002 Heron Hill, New York (Atlantic Northeast, $25) *Sleek and lovely. Bracing acidity supports an exciting abundance of lime, melon, and mineral flavours. Ultra-dry to the point of being austere, but enhanced by enough fruit and minerals to keep it from being tart.* Sandra Silfven
Much richer than Heron Hill's painting-by-numbers Ingle Vineyard Riesling from the same vintage. Tom Stevenson

Reserve Dalliance Sparkling Chardonnay 1998 Hungerford Hill (Australia, A$26) *Hungerford Hill is a reborn company and it is extremely rare to find sparkling wine of this calibre from a smaller producer in Australia, let alone an ostensibly new one. This bubbly overdelivers in a big way and has real class: layers of toast, hazelnut, bread, and Vegemite-yeast autolysis complexities, with fine balance and plenty of nuance on the palate. It shows considerable age without sacrificing delicacy or subtlety.* Huon Hooke
If Bollinger made a blanc de blancs it would be something like this in every respect except acidity and age. The acidity would be much higher, and it would take two or three times as long to reach this stage in its evolution. Tumbarumba is starting to live up to its potential, but it still has a long way to go. Tom Stevenson

Irancy Vieilles Vignes 2002 Domaine
Anita, Stéphanie & Jean-Pierre Colinot
(Burgundy, €9.50) *A crisp, youthful,
medium-bodied, elegant wine. Very
petits fruits rouges in flavour. Can
be kept.* Clive Coates MW
*Very perfumed. Can be kept
(lovely acids), but will it get better?*
Tom Stevenson

Chardonnay Blauw 2000
Wijnkasteel Genoels-Elderen, Belgium
(Belgium, Netherlands & Scandinavia,
€9.90) *The 'face' of the estate. One-
third vinified in wood. Light gold-yellow,
complex nose, with vanilla, ripe fruit,
minerals, and nervous citric acidity.
Wood well integrated. Rather powerful
and rich (13 per cent alcohol).
Character and finesse. Like a well-
made Chablis.* Gert Crum
*Cleaner and better-focused than
Genoels-Elderen's Chardonnay Wit.*
Tom Stevenson

Riesling 2002 Apostelhoeve,
Netherlands (Belgium, Netherlands &
Scandinavia, €9) *From 30-year-old
vines. Vinified in stainless steel. Pale,
with very flowery flavours. Juicy, fine,
and elegant on the palate, with
mineral accents – very, very light CO_2
– and at the same time very subtle
goût de pétrole. It is the special,
chalky terroir of the Louwberg you
taste. Rather dry. Good as an apéritif
and very fine with sauerkraut and
Asian food.* Gert Crum
*I could not find the petrolly character,
Gert, but I agree with the rest of your
notes. Although there are a lot of
better Rieslings at this price from
elsewhere in the world, the fact that
you can get a half-decent Riesling
from the Netherlands does deserve
a mention.* Tom Stevenson

Porfyros 2000 Domaine Spiropoulos,
Greece (Organic & Biodynamic Wines,
€12.50) *Unusual combination of
Cabernet Sauvignon and the Greek
St George grape.* Monty Waldin

*Also contains Merlot, but the
Agiorgitiko grape is dominant. The
tannins are a bit pushy, considering
the fruit and acidity levels, but a good
wine nonetheless.* Tom Stevenson

Syrah 2002 Domaine Wardy (Lebanon,
LL 11,000) *Pungent and spicy on the
nose, full-bodied, awash with black
cherries and liquorice on the palate,
and deliciously long. This is Lebanon's
only Syrah, Lebanon's best varietal, and
Domaine Wardy's best wine. It is also
a bargain.* Michael Karam
*Although this immediately appeals on
the nose, the expansive Syrah aromas
are let down by a lack of acidity on
the palate. This may mean that it is
true to its terroir and other better-
balanced Lebanese are not, but it
does not make it a better wine.
However, it is early days for Syrah in
the Middle East, thus it must squeeze
into the Top 100.* Tom Stevenson

Chardonnay Unfiltered 2002
Domaine Sogga, Hideo Vineyard,
Obuse Winery, Japan (Asia, ¥5,000)
*An interesting style interpretation
from an innovative newcomer: neither
burgundian nor New World. It took one
of only two gold medals awarded at
Japan's first domestic wine competition
in 2003. Intriguing hints of kumquat
and marmalade.* Denis Gastin
*For me, it clearly has the toasty-oak
aromas of a New World or, indeed,
international Chardonnay, but it lacks
the weight, fruit, and mouthfeel of
the genuine article. If it is to be taken
as a very individual expression of
Chardonnay (which I have absolutely
no qualms about), then there should
be much less oak. As it is, it falls
between two stools, yet wins one of
only two gold medals, which probably
says more about the competition than
it does about this particular wine. For
the same reason, I feel it deserves
at least a place in this Top 100.*
Tom Stevenson